Improving animal traction technology

Proceedings of the first workshop of the
Animal Traction Network for Eastern and Southern Africa (ATNESA)
held 18–23 January 1992, Lusaka, Zambia

Edited by

Paul Starkey, Emmanuel Mwenya and John Stares

An ATNESA publication
made possible with the assistance of
Directorate General for International Cooperation (DGIS), The Netherlands
Technical Centre for Agricultural and Rural Cooperation (CTA)
Deutsche Gesellschaft für Technische Zusammenarbeit GmbH (GTZ), Germany

Citation of this publication

Starkey P, Mwenya E and Stares J, 1994. *Improving animal traction technology.* Proceedings of the first workshop of the Animal Traction Network for Eastern and Southern Africa (ATNESA) held 18–23 January 1992, Lusaka, Zambia. Technical Centre for Agricultural and Rural Cooperation (CTA), Wageningen, The Netherlands. 490p.

Publication sponsored by

Directorate General for International Cooperation (DGIS), The Hague, The Netherlands
Technical Centre for Agricultural and Rural Cooperation (CTA), Wageningen, The Netherlands
Deutsche Gesellschaft für Technische Zusammenarbeit GmbH (GTZ), Eschborn, Germany

Published on behalf of the Animal Traction Network for Eastern and Southern Africa (ATNESA) by

Technical Centre for Agricultural and Rural Cooperation (CTA)
Postbus 380, 6700 AJ Wageningen, The Netherlands

Book preparation

This book was prepared ("desk-top published") to the stage of camera-ready copy by
Paul Starkey, Animal Traction Development, 64 Northcourt Avenue, Reading RG2 7HQ, UK

Printed by
Mills Litho, Maitland, Cape Town, South Africa

Published 1994
ISBN 92–9081–127–7

Paul Starkey, Emmanuel Mwenya and John Stares (editors)

Improving animal traction technology

Proceedings of the first workshop of the
Animal Traction Network for Eastern and Southern Africa (ATNESA)
held 18–23 January 1992, Lusaka, Zambia

Technical Centre for Agricultural and Rural Cooperation
(ACP–EU Lome Convention)
Wageningen, The Netherlands

1994

Contents

Animal-powered tillage and weeding technology

The supply and distribution of implements for animal traction

Women and animal traction technology

The transfer of animal traction technology

Animal-powered transport

Diversifying operations using animal power

Country experiences and constraints

Index

Preface and acknowledgements

Workshop organisation and support

This publication is the proceedings of the first ATNESA workshop which was held from 18 to 23 January 1992 in Lusaka, Zambia. The workshop was attended by 107 people from 17 countries. More than 80 papers relating to animal traction were submitted and these form the basis of this publication.

The organisation of a major workshop and the publication of a thick volume of proceedings depends on the help and cooperation of a large number of people in many organisations. The ATNESA Steering Committee would like to thank all those who assisted, participated in or supported the workshop and this follow-up publication.

This first ATNESA workshop was made possible thanks to the workshop hosts and local organising committee which included representatives of the Zambian Department of Agriculture and several Zambian organisations, institutions and donor-assisted projects involved with animal draft power. Cooperation between the local organisers and the international members of the ATNESA steering committee was exemplary. Members of the local committee who are to be thanked and congratulated included E Mwenya (Chair), M Bwalya, B Chanda, H Dibbits, H Drechsel, R Meijer, G Phiri, E Sakala, H Sichembe, M Tambatamba, H van Slooten and H Vroom, with further support provided by P Jabani, F Kruit and P Stevens.

Following planning discussions involving staff of the Royal Netherlands Embassy in Lusaka, the Directorate General for International Cooperation (DGIS) of The Netherlands provided the "core costs" of the workshop and made this publication possible. With sponsorship from DGIS, organisational support was provided by the Institute of Agricultural and Environmental Engineering (IMAG-DLO) of The Netherlands, notably by H Dibbits and A Wanders, and also by consultant P Starkey.

Many external and local workshop participants were sponsored by their own organisations or by agencies within their own countries. Such local assistance to participants from eastern and southern Africa was vital in allowing workshop attendance and the preparation of papers. This clearly demonstrated the user-supported nature of ATNESA.

The ATNESA Steering Committee would like to convey its thanks to all the local, national, regional and international organisations that supported participants, directly and indirectly. In the papers published in these proceedings, the names of many of the organisations concerned are cited. Institutions outside the region that sent participants included the Commonwealth Secretariat, the Food and Agriculture Organization of the United Nations (FAO), Deutsche Gesellschaft für Technische Zusammenarbeit (GTZ), the International Livestock Centre for Africa (ILCA), IMAG-DLO, Intermediate Technology Development Group, IT-Transport, Larenstein International Agricultural College, Silsoe Research Institute, Tool (an NGO based in The Netherlands), the Universities of Ahmadu Bello, Edinburgh, Hohenheim, Uppsala and Warwick and the West Africa Animal Traction Network.

Several participants were sponsored by the Technical Centre for Agricultural and Rural Cooperation (CTA), Ede-Wageningen, The Netherlands, by the International Development Research Centre (IDRC) of Canada and by DGIS. The assistance provided by these sponsors is gratefully acknowledged.

Workshop reporting

Workshop plenary sessions and group discussions involved active participation of many people who acted as chairpersons, discussion leaders, group facilitators or rapporteurs. E Sakala was the Chief Rapporteur. The Steering Committee would like to thank him and the many people who contributed towards reports, including A Aganga, M Anderson, A Astatke, M Bwalya, B Chanda, S Chikura, B Chikwanda, R Connor, S Croxton, H Dibbits, K Dippon, J Doran, H Drechsel, D Dube, C Ekemu, J Ellis-Jones, F Emhardt, R Fischer, J Francis, A Galema, J de Graaf, M Guntz, J Hagmann, L Handia, H Helsloot, F Inns, J Jansen, P Jones, J Kahumbura, C Kalima, H Kamphuis, A Kayumbo, F Kruit, W Kumwenda, E Kwiligwa, C Löffler, M Lombe, P Maina, A Makwanda, K Marshall, R Meijer, R Mpande, F Mujemula, I Mukuka, A Muma, J Muthama, G Muwanga, E Mwenya, G Mwakitwange, W Mwenya, M Mwinjilo, H Ojirot, A Okuni, J Olukosi, J Omoding, G Oodally, C Oram, K Owen, A Panin, A Pearson, G Phiri, R Shetto, H Sichembe, C Sikanyika, T Simalenga, R Simuyi, L Singogo, M Sizya, H Sosovele, P Starkey, P Stevens, L Sylwander, A Tembo, H Vroom, A Wanders and H Zaugg.

Proceedings preparation and editing

Support relating to the preparation, printing and distribution of these publication was provided by

DGIS, GTZ and CTA. The ATNESA Steering Committee and the editors of these proceedings extend their warm thanks to DGIS, IMAG-DLO, GTZ and CTA for all their assistance.

The members of the ATNESA Steering Committee would also like to thank the proceedings editors for the impressive amount of hard work that has been invested in this publication. The ATNESA Technical Adviser, Paul Starkey, has had overall responsibility for the editing and desktop publication of the proceedings. At the time of the workshop, Emmanuel Mwenya was chairperson of both the ATNESA Steering Committee and the Local Organising Committee which made the workshop possible. John Stares, a professional scientific and English language editor and Freda Miller, Research Fellow of the Centre for Agricultural Strategy of the University of Reading, provided additional editorial support. Malcolm Starkey assisted with desktop publishing and the preparation of tables, illustrations and the index.

The ATNESA Steering Committee hopes that this volume of proceedings will be one of many valuable resource documents that will be produced by ATNESA and its member organisations in the coming years. These should help achieve the important ATNESA goal of better information exchange between all those involved in improving animal traction research, development, extension, policy formulation and actual use.

The ATNESA Steering Committee warming thanks everyone who has been involved in the planning, implementing and supporting of this workshop and the various follow-up ATNESA activities. The Steering Committee looks forward to further close collaboration with individual members, national animal traction networks, supporting organisations and other networks.

The ATNESA Steering Committee

Dr T E Simalenga, ATNESA Chair, *Tanzania*

Dr A A Aganga, *Botswana*

Ato Kebede Desta, *Ethiopia*

Mr Manfred Guntz, *GTZ, Germany*

Dr Pascal Kaumbutho, *Kenya*

Mr Emmanuel Mwenya, *Zambia*

Mr Raymond Nazare, *Zimbabwe*

Mr John Olupot, *Uganda*

Ms Lotta Sylwander, *AGROTEC, Zimbabwe*

Mr Paul Starkey, *Technical Adviser, UK*

ATNESA: an introduction and update

Introduction to ATNESA

The Animal Traction Network for Eastern and Southern Africa (ATNESA) was formed in 1990 to improve information exchange and regional cooperation relating to animal draft power. The network aims to unite researchers, manufacturers, development workers, institutions and the users of animal traction in the region. Membership of the network is open to all individuals and organisations interested in the objectives of ATNESA.

The Network is coordinated by a Steering Committee comprising specialists from six African countries and representatives of two supporting organisations, together with invited resource persons. The committee plans, initiates, stimulates and facilitates a variety of networking events. The network has no full-time staff or secretariat and responsibility for implementing network activities is delegated to ATNESA members in different countries.

First ATNESA workshop

The first ATNESA workshop was held on 18–23 January 1992 in Lusaka, Zambia. The workshop was attended by 107 people from 17 countries. Full details of this workshop are to be found in this publication, together with reports of the first two ATNESA General Assembly meetings at which the ATNESA statutes were agreed. An outline is also given of the work programme the Steering Committee adopted at the end of this workshop.

Since the first ATNESA workshop reported here, there has been much progress and several follow-up activities. Full details will be contained in future network proceedings and resource documents, but mention can be made here.

National networks

National animal traction networks, affiliated to ATNESA, have been launched in Kenya, Tanzania, South Africa and Ethiopia, with national workshops attended by colleagues from other ATNESA countries. Elsewhere, for example in Zambia, Uganda, Malawi, Botswana and Zimbabwe, informal animal traction networking and some formal activities have been encouraged by ministry of agriculture, project, university or NGO structures. In several countries directories of those involved in animal traction have been prepared.

Thematic workshops

At an international level, ATNESA has held three follow-up workshops on particular themes highlighted during the 1992 workshop.

Gender issues and animal traction was the subject of an ATNESA workshop held in Mbeya, Tanzania, in June 1992. The workshop, hosted by the Mbeya Oxenization Project, was attended by 32 people from Tanzania, Zambia and Zimbabwe. The participants reviewed project experiences relating to gender and animal traction and discussed ways in which women can gain more from animal traction.

Design, testing and manufacture of animal-drawn carts was the topic of a workshop held in January 1993 in Harare, Zimbabwe. The workshop, hosted by the Institute of Agricultural Engineering, was attended by 40 people from 10 countries. The participants reviewed successful and unsuccessful cart designs, and drew up guidelines for large-scale and artisanal cart manufacture. Recommendations were made relating to harnessing, standardised cart testing, credit provision and policy issues.

Animal power for weed control was the subject of an ATNESA workshop held in November 1993 in Tanga, Tanzania, in collaboration with the Animal Traction Network Tanzania (ATNET). It was attended by 64 people from 14 countries. The workshop provided an overview of national, regional and international experiences relating to animal-drawn weeding. Participants discussed weeding issues with farmers and assessed 20 weeding implements, pulled by oxen and donkeys. Multidisciplinary groups established guidelines on weeder design, testing, manufacture and distribution. Specific follow-up proposals covered extension programmes, collaborative testing and improved implement supply and logistical backup.

Planned workshops

The ATNESA Steering Committee has plans to hold another focused thematic workshop on "Improving donkey utilisation and management". It is envisaged that this may be held in Ethiopia in 1995 or 1996 in collaboration with the Ethiopian Network for Animal Traction (ENAT). Planning is underway for the next broadly-based ATNESA workshop on the theme of "Meeting the challenges of animal traction". This is expected to be held in cooperation with the Kenya Network for Draught Animal Technology (KENDAT) in 1995.

ATNESA Steering Committee Members
and Network Contacts, 1994

Dr T E SIMALENGA *(ATNESA Chair)*
Training Officer, AGROTEC
PO Box BW 540, Borrowdale, Harare
ZIMBABWE

Tel: + 263-4-860009
Fax: + 263-4-860009
Tlx: 24668 UNDEV ZW

Dr (Mrs) Adeolu Ademitu AGANGA
Senior Lecturer
Department of Animal Health and Production
Botswana College of Agriculture,
Private Bag 0027, Gaborone, BOTSWANA

Tel: + 267-352381
Fax: + 267-314253
Tlx: 2752 SACCAR BD

Ato KEBEDE DESTA *(ENAT Secretariat)*
Agricultural Implements and Equipment Division
Rural Technology Promotion Department
Ministry of Agriculture
PO Box 7838, Addis Ababa, ETHIOPIA

Tel: + 251-1-513753
Fax: + 251-1-512345
Tlx: 21390 ET

Mr Emmanuel MWENYA
National Animal Draft Power Coordinator
Agricultural Engineering Section
Department of Agriculture
PO Box 50291, Lusaka, ZAMBIA

Tel: + 260-1-252824
Fax: + 260-1-262820
Tlx: 43950 ZA

Mr John OLUPOT
National Animal Traction Coordinator
Ministry of Agriculture
PO Box 102, Entebbe, UGANDA

Tel: + 256-42-20981
Fax: + 256-42-21047
Tlx: 61287 UG

Mr Manfred GUNTZ
GTZ Dep 421
Deutsche Gesellschaft für Technische Zusammenarbeit
D-65726 Eschborn, GERMANY

Tel: + 49-6196-791340
Fax: + 49-6196-797130
Tlx: 4075010 D

Ms Lotta SYLWANDER
Socio-Economist, AGROTEC
PO Box BW 540, Borrowdale, Harare
ZIMBABWE

Tel: + 263-4-860009
Fax: + 263-4-860009
Tlx: 24668 UNDEV ZW

ATNESA Technical Adviser
Mr Paul H STARKEY
Animal Traction Development
Oxgate, 64 Northcourt Avenue
Reading RG2 7HQ, UNITED KINGDOM

Tel: + 44-1734-872152
Fax: + 44-1734-314525
E-mail: *P.H.Starkey@reading.ac.uk*
Tlx: 94011615 OXEN G

Invited resource person (First ATNESA Chair)
Mr Raymond NAZARE
Chief Agricultural Engineer
Agritex Institute of Agricultural Engineering
PO Box 330, Borrowdale, Harare
ZIMBABWE

Tel: + 263-4-725936
Fax: + 263-4-725342
Tlx: 22455 ZW

Invited resource person (KENDAT Chair)
Dr Pascal KAUMBUTHO, Chair,
Kenya Network for Draught Animal Technology
(KENDAT)
Department of Agricultural Engineering
University of Nairobi
PO Box 30197, Nairobi, KENYA

Tel: + 254-2-593465
Fax: + 254-2-593465

SANAT contact
Mr A B D JOUBERT
Secretary, South Africa Network on Animal Traction
(SANAT)
Faculty of Agriculture, University of Fort Hare
Private Bag X1314 Alice, Ciskei
SOUTH AFRICA

Tel: + 27-404-22085
Fax: + 27-404-31730

ATNET contact
Animal Traction Network Tanzania (ATNET) Secretariat
Department of Agricultural Engineering
Sokoine University of Agriculture
PO Box 3003, Morogoro, TANZANIA

Tel: + 255-56-3259
Fax: + 255-56-3599
Tlx: 55308 UNIVMOG TZ

Acronyms and abbreviations

ACEMA   Association Euro-Africaine des Centres de Mécanisation Agricole, Cameroon and France

ACIAR   Australian Centre for International Agricultural Research, Australia

ACIAR-DAP ACIAR Draught Animal Power Project, Townsville, Australia

ACP   Africa, Caribbean and Pacific

ACREMA   Atelier de Construction et de Réparations de Matériel Agricole, Niger

ADB   African Development Bank

ADD   Agricultural Development Division

ADMARC   Agricultural Development and Marketing Corporation, Malawi

ADP   Animal Draft Power (Animal Draught Power)

ADPRDP   Animal Draft Power Research and Development Project (subsequently Programme), Magoye, Zambia

AED   Agricultural Extension Department

AES   Agricultural Engineering Section, Department of Agriculture

AETC   Agricultural Engineering Training Centre, Zimbabwe

AFRC   Agriculture and Food Research Council, UK. AFRC-Engineering: AFRC Institute of Engineering Research (formerly NIAE, now Silsoe Research Institute), Silsoe, UK

AFVP   Association Française des Volontaires du Progrès, France

AGROTEC   Agricultural Operations Technology for Small Holders in East and Southern Africa, Zimbabwe

AGS   Agricultural Services Division of FAO, Italy

AIRIC   Agricultural Implement Research and Improvement Centre, Nazareth, Ethiopia

ALDEP   Arable Lands Development Programme, Botswana

AMRDU   Agricultural Machinery Research and Development Unit, Zambia

APTP   Animal Power Technology Project (GATE/GTZ regional project)

ARAP   Accelerated Rainfed Arable Programme, Botswana

ARDU   Arsi Rural Development Unit, Ethiopia

ARMA   Cellule de l'Artisanat Rural et Machinisme Agricole, Niger

ARNAB   African Research Network for Agricultural Byproducts, Addis Ababa, Ethiopia

AT   animal traction; appropriate technology

ATIP   Agricultural Technology Improvement Project, Botswana

ATNESA   Animal Traction Network for Eastern and Southern Africa

ATNET   Animal Traction Network Tanzania

ATOL   Aangepaste Technologie Ontwikkelingslanden, Leuven, Belgium

BBF   Broad-bed and furrow (system of cultivation)

BDPA   Bureau pour le Développement de la Production Agricole, France

BTC   Botswana Technology Centre, Botswana

Camartec Centre for Agricultural Mechanization and Rural Technology, Tanzania

CBPP   Contagious Bovine Pleuropneumonia

CEEMAT   Centre d'Etudes et d'Expérimentation du Machinisme Agricole Tropical, France

CFA   West African franc

CGOT   Compagnie générale des oléagineux tropicaux, France

CIAE   Central Institute of Agricultural Engineering, Bhopal, India

CIDA   Canadian International Development Agency, Hull, Quebec, Canada

CIDARC   Centre d'Information et de Documentation en Agronomie des Régions Chaudes, Montpellier, France

CIMMYT   Centro Internacional de Mejoramiento de Maíz y Trigo, Mexico

CIPEA   Centre International pour l'Elevage en Afrique (ILCA), Ethiopia

CIRAD   Centre de coopération internationale en recherche agronomique pour le développement, France

cm   centimetre (unit of length)

CMA   Christian Mission Aid, Kenya

CMDT   Compagnie Malienne pour le Développement des Textiles, Mali

CMG   crushed maize grain

ConTil   Conservation Tillage for Sustainable Crop Production Systems Project, Zimbabwe

COOPIBO   Coopération au Développement Ibo, Belgium (NGO)

CTA   Technical Centre for Agriculture and Rural Cooperation, The Netherlands

CTVM   Centre for Tropical Veterinary Medicine, Edinburgh, UK

CUSA   Credit Union and Savings Association

DANIDA   Danish International Development Agency

DAP   draft (or draught) animal power

DGIS   Directorate General for Development Cooperation, Ministry of Foreign Affairs, The Hague

DM   dry matter

dN   decanewton (unit of force approximately equivalent to 1 kg weight)

DRP   Drought Relief Programme, Botswana

DVTCS   Department of Veterinary and Tsetse Control Services

EC   European Community

ECF   East Coast Fever

ETSP   Extension Training Support Programme, Zambia

ENDA   Environment and Development in the Third World (international NGO)

FAO   Food and Agriculture Organization of the United Nations, Rome, Italy

FCFA   West African franc

FFW   Food for Work

FINNIDA   Finnish International Development Agency, Finland

FIT   Farm Implements and Tools Project, The Netherlands

FMDU   Farm Machinery Development Unit, Botswana

FMU   Farm Machinery Unit, Malawi

FSR   Farming Systems Research

FSRU   Farming Systems Research Unit, Zimbabwe

FSSP	Farming Systems Support Project, Gainesville, Florida, USA	kN	kilonewton (unit of force approximately equivalent to 100 kg weight)
FTC	Farmer Training Centre	kph	kilometres per hour
FTSS	Farmer Technical Service Station	KSDP	Kabwe Smallholder Development Project, Zambia
g	gram (unit of mass)		
GATE	German Appropriate Technology Exchange, GTZ, Germany	LENCO	Lusaka Engineering Company, Zambia
GFA	Gesellschaft für Agrarprojekte mbH, Hamburg, Germany	LIAC	Larenstein International Agricultural College, Deventer, The Netherlands
GNP	Gross national product	LPDP	Lokitaung Pastoral Development Project, Kenya
GRZ	Government of the Republic of Zambia	m	metre
GTZ	Deutsche Gesellschaft für Technische Zusammenarbeit GmbH, Germany	MAAIF	Ministry of Agriculture, Animal Industry and Fisheries
h	hour	MALD	Ministry of Agriculture and Livestock Development
ha	hectare		
HABITAT	United Nations Centre for Human Settlements	MATI	Ministry of Agriculture Training Institute
Hata	houe à traction asine (donkey cultivator)	MAWD	Ministry of Agriculture and Water Development
HIMA	Iringa Soil and Water Conservation Project		
IAE	Institute of Agricultural Engineering, Zimbabwe	MAWRD	Ministry of Agriculture, Water and Rural Development
IAR	Institute of Agricultural Research, Ethiopia	MDM	Name of an engineering company based in Kitwe
IBRD	International Bank for Reconstruction and Development (World Bank), Washington DC, USA	ME	metabolisable energy
		MEDA	Mennonite Economic Development Associates
ICRISAT	International Crops Research Institute for the Semi-Arid Tropics, India	MEIDA	Metal Engineering and Industrial Development Association
IDRC	International Development Research Centre, Ottawa, Canada	MIFIPRO	Mixed Farming Improvement Project, Mwanga, Kilimanjaro, Tanzania
IEMVT	Institut d'Elevage et de Médecine Vétérinaire des Pays Tropicaux, France	MJ	megajoule (unit of energy or work)
		mm	millimetre
IFAD	International Fund for Agricultural Development, Rome, Italy	MoA	Ministry of Agriculture
IITA	International Institute of Tropical Agriculture, Nigeria	MOP	Mbeya Oxenization Project, Tanzania
		MSc	Master of Science, university degree
ILCA	International Livestock Centre for Africa, Ethiopia	N	newton (unit of force approximately equivalent to 0.1 kg weight)
ILO	International Labour Office (Organisation), Switzerland	NALERP	National Agriculture and Livestock Extension and Rehabilitation Programme
IMAG-DLO	Instituut voor Mechanisatie, Arbeid en Gebouwen - Dienst Landbouwkundig Onderzoek (Institute of Agricultural Engineering), Wageningen, The Netherlands	NAMA	Network for Agricultural Mechanisation in Africa
		NATSC	National Animal Traction Steering Committee
IPI	Institute of Production Innovation, University of Dar es Salaam, Tanzania	NEI	Nederlands Economisch Instituut (Netherlands Economics Institute)
IRDP	Integrated Rural Development Programme	NGO	Non-governmental organisation
ISRA	Institut Sénégalais de Recherches Agricoles, Senegal	NIAE	National Institute of Agricultural Engineering, UK (subsequently Silsoe Research Institute)
IT	Intermediate Technology		
IT-Transport	Intermediate Technology Transport, UK	Nm	newton metre (unit of work or energy equivalent to 1 joule)
ITDG	Intermediate Technology Development Group, UK	NORAD	Norwegian Agency for International Development
J	joule (unit of work or energy)	NRDC	National Resources Development College, Lusaka, Zambia
K	Kwacha currency		
KADICU	Kaoma District Cooperative Union	NRDP	National Rural Development Programme, Malawi
KAEC	Katapola Agricultural Engineering Centre		
KENDAT	Kenya Network for Draught Animal Technology, Nairobi, Kenya	NRI	Natural Resources Institute, Chatham, UK
		NS	not significant
kg	kilogram	NUC	Njala University College, Sierra Leone
kgf	kilogram force (unit of force approx. equivalent to 1 kg weight or 10 N)	NWCU	North Western Cooperative Union
		NWIRDP	North Western Integrated Rural Development Programme
KIT	Koninklijk Instituut voor Tropen (Royal Tropical Institute), Amsterdam, The Netherlands	OAU	Organization of African Unity
		ODA	Overseas Development Administration, London, United Kingdom
kJ	kilojoule (unit of work or energy)		
km	kilometre	P	probability

PAFSAT	Project for Promotion of Adapted Farming Systems based on Animal Traction, Cameroon
PARC	Pan-African Rinderpest Campaign
PCV	packed cell volume
PhD	Doctor of Philosophy, university degree
PRIVAT	Projet participatif pour le renforcement des institutions villageoises pour le développement de l'agriculture à Tahoua, Niger
PROPTA	Projet pour la Promotion de la Traction Animale, Togo
PTA	Preferential Trade Area (eastern and southern Africa)
PV	bearing pressure in relation to the sliding velocity between bearing and axle
PVC	polyvinyl chloride (synthetic material)
RDP BV	Name of a consultancy company based in The Netherlands
RDP	Rural Development Project/Programme
revs/min	revolutions per minute, rpm
RIIC	Rural Industries Innovation Centre, Botswana
RNAM	Regional Network for Agricultural Machinery, Pasay City, Philippines
RRM	rural roads maintenance
RTC	Rural Technology Centres
RTDU	Rural Technology Development Unit, Kenya
RTPC	rural technology promotion centre
RTPD	Rural Technology Promotion Department, Ethiopia
s	second
SACCAR	Southern African Centre for Cooperation in Agricultural Research, Botswana
SADCC	Southern Africa Development Coordination Conference
SAFGRAD	OAU Semi-Arid Food Grain Research and Development, Burkina Faso
SAFIM	Southern African Farming Implements Manufacturers, South Africa
SD	Standard deviation
SDP	Smallholder Development Project
SEMA	Secteur expérimental de modernisation agricole, Senegal
SFMP	Small Farm Mechanization Programme, Nakuru, Kenya
Siammco	Soroti Agricultural Implement Machinery Manufacturing Company, Uganda
SIDA	Swedish International Development Authority, Stockholm, Sweden
SIDO	Small Industrial Development Organization
Siscoma	Société Industrielle Sénégalaise de Constructions Mécaniques et de Matériels Agricoles, Senegal
Sismar	Société Industrielle Sahélienne de Mécaniques, de Matériels Agricoles et de Représentations, Senegal
SKF	Name of a multinational engineering and bearing company, based in Sweden
SMECMA	Société Malienne d'Etude et de Construction de Matériel Agricole, Mali

SNV	A development and volunteer organisation based in The Netherlands
SUA	Sokoine University of Agriculture, Morogoro, Tanzania
SUAS	Swedish University of Agricultural Sciences, Uppsala, Sweden
t	tonne
TAMTU	Tanganyika/Tanzania Agricultural Machinery Testing Unit, Tanzania
TDAU	Technology Development Advisory Unit, University of Zambia, Lusaka
TFNC	Tanzanian Food and Nutrition Centre, Dar es Salaam, Tanzania
TIRDEP	Tanga Integrated Rural Development Programme, Tanga, Tanzania
TOOL	Technologie Overdracht OntwikkelinsLand, The Netherlands
TSh	Tanzanian shilling
UAC	Uyole Agricultural Centre, Mbeya
UCOMA	Unité Construction Matériel Agricole, Niger
UFI	Ubungo Farm Implements, Dar es Salaam, Tanzania
UK	United Kingdom (of Great Britain and Northern Ireland)
UN	United Nations
UNDP	United Nations Development Programme, New York, USA
UNECA	United Nations Economic Commission for Africa, Addis Ababa, Ethiopia
UNICEF	United Nations Children's Fund, New York, USA
UNIDO	United Nations Industrial Development Organization, Vienna, Austria
UNIFEM	United Nations Development Fund for Women, New York, USA
UNZA	University of Zambia, Lusaka
UPROMA	Unité de Production de Matériel Agricole, Togo
US$	United States dollar
USA	United States of America
USAID	United States Agency for International Development, Washington DC, USA
VAP	Village Agricultural Programme
VITA	Volunteers in Technical Assistance, USA
W	watt (unit of power)
WAATN	West Africa Animal Traction Network
WACU	West Acholi Cooperative Union Ltd, Uganda
WADA	Wum Area Development Authority, Cameroon
WAFSRN	West African Farming Systems Research Network
Z$	Zimbabwe dollar
ZAFFICO	Zambia Forestry and Forest Industries Corporation
ZCF	Zambia Cooperative Federation (FS: Financial Services Division)
ZK	Zambian Kwacha
ZZK	Zana za Kilimo, Mbeya, Tanzania

Photograph opposite
Participants at the First ATNESA Workshop, Lusaka, Zambia

"Improving animal traction technology"

Improving animal traction technology

Workshop reports

An overview of the workshop

Report by P Starkey. Photographs by P Starkey and L Sylwander

Objectives

The overall aim of the workshop was to bring together a wide range of people of various disciplines involved in research, development, extension, training, planning and infrastructural support for the use of animal power in the region in order to stimulate the exchange of information and experiences and to facilitate collaboration and cooperation.

Themes

The overall workshop theme was **"Improving animal traction technology"**. This broad topic was chosen as a development-oriented framework for analysing and discussing research and extension experiences concerning animal draft power. Seven interrelated themes were selected to allow contributors and discussion groups to focus on particular research and development topics:

- Improving the profitability of animal traction
- Improving draft animal management
- Improving tillage and weeding technology
- Improving implement supply and distribution
- Women and animal traction technology
- Transfer of animal traction technology
- Improving animal-powered transport.

Participants

The workshop was open to all persons actively concerned with animal traction who were prepared to submit a paper. A total of 107 people from 17 countries participated. Most were African nationals occupying senior positions in organisations concerned with animal power research, development and extension. About half the participants had an agricultural engineering background, 20 were social scientists or economists, 15 were animal scientists or veterinarians and 15 had an agronomic or general

agricultural background. Thirteen participants were women and 94 were men. The names of participants and the addresses of their organisations are provided on pages 61–64.

Hosts, location and sponsorship

The workshop was hosted by a local organising committee which included representatives of the Zambian Ministry of Agriculture and several Zambian organisations, institutions and donor-assisted projects involved with animal draft power. The workshop was held in Lusaka at the Intercontinental Hotel. It had been a condition of registration that all participants stayed in this hotel, and this was realistic due to specially-negotiated rates for accommodation and board.

Most external and local workshop participants were sponsored by their own organisations or by agencies within their own countries. Several participants were sponsored by the Technical Centre for Agricultural and Rural Cooperation (CTA), the International Development Research Centre (IDRC) and the Directorate General for International Cooperation (DGIS) of The Netherlands. DGIS, in cooperation with IMAG-DLO, funded the workshop secretariat and provided organisational support.

Workshop methodology

In planning the workshop, the ATNESA Steering Committee and the Zambian workshop organising committee had discussed the experiences of the West Africa Animal Traction Network. In particular, they had noted the feedback provided by participants through evaluations of previous workshops. This suggested that the workshops should aim to provide a stimulating framework for informal information exchange, with emphasis on participatory activities rather than long plenary sessions. There should be

Workshop plenary session

Workshop discussion group

Workshop opening ceremony
ATNESA introduction: J Omoding (left). Opening speech: Hon Dr G Scott, Zambian Minister of Agriculture (right)

some keynote reviews of important topics, on-farm discussion with smallholder farmers and detailed analysis of specific issues in small working groups.

A workshop programme was planned to provide a conducive and stimulating framework that allowed as much as possible to be achieved in the time available. Several early programme activities were designed to stimulate subsequent informal interactions (participant introductions, networking announcements, reception). A wide-ranging technical review was then to presented, in the form of thematic keynote papers. Background information was to be given on animal traction in the host country. Participants then visited farms in small groups, whose composition had been chosen to ensure maximum mixing of countries and disciplines. These groups were asked to work separately towards a common purpose, that of understanding and defining many of the farm-level problems and constraints in terms of the workshop themes. The *ad hoc* field visit groups reported to each other, before people joined with others with similar special interests to undertake in-depth, critical analyses of the main thematic issues. It was anticipated that all groups would engage in

constructive information exchange, leading to better understanding of the topic by all involved. It was anticipated that some groups might also be able to make recommendations or highlight specific needs or areas for further network attention. It was hoped that workshop interactions and working together would generate a momentum during the week, culminating in a final synthesis and summary.

Interwoven into the technical workshop programme, would be a series of network meetings, designed to firmly establish ATNESA, bond special-interest groups and result in a new steering committee with a mandate to implement a network programme based on the needs expressed by the participants.

The unusual decision to hold a six-day workshop running from Saturday to Thursday had been a practical one, made following a study of airline timetables. Most external participants were able to arrive and depart on a Friday. The organisers determined that all participants should stay in the same hotel as this would encourage informal interactions between the different countries and organisations and would allow various interest-groups to meet together easily.

Programme elements

Opening ceremony and keynote presentation

Welcoming and introductory remarks were made by the acting ATNESA chairman, J Omoding, and the chairman of the local committee, E Mwenya. The workshop was formally opened by the Zambian Minister of Agriculture, Hon Dr G Scott who, in addition to his prepared speech, reflected on some of his experiences as a commercial farmer and on the continuing importance of animal traction.

A keynote slide presentation was given by P Starkey, with colourful images from around the world that illustrated the many systems of animal

Keynote slide presentation: P Starkey

Workshop programme

Friday 17 January

Arrival of participants and registration

1930 Welcoming reception

Saturday 18 January

0700 Working breakfast for network steering committee

0900 Organisational matters and announcements

0930 Opening ceremony

1100 Keynote presentation

1400 Open session of introductions and networking announcements

1600 First ATNESA General Assembly Meeting

2000 Optional evening session: project videos

Sunday 19 January

0800 Invited presentations on workshop themes

Improving the profitability of animal traction

Women and animal traction technology

Improving draft animal management

Improving tillage and weeding systems

Improving the supply and distribution of implements

Improving animal-drawn transport

Transfer of animal traction technology

1445 Presentation of Zambian animal traction experience

1630 Outline of field visits and discussions

2000 Optional evening session: farming systems interest group

Monday 20 January

0630 Field visits in small groups to different villages to see animal traction operations and hold discussions with farmers

1400 Field visits to Zambian animal traction programmes, manufacturers and training centres

2000 Optional panel discussion with large-scale, commercial farmers using animal traction

Tuesday 21 January

0800 Small group discussions relating to field visit findings. Preparation of flip-chart or overhead projector presentations of reports and recommendations

1400 Presentations of reports of small groups followed by plenary discussions

1600 Small group discussions on workshop themes

2000 Optional evening session: project videos

Wednesday 22 January

0800 Small group discussions relating to workshop themes. Preparation of flip-chart or overhead projector presentations of recommendations

1200 Presentations of reports of small groups followed by plenary discussions

1400 Presentations of reports of small groups followed by plenary discussions

1600 Second ATNESA General Assembly Meeting
Election of new ATNESA Steering Committee

2000 Optional evening session: panel discussions with implement manufacturers

2000 Working dinner for new and old Steering Committees and resource organisations

Thursday 23 January

0830 Invited keynote analysis of workshop findings and conclusions
"Improving animal traction technology in eastern and southern Africa: progress, needs and priorities in the light of workshop presentations and discussions"
Final plenary discussion

1000 Workshop evaluation
Closing statements

1100 End of workshop

1400 Optional visits to Lusaka

Friday 24 January

Departures

Networking announcements: J Kahumbura

Keynote papers: A Wanders

traction use in the different continents. This is summarised on pages 66–81. The presentation concluded with an introduction to the workshop themes and programme.

Networking announcements

During an open networking session, all participants introduced themselves, summarising their work, their interests and ways in which they, or their organisations, could contribute to, and benefit from, the network (see pages 27–31).

Keynote papers

Discussion papers in each of the seven themes were presented by subject matter specialists. It had originally been hoped that all papers could have been jointly prepared by an expert from an ATNESA country and an expert from outside the region, but in many cases collaboration proved difficult in the time available. The authors had been asked to prepared in-depth review papers for circulation during the workshop and subsequent publication. During presentations authors were expected to highlight the main points only, and allow time for a few questions and clarifications.

The first presentation was collaborative, and Dr A Panin and J Ellis-Jones jointly introduced their paper on "Increasing the profitability of animal draft power" (see page 94). This was followed by the lead presentation of L Sylwander on "Women and animal traction technology", which had been prepared in consultation with colleagues in Tanzania and Swaziland (see page 260). Dr A Pearson summarised the lead paper on "Improving draft animal management" (see page 122). P Stevens highlighted the conclusions of his paper on "Improving animal-powered tillage systems and weeding technology", prepared in consultation with R Shetto (see page 168). The keynote paper on "Improving the supply and distribution of implements" was presented by A Wanders.

M Anderson summarised her review papers relating to "Improving animal-powered transport" prepared in cooperation with R Dennis (see pages 378 and 396). The final thematic presentation was by R Fischer on the topic of "Transfer of animal traction technology" (see page 296).

Animal traction in Zambia

The host country had been invited to make a presentation on animal traction in Zambia. The aim was to introduce, prior to the field visits, the organisations involved and some key issues. Several people cooperated in planning the Zambian synthesis, including E Mwenya, H Dibbits and others whose personal papers relating to Zambian experience are included in the thematic sections in these proceedings. Dr W Mwenya made the presentation (see page 469).

Field visits

The third day was devoted to field visits, made in small, multidisciplinary, multinational groups, to a total of 32 villages. The groups were small enough to allow detailed discussions with male and female farmers. The aims of the visits had been given by H Dibbits and P Starkey, and background information on the various villages had been prepared by members of the local organising committee. At precisely 0600, 16 vehicles left the hotel to travel to the various villages. Each group had the opportunity to visit two different farmers, and pose questions on their particular farming systems. Unfortunately, weather conditions made the planned practical demonstrations difficult in some cases, but the heavy rain was welcomed by the farmers.

In the afternoon, participants visited various animal traction organisations including Palabana Training Centre, Magoye Agricultural Engineering Station,

Working groups

the Kasisi Project (run by a local NGO) and the manufacturers Lenco and Gameco.

The following day the same, small multidisciplinary groups discussed their observations on animal traction in the Zambian farming systems, noting the major constraints and the implications of these for the country, the region and the network. The various group conclusions were shared in a plenary session (see pages 32–33).

Working groups on workshop themes

Workshop participants regrouped to allow people to choose the workshop theme most relevant to their work. This allowed detailed discussions between colleagues involved in similar areas of research, development, extension or infrastructural support. The conclusions of each group were presented and discussed in plenary sessions (see pages 34–47).

Workshop conclusions

An invited speaker, M Guntz of GTZ, had been asked to bring together the main issues arising from workshop papers, visits and discussions in a final presentation on the last day. He undertook this work in collaboration with a multidisciplinary group of participants, who met several times and worked

though much of the final night to try to highlight the main points that had been made during the week. The overview and concluding synthesis that was presented is printed on pages 23–26.

ATNESA General Assembly

During the workshop, two open General Assembly meetings were convened. At the first meeting, background information was given on networking and the history of ATNESA. Draft statutes and organisational arrangements for the network were presented and discussed. A nominated committee reviewed these. At the second meeting, the statutes were formally approved and adopted. A new steering committee was elected and given a mandate to draw up and implement a programme of activities based on the workshop recommendations (see pages 48–51).

Workshop papers and exhibits

A total of 80 technical papers had been prepared for the workshop. All participants received copies of these, but only the invited keynote papers were presented in plenary sessions. There were at least five written contributions per theme, with emphasis on technology transfer, tillage and weeding, gender

Workshop conclusions: M Guntz

ATNESA General Assembly: L Singogo, Chair

Informal networking

issues and draft animal management. Edited versions of all the papers circulated are to be found in these proceedings.

Throughout the workshop, several poster and photographic displays were exhibited. One exhibition, by P Starkey, provided a world-wide view of animal traction. F Inns mounted a poster on harnessing systems. Projects and institutions providing details of their work included the Animal Power Technology Project, the ConTil Project, Mbeya Oxenization Project, the Rural Technology Promotions Department and the universities of Hohenheim, Kassel and Warwick.

A variety of animal traction books and resource publications were exhibited, including publications of CTA, GTZ and ILCA. Several participants, including J Nolle (France) and H Ojirot (Uganda), brought videos relating to their work, and these were shown during evening sessions.

Animal traction implements on show included some made by Lenco, Bulawayo Steel and J Nolle. Some harnessing systems were exhibited by H Dibbits.

Special groups and panels

Various groups of participants with specialised interests met during the workshop to coordinate activities and plan collaboration. Among the groups were people interested in farming systems research and extension, gender issues, local manufacture of implements, donkey power, cart design and animal-powered systems. Other optional sessions included panel discussions with manufacturers from

several countries and with some large-scale Zambian commercial farmers who use animal traction.

Informal networking

Throughout the workshop, informal networking was taking place during meal times, coffee breaks and in the evenings. Towards the end of the workshop, an attempt was made to see whether the informal networking that was going on might lead to any follow-up exchanges. Thus, after one workshop session, people were requested to list specific examples of information exchange that had taken place or cooperation that was being planned.

The results were staggering, for within a short period of time there was a list of over 200 different specific interactions that had already been discussed. For example, Coopibo (Tanzania) was to visit Palabana (Zambia) and obtain training manuals. The Animal Power Technology Project (Zambia) was to liaise with interested colleagues in Tanzania, Zimbabwe, The Netherlands and UK. The conservation tillage project in Zimbabwe was to discuss collaboration with Tanga Project (Tanzania) and Magoye (Zambia). The Tanga Project (Tanzania) was to contact Binga (Zimbabwe) in relation to donkeys. Tool (The Netherlands) was to send information to colleagues in Ethiopia, Zambia, Germany and UK. Organisations involved in cart bearing development in Tanzania, Zambia, Zimbabwe and UK were to exchange information and discuss collaboration and a possible follow-up workshop. Several individuals involved in gender issues in Zambia, Zimbabwe, Tanzania, UK and The

Informal networking

Netherlands agreed to exchange information and, if possible, plan a follow-up workshop. Propta (Togo) was to obtain information on use of cows from ILCA (Ethiopia). The University of Edinburgh and GTZ had lists of people to whom publications would be sent. The many other similar interactions listed were probably only the tip of an information exchange iceberg. Subsequent reports suggest that a very large number of these proposals were actually implemented, with publications exchanged, visits undertaken and collaborative programmes started.

Evaluation

Just before the closing ceremony, 100 participants completed anonymous evaluation forms allowing them to rate and comment on all aspects of workshop and organisation. The results (which were generally very positive) are presented and discussed on pages 52–60.

Workshop outputs

This brief overview of the workshop has summarised an intensive week in which more than 100 people from many countries, backgrounds and disciplines interacted and discussed in formal and informal sessions, exchanging information, identifying priorities and planning follow-ups. The workshop outputs were many and varied, individual and joint.

Some workshop conclusions are presented in the specific summaries, reports and papers that have been referred to in the preceding paragraphs, including the workshop synthesis, thematic group outputs, the network report and participant evaluation comments. These are complemented by the many experiences described in the edited papers. However, the output of the workshop was much greater than all the ideas, experiences and information contained in this volume. About 100 participants returned to their work more highly

Equipment display

motivated and with fresh ideas and approaches. Many organisations and individuals that made contact as the result of the workshop have continued to exchange information and to collaborate. Affiliated national animal traction networks have been formed and ATNESA has held several follow-up workshops.

This volume of workshop proceedings is but one tangible output of the workshop. The main workshop outputs are there to be seen among the individuals and organisations working with animal traction in the ATNESA region.

Final workshop analysis: progress, needs and priorities

Invited keynote synthesis of workshop presentations, discussions and conclusions. Prepared by M Guntz

Improving animal traction technology

During the six days from 18 to 23 January 1992, 107 professionals directly or indirectly involved in promoting animal traction in eastern and southern Africa met in Lusaka, Zambia, for the first workshop of the Animal Traction Network for Eastern and Southern Africa (ATNESA).

This synopsis is based on an analysis of the papers, presentations and discussions (informal as well as formal).

The workshop

The workshop was characterised by a balanced representation of participants with a wide spectrum of professional backgrounds. This facilitated cross-linkages between various issues in animal traction. The multidisciplinary discussion groups exposed individual participants to different perspectives. Besides "broadening the horizons" of participants, this resulted in mutually beneficial "cross-fertilisation".

No profession was over-represented or dominated the discussions. In fact, all participants emphasised the pleasant atmosphere and excellent personal relationships which developed during the workshop. This environment greatly facilitated cooperation among the participants and resulted in constructive and productive group sessions dealing with common problems.

The workshop organisers found an appropriate balance between formal presentations and informal discussions and activities, which was commended by participants. The field visits, organised in small groups, were stimulating and strongly reinforced the farmers' perspective during the workshop. They provided an opportunity for many participants to gain hands-on experience in, for example, harnessing oxen or walking behind a plow. The field visits also made many participants aware of their own inability to provide solutions to the farmers' pressing problems.

After the seven keynote presentations and the field visits, the following themes were discussed in small groups:

○ Animal management
○ Profitability
○ Tillage and weeding
○ Implement supply and distribution
○ Gender issues
○ Transfer of technology
○ Transport

These topics are priority issues in the ATNESA region. Other important topics, such as institutional aspects, credit, marketing, access to information and child labour, could not be covered.

Every participant prepared a paper on one of the workshop sub-themes. Not all the papers could be presented during the sessions, but they constitute a unique and up-to-date source of information. All contributions have been professionally edited for the proceedings, which will act as a regional resource book on animal traction.

Illustrative quotations

The following quotations were collected by the author during the formal and informal workshop activities. They are included here to assist reflection on some key issues before proceeding to a discussion of identified needs and conclusions.

"The West Africa Animal Traction Network (WAATN) has flourished for more than five years despite the absence of a permanent secretariat"

"There has been a huge change in information exchange relating to animal traction in West Africa in recent years, much of which is directly, or indirectly, attributable to the activities of the West Africa Animal Traction Network"

"Labour productivity in the ATNESA region is extremely low"

"Draft animals are by far the most economic power source for agricultural production in the region"

"75% of agricultural work in the region is done by women; we have a female farming system"

"Women do not have much access to animal traction"

"Traditional beliefs and local customs hamper the introduction and use of draft animal power"

"Let's be realistic. Donor support will be required for a long time to come to firmly establish animal draft power in the region"

"When I started four years ago I had 22 cattle and 2 wives. Now I have 2 cattle and 4 wives"

"The cattle just die even though I spray every week. Neither the government nor anyone else helps me"

"This planter is still in good condition, but I cannot use it because I cannot get a replacement of the metering disk. I have to buy a new planter"

"There are often no credit facilities to purchase animals and implements"

"Donkey power is a potential, yet gravely neglected, technology"

"The network should ensure that government policies favour animal traction technology"

"The extension service is unsatisfactory"

"You can see that the machines work perfectly. Yet it has been written that they have been rejected"

"We saw very little evidence of any recent improvement in animal traction on the farm: indeed the contrary was the case"

"Animal traction cannot be viewed in isolation. It must be part of the system"

Progress

Animal traction plays an important role in the eastern and southern African region. It is recognised as an appropriate, affordable and sustainable technology requiring few external inputs. It is used mainly for crop production (plowing, weeding) and transport. These applications result in the highest economic returns for investment in animal traction.

Workshop participants estimated that animal traction technology is used by approximately 40 % of the farmers in the ATNESA region. However, its application varies from approximately 5 % in the Tanga region of Tanzania to about 95 % in smallholder systems in southern Zambia and Botswana.

The use of animal traction is reported to have increased by about 5 % annually, ie, the animal power growth rate has been higher than the population increase in the region.

Despite expansion, progress achieved in animal traction during the past decade or so has not fulfilled expectations. The major reasons for the shortfall are highlighted below and covered in detail in the workshop papers.

Major constraints

The overall economic and infrastructural environment has a significant impact on animal traction technologies. Economies and national infrastructures have been deteriorating in many countries in recent years. The overall economic situation has increasingly been a constraint to the introduction and/or expansion of animal traction technologies.

As a consequence, many small-scale farmers do not get sufficient incentives, through agricultural prices, to produce more than their subsistence requirements. Added constraints have been imposed by the severe droughts in most parts of the region during the past few years.

Government policies do not sufficiently encourage the adoption and use of animal traction. If governments proclaim support for animal traction then this is often limited to "lip service" rather than to actual support in terms of credit, extension, veterinary services, etc. However, changes in attitudes on this aspect have become evident during the past year or so.

Farmers keen on adopting animal traction face serious input constraints. The limited availability of animals, as well as of suitable implements and spare parts, restricts wider application.

Lack of animal health services is yet another problem in some areas. Insufficient awareness, lack of know-how and poor availability of suitable chemicals and drugs, especially among the small marginal farmers, can cause heavy economic losses. (One farmer in Zambia reported losing 20 of his herd of 22 cattle within four years; this was not exceptional.) However, large-scale commercial farmers demonstrate that health risks can be minimised through proper management.

Donor interventions can themselves impose constraints on the transfer of animal traction technology. Examples were cited where donors supplying large numbers of implements have forced local production companies to cease business.

Future Needs

Local

When investing in animal traction technology, farmers expect to improve their living standards through increased agricultural production and increased profitability. Other desirable effects, from the farmers' viewpoint, include reduced drudgery, improved productivity and improved timeliness.

The farmers' principal needs are good prices for their produce and access to essential services. These include marketing, credit and veterinary services as well as a reliable supply of spares, equipment, information and infrastructural facilities such as roads and communications.

Special mention was made of the need to help farmers to articulate their needs to partners, government institutions and development organisations. This will be particularly important in the coming years, in view of expected future financial constraints throughout the region in the public sector(s). There will be an increased need to use limited resources more effectively. Structural adjustment programmes will have consequences for farmers through cuts in subsidies, extension and veterinary services.

National

In order to facilitate the use of animal traction technologies, there is a need to create a suitable economic climate that favours investment in animal traction. In addition, the following improvements are needed at national level.

The national policy environment should encourage the use and adoption of animal traction. National "pressure groups" might be formed for this purpose. Policies should stimulate the production of equipment based on locally available resources.

There is a need to improve coordination of animal traction activities and programmes at a national level. There should be more exchange of know-how, more learning from regional experience and greater coordination among the various donor organisations.

National planners need to be encouraged to formulate realistic and sustainable goals for animal traction and to identify the resources required to achieve these goals. Requests for external inputs can often be forwarded to donors who appreciate and value such local participation.

Regional

Information exchange is seen as a practicable and highly desirable regional need. Effective information exchange and successful coordination will, to a large extent, depend on the formation of national networks to facilitate networking within and between the member countries.

The regional ATNESA network must facilitate collaboration, linkages and the exchange of know-how. ATNESA should become a highly influential organisation in order to support and strengthen national networks and achieve relevant and consistent animal traction policies throughout the region. The workshop decided, as an immediate activity, to create a data bank of animal traction resource persons, institutions, manufacturers and others involved in animal traction in eastern and southern Africa.

Recommendations

The following recommendations summarise the output of the workshop sub-theme discussion groups. They reflect the priorities identified by the groups, the plenary reaction to their presentations and their subsequent endorsement by the workshop.

Management

○ Disease is a fundamental issue in the region, (although not specific to animal traction) and needs to receive prime attention

○ Feeding is not perceived as a major problem. However, most draft animals would increase power output if they were better fed. Work on grazing systems needs to be intensified and introduced to improve fodder quality and controlled grazing

○ Awareness needs to be created of the valuable role donkeys can play in animal traction

○ Cows are increasingly used for work. This is an important and entirely farmer-led process, of which researchers and extension workers seem largely unaware.

Profitability

○ Profitability is an overriding issue affecting all other factors relating to animal traction. Animal traction will be sustainable only if it is profitable to all concerned (including equipment manufacturers and parts suppliers).

Tillage

○ Tillage systems are not a major constraint: a wide range of implements is available which achieve acceptable results. Design work should therefore not focus on new developments but on the adaptation of existing solutions to suit local agronomic conditions and manufacturing capabilities

○ Animal-drawn weeding provides an important scope for expansion. Not all farmers who plow with animals also use animals for weeding.

Supply and distribution

○ There are severe marketing constraints as a result of farmers' lack of purchasing power

○ The supply and distribution systems for animal traction technology and the marketing infrastructure in eastern and southern Africa need improvement

○ More local blacksmiths need to be trained in the production of tools and implements

○ The supply of raw materials to manufacturers and blacksmiths needs to be improved

○ Emerging private industries need to be protected from international trade distortions

○ Governments need to ensure that donor activities (including supply of equipment through projects) strengthen, rather than weaken, local industries and distribution systems.

Gender

○ Gender implications in animal traction technology have in the past been neglected. They should be considered sensitively in all future programmes and methodologies

○ More information on gender issues is required, especially on aspects of specifically addressing women and on how to make animal traction technology more accessible to them.

Transfer of technology

○ There should be no "blind" transfer of technologies. More information needs to be shared on systematic technology transfer approaches and the Hows and Whys of introducing animal power

○ As most technology is transferred informally between generations, families and migrants, more attention should be paid to this

○ In areas of widespread use of animal traction, formal extension services appear to have minimal effect. Formal extension agents are more effective during the introductory phase and should therefore focus their limited resources in these areas

○ Extension services, research institutions and manufacturers of equipment need to pay more attention to farmers' needs and constraints in order to be more effective

○ Extension agents should be trained in participatory methods and the farming systems research/extension approach.

Transport

○ Animal transport is a fundamental and major aspect of animal traction, bringing cash returns and social and agricultural benefits

○ Animal-based transport offers much potential for further expansion and development

○ There is a mutually beneficial synergy between animal transport and agriculture that needs to be emphasised and encouraged

○ Animal-based transport in the region has primarily been a farmer-led activity, using carts based on scrap axles

○ Governments and donor-supported projects have been largely unsuccessful in promoting "appropriate technology" carts using wooden wheels and bearings. In contrast, expansion of animal-based transport has occurred when carts using machined bearings and pneumatic tyres have been promoted

○ Future needs should focus on the dissemination of known and proven technologies rather then on "reinventing the wheel"

○ The artisanal sector needs support to overcome the chronic shortage of wheels and axles.

Networking priorities

Networking appears to be a most efficient and cost-effective means of supporting animal traction in eastern and southern Africa. The following issues have been identified as priorities for immediate attention. ATNESA should:

○ influence the national and regional policy environment to encourage the enhanced use of animal traction

○ encourage exchange of information and proven technologies

○ facilitate personal contacts and animate professionals to organise regional group meetings and discussions on common problems and topics of interest and benefit to the region

○ facilitate regional collaboration and coordination of national and regional activities, and those supported by donor agencies

○ provide encouragement and appropriate support to national networks.

The above recommendations and priorities resulted, at the end of the workshop, in the definition of the following activities. Some will be dealt with in informal working groups and others will be coordinated by national network representatives.

○ Formation of national networks

○ Preparation of a regional directory of animal power organisations, individuals and resources

○ Formation of formal or informal groups to further consider policy, transport and gender issues and the need for pressure groups.

Based on the positive experience of the WAATN, ATNESA too will be rooted in existing national administrative structures and not have a permanent secretariat. It will therefore be less dependent on outside support.

This strong local involvement and participatory approach is expected to enable ATNESA to mobilise existing local know-how and resources, be need oriented and produce sustainable results.

Networking introductions, announcements and resources

(For the addresses of these organisations, please refer to the address list on pages 61–64)

AGROTEC (Agricultural Operations Technology for Small Holders in East and Southern Africa) is a regional programme of UNDP (United Nations Development Programme). Based in Zimbabwe, it is funded by the Swedish International Development Authority (SIDA) and operates in Lesotho, Kenya, Tanzania, Uganda, Zambia and Zimbabwe. It is funding small agricultural engineering research programmes in the six countries, which are monitored by regional reference groups. It holds training workshops and will help establish a regional MSc course. One of its areas of interest is animal traction. It was at an AGROTEC workshop in Harare that ATNESA was launched. It produces a newsletter and will publish manuals relating to animal-drawn implements and transport. Publications include:

Kalisky J (ed), 1990. *Proceedings of a regional course on planning an integrated animal draught programme, held Harare, Zimbabwe from 5–13 November 1990.* Bulletin No 2. AGROTEC (Agricultural Operations Technology for Small Holders in East and Southern Africa), Harare, Zimbabwe. 235p.

The *Centre for Tropical Veterinary Medicine (CTVM)* of the University of Edinburgh is carrying out research on the nutritional and physiological implications of draft work, using cattle, buffaloes, horses and donkeys. Equipment had been developed that allows the measurement and logging of many factors associated with animal work, including force, distance travelled, animal temperature and oxygen consumption. At CTVM, this equipment can be used with treadmills and climate chambers. Portable versions of the equipment have been used in the field in several countries. Staff of CTVM have published many scientific papers relating to animal power. CTVM publishes *Draught Animal News* twice a year and welcomes contributions from ATNESA members. CTVM offers MSc degrees in Tropical Animal Production and cooperates with Larenstein International Agricultural College in Deventer, The Netherlands, in the holding of more practical courses on animal traction. In 1990, CTVM hosted an international colloquium on working equines in tropical agriculture, the proceedings of which were published as:

Fielding D and Pearson R A (eds), 1991. *Donkeys, mules and horses in tropical agricultural development.* Centre for Tropical Veterinary Medicine, University of Edinburgh, Edinburgh, UK. 336p.

The *Commonwealth Secretariat* is aware that animal traction is important in Commonwealth countries. For some time, the Agriculture and Rural Development Division has been concerned with the closely related issues of appropriate technology and agricultural mechanisation. It organised meetings which aim to establish a Network for Agricultural Mechanisation in Africa (NAMA), and it hopes there will be scope for valuable collaboration between NAMA and ATNESA. Publications include:

Commonwealth Secretariat, 1991. *Agricultural mechanization in Commonwealth Africa.* Report of a workshop held 13–17 August 1990, Zaria, Nigeria. Commonwealth Secretariat, London, UK. 80p.

FAO, the Food and Agriculture Organization of the United Nations, has for many years been supporting projects and initiatives in the region concerned with animal traction. Over the years, FAO has produced a variety of animal traction publications, and it is presently preparing an animal traction training manual in consultation with an FAO-supported project in Malawi.

The *Farming Systems Programme* is a regional programme, based in Botswana, that is supported by FAO and SIDA. While it does not specialise in animal traction, draft animals are important in many farming systems in the region. It would like to see the formation of a regional farming systems network which could collaborate with ATNESA in activities and topics of mutual interest.

GTZ (Deutsche Gesellschaft für Technische Zusammenarbeit) is financing several projects in Africa undertaking research and development on animal traction. The *German Appropriate Technology Exchange (GATE)* is a specialised division of GTZ that is supporting research and development on animal powered gears, mills and water-lifting devices in several countries, including Zambia (see paper by H Dreschel and C Löffler, p 440). GATE publishes the journal *GATE: Questions, Answers, Information* which sometimes includes articles relating to animal traction. GATE normally supplies its journal and publications free-of-charge to people working in developing countries. Among the publications available are:

Boie W, 1989. *Introduction of animal-powered cereal mills.* Vieweg for German Appropriate Technology Exchange, GTZ, Eschborn, Germany. 70p.

Schmitz H, Sommer M and Walter S, 1991. *Animal traction in rainfed agriculture in Africa and South America.* Vieweg for German Appropriate Technology Exchange, GTZ, Eschborn, Germany. 311p.

Starkey P H, 1988. *Animal traction directory: Africa.* Vieweg for German Appropriate Technology Exchange, GTZ, Eschborn, Germany. 151p.

Starkey P H, 1988. *Perfected yet rejected: animal-drawn wheeled toolcarriers*. Vieweg for German Appropriate Technology Exchange, GTZ, Eschborn, Germany. 161p.

Starkey P H, 1989. *Harnessing and implements for animal traction*. Vieweg for German Appropriate Technology Exchange, GTZ, Eschborn, Germany. 245p.

The *International Development Research Centre (IDRC)* has funded several animal traction research and development projects in Africa and has supported animal traction and farming systems networking activities in West Africa. It maintains an interest in these fields and supported several participants at this workshop. Although the head office of IDRC is in Canada, correspondence relating to eastern and southern Africa should be addressed to the IDRC regional office in Nairobi.

The *International Livestock Centre for Africa (ILCA)* has its headquarters in Ethiopia. Animal traction has been one of its "research thrusts". ILCA received a grant from the European Community to assist networking activities relating to animal traction research in sub-Saharan Africa, and this has concentrated on activities in West Africa, including the development of animal traction research protocols and support to the 1990 workshop of the West Africa Animal Traction Network. In the highlands of Ethiopia, ILCA is undertaking research on the effect of work on the fertility and milk production of crossbred cows (see paper by E Zerbini et al, p. 130) and the use of simple animal-drawn implements in vertisols (see paper by A Astatke and M Mohammed-Saleem, p. 301). ILCA publishes a newsletter (available free-of-charge) and the journal *African Livestock Research*. ILCA has published an annotated bibliography on animal traction containing 1350 entries in the form of a book and a searchable computer database. ILCA publications, which are normally available free-of-charge to scientists in Africa, include:

Starkey P H, Sirak Teklu and Goe M R, 1990. *Animal traction: an annotated bibliographic database*. International Livestock Centre for Africa (ILCA), Addis Ababa, Ethiopia. 203p

Lawrence P R, Lawrence K, Dijkman J T and Starkey P H (eds), 1993. *Research for development of animal traction in West Africa*. Proceedings of fourth workshop of West Africa Animal Traction Network held 9–13 July, 1990, Kano, Nigeria. International Livestock Centre for Africa (ILCA), Addis Ababa, Ethiopia. 322p.

IMAG-DLO is an agricultural engineering institute based in The Netherlands. It has provided technical support to several animal traction programmes in Africa, notably in Mali and Zambia. Its publications include:

Starkey P H, Dibbits H J and Mwenya E, 1991. *Animal traction in Zambia: status, progress and trends*. Ministry of Agriculture, Lusaka, Zambia and IMAG-DLO, Wageningen, The Netherlands. 105p.

Dibbits H J and Mwenya E, 1993. *Animal traction survey in Zambia*. Ministry of Agriculture, Lusaka, Zambia and IMAG-DLO, Wageningen, The Netherlands. 105p.

The *Intermediate Technology Development Group (ITDG)* is a British NGO involved with "appropriate technology". Over the years, emphasis has moved away from the mere development of hardware prototypes to socially sensitive, participatory development initiatives, including animal traction projects in Sudan and Kenya (reported here by S Croxton, p. 280). Publications include the quarterly journal *Appropriate Technology*.

IT Transport is a British consultancy organisation affiliated to ITDG. It has carried out consultancies relating to animal-powered transport for many different development agencies. It helps to coordinate the International Forum for Rural Transport and Development which publishes a newsletter. Some work of its staff has been published in books by IT Publications, including:

Barwell I and Hathway G, 1986. *The design and manufacture of animal-drawn carts*. Technical memorandum prepared for the International Labour Office (ILO) and UN Centre for Human Settlements (HABITAT). IT Publications, London, UK. 72p.

Larenstein International Agricultural College (LIAC), based at Deventer in The Netherlands, organises several courses relating to tropical agriculture. In cooperation with the University of Edinburgh it has organised courses specifically relating to draft animal power and harnessing techniques. LIAC would be interested in discussing possible collaboration with partner organisations in Africa. In 1990, in conjunction with CTVM, it organised a workshop on draft animal technology, the proceedings of which were published as:

den Hertog G and van Huis J A (eds). *The role of draught animal technology in rural development*. Proceedings of an international seminar held 2–12 April 1990, Edinburgh, Scotland. Pudoc Scientific Publishers, Wageningen, The Netherlands. 233p.

The French agricultural engineer *Jean Nolle*, who died in 1993, worked for many years developing animal-drawn implements for small farmers in Africa (see p. 247). Among his many designs were the *Houe Sine, Ariana, Tropicultor* and *Kanol* (on display). His experiences have been recorded in several videos (shown during the workshop) and in the book:

Nolle J, 1986. *Machines modernes à traction animale*. Harmattan, Paris, France. 478p.

Rumptstad is a commercial agricultural equipment manufacturer based in The Netherlands. Its Agricultural Tropical Machinery division has cooperated with local workshops producing animal traction implements in several countries, including Mali, Kenya and Zambia.

Silsoe College of Cranfield University is involved in teaching and research on agricultural engineering, including animal traction. Prof F Inns has retired, but continues to research on harnessing systems.

Silsoe Research Institute of UK has been working on animal traction topics for many years (formerly as AFRC-Engineering). It has collaborated with many organisations in Africa. Recent emphasis has been on instrumentation for measuring and logging the mechanical and physiological parameters associated with animal draft power. Staff members have published results from research studies in several scientific journals. Silsoe Research Institute will arrange an international workshop on a topic related to animal power in the region in 1993, and would welcome involvement of ATNESA members.

The *Swedish University of Agricultural Sciences (SUAS)* is based in Uppsala. It provides technical support services to several farming systems and agricultural engineering projects in the regional, including AGROTEC and the Farming Systems Project. Research at SUAS includes mechanical studies on animal-drawn plows. Publications include:

Gebresenbet G, 1992. *A literature search for agricultural system engineering education in developing countries: selected bibliography.* Report 160. Department of Agricultural Engineering, Swedish University of Agricultural Sciences, Uppsala, Sweden. 82p.

The *West Africa Animal Traction Network* (WAATN) organises animal traction workshops and information exchange in West Africa. Since 1986, it has invited people from eastern and southern Africa to participate in its workshops and is pleased that this influenced the decision to form ATNESA. It looks forward to close cooperation and collaboration with ATNESA. People working on animal traction in Africa can generally obtain the proceedings of its past workshops free-of-charge from the respective publishers listed here: *Animal power in farming systems* (1986 workshop) from GATE/GTZ; *Animal traction for agricultural development* (1988 workshop) from CTA; *Research for development of animal traction* (1990 workshop) from ILCA.

The *West African Farming Systems Research Network* (WAFSRN) organises workshops, produces a bulletin and journal and is developing databases and a documentation centre. Farming systems and animal traction networks have much in common and there is scope for joint activities. WAFSRN would welcome the formation of a farming systems network for eastern and southern Africa and the holding of an all-Africa farming systems workshop.

The *Technical Centre for Agricultural and Rural Cooperation (CTA)*, financed by the European Community under the Lomé Convention with ACP (Africa, Caribbean and Pacific) countries is based in The Netherlands and is actively involved in gathering and disseminating information relating to rural development in tropical Africa and elsewhere. Animal traction is an area of interest of CTA, which has co-sponsored several animal traction workshops in Africa, including this one. CTA has co-funded the publication of some French-language annotated bibliographies on animal traction and the proceedings of the 1988 WAATN workshop which are normally available free-of-charge from CTA.

Starkey P and Faye A (eds), 1990. *Animal traction for agricultural development.* Proceedings of workshop held 7–12 July 1988, Saly, Senegal. Technical Centre for Agriculture and Rural Cooperation (CTA), Ede-Wageningen, The Netherlands. 475p.

Marti A, Second C, Lhoste P et le Thiec G, 1988. *Traction animale et développement agricole des régions chaudes: bibliographie annotée.* No 1, Expériences et bilan. No 2, Les outils: fabrication, conduite et entretien. No 3, Les animaux. Centre technique de coopération agricole et rurale (CTA), Wageningen, The Netherlands et Centre d'Information et de Documentation en Agronomie des Régions Chaudes (CIDARC), Montpellier, France. 254p. 421p. 240p.

Tool is an NGO based in The Netherlands whose work includes the Farm Implements and Tools (FIT) Project with funding from ILO (see paper by H Helsloot p. 374). Publications include:

FIT, 1992. *Small-scale tools and implements for agriculture and food processing in sub-Saharan Africa: an annotated bibliography.* Farm Implements and Tools Programme (FIT), Tool, Amsterdam, The Netherlands with International Labour Organisation (ILO), Geneva, Switzerland. 72p.

The Regional *Tsetse and Trypanosomiasis Control Programme* is based in Zimbabwe. With support from the European Community, it is engaged in work in several countries including Malawi, Mozambique, Zambia and Zimbabwe. As animal power provision is an important function of cattle in the target countries, and draft work is affected by trypanosomiasis, the programme is interested in exchanging information and collaborating with animal traction programmes in the region (see paper by R Connor p. 155).

The United Nations Development Fund for Women *UNIFEM* is concerned with numerous aspects of women in development. In Zimbabwe, UNIFEM commissioned a study relating to women's access to animal power (see paper by J Doran p. 272). UNIFEM is to produce a source book covering rural transport issues, including sledges, carts and packing.

Staff of the *University of Hohenheim* in Germany have carried out several studies relating to animal traction in Niger and elsewhere. Research has included measurement of power of draft animals and the draft forces imposed by different implements. A simple donkey-drawn weeding implement has been developed (see paper by F Emhardt p. 210) and some animal-powered systems have been tested (see paper of K Dippon, p. 436).

The Development Technology Unit of the *University of Warwick* in UK has carried out research and development work on the use of animal power to drive stationary machinery, such as that used for water-lifting and crop processing. It has developed prototypes including a rope engine and a simple gear system. Research is also being undertaken on various bearings suitable for animal-drawn carts, and methods of testing and evaluating these. It is interested in testing and evaluating these technologies with partner organisations in Africa (see paper by C Oram, p. 428).

National programmes in Africa

In *Botswana* teams of oxen are widely used for cultivation, and animal traction has been assisted by several government-sponsored credit schemes (see paper by A Panin et al, p. 104). The *Botswana College of Agriculture* has staff from several African countries and people in various departments are interested in animal traction research, with topics including socioeconomic issues, mechanisation policies and donkeys (see paper by A Aganga and K Maphorisa, p. 146). The *Rural Industries Innovation Centre* at Kanye has been working on appropriate technologies for several years, and areas of interest include animal-powered pumps and gear systems and animal-drawn carts.

In *Ethiopia* most farmers employ oxen for plowing and pack donkeys are very widely used. The *Rural Technology Promotion Division* of the Ministry of Agriculture is working on implement and cart design and testing (see papers by Kebede Desta, p. 454 and Oumer Taha, p. 292). The Selam Vocational Training Centre in Addis Ababa is an NGO with an interest in developing local production of steel implements (see paper by H Zaugg, p. 244)

In *Kenya* animal traction research is being carried out at the Department of Agricultural Engineering of the *University of Nairobi* (see paper by L Oudman, p. 422). Staff of this department have been cooperating with the NGO *Christian Mission Aid* on regional and national animal traction networking initiatives, and a national workshop on draft animal technology is scheduled. The *Ministry of Agriculture* has been involved in the development and testing of animal traction implements and farming systems research (see papers by P Maina, p. 110, and J Kahumbura, p. 222). The Dutch firm *Rumptstad* is establishing a joint-venture company to manufacture animal traction implements in Nairobi. Other organisations interested in animal traction include *Egerton University*.

Animal traction is increasingly being used in *Malawi*, notably in the northern and central areas. For many years, staff of the *Chitezde Research Station* have been involved in the development and testing of animal-drawn implements (see paper by W Kumwenda and P de Roover, p. 340). FAO has been supporting the national *Animal Power Utilisation Project*, and activities have included training staff of local Agricultural Development Divisions. A simple wooden ox cart has been developed. The *Forestry Department* uses oxen for logging in several plantations (see paper by D Singa, p. 460). Several staff of Bunda College of the University of Malawi are interested in animal traction research (see paper by M Mwinjilo, p. 456).

In *Mozambique* the *Agro-Alfa* factory is manufacturing animal-drawn equipment and is looking for export markets. Present implements are similar to *Safim* designs, but the company hopes for product development and diversification.

In *Tanzania* a national network has been formed to link the many organisations involved in animal traction, and a national animal traction workshop was held in 1991. The *Animal Traction Network Tanzania (ATNET)* receives support from the *Mbeya Oxenization Project* (MOP), a development programme in the south-west highlands that is actively involved in implement and cart production and testing and the analysis of gender, marketing and credit issues (see papers by K Marshall and M Sizya, p. 266, and J Jumbe, p. 256). The ATNET secretariat is based at *Sokoine University of Agriculture*, where animal traction is an area of particular concern of the Department of Agricultural Engineering (see papers by G Mgaya et al, p. 139, and A Luzigo et al, p. 136). The *Uyole Agricultural Centre* in Mbeya is a research and training institution that has been undertaking research on animal-drawn weeding technologies (see paper by E Kwiligwa et al, p. 182). Uyole has also has been cooperating with MOP and the Usangu Irrigation Project (see paper by M Lecca et al, p. 218). The Ministry of Agriculture has been responsible for a national extension programme involving oxen training centres (see papers by A Kayumbo, p.191–197). The Ministry of Industry has responsibility for the parastatal implement factories, notably *UFI*, and for *Camartec* (Centre for Agricultural Mechanisation and Rural Technology). Camartec is an appropriate technology organisation charged with developing and testing animal traction implements and carts (see paper by F Mujemula, p. 414). At the University of Dar es Salaam, the *Institute of Production Innovation* has been working on animal-drawn carts (see paper by J Wirth, p. 405), while the *Institute of Resource Assessment* has been studying socioeconomic aspects of animal power (see paper by H Sosovele, p. 318). Among the many area-specific development programmes with animal traction components are *Mifipro* and *Tanga* in the north-east and *Mbozi* in the south-west (see papers by A Galema, p. 321, R Fischer, p. 296, A Makwanda, p. 276, and G Mwakitwange, p. 328). Publications include:

Simalenga T E and Hatibu N (eds), 1992. *Proceedings of an animal traction workshop held 8-10 April 1991, Morogoro, Tanzania*. Mbeya Oxenization Project, Mbeya, Tanzania. 57p.

In *Togo*, *PROPTA* (Projet pour la Promotion de la Traction Animale) provides a national service to undertake and coordinate research, development, monitoring and evaluation work relating to animal traction. Topics of interest include the use of draft cows, harnessing single animals and animal power for tuber crops. PROPTA publishes *Force Animale*, a quarterly animal traction newsletter, in French.

In *Uganda* animal traction is being promoted by the *Ministry of Agriculture* and by several NGOs (see papers by A Akou, p. 331, J Omoding, p. 334, A Okuni, p. 468, and E Ojirot, p. 338). A dairy project supported by FAO has been promoting the use of draft animals and has produced a video (shown at the workshop). In recent years, animal traction implements have been imported, and have tended to be of poor quality. *Saimmco* in Soroti has recently started the local manufacture of implements.

In *Zambia*, the national *Draft Animal Power Coordination Programme* is based within the Agricultural Engineering Section of the Department of Agriculture (see paper by E Mwenya et al, p. 469). The *Draft Animal Power Research and Development Programme* based in Magoye has been engaged in the on-station and on-farm testing of animal-drawn carts, implements and tillage systems. It has published many test reports, and its work is mentioned in the papers by P Stevens (p. 168) and R Meijer (p. 369). The *Palabana Draft Animal Power Training Centre* conducts in-service training courses for extension workers, and is starting an outreach programme. It is developing training manuals and training videos (see papers by

M Bwalya, p. 350 and J de Graaf, p. 116). Several departments of the *University of Zambia* have an interest in animal power including *TDAU* which has been working on animal-drawn carts (see paper by H Vroom, p. 418). The parastatal company *Zaffico* is using oxen for logging operations (see paper by C Kalima, p. 445). Some large-scale commercial farmers use animal power (see paper by B Dankwerts, p. 108. The manufacturing firm *Lenco* has been collaborating with Rumptstad in producing a range of implements. The bearing company *SKF-Zambia* has designed and manufactured axles for ox carts. Within Zambia there are many area-specific programmes and projects with animal traction components, concerned with a variety of issues including implement and cart supply, credit, gender issues and animal health. Among those represented at the workshop were programmes in Copperbelt (see paper by A Mkandawire, p. 364), Luapula Province (see paper by S Lubumbe, p. 366), Northern Province (see paper by M Lombe et al, p. 284), North-Western Province (see papers by C Löffler, p. 354, and I Mukuka, p. 293) and Western Province (see papers by H Kamphuis, p. 360 and C Hocking, p. 288). The various projects and programmes in Zambia are very aware of the need to exchange information relating to animal traction and are keen to participate in networking activities in the region.

In *Zimbabwe*, animal traction is an integral part of most smallholder farming systems. The national agricultural extension service *Agritex* with technical cooperation from GTZ has developed an Agricultural Extension Training Centre *(AETC)* which holds courses on draft animal technology and blacksmithing. Agritex, with support from GTZ, is also investigating soil and water conservation on farms where draft animals are employed (see paper by J Hagmann, p. 198). At the *University of Harare* and *Makoholi Experimental Station* research is being carried out on the nutrition of draft animals, as described in papers by J Francis et al (p. 158) and V Prasad et al (p. 164). Animal traction has been an area interest of the *Farming Systems Research Unit* of the Ministry of Agriculture (see papers of S Chikura, p. 162 and p. 203). There is increasing interest in the use of donkeys for work in Zimbabwe (see papers of P Jones, p. 426, and R Mpande, p. 150). *Bulawayo Steel* is one of the Zimbabwean manufacturers of animal traction equipment. Publications of the AETC include:

Jones P A, 1991. *Training course manual on the use of donkeys in agriculture in Zimbabwe*. Agritex Institute of Agricultural Engineering, Harare, Zimbabwe. 81p.

Field visit observations

Plenary session rapporteurs: H Helsloot and F Kruit

Sixteen separate groups of five to seven participants visited different smallholder farmers. The farmers (at least two per group) differed in many respects, including gender, wealth, farm size, ownership of animals, experience of using draft animals, formal education or training and relationship with local extension services. Although the farming systems differed in several ways, all were within a two-hour drive of Lusaka, and so were not representative of all the provinces and agro-ecological zones in Zambia, let alone the whole ATNESA region. This limitation was acknowledged from the outset.

The groups had been asked to bear in mind the seven workshop themes when holding discussions with the farmers. In addition to noting the major problems and constraints to using animal traction in those farming systems, the groups tried to identify ways in which animal traction had been improved in recent years, or ways in which it could be improved. In their subsequent deliberations, the groups also reflected on whether their observations had relevance for other countries and whether there were any obvious implications for the network arising from the visits and discussions.

General

It was noted that the time spent with farmers was insufficient for the workshop groups to obtain a full understanding of the unfamiliar farming systems, and to draw valid conclusions. Nevertheless, it was agreed that, provided the field visits were viewed as a workshop participatory exercise and not a structured rapid rural appraisal survey, the group findings could be of value. Although some observations were specific to the individual farms or local farming systems, many of the identified constraints and findings were likely to have close parallels in other countries in the ATNESA region.

Economic and profitability issues

The groups noted that many constraints to the farming systems were of a general economic nature. Farm income was low and limited by poor marketing and payment systems. Farmers seldom had cash available for investment in technology or access to affordable credit. Inflation was high. Rural infrastructure was poor, and farmers could not depend on a timely supply of appropriate agricultural inputs or services. Farmers did not feel they were benefiting from government services or policies (recent political changes at a national level had not yet had an effect on farm economies). Most farmers claimed animal traction was profitable, but this was not always clearly apparent to the groups. Time and labour were often limiting factors. Some animals appeared underutilised.

Animal management issues

Animal health constraints were frequently mentioned, notably the recent problems with the tick-borne "corridor disease" (a form of *theileriosis*). Some of the farms visited were in areas where cattle ownership had not been common. In these areas, lack of knowledge of cattle husbandry and poor availability of cattle were cited as constraints. Veterinary services were generally unavailable in the villages or inadequate. Some groups noted that there was some farmer interest in the use of donkeys, although the zone visited was not one where donkeys are commonly seen.

Supply of implements and spares

Many farmers commented on the difficulties in obtaining equipment and spare parts. They were generally available only in the towns. Farmers were generally unaware of the existence of different types of plow, or of the use of weeders or ridgers. Much equipment was old (some more than 20 years old) and in need of maintenance and spare parts. Most plows had had their regulators removed. Blacksmith services were few, and blacksmiths complained about lack of raw materials. The groups who visited

Workshop participants question a farmer about his plow and availability of spares

Workshop participants discuss credit availablity and other issues with a farmer

blacksmiths felt these artisans would benefit from training and more equipment.

Animal-powered transport

Few farmers owned carts, and carts were generally difficult to obtain in the rural areas. Those carts that were owned were generally in need of maintenance and/or spare parts. Some appeared underutilised although transport appeared profitable. Most farmers expressed interest in cart ownership.

Transfer of technology

Most transfer of technology relating to animal traction had taken place through the family, neighbours and migrants. There were very few examples of knowledge or skills being obtained from the extension services (which were judged as rather irrelevant, unavailable or poor).

Tillage and weeding technology

Few farmers mentioned, or complained about, any inadequacies in their tillage systems. Some workshop participants, however, perceived possibilities for improvements. Few farmers mentioned animal-drawn weeding, although manual weed control was perceived as a problem. Animal-drawn weeders or ridgers were not generally available, or known.

Gender and age issues

Both male-headed and female-headed households were visited, and several conversations were held with wives of male farmers. It appeared that women generally had access to animal traction, but not necessarily control over the technology. Although plowing with draft animals was mainly a male domain, women generally claimed to be able to plow and some women assisted with or undertook animal traction operations. Children were extremely important in animal traction operations. Often they were the main operators of draft animal technology.

Recent improvements

Most groups were unable to identify recent improvements in animal traction. The technology, animal management and operational systems seemed similar to those used by the past generation. Some farmers had adopted animal traction in recent years, but the technology itself (transferred from other farmers) was not new. Some groups reported that farmers used cows for work, something that had never been recommended by the extension services.

Need for improvements

The groups felt that animal traction systems could best be improved by:

- improved supply of implements, spares and carts
- better repair facilities for implements
- availability of veterinary services and disease control methods
- some supplementary feeding of animals
- farmer-training in animal traction technologies
- different extension methodologies.

Implications for ATNESA

Most of the farm-level problems and recommendations were country-specific. ATNESA, as a regional organisation, should work with and through local bodies in order to influence those government policies that might assist the development of animal traction. For example, research and extension services should develop more participatory, gender-sensitive, farming-systems approaches. More attention should be given to promotion of self-help, traditional or private sector solutions to existing problems, including the supply and distribution of equipment.

ATNESA should be an accessible resource for those involved in animal traction research, development and extension. It should facilitate curriculum development and the training of extension workers. It should promote national-level networking, which should include farmers and field-based extension workers.

Some workshop participants have an opportunity to weed with draft animals at Magoye

Gender and animal traction technology

Group leader: K Marshall. Rapporteur: L Sylwander

The problem

Technological changes, such as the introduction of animal traction, affect women and men differently. Improved technologies are usually adopted and used by men according to the traditional gender-specific division of work. In most cases women have not benefited directly from the adoption of animal draft power because they have not had control of, or access to, draft animals.

Projects and programmes related to animal traction have often neglected the gender aspect and no special attention has been given to women in either the planning or the implementation stage.

Targets

An overall target of animal traction development work should be to ensure that women benefit from the use of draft animals. This should be a minimum condition for all programmes.

The primary target should be to provide women with access to draft animals. Access can be both indirect and direct. *Indirect access* to draft animals can be when draft animals benefit women when they are used for women's tasks (eg, transporting water), but the animals are not necessarily worked by the women themselves. *Direct access* to draft animals implies that women are the users of the technology and have the skills and knowledge to handle the draft animals and implements.

A long-term target should be to make it possible for women to have *control* of draft animals by owning animals and implements and having decision-making power over the technology. In the socio-cultural and economic setting of most African communities this could be a difficult aim to accomplish and might meet much cultural resistance instead of benefiting women.

The discussion group felt that women's indirect and direct access to (rather than control of) animal draft power is probably a more feasible target, at present, for development programmes and research projects in eastern and southern Africa.

Constraints

The group identified specific constraints for women in obtaining access to animal draft power.

Lack of time

Time is a scarce resource for women, especially for women in female-headed households. This might constrain women from learning and being trained in the use of animal draft power.

Recommendation

An understanding of women's time allocation for different productive and reproductive (domestic) tasks should be developed in order to design projects according to women's needs and preferences.

Lack of self-confidence of women

Lack of self-confidence hampers women from asserting their needs and wants. Women can gain self-confidence by being involved and participating in development activities.

Recommendations

Development programmes should endeavour to:

o provide training for women according to their needs and wants
o involve women in all aspects of planning and decision making
o develop special women's groups where women can talk and work together
o provide women with skills in related fields.

Legal and credit constraints

Women often lack the legal and/or traditional right to own resources such as land and cattle. This affects women's prospects for acquiring loans because they lack suitable collateral property.

Recommendations

Development programmes should endeavour to:

o develop credit schemes for women that are not tied to specific activities. Women should determine when credit is due
o develop credit schemes that make credit available to both individuals and groups
o encourage saving schemes, both formal (eg, through banks or credit institutions) and informal (eg, through community groups)
o influence credit institutions to adjust their policies to take account of the needs and constraints of small-scale farmers and especially those of women.

Cultural constraints

Culture can in some cases deny women access to animal traction technology. Cultural constraints are often overlooked and not dealt with in the planning and implementation of projects and programmes. However, farming communities are not stagnant and will change and adopt new technologies if it is felt that they are profitable and beneficial to the society.

Recommendations

Research, training, development and extension organisations and programmes should endeavour to:

○ train planners and implementers to consider and recognise cultural aspects that can influence technology transfer and development

○ sensitise the whole community to the particular cultural practices that might constrain women's access to animal draft power.

Approaches and strategies

Constraints women face in animal traction cannot be viewed in isolation from other aspects of their lives. Specific strategies have been suggested to overcome constraints and a more holistic approach to solving women's constraints in acquiring access to and/or control of draft animals was proposed by the discussion group.

Recommendations

Further studies and the development of strategies and methodologies for women's participation in animal traction adoption should focus on:

○ understanding the position, status and roles of women and men in the particular farming system and community

○ gender interaction analysis of productive and reproductive (domestic) tasks

○ analysis of gender issues relating to the control of resources and access to resources

○ involvement of the whole farming family in the activities of projects and programmes

○ giving special attention to female-headed households in analysis, methodologies and implementation.

Research

Research programmes relating to animal traction have seldom considered or included socioeconomic and gender issues. Women seldom participate in current on-farm trials and research although they are very much involved in farm production.

Recommendations

Research organisations and programmes should:

○ encourage and facilitate socioeconomic and gender-sensitive research in animal traction

○ ensure end-user involvement in research and trials so that both female and male farmers participate.

Extension and training systems

There is a general lack of gender-sensitivity among planners, policy makers, project staff and extensionists. Most training and extension is designed for male farmers and carried out by male trainers or extensionists. Personnel are not appropriately trained and the training they receive is based on inadequate extension methods.

Recommendations

Training organisations and extension programmes should endeavour to:

○ provide gender-sensitivity training to extension staff and trainers

○ ensure that women have equal access to training and encourage their participation

○ develop extension methods that are more appropriate and address the whole farming family

○ recognise and make use of informal local diffusion of animal traction technology

○ influence policy makers and planners on gender issues.

Project strategies for gender sensitivity

Project surveys and designs should:

○ ensure that gender is considered whenever data collection is planned and implemented

○ ensure that women's needs will be identified and addressed

○ ensure the participation of all the community.

Project planning should:

○ ensure that planners are aware of the gender implications of the projects

○ ensure that gender-sensitivity training is conducted for all staff

○ ensure that women are involved in all stages of project planning, implementation and monitoring

○ ensure that budget allocation to involve women is adequate.

Project implementation should:

○ ensure that a gender perspective (ie, both a female and a male perspective) is considered in all activities, including monitoring and evaluation

○ ensure the active participation of women in project activities.

Tillage technology

Group leader: P Stevens. Rapporteur: F Emhardt

Review of tillage options

The tillage system was considered as the combination of different cultivation methods for land preparation over the whole farming season.

Plowing

Plowing has several advantages, notably:

o   weed control
o   soil loosening
o   increased infiltration
o   moisture conservation
o   incorporation of organic matter.

However, it also has disadvantages, notably:

o   power requirements are high
o   erosion may be accelerated
o   it is time-consuming
o   loss of soil and moisture is increased
o   soil structure is disturbed
o   plow pans may form
o   organic matter which is incorporated becomes unavailable as a mulch (a temporary advantage).

Direct hand planting

Planting by hand without primary cultivation has several advantages including:

o   little disturbance of the soil structure
o   few erosion problems
o   crop residues can remain on surface
o   no investment necessary.

However, it also has disadvantages, notably that:

o   it is labour intensive
o   much drudgery is involved
o   it is slow, which results in a long planting period
o   weeding is difficult
o   water infiltration is low.

Ranking of options

The group decided that the main tillage options were:

o   plowing
o   direct hand planting
o   ridging
o   tied-ridging
o   ripping
o   direct sowing by seeder
o   cultivation (tine tillage).

The group tried to assess the various options by giving them rough relative scores (good, medium and poor) for each of 12 criteria. These are summarised in Table 1. A simple (unweighted) overall score was obtained by considering all criteria

Table 1: Comparisons of some tillage options based on subjective scoring by discussion group members

Criteria for improvement	Plowing	Hand planting	Ridging	Tied-ridging	Ripping	Planter	Cultivation
Labour reduction	C	C	B	C	B	A	C
Weed control	A	C	A	A	C	C	B
Suited to available power	C	A	B *	B *	A	A	B
Environmental protection	C	A *	A	A	A *	A	C
Moisture conservation	B	C *	A	A	C *	C *	B
Low risk	B	A	C *	C *	A *	C	C
Simplicity	B	A	C	C	A	C	B
Flexibility	B	B	C	C	B	C	C
Yield stability	–	–	–	–	–	–	–
Sustainability	–	–	–	–	–	–	–
Suitable for soil and crop	–	–	–	–	–	–	–
Acceptability	–	–	–	–	–	–	–
Unweighted "score" [1]	18	15	16	17	14	18	20
Weighted "score" [2]	17	15	9	10	14	13	17

Key and notes

A = Relatively good; B = Medium; C = Relatively poor; – = Very site-specific

* *The discussion group was not unanimous in these judgements*

[1] *Raw score using all criteria and giving 1 for A, 2 for B, and 3 for C. The lower the score the better*

[2] *Weighted score giving 1 for A, 2 for B, and 3 for C for the first three listed criteria and 2 for A, 4 for B, and 6 for C for criteria four and five on list, with the other criteria ignored. The lower the score the better*

to have equal importance. Using this, ripping came out as most desirable, with plowing, cultivating and direct sowing appearing poor. A weighted score was then obtained, by giving high importance to labour reduction, weed control and suitability for the available power source. Higher scores were given to environmental protection and moisture conservation, and the scoring effectively penalised the systems that were poor in these aspects. In this case, ridging and tied-ridging came out as most suitable, and plowing again was among the least desirable options. The group stressed that its methodology and procedure had not been scientific or objective, but had helped the members of the group to reassess some of their widely-held conceptions.

Conclusions

There is no overall solution or general prescription. Tillage systems have to be adapted to local circumstances.

The group concluded there may be advantages in moving from conventional plowing to other systems.

Present research appears to be moving in the right direction.

Profitability of animal draft power

Group Leaders: J Ellis-Jones and A Panin

Aims

The group identified a need to ensure that participants had a sound understanding of the interrelationships of the factors affecting profitability and to identify priority areas where action should be taken to increase profitability.

Farmer objectives

Before analysing the farming environment, it was felt necessary to ascertain farmers' objectives. These are likely to include a combination of:

o   provision of subsistence needs
o   risk minimisation
o   profit maximisation
o   drudgery reduction.

Interrelationships with farming systems

A number of different sub-systems, each with their own costs and benefits, operate within the farming system. These interrelate with each other and changes in a single component of a sub-system can act adversely or positively on another.

At the centre of the farming system are three sub-systems relating to the draft animal, to the implement it pulls and to the operator. The costs and benefits and other factors affecting profitability are as follows:

Draft animal system

Costs	Benefits
Acquisition	Power
Nutrition	Meat
Health	Milk
Training	Manure
Shelter	Social/cultural

Implement system

Costs	Benefits
Acquisition	Tillage etc
Maintenance	Transport
The operator	

Operator system

Labour productivity
Health
Nutrition
Training
Gender issues

These three sub-systems operate within the total **farming system** where other factors come into play. Of greatest significance is the cropping system. Associated with this, various soil and water conserving technologies can be very important in the medium and long term. There are many input–output relationships which contribute to costs and benefits including:

Crop system

Costs	Benefits
Seed	Crop yields
Fertiliser	Crop residues
Chemicals	
Hired labour	

Household economy system

The needs of the household for firewood, water, housing, food, health and education further impact on the farming system.

National policy and infrastructure

Both the household economy and the farming system are affected by national policies and institutional framework. The major components are:

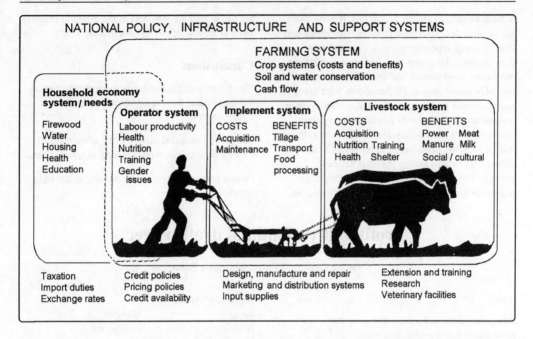

Figure 1: Farm systems model relating to the profitability of draft animal power adoption and use

Fiscal policy
o   taxation
o   import duties
o   exchange rates
o   credit policies

Infrastructure and support systems
o   implement design, manufacture and repair
o   marketing
o   input supplies
o   distribution systems
o   credit availability
o   extension and training
o   research
o   veterinary facilities

A model demonstrating the interrelationships of these factors was drawn up and illustrates the complexity of the system (Figure 1).

Financial and economic appraisal of the whole or parts of the system can be undertaken using a variety of different methods, including gross-margin analysis, partial budgets, whole farm analysis to determine profits and cash flows and detailed cost-benefit analysis.

Priority areas for further consideration

Areas of particular concern were identified within each of the various systems or sub-systems that should be given priority attention in order to make use of draft animals more profitable. These include:

Animal system
o   animal availability
o   animal health

Implement system
o   high cost of implements
o   availability of parts and repair facilities

Operator system
o   training in draft animal technology

Farming system
o   integration of cash crops
o   tillage systems to promote soil and water conservation

National policy and institutional framework
o   fiscal policies
o   crop marketing systems
o   access to credit
o   availability of raw materials
o   extension and training
o   research

Recommendation

It is recommended that ATNESA gives attention to these identified priority areas and consider them in detail within small, focused workshops.

Improving animal management

Group leader: A Pearson. Rapporteur: A Aganga

Introduction

Eleven people from eight countries discussed ways to improve the management and husbandry of draft animals. The wide-ranging discussions drew on experiences from the different countries and the information obtained from Zambian farmers and extension workers during the field visits. The following recommendations were put forward during group discussions and the subsequent plenary session. The points are **not** listed in order of priority.

Recommendations

General

° animals should have adequate quality and quantity of feed available
° they should have easy access to water
° there should be appropriate strategies to control the relevant diseases in the ATNESA area
° indigenous breeds tend to be well-adapted and their use should be encouraged
° animals should be treated humanely
° in areas where farmers work cows there is a particular need to monitor animal productivity and welfare.

District level

Where appropriate, efforts should be made to:

° improve farmer knowledge of appropriate management technologies by strengthening the extension service and encouraging self help and greater farmer responsibility
° increase the emphasis on animal husbandry in the extension services
° encourage the establishment of breeding herds in areas where supply is a problem
° improve the availability of veterinary drugs at village level.

Farm level

Where appropriate, efforts should be made to:

° encourage better use of crop residues, tree fodder and industrial byproducts to complement grazing to ensure a more reliable supply of animal feeds
° improve availability of water on the farm for the animals
° learn fodder conservation techniques, storage of residues and alley cropping

° encourage farmers to practise simple management/husbandry techniques for disease prevention
° encourage better kraal construction and management
° increase awareness of the value and role of donkeys.

Points of emphasis

Disease control is a fundamental problem associated with ownership of animals in general, not just draft animals and needs to be treated as such.

Simple, affordable animal husbandry practices that do not require the use of chemicals should be promoted to ensure health and help prevent diseases, particularly for farmers who keep small numbers of animals and can give them close individual attention.

Feed supply and availability are not perceived to be a problem by many of the Zambian farmers. However, most of the draft animals would benefit from supplementary feeding if farmers could provide it.

In the present economic climate, some commercial farmers in the ATNESA region are finding animal power a more attractive option than tractor power for some farm tasks. These people are likely to have more financial scope to practise improvements in animal management than many of the smallholder farmers. This sector should not be forgotten in considering "improved animal management".

Farmers in the ATNESA region are increasingly using cows for work. In Zambia, at least, this appears to be very much a farmer-led innovation. Many extension workers appeared to be unaware of the extent of use of draft cows in their areas. There is a fairly urgent need to look more closely at the role of working cows in the region. The implications of using cows for work in terms of productivity, lactation, reproduction and feeding in the region should also be investigated.

Donkeys are considered to be a relatively untapped source of animal power in the region, cheaper than oxen. It was thought that their use should increase. Where donkeys are being used in land cultivation and transport there is an urgent need to discourage the use of yokes and promote appropriate harnessing, more suited to the conformation of the donkey. This is not only an issue of welfare but will enable donkeys to work more effectively.

Improving animal-based transport

Group leader: M Anderson. Rapporteur: F Mujemula

Introduction

Participants in the group represented a wide range of disciplines, from engineers who wanted to discuss technical problems, to socioeconomists who wanted to focus more on farmer perceptions and the process of social change. The outcome was an attempt to integrate these two approaches, which generated a valuable debate on both technical and socio-economic issues relating to transport.

The size and enthusiasm of the group underlined the view that animal-based transport is seen as playing a very important role in farming systems. There was consensus that animal transport can reduce the time and effort required to move goods at farm and village level. The use of oxen, donkeys, horses or camels for transport purposes can be almost more significant than tillage in terms of the extent of animal use throughout the year, and it can bring economic as well as social benefits.

Farming households and transport

The group agreed that the perspective of the farming households should be paramount in assessing how animal-based transport can be improved. From a farming household's viewpoint, animal-based transport technology should be:

○ convenient and efficient

○ readily available and affordable

○ reliable (risk is not high)

○ based on a technology which is well-known and understood, so that households can maintain and, if appropriate, produce it themselves

○ acceptable to household members in terms of status and cultural image

○ acceptable in terms of impact on the rest of the farming system, including animal health and feeding requirements

○ accessible to, and open to control by, the household and by individual household members, for subsistence and agricultural uses

○ developed and introduced through processes involving the whole farming household.

The group then discussed how the main types of animal-based transport relate to these farmer-centred objectives and examined how transport technology could be improved to meet these objectives.

Sledges

Farmer viewpoint

Sledges are widely used by ox-owning farmers to move moderate loads over short distances. The technology involved is simple so farmers can readily make their own sledge at minimal cash cost. Sledges therefore have the advantages of being affordable, available, well-known, understood and directly controlled by the farming household. Disadvantages are that they are difficult for oxen to pull and are believed to cause some erosion of paths and tracks (eg, at commonly-used road crossings). These erosion effects have caused sledges to be banned in Zimbabwe since before independence, but sledges still play an important role in Zambia, Tanzania and other countries.

Recommendations

○ Banning sledges seems inappropriate while carts remain inaccessible to many poor farmers.

○ No policy decision on sledges should be taken before weighing the economic costs and benefits to users and the community at large and before examining carefully whether erosion is in fact a problem and whether it can be alleviated in any way.

○ Research could be undertaken to improve sledge design. This is regarded as a fairly low priority and should not involve any recommendations which put sledge ownership or production beyond the reach of poor farmers.

Pack animals

Farmer viewpoint

Even where animal traction is not being used for tillage, the use of donkeys (and in parts of Africa horses, mules and camels) as pack animals can play an important role in meeting rural transport needs. In Botswana and other parts of southern Africa, donkeys are playing an increasingly important role in assisting women with agricultural and subsistence transport tasks. The technology of donkey packs and harnessing is relatively simple, generally requiring only local materials such as leather and wood, and the feed requirements of donkeys are much less than those of oxen. However, donkeys are new to many parts of southern and eastern Africa, so many farmers lack the knowledge and understanding required to train, harness and care for them.

Recommendations
- Planners, policy makers and NGOs should share and disseminate information on donkey use, care and harnessing, including guidelines for load-carrying limits.
- Farmers' access to information about donkeys should be improved, through extension services and projects.
- Particular care should be given to animal health and disease when introducing donkeys to new areas.

Animal carts

Farmer viewpoint

Increased cart ownership among animal traction farmers is a high priority, because carts are generally by far the most efficient and convenient type of animal-based transport for moving larger loads. However, carts are expensive and difficult to obtain relative to other animal-based means of transport. Hire markets can play an important role in enabling poorer households to use carts, but the hiring household obviously has less control over the timing and extent of cart use. Women's access to carts is limited in many parts of Africa, as the carts are often controlled by men in the household. However, young men and boys have been observed to use carts for firewood and water collection, so the cart can effectively transfer transport responsibilities away from women. It is less common for a cart to be hired specifically for subsistence purposes (wood and water) than for cash-related activities such as harvesting or marketing.

Cart wheel and axle components are relatively complex to make, often requiring use of steel and other imported materials. This means that farming households can rarely undertake the production and repair of carts themselves and are reliant on the availability of supporting services. The group considered different options for cart design from the perspective of farming households, focusing on the two most problematic cart components—wheels and bearings. Other aspects of cart design (brakes, suspension and body design) were identified but could not be discussed due to lack of time.

Improvement of wheels

The group discussed three main options: pneumatic, steel and wooden wheels.

Pneumatic wheels are generally preferred by farmers except in areas where punctures pose a major problem. Although they are difficult to produce locally and are very difficult to obtain in rural areas, they offer high performance on rough surfaces and appear to have good status value. High priorities for improvement are to:

- improve the supply of second-hand pneumatic rims by commercial manufacturers and importers
- improve the supply of reconditioned tyres, particularly radial tyres with inner steel mesh
- develop and field-test low-cost technology for decentralised production of pneumatic rims
- develop and field-test technology for puncture prevention
- encourage the development of puncture repair workshops
- improve the distribution of materials and components for pneumatic wheels to rural workshops.

Steel wheels are preferred by some farmers, particularly where punctures are very frequent (eg, in areas with many thorns) or where repairs are difficult (ie, in more remote areas). They can be produced relatively easily from basic raw materials by metal workshops. The main technical problem is weld failures caused by impact loads on rough roads. Priority areas for improvement are to:

- encourage the development of blacksmith workshops that have welding equipment
- develop and field-test simple suspension systems to reduce impact loading (eg, rubber cushioning).

Most attempts in Africa to cushion impact by nailing or otherwise attaching solid rubber around a steel wheel have not been successful. However, channel-section steel has been successfully used on many Asian carts to hold a strip of rubber around a solid wheel.

Wooden wheels have been developed by a large number of projects, which have attempted to make simple wheels from locally-available materials. Despite the apparent attraction of this approach, wooden wheels have not been adopted on any significant scale in Africa, except in areas such as Madagascar which have a long tradition of carpentry and wheel-making. The reasons for this failure appear to be the "low-tech" image and low status of wooden wheels and the difficulty of making strong and durable wheels, which require skilled carpenters and good timber. Wooden wheels are not viewed as an acceptable option for carts in most parts of Africa.

Improvement of hubs and bearings

Two options for hubs and bearings were discussed; hubs with rolling contact bearings or wooden bushes.

Hubs using roller or ball bearings have, like pneumatic wheels, proved the most popular system for animal-drawn cart axles in Africa. The bearings themselves have to be imported, and are consequently costly and often difficult to obtain in rural areas. Hubs using roller or ball bearings are highly durable and need very little maintenance, but if they fail, some bearing elements usually need to be replaced. This requires access to a skilled workshop and poses major problems because of the limited availability of imported bearings. Improvements which are high priority are to:

○ improve the supply and distribution of imported bearings, for hub repair and production

○ improve the supply and distribution of manufactured hubs using rolling contact bearings, from importers and centralised local producers

○ encourage the production and use of integrated hubs units, which can be removed and replaced by a relatively unskilled workshop (used hubs could then be reconditioned and resold by a central producer)

○ improve the standard of seals to keep dust out and hence reduce wear

○ develop and field-test low-tech roller bearings suitable for decentralised production.

Wooden bushes and other types of bush bearings are much easier to produce than roller bearings and can usually be made from locally available materials. Despite their low cost and ease of supply, wooden bearings have not proved popular with farmers. This appears to be because frequent lubrication is required; many farmers let their bearings dry out, with consequent increase in wear rates. Improvement of wooden bearings is of a moderate priority and should attempt to:

○ develop and field-test oil-soaked and self-greasing bearings (eg, spring-loaded grease applicators)

○ improve the supply and distribution of lubricants to rural areas

○ develop and field-test other bush bearing materials which are durable and locally available.

Policy issues

Networking on cart design

In terms of cart design, which was a major focus of debate within the group, there is a need for better sharing of information on experiences of different projects. These experiences can shed light on the ongoing debate between "low-tech/decentralised" and "high-tech/centralised" approaches, by revealing what has and has not worked in different circumstances, for different cart components. It was recommended that a mechanism be found through ATNESA to share the extensive field experience of different group members. The aim of this exercise would be to develop and publish guidelines for cart design, and provide an ongoing mechanism for sharing experience. The group participants agreed to communicate after the conference to pursue this suggestion.

Increasing access to carts

It was agreed that there is a need for increased recognition by policy makers of the profitability and importance of animal-based transport within many farming systems. This should be reflected in the improvement of supply and distribution systems for cart materials and components, in the provision of credit for cart purchase and the facilitation of group use for poorer farmers and for women who have restricted access to carts. Designs for donkey carts and harnesses should be more widely disseminated.

Beyond the ox cart

Policy initiatives on animal transport should not be restricted to carts. Policy makers should recognise that while sledges and pack animals have their own limitations, they may be more appropriate than carts in some farming systems, being cheaper, easier to obtain and often more accessible to women for time-consuming subsistence tasks.

Transfer of technology

Group leader: R Fischer. Rapporteur: P Jones

The group discussing technology transfer was large, and their deliberations were wide-ranging. They considered the different groups involved in technology transfer and their relationships to each other and their respective influences. They also consider the information available and the technologies.

Current technology transfer problems

Farmers do not receive sufficient information on alternative technologies to enable them to make rational choices themselves.

Smallholder farmers have little or no influence on animal traction research programmes or the decisions of implement manufacturers.

Farmers are often ignored, misunderstood and stereotyped by research and extension staff and by manufacturers. Sometimes farmers are even dismissed as conservative and ignorant.

Smallholder farmers have insufficient influence on authorities and information sources and they tend to be marginalised both politically and economically.

The existing formal agents of change (extension workers and researchers) may face a conflict of interests if they attempt to meet the needs of the farmers. They generally find it easier to be oriented towards their urban-based supervisors, on whom their future depends.

Recommendations

Research and extension should start with farmers' problems.

Research and extension should consider the whole farming system, not isolated elements.

Research and extension should be flexible, participatory, holistic and adaptive.

Farmers must take more responsibility for their extension requirements. They should be more assertive concerning their real needs and problems, perhaps though participation in pressure groups.

Extension workers need training in participatory methods and approaches. School, college and university curricula need to be made more relevant.

National policies need to be modified to facilitate these changes.

The supply and distribution of animal traction implements

Group leader: A Wanders. Rapporteur: E Sakala

Introduction

The group tried to gain an overview of the present situation in the five countries represented in the group (Kenya, Malawi, Tanzania, Uganda and Zambia). To provide a theoretical framework, use was made of the models presented in the keynote paper on the subject by A Wanders. Although the situation in each country is complex, the issues considered to be of greatest significance are summarised in Tables 1–3, which cover supply scenarios, distribution systems and key constraints.

As these tables were produced, it became clear that the situations in the various countries were very different, although there were some striking similarities. In order to discuss concrete examples of the problems and possible solutions, the group decided to concentrate on the situation in Zambia,

which had been highlighted during plenary sessions and the field visits. It was agreed that the general constraint was the non-availability and/or untimely distribution in the rural areas of a range of animal traction implements (and spares) adapted to local conditions. The group then highlighted the following associated constraints and possible solutions. Although they concern Zambia, many of the problems and possible solutions are likely to be relevant in other countries in the region.

Distribution constraints in Zambia

Constraints relating to demand by farmers

○   Poor profitability of food crop farming. Poor farm prices and marketing systems. Absence of credit. Late payment for produce.

○ Poor awareness by farmers of new or existing equipment options and techniques for tillage and weeding.

○ Weak position of farmers. Poor representation within supplying cooperative societies leading to top-down and arbitrary decisions relating to the type, origin, quality and price of equipment supplied to farmers.

Possible solutions and recommendations

○ Improve rural marketing and credit systems.

○ Increase and intensify on-farm implement trials and extension programmes using trained extension staff (supported by local development programmes and Magoye/Palabana outreach).

○ Strengthen the position of farmers through organisation of farmers' animal draft power groups to provide adequate feedback on actual needs and acceptability of the present supply.

○ Proper marketing and advertising of implements based on implement qualities and prices (with possible role for independent "seal of approval" following testing by Magoye/Palabana).

○ Regular update by Department of Agriculture of "profiles" of farmers' production systems with trends in use of (demand for) different animal traction implements. Dissemination of such information to suppliers and manufacturers to assist market forecasts.

Distribution-side constraints

○ Within governmental and parastatal sectors, there are financial crises and an inefficient top-down distribution system to rural areas and within rural areas.

○ For local development programmes in areas of animal traction introduction there are major problems of logistics and infrastructure.

○ There is a lack of sustainable credit at realistic rates.

○ The private sector does not have efficient retailer/dealer/agent networks in the rural areas and there are problems of costs, risks and logistics of setting up a new system of agents.

○ Assembly workshops do not exist in rural areas and transport costs for supplying such workshops would be very high.

○ Existing small rural workshops face constraints with capital and supply of raw materials.

Possible solutions and recommendations

○ Government agencies to implement a more effective and farmer-oriented distribution system with depots within the rural areas (this is in line with proposed government reforms under discussion).

○ Establish a distribution system with depots in areas of new introduction (with potential for private sector involvement)

○ Investigate feasibility of area development projects providing credit with non-monetary "in kind" or barter systems of repayment through local development programmes.

○ Establish a private sector marketing and distribution system in the main animal traction areas.

○ Development of manufacturers' marketing strategies and marketing investment, with investigation of possible systems for prefinancing rural stocks (eg, bank guarantees).

○ Manufacturers to take initiatives to establish basic, equipped rural workshops for local manufacture or assembly in combination with agents.

○ Investigate support for initial working capital for improving rural workshop capacity (eg, for producing or assembling ox carts) with reference to the recent programme of the Small Industries Development Organisation (SIDO).

○ Support for market research, market forecasts and feasibility studies.

○ Creation by government of favourable conditions for initiatives of the emerging private sector.

Blacksmiths

The present role of rural blacksmiths is poorly developed in both numbers and capacity and blacksmiths have poor access to spare parts and scrap materials

Possible solutions and recommendations

○ Provide blacksmith training relating to techniques and business management (by local development programmes and training centres).

○ Provide support to selected blacksmiths in provision of tools and equipment (by local development programmes).

○ Improve supply of scrap materials in rural areas

○ Establish and logistically assist effective links between blacksmiths and regional assembly workshops and spare-part outlets.

Table 1: Summary of implement supply scenarios in Zambia, Kenya, Uganda, Malawi and Tanzania

	Zambia	*Kenya*	*Uganda*	*Malawi*	*Tanzania*
Imports					
Proportion	75% imports	60% imports	75% imports	0% imports	50% imports
Equipment imported	Mainly Zimbabwe plows and some cultivators, ridgers and planters. Some imports from India, The Netherlands Italy, and Tanzania (cross-border)	Mainly plows from India, Korea and Tanzania	Indian plows (Cossul) and some ox carts		Plows, ridgers and cultivators from India and Zimbabwe
Centralised manufacture					
Monopoly situation	Until 1986, Northland plow monopoly plus small manufacturing of harrows and cultivators in Copperbelt		WACU–Acord monopoly in north and north-east	Agrimal Company	
Competing manufacturers	Since 1986, three main manufacturers: Lenco, Gameco and Northland		Saimmco, Peko and NGOs		UFI (main), Zana Za Kilimo, Mbeya and Camartec
Range of implements	Essentially plows with few ridgers, cultivators and harrows	Mainly plows, cultivators and spike harrows		Plows, ridgers, harrows and chains	Mainly plows
Ox cart manufacture	Presently only conventional carts or axle/bearing/tyre assemblies in small numbers by SKF, Lenco and T&M. Previous attempts with alternative designs failed (metal and solid rubber wheels)	No centralised ox cart manufacture.	Ox carts manufactured by Saimmco on order	Ox carts made by Petroleum Services and by Brown and Clapperton	Some ox carts produced by Camartec
Decentralised manufacture					
Manufacture in provinces	Non-existent at present, but local development projects have supported ox cart initiatives (small numbers only)	Non-existent	Private and NGOs	A few activities by Petroleum Services	Some rural craft workshops
Private-sector initiatives in provinces	Non-existent at present except ox carts made from scrap axle/bearings and wheels mainly in "line-of-rail" (scarce supply)	Ox carts from scrap axles by small workshops (scarce supply)	Peko and blacksmiths	Some ox carts	Mainly ox carts
Spare part provision					
Imported equipment	Negligible		Non-existent		15% of imports are spare parts
Local implements	Generally neglect of spares and poor standardisation. 40% of implements need repairs and spare parts	Neglected and poor quality	Non-existent	Available but poor distribution	Manufactured but poor distribution and standardisation
Blacksmiths					
Manufacturing	Poorly developed. Some cart production. Some implements made in Eastern Province			Limited	Poorly developed and neglected area
Repairs and spare parts	Limited as there are few blacksmiths and severe problems obtaining scrap and raw materials	Available but small market. Problems obtaining materials	Mainly in north and east but lack of training and raw materials	Mainly blacksmiths' own initiatives. Lack of facilities	Lack of market information and raw materials

Table 2: Summary of animal traction implement distribution scenarios in Zambia, Kenya, Uganda, Malawi and Tanzania

	Zambia	Kenya	Uganda	Malawi	Tanzania
Government and parastatal systems					
	Main distribution through cooperative unions and parastatal dealers (eg, Afe) based mainly on batch imports	Distribution by cooperatives and private companies	Distribution by cooperatives and projects	Parastatal distribution and credit provision suspended	Distribution mainly through cooperatives and parastatals
Present constraints	Financial crises and collapse of old centralised/top-down system. Distribution inside rural areas non-existent or untimely (depots exist but are poorly managed)	Target farmers have low purchasing power; high prices, notably for spares	Same constraints as cited for Zambia	Lack of materials at correct time Lack of distributor commitment	Top-down system inefficient. Rural depots ineffective
Local development programmes and projects					
	In areas of new introduction of animal traction local programmes with donor assistance have established depots and distribution systems with credit links (eg, Kabwe, Pongwe, Kaoma)	Production and local demonstrations by Rural Technology Centres	Acord (Nebbi) and Lutheran World Federation (Moyo, Karamoja)	Donor funding for training and extension and a revolving fund for veterinary products	Several donor-supported programmes and projects
Present constraints	Non-sustainable credit system, poor rural communications and infrastructure	Poor credit system	Poor credit systems; lack of funding for training	High interest rates for credit; poor credit monitoring	Poor infrastructure and no continuity
Private-sector distribution					
	Hardly exists in rural areas, except for some district hardware stores with small stocks of plows	Available in markets in some regions	Hardly exists	Available but not consistent	Few private dealers in rural areas
Present constraints	Lack of dealer or agent network in rural areas (initiatives required by manufacturers) No market studies or forecasts	Low demand due to low farmer income	Lack raw materials	Distributors reluctant to invest capital in slow-moving seasonal stocks	Prices set high Difficult logistics
	High costs and difficult logistics to establish a dealer or agent network		Difficult logistics	Needs more distributors	Lack market information
Assembly at workshops in the regions					
	There are no assembly workshops linked with or supported by central manufacturers	Non-existent	Non-existent	Manufacturer tried but failed	Past attempts by UFI, ZZK and Camartec
Present constraints	Lack of manufacturers' initiatives. Uncertain economic feasibility and logistics	Market not yet developed	Saimmco production too low at present	Manufacturer says system expensive	Logistics and infrastructure problems

Acronyms used in Tables 1–3

NGO	Non-governmental organisation	UFI	Ubungo Farm Implements
Saimmco	Soroti Agricultural Implement Machinery Manufacturing Company	WACU	West Acholi Cooperative Union Ltd
		ZZK	Zana Za Kilimo
SIDO	Small Industries Development Organisation		

Table 3: Some key constraints to animal traction implement supply systems in Zambia, Kenya, Uganda, Malawi and Tanzania

	Zambia	Kenya	Uganda	Malawi	Tanzania
Demand by farmers	Poor profitability of food crop farming. Poor farm prices and marketing systems. Absence of credit. Late payment for produce	Poor quality of implements so farmers reluctant to purchase	High price of donor-supplied equipment; poor marketing of farm produce	Low demand is *not* a problem (high demand from farmers)	Poor marketing of farm produce; low farm incomes
	Limited awareness by farmers of existing or new implements for tillage and weeding systems, associated with weak or under-resourced extension services and credit agencies and lack of supplier extension (few demonstrations; little display stock in rural areas)	Farmers unaware of present and alternative animal traction implements and lack resources to acquire them	Low effectiveness of extension services due to inadequate logistical support		Farmers lack information on new equipment Equipment often available only in urban centres
	Lack of availability of implements and spares in the rural areas	Low level of agricultural training and education	Cattle rustling reduces demand for animal traction		Poor credit systems and after-sales services
Supply by manufacturers	Until recently, no local developments but copying imported Safim-type plows and relatively heavy ridgers and cultivator	Little change during past decade with no new inventions or adaptations	Lack of raw materials for local equipment	Manufacturing capacity too low for demand	Lack of raw materials
	Lack of diversification of animal traction implements. No adaptation of ranges to area-specific requirements	Little profit for engineers from innovations	Supply dependent on donor support for importations		Manufacturers do not diversify ranges as risks high
	Little or no feedback from regions on farmers' needs and implement acceptability (lack of marketing strategies and rural distribution networks)	Poor distribution system; farmers sometimes appear conservative			Low feedback from regions
Support by public-sector institutions	In past, little impact of government-funded research, testing and extension services (funding and communication constraints). Since 1989, the Magoye implement testing and on-farm trial and demonstration programme has aimed to increase farmers' awareness of different tillage and weeding practices (and implements) and to improve feedback to manufacturers	Efforts being made through extension services and farmers training centres	Limited training of both farmers and staff	Some research and development of new equipment	Manufacturers and distributors are largely government-owned but not efficient
	The government-established cooperative unions and credit system have proved largely ineffective in bridging the gap between actual farmers' need and implement supply		Research and development programmes have not been effective	Promising imported designs are tested	Cooperative unions and banks not providing sufficient support to farmers to stimulate demand

ATNESA Network Meetings

During the workshop there were two ATNESA General Assembly Meetings, as well as several meetings of committees.

First ATNESA General Assembly

The First General Assembly Meeting was held in the afternoon of the first working day (Saturday 18 January). It was chaired by L P Singogo (Farming Systems Programme), the rapporteurs were R Shetto and T Simalenga, and most workshop participants attended.

The meeting started with a review of animal traction networking activities in Africa. This was introduced by the ATNESA Technical Adviser, P Starkey, who presented a paper describing and analysing recent experiences and organisational arrangements (see page 82). Dr K Apetofia of Togo highlighted some of the benefits of the West Africa Animal Traction Network, of which he was a steering committee member. The ATNESA steering committee member from Uganda, J Omoding, then described how an initial ATNESA Steering Committee had been formed in November 1990, during a meeting in Harare organised by AGROTEC (Agricultural Operations Technology for Small Holders in East and Southern Africa). The steering committee comprised:

- R Nazare, Zimbabwe, *Chair*
- E Mwenya, Zambia, *Secretary*
- E Kayumbo, Tanzania
- C Mbara, Kenya
- J Omoding, Uganda
- S Tlhaole, Lesotho
- L Sylwander, AGROTEC
- C Schmieg, GTZ
- P Starkey, UK, *Technical Adviser*

The committee had met in Lusaka in April 1991, to plan the present workshop and discuss formal network statutes. J Omoding had been given the task of drawing up draft statutes based on those of the West Africa Animal Traction Network. These were presented to the General Assembly and several points were discussed. The General Assembly then approved the formation of a small committee to review the statutes, in the light of the points raised, and prepare a revised draft for submission to the Second General Assembly, scheduled for the fifth day of the workshop. The committee was also to make appropriate arrangements for the election of a new Steering Committee, and to consider suggestions for future network activities.

Second ATNESA General Assembly

The Second General Assembly Meeting was held on the penultimate day. It was Chaired by A Muthama (Commonwealth Secretariat), the rapporteur was M Sizya and the meeting was attended by most workshop participants.

J Omoding, who had chaired the working group, presented the revised network statutes. After discussion and slight modification, the statutes were accepted by the general assembly (see page 50).

Reports of the progress of national networking activities were given for Uganda, Zimbabwe, Malawi, Kenya, Zambia and Tanzania. Some suggestions were made for future ATNESA activities.

The Chairman introduced the procedures for the Steering Committee election proposed by the working group. It had been agreed that the Steering Committee should have a geographical, disciplinary, gender and institutional diversity. As the committee was to be small, not all ATNESA countries would be able to have one of their nationals on the committee. Thus, in order to achieve geographical diversity, and ensure all countries were *represented* on the committee, it had been proposed have one committee member per broad geographical area within the ATNESA region. The committee members should be concerned about the animal traction interests of several countries. For the purposes of this election (and taking into account the countries then present), it was suggested and agreed that there be a minimum of one member from the Horn of Africa (including Ethiopia, Somalia, Sudan), one from eastern Africa (including Kenya, Tanzania, Uganda), one from Central Africa (including Malawi, Zambia, Zimbabwe) and one from southern Africa (including Angola, Botswana, Lesotho, Mozambique, Namibia, Swaziland).

Eight people were nominated and given a chance to introduce themselves to the General Assembly. Six of these candidates were then elected onto the committee. Three people were nominated for the two committee positions reserved for donor agencies or international institutions. Following discussions, it was agreed that two of these would be committee members, and the third would act as an invited resource person (the committee was empowered to invite relevant individuals and organisations to assist its planning and deliberations). The General Assembly agreed that P Starkey should continue to act as ATNESA Technical Adviser. The new committee comprised:

- A Aganga, *Botswana*
- R Mpande, *Zimbabwe*
- E Mwenya, *Zambia*
- J Omoding, *Uganda*
- T Simalenga, *Tanzania*
- O Taha, *Ethiopia*
- L Sylwander, *AGROTEC*
- M Guntz, *GTZ*

Resource persons

- P Starkey, *UK (Technical Adviser)*
- H Helsloot, *The Netherlands*

Steering Committee plans

The new Steering Committee met immediately after the workshop, and asked E Mwenya to act as its new chairman. The committee stressed that while it would help to stimulate, coordinate and facilitate arrangements, the actual responsibility for implementing network activities would have to lie with individual ATNESA members in several countries (perhaps with support from resource organisations).

In the light of workshop discussions, the committee proposed that ATNESA members should undertake the following networking activities in the coming years.

- Form informal or formal national animal traction networks in as many countries in the region as possible. The success of ATNESA regional networking will depend on the effectiveness of these. The Tanzanian animal traction network will prepare and circulate a paper on its experiences.

- Collect and collate information on organisations and individuals involved in animal traction in all countries in the region. Such information will be used in national and regional mailing lists and will form the basis of an ATNESA directory.

- Increase awareness of the existence, aims and objectives of ATNESA through publicity materials and announcements in newsletters.

- Prepare a report of the workshop and edit and publish the papers prepared for the first ATNESA workshop.

- Collaborate with Silsoe Research Institute in the planning and implementation of a regional workshop relating to animal draft power in 1993.

- Facilitate the holding of a small regional workshop on gender issues in animal traction.

- Facilitate the holding of a small regional workshop on animal-drawn transport, concentrating on issues of cart design.

- Facilitate the holding of a small regional workshop on the use of donkeys.

- Facilitate the holding of a small regional workshop relating to the design, manufacture and distribution of tillage implements.

- Identify a suitable venue and host for the next large ATNESA workshop, anticipated to be held in 1994.

Statutes of the Animal Traction Network for Eastern and Southern Africa (ATNESA)

Section 1: Name and objectives

Article 1

A regional network has been formed to link organisations and individuals involved in the application and development of animal traction technology. The name of the network shall be the Animal Traction Network for Eastern and Southern Africa (ATNESA).

Article 2

The objectives of ATNESA are to:

○ promote environmentally sound and sustainable systems of using animal traction in the region

○ promote a farming systems, farmer-oriented, and gender-sensitive approach to animal traction development and research

○ strengthen and promote links between individuals and organisations engaged in using draft animals and those carrying out animal traction research, extension, training, manufacture and other related activities

○ stimulate and promote the dissemination and exchange of information, research findings and experiences in animal traction

○ promote coordination and collaboration in development and research activities

○ encourage and stimulate the formation of national animal traction networks

○ enhance the performance and professional development of researchers and technical personnel involved in animal traction activities through appropriate training initiatives

○ facilitate assistance to network members on technical and organisational matters relating to the planning, preparation, funding, implementation and evaluation of their animal traction programmes

○ stimulate linkages between members and organisations capable of providing financial and/or technical support

○ organise regional activities including biennial workshops, seminars, study tours and professional visits

○ act as a catalyst for the development of animal power in the region and assist in the development of appropriate animal traction policies

Section 2: Composition and language

Article 3

The network shall be open to all individuals and organisations interested in the network objectives. There are three main categories of members.

(i) Eastern and southern African members comprise individuals, farmers' associations, government ministries, research institutes, educational establishments, agricultural development projects, non-governmental organisations, manufacturers and other national or international organisations in the region involved with animal traction technology

(ii) Donor members comprise organisations and institutions who provide funding or comparable support to ATNESA

(iii) Associate members comprise individuals, organisations or complementary networks based outside the region.

Article 4

English shall be the official language of the network. Where practicable, sympathetic consideration will be given to network members whose working language is Portuguese, French or an indigenous language and for whom communication in English may be difficult.

Section 3: General Assembly and Voting

Article 5

The General Assembly of ATNESA will be convened every two years, during a workshop that has been widely publicised and which has a wide participatory base. The General Assembly will:

○ approve the adoption and modification of the statutes by a majority of at least two thirds of the voting members present

○ discuss and adopt the report of the network Steering Committee and proposed action plans for forthcoming activities

○ approve the network financial report

○ elect members of the Steering Committee.

Article 6

(i) Voting rights will be restricted to eastern and southern African members and donor members (Article 3 categories i and ii)

(ii) At a General Assembly meeting, no single country or organisation is entitled to more than one fifth of the voting power.

Section 4: Steering Committee

Article 7

The Steering Committee will comprise:

○ Six (6) elected members from eastern and southern African countries

○ Two (2) members representing donor agencies or international institutes, as approved by the General Assembly.

If the Steering Committee appoints a Network Coordinator, Network Administrator or Technical Adviser, these will normally be expected to participate in Steering Committee Meetings.

The Steering Committee members may invite the participation of relevant individuals or organisations that may assist their planning and deliberations.

The Steering Committee will elect its own chairperson.

Article 8

Steering Committee members are elected at a General Assembly, and serve until the next General Assembly, normally a period of two years. If they so wish, they may stand for re-election for a second and final term.

When elections are held, the General Assembly should strive to ensure that a geographical, gender, disciplinary and institutional diversity is maintained on the committee and that no one interest group dominates (eg universities, government ministries, researchers). In normal circumstances, no two elected committee members should be from the same country. The General Assembly should aim to ensure that some continuity is maintained between the outgoing and the new committee.

Article 9

The Steering Committee will meet at least once a year to:

○ review the work of the network

○ plan network activities and arrange for the implementation of decisions taken by the General Assembly

○ discuss and approve network financial matters

○ delegate responsibilities for action to network members and appointed persons.

Section 5 Network coordination

Article 10

The network will function largely through the interaction of the autonomous national animal traction networks and direct contacts between the different programmes in the region.

The General Assembly will delegate responsibility for coordinating the network to the Steering Committee. The Steering Committee will delegate day-to-day responsibility for particular activities and actions to network members and appointed persons.

In the first instance, the network secretariat will be operated on a voluntary basis by the organisation that is about to host, or has just hosted, a major workshop. In the longer term a permanent secretariat may be established alongside a national programme or international centre.

Article 11

The Steering Committee may appoint people to undertake particular responsibilities, on a full-time, part-time or intermittent basis. These may include:

○ a network coordinator

○ a network administrator

○ a technical adviser.

Appointed persons will be responsible to the Steering Committee, who will determine their terms of reference. Conditions of appointment will be determined in liaison with the relevant funding agencies.

Section 6: Funding arrangements

Article 12

ATNESA funds may come from:

○ workshop fees or other dues recommended by the Steering Committee and/or the General Assembly

○ contributions from member organisations or individuals

○ grants from donors for network coordination or specific network activities

○ ATNESA fund-raising and income-generating activities.

Article 13

The network will establish a network bank account, in association with an internationally recognised institution. The account will be administered by that institution, acting on behalf of the Steering Committee. The Steering Committee will prepare annual financial reports for the General Assembly.

Those delegated with undertaking network-funded activities, such as workshops, may open temporary local bank accounts in the name of the relevant activity. They will be expected to follow internationally acceptable financial control procedures, and submit financial statements and reports to the Steering Committee.

Workshop evaluation

Reported by P Starkey, E Mwenya and M Starkey

Introduction

On the final day, participants were given evaluation forms, which they filled in and submitted anonymously. A total of 100 completed forms were returned. There were 45 questions about specific aspects of the workshop programme and organisation. Participants were asked to grade each programme element on the scale A to E, with A equivalent to "very good", C "acceptable" and E "very poor". There then followed 12 open-ended questions and a space for any additional comments.

All the answers to the 45 fixed-response questions are shown in Bar charts 1–45 on the following pages. The charts include a bar for the numbers of participants who left the question blank (probably because they were not present or the question did not concern them). Some participants wrote additional comments concerning the programme elements, and these have been included in the analysis of the open-ended questions.

To compare the overall popularity of the different programme elements, the responses were assigned scores and the average scores were calculated. By giving 10 for A, 7 for B, 5 for C, 3 for D and 0 for E, equal importance was assigned to the positive and negative categories, but the strongly positive and negative responses were given slightly more weight than the milder reactions. The average scores are shown in ranked order in Bar chart 46. The aim of the bar charts is simply to provide a rapid visual impression of participant reaction to the different workshop elements: there has been no analysis for statistical significance.

Evaluation of programme elements

Bar charts 1–31 show participant responses to the various elements of workshop programme, and the average responses are ranked in Bar chart 46. The visits to farmers received the highest acclaim, followed by two keynote presentations (Guntz et al and Starkey) and the opening ceremony. Also very popular were the field visits to organisations and the small group discussions relating to the visits and to the themes. Three other plenary presentations were very popular (Dibbits/Starkey, Wanders and Pearson), as were three of the workshop evening meetings (commercial farmers, Nolle videos and manufacturers). Next in overall popularity were the

final discussions, self-introductions and two other thematic presentations (Mwenya et al and Anderson).

The less popular programme items (but still rated quite highly—nearer "good" than "acceptable") were the network planning meetings, some other thematic presentations and the reports of the field group discussions.

Evaluation of workshop organisation

Bar charts 32–44 show the responses to many aspects of workshop organisation. Participants were very positive, and all elements save one received an average score better than "good". The organisation of general and social activities had relatively low approval ratings, probably because there were few entirely social arrangements: the day programme was full and there were optional activities and meetings each evening. The highest score (and highest for the whole evaluation) went to the organisation of the field trips. The hotel accommodation and facilities were considered good, although several people (12) wrote on their forms that the ventilation in the main workshop room was poor. Participants were happy with the exhibitions the provision of editorial advice during the workshop (Stares).

Open-ended questions

The open-ended questions gave participants a chance to comment on workshop strengths and weaknesses and to make comments relating to future workshops. Many questions elicited responses that showed several areas of widespread agreement. There were clear "clusters" of responses, in which participants expressed similar ideas, with slight differences in wording. These are all reported here together with the number of citations (given in brackets). As there were 100 returned evaluation forms, the number of citations approximates to a percentage figure. There were also some points made by a few people, or by just one individual, which tended to reflect their specific interests, needs, perceptions or (occasionally) personal grievances. These are also reported.

There was inevitably overlap between the areas covered by the questions, and respondents used different questions to express their views on aspects of the workshop. While some people made pertinent comments at the first relevant question, and did not repeat them, others repeated the same strongly-held point several times. In some questions the total number of citations reported is greater than the number of respondents, for when people referred to two separate issues or topics, both were included in this analysis.

Most useful aspect

In response to this question, the majority of participants did not cite specific programme elements, but rather gave responses that suggested that the entire combination of the multifaceted workshop, the varied participants and the stimulating atmosphere was "most useful". The workshop provided a favourable environment for making contacts and information exchange between professionals from different African countries and resource organisations (46), resulting in new contacts and exchanges (18) and greater knowledge of other experiences in the region and available literature and resources (10). People considered it useful that the workshop involved a balanced, multidisciplinary group of people from many countries (15). The stimulating atmosphere of teamwork provided inspiration and wider horizons (5), with integrated analysis of constraints and solutions (4) allowing people to see things from other people's perspectives (3). A few people simply said all was useful (3).

For those participants who did cite programme elements, the discussions with farmers and the field visits were most popular (23), followed by the small group discussions (14). Some individuals found the lead presentations (3) most useful, the thematic presentations (2 for transfer and gender, 1 each for the others), the videos (2) and information on donkeys and harnessing (1).

Help provided by workshop

Participants were asked in what way (if any) the workshop had helped them. Most people responded very positively, stressing overall networking benefits. Particular mention was made of information exchange and new contacts gained (55). Some participants specifically cited future collaboration as a result of the contacts (5) and others mentioned the benefits of acquired knowledge of further literature and information sources (7). Many people commented on new and broader perspectives gained from learning of other animal traction situations and problems (28). Specific mention was made of increased inspiration and motivation (7), greater understanding (5) and self-evaluation (2). Some people mentioned they had gained in personal skills relating to animal traction, including strategy formulation and planning (3) and

problem solving (3). Some participants said they had gained from new technical knowledge (6), while others mentioned particular topics including: implements (2), extension (2), research (1), transport (1), weeding (1), animal disease (1), farmer-innovations (1) and blacksmiths (1). Some people acquired greater gender sensitivity (2) or knowledge that gender issues can be threatening (1).

Least useful aspect

On the question of the weakest aspect of the workshop there were no overriding issues. Some participants left this blank (10) or specifically said there were no items of low value (19). Various programme items were mentioned by a few people including the network meeting and elections (7), presentation of field visit discussions (5), group discussions on the field visits (4), the gender theme (4) and evening meetings (2). Some people referred to the tightness of the programme, rushed presentations and lack of time for reflection, rest or social activities (7). Some of the lead thematic papers were felt to be weak, complicated or lacking in scientific detail (4) and some felt the themes did not address their interests (2). Too much prominence was given to donors and expatriates (2). Individuals also mentioned poor ventilation in the hall (1), posters (1), too many papers (1), poor timekeeping (1), commercial farmer panel (1), tillage theme (1), field visits (1) and examples of complicated technologies (1).

Possible improvements

On the subject of how the workshop could be improved, some said there was nothing to improve (6) and some left the question blank (4). However, most people provided specific suggestions. Many related to having more time during the workshop in general (8), for the key presentations and discussions (8), for small-group discussions (8), for planning action programmes (3), for informal networking (1) and for recreation (2). There could also have been more field visits (5), including visits to farmers not using animal traction (3) and blacksmiths (1), and information on how to hold interviews with farmers (1). There were no clear suggestions on where the extra time could come from, although there was some mention of less time for discussions (1) and self-introductions (1). Several people felt the workshop could have benefited from more focused discussions with less generality (6), fewer subthemes (6) and more highly selected, expert participants (5). There could have been better and more animated thematic presentations (3) and these could have been spaced out during the week (2) with more emphasis on indigenous experts (3). Some people wanted an opportunity to present their papers (4) or discuss them in groups (4). Mentions were made of the desirability of more decision-makers (2), a rural environment for the workshop (1) and the circulation of an address list at the start of the workshop (1).

Among the other comments were observations that personal name tags should be larger (2) but that photo credits should be smaller (2). More people should have been involved in producing poster displays and photo exhibitions (4).

Workshop participation, length and cuts

Nobody thought there were too few participants. Most people thought the numbers were acceptable (69), but some thought there were too many (10), particularly for detailed information exchange. A few people noted there could have been a better balance between countries (1), with fewer host-country participants (1).

Most people thought the length of the workshop was appropriate (64) even though some added it was very full (2). Some thought it was too short (12) and a few too long (5).

When asked what could have been cut from the full programme many people said "nothing!" (32) or left this question blank (9). Some said instead of cutting content, the workshop should have been extended to relieve the time-pressure (4). Some people thought time could have been saved on the presentation of group reports on the field visits (8), the self-introductions (3), the network assembly meetings (2), general discussions (2), the thematic papers (2) and evening videos (1). Some people thought there should have been one free evening (2) and/or an afternoon free for seeing Lusaka and shopping (3).

Further ATNESA workshops

Almost all participants felt there should be another ATNESA workshop (79), with some noting it should be different (9) and held after 3–4 years (1). One person thought it should only be held if real African experts were brought together. There was no clear consensus of the next host country. Some people said anywhere in the region that was suitable (8), with good transport connections (4), cheap (2) and in a rural setting (1). Mentions were made of East Africa (5), Central Africa (2) and the Horn of Africa (1). The specific countries suggested were Tanzania (17), Zimbabwe (13), Botswana (11), Kenya (8), Uganda (6), Malawi (4), Swaziland (3), Ethiopia (2), Mozambique (2), South Africa (2), Zambia (2) and Lesotho (1).

A wide variety of themes was suggested, with no clear consensus emerging. Several people suggested the same theme of "improving animal traction technology" (6) or a similar general theme (2) perhaps relating to innovations and progress (4). Specific mention was made of sustainable systems (6), farming systems (4) and small-scale farmers (2) and the *impact* of animal traction on households (including women and children), farming systems, the environment and rural development (11).

Several suggestions were made for specific themes (or subthemes) and most of the present workshop subthemes were mentioned. Themes suggested with several advocates included technology transfer and dissemination, project experiences and reasons for non-adoption (10 in total), economics and credit issues (6), the specific problems of areas of introduction with few cattle (4) and problems of implement supply and manufacture (4). Other issues mentioned included participatory methods (3), animal management and welfare (2), policy issues (2), donkeys (2), transport (1) and tillage (1).

Various suggestions were made for future workshop methodology, and these generally reinforced the comments already made about ways this workshop could have been improved. A number of people thought a similar methodology should be used (8), while allowing it to evolve with time (1). Others thought the methodology should be more participatory (2) and farmer-oriented (2), with greater emphasis on the role of African experts (4), although outsiders can be useful for identifying "hidden problems". There should be more time for field visits (3) and lead presentations (3). Some people thought more participants should be given time to present their papers (2), perhaps in parallel sessions (3), allowing for more discussion time (1). There should be guidelines on paper preparation and presentation (2), papers should be circulated in advance (1). There should be more policy makers (4) and greater farmer involvement (3). Analysis should be more rigorous (2), with a more self-critical approach to the benefits (or otherwise) of animal traction (1). One person thought ATNESA should consider making payments to those presenting papers (1).

Any other comments

Several participants (26) used this space to express satisfaction at the workshop, thank the organisers and wish the steering committee well. Most other comments placed in this space in the evaluation forms related to previous questions (such as future workshop themes or ways of improving the workshop). For clarity and to avoid repetition, these comments have been included in the responses already reported.

It was suggested that ATNESA should establish a permanent secretariat (2) and should develop and disseminate guidelines relating to animal traction policy and extension practices (1). ATNESA should assist the development of national networks (1), but continue to emphasis the value of informal networking (1).

Conclusion

The workshop evaluation was extremely positive. No one gave the workshop a poor overall rating, and 82 out of 100 respondents said it was good or very good. There were very few poor ratings on any aspect of the workshop programme or organisation (fewer than 5%, overall). The very positive results are quite remarkable, given that 100 people of very different educational background, discipline, professional seniority, tradition and nationality all participated in the same programme for five intensive days, and had been given the opportunity to comment freely and anonymously on their likes and dislikes. The general consensus of satisfaction despite obvious diversity is well illustrated by reaction to the farm visits. These were rated as good or very good by 81 respondents, yet one participant considered them "very poor" and the least useful part of the workshop, for him or her.

People clearly felt they had benefited from the workshop. In particular they had gained from many new contacts and fresh insights into other people's experiences.

Most people felt that the length of the workshop and the number of participants had been about right. The programme was very full, but most people accepted that this was inevitable in the circumstances—there was no consensus on what could have been left out. People would have appreciated a little more free time, but not at the expense of cutting out programme elements or increasing the length of the workshop. A small number of participants commented that they would have liked an opportunity to present their papers in plenary sessions, parallel sessions or groups, as happens at academic conferences. This was certainly not the majority view and given the time constraints and general low popularity of long plenary sessions, this would not have been realistic.

The most popular elements of the programme (considered by more than 75 people to have been good or very good) were (in chronological order) the opening ceremony, the keynote address, field visit briefings, visits to farmers, small group discussions on field visits, plenary discussions on workshop themes and the keynote synthesis. Also rated highly (over 75% good or very good) were the posters and photos, the workshop content and methodology, workshop publicity, briefing notes, pre-workshop liaison, registration, paper reproduction, field visit information and field visit organisation. One innovation at the workshop proved popular—the provision of an editor to advise participants on the style and content of their papers.

There were just five items which were considered by at least 10% of the respondents to have been poor. These included two lead papers (profitability and technology transfer), reports of field visits, the second network general assembly meeting and arrangements for social activities. To put the *relatively* poor ratings of some lead papers in perspective, it should be noted that many more people rated these papers positively than negatively (eg, 64 good vs 14 poor for profitability). The probable reason why the field visit reports were rated poorly is that all groups were given a chance to present their results: participants were frustrated by the inevitable repetition (and some weak presentations). In future it might be better to combine similar reports, or present them simultaneously as poster displays. The network meeting involved discussion of network statutes and election procedures, which some people found tedious.

The overall evaluation results are very much in line with those of the workshops of the West Africa Animal Traction Network, although there were fewer negative comments and complaints than have been expressed in West Africa. Participants at these workshop also tended to like a few good key presentations, visits to farmers and some intense discussions in small groups. They also did not favour a large number of paper presentations or long plenary sessions.

The workshop evaluation has given ATNESA much useful information concerning participant ideas, reactions and preferences that will be of assistance in planning future workshops.

Bar charts 1–12: Numbers of responses to the workshop evaluation questions

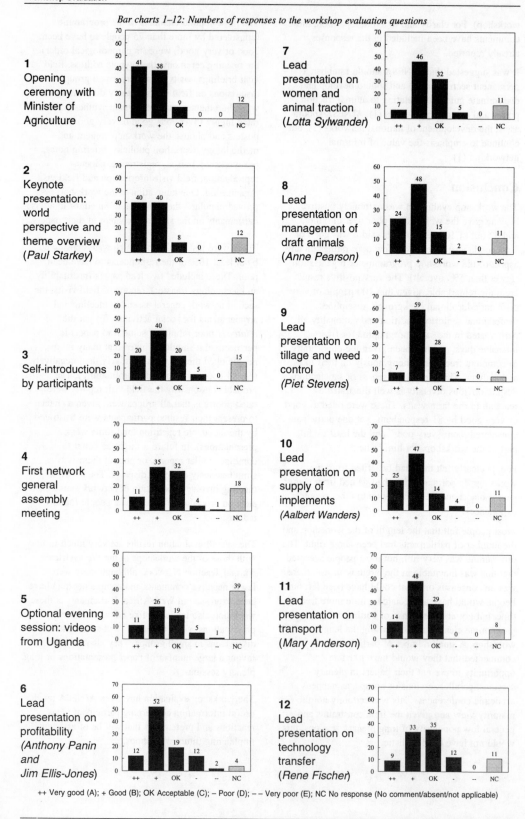

1 Opening ceremony with Minister of Agriculture

2 Keynote presentation: world perspective and theme overview (*Paul Starkey*)

3 Self-introductions by participants

4 First network general assembly meeting

5 Optional evening session: videos from Uganda

6 Lead presentation on profitability (*Anthony Panin and Jim Ellis-Jones*)

7 Lead presentation on women and animal traction (*Lotta Sylwander*)

8 Lead presentation on management of draft animals (*Anne Pearson*)

9 Lead presentation on tillage and weed control (*Piet Stevens*)

10 Lead presentation on supply of implements (*Aalbert Wanders*)

11 Lead presentation on transport (*Mary Anderson*)

12 Lead presentation on technology transfer (*Rene Fischer*)

++ Very good (A); + Good (B); OK Acceptable (C); – Poor (D); – – Very poor (E); NC No response (No comment/absent/not applicable)

Bar charts 13–24: Numbers of responses to the workshop evaluation questions

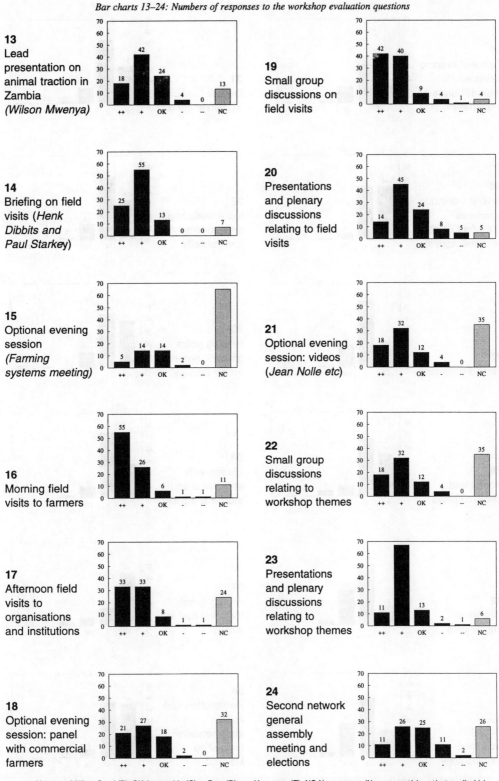

13
Lead presentation on animal traction in Zambia *(Wilson Mwenya)*

14
Briefing on field visits *(Henk Dibbits and Paul Starkey)*

15
Optional evening session *(Farming systems meeting)*

16
Morning field visits to farmers

17
Afternoon field visits to organisations and institutions

18
Optional evening session: panel with commercial farmers

19
Small group discussions on field visits

20
Presentations and plenary discussions relating to field visits

21
Optional evening session: videos *(Jean Nolle etc)*

22
Small group discussions relating to workshop themes

23
Presentations and plenary discussions relating to workshop themes

24
Second network general assembly meeting and elections

++ Very good (A); + Good (B); OK Acceptable (C); – Poor (D); – – Very poor (E); NC No response (No comment/absent/not applicable)

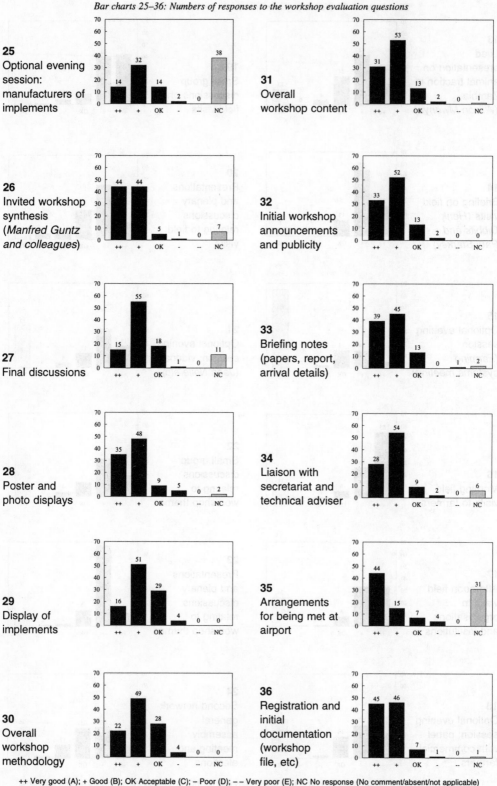

Bar charts 25–36: Numbers of responses to the workshop evaluation questions

25 Optional evening session: manufacturers of implements

26 Invited workshop synthesis (*Manfred Guntz and colleagues*)

27 Final discussions

28 Poster and photo displays

29 Display of implements

30 Overall workshop methodology

31 Overall workshop content

32 Initial workshop announcements and publicity

33 Briefing notes (papers, report, arrival details)

34 Liaison with secretariat and technical adviser

35 Arrangements for being met at airport

36 Registration and initial documentation (workshop file, etc)

++ Very good (A); + Good (B); OK Acceptable (C); – Poor (D); – – Very poor (E); NC No response (No comment/absent/not applicable)

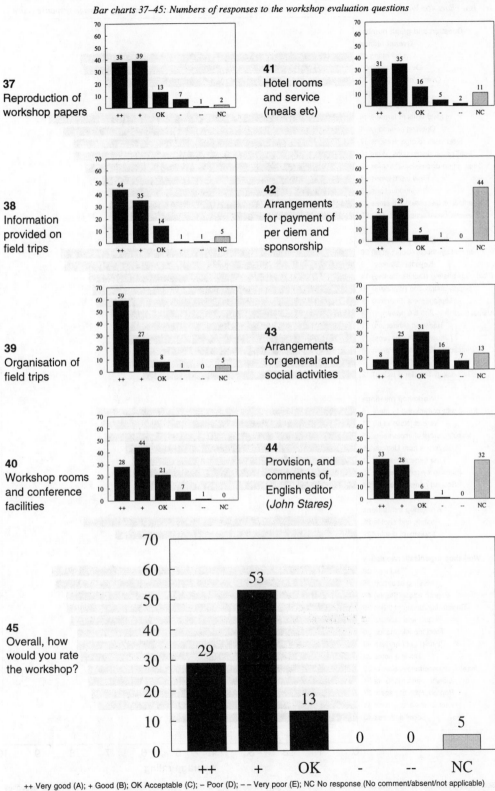

Bar charts 37–45: Numbers of responses to the workshop evaluation questions

37 Reproduction of workshop papers

38 Information provided on field trips

39 Organisation of field trips

40 Workshop rooms and conference facilities

41 Hotel rooms and service (meals etc)

42 Arrangements for payment of per diem and sponsorship

43 Arrangements for general and social activities

44 Provision, and comments of, English editor (*John Stares)*

45 Overall, how would you rate the workshop?

++ Very good (A); + Good (B); OK Acceptable (C); – Poor (D); – – Very poor (E); NC No response (No comment/absent/not applicable)

Bar chart 46: Workshop evaluation questions, sorted by question topics and then ranked by average response score

Question and graph number
Overall ratings
Overall rating 45
Overall content 31
Overall methodology 30

Workshop activities
Field visits to farmers 16
Opening ceremony 1
Field visits to organisations 17
Small group discussions: visits 19
Small group discussions: themes 22
Final discussions 27
Self-introductions 3
Presentations/discussions: themes 23
Presentations/discussions: visits 20

Workshop presentations
Invited synthesis (Guntz et al) 26
Keynote (Starkey) 2
Field visits briefing (Dibbits/Starkey) 14
Supply/distribution (Wanders) 10
Management (Pearson) 8
Animal traction in Zambia (Mwenya) 13
Transport (Anderson) 11
Tillage/weeds (Stevens) 9
Profitability (Ellis-Jones/Panin) 6
Women (Sylwander) 7
Technology transfer (Fischer) 12

Workshop meetings
Panel with commercial farmers 18
Videos (Nolle et al) 21
Manufacturers of implements 25
Videos from Uganda 5
First general meeting 4
Farming systems meeting 15
Second general meeting 24

Workshop exhibitions
Posters and photos 28
Implement display 29

Workshop organisation/logistics
Field trips 39
Meeting at airport 35
English editor (Stares) 44
Registration/documentation 36
Rooms and facilities 40
Field trip information 38
Payment of per diem 42
Briefing notes 33
Initial announcements/publicity 32
Liaison with organisers 34
Reproduction of papers 37
Hotel rooms and service 41
Social activities 43

0 1 2 3 4 5 6 7 8 9 10
Average rating

Scores: Very poor (E), 0; Poor (D), 3; Acceptable (C), 5; Good (B), 7; Very good (A), 10. No response excluded—mean is average of responses

"Improving animal traction technology"

Addresses of workshop participants

Botswana

Dr (Mrs) Adeolu A AGANGA
Senior Lecturer
Dept Animal Health and
Production
Botswana College of Agriculture
Private Bag 0027, Gaborone
BOTSWANA
Tel: + 267-352381
Fax: + 267-314253
Tlx: 2752 SACCAR BD

Dr Anthony PANIN
Lecturer
Dept Agricultural Economics
and Extension
Botswana College of Agriculture
Private Bag 0027, Gaborone
BOTSWANA
Tel: + 267-352381
Fax: + 267-314253
Tlx: 2752 SACCAR BD

Mr Martin S SEBONEGO
Design Engineer
Rural Industries Innovation
Centre (RIIC)
P Bag 11, Kanye
BOTSWANA

Mr Lingston SINGOGO
Assistant Co-ordinator
Farming Systems Programme
(FAO)
c/o UNDP, Box 54, Gaborone
BOTSWANA
Tel: + 267-359740
Fax: + 267-359740
Tlx: 2412 BD

Ethiopia

Mr ABIYE ASTATKE
Agricultural Engineer
International Livestock Centre
for Africa (ILCA)
PO Box 5689, Addis Ababa
ETHIOPIA
Tel: + 251-1-613215
Fax: + 251-1-611892
Tlx: 21207 ILCA ET

Mr ABEDE BELAYNEH
WORKNEH
Agricultural Engineer
Rural Technology Promotion
Department
Ministry of Agriculture
PO Box 7838, Addis Ababa
ETHIOPIA
Tel: + 251-1-150364
Fax: + 251-1-654388
Tlx: 21390 MINAG ET

Mr OUMER TAHA
Agricultural Engineer
Asela Rural Technology
Promotion Centre
Ministry of Agriculture
PO Box 6, Asela
ETHIOPIA
Tel: + 251-2-311731
Fax: + 251-1-654388
Tlx: 21390 MINAG ET

Mr Hans ZAUGG
Workshop Supervisor
Farm Implements Section
Selam Children's Village
PO Box 8075, Addis Ababa
ETHIOPIA
Tel: + 251-1-188120
Fax: + 251-1-610388

France

M Jean NOLLE
Conseiller Technique en
Machinisme Agricole
19 Avenue du Général LeClerc
75014 Paris, FRANCE
Tel: + 33-1-43 21 42 96
(M Nolle died in 1993)

Germany

Mr Klaus DIPPON
Institut für Agrartechnik
Universität Hohenheim
Postfach 700562
Garbenstraße 9
70599 Stuttgart, GERMANY
Tel: + 49-711-459-2532
Fax: + 49-711-459-2519
Tlx: 7255202 ATHO D

Mr Frank EMHARDT
Institut für Agrartechnik
Universität Hohenheim
Postfach 700562
Garbenstraße 9
70599 Stuttgart, GERMANY
Tel: + 49-711-459-2532
Fax: + 49-711-459-2519
Tlx: 7255202 ATHO D

Mr Manfred GUNTZ
Planning Officer Agricultural
Mechanization, Dept 421
Deutsche Gesellschaft für
Technische Zusammenarbeit
(GTZ)
Postfach 5180
D-65726 Eschborn
GERMANY
Tel: + 49-6196-791340
Fax: + 49-6196-797130
Tlx: 407501-0 GTZ D

Mr Christian LOFFLER
Socio-Economist
Animal Power Technology
Project (Zambia)
OEKOTOP Ltd, Binger Str 25a
D-14197 Berlin, GERMANY
Tel: + 49-30-824-2082
Fax: + 49-30-823-1510
Tlx: 184452 OEK D

Italy

Mr Goolam OODALLY
Agricultural Engineer
Agricultural Engineering Service
Food and Agriculture
Organization (FAO)
Via delle Terme di Caracalla
00100 Rome, ITALY
Tel: + 39-6-57974614
Fax: + 39-6-57973152
Tlx: 610181 FAO I

Kenya

Mr Simon BARASA
Animal Draught Coordinator
Oxfam/LPDP
PO Box 40680, Nairobi, KENYA
Tel: + 254-2-442122

Mr James KAHUMBURA
Head of Agricultural
Engineering Programme
Kenya Agricultural Research
Centre, Muguga
PO Box 30148, Nairobi
KENYA
Tel: + 254-154-32885
Fax: + 254-2-747986 c/o

Mr Yoram LAZAR
Agricultural Engineer and
Manufacturer
PO Box 58752, Nairobi
KENYA
Tel: + 254-2-534143
Fax: + 254-2-534144

Mr Paul M MAINA
Managing Director
Farming Systems Kenya
PO Box 2816, Nakuru
KENYA
Tel: + 254-37-41201

Malawi

Mr Wells F KUMWENDA
Senior Agricultural Engineer
Farm Machinery Unit
Chitedze Research Station
Ministry of Agriculture
Box 158, Lilongwe, MALAWI
Tel: + 265-767222
Fax: + 265-730514
Tlx: 44648 MINAGRIC MI

Dr Macdonald L MWINJILO
Senior Lecturer
Department of Agricultural
Engineering
Bunda College of Agriculture
University of Malawi
P O Box 219, Lilongwe 3
MALAWI
Tel: + 265-277222
Fax: + 265-277251
Tlx: 43622 MI

Subsequent address
Dr Macdonald MWINJILO
Senior Lecturer
Faculty of Agriculture
Africa University
PO Box 1320, Mutare
ZIMBABWE
Tel: + 263-20-60026
Fax: + 263-20-61785

Mr Darwin D SINGA
Commodity Team Leader
Department of Agricultural
Research
Chitedze Research Station
P O Box 158, Lilongwe
MALAWI
Tel: + 265-767222
Fax: + 265-730514
Tlx: 44648 MI

Mozambique

Mr Nelson Lucas NKINI
Agro-Alfa Export Manager
Fábrica de Alfaias Agrícolas
Av 24 Julho 2755
CP 1318, Maputo
MOZAMBIQUE
Tel: + 258-1-422341
Fax: + 258-1-30889
Tlx: 6405 AGRAL MO

Mr Jacinto Sabino MUTEMBA
Product Development Manager
Agro-Alfa
Fábrica de Alfaias Agrícolas
Av 24 Julho 2755
CP 1318, Maputo
MOZAMBIQUE
Tel: + 258-1-422341
Fax: + 258-1-30889
Tlx: 6405 AGRAL MO

The Netherlands

Mr Klaas B van DAM
Director
Agricultural Tropical Machinery
Rumptstad BV
PO Box 1
3243 ZG Stad aan't Haringvliet
THE NETHERLANDS
Tel: + 31-1871-6133
Fax: + 31-1871-2358
Tlx: 22585 NL

Mr Henk DIBBITS
IMAG-DLO (Instituut voor
Mechanisatie, Arbeid en
Gebouwen)
Mansholtaan 10–12, Postbus 43
6700 AA Wageningen
THE NETHERLANDS
Tel: + 31-8370-76350
Fax: + 31-8370-75670
Tlx: 45330 CTWAG NL

Mr Hans HELSLOOT
Farm Implements and Tools
(FIT) Section
TOOL Consultancy Department
Sarphatistraat 650
1018 AV Amsterdam
THE NETHERLANDS
Tel: + 31-20-6264409
Fax: + 31-20-6277489

Subsequent address
Hans HELSLOOT
Havensingel 70
5211 TZ Den Bosch
THE NETHERLANDS
Tel: + 31-73-135145
+ 31-73-135145

Mr Wilhelm JANSSEN
Lecturer
Larenstein International
Agricultural College
Brinkgeversweg 69, PO Box 7
7400 AA Deventer
THE NETHERLANDS
Tel: + 31-5700-84600
Fax: + 31-5700-84608
Tlx: 49517 TGCON

"c/o" after a fax or telex indicates that the recipient's full name and address should be given in any communication

Mr Aalbert A WANDERS
IMAG-DLO (Instituut voor
Mechanisatie, Arbeid en
Gebouwen)
Mansholtaan 10–12, Postbus 43
6700 AA Wageningen
THE NETHERLANDS
Tel: + 31-8370-76350
Fax: + 31-8370-75670
Tlx: 45330 CTWAG NL

Nigeria

Dr James O OLUKOSI
Interim Coordinator
West African Farming Systems
Research Network
Department Agricultural
Economics
Institute for Agricultural
Research
Ahmadu Bello University
PMB 1044, Zaria, NIGERIA
Tel: + 234-69-51048
Tlx: 75248 NITEZ NG

Sweden

Mr Jan JANSEN
Research Officer
International Rural Development
Centre
Swedish University of
Agricultural Sciences
PO Box 7005
S-75007 Uppsala, SWEDEN
Tel: + 46-18-671846
Fax: + 46-18-673420
Tlx: 195068 UNRUDEV S

Tanzania

Mr René FISCHER
GTZ Project Manager
Tanga Draft Animal Project
PO Box 5047, Tanga
TANZANIA
Tel: Korogwe 187
Fax: + 255-51-46454 c/o
Tlx: 45155 TIRDEP TZ
Subsequent address
 Mr René FISCHER
 PO Box 5047, Tanga
 TANZANIA
 Fax: + 255-51-46454 c/o
 Tlx: 45155 TIRDEP TZ

Mr Anno H Y GALEMA
Coopibo Agricultural Project
Adviser, Mifipro
PO Box 183, Mwanga
Kilimanjaro Region
TANZANIA
Tlx: 43095 ZITA TZ

Mr A K KAYUMBO
Agricultural Officer
Mechanization
Ministry of Agriculture
PO Box 9071, Dar es Salaam
TANZANIA
Tel: + 255-51-29481
Tlx: 41246 KILIMO TZ

Mr Emmanuel M B KWILIGWA
Senior Research Officer
Uyole Agricultural Centre
PO Box 400, Mbeya
TANZANIA
Tel: + 255-65-3081
Tlx: 51039

Mr Andrew MAKWANDA
Counterpart Project Manager
Tanga Draft Animal Project
Ministry of Agriculture
PO Box 228, Korogwe, Tanga
TANZANIA
Tel: Korogwe 187
Fax: + 255-51-46454 c/o
Tlx: 45155 TIRDEP TZ

Ms Kathy MARSHALL
Gender Issues Coordinator
Mbeya Oxenization Project
PO Box 2904, Mbeya
TANZANIA
Tel: + 255-65-3371
Fax: + 255-65-2279
Tlx: 51312 ZANKIL TZ
Subsequent address
 Ms Kathy MARSHALL
 28 Hearn Avenue, Guelph
 Ontario N1H 5Y4, CANADA

Mr Felix K MUJEMULA
Principal Technologist
Centre for Agricultural
Mechanization
and Rural Technology
(Camartec)
PO Box 764, Arusha
TANZANIA
Tel: + 255-57-8357
Fax: + 255-57-8250
Tlx: 42115 TZ
Subsequent address
 Mr Felix K MUJEMULA
 PO Box 464, Usa River, Arusha
 TANZANIA

Mr Godfrey J MWAKITWANGE
Agriculturalist
Mbozi Agricultural
Development Project
PO Box 204, Mbozi, Mbeya
TANZANIA
Tel: Mbozi 95

Mr Richard SHETTO
Head of Agricultural Engineering
Uyole Agricultural Centre
PO Box 400, Mbeya
TANZANIA
Tel: + 255-65-3081
Tlx: 51039

Dr T E SIMALENGA
Chairman, National Animal
Traction Steering Committee
Department of Agricultural
Engineering
Sokoine University of
Agriculture
PO Box 3003, Morogoro
TANZANIA
Tel: + 255-56-3259
Fax: + 255-56-3259 or 4562
Tlx: 55308 UNIVMOG TZ
Subsequent address
 Dr T E SIMALENGA
 Training Officer
 AGROTEC (UNDP-OPS)
 PO Box BW 540, Borrowdale,
 Harare, ZIMBABWE
 Tel: + 263-4-860009
 Fax: + 263-4-860009
 Tlx: 24668 UNDEV ZW

Ms Mwajuma G SIZYA
Extension Officer
Mbeya Oxenization Project
PO Box 2904, Mbeya
TANZANIA
Tel: + 255-65-3371
Fax: + 255-65-2279
Tlx: 51312 ZANKIL TZ

Dr Hussein SOSOVELE
Institute of Resource Assessment
University of Dar es Salaam
PO Box 35097, Dar es Salaam
TANZANIA
Tel: + 255-51-49039
Tlx: 41327 UNISCIE TZ

Togo

Dr Kossivi APETOFIA
Directeur
Projet pour la Promotion de la
Traction Animale (PROPTA)
BP 37, Atakpamé, TOGO
Tel: + 228-400204
Fax: + 228-400033 c/o

Uganda

Mr Alphonse AKOU
Head of Oxen Unit
Serere Research Station
PO Private Bag, Soroti
UGANDA
Subsequent address
 Mr Alphonse AKOU
 PO Box 99, Soroti
 UGANDA

Ms Christine A EKEMU
Public Relations Officer
National Environment Action
Plan
Karamoja Development Agency
PO Box 3912, Kampala
UGANDA
Tel: + 256-41-254670
Fax: + 256-41-232175 c/o

Mr Henry E S OJIROT
Project Coordinator
Animal Draft Power Training
Programme
Animal Traction Development
Organization
PO Box 9112, Kampala
UGANDA
Fax: + 256-41-232175 c/o
Tlx: 61125 UG

Mr Asanasio A OKUNI
Agriculture Engineer
Ministry of Agriculture, Animal
Resources and Fisheries
Busitema NCAM
PO Box 236, Tororo
UGANDA

Mr Japheth O Y OMODING
Assistant Commissioner for
Agriculture
Ministry of Agriculture, Animal
Industries and Fisheries
PO Box 102, Entebbe
UGANDA
Tel: + 256-42-20981
Fax: + 256-42-21047
Tlx: 61287 NATURE UG

United Kingdom

Ms Mary E ANDERSON
Transport Programme
Co-ordinator
IT Transport Ltd
Old Power Station, Ardington
Nr Wantage, Oxon OX12 8QJ
UNITED KINGDOM
Tel: + 44-1235-833753
Fax: + 44-1235-832186
Tlx: 838055 ITTRAN G

Mr Simon P CROXTON
Agricultural Engineer
Intermediate Technology
Development Group (ITDG)
Myson House, Railway Terrace
Rugby CV21 3HT
UNITED KINGDOM
Tel: + 44-1788-560631
Tel: + 44-1788-540270
Tlx: 317466 ITDG G

Mr Jim ELLIS-JONES
Agricultural Economist
Overseas Division
Silsoe Research Institute
Wrest Park, Silsoe
Bedford MK45 4HS
UNITED KINGDOM
Tel: + 44 1525 860000
Fax: + 44 1525 860156
Tlx: 825808 G

Prof Frank INNS
Consultant Agricultural and
Mechanical Engineer
53 Alameda Road, Ampthill
Bedford MK45 2LA
UNITED KINGDOM
Tel: + 44-1525-402508
Tel: + 44-1525-406373 c/o

Mr J K MUTHAMA
Director, Food Production and
Rural Development Division
Commonwealth Secretariat
Marlborough House, Pall Mall
London SW1Y 5HX
UNITED KINGDOM
Tel: + 44-171-839-3411
Fax: + 44-171-930-0827
Tlx: 27678 G

Dr Colin ORAM
Teaching Fellow
Development Technology Unit
Department of Engineering
University of Warwick
Coventry CV4 7AL
UNITED KINGDOM
Tel: + 44-1203-523523 (x 2128)
Fax: + 44-1203-418922
Tlx: 311904 UNIVWK G

Dr Anne PEARSON
Research Fellow
Centre for Tropical Veterinary
Medicine
Easter Bush, Roslin
Midlothian EH25 9RG, Scotland
UNITED KINGDOM
Tel: + 44-131-650-2617
Fax: + 44-131-445-5099
Tlx: 727442 UNIVED G

Mr John STARES
7 Cheney Hill
Heacham, King's Lynn
Norfolk PE31 7BL
UNITED KINGDOM
Tel: + 44-1485-572227
Fax: + 44-1485-570330 c/o

Mr Paul H STARKEY
ATNESA Technical Adviser
Animal Traction Development
Oxgate, 64 Northcourt Avenue
Reading RG2 7HQ
UNITED KINGDOM
Tel: + 44-1734-872152
Fax: + 44-1734-314525
Tlx: 842029 PANLIV G c/o
Email:
P.H.Starkey@reading.ac.uk

Zambia

Mr Michael BECKETT
Managing Director
Momba Farms Ltd
PO Box 630022, Choma
ZAMBIA
Tel: + 260-32-20374
Fax: + 260-32-20374
Tlx: 24650 ZA

Mr Martin BWALYA
Head of ADP Training
Department
Palabana Animal Draft Power
Project
Private Bag 173, Woodlands
Lusaka, ZAMBIA
Tel: + 260-1-264560
Fax: + 260-1-264560
Tlx: 43950 ZA

Mr Bonwell CHANDA
Agricultural Engineer
Ministry of Agriculture
Magoye Regional Research
Station
PO Box 11, Magoye, ZAMBIA
Tel: + 260-32-30377
Fax: + 260-32-30628
Tlx: 24560 BMAGO ZA

Mr Webby CHANDA
Development Manager
Lusaka Engineering Company
Limited (LENCO)
PO Box 33455, Lusaka
ZAMBIA
Tel: + 260-1-287558
Fax: + 260-1-289427
Tlx: 41720 ZA

Mr Dan DAHLIN
Cattle Development Adviser
Luapula Rural Development
Programme
PO Box 710134, Mansa
ZAMBIA
Tel: + 260-2-821798
Tlx: 59050 IRDPLP ZA

Mr Jacques DE GRAAF
ADP Development and Training
Officer
Palabana ADP Training Project
c/o Royal Netherlands Embassy
PO Box 31905, Lusaka
ZAMBIA
Tel: + 260-1-262520
Fax: + 260-1-250200
Tlx: 42690 ZA

Mr Hans DRECHSEL
Project Coordinator
Animal Power Technology
Project
GTZ-PAS, P/Bag RW 37X,
Lusaka, ZAMBIA
Tel: + 260-1-222876
Fax: + 260-1-222875
Tlx: 40246 GTZ ZA

Mr Lloyd C HANDIA
Production Manager
SKF (Zambia) Ltd
PO Box 20133, Kitwe
ZAMBIA
Tel: + 260-2-223333
Tel: + 260-2-226219
Tlx: 40020 ZA

Mr Traugott HARTMANN
District Agricultural Adviser
Kabwe Smallholder
Development Project (EC)
Department of Agriculture
PO Box 81110, Kabwe
ZAMBIA
Tel: + 260-5-223511
Fax: + 260-5-223512
Tlx: 81396 AGRIC ZA

Mr Jan Pieter HEIJBOER
Production Manager
Lusaka Engineering Company
Limited (LENCO)
PO Box 33455, Lusaka
ZAMBIA
Tel: + 260-1-264770
Fax: + 260-1-289427
Tlx: 41720 ZA

Dr D HESSELLBACH
GTZ Agricultural Adviser
Siavonga Agricultural
Development Project
PO Box 92, Siavonga
ZAMBIA
Tel: + 260-?-511303
Fax: + 260-1-222875 c/o
Tlx: 40246 GTZ ZA

Mr Christopher KALIMA
Logging Superintendent
ZAFFICO
Zambia Forestry and Forest
Industries Corporation Ltd
PO Box 21871, Kitwe
ZAMBIA
Tel: + 260-2-733087
Tlx: 30000 ZA

Mr Herman G KAMPHUIS
Team Leader
Western Province Animal Draft
Power Programme
Department of Agriculture
PO Box 910067, Mongu
ZAMBIA
Tel: + 260-7-221215
Subsequent address
Mr Herman G KAMPHUIS
RDP Livestock Services BV
Steylaan 19F, PO Box 523
3700 AM Zeist
THE NETHERLANDS

Mr Fred KRUIT
Project Officer Magoye
Animal Draft Power Research
and Development Project
c/o Royal Netherlands Embassy
PO Box 31905, Lusaka
ZAMBIA
Tel: + 260-32-30377
Fax: + 260-1-250200
Tlx: 42690 ZA

Mrs Margaret K LOMBE
Deputy Animal Draft Power
Coordinator
Department of Agriculture
(Northern Province)
PO Box 410018, Kasama
ZAMBIA
Tel: Kasama 221071

Mr Stanislaus Lungo LUBUMBE
Provincial Animal Husbandry
Officer
Department of Agriculture
(Luapula Province)
PO Box 710072, Mansa
ZAMBIA
Tel: + 260-2-821251
Tlx: 59050 IRDPLP ZA

Mr Roelof A MEIJER
Project Coordinator
Animal Draft Power Research
and Development Programme
PO Box 11, Magoye, ZAMBIA
Fax: + 260-32-30628 c/o
Fax: + 260-1-262517 c/o
Tlx: 24560 ZA
Subsequent address:
Mr Roelof A MEIJER
Paddepoelseweg 1
6532 ZG Nijmegen
THE NETHERLANDS

Mr Aaron MKANDAWIRE
Agricultural Engineering Officer
Kabwe Smallholder
Development Project
Ministry of Agriculture, Food
and Fisheries
PO Box 80434, Kabwe
ZAMBIA
Tel: + 260-5-223927
Fax: + 260-5-223512
Tlx: 81396 AGRIC ZA

Mr Isaac MOREITHI
Deputy Resident Representative
World Bank
PO Box 35410, Lusaka
ZAMBIA
Tel: + 260-1-229046

Mr Ivor MUKUKA
Agricultural Engineer
Department of Agriculture
(North Western Province)
PO Box 110041, Solwezi
ZAMBIA
Tel: + 260-8-821320
Fax: + 260-8-821655

Mr Andrew K MUMA
District Animal Draft Power
Coordinator
Department of Agriculture
PO Box 940007, Kaoma
ZAMBIA
Tel: + 260-7-360089

Mr Chanda Charles MULENGA
Provincial Agricultural Engineer
Department of Agriculture
PO Box 410018, Kasama
ZAMBIA
Tel: + 260-4-221071
Fax: + 260-4-221553
Tlx: 65004 ZA

Ms Grace MUWANGA
Lecturer Biomedical Sciences
School of Veterinary Medicine
University of Zambia
PO Box 32379, Lusaka
ZAMBIA

Mr Emmanuel MWENYA
National Animal Draft Power
Coordinator
Agricultural Engineering Section
Department of Agriculture
PO Box 50291, Lusaka
ZAMBIA
Tel: + 260-1-252824
Fax: + 260-1-264281
Tlx: 43950 ZA

Dr Wilson N M MWENYA
Department of Animal Science
University of Zambia
PO Box 32379, Lusaka
ZAMBIA
Tel: + 260-1-223721
Fax: + 260-1-250587
Tlx: 44370 ZA

Mr Mulugeta NEGASSA
FINNIDA Senior Agricultural
Adviser
Luapula Rural Development
Programme
PO Box 710134, Mansa
ZAMBIA
Tel: + 260-2-821798
Tlx: 59050 IRDPLP ZA

Mr Gert Jan NIEUWHOF
Animal Scientist, SNV
PO Box 710151, Mansa
ZAMBIA

Mr Roy Chileya NKANDU
Livestock Development Officer
Smallholder Development
Project
PO Box 90793, Luanshya
ZAMBIA
Tel: + 260-2-510497
Fax: + 260-2-510539
Tlx: 56760 ZA

Mr Gervazio B M PHIRI
Chief Animal Husbandry Officer
Department of Agriculture
PO Box 50291, Lusaka
ZAMBIA
Tel: + 260-1-251442
Tlx: ZA 43950

Mr Keith OWEN
Agricultural Inputs, Credit and
Marketing Specialist
EC/GRZ Smallholder
Development Project
PO Box 90793, Luanshya,
ZAMBIA
Tel: + 260-2-510497
Fax: + 260-2-510539
Tlx: 56760 ZA

"c/o" after a fax or telex indicates that the recipient's full name and address should be given in any communication

Mr Gerhard RITTER
District Agricultural Adviser
Kabwe Smallholder
Development Project (EC)
Department of Agriculture
PO Box 81110, Kabwe
ZAMBIA
Tel: + 260-5-223511
Fax: + 260-5-223512
Tlx: 81396 AGRIC ZA

Mr Emmanuel A SAKALA
Dept Agricultural Engineering
Natural Resources Development
College (NRDC)
PO Box 310009, Lusaka
ZAMBIA
Tel: + 260-1-224610

Mr Henry SICHEMBE
Acting Head
Agricultural Engineering Section
Department of Agriculture
PO Box 50291, Lusaka
ZAMBIA
Tel: + 260-1-252824
Fax: + 260-1-262517
Tlx: 43950 ZA

Ms Christine SIKANYIKA
Senior Agricultural Supervisor
Female Extension Section
Department of Agriculture
PO Box 50291, Lusaka
ZAMBIA
Tel: + 260-1-251442
Tlx: 43950 ZA

Mr Ronald SIMUYI
Provincial Agricultural Engineer
Department of Agriculture
PO Box 80434, Kabwe
ZAMBIA
Tel: + 260-5-223927
Fax: + 260-5-223512
Tlx: 81396 AGRIC ZA

Mr Piet STEVENS
Agricultural Engineer
Animal Draft Power Research
and Development Project
Magoye Regional Research
Station
c/o Royal Netherlands Embassy
P O Box 31905, Lusaka
ZAMBIA
Tel: + 260-1-264560
Fax: + 260-1-264560

Dr Chris TAUPITZ
Mining Adviser, SADCC
Mining Coordinating Unit
Small Scale Mining Subsector
c/o GTZ, P Bag RW 37X,
Lusaka, ZAMBIA
Tel: + 260-1-251264
Fax: + 260-1-252095
Tlx: 40246 GTZ ZA

Ms Annie Nawa TEMBO
Senior Female Extension officer
Female Extension Section
Department of Agriculture
PO Box 50291, Lusaka
ZAMBIA
Tel: + 260-1-251442
Tlx: 43950 ZA

Mr Hermannus J VROOM
Project Engineer
Technology Development and
Advisory Unit (TDAU)
University of Zambia
PO Box 32379, Lusaka
ZAMBIA
Tel: + 260-1-213221 (x 1524)
Fax: + 260-1-253952
Tlx: 44370 ZA

Zimbabwe

Mr Samuel CHIKURA
Research Officer
Farming Systems Research Unit
Department of Research and
Specialist Services (DRSS)
Ministry of Agriculture
PO Box 8108, Causeway, Harare
ZIMBABWE
Tel: + 263-4-704531

Mr Basilioh Bunu
CHIKWANDA
Training Officer
Agritex Institute of Agricultural
Engineering
PO Box 330, Borrowdale, Harare
ZIMBABWE
Tel: + 263-4-725936
Fax: + 263-4-302529
Tlx: 22455 AGRIC ZW

Dr Robert J CONNOR
Regional Tsetse and
Trypanosomiasis Control
Programme
PO Box A 560, Avondale, Harare
ZIMBABWE
Tel: + 263-4-707683
Fax: + 263-4-725360 c/o
Tlx: 22174 RTTP ZW

Subsequent address
Prof Robert CONNOR
Head of Department of
Veterinary Tropical Diseases
University of Pretoria
Private Bag X04
0110 Onderstepoort
SOUTH AFRICA
Tel: + 27-12-5460645
Fax: + 27-12-5463102
Tlx: 3-22723 SA

Ms Joanna DORAN
Associate Expert, Technology
UNIFEM (United Nations
Development Fund for Women)
7th Floor, Takura House
67 Union Avenue
PO Box 4775, Harare
ZIMBABWE
Tel: + 263-4-728691
Fax: + 263-4-728695
Tlx: 24668 ZW

Subsequent address
Ms Jo DORAN
Rural Transport Adviser
ITDG-Kenya
PO Box 39493, Nairobi
KENYA
Tel: + 254-2-442108
Fax: + 254-2-445166

Mr Dumezwsai DUBE
Director, Sales and Marketing
Bulawayo Steel Products
PO Box 1603, Bulawayo
ZIMBABWE
Tel: + 263-9-69103/62671
Fax: + 263-9-62283
Tlx: 33257 ZW

Subsequent address
Mr Dumezwsai DUBE
International Trade and
Development Consultants
Kurima House
PO Box 2738, Harare
ZIMBABWE

Mr Joseph FRANCIS
Research Fellow
Department of Animal Science
University of Zimbabwe
PO Box MP 167 Mount
Pleasant, Harare, ZIMBABWE
Tel: + 263-4-303211 (x 1157)
Fax: + 263-4-732828
Tlx: 26580 UNIV ZW

Mr Jürgen HAGMANN
GTZ Soil Conservation
Specialist
Conservation Tillage Project
PO Box 790, Masvingo
ZIMBABWE
Tel: + 263-39-63255
Fax: + 263-39-64035
Tlx: 91111 GTZMAS ZW

Dr Peta A JONES
Private Bag 5713, Binga
ZIMBABWE

Mr Rodger L MPANDE
Project Manager,
Entrepreneurship amongst Rural
Women
Ministry of Community and
Cooperative Development
St Andrews House
Samora Michel Avenue, Harare
ZIMBABWE
Subsequent address
Mr Rodger L MPANDE
Zero Regional Network of
Environmental Experts
44 Edmonds Avenue,
Belvedere, Harare
ZIMBABWE
Tel: + 263-4-791333
Fax: + 263-4-732858

Ms Lotta (A-C) SYLWANDER
Socio-Economist
AGROTEC (UNDP-OPS)
PO Box BW 540, Borrowdale,
Harare, ZIMBABWE
Tel: + 263-4-860009
Fax: + 263-4-860009
Tlx: 24668 UNDEV ZW

Subsequent address
Ms Lotta (A-C) SYLWANDER
Lövholmsvägen 21
S - 117 65, Stockholm
SWEDEN
Tel: + 46-8-198242

Resource organisations

CTA
Technical Centre for
Agricultural and Rural
Cooperation
Galvanistraat 9, Ede
Postbus 380
6700 AJ Wageningen
THE NETHERLANDS
Tel: + 31-8380-60400
Fax: + 31-8380-31052
Tlx: 30169 CTA NL

DGIS
Ministerie van Buitenlandse
Zaken
Postbus 20061
2500 EB The Hague,
THE NETHERLANDS

GTZ
Deutsche Gesellschaft für
Technische Zusammenarbeit
Postfach 5180
D-65726 Eschborn, GERMANY
Tel: + 49-6196-79-0
Fax: + 49-6196-797130
Tlx: 407501-0 GTZ D

IMAG-DLO
Instituut voor Mechanisatie,
Arbeid en Gebouwen
Mansholtaan 10–12, Postbus 43
6700 AA Wageningen
THE NETHERLANDS
Tel: + 31-8370-76350
Fax: + 31-8370-75670
Tlx: 45330 CTWAG NL

IDRC
International Development
Research Centre
PO Box 62084, Nairobi
KENYA
Tel: + 254-2-330850
Fax: + 254-2-214583
Tlx: 23062

Photograph opposite
Pack donkey carrying manure, Egypt

Improving animal traction technology

Overview papers

A world-wide view of animal traction highlighting some key issues in eastern and southern Africa

Keynote paper and photographs by

Paul Starkey

ATNESA Technical Adviser
Animal Traction Development, Oxgate, 64 Northcourt Avenue, Reading RG2 7HQ, UK

Abstract

The paper reviews the use of draft animals throughout the world, citing examples of the use of oxen, bulls, cows, buffaloes, horses, mules, donkeys and less common work animals. In most parts of the world, including Asia, Europe, the Americas, North Africa and Ethiopia there have been hundreds or even thousands of years of experience of using animal traction. Common to several regions are simple ard plows with long wooden beams, with the animals and implement controlled by one person.

In most of sub-Saharan Africa, animal traction has been introduced this century, and the processes of introduction are continuing. There has been relatively little time for indigenous support systems to develop and evolve, and past interventions by government agencies and donor-assisted projects have tended to be "top-down". Factory-made steel implements pulled by chains have been supplied, and two or more people usually work with animals. Oxen are the main work animals, but donkeys are increasingly used for transport and some cultivation in the semi-arid areas.

The paper goes on to raise some animal traction issues relating to profitability, animal management, tillage systems, implement supply, women, technology transfer and transport.

Introduction

In many parts of the world animal traction is an appropriate, affordable and sustainable technology. Work animals can be used to reduce drudgery and intensify agricultural production, so raising living standards throughout rural communities, benefiting men and women, young and old. Cattle, buffaloes, donkeys, mules, horses, camels and other working animals can provide smallholder farmers with vital power for crop cultivation and transport. Draft animals can also be used for other activities including water-raising, milling, logging, land-levelling and road construction.

This paper draws mainly on professional visits to many countries in Africa and the rest of the world. It starts by providing a global overview of animal traction and goes on to highlight some pertinent issues relating to the workshop themes.

Animal traction in Asia

Draft animals have been used in Asia for thousands of years. To this day, animal traction technology remains a widely used, highly persistent and economically essential component of many Asian smallholder farming systems. Cattle are the main work animals, and they are generally worked in pairs with withers yokes. It is rare for more than one person to work with a pair of draft animals. They are used for plowing and levelling rice swamps (Photo 1), and for plowing and harrowing upland soils (Photo 2). Most implements are pulled by a long wooden beam. They are made in villages largely from wood, but with steel shares. The use of steel mouldboard plows is gradually increasing, but wooden ard plows are very persistent. In India, wooden-beamed ards remain much more common than the inexpensive steel plows which have been available for decades (Photo 3). Simple seeders and weeders are also quite common, and in India blade

Photo 1: Cows pulling simple wooden leveller in a rice field, Indonesia

Photo 2:
Woman sows while man uses wooden ard plow, India

Photo 3: Contractors using oxen and simple wooden ard plows to cultivate rice field, India

Photo 5: Single buffalo levelling rice field, Philippines

Photo 6:
Buffalo pulling wooden sledge, Philippines

harrows, implements with broad shares, are employed for secondary cultivation.

In Asia, oxen are commonly used to pull carts (Photo 4). In rural areas, the traditional designs tend to have two large wooden wheels. In urban centres, four-wheel trailers are more common, and these generally have pneumatic tyres.

Water buffalo are worked in some south-east Asian countries (Photo 5). They are particularly well-adapted to the cultivation of rice swamps, with large feet and the ability to thrive on diets based mainly on rice straw. They are used in pairs, or singly, for swamp rice cultivation. Although buffaloes are mainly employed for rice cultivation, they can be used for upland plowing and for pulling carts or sledges (Photo 6). They are less adapted to such operations than cattle, being less efficient at thermoregulation. The wallowing for which they are famous is a means of cooling themselves. In most Asian countries, working cattle are numerically more important than working buffaloes.

Female working animals are very common in Asia. In Indonesia it has been estimated that 80% of working animals are cows or female buffaloes (Photo 1).

In the drier parts of Asia (including the Middle East) horses, donkeys and mules are employed. They tend to be used mainly for transport (Photo 7), but they may perform some cultivation (Photo 8).

Camels are used for pack transport and pulling carts. They are also used for cultivation, particularly in the Indian state of Rajasthan. Camels are worked singly. Around the Himalayas, yaks are employed for pack transport. In some countries of south-east Asia, elephants assist with logging.

Photo 4: Ox carts with large wooden wheels, India

Photo 7: Horses in tandem pulling cart, China

Photo 8: Plowing with a donkey, Palestine

Animal traction in the Americas

Animal traction was introduced into the Americas by the early colonialists, and some countries have been using animal power for hundreds of years.

In the tropical zone, work cattle are the main draft animals. These are usually worked in pairs, using horn/head yokes (Photo 9). Most animals are oxen or uncastrated bulls (Photo 10). It is rare to see more than one person working with a pair of animals. The traditional long-beamed, wooden ard plows are widely used. Traditional carts with two large wooden wheels (Photo 11) are slowly being replaced by carts with pneumatic tyres. In Central America, animal-powered mills made from wood or steel are used to crush sugar cane (Photo 12).

In parts of the Andes, llamas are used as pack animals. In the north-east hills of the Dominican Republic, uncastrated bulls are employed for pack

Photo 9: Ridging with bulls fitted with horn/head yoke and muzzles, Guatamala

Photo 10:
Bulls pulling seeder on a long-beamed ard, Honduras

Photo 11: Large oxen pulling wooden-wheeled cart, El Salvador

Photo 12: Oxen turning sugar-cane crusher, Honduras

transport. In one area of Honduras, goats fitted with horn/head yokes pull carts of water along flat roads (Photo 13).

In the highland and temperate areas of north and south America, horses, mules and donkeys tend to be preferred to oxen. They walk faster, can give greater bursts of power and are well suited for transport operations. Horses, donkeys and mules are employed by some smallholder farmers for cultivation in Mexico, Chile and Argentina. In other countries they are mainly used for riding, carting and pack transport.

In the last century, oxen were important draft animals for farm cultivation in north America. Withers yokes, with broad bows were often employed, although some farmers, notably those in Quebec, used horn/head yokes. One person worked with a team of animals. Heavy horses (Photo 14) and mules steadily replaced oxen as farm equipment

Photo 13:
Goats pulling cart for collecting water, Honduras

Photo 14: Heavy horses pulling seeder, USA

Photo 17: Heavy horses mowing hay, UK

Photo 15: Amish farmer cultivating with horse, USA

Photo 18: Donkey cart for hay transport, Spain

diversified and harvesting implements with large power requirements were developed. Factory-made steel equipment pulled by traction chains superseded the more traditional, artisan-made implements. Horses were themselves gradually replaced by tractors in most farming systems. Nevertheless, even today, amid the modern farming systems of the United States of America, several thousand Amish farmers profitably make use of horses for all farm operations (Photo 15). Oxen are still used by smallholder farmers for winter logging operations. In New England ox-pulling contests remain popular (Photo 16).

Photo 16: Oxen training and pulling competition, USA

Animal traction in Europe

Europe has had centuries of tradition of using draft animals. Oxen were the original work animals, and these were worked with withers yokes in northern Europe and head/horn yokes in southern and western Europe. Oxen were mainly worked in pairs. One person controlled the oxen and a long-beamed wooden plow. Wagons, fitted with four large wooden wheels, replaced traditional two-wheeled carts for on-farm, rural and urban transport. Following the industrial revolution, farmers increasingly used factory-made, steel implements, pulled by traction chains.

Horses, fitted with collars, tended to supersede oxen in the northern and eastern countries of Europe (Photo 17). Horses were the preferred animals for transport operations in most of Europe. Wooden wheels gave way to pneumatic tyres.

During the present century, tractors have been replacing horses and oxen in European countries. Work oxen are still employed for cultivation and carting in some smallholder farming systems in southern Europe, and donkeys are quite widely maintained for transport (Photo 18). Heavy horses are used in several countries, notably Poland. For environmental and economic reasons, horses remain important for logging in Belgium and Scandinavia.

Photo 19: Donkey carrying forage, Egypt

Photo 21: Camel and mule plowing with ard, Morocco

Photo 20: Horse and donkey plowing together, Morocco

Photo 22: Boy plowing with a cow and a donkey, Morocco

North Africa and Ethiopia

In North Africa animal traction has been used since the time of the Egyptian pharaohs (illustrations of oxen plowing are common in ancient Egyptian tombs and temples). Along the north African coast cows, donkeys, mules, horses and camels are widely used for cultivation, pack transport and pulling carts (Photo 19). In Morocco, these different species are even worked together in a variety of combinations using traditional belly yokes (Photos 20–22). In the Nile valley and delta, cows (female animals) and water buffaloes are also used for plowing (Photo 23). Donkeys, cattle, buffaloes and camels are used to power the *sakia* irrigation wheels (Photo 24). The use of four-wheel trailers for urban and rural transport is common throughout north Africa (Photo 25). Pneumatic or solid rubber tyres are becoming more common, although traditional wooden-spoked wheels are still widespread.

Ethiopia has had generations of experience of using draft animals. Work oxen and pack donkeys (Photo 26) have been part of Ethiopian farming systems for centuries. Farmers cultivate with pairs of oxen, using a withers yoke and a long-beamed *maresha* ard plow (Photo 27). The *maresha* plows are made by the farmers themselves, with local blacksmiths supplying the steel point and attachment ring. The plows are light enough for the farmer to carry to the field. Farmers work alone with their pair

Photo 23: Plowing with two cows (females) and a traditional wooden ard, Egypt

Photo 24: A milk cow turning a traditional sakia water-lifting device, Egypt

Photo 25: Donkey with collar pulling four-wheel trailer with rubber tyres, Egypt

"Improving animal traction technology"

Photo 26: Pack donkey, Ethiopia

Photo 27: Plowing with oxen and a long-beamed maresha *ard, Ethiopia*

Photo 28: Locally designed donkey cart, Ethiopia

of oxen. The use of cows or bulls is most unusual, and oxen are seldom used to pull carts.

Large numbers of pack donkeys are used in Ethiopia, particularly in the highland areas. They carry fuel wood, building materials, fodder for animals and goods for marketing. Carts, pulled by horses, mules or donkeys, are used in some towns. In a few rural areas, simple and inexpensive donkey carts are spreading (Photo 28).

Sub-Saharan Africa

Animal traction in sub-Saharan Africa (excluding Ethiopia) differs greatly from that in other regions of the world because there has not been such a long tradition of animal power use. In most of sub-Saharan Africa, animal power for crop cultivation has been introduced during the present century (Starkey, 1991a).

There have been some long-standing uses of animal power. Certain pastoralists in West Africa and eastern Africa have had a long tradition of using cattle and donkeys as pack animals (Photo 29). The riding of horses and camels, and the use of pack transport has had a long tradition in the Sahelian zone of West Africa. As ports developed around Africa's west and east coast, work animals tended to be employed to assist local transport operations. In the islands to the east (Madagascar, Zanzibar and Pemba) cart transport was introduced long ago, and traditional skills in making wooden wheels remain to this day (Photos 30–31). In the south of the continent, the early European settlers started using oxen for transport and for farming.

Photo 29:
Traditional panniers used by pastoralists, Kenya

Photo 30:
Two oxen pulling wooden-wheeled cart, Madagascar

Photo 31:
Single ox pulling cart with wooden wheels, Zanzibar

Photo 32: Direct ridging with uncastrated bulls, Nigeria

Photo 34: Carrying manure in a single-donkey cart, Mali

Photo 33: Long-horned, zebu bulls making ridges with a plow, Tchad

Photo 35: Early weeding with a donkey and Houe occidentale cultivator, Senegal

In much of Africa, crop farming and cattle herding have tended to be separate activities, carried out by different tribal groups. Traditional cropping systems have been based on shifting cultivation. Roots of trees and shrubs have been maintained in the soil, as land has been temporarily cropped for a season or two. These factors reduced the potential for animal power to spread among traditional cropping systems (Pingali, Bigot and Binswanger, 1987).

Animal power was introduced into the smallholder farming systems of sub-Saharan Africa in relatively recent times. Although there were a few introductions before the 1920s, in most villages in West, Central, southern and eastern Africa, animal traction was introduced during the lifetime of the present village elders. The technology has been spreading, rapidly in some areas, more slowly in others. Formal and informal introductions have been continuing. In many countries there are areas where animal power was first introduced in the 1950s, 1960s, 1970s and 1980s. There are some villages that have started using animal power for the first time this year.

Animal traction in West Africa

West Africa can be divided into four broad agro-ecological zones which greatly influence the uses of animal traction. The most northerly zone,

including the south of the Sahara desert and its arid fringes, there is little or no tillage for crop cultivation. Some work animals, notably camels, donkeys and horses, are used for riding and for pack transport. Water is the major constraint, and animal power may be used to pull water from wells, and to transport it on carts.

South of this zone is the Sahel region where annual rainfall is 400–1000 mm. This zone runs from Senegal and The Gambia in the west, to northern Nigeria, northern Cameroon and southern Tchad in the east; the Sahel zone encompasses southern Mali, southern Niger and much of Burkina Faso and includes areas where animal traction has been promoted by companies or projects developing the production of cotton and groundnuts. Humped zebu oxen are particularly important for farm power (Photos 32–33). They are worked in pairs, with withers yokes, and it is common for two or three people to work with a pair of animals (Photo 33). The long-beamed, wooden implements seen in other regions of the world are not used in West Africa. Oxen pull on a traction chain, attached to their yoke, to draw factory-made steel equipment. The first implements introduced to the region were plows and ridgers, manufactured in Europe. Plows remain the dominant implement in the south (higher rainfall areas) of the animal traction zone. In northern

Photo 36: Tine tillage with a donkey, Mali

Photo 38: Horse turning sugar cane crusher, Nigeria

Photo 37: Direct planting with horse and Super-eco seeder, Senegal

Photo 39: Training oxen of the small N'Dama breed, Guinea Bissau

Nigeria, farmers prefer ridgers, as direct ridging in light soils is quicker than plowing (Photo 32). In the more arid areas, farmers increasingly use cultivation tines for tillage, and in some areas, notably in Senegal, direct seeding is practised.

Although oxen are the main work animals in West Africa, cows are increasingly being used for work, for example in Sine Saloum, Senegal (Reh and Horst, 1982). In Tchad and northern Nigeria, farmers use uncastrated work bulls (Photos 32–33). There is general movement of cattle southwards, from breeding herds in the north to markets in the south. Farmers tend to buy young bulls, work them for one or two seasons and then sell them to butchers, having profited from their weight gains.

Oxen and donkeys are very important for transport in semi-arid areas. Large numbers of donkey carts with pneumatic tyres and factory-made axles are used in Sahelian countries (Photo 34). In Nigeria and Ghana, ox carts made from motor vehicle axles are common.

Donkeys are increasingly used for tine tillage, direct seeding and weeding (Photos 35–36). Horses are mainly kept for prestige purposes and high-value urban and rural transport. In the groundnut area of Senegal transport horses are employed to pull cultivators and planters (Photo 37). A few horses turn sugar cane mills in Nigeria (Photo 38).

South of the semi-arid zone is the semi-humid agro-ecological zone that runs eastwards from southern Senegal and Guinea, through northern parts of Sierra Leone, Côte d'Ivoire, Ghana, Togo and Benin. The higher rainfall in this zone is associated with thicker bush than that of the semi-arid zone. The de-stumping of farms to allow plowing can be a constraint to the spread of animal traction and the thick bush growth near paths can restrict the utility of carts. The dominant animals in this zone are humpless, trypanotolerant cattle, such as the N'Dama. These cattle can resist moderate challenges of trypanosomiasis, a disease transmitted by tsetse flies. Trypanotolerant cattle tend to be small, but they can usefully be employed (Photo 39). They are often fitted with horn/head yokes. Steel mouldboard plows are the main implements in this zone.

There are no distinct boundaries between the semi-arid and semi-humid zone, and in the transitional areas the humpless cattle coexist and crossbreed with humped zebu animals. The zebu cattle are preferred for their larger size, and the trypanotolerant cattle for their disease resistance. In the more humid areas donkeys seldom flourish.

Further south, in the coastal regions of Sierra Leone, Liberia, Côte d'Ivoire, Ghana, Togo, Benin, Nigeria and Cameroon, there are very few cattle and no donkeys. Animal traction is almost nonexistent.

Photo 40: A water buffalo being assessed, Senegal

The animal traction zones mentioned are not static, but are gradually moving southward. This may be associated with regional changes in climate, increased deforestation and human population density and decreased disease challenge. The southern limits of the trypanotolerant cattle, the zebu cattle and donkeys seem to be extending southward year by year. For example, 30 years ago, donkeys were relatively uncommon in The Gambia. Now they are the dominant work animals. Donkeys are gradually moving southward in many countries including Senegal, Burkina Faso and Mali. Cattle are increasingly being brought into the coastal area, and animal traction is steadily spreading southward in most countries in West Africa.

Camels in West Africa are mainly kept for pack transport, but they are sometimes used for crop cultivation in the Sahelian zone. Surprisingly there is also one area in central Nigeria where camels are quite commonly employed for plowing. One project in northern Senegal has attempted to introduce water buffalo (Photo 40). Although they are larger than local cattle, they are less well adapted and unlikely ever to become common.

Southern and eastern Africa

Comparable agro-ecological zoning of animal traction also occurs in southern and eastern Africa, but the pattern is more patchy and less distinct than in West Africa. The areas of high animal traction include the Machakos area of southern Kenya, the cotton zone of northern Tanzania, the maize belts of southern Zambia and central Malawi and the

Photo 41: Plowing with three oxen and one cow, Zambia

communal areas of Zimbabwe, southern Mozambique and northern Namibia. In these areas the great majority of farmers use animal traction. They are mainly semi-arid areas, with rainfall of 600–1200 mm with local cattle-keeping traditions. Areas without animal traction tend to be high rainfall zones (eg, northern Zambia), tsetse infested areas with few cattle (eg, southern Tanzania and northern Mozambique) or arid areas with little crop cultivation (eg, northern Kenya, southern Namibia and the Masai steppe of Tanzania).

Cattle are the main work animals. Oxen are most common, but cows are increasingly used in several countries. Cattle are yoked in pairs using withers yokes. In many countries it is common for two pairs to be linked and worked as teams of four (Photo 41). Six animals are sometimes used, and in Botswana it is common for eight or more animals to be hitched together (Photo 42).

Factory-made mouldboard plows are the most common implements. Throughout the region, the designs are broadly similar, and unlike those of West Africa, they have I-section beams. The "Safim" designs of southern Africa are widely used, but in most cases the farmers remove the hake adjustment mechanism.

Many farmers own simple sledges, made from tree branches (Photo 43). These provide low-cost transport, although they have been banned in some countries due to erosion problems. Interestingly, a similar widespread use of sledges has not developed in West Africa. Animal-drawn carts made from old vehicle axles are common in some areas (Zimbabwe, Botswana, Namibia, central Malawi, north-central Tanzania). Seed planters are not common, and many farmers plant in the furrow at

Photo 42: Eight thin animals training for work, Botswana

Photo 43: Four oxen pulling sledge, Namibia

Photo 44: Planting every third furrow while plowing, Zambia

Photo 45: Donkey cart used for rural transport, Zimbabwe

the time of plowing (Photo 44). The use of inter-row weeders is quite common in Zimbabwe. Elsewhere weeders are unusual, but in several countries there are signs that farmers are likely to adopt inter-row weeding soon.

Donkeys are increasingly used for cart transport (Photo 45) and, to a lesser extent, for packing and for cultivation (Photo 46). Their geographical range is spreading in many countries, including

Zimbabwe, Namibia and Tanzania. Their low cost, ease of management and ability to withstand drought has encouraged their use.

Some key issues in southern and eastern Africa

Profitability

Animal traction is presently increasing in most countries in sub-Saharan Africa. This suggests that it must be profitable, although the economics are not always clear to the outsider. Within societies, animal traction may not benefit all members of society equally. Those who invest in animal traction themselves will have greatest access to it (with associated benefits of timeliness), but they also have more risk and more year-round labour. Indeed, animal traction is often seen as labour-shifting rather than labour-saving. Benefits of timeliness (with possible yield increases or risk reduction) may have to be paid for with out-of-season labour, and possibly the labour of the children delegated to look after the animals (Starkey, 1987a).

Animal transport can be crucial for the profitability of animal traction. One farmer in Malawi reported his first investment in animal traction was a pair of oxen and a plow. After three seasons spent plowing with his animals, he invested in a cart. The following season he reverted to manual cultivation of his fields (using hired labour) for his oxen earned more in transport fees than the cost of hired labour (Starkey, 1985). At harvest, income from carting can be particularly high, for hire rates such as "one bag kept for six bags carried" may represent 15% or more of harvest value, merely for transport.

Animal transport can stimulate marketing and economic activity, for headloading places severe limits on the weight of goods that can be carried to and from market (Photo 47). Animal transport also increases profitability through the greater use of manure and crop residues.

Photo 46: Donkeys plowing, Zimbabwe.
This was the first year the farmer had tried to plow with donkeys using home-made collars

Photo 47: Farmer selling tomatoes from ox cart, northwest Zambia. The farmer said the cart improved marketing and this had allowed production to increase

*Photo 48: Forage for animals collected by cart
and stored in a tree, Namibia*

Animal management

As the problems of drought have hit Africa, donkeys have become increasingly popular, for they can survive in arid and over-grazed conditions better than cattle. Drought conditions also exacerbate the serious problem of animal condition at the start of the plowing season. One low-cost method of improving animal condition is the stocking of crop residues, and this becomes increasingly feasible once animal-drawn carts are available (Photo 48).

As farming systems become more intensive, cows tend to be increasingly used for work. When insufficient oxen are available, cows are sometimes used to make up numbers in a team of four animals. Lack of harmful results may then lead to the practice continuing. However, if nutritional levels are inadequate (which is common) reproductive performance may be adversely affected. Nevertheless, farmers may find that even with mediocre reproductive performance, the use of cows for light work may be more profitable than maintaining oxen. For heavier work and regular transport, oxen are likely to be preferred.

Tillage systems

Despite research on alternative tillage systems in several countries, the mouldboard plow remains the dominant implement in eastern and southern Africa.

In Zambia, and elsewhere, plows tend to be used (against all extension advice) without an adjustable hake (Photo 41). They are generally held at an angle during work. In this way, they do not operate like the classic, well-adjusted, asymmetrical mouldboard plows shown in most extension manuals. In some ways they become a little more like the symmetrical ard plows widely used elsewhere in the tropics

Research in the region continues on alternative tillage systems, including ridging systems, tied-ridging, conservation tillage, direct planting and tine tillage. Farmers seem to want tillage systems with low power requirements, partly because their cattle are in poor condition and their donkeys are weak. However, they also want good weed control, and this has been a weak point for several alternatives to the mouldboard plow.

It appears that animal-drawn weeding technology is likely to spread quite rapidly in the coming decade, provided weeding implements are available in the rural areas (Photo 49). In some cases, the low level of animal-drawn weeder adoption seems due to farmer (and extensionist) unfamiliarity with the techniques and the length of yokes required. Another major constraint is fear that animals could damage the growing crops. In Guinea and Mali, special village-level training sessions have been held (Photo 50), with animals and their handlers practising on rows of sticks, before entering the crop fields (Sangaré et al, 1988). Such simple and rapid training of animals has given the owners of oxen the necessary confidence to start mechanical inter-row weeding.

Supply and distribution

In much of the world, including North Africa and Ethiopia, animal-drawn implements are made in villages. Close links between blacksmiths and farmers have led to acceptable equipment specifications and sometimes innovations. In Europe, most present-day large farm-equipment

Photo 49: Weeding cotton using oxen, Zimbabwe

Photo 50: Training oxen to weed between rows, Guinea

companies had their origins in small blacksmith workshops. As they expanded, they established networks of dealers, ensuring local depots of equipment and spare parts.

In several countries in Africa, including Madagascar, Mali and Nigeria, some blacksmiths have started to make innovative designs of animal traction equipment. More commonly, blacksmiths tend to concentrate on making spare parts and repairing (or rebuilding) implements. Rural weekly markets are important for marketing artisanal products, such as spare parts (Photo 51). Blacksmiths tend to be severely constrained by lack of raw materials and may be unaware of techniques and tools that might assist implement production. In some areas, there are very few blacksmiths, making it difficult for farmers to obtain spares.

In sub-Saharan Africa, centralised systems for the production and distribution of implements have tended to inhibit village-level implement production and the development of close farmer–manufacturer relationships. Donor-assisted projects have tended to order equipment from abroad with large contracts for the successful tendering firms. This has often led to large stockpiles of centrally-purchased equipment that farmers perceive as being technically inappropriate (Photo 52) or of poor quality (Starkey, 1989). Zambia and Mozambique have both suffered from such donor-controlled inappropriate equipment provision. In Tanzania, the main Ubungo Farm Implements (UFI) factory had to cease plow production for several years, as large numbers of donor-funded imported plows saturated the market.

Photo 51: *Products made by blacksmiths and by factories on sale at a weekly market, Mali*

Photo 52: *Numerous unsuitable seeders ordered by international tender but lying unused, Mali*

Local production can be an answer, provided the equipment manufactured is considered appropriate to farmers. This might seem self-evident, but this has not always been the case with the top-down approach of certain donor-assisted projects. In Tanzania, external "experts" and their counterparts in Zana za Kilimo (ZZK) were responsible for the manufacture of several hundred unpopular plows concerning which there had been inadequate farmer consultation and market assessment (Starkey, 1989).

The successful supply of animal traction implements depends not only on appropriate hardware, but also on the necessary supporting infrastructure, including credit provision. In Senegal, the large Siscoma factory was making a range of implements and spare parts that appeared acceptable to farmers. However, when the government changed its policy on agricultural credit, sales slumped and stockpiles grew, forcing the firm into bankruptcy (Starkey, 1989).

Some projects have used credit to promote one particular type of implement. This top-down approach can be dangerous, for farmers without available cash may purchase sub-optimal equipment simply to make use of the credit. This was seen in Guinea Bissau, where almost all sales of heavy *Arara* implements and ox carts involved credit. Farmers who had cash available tended to buy lighter cultivators and donkey carts, which they generally preferred (Starkey, 1991b).

Women and animal traction

Historically, animal power in Africa has been a male-dominated technology. Cattle are commonly owned, or controlled, by men and most animal traction operations tend to be performed by men and boys, provided male labour is readily available. Women increasingly have access to, and control over, animal traction. The migration of male labour to urban centres means that many rural households are female-headed or female-managed. Lack of rural

Photo 55: Farmers in first year of using work oxen in Zambia: the technology had been introduced into the area by a donor-assisted project but these people learned it from other farmers

Photo 53: Women weeding maize with oxen, Zaire

male labour means that women increasingly handle draft animals and implements (Photos 53–54).

In several countries, women's groups have purchased their own draft animals. This has not always been easy, because the management of work animals can be labour-intensive, and women are normally extremely busy fulfilling numerous time-consuming domestic tasks. In Sierra Leone, a women's group successfully used girls to work their animals, but the girls had to be replaced when they married. Eventually the women became tired of training girls, and hired a man to look after their animals. Other women's groups have also handed over daily responsibility for their animals to men, who sometimes exploit the situation and begin to control access to them.

In some societies, women have primary responsibility for weeding operations. In such cases, the extensification associated with animal traction could increase the work load of women. Similarly, the adoption of animal-drawn weeders could help diminish the work load of women, particularly if men operate the weeding implements.

Rural women often have major transport roles. The carrying of domestic water, wood and crop harvests

Photo 54:
Women weeding with draft cows, Zimbabwe

is often the responsibility of women. The use of pack animals or animal-drawn carts can have particular benefits for women. If work animals are available, women may be able to delegate work relating to water transportation to children, who may even consider the task recreational.

If women can use animal power to release them from the size and weight limits of headloads, they can take more to and from market, increasing their marketing potential and stimulating the rural economy. Where men own animal-drawn carts, women may delegate some of their marketing duties to their husbands, although this has the risk that women lose control over the income generated by produce marketing. The purchase of animal-drawn carts often requires credit, but women generally have less access to credit than men. Increasing credit provision for carts for women could bring many social, economic and agricultural benefits.

The increasing adoption of donkeys as draft animals in the region may improve women's access to animal transport. Donkeys are particularly good for domestic transport operations and they can easily be managed by children. They also have fewer traditional associations with male ownership and dominance than do cattle.

Transfer of technology

Two very distinct types of technology transfer have been taking place in sub-Saharan Africa: formal and informal. The national extension services have generally provided relatively formal, top-down training. This has effectively taught farmers to start to use work animals in areas where animal traction was unknown. Credit provision to allow the acquisition of technology has sometimes been associated with such success.

Once animal traction has started in a region, much transfer has been informal, within families, from farmer to farmer or from regional immigrants to local farmers (Photo 55). Farmer-led innovation has often been much more significant than formal extension advice. For example, in The Gambia, animal traction was not widely used prior to the 1950s. A formal extension process during the 1950s and 1960s successfully introduced the use of pairs of yoked oxen to pull ridgers and plows. During the 1970s and 1980s, the farmers themselves gradually switched to a very different system using single donkeys with breastband harnesses and light cultivators. Formal extension was important for introduction, but thereafter it did not keep up with the evolution of farming systems (Starkey, 1987b).

Similar examples can be seen in eastern and southern Africa. The more successful animal traction extension programmes have tended to be in the areas of new introduction. In areas where draft animals are already widely used, extension programmes seem to have had little success.

One problem has been the old transfer model. Public-sector researchers have developed "improved" animal traction technologies on research stations. These have then been promoted by the extension services, often to be rejected by farmers as technically or economically inappropriate to their farming systems. In most countries in the region, development programmes have tried to promote animal-drawn wheeled toolcarriers (Photo 56), but the transfer process has not succeeded: the technology has been "perfected yet rejected" (Starkey, 1988). Other examples of disappointing formal attempts at technology transfer include the single-ox harness in Ethiopia, water buffaloes in Senegal and Tanzania, good-but-heavy plows in Zambia and animal-powered gear systems in several countries (Gryseels et al, 1984; Starkey, 1990; Starkey, Dibbits and Mwenya, 1991; Abiye Astatke and Mohammed-Saleem, 1994). In contrast, successful farmer-to-farmer transfer appears to have been responsible for the increase in the use of donkeys and working cows in several countries in

Photo 57: Farmer trying out his idea of using a prototype over-the-row seeder as a furrow opener, Mbeya, Tanzania

southern Africa. This adoption has sometimes been against the advice of extension agents.

In order to become more relevant, researchers are beginning to adopt more farmer-centred approaches, emphasising on-farm research–development. There is also a trend for projects to move away from formal farmer training to more participatory methods that build on farmer innovation and farmer-to-farmer transfer processes. For example, the Mbeya Oxenization Project tried to introduce an over-the-row weeder, believing this to be better than an inter-row model. The farmers did not seem convinced, but one felt the innovative equipment might have value as a furrow-opener (Photo 57). The technology may or may not be successful, but the process appears applicable to many animal traction situations—a motivated team working closely with farmers on their farms, offering them different alternatives and options, rather than prescriptions (Loewen-Rudgers et al, 1990; Mkomwa, 1992)

Transport

Observed trends suggest that animal-powered transport is likely to increase significantly in sub-Saharan Africa in the coming years. In many countries, donkey carts are becoming increasingly common. As noted above, this trend should have major social and economic benefits, particularly for women. Increasing use of animal carts is likely to improve both animal nutrition and the recycling of nutrients, as crop residues and manure are transported. It will also stimulate local economies, as people find it easier to transport and market produce. The larger circles of production and trade associated with animal transport will stimulate the

Photo 56: Wheeled toolcarrier fitted with sweeps on a research station where it was developed, Botswana

Photo 58: Wooden-wheeled carts rejected by farmers in north-western Zambia. The farmers eventually accepted carts with roller bearings and pneumatic tyres

Photo 60: Harnessing system commonly used for donkeys in Namibia and elsewhere in the region. The weight of the beam is supported by a thin rope on the neck of the donkey

growth of animal traction support services. Although initial adoption of animal-drawn carts may be difficult (with problems of repairs and punctures), once a critical mass of carts is used in an area, a virtuous circle may well develop, with support services making further adoption easier.

The success of animal-drawn carts in West Africa has been associated with the use of roller-bearings and pneumatic tyres. In many countries factory-made axles have been available, and use has been made of old vehicle axles. In several countries in eastern and southern Africa, organisations have placed emphasis on "appropriate technology" solutions, with wooden wheels and bearings. In the 1980s, a project in eastern Zambia tried to promote such carts for many years, with minimal success. About the same time, another project, this time in north-western Zambia, started with a similar cart designs, but noticed the distinct lack of farmer enthusiasm for the "flintstone" models (Photo 58). The project tried various other options, and eventually settled for axles with roller bearings and pneumatic tyres. The number of these carts rapidly

increased. The provision of suitable cart axles and credit appears to have been instrumental in stimulating rural transport and trade in that area (Starkey, Dibbits and Mwenya, 1991; Löffler, 1994).

In much of eastern and southern Africa, animal transport has been based largely on simple chain-drawn sledges and ox carts, equipped with a single draw bar. When donkeys have first been employed for carting (usually a farmer-led innovation) they have often been yoked, like oxen (Photo 59). Subsequently, donkey yokes have tended to be replaced by harnesses, often made from tyre rubber or machine belts. These have caused problems when the cart weight has been taken on the necks of the animals (Photo 60). This problem has been avoided in West Africa and elsewhere by using a two-shaft cart with a simple back saddle to take the weight of the cart (Photos 7, 25 and 34) . Some projects have experimented with similar designs in eastern and southern Africa (Photo 61), but these are not yet widely used. There still seems much scope for improving donkey harnesses throughout the region.

Photo 59: Two pairs of yoked donkeys pulling a cart made from an old pickup, Namibia

Photo 61: Prototype donkey cart in Malawi: the load from the two shafts is taken on the donkey's back

Conclusions

There was a time when animal traction was perceived by politicians and researchers as a backward technology that would be rapidly superseded. It is now increasingly seen as an economically and ecologically appropriate technology that will remain highly relevant in smallholder farming systems for the foreseeable future. Within southern and eastern Africa, it seems likely it will continue to spread, and diversify.

In general, development agencies have proved more successful at introducing animal traction technology than improving it. Progress is likely to be faster with the adoption of more farming-systems, farmer-centred, participatory processes and activities.

Regional farmer-led trends include greater use of donkeys and carts, increasing use of work cows and greater involvement of women in animal traction. There seems much scope in the region for improvements in harnessing and animal-drawn carts, greater use of animal-drawn weeders, greater conservation of crop residues to feed to work animals and improved access in rural areas to implements, cart axles, spares and credit.

Support to new animal traction initiatives from national governments and aid agencies is likely to be highest in areas where the technology can be seen to reduce environmental degradation, improve the quality of life of women and increase sustainable, private-sector agricultural production. All these important topics would be well tackled through a networking approach to improving animal traction.

References

Abiye Astatke and Mohammed-Saleem M A, 1994. Experiences with the use of a single ox for cultivation in the Ethiopian highlands. pp. 301–305 in: Starkey P, Mwenya E and Stares J (eds), *Improving animal traction technology*. Proceedings of the first workshop of the Animal Traction Network for Eastern and Southern Africa (ATNESA) workshop held 18–23 January 1992, Lusaka, Zambia. Technical Centre for Agriculture and Rural Cooperation (CTA), Ede-Wageningen, The Netherlands. 490p.

Gryseels G, Abiye Astatke, Anderson F M and Assamenew G, 1984. The use of single oxen for crop cultivation in Ethiopia. *ILCA Bulletin* 18:20–25. International Livestock Centre for Africa (ILCA), Addis Ababa, Ethiopia.

Loewen-Rudgers L, Rempel E, Harder J and Klassen Harder K, 1990. Constraints to the adoption of animal traction weeding technology in the Mbeya region of Tanzania. pp. 460–471 in: Starkey P and Faye A (eds), *Animal traction for agricultural development*. Proceedings of workshop held 7-12 July 1988, Saly, Senegal. Technical Centre for

Agriculture and Rural Cooperation, Ede-Wageningen, The Netherlands. 475p.

Löffler C, 1994. Transfer of animal traction technology to farmers in the North Western Province of Zambia. pp. 354–359 in: Starkey P, Mwenya E and Stares J (eds), *Improving animal traction technology*. Proceedings of the first workshop of the Animal Traction Network for Eastern and Southern Africa (ATNESA) workshop held 18–23 January 1992, Lusaka, Zambia. Technical Centre for Agriculture and Rural Cooperation (CTA), Ede-Wageningen, The Netherlands. 490p.

Mkomwa S, 1992. Research and development experiences of the Mbeya Oxenization Project in animal draft technologies. pp. 31–33 in: Simalenga T E and Hatibu N (eds). *Proceedings of an animal traction workshop held 8-10 April 1991, Morogoro, Tanzania*. Mbeya Oxenization Project, Mbeya, Tanzania. 57p.

Pingali P, Bigot Y and Binswanger H P, 1987. *Agricultural mechanization and the evolution of farming systems in sub-Saharan Africa*. Published for World Bank by Johns Hopkins Press, Baltimore, Maryland, USA. 216p.

Reh I and Horst P, 1982. Possibilities and limits of the use of trypanotolerant cattle for draught purposes. pp. 217–222 in: Karbe E and Freitas E (eds), *Trypanotolerance: research and implementation*. GTZ, Eschborn, Germany. 314p

Sangaré M I, Ladrette C, Mungroop R R and Berthé A, 1988. Contraintes et améliorations de la traction animale en Mali-sud: l'expérience de la DRSPR. pp. 191–211 in: Starkey P and Ndiamé F (eds), *Animal power in farming systems*. Proceedings of networking held 17–26 September 1986 in Freetown, Sierra Leone. Vieweg for German Appropriate Technology Exchange, GTZ, Eschborn, Germany. 363p

Starkey P H, 1985. *Animal power utilization in Malawi*. Report of consultancy mission 7–21 September 1985. Food and Agriculture Organization of the United Nations (FAO), Rome, Italy. 26p.

Starkey P, 1987a. Animal power in development: some implications for communities. *Community Development Journal* 22(3):219–227.

Starkey P H, 1987b. Brief donkey work. *Ceres* 20, 6:37–40.

Starkey P H, 1988. *Perfected yet rejected: animal-drawn wheeled toolcarriers*. Vieweg for German Appropriate Technology Exchange, GTZ, Eschborn, Germany. 161p.

Starkey P H, 1989. *Harnessing and implements for animal traction*. Vieweg for German Appropriate Technology Exchange, GTZ, Eschborn, Germany. 244p.

Starkey P H, 1990. *Water buffalo technology in northern Senegal*. Report prepared for USAID-Dakar (contract 685-0281-000-0199-00) and Projet Buffle, Saint Louis, Senegal. Tropical Research and Development Inc, Gainesville, Florida, USA. 37p.

Starkey P, 1991a. Animal traction: constraints and impact among African households. pp. 77–90 in: Haswell M and Hunt D (eds), *Rural households in emerging societies*. Berg, Oxford, UK. 261p.

Starkey P H, 1991b. *Animal traction in Guiné-Bissau: status, trends and survey priorities*. Report of a consultancy from 22 February to 5 March 1991 in association with Pan Livestock Services, Reading University and Gaptec, Lisbon Technical University. Animal Traction Development, Reading, UK. 22p.

Starkey P H, Dibbits H J and Mwenya E, 1991. *Animal traction in Zambia: status, progress and trends*. Ministry of Agriculture, Lusaka in association with IMAG-DLO, Wageningen, The Netherlands. 105p.

Animal traction networks in Africa: background, lessons and implications

by

Paul Starkey

ATNESA Technical Adviser
Animal Traction Development, Oxgate, 64 Northcourt Avenue, Reading RG2 7HQ, UK

Abstract

Animal traction is increasingly used in the farming systems of sub-Saharan Africa. In most countries, animal traction is now recognised as an appropriate, affordable and sustainable technology requiring few external inputs. Adoption of draft animals can lead to increases in crop production, reduction of drudgery and the many social and economic benefits of cart transportation.

The West Africa Animal Traction Network was formed in 1985. For six years it has been an open, informal and active network with a multidisciplinary, farming systems perspective. Network workshops have been attended by over 200 people from 30 countries. During workshops, small-group discussions in villages with farmers have been educative and very popular. Over 140 papers concerning animal traction have been circulated and/or published. There have been improvements in information exchange relating to farming systems research, development, extension, training, implement production and policy implications. Practical collaboration between national animal traction programmes in West Africa has increased.

Research and development workers from other regions of Africa have also participated in the activities of the West Africa Animal Traction Network. In November 1990 they launched the Animal Traction Network for Eastern and Southern Africa (ATNESA), which will build on the experience of the West Africa Network.

This paper reviews the background, establishment and organisation of these animal traction networks. Lessons derived from the problems and the successes of the West Africa Network are discussed. Network continuity has been assisted by member enthusiasm, flexible communications channels and multi-donor support. The network has not been controlled by researchers, development workers or members of any one discipline and has flourished despite the absence of a permanent secretariat. The institutionalisation of the network has been controversial: some support has been offered by an international centre and by another network. Close association with either should lead to improved coordination, but might also reduce the autonomy and independence of the network.

Animal traction in Africa

In many parts of the world, animal traction is an appropriate, affordable and sustainable technology, requiring few external inputs. Work animals can be used to reduce drudgery and intensify agricultural production, so raising living standards throughout rural communities, benefiting men and women, young and old. Cattle, buffaloes, donkeys, mules, horses, camels and other working animals can provide smallholder farmers with vital power for crop cultivation and transport. Draft animals can also be used for other activities including water-raising, milling, logging, land-levelling and road construction.

In North Africa and the Nile valley there has been a very long history of animal traction. A large number of draft animals, including oxen, cows, bulls, donkeys, mules, horses, buffaloes and camels have been used for soil tillage and transport. There has also been a long tradition of using work animals in parts of the horn of Africa. In Ethiopia, which has the highest population of draft animals in Africa, traditional cropping systems almost invariably involve the use of the wooden *maresha* ard plow, pulled by pairs of work oxen. Pack donkeys and mules are also widely used in Ethiopia. Elsewhere in sub-Saharan Africa, animals have long been employed for transport by certain pastoralists and traders, but animal-drawn implements have not been used in traditional farming systems.

Animal traction for tillage and for wheeled transport was introduced into sub-Saharan Africa during the colonial period. Indeed, in most African countries the technology was pioneered during the lifetime of the present elders. The animal traction technology, usually involving pairs of work oxen and imported metal implements, slowly spread during the first half of this century. There was great variation in adoption rates between areas and countries, with fastest adoption in areas with relatively developed marketing systems, particularly for cotton and groundnuts.

During the 1960s and early 1970s animal traction received relatively little attention from newly independent governments. This was a period when many people thought that the rapid tractorisation recently seen in Europe and North America would take place in African countries. Animal traction had dropped out of the curriculum in Europe, and it was also often omitted in sub-Saharan Africa. A generation of agricultural students graduated with little or no formal training relating to animal traction. These agriculturalists were often rapidly promoted within ministries and research organisations and became responsible for planning and implementing agricultural projects and programmes.

By the late 1970s higher oil prices, foreign exchange shortages and numerous failed tractor schemes suggested that rapid motorisation was not, after all, practicable. Animal traction started to be perceived by governments and donors as an appropriate, affordable and sustainable technology. It became increasingly recognised that animal traction could reduce drudgery and increase crop production (mainly through area expansion). Furthermore, many social and economic benefits could come from the employment of animal-drawn carts. Animal traction started to be seen in many countries as a serious, but neglected, development option.

With the inflow of donor funds that followed the well-publicised Sahelian droughts, many donor-assisted projects were established in Africa to introduce (or re-introduce) and/or research animal traction technologies. These projects tended to work in isolation, unaware of each other. Many were oriented to solving technological constraints, and often ignored social and economic factors. Several experienced serious problems, because those implementing the projects did not really understand all the technical, social and economic implications of using animal traction technology in the target farming systems (Sargent et al, 1981; Munzinger, 1982; Starkey, 1986).

International information exchange

In 1982, the Food and Agriculture Organization of the United Nations (FAO) convened an expert consultation on animal traction. This concluded that improved information exchange concerning animal draft power was extremely important (FAO, 1982; 1984). As a follow-up, FAO, in conjunction with the International Livestock Centre for Africa (ILCA), then commissioned a series of missions to 12 African countries in 1983, 1984 and 1985 to investigate the possibilities of establishing an animal traction network in Africa (Imboden, Starkey and Goe, 1983; Starkey and Goe, 1984; 1985).

The missions found that there was very little information exchange taking place between animal

traction programmes within countries, let alone between countries. There were far too many cases of projects, a short distance from each other, "re-inventing the wheel" (or redesigning an implement) in almost total isolation. The missions concluded that a network was not only extremely desirable, it was also very feasible. There existed strong support for the idea both at project/ institutional level and in the national ministries. It was suggested that it might be most practicable if a network were to be launched in West Africa, to be quickly followed by complementary initiatives in Southern and Eastern Africa (Starkey and Goe, 1984; 1985).

Launch of the West Africa Network

Although the FAO/ILCA proposals had stimulated interest in the creation of a network, for various institutional and organisational reasons there was no immediate follow-up. ILCA submitted a budget proposal to one of its funding agencies to allow it to coordinate an "animal traction research network". These succumbed to donor bureaucratic delays and by the time this proposal was approved, the West Africa Animal Traction Network (WAATN) encompassing both research and development had already been formed in West Africa (Figure 1). ILCA therefore decided to implement its animal traction research networking project within the context of this broader network.

The practical initiative that led to the creation of the network was a small workshop organised in March 1985 by the Farming Systems Support Project (FSSP) of the University of Florida, USA. FSSP had identified animal traction as one area in which a farming systems perspective was desirable, and one means by which crop and livestock farming systems (which were often separated in West Africa) could

Figure 1: Logo of West Africa Animal Traction Network (WAATN)

become more integrated. The workshop was hosted by a USAID-funded animal traction project in Togo.

This 1985 "networkshop" was the probably the first time that people from several anglophone and francophone countries in West Africa had come together specifically to discuss animal traction technology, and review it from a farming systems perspective. The 30 participants highlighted technical, economic and infrastructural constraints and debated the preconditions for the successful development of animal traction (Poats et al, 1985). The participants regarded the workshop as extremely useful, and resolved to hold a follow-up workshop which would allow further in-depth analysis of the issues and enable more countries in West Africa to exchange information.

A steering committee was elected, comprising representatives from animal traction programmes of five West African countries. They were joined on the committee by a representative of the main resource organisation (University of Florida) and a facilitating technical adviser. The steering committee subsequently met later in 1985, in The Gambia, and invited Sierra Leone to host the next "networkshop". The committee also recommended several activities designed to improve information exchange between countries and between other networks. For example, two committee members took part in a study tour of Nepal and Indonesia, and circulated a report on the implications of this for animal traction programmes in West Africa (Starkey and Apetofia, 1986).

Workshops and their methodology

Among the main, visible activities of the West Africa network have been the major workshops. In 1986, the workshop on "Animal power in farming systems" was held in Sierra Leone. This was attended by 73 people from 20 countries, with 34 papers written by 51 people active in animal traction being circulated, and published in the proceedings (Starkey and Ndiamé, 1988).

This was followed by the workshop on "Animal traction for agricultural development" held in Senegal in 1988. It was attended by 78 people from 24 countries. A total of 60 papers prepared by 84 people working in animal traction were circulated and published in the proceedings (Starkey and Faye, 1990).

In 1990, the workshop "Research for development of animal traction" was held in Nigeria, and was attended by 93 people from 19 countries. Circulated at this workshop were 52 papers prepared by 75 people working in animal traction (Starkey, 1990a).

The proceedings were edited and published in association with ILCA (Lawrence et al, 1993).

Thus, to date, network workshops have been attended by over 200 people. Furthermore, the workshops have directly stimulated the preparation and publication of over 140 papers covering a wide variety of issues and experiences concerning animal traction in different farming systems and related research, development, extension, training, implement production and policy implications.

The workshops have proved extremely popular, and participants have considered them interesting, helpful and professionally valuable. The detailed evaluations conducted at the end of each workshop have allowed the organisers to learn which aspects of the workshop have been most appreciated. The workshops have used the same general approach and methodology, with variations based on local conditions and on the participant feedback from the previous evaluation.

The workshops have been well-publicised in advance, with an "open" invitation to all those working in the field of animal traction, in West Africa and elsewhere. This open approach has encouraged a broad range of people to attend. This has been in contrast to the "closed" international workshops more common in Africa, where attendance is only by specific invitation to individuals or official, nominated representatives.

Although the invitation has been open, certain conditions have had to be met, including the preparation and submission of a suitable paper. Furthermore, when an excessive number of people from the same country applied to attend a workshop, selections were made based on quality of papers, and the balance of organisations and disciplines.

As a result of the open invitations, the workshops have been thoroughly multidisciplinary with agricultural engineers, economists, animal scientists, agronomists, sociologists and others meeting together. Furthermore, the participants have come from different professional fields, with researchers, extension workers, administrators, producers and donor representatives all closely interacting.

Although participants have received copies of all the papers prepared, they have not spent much time sitting through long sessions of paper presentations (which people tend to find tedious). Rather, there have been a few selected key papers, designed to stimulate discussion. Informal discussion has also been stimulated by "networking announcements" in which people could briefly summarise their work and interests, and the topics on which they would like to exchange information during the week. Sometimes these have led to special evening sessions for those with particular interests, and these have resulted in subsequent collaboration. For example, at the 1990 workshop in Nigeria, participants from eastern and southern Africa met in one special session to discuss the formation of an animal traction network for that region.

Without doubt, the most popular elements of each workshop have been the field visits. People who have been to conferences where the field visits have involved large groups slowly straggling around research sites may be surprised at this. The popularity of the network field visits appears to be due to the fact they have been in small groups of five to eight people from different countries, who have gone to villages, to watch work animals in use, and to talk directly with farmers. Such in-depth talking with farmers is accepted as an integral part of the farming systems approach, but has often been a new experience for participants. They have often felt free to ask farmers questions they would never dare to ask in their own countries, for fear that their juniors would laugh at them. The small groups have also visited village blacksmiths. Some groups, returning from the villages, have briefly visited project sites, research stations and implement producers.

In the day following the field visits, the small groups have sat down to discuss in detail their observations and findings, and to discuss also specific workshop themes highlighted in the lead papers. The groups have then reported back to all the other participants, in preparation for open discussion on the key issues raised. The small group discussions have proved almost as popular as the field visits.

The workshops have also provided an opportunity for a network business meeting, to discuss plans for the network, and elect a new steering committee to supervise the forthcoming programme.

Network publications

A further important element of the workshops has been the publication of the proceedings in an attractive format. These have been made available free-of-charge to people working in Africa. As there are no specific animal traction journals, people have tended to publish their experiences in the periodicals of their particular discipline, including journals of anthropology, agricultural engineering, economics and animal science. Unfortunately, even in countries blessed with well-stocked libraries, these are seldom read by their colleagues of different disciplinary

backgrounds who are also working with animal traction. In Africa, such specialised professional journals are only rarely available to people actually engaged in animal traction research and development. Thus to have workshop papers in one volume has provided useful and easily accessible resource documents for those working in this field. Furthermore, non-participants, seeing such proceedings, have been encouraged to put their own experiences in writing for subsequent workshops. To date three proceedings have been published (Poats et al, 1985; Starkey and Ndiamé, 1988; Starkey and Faye, 1990) and one is currently being prepared.

The German Appropriate Technology Exchange (GATE) has also published a series of other animal traction resource books based largely on the networking experiences and approach, including the Animal Traction Directory: Africa (Starkey, 1988a). ILCA has published an animal traction bibliographic database, made possible by the same networking approach (Starkey, Sirak Teklu and Goe, 1991). These publications have been made available free-of-charge to network members in Africa.

Other network activities

Between the main workshops, the steering committee has met once or twice a year, as far as possible each time in a different country. As these meetings have been combined with field visits, they have been, in effect, small group study tours, with mutually beneficial interactions between the committee members and the host country.

Other activities have been carried out by two or more country programmes themselves, and by the members of particular interest groups. For example, in 1989, ILCA hosted a planning workshop for WAATN members specifically interested in collaborative research. This was held to develop consistent research protocols for implementation in West Africa (ILCA, 1990). For various reasons, the wide-ranging collaborative research programme envisaged has yet to be implemented. However, ILCA is cooperating with animal traction programmes in several countries, and has a full-time animal traction network research scientist based in West Africa (initially at ILCA-Ibadan and more recently at ILCA-Niger). This network research coordinator also represents ILCA on the network steering committee.

As with all members of the network, the research coordinator is free to communicate directly with other members, and this illustrates again the open and informal nature of the network. In a similar way, visits and collaboration have been arranged between (for example) Sierra Leone and Togo, Senegal and The Gambia, Guinea and Mali. Collaborative programmes have also been arranged between (for example) the French Centre d'Etudes et d'Expérimentation du Machinisme Agricole Tropical (CEEMAT) and research organisations in Senegal and Burkina Faso, and between GATE and Senegal. These activities have been arranged directly between members of the network, and may, or may not, have been stimulated by contacts made during network workshops. They are considered within the network umbrella in that they involve collaboration between members with the information produced likely to be reported in subsequent network workshops and also diffuse informally through other networking contacts.

There is no official network newsletter. ILCA started an Animal Traction Research Network Newsletter, with English and French editions, but, for internal reasons, it was discontinued after just one issue (ILCA, 1988; CIPEA, 1989). One country, Togo, produces a national animal traction newsletter "Force Animale", which it circulates to several other network members (PROPTA, 1991). Most other document exchange continues on an individual to individual, or organisation to organisation, basis. Thus documents produced in Mali, Sierra Leone, Togo and Senegal (for example) are now quite commonly found in other countries in the region. This was not the case seven years ago, when the network was launched.

Eastern and southern Africa network

In 1987, the Southern African Centre for Cooperation in Agricultural Research (SACCAR) arranged a regional animal traction workshop in Maputo, Mozambique. At this it was resolved that a regional information-sharing network should be established under the auspices of SACCAR (Namponya, 1988). For institutional reasons, there was no immediate follow-up to this, but several individuals from eastern and southern Africa participated in animal traction workshops organised in 1988 (Senegal), 1989 (Indonesia) and 1990 (Scotland and Nigeria). On each occasion, the participants from the region affirmed that they should form their own animal traction network.

As a direct result of the 1990 workshops, two separate networking initiatives in eastern and southern Africa were started. For a few months they coexisted as parallel schemes, but they came together in 1991. One was initiated by staff of Christian Mission Aid (CMA), a non-governmental

organisation based in Kenya. The other involved animal traction specialists in Zambia and Zimbabwe.

A valuable opportunity to launch the animal traction network for Eastern and Southern Africa came in November 1990. The setting was a regional course on planning integrated animal draft programmes, held at the Agricultural Engineering Training Centre (AETC) of the Institute of Agricultural Engineering in Harare, Zimbabwe. The course was arranged by AGROTEC (Programme on Agricultural Operations Technology for Small Holders in East and Southern Africa) a regional project of the United Nations Development Programme (UNDP), funded by the Swedish International Development Authority (SIDA). During the course, there had been much discussion about networking, and the experience of the West Africa Animal Traction Network had been presented. The course participants therefore selected six people from different countries to form a committee to discuss organisational details and prepare an action plan for the network. Representatives of AGROTEC, GTZ (Deutsche Gesellschaft für Technische Zusammenarbeit) and a consultant resource person (Technical Adviser) were invited to join the committee. The decision of this committee to launch the network and arrange a major workshop were endorsed by the final plenary session of the AGROTEC course (Kalisky, 1990).

The provisional steering committee of the new Animal Traction Network for Eastern and Southern Africa (ATNESA) met again in Zambia in April 1991, to discuss network organisation and to plan the first major open workshop. The chairman of the committee had prepared a paper on possible ways of coordinating the network, and another member had prepared draft statutes, based on those of WAATN. The committee decided to adopt an informal system of network management, based on national networks linked through a regional steering committee. A network logo was approved (Figure 2).

The organisational strategy of ATNESA was subsequently discussed at the first open workshop of ATNESA which was held in Zambia in January 1992 with the theme of "Improving animal traction technology". This was attended by 107 people from 17 countries and 77 technical papers were circulated. Most external and local workshop participants were sponsored by their own organisations or by agencies within their own countries. This demonstrated the user-supported nature of the network and workshop. The core costs of workshop planning and implementation were provided by the Directorate General for International Cooperation (DGIS) of The

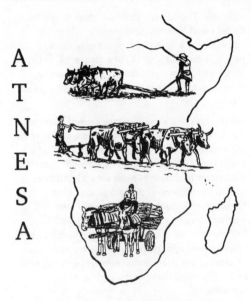

A
T
N
E
S
A

Figure 2: Logo of the Animal Traction Network for Eastern and Southern Africa (ATNESA)

Netherlands, in cooperation with the Dutch agricultural engineering institute (IMAG-DLO).

The workshop followed the pattern established by the West Africa network, with emphasis on field visits and small group discussions. Where possible, invited lead papers were prepared collaboratively, with experts in two or more countries (or resource organisations) combining their experiences prior to the workshop. The workshop was also offered as a means whereby members with specialised interests could meet to coordinate activities and plan collaboration. Among these groups were people interested in farming systems research and extension, gender issues, local manufacture of implements, donkey power, cart design and animal-powered systems.

Some lessons from the networks

Structure or function

One clear lesson that emerges is that network activities are more important than formal structures. Despite its lack of a formal secretariat, WAATN has been active for about six years, and it has much to show for its work. While network members agree that a strong, active coordination unit would be highly desirable, the absence of this should not prevent a network from flourishing, provided the members are themselves active.

Another lesson is that the network is informal and open to all persons and organisations sympathetic

with the aims and objectives of the network, whatever their discipline and whatever their role in animal traction development. Thus researchers are members of the network, but the network is not limited to research interests. Planners, extension workers, veterinarians and implement manufacturers are all active members of the network which is open to government services, non-governmental organisations, cooperatives and private companies. In principle, farmers or farmers' groups could be involved, but in practice farmers' interests are represented by those individuals and organisations working with, or for, farmers (directly or indirectly; perfectly or imperfectly).

By keeping the network open and informal, communication channels have tended to be reliable and efficient. Naturally, respect has been given to national and institutional protocols, but within such limitations, network members have been encouraged to correspond directly with their colleagues in other countries. Such direct contact, combined with copying relevant correspondence to interested parties, has proved very effective.

Communication channels

There have been some network members who have argued that all communications should be channelled through a central secretariat and/or through "focal points" within each country or resource organisation. However, practical experience has shown that both individuals and institutions can suddenly change from being facilitators to become communications "bottlenecks". Whatever the good intentions of nominated representatives, they can, with little or no warning, be promoted to a different post, sent on study leave or be incapacitated by illness or an accident. Within national and international institutions, managements can change or shift priorities, work loads can suddenly increase, key staff may leave and budgets can suddenly be cut. In such circumstances, network correspondence can be neglected. This may not be too critical if just one individual or organisation is involved, but if network members rely on that "focal point" to disseminate information, several network members could be deprived of information.

Lack of domination

Perhaps the strongest feature of the two networks is that they are informal African organisations. They did not arise from project documents of donors, nor were they created by any one resource institution. They have grown up from strong member interest and close collaboration with a variety of donor organisations. The networks have received support from several donors and international institutions, but they are not dependent on, or controlled by, any single one of these. Such flexible structures should allow the networks to survive the inevitable changes in the policies and financial support strategies of particular resource organisations. The multi-donor support also reduces the genuine risk of any one funding agency using its financial muscle to impose its particular policies and priorities on the network.

To date, the networks have had no financial resources of their own. They have found that sufficient funds can generally be obtained for specific network activities that have clear objectives, such as workshops and study tours. Often, when the networks have taken an initiative and arranged an activity, costs of travel and participation have been largely met by projects within the member countries.

At all the workshops held so far, the majority of participants have been funded from sources (often donor-assisted projects) within their own countries, and not from the central workshop budget. This makes workshop organisation easier and cheaper, and emphasises the user-supported nature of the networks. When applications for sponsorship have been received by the workshop committee, it has often been possible to put that applicant in touch with a sponsoring organisation within his/her country, so initiating useful and beneficial contacts.

In the past, the networks have received specific support from the FSSP, GTZ, GATE, ILCA, AGROTEC, the International Development Research Centre (IDRC), the Technical Centre for Agriculture and Rural Cooperation (CTA), the International Institute for Tropical Agriculture (IITA), Environment and Development in the Third World (ENDA) and Directorate General for International Cooperation (DGIS) of The Netherlands and several national organisations and projects within Africa.

Some problems experienced

The networks have experienced various operational and organisational problems. Postal services and telecommunications between African countries can be slow, difficult and unreliable. Indeed, because intra-Africa communications can be difficult compared to Europe–Africa links it has sometimes proved pragmatic to communicate via Europe. Although this was not planned, the fact that the Technical Adviser has had an office in Europe has frequently proved valuable in facilitating network liaison and information dissemination.

Air schedules and connections within Africa are such that committee members or workshop participants can seldom all arrive and depart on the same day. Two or even three days may be needed for air travel between some countries. Thus attendance at a three-day meeting may require people to sacrifice a week from their work. Difficult air schedules can significantly increase meeting costs, as provision has to be made for additional *per diem* payments.

During workshops and meetings network members can devote themselves fully to network activities. In the enthusiasm of a workshop, participants find it easy to offer to take on responsibilities. However, well-meant intentions to assist network activities tend to be relegated to the background when members return to their families, and to the practicalities of their own demanding jobs. Furthermore, not all members involve themselves in national-level networking activities. A combination of national and international networking is essential to maximise and multiply the benefits of the networks.

One possible danger with any network is the tendency for it to become "inbred", for familiarity tends to diminish the intensity of technical communication when colleagues meet each other frequently. This pitfall has largely been avoided at WAATN workshops by attracting many new people to each workshop—a policy that has necessitated large workshops. If workshops were smaller, perhaps restricted to just one or two participants per country, the same individuals specialising in animal traction or leading national networks would tend to be involved each time.

The membership of the steering committee of WAATN has been fairly constant since its inception. This has given valuable continuity and stability, but the limited turnover of committee members has restricted opportunities for fresh vision and new dynamism. To avoid this, the provisional ATNESA committee decided to recommend that no ATNESA committee member should serve for more than two terms of two years.

It has proven very difficult to bring together all members of the steering committee at the same time. For example, in 1990 and 1991 there were a total of three meetings of the WAATN steering committee, but at none of the meetings did the committee members feel that they had enough members present to make binding decisions on the future organisation of the network. At each meeting, one or more of the individuals crucial to the topic were unavoidably absent, due to conflicting activities, communication difficulties, travel problems, illness, political upheavals or other unforeseen circumstances.

Some resource organisations have tended to be rather fickle—sometimes supporting the networks strongly and at other times appearing rather cool. Such inconsistencies may have been brought about by changing institutional policies or by different budgetary situations. Other inconsistencies have been attibutable to the whims of particular individuals. Whatever the stated position of a resource organisation, practical support for the networks depends largely on the enthusiasm (or otherwise) of one, or more, key individuals within each organisation. Whether or not an activity is supported often depends on the prevailing work load, mood or self-interest of the contact individual.

Network organisation

The networks have been run on a voluntary basis, with no full-time staff. When activities, such as workshops, have been arranged, or papers have to be written or edited, the host institutions have given permission for their staff to spend time on these jobs. However, they have not reduced their other work loads, and individuals have often been quite stressed. The work of the Technical Adviser has also been largely on a voluntary basis, with no budget available for professional time and communication costs. For some major organisational or editorial tasks, sponsors have provided short-term consultancy assignments.

The networks have not had central budgets or accounts. All the day-to-day costs of networking have been met by individuals or their organisations. Specific activities, such as network committee meetings, study tours and workshops, have been funded by one or more donors, and participants have generally claimed relevant expenses from the activity account or one of the sponsors. Most activities have been organised in faith, with expenditure coming long before a refund, placing financial strain on facilitators and participants.

Institutionalisation of WAATN

While the informal WAATN management system has clearly been able to achieve results, it has been far from ideal. Various proposals have been made to institutionalise WAATN, and the WAATN steering committee has twice prepared ambitious project documents. These have had budgets large enough to hire and house a full-time network coordinator (assumed to be a West African with an international salary), equip a secretariat and provide operating expenses. Donors have rejected these as being too expensive. One point raised (partly as a joke and partly as a serious point) was that the animal

traction network had operated effectively for several years without a large budget. Thus it seemed difficult to justify major financial provision if the network seemed capable of working well without it. The relative success of enthusiastic volunteers and part-time amateurs had actually made it more difficult to obtain the services of full-time professionals.

Attempts were made to try to combine the benefits of voluntary work with longer periods of committed time. One donor, IDRC, offered to provide funds that would provide financial inducements to allow committee members to take time off from their main jobs, and work for a few months on specific network activities. This creative proposal was received by the steering committee with mixed enthusiasm. It was perceived by some as a distinctly second-best alternative to the requested full-time coordination, rather than as an improvement on the existing system.

One resource organisation, ILCA, offered in 1988 to coordinate an animal traction research network from its headquarters in Addis Ababa. This was to be a formal research network that would draw on human resources and linkages identified by the informal WAATN. A steering committee would have had overall responsibilities for the network, but day-to-day coordination would have been undertaken (and paid for) by ILCA (Goe, 1988). This offer was put to the WAATN general assembly in 1988, but was politely declined, mainly because of fears of losing control of the network to one member institution, with its own goals and priorities. People were under the impression that international research centres had, in the past, used networks to promote their own interests, rather than those of the network members. Furthermore, international research centres had mandates clearly limited to research, while the animal traction network had been established to link not only researchers, but also those more concerned with development, extension and implement production.

Negotiations were entered into to associate the animal traction network with the West African Farming Research Network (WAFSRN). This had moved out of an international research centre (IITA), and had established an independent secretariat in Ougadougou under the umbrella of SAFGRAD, the Semi-Arid Food Grain Research and Development programme of the Organisation of African Unity. Draft protocols of understanding were drawn up with both WAFSRN and SAFGRAD, and it was envisaged that the animal traction network would continue to operate as a fully independent network, under SAFGRAD, sharing offices with the farming systems network, WAFSRN.

The steering committee of WAFSRN subsequently, in 1990, decided that if the animal traction network wished to share WAFSRN facilities, it should become a *sub*-network of WAFSRN. The animal traction network committee did not want to become a subcommittee. It was worried that its network might be swallowed up by WAFSRN, and the animal traction network would lose its name, logo and corporate identity that had been built up over the years.

ILCA then offered to host the animal traction network secretariat at its offices in Kaduna, Nigeria. Although the secretariat would be located at ILCA-Kaduna, network independence was promised. In this case, there was no need for down-grading to a sub-network: the full network name could be retained. The offer had definite attraction, although Kaduna had poor international communications. There was still some concern that the network would lose its autonomy and that, in practice, its future programme and priorities would be largely determined by ILCA.

No final decision was taken by the WAATN steering committee in 1991, partly because no quorum of committee members could be formed. Then, the situation of the possible host institutions altered significantly in 1991/92. The WAFSRN network coordinator resigned and two key ILCA animal traction personnel moved from Nigeria to Ethiopia and to Niger. The WAATN steering committee, which had started to rely on its possible partner institutions, ILCA and WAFSRN, to instigate planning meetings, was not convened in the first half of 1992. The momentum of the steering committee for establishing a coordination unit, and planning a programme of activities, had reached a low point.

Ascertaining the benefits of the networks

While all those associated with the network can point to the advantages to individuals and to programmes of improved knowledge and understanding, it is extremely difficult to actually measure the benefits.

If one looks back to the years of work "wasted" in the past on unsuitable technologies in Africa (such as wheeled toolcarriers which were "perfected yet rejected"), one can see the great potential for savings through networking (Starkey, 1988b). For example, one project in West Africa has recently spent about two million dollars attempting to introduce Asian water buffaloes for work in part of the Sahelian zone of West Africa (Starkey, 1990b). This animal traction project (which was planned before the start of the network) lacked a farming systems orientation. It also did not benefit from networking interactions with colleagues familiar with other attempts to introduce exotic work animals into sub-Saharan Africa. In retrospect, it seems likely that the money allocated to the project could have been better utilised had those responsible for planning and implementation been exposed to the experiences and perspectives of network members.

Other comparable project initiatives may well have already been made more relevant and productive because people recently have been able to learn from the network. It is impossible to know how many programmes and projects have benefited, but some clear examples of network influence can be documented.

To illustrate the genuine yet elusive nature of the benefits, one can take one recent example of an animal traction project in Guinea that has not yet itself participated in any "formal" network activity such as a workshop. The leaders of this project recently made use of some of the network publications mentioned here, to learn of, and then to contact, colleagues working in Mali, Senegal and Sierra Leone. This led to one three-week training visit in Mali, the testing of Senegalese and Sierra Leonean implements in Guinea, detailed discussions on technical, economic and organisational issues and the obtaining by the project of documents on a wide variety of topics. Moreover, each contact led to others: for example, the people in Mali were able to discuss the experiences of their colleagues in Togo, whom they had met at a networkshop. This project acknowledges that its contacts were made as an indirect result of the formal network activities and publications. Such information exchange would have been almost impossible a mere five years before, simply because people in one country were almost completely unaware of each others' activities. As a result of its networking and its dynamism, the project implemented some well-proven strategies, and so achieved in two years an output that, in more "normal" circumstances, might well have taken a project three to four years (Starkey, 1991). The suggestion is that significant savings in time and costs were achieved in this one project through networking.

While all involved in this Guinea project believe they saved time and money, it would be difficult to objectively "prove" a cause and effect relationship, since so many other factors were involved. It would also be difficult to measure the specific economic benefits, as the "time saved" could not be quantified without a "control". Similarly, it is impossible to quantify the benefits of numerous similar exchanges that are now taking place within the region, and with other regions. While the genuine value of networking can be seen in the improvements in knowledge, understanding and programme implementation, it will remain difficult to estimate the total benefits to the region.

Conclusions

There has been a huge change in information exchange relating to animal traction in West Africa in recent years, much of which is directly, or indirectly, attributable to the activities of WAATN. There are also increasing numbers of examples of collaboration between programmes, notably in areas of research, training and implement testing. ATNESA has started to achieve similar benefits in eastern and southern Africa.

While the large general workshops are likely to remain popular for some time, particularly for those for whom they are a completely new experience, it is probable that the networks will put increasing efforts into events for special interest groups within the network. For example, intensive seminars may be held for researchers working on similar topics (eg, the use of draft cows), or for development projects involved in similar work (eg, the use of animal traction for rice production) or for the many implement manufacturers in the two regions. Such activities may in the future be arranged by a network secretariat, or may continue to be organised by one or more of the network members.

It is likely that the combination of member enthusiasm, open membership, flexible communication channels and multi-donor support will ensure the continuing effectiveness of both the animal traction networks. These networks should therefore continue to promote the development of animal traction in sustainable, low-external input agricultural systems in Africa in the coming years.

References

CIPEA, 1989. *Bulletin du réseau de recherche sur la traction animale.* No 1. Centre international pour l'élevage en Afrique (CIPEA). International Livestock Centre for Africa (ILCA), Addis Ababa, Ethiopia. 24p

FAO, 1982. *Report of the FAO Expert Consultation on the appropriate use of animal energy in agriculture in Africa and Asia held Rome, 5–19 November 1982.* Food and Agriculture Organization of the United Nations (FAO), Rome, Italy. 44p.

FAO, 1984. *Animal energy in agriculture in Africa and Asia.* Animal Production and Health Paper 42, Food and

Agriculture Organization of the United Nations (FAO), Rome, Italy. 143p.

Goe M R, 1988. *Animal traction research network: proposed implementation and operation.* Unpublished paper prepared for discussion at the West Africa Animal Traction Network Workshop held 7–12 July 1988, Saly, Senegal. International Livestock Centre for Africa (ILCA), Addis Ababa, Ethiopia. 8p.

ILCA, 1988. *Animal traction research network newsletter.* No. 1. International Livestock Centre for Africa (ILCA), Addis Ababa, Ethiopia. 25p.

ILCA, 1990. *Annual report 1989.* International Livestock Centre for Africa (ILCA), Addis Ababa, Ethiopia. 144p.

Imboden R, Starkey P H and Goe M R, 1983. *Report of the preparatory consultation mission for the establishment of a TCDC network for research, training and development of draught animal power in Africa.* Animal Production and Health Division (AGA) Consultancy Report, Food and Agriculture Organization of the United Nations (FAO), Rome, Italy. 115p.

Kalisky J (ed), 1990. *Proceedings of a regional course on planning an integrated animal draught programme, held Harare, Zimbabwe from 5–13 November 1990.* Bulletin No. 2. AGROTEC (Agricultural Operations Technology for Small Holders in East and Southern Africa), Harare, Zimbabwe. 235p.

Lawrence P R, Lawrence K, Dijkman J T and Starkey P H (eds), 1993. *Research for development of animal traction in West Africa.* Proceedings of fourth workshop of West Africa Animal Traction Network held 9–13 July, 1990, Kano, Nigeria. Published on behalf of the West Africa Animal Traction Network by International Livestock Centre for Africa (ILCA), Addis Ababa, Ethiopia. 322p.

Munzinger P (ed), 1982. *Animal traction in Africa.* Deutsche Gesellschaft für Technische Zusammenarbeit (GTZ), Eschborn, Germany. 490p.

Namponya C R (ed), 1988. *Animal traction and agricultural mechanization research in SADCC member countries.* Proceeding of workshop held August 1987, Maputo, Mozambique. SACCAR Workshop Series 7, Southern African Centre for Cooperation in Agricultural Research (SACCAR), Gaborone, Botswana. 87p.

Poats S V, Lichte J, Oxley J, Russo S L and Starkey P H, 1985. *Animal traction in a farming systems perspective.* Report of networkshop held Kara, Togo, March 3–8 1985. Network report no. 1, Farming Systems Support Project (FSSP), University of Florida, Gainesville, Florida USA. 187p.

PROPTA, 1991. *Force animale.* Bulletin technique trimestriel du projet pour la promotion de la traction animale (PROPTA), Atakpamé, Togo. 20p.

Sargent M W, Lichte J A, Matlon P J and Bloom R, 1981. *An assessment of animal traction in francophone West Africa.* Working Paper 34. Department of Agricultural Economics, Michigan State University, East Lansing, Michigan, USA. 101p.

Starkey P, 1986. *Draught animal power in Africa: priorities for development, research and liaison.* Networking Paper 14, Farming Systems Support Project (FSSP), University of Florida, Gainesville, USA. 40p.

Starkey P, 1988a. Animal traction directory: Africa. Vieweg for German Appropriate Technology Exchange, Deutsche Gesellschaft für Technische Zusammenarbeit (GTZ), Eschborn, Germany. 151p.

Starkey P, 1988b. *Perfected yet rejected: animal-drawn wheeled toolcarriers.* Vieweg for German Appropriate Technology Exchange, Deutsche Gesellschaft für Technische Zusammenarbeit (GTZ), Eschborn, Germany. 161p.

Starkey P, 1990a. *Research for development of animal traction: a report of the fourth workshop of the West Africa Animal Traction Network held 9–13 July 1990, Kano Nigeria.* Animal Traction Development, Reading, UK. 53p.

Starkey P, 1990b. *Water buffalo technology in northern Senegal. Report prepared for USAID-Dakar (contract 685-0281-000-0199-00) and Projet Buffle, Saint Louis,*

Senegal. Tropical Research and Development Inc, Gainesville, Florida, USA. 37p.

Starkey P, 1991. *The revival of animal traction in Kindia Region of Guinea Conakry (Relance de la traction bovine dans la région de Kindia, Guinée Conakry)*. Report of evaluation of project ONG/78/89/B Guinea Conakry. Commission of the European Communities, Brussels, Belgium. 43p.

Starkey P and Apetofia K, 1986. *Integrated livestock systems in Nepal and Indonesia: implications for animal traction programs in West Africa*. Farming Systems Support Project (FSSP), University of Florida, Gainesville, Florida, USA. 64p.

Starkey P and Faye A (eds), 1990. *Animal traction for agricultural development*. Proceedings of workshop held 7g12 July 1988, Saly, Senegal. Technical Centre for Agriculture and Rural Cooperation, Ede-Wageningen, The Netherlands. 475p.

Starkey P and Goe M R, 1984. *Report of the preparatory FAO/ILCA mission for the establishment of a TCDC network for research, training and development of draught animal power in Africa*. Animal Production and Health Division (AGA) Consultancy Report, Food and Agriculture Organization of the United Nations (FAO), Rome, Italy. 82p.

Starkey P and Goe M R, 1985. *Report of the third joint FAO/ILCA mission to prepare for the establishment of a TCDC network for research, training and development of draught animal power in Africa*. Animal Production and Health Division (AGA) Consultancy Report, Food and Agriculture Organization of the United Nations (FAO), Rome, Italy. 85p.

Starkey P and Ndiamé F (eds), 1988. *Animal power in farming systems*. Proceedings of networkshop held 17–26 September 1986 in Freetown, Sierra Leone. Vieweg for German Appropriate Technology Exchange, Deutsche Gesellschaft für Technische Zusammenarbeit (GTZ), Eschborn, Germany. 363p.

Starkey P, Sirak Teklu and Goe M R, 1991. *Animal traction: an annotated bibliographic database*. International Livestock Centre for Africa (ILCA), Addis Ababa, Ethiopia. 255p.

Photograph opposite
Ox cart used for marketing farm produce and other income-generating activities in north-western Zambia

The profitability of animal traction

Increasing the profitability of draft animal power

by

A Panin[1] and J Ellis-Jones[2]

[1] *Department of Agricultural Economics and Extension*
Botswana College of Agriculture, Private Bag 0027, Gaborone, Botswana
[2] *Silsoe Research Institute, Wrest Park, Silsoe, Bedford MK45 4HS, UK*

Abstract

This paper examines the existing use and potential for draft animal power in sub-Saharan Africa. Regional differences are identified and indicative costs of human, animal and tractor power are compared. Animal traction is considered an appropriate technology, whose adoption and profit potential are limited by political, social, technical, economic and institutional constraints. These are critically analysed in the light of the urgent need to increase both productivity and sustainability of existing farming systems. It is concluded that draft animal power should play an increased role in the development process in the region and every effort should be made to alleviate the constraints to increased profitability.

Introduction

Animal traction has a long history in agricultural production. It has played, and still plays, an important role in meeting the power requirements of farming systems in many parts of the developing world.

The total world population of draft animals is estimated at 400 million, of which less than 5% are found in sub-Saharan Africa (Ramaswamy, 1988; Mrema, 1991).

The overall low level of use of animal traction technologies in sub-Saharan Africa raises doubts about its profitability and sustainability in small farming systems. Yet participants in a workshop on "Animal traction for agricultural development", held in Senegal in 1988, noted that the persistence of draft animal power and its spread in Africa suggest that animal traction can be profitable.

This observation requires study of the factors mitigating against increased profitability of draft animal power, in order to stimulate its increased adoption in sub-Saharan Africa. This paper analyses the problems associated with improving the profitability of animal traction.

The existing situation

Historical perspective

In much of sub-Saharan Africa draft animal power was initially introduced through European settler farmers, early development programmes and the migration of workers within the region. Although the technology was introduced over 70 years ago, its adoption has been patchy; it is used on less than 15% of arable land, mostly in the arid and semi-arid areas.

Oxen were the main draft animals introduced, although occasionally cows were used to make up teams. Donkeys, mules and horses were used where they were available.

Tractors were introduced from the 1940s onwards, in the periods leading up to independence and immediately thereafter. They were first used in the commercial (white) farm sector, but they spread quickly as tractor hire schemes for small farmers were promoted by aid agencies, donor countries and tractor manufacturers.

During this time tractors were considered the key to successful agricultural development and a natural progression from hand and draft animal power. Tractor schemes were taken as good examples of mechanised agriculture by the emerging African elites who were engaged in the political struggle for independence. Political leaders were unlikely to refuse assistance based on increased use of tractors. Consequently, large-scale tractorisation schemes were initiated in most sub-Saharan African countries in the 1960s. In Tanzania, for instance, 60% of government investment in settlement schemes was in the form of agricultural machinery, implements and vehicles, with heavy reliance on expatriate managers (Mrema, 1991a; 1991b).

Similar policies were initiated in the nominally independent homelands of South Africa during the late 1970s and early 1980s (Ellis-Jones, 1991).

This large-scale introduction of tractors, be it through government hire schemes or state, settlement or cooperative farms, was not successful. The failures are still having a pronounced influence on agricultural mechanisation policies.

Duality of agricultural production

Agricultural production is, and is likely to continue to be, undertaken in a dual structure of medium to large commercial and peasant smallholder farms, often referred to as the formal and informal sectors. Pressures on egalitarian grounds for land redistribution to promote smallholder production will continue, especially in South Africa and to a lesser extent in Zimbabwe and other countries having a substantial large-farm sector. It is important that the two sectors are accurately defined, through the use of farm surveys, so that appropriate strategies for each can be developed.

In parts of sub-Saharan Africa there are large differences arising from the history of white settlement and the interests of large commercial companies, whose management systems are comparable with those found in the USA and the European Community.

Typically one can find sub-subsistence farmers (especially where there are large numbers of migrant workers, whose families scratch a living on small rural plots), subsistence farmers, emerging commercial farmers, small-, medium- and large-scale commercial farms and plantation cropping estates. Larger farms can be organised as communes, cooperatives, parastatal or private commercial entities. In reality most forms of agricultural organisation exist in the same country, regardless of that country's political ideology.

In most cases large farms, regardless of ownership, have adopted tractor technologies, whereas small farms use a variety of power sources, sometimes only hand tools, sometimes draft animal power or tractors, and often a mixture of all three.

Increasing farm size has been associated with a transition from hand tools through animals to tractor-based mechanisation technology. However, hand tools are required in all farming systems, and a combination of tractors and draft animal power is increasingly being considered by commercial farmers.

Table 1: Proportional contribution (%) of total power use in 93 developing countries

Area	Human	Animal	Tractor
North Africa	69	17	14
Sub-Saharan Africa	89	10	1
Asia (excl China)	68	28	4
Latin America	59	19	22
Overall	71	23	6

Source: FAO (1987)

Importance of draft animal power

Review of the present use of animals

Animals are used within a range of farming systems, where the output is often multi-purpose providing milk, meat, manure (for fertiliser or fuel), hides, skins and horns, replacement animals, draft power and social needs (status in the community, capital accumulation, rituals, *lobola*, etc).

The cost of keeping stock can therefore be spread over a number of uses. The greater the spread, the lower will be the cost of providing draft animal power.

Importance of animals as a power source

The contributions of different power sources in the production of food in developing countries vary widely, as shown in Table 1. Sub-Saharan Africa ranks lowest in the use of both tractors and animals, and highest in human power sources. Clearly there is great potential for increasing the use of draft animal power in this region.

Although considerable variation occurs, depending on individual circumstances, most studies indicate that it costs more than twice as much to prepare a hectare of land using a tractor as it does using draft animal power (Table 2). Hand labour can be the cheapest power source, but the maximum area for which it can be used is 2 ha.

Relevance of improving draft animal traction profitability in Africa

Despite the limitations of available data, it is clear that agricultural performance in sub-Saharan Africa has deteriorated in recent years (Eicher, 1984; Lele, 1984). Annual rates of increase of food crop production in the region lag behind those of the population, resulting in a decline in per capita output. A large proportion of Africa's population is either undernourished or chronically malnourished.

Table 2: Workrates, daily outputs and plowing costs using different power sources

	Tractor 50 kw	Animal 2 oxen	Human 1 man
Work rate (hours/ha)	2–3	25	100
Work day length (hours)	8–16	5	5
Daily output (ha/day)	3–7	0.2	0.05
Cost[1] (US$/ha)	100	30–50	50–100

[1] These are approximate costs for comparison. They will vary considerably depending on actual and opportunity labour costs
Source: Morris (1983)

One of the main features of African agriculture is its low productivity. This has resulted from a combination of socioeconomic factors of which dependence on human labour for most farm operations is crucial. As noted by many writers (ILCA, 1981; Lele, 1984), increases in crop production in Africa result from increases in the area under cultivation, rather than from gains in productivity per unit of input. With current rates of population growth, the main way to avoid food shortages is to focus attention on technologies that raise productivity of labour.

Most African countries have attempted to mechanise agriculture through the use of tractors. The results have been disappointing. Attempts with draft animal power have also experienced problems. However, the high cost of imported machinery and spare parts, disappointing experience with tractorisation and the ever-increasing foreign exchange problem, have motivated many African countries to redirect their agricultural policies to include draft animal power (Dibbits, 1988; Sindazi, 1988; Silumesii and Musonda, 1991; Twum and Gyarteng, 1991), and to actively encourage its use (Starkey, 1988a). Yet the use of draft animal power is still limited in sub-Saharan Africa. There are marked regional concentrations resulting from historical differences, farmer attitudes and the spread of livestock diseases; intensity of use is highest in eastern Africa, followed by southern Africa (Jahnke, 1982).

Efforts to improve the image and profitability of draft animal power are being supported by national and international aid agencies. The World Bank strongly recommends the use of this technology in order to raise the productivity of labour (IBRD, 1989).

Draft animal power is potentially an appropriate technology. It is relatively inexpensive, not too complicated, and can help to increase productivity (Norman, Newman and Onedradago, 1981). Experience in various sub-Saharan African countries (Sindazi, 1988), suggests that animal traction is increasing.

Means of improving profitability of draft animal power

Many factors affect the profitability of draft animal power in sub-Saharan Africa. Prominent among these are farmers' attitudes and economic, technical and institutional issues.

Farmers' attitudes, choices and perceptions

Although draft animals are the most cost-effective source of farm power, farmers' perceptions can have an important bearing on the choice of power source.

A decision to purchase a draft animal is not made only on business grounds. Reduction in drudgery, provision of family transport and increased status are other factors that farmers consider. Farmers' attitudes may also limit the use of draft animal power. For instance, when fodder and grazing are a constraint, tractors may be used, even if it is more cost-effective to use animals and pay for feed. Such attitudes tend to favour use of tractors where these are available.

Economic factors

Attempts to increase the use of draft animal power have often concentrated on removing the technical constraints and increasing the physical supply of draft animals, without adequate consideration of the economic realities faced by small farmers.

The demand from farmers tends to be for power *per se*, regardless of source. The amount of power demanded is unlikely to be changed by price changes.

It is therefore sensible to identify those factors which have significant effects on the supply of draft animal power relative to other types of farm power. Gregory (1989) identified these as being:

○ the relative costs of different sources of farm power. Draft animals are the least costly sources of farm power and increased use would increase small farm incomes and improve the economic efficiency of agricultural production. However, overvalued exchange rates, low import duties for tractors relative to other goods and the availability of cheap loans for tractors are factors that make tractors cheaper. These factors mitigate against draft animal power

○ the proportion of the cost of the draft animal which has to be covered by its farm work. Greater use of animals will reduce the proportion of capital and maintenance costs of draft work per unit of land. There is a great demand in most rural areas for transport (of firewood, water, building materials and harvested crops). In fact, transport contracting offers great income-generating opportunities

○ the work output and efficiency of the draft animal during the land preparation season. Increasing draft efficiency by using cost-neutral technologies will decrease the relative cost of draft animal power. This is likely to be attractive to farmers, who will probably reject technologies that increase costs. Technical initiatives to promote draft animal power should concentrate on those factors which offer the greatest return.

Technical factors

Integration of cash crops into farming systems

Attempts to introduce draft animal power into agriculture have not always taken account of the complexity of the farming systems and the interactions between them and the social, political and ecological systems, as well as the ability of farmers to manage new elements in their farming system.

Resources (such as land and labour) in rural farming communities are generally allocated with strong emphasis on meeting households' subsistence needs and minimising the risks involved in production. In most cases, households only give attention to cash crops after they are sure that their own needs can be satisfied.

It has been suggested that draft animal power leads to increased production of cash crops. Certainly this has been the case in areas where draft animal power has been introduced and promoted as a development project aimed at increasing cash crop production. However, some surveys have indicated that the introduction of draft animal power has not induced any significant changes in the traditional cropping patterns (Barett et al, 1982; McIntire, 1983; Panin, 1986).

Staple food crops, which still dominate as farmers adopt draft animal power, can suffer from internal market forces. Production which is surplus to household requirements is offered to the market at relatively low prices, whereas the prices farmers have to pay for their inputs can be very high; this reduces the potential profitability of draft animal power investment. Mwinjilo (1991), observed that the overall aggregate price increase of the draft animal power package and inputs used in Malawi between 1978 and 1982 far exceeded crop price increases, leading to reduction in gross margin.

The use of draft animal power substantially increases the financial burden on farmers, particularly during the early years of adoption (Reddy, 1988; Panin, 1989). This can make the investment unattractive. One way to overcome this problem is to embark on some cash cropping. Groundnuts and other cash crops can increase the profitability of draft animal power more than staple food crops such as millet, maize and sorghum

(Delgado and McIntire, 1982; Panin, 1987). However, care needs to be taken in selecting the types of cash crop and the amount of land to be allocated to them, because production of staple food crops must still be sufficient to meet household requirements.

Draft animal power in isolation should not be regarded as the "optimal solution" to the productivity problem.

Raising crop yields

The use of animal traction can increase crop yields through either intensification or extensification of land use systems. Draft animal power enables farmers to work faster and undertake additional agronomic practices such as deeper ridging, mulching, application of fertilisers and better weed control, all of which considerably improve agricultural productivity (Normal, Newman and Onedradago, 1981). In areas where arable land is abundant, animal traction is often used to expand the cultivated area (Barett et al, 1982; Francis, 1988; Sumberg and Gilbert, 1992). This implies that there is a positive correlation between the land area farmed by a household and the use of draft animal power. That notwithstanding, it is inappropriate to attribute the increased area totally to the use of draft animal power; in many cases households which use draft animal power have a larger labour force than households which do not (Panin, 1987; Sumberg and Gilbert, 1992).

Although there seems to be a consensus in the literature on the relationship between the use of draft animal power and the total cultivated area per household, the same cannot be said for the effects of draft animal use on crop yields (Singh, 1988). Reports from experimental stations show that yields increase substantially on draft animal power farms (Eicher and Baker, 1982; Pingali, Bigot and Binswanger, 1987), but evidence from farmers' fields indicates only modest yield increases (Lassiter, 1982; Panin, 1987). On experimental stations, animal traction is complemented by improved seeds, fertiliser, pesticides and other inputs, whereas on farmers' lands this is often not the case. Also, the level of management is usually greater on experiment stations. However, on-station results clearly indicate a potential for increasing crop yields at the farm level. The question that still remains is how lessons drawn from experiment stations can be carried over to the farmers. Research on agronomic practices leading to intensification of land use systems should be encouraged in order to exploit appropriate methods suitable to the farming conditions.

Animal nutrition

Throughout sub-Saharan Africa traditional animal management systems are extensive. The use of communal, often over-utilised grazing, with limited access to crop residues during the dry season or winter months, is the norm. This adversely effects both the quantity and quality of feed available.

Without proper nutrition work animals cannot provide the power required from them. Guma (1988), Rocha (1988) and Tembo and Elliot (1988) cite weakness of draft animals at the beginning of the cultivation period as one of the major factors limiting draft animal productivity in Swaziland, Mozambique and Zimbabwe. Unfortunately, forage is in short supply during this period, and the animals are often in poor condition, and likely to remain so. Undernourished animals can work, but timeliness is likely to suffer.

One solution is to establish low-cost feeding systems, especially in arid and semi-arid areas. Maize stover, groundnut or bean hay and, occasionally, cottonseed cake have been used in this way when they are available.

Another strategy to improve nutrition of work animals is to introduce fodder production into the farming systems. Successful alley farming methods which have emerged from national and international research stations should be introduced to farmers, and wide-scale adoption should be encouraged.

Alternatively, major farm operations could be undertaken when animals are still in good condition. Plowing and ridging could be done immediately after harvest when soils have sufficient residual moisture for deep plowing. This system, despite its associated problems, has had a good response among communal farmers in Zimbabwe (Tembo and Elliot, 1988).

Cows as draft animals

Development programmes initially concentrated on selecting the most powerful animals for the most demanding tasks. Other characteristics such as resistance to disease, low maintenance, quiet temperament, ease of handling and training are now receiving increased attention.

Oxen still comprise the greatest number of work animals in sub-Saharan Africa. Cows, although they dominate the cattle population, are seldom used for draft. However, the cost of maintaining oxen only for work can easily exceed the benefits. For example, it has been estimated in Sierra Leone that, on average, oxen work for only 41 days each year (Corbel, 1988). Under such circumstances the use of female animals, particularly cows, for draft has

many advantages. Benefits such as milk and progeny will reduce the costs of draft animal power. Experience shows that cow traction is technically feasible and is a means of raising net farm incomes (Matthewman, 1987; Panin and Brokken, 1992).

Additional benefits arising from the adoption of cow traction include the earlier sale of male animals, thereby reducing the total number of livestock and increasing the feed available for the remaining animals.

However, successful cow traction requires improved management skills of farmers. Cows should not be used in the last month before calving or in the first month of lactation. Research is required to optimise the production of draft animal power, progeny and milk.

Increasing the meat value of the animal

The profitability of draft animal power is affected by the value (as meat) of the animal at the end of its working life. Residual values of donkeys, mules and horses (which, in most of sub-Saharan Africa, are not eaten) are low, which may mitigate against their increased use as draft animals.

Empirical evidence indicates that the salvage values of draft animals can exceed the purchase prices (Barett et al, 1982; Panin, 1987), particularly when the animal is in good condition. This could itself encourage additional feeding of draft animals.

In some countries in sub-Saharan Africa draft animal power reduces the practice of keeping cattle too long (Starkey, 1990). Thus the payback period of the investment is shortened and liquidity problems are reduced, as also are the risks involved in keeping the animals on the farm for several years. Farmers should be made aware of the potential benefits from this.

Animal health

In large parts of sub-Saharan Africa tsetse infestation and animal trypanosomiasis limit livestock production. The introduction of trypanotolerant breeds, largely in West Africa, has had some success, but the power output of these breeds is lower than that of non-tolerant breeds. Other endemic diseases (foot and mouth, blackquarter and septicaemia), and problems of a local or sporadic nature (tick-borne diseases, brucellosis, internal parasites, etc), can also have a serious impact on the availability and utility of draft animals.

Protection against many of these diseases is possible, provided there are adequate distribution systems to deliver the appropriate veterinary product—hence the importance of appropriate infrastructure and improved veterinary services.

There is, however, a need to ascertain the economic importance of these diseases in the draft animal population, in particular the interactions between diseases and parasites and the effect these have on the work output of draft animals.

Equipment availability

A great deal of equipment has been developed for use with draft animals. The implements most commonly adopted are plows, ridgers and carts. Starkey (1988b), in his book "Perfected yet rejected", has clearly shown that some of the technologies developed over the past three decades have not been adopted. One reason is that the technologies did not develop to solve problems identified on the farm, but rather from engineers' perceptions of what was required.

However, Starkey (1988b) has also argued that better circulation of available technology to researchers and extension agents could lead to greater profitability. Better identification of farmers' constraints, and farmer participation in research and development, are likely to lead to technologies that are more affordable. Research should consider the animal, harness, implement and operator as a system rather than concentrate on one aspect in isolation (O'Neill, 1990).

With increased attention being paid to improvements in draft animal power, particularly feeding and health, better use of the increased power will require a greater range and improved quality of the equipment. By offering implements for land preparation, planting, weeding and other crop care operations, water pumping and improvement in ox cart design, greater profitability of draft animal power may be achieved. Transport is a major area where profitability can be enhanced.

Labour productivity

The productivity of labour in African agriculture is very low. Often two or three people work with a team of two oxen, whereas in most parts of Asia only a single person is required.

Barett et al (1982) and Singh (1988) show that the use of draft animal power may not increase the area cultivated per active worker. This implies that draft animal power, as used in many African countries does not substitute for labour. From this observation, the low profitability of animal traction resulting from the low labour productivity should not come as a surprise. Rather, the causes of this poor performance need further investigation.

Expansion of cultivated area by households using draft animal power can be constrained by a lack of implements for weeding and harvesting. The most common use of draft animal power in Africa is for primary tillage and transport (Reddy, 1988); its application to weeding and harvesting is limited. However, a positive correlation has been found between cultivated area and total annual labour input for weeding and for harvesting (Panin, 1987). The selective use of animal traction technology shifts the labour demand for these two operations. The effective execution of both operations depends mainly on the available household labour. This explains why the land-to-worker ratio is generally the same for households which do and do not use draft animal power. Hence, in order to achieve higher yields through extensification of land use, appropriate weeding and/or harvesting equipment should be included in the animal traction package offered to farmers.

Institutional factors

The profitability of draft animal power is heavily dependent on support services and infrastructure. Appropriate research and development, extension, credit, input and service supplies and manpower development are all essential ingredients that require careful planning and coordinating in promoting the use of animal traction.

Improving research and development

Research programmes and development work in animal production and draft animal power tend to proceed independently; they are often uncoordinated and consultation between interested groups is inadequate. Emphasis should be given to problem-orientd research determined in the context of farmers' needs. Appropriate technologies should be screened using technical, environmental and socioeconomic criteria. Research should be integrated closely with credit, input supply, extension and training activities.

The following coordinated research and development activities need to be intensified:

o   farming systems research to identify the role and potential profitability of draft animal power

o   adaptation, development and design of draft animal technologies, to remove the present constraints. The approach should be multi-disciplinary and should include the farmers, the implements, the animals and the effects on the environment

o   development of methods to encourage adoption and diffusion of innovation by both farmers and manufacturers

° formulation, monitoring and evaluation of draft animal power activities, especially the status and performance of credit, extension, manufacturing facilities and government policy instruments (import licensing, tariff regulations, etc).

Extension

Extension efforts will be required to support a draft animal power programme providing inputs for selecting, rearing, training, care and use of work animals, as well as selection and use of equipment. This should be an integrated programme involving livestock specialists, vets, agricultural engineers and socioeconomists.

Industrial extension will be required to provide local manufacturers with assistance in assessing market needs, skills training and business management. Promotional support and assistance with demonstrations and audio-visual material should be provided to help market completed products.

For draft animal power to be sustained, adequate repair facilities, skills, materials, parts and consumables need to be made available. Repair and servicing networks must be close to farmers in the rural areas and not restricted to the main urban centres. This is likely to require the support of local artisans and blacksmiths.

Credit availability

Agricultural credit is a development resource which can give a high degree of direction to both the pace and the form of mechanisation.

In the past, public credit institutions often provided loans for tractors and equipment at subsidised rates. As a result, tractor sales soared, and draft animal power and labour were displaced. Such practices cause market distortions, which are ultimately not sustainable.

Credit facilities for the purchase of animals and equipment packages need to be formulated according to farmers' needs and ability to repay. Rates and terms should reflect a balance between the desire to promote draft animal power and the need to maintain a realistic relationship with rates for the purchase of other agricultural inputs.

Suitable credit packages for local manufacturers should include finance for buildings, plant and equipment and working capital for development, manufacture and marketing.

Personnel development

A wide range of personnel is required to formulate and implement a draft animal power programme. These include farmers, extension agents and researchers, who need training aimed specifically at improving the use of work animals in existing farm systems. Technicians, managers and administrators need training in manufacturing, maintenance and repair on the one hand and in commercial administrative skills on the other.

Transport, communications and infrastructure

Transport and communications directly influence the acquisition, delivery, operation and maintenance of draft animal power. A strategy to promote animal traction must recognise the limitations of existing facilities. It may be necessary to improve infrastructure directly to establish new rural workshops with better communications for distributors and manufacturers.

Evaluation of draft animal power investments

At farm level

An investment in draft animals and implements represents both a capital (acquisition) cost and maintenance costs over the working life of the animal. Evaluation of such an investment involves detailed cash flow analysis as well as consideration of opportunity costs of capital.

For the investment to be attractive to farmers, the anticipated benefits should be considerably greater than the costs. As pointed out by Binswanger (1986), farmer adoption of a technological innovation will depend on the degree to which the innovation reduces the unit costs of inputs used in the production process. Also, one of the findings of a group discussion in a workshop on "Animal power in farming systems", held in Sierra Leone in 1986, was that unfavourable terms of trade between the costs of inputs and those of the outputs affect profitability of animal traction (Starkey, 1988a).

The benefits of animal traction accrue from increased crop production, services (eg, hiring and transportation), the salvage value of the animals and reduced costs of inputs.

The methodology most often used in draft animal power studies is cross-sectional comparison of various types of animal traction farms with the predominantly hand-hoe farms at a given moment in time. However, such cross-sectional data do not provide an accurate and realistic representation of essential time related production issues, such as: changes in investment outlays on the farm; the critical learning period required by new adopters; changes in net production value arising from variations in crop mixtures and yields; and liquidity requirements of the investment.

Starkey (1990) points out that time series data should be used for the analysis of economic impacts of animal traction, in order to ensure that observed trends in production are not spurious. Unfortunately, there is not a single known case of a farm level study on the economics of animal traction in Africa which has used time series data extending over a period of two years. Attempts to remedy this situation are made by using projections based on average figures (Lassiter, 1982; Panin, 1989).

Another problem in assessing animal traction profitability is that profitability measures used in most studies have been derived from gross margin analysis. Gross margin comparisons refer to one aspect of the farm enterprise, thus isolating animal traction activities from the rest of the farm business. Yet is necessary to look at the total profitability of the farm because the use of animal traction technology for one enterprise in the farm can have positive multiplicative effects on all other enterprises of the farm business.

At a national level

What appears financially attractive to a farmer may not be suitable or sustainable in the overall economy of a country. An evaluation of draft animal power investments at a national level requires a substantiation of the values of the costs of the manpower, financial and natural resources allocated to the programme. It would take account of any subsidies or incentives to farmers, a credit programme or tax exemptions, as well determination of any foreign currency component. Likewise the value of the direct and indirect benefits would be assessed. Direct benefits include increased farm incomes, an increase in agricultural production, reduction in imports and increased employment. Indirect benefits include institutional and infrastructural development (training, extension, skilled manpower, transport, communications), impacts on the industrial sector (local production of implements), increased food supplies and security, and possibly lower consumer prices.

Conclusions

Profitability and adoption of draft animal power are interlinked. If farmers perceive technology to be profitable, by either reducing costs or increasing income, without necessitating major changes in farming systems, they are likely to adopt that technology.

The profitability of draft animal power in sub-Saharan Africa can be substantially increased. However, this is not the complete answer to the

agricultural mechanisation problem. The limited adoption of animal traction, despite 70 years of extension effort and its apparent advantage over hand tool technology, indicates that there are still serious technical and socioeconomic problems to be overcome. Promotion of draft animal power technologies must be based on sound financial and economic analysis.

Animal traction needs to be supported by sound fiscal policies (exchange rates, credit policies, taxation, import duties and pricing policies) which, if used correctly, can have major benefits on promoting draft animal power in a balanced way. However, to bias such measures in favour of draft animal power in the short term will not ensure long-term sustainability.

Recommendations

To allow draft animal power to play its rightful role in the development process the following actions should now be given priority.

○ Detailed farming systems research needs to be carried out to establish the technical, economic, social and political constraints to improving the profitability of draft animal power
○ Improved coordination and communication between aid agencies, research programmes, extension services, farmers and private sector manufacturers and distributors should be promoted, with emphasis being given to formulating appropriate mechanisation strategies
○ Research and extension must be improved. Priority should be given to adaptive research and dissemination of existing technology
○ Intensified training efforts should be promoted to provide the manpower for draft animal power
○ Government policy instruments for credit, taxation, exchange rates and import duties should be closely examined to ensure that they do not mitigate against draft animal power.

References

Barett V, Lassiter G, Wilcock D, Baker D and Crawford E, 1982. *Animal traction in eastern Upper Volta: a technical, economic and institutional analysis*. International Development Paper 4. Michigan State University, East Lansing, Michigan, USA.

Binswanger H, 1986. Evaluating research system performance and targeting research in land abundant areas of sub-Saharan Africa. *World Development* 14(4):469–475.

Corbel H, 1988. The economics of animal power in Koinadugu District, Sierra Leone: a case study of the work oxen introduction and credit programme. pp. 299–310 in: Starkey P and Ndiamé F (eds), *Animal power in farming systems*. Proceedings of the Second West African Animal Traction Networkshop held 17–26 September 1986 in Freetown, Sierra Leone. Vieweg for German Appropriate Technology Exchange. Deutsche Gesellschaft für Technische Zusammenarbeit (GTZ), Eschborn, Germany. 363p.

Delgado C L and McIntire J, 1982. Constraints on oxen cultivation in the Sahel. *American Journal of Agricultural Economics* 64(2):188–196.

Dibbits H K, 1988. The state of national animal draught power programme in Zambia. pp. 51–56 in: Namponya C R (ed), *Animal traction and agricultural mechanisation in SADCC member countries*. Proceedings of workshop held in August 1987, Maputo, Mozambique. SACCAR Workshop Series 7. Southern Africa Centre for Cooperation in Agricultural Research (SACCAR), Gaborone, Botswana. 87p.

Eicher C K, 1984. Facing up to Africa's food crisis. pp. 453–479 in: Eicher C K and Staatz J M (eds), *Agricultural development in the Third World*. Johns Hopkins University Press, Baltimore, Maryland, USA, and London, UK. 491p.

Eicher C K and Baker D C, 1982. *Research on agricultural development in sub-Saharan Africa: a critical survey*. International Development Paper 1. Michigan State University, East Lansing, Michigan, USA.

Ellis-Jones J, 1991. *Agricultural development in a post-apartheid Transkei: towards a brighter future*. Paper presented at the Conference on Political Transition and Economic Development in Transkei held November 1991, Rhodes University, Grahamstown, South Africa. (Unpublished, but available from Overseas Dvision, Silsoe Research Institute, Wrest Park, Silsoe, Bedford MK45 4HS, UK.) 10p.

FAO, 1987. *African agriculture: the next 25 years*. Food and Agriculture Organization of the United Nations (FAO), Rome, Italy.

Francis P A, 1988. Ox draught power and agricultural formation in Northern Zambia. *Agricultural Systems* 27:15–28.

Gregory M, 1989. *Economic issues in draft animal power in Sri Lanka*. Paper presented at the Sri Lankan Association for the Advancement of Science Seminar, Sri Lanka. (Unpublished, but available from Overseas Dvision, Silsoe Research Institute, Wrest Park, Silsoe, Bedford MK45 4HS, UK.)

Guma F, 1988. State of mechanisation in Swaziland. pp. 48–50 in: Namponya C R (ed), *Animal traction and agricultural mechanisation research in SADCC member countries*. Proceedings of workshop held in August 1987, Maputo, Mozambique. SACCAR Workshop Series 7. Southern Africa Centre for Cooperation in Agricultural Research (SACCAR), Gaborone, Botswana. 87p.

IBRD, 1989. *Sub-Saharan Africa—from crisis to sustainable development: a long term perspective*. International Bank for Reconstruction and Development (IBRD), The World Bank, Washington, DC, USA. 300p.

ILCA, 1981. Animal traction in sub-Saharan Africa. *ILCA Bulletin* 14:2–8. International Livestock Centre for Africa (ILCA), Addis Ababa, Ethiopia.

Jahnke H E, 1982. *Livestock production systems and livestock development in tropical Africa*. Kieler Wissenschaftsverlag Vauk, Kiel, Germany, 253p.

Lassiter G C, 1982. *The impact of animal traction on farming systems in eastern Upper Volta*. PhD Thesis. Department of Agricultural Economics, Cornell University, Ithaca, NY, USA. University Microfilms International, Ann Arbor, Michigan, USA.

Lele U, 1984. Rural Africa: modernisation, equity and long term development. pp. 436–452 in: Eicher C K and Staatz J M (eds), *Agricultural development in the Third World*. Johns Hopkins University Press, Baltimore, Maryland, USA, and London, UK. 491p.

Matthewman R W, 1987. Draught animals and the role and future potential of draught cows in African farming systems. *Draught Animal News* 8:23–29.

McIntire J, 1983. *Two aspects of farming in SAT Upper Volta: animal traction and mixed cropping*. Progress Report 7. International Crops Research Institute for the Semi-Arid Tropics (ICRISAT) Economics Programme, Ougadougou, Burkina Faso. 48p.

Morris J, 1983. Smallholder mechanisation: man, animal or engine? *Outlook on Agriculture*. 12(1):28–33.

Mrema G C, 1984. Agricultural mechanisation in Tanzania: constraints and prospects. pp. 199–209 in: Moens and Siepman (eds), *Development of agricultural machinery industry in developing countries*. Pudoc, Wageningen, The Netherlands.

Mrema G C, 1991a. An overview of agricultural mechanisation in the world. pp. 1–14 in: Mrema G C (ed), *Agricultural mechanisation policies and strategies in Africa: case studies from Commonwealth African countries*. Proceedings of the workshop held at the Institute of Agricultural Research, Ahmadu Bello University, 13–17 August 1990, Zaira, Nigeria. Food Production and Rural Development Division, Commonwealth Secretariat, London, UK. 313p.

Mrema G C, 1991b. Synthesis of African experience in agricultural mechanisation. pp. 250–287 in: Mrema G C (ed), *Agricultural mechanisation policies and strategies in Africa: case studies from Commonwealth African countries*. Proceedings of the workshop held at the Institute of Agricultural Research, Ahmadu Bello University, 13–17 August 1990, Zaira, Nigeria. Food Production and Rural Development Division, Commonwealth Secretariat, London, UK. 313p.

Mwinjilo M L, 1991. The role of animal draught in smallholder farming systems in Malawi, pp. 30–33 in: Namponya C R (ed), *Animal traction and agricultural mechanisation research in SADCC member countries*. Proceedings of workshop held in August 1987, Maputo, Mozambique. SACCAR Workshop Series 7. Southern Africa Centre for Cooperation in Agricultural Research (SACCAR), Gaborone, Botswana. 87p.

Norman D W, Newman M D and Onedradago I, 1981. *Farm and village production systems in the semi-arid tropics of West Africa*. Research Bulletin 4 (Vol 1). International Crops Research Institute for the Semi-Arid Tropics (ICRISAT), Patancheru, Andhra Pradesh, India.

O'Neill D H, 1988. *Ergonomics in agricultural and rural development*. Paper presented at South East Asian Ergonomics Society, Denarper, Bali, Indonesia 27–29 July 1988. (Unpublished, but available from Overseas Dvision, Silsoe Research Institute, Wrest Park, Silsoe, Bedford MK45 4HS, UK.) 2p.

Panin A, 1986. *A comparative socio-economic analysis of hoe and bullock farming systems in Northern Ghana*. PhD Thesis. University of Goettingen, Germany, 199p.

Panin A, 1987. The use of bullock traction technology for crop cultivation in Northern Ghana: an empirical economic analysis, *ILCA Bulletin* 29: 2–8. International Livestock Centre for Africa (ILCA), Addis Ababa, Ethiopia.

Panin A, 1989. Profitability assessment of animal traction investment: the case of Northern Ghana. *Agricultural Systems* 30:173–186.

Panin A and Brokken R, 1992. Effects of alternative animal systems on farm output and income for smallscale farmers in the Ethiopian highlands. *Quarterly Journal of International Agriculture* 31(2):162–174.

Pingali P, Bigot Y and Binswanger H, 1987. *Agricultural mechanisation and the evolution of farming systems in sub-Saharan Africa*. Johns Hopkins University Press, Baltimore, Maryland, USA.

Ramaswamy N S, 1988. Draught animal socio-economic factors. pp. 26–31 in: Copland J W (ed), *Draught animal power for production*. ACIAR Proceedings Series 10. Australian Centre for International Agricultural Research (ACIAR), Canberra, Australia. 170p.

Reddy S K, 1988. Use of animal power in West African farming systems: farm level problems and applications of research: perspectives from Mali. pp 182–190 in: Starkey P and Ndiamé F (eds), *Animal power in farming systems*. Proceedings of the Second West African Animal Traction Networkshop held 17–26 September 1986 in Freetown, Sierra Leone. Vieweg for German Appropriate Technology Exchange, Deutsche Gesellschaft für Technische Zusammenarbeit (GTZ), Eschborn, Germany. 363p.

Rocha A, 1988. The importance of animal power in a mixed farming system of the traditional sector of southern

Mozambique. pp. 38–47 in: Namponya C R (ed), *Animal traction and agricultural mechanisation research in SADCC member countries*. Proceedings of workshop held in August 1987, Maputo, Mozambique. SACCAR Workshop Series 7. Southern African Centre for Cooperation in Agricultural Research (SACCAR), Gaborone, Botswana. 87p.

Silumesii G M, and Musonda N G, 1991. An overview of agricultural mechanization strategies in Zambia. pp 160–176 in: Mrema G C (ed), *Agricultural mechanisation policies and strategies in Africa: case studies from Commonwealth African countries*. Proceedings of the workshop held at the Institute of Agricultural Research, Ahmadu Bello University, 13–17 August 1990, Zaira, Nigeria. Food Production and Rural Development Division, Commonwealth Secretariat, London, UK. 313p.

Sindazi M, 1988. Animal draught power programme in Zambia. pp. 57–60 in: Namponya C R (ed), *Animal traction and agricultural mechanisation research in SADCC member countries*. Proceeding of workshop held in August 1987, Maputo, Mozambique. SACCAR Workshop Series 7. Southern African Centre for Cooperation in Agricultural Research (SACCAR), Gaborone, Botswana. 87p.

Singh R D, 1988. *Economics of the family and farming systems in sub-Saharan Africa: development perspectives*. Westview Press, Boulder, Colorado, USA, and London, UK.

Starkey P, 1988a. The introduction, intensification and diversification of the use of animal power in West African farming systems: implications at farm level. pp. 97–115 in: Starkey P and Ndiamé F (eds), *Animal power in farming systems*. Proceedings of the Second West African Animal Traction Networkshop held 17–26 September 1986 in Freetown, Sierra Leone. Vieweg for German Appropriate Technology Exchange, Deutsche Gesellschaft für Technische Zusammenarbeit (GTZ), Eschborn, Germany. 363p.

Starkey P, 1988b. *Perfected yet rejected: animal drawn wheeled tool carriers*. Vieweg for German Appropriate Technology Exchange, Deutsche Gesellschaft für Technische Zusammenarbeit (GTZ), Eschborn, Germany. 161p.

Starkey P, 1990. Animal traction for agricultural development in West Africa: production, impact, profitability and constraints. pp. 90–114 in: Starkey P and Faye A (eds), *Animal traction for agricultural development*. Proceedings of the Third Workshop of the West African Animal Traction Network held 7–12 July 1988, Saly, Senegal. Published on behalf of the West African Animal Traction Network by the Technical Centre for Agricultural and Rural Cooperation (CTA), Ede-Wageningen, The Netherlands. 479p.

Sumberg J and Gilbert E, 1992. Agricultural mechanisation in The Gambia: drought, donkeys and minimum tillage. *African Livestock Research* 1:1–10. International Livestock Centre for Africa (ILCA), Addis Ababa, Ethiopia.

Tembo S and Elliot K M, 1988. The state of use and on going research on draught animal power (DAP) in Zimbabwe. pp. 61–70 in: Namponya C R (ed), *Animal traction and agricultural mechanisation in SADCC member countries*. Proceedings of workshop held in August 1987, Maputo, Mozambique. SACCAR Workshop Series 7. Southern African Centre for Cooperation in Agricultural Research (SACCAR), Gaborone, Botswana. 87p.

Twum A and Gyarteng O K, 1991. Agricultural mechanisation in Ghana: an overview. pp. 59–76 in: Mrema G C (ed), *Agricultural mechanisation policies and strategies in Africa: case studies from Commonwealth African countries*. Proceedings of the workshop held at the Institute of Agricultural Research, Ahmadu Bello University, 13–17 August 1990, Zaira, Nigeria. Food Production and Rural Development Division, Commonwealth Secretariat, London, UK. 313p.

Government financial assistance programmes to improve the profitability of animal traction in Botswana

by

A Panin, M Mrema and M Mahabile

Department of Agricultural Economics and Extension
Botswana College of Agriculture, Private Bag 0027, Gaborone, Botswana

Abstract

This analysis evaluates the effects of government financial assistance programmes on animal traction profitability in Botswana. Using secondary data, it compares variables such as area planted and harvested, crop productivity and ownership of various technological packages for two groups of farmers using animal traction—one receiving government financial assistance and the other not. The overall results indicate that government financial assistance programmes are important to animal traction. They enable resource-poor farmers to overcome the major impediments to the adoption of animal traction and other technologies and thereby increase productivity. The analysis further supports the notion that small farmers are, and can be, efficient and productive if they are financially assisted. It is therefore recommended that other African governments should learn from Botswana's experience. Financial assistance programmes designed for animal traction projects should encompass all equipment associated with the use of draft animals.

Introduction

Unlike many other African countries, Botswana has a long history of animal traction, covering more than 80 years (Baker, 1988). The technology is popular and is used extensively in the traditional farming systems.

Almost all traditional farming households rely on animal traction for plowing. Over the past few years there has been a trend towards the use of tractors, largely as a result of plowing grants which were made available to farmers during the drought period of 1981–86. However, available evidence (MoA, 1991) indicates that animal traction technology is more efficient, economically, than tractors, and because most farmers cannot afford to buy tractors, animal traction will continue to play a crucial role in arable farming in Botswana for the foreseeable future. The total number of draft animals is estimated at 350 000, of which 200 000 are oxen and 150 000 donkeys (Poulsen and Purcell, 1989).

As in many parts of sub-Saharan Africa, lack of capital and draft animals are the main factors limiting profitability and sustainability of animal traction (Srivastava, 1991).

Since 1981, the government, in line with its policy of assisting farmers to increase agricultural production and productivity, has introduced financial assistance programmes such as the Drought Relief Programme (DRP), the Accelerated Rainfed Arable Programme (ARAP) and the Arable Lands Development Programme (ALDEP). Both DRP and ARAP, introduced in 1982/83 and 1985/86, respectively, have been phased out. ALDEP, also introduced in 1982/83, is still operational and figures prominently in the National Development Plan 7 (MoF, 1991). ALDEP is supported by loans from the African Development Bank (ADB) and the International Fund for Agricultural Development (IFAD). The envisaged value of the project at the time of its formulation in 1981 was 23 million Pula (then about US$ 22 million).

The main objective of this paper is to evaluate the performance of ALDEP in order to find out whether or not animal traction profitability improves with government financial assistance. The analysis uses secondary data on animal traction farming systems in Botswana. It compares cropped area, area harvested, crop productivity and number of animal traction packages used by ALDEP-aided farmers and non-aided farmers.

Agriculture in Botswana

About 76% of Botswana's 1.3 million people live in the rural areas and derive their subsistence from mixed crop and livestock farming (MoA, 1989). Livestock are the major source of farm income. However, cattle distribution is very skewed; about 40% of the farming households own no cattle, while over 60% of the national herd, 2.3 million head, are owned by less than 10% of the farming households.

Low crop productivity is the primary agricultural problem (MoA, 1991). Yields of cereal crops (sorghum and maize), the main staple food of the country, are very low, ranging between 200 and

400 kg/ha. Because of this, most of the annual staple food requirements of the country are imported. Imports amount to about 60% of the total grain requirement in good years and as much as 90% in bad years. Because of the importance of agriculture in the economy, even though its share of GNP is 4% (MoA, 1991), development of this sector and rural areas is a major concern of the government.

Climate

Botswana is a semi-arid country. It is characterised by high pressure, which results in dry air with temperatures reaching as high as 39°C in summer and frost at night during winter. As a result the country is prone to recurrent drought.

The average rainfall is 475 mm per year, ranging from 600 mm in the north to 250 mm in the south-west. This rain, which falls in summer, is erratic, poorly distributed and unreliable; it falls in short heavy showers and most of it is lost through run-off. Coupled with this problem, much of the soil moisture is lost through a high rate of evaporation, which far exceeds the incoming rainfall. This has left Botswana with very little surface water or perennial rivers, making even irrigation a very costly exercise.

Evapotranspiration during the growing season (October to April) reaches as high as 1800 mm or four times the seasonal rainfall (Cooke, 1978; MoA, 1991). The soils are sandy and characterised by low levels of minerals, especially nitrogen and phosphorus. This makes arable farming very risky, and so farmers prefer livestock to arable farming.

Aims of ALDEP

The Arable Lands Development Programme (ALDEP) is designed to assist farmers. The main beneficiaries are poor smallholders who comprise about 70–75% of the traditional farmers (Mokone and Sebolai, undated; MoA, 1991). However, they cannot produce enough food to satisfy their subsistence requirements. The rationale behind the introduction of ALDEP was the recognition by the government that most of the smallholders, if left unassisted, will languish in a technical and economic equilibrium trap. The main aims of the project are:

∘ to achieve household food self-sufficiency by addressing some of the known constraints of small farmers

∘ to free small-scale farmers from dependence on large-scale farmers for the supply of inputs, by providing essential inputs to small producers that will enable them to undertake timely

plowing and planting operations for full utilisation of the available moisture which is so essential in semi-arid conditions of Botswana.

Types of assistance

ALDEP assistance designed for the farmers should enable them to acquire farm investment goods which are crucial to improving crop productivity, and thereby increase agricultural production in the country. The assistance covers the following on-farm investment packages (MoA, 1991).

Draft animals, including donkeys, oxen and mules. A farmer can get a maximum assistance of 1400 Pula (about US$ 700 in 1991) and 2400 Pula (about US$ 1200) for the purchases of donkeys and oxen, respectively. The aim of providing draft power and plows is to enable farmers to plow and plant early in order to take advantage of the short-lived soil moisture following rain.

Animal drawn implements, including plows, planters, cultivators and harrows. The amounts granted for these vary according to implement. Planters are used for row planting, and they are provided to encourage farmers to plant in straight rows. Cultivators are meant for effective weeding in row-planted fields.

Fencing materials (a maximum value of 4500 Pula). This assistance will encourage farmers to put up a fence to keep their livestock within their premises and to keep wild animals out.

Water catchment tank (a maximum value of 3600 Pula). The purpose of the water tank is to provide draft animals with water and hence help in timely plowing and planting. Without such a facility animals have to trek long distances in search of water.

Animal-drawn carts (a maximum value of 1900 Pula—about US$ 950 in 1991). The purchase of these will facilitate transport of farm inputs and outputs.

Fertilisers (a maximum value of 100 Pula). These will obviously increase crop productivity when applied at the right time.

As a result of changes in input prices, the maximum amounts granted under each item are revised from time to time.

Implementation of ALDEP

When ALDEP was first introduced farmers were offered assistance in the form of loans and subsidies. This scheme was not successful, probably because resource-poor farmers lacked collateral for the loans.

Table 1: Draft animal ownership by ALDEP aided and non-aided farmers (1982–88)

| Period | Aided farmers | | Non-aided farmers | |
	Number sampled	% owning draft animals	Number sampled	% owning draft animals
1982/83	1 284	69.4	na	na
1983/84	1 181	64.3	na	na
1984/85	4 890	62.9	4 890	40.8
1985/86	11 249	42.2	11 235	44.3
1986/87	15 825	55.2	15 809	40.1
1987/88	20 760	50.4	na	na
Average[1]		57.4		41.7

na = not available

[1] Present authors' calculations

Source: Adapted from Srivastava (1991)

After 18 months, therefore, the form of assistance was changed to grants and downpayments.

The new arrangement, intended to favour all potential beneficiaries, has no loan component, but the subsidy component has been raised to 85% of the value of each package. Farmers are therefore required to find only the remaining 15%. The only exception to this regulation is that a farmer with 11–20 cattle, who wants to acquire draft oxen through the programme, is requested to contribute 40% of the total value.

To qualify for ALDEP assistance, a farmer has to satisfy the following conditions:

o the farmer must own fewer than 40 head of cattle. (Judged by this criterion alone, about 85% of traditional farmers qualify for ALDEP assistance)

o the annual income of the farmer must be less than 7500 Pula (about US$ 3750).

Effects of ALDEP

Draft animal ownership

ALDEP's effect on draft power ownership is demonstrated in Table 1. Between 1982 and 1988, almost 60% of ALDEP-aided farmers managed to acquire their own draft animals, compared with about 40% of non-aided farmers. It is worth noting that the difference would have been greater if ARAP had not been introduced in 1985/86. The maximum potential effect of ALDEP is distorted by ARAP because most of farmers not aided by ALDEP received grants from ARAP. It is clear that government financial assistance programmes such as ALDEP are crucial in helping farmers to acquire their own draft animals.

Crop production

Crop productivity was higher for ALDEP-aided farmers than for non-aided farmers (Table 2). While the average productivity of aided farmers is surprisingly low, it is still 65% higher than that of non-aided farmers. Also, aided farmers planted and harvested larger areas of land than their counterparts. The relatively better performance of the aided farmers can be attributed to the acquisition of the various technological packages made available to them through ALDEP. Of course, the use of such technologies might have influenced the timely execution of farming operations which are directly related in increasing crop productivity.

Table 2: Planted and harvested area and production by ALDEP-aided and non-aided farmers, 1984–88

		Number of farmers	Average area planted per farm (ha)	Average arable area harvested (ha)	Average production per farm (kg)	Average yield (kg/ha)
1984/85	Aided	4 890	4.6	3.6	616	171
	Unaided	4 890	3.6	3.0	397	132
1985/86	Aided	11 249	5.0	4.5	616	137
	Unaided	11 235	4.1	3.9	462	118
1986/87	Aided	15 825	6.7	6.2	811	131
	Unaided	15 809	4.5	4.0	341	85
1987/88	Aided	20 760	6.4	6.2	1859	300
Total average yield[1]	Aided					184.7
	Unaided					111.7

[1] Present authors' calculations

Source: Adapted from Srivastava (1991)

Table 3: Effects of number of technological packages on area cropped and productivity, 1987/88

	Sample size		Area planted per farm	Average yield
Number of packages	Number of farmers	Percentage	(ha)	(kg/ha)
One	12 871	62	5.8	282
Two	5 398	26	6.3	322
Three	1 453	7	8.3	340
Four or more	1 038	5	11.3	317
Total	**20 760**	**100**		

Source: Adapted from Srivastava (1991)

Number of technological packages and crop production

Table 3 shows the effects of the combined application of more than one technological package (ie, draft power, plow, planter, harrow and water tank) on area planted and crop yields. There is a positive linear correlation between the number of packages available to a farmer and the area planted and the crop yields. The only deviation from this trend is found where farmers use four or more packages, when productivity seems to decline slightly. There seems to be no obvious explanation for this anomaly.

Conclusions

The overall results indicate that government financial assistance programmes are crucial to animal traction. They enable resource-poor farmers to overcome the major impediments to the adoption of animal traction and other technologies. If small farmers are financially assisted they can be efficient and productive. In the particular case of Botswana, government financial assistance has enabled farmers to purchase the necessary inputs for enhancement of productivity. In this connection, ALDEP has played a useful role through three major approaches:

○ helping farmers to acquire their own draft animals. This has increased the number of farms owning draft animals and reduced the number of farmers who have to hire such animals

○ increasing crop productivity. This is a consequence of the first approach

○ increasing the area planted to crops.

Botswana has useful lessons for other countries that intend to increase farmers' productivity through animal traction farming systems.

Acknowledgement

We wish to thank Mr S K Karikari of the Crop Science Department, Botswana College of Agriculture, for his valuable input.

References

Baker B, 1988. *Traction use in Shoshong Agricultural Technology Improvement Project (ATIP)*. ATIP WP-22. Department of Agricultural Research, Ministry of Agriculture, Gaborone, Botswana. 53p.

Cooke H J, 1978. Botswana: present climate and evidence from past change. In: Hinchey M T (ed), *Symposium on drought in Botswana*. Proceedings of a workshop held in Gaborone, Botswana, on 5–8 June 1978. The Botswana Society in collaboration with Clark University Press, Worcester, Massachusetts, USA. 305p.

MoA, 1989. *Agricultural sector assessment: a strategy for development of agriculture in Botswana*. Ministry of Agriculture (MoA). Government Printer, Gaborone, Botswana. 239p.

MoA, 1991. *Botswana's agricultural policy: critical sectoral issues and future strategy for development*. Ministry of Agriculture (MoA). Government Printer, Gaborone, Botswana. 28p.

MoF, 1991. *National Development Plan 7, 1991–96*. Ministry of Finance (MoF). Government Printer, Gaborone, Botswana. 507p.

Mokone F S and Sebolai M K, (undated). *Information for small projects: revised version for use by extension workers and entrepreneurs*. Ministry of Finance and Development Planning. Government Printer, Gaborone, Botswana. 98p.

Poulsen E and Purcell R A, 1989. *Relative economics of different draft power applications in Botswana: a review of current situation and recommendations for future policy*. Ministry of Agriculture. Government Printer, Gaborone, Botswana. 71p.

Srivastava P D, 1991. *Nine years of arable lands development programme 1982–1991*. Ministry of Agriculture. Government Printer, Gaborone, Botswana. 82p.

A note on improving the profitability of a large-scale commercial farm in Zambia through the use of oxen

Bruce Danckwerts

New Venture Farm, PO Box 630021, Choma, Zambia

Abstract

This brief paper gives information on the use of oxen on a commercial farm in Zambia. About 40 pairs of oxen are profitably employed and provide year-round, low-cost on-farm transport for little management effort. By using oxen, the farm saves at least 15 000 litres of diesel fuel each year. Although oxen have been used for various cultivation operations, lack of suitable equipment and need for speed and timeliness hinder the prospects for expanding these areas. Personal observations are presented concerning limiting factors and areas that can be expanded.

Introduction

My father farmed in Zimbabwe, and until 1960 he used oxen for the majority of his farm work there. During the period 1960 to 1964 he had one tractor but continued to use oxen. In 1965 he bought the farm in the Southern Province of Zambia that I am now managing. At that time the farm was tractor-oriented and had no working teams of oxen. It had always been my father's intention to reintroduce oxen but his deportation in 1975 put a stop to his plans. Partly as a result of his wishes and partly through the interest in appropriate technology that I acquired at university, I was determined to restart using oxen on the farm.

In 1978, I used my father's idea of an animal-drawn wheeled toolbar or forecart to act as the drawbar to which a four-wheel four-tonne tractor trailer could be attached. This would allow a quick interchange between oxen and tractors should the need arise. In my ignorance we started with a team of six raw oxen and inexperienced ox drivers. It was a near disaster, for the inexperienced oxen destroyed several gates. Steering six oxen was difficult on the curved reaping roads in the tobacco fields and in the narrow alleyways between barns. Since then we have made some progress and now use about 40 pairs of oxen on the farm.

Appropriate technologies

New Venture Farm has many appropriate technologies, some simple, some complicated. For example, this paper was prepared on one computer while a second computer processed farm data. The farm has tractors, mains electricity, sprinkler irrigation, a workshop and lathe and a continuous tobacco curing process using forced-air. Thus the farm may be considered a "high technology" one by Zambian standards. Some people think it strange to see oxen working on such a farm.

The main and most successful use of oxen has been for transport. Two labourers are used with each set of oxen, one to drive and one to lead (the leader is useful when negotiating tight turns or when walking among valuable tobacco plants). Pairs of oxen pull a disselboom (shaft) that fits into a socket on the four-wheel trailers. They generally manage loads of 3 tonnes for distances of up to 15 km. On slopes steeper than about 4%, a second team may be connected to help them up the hill.

Smaller, two-wheel "scotch carts" are used to transport molasses to cattle, sand to builders and water to sprayers operating in the fields. Other animal-powered farm operations tried have included:

o   raking hay using a four-wheel Vicon side-delivery rake
o   heaping hay using a buck rake
o   cultivating tobacco using a single-row "pot-holer" which leaves tied ridges to catch the rain
o   spraying herbicide when the land was too wet for tractors. The oxen pulled a four-row boom on wheels, a pressurised 200 litre drum and a foot pump to boost pressure at each headland
o   plowing fireguard strips
o   pulling logs off newly cleared land.

However, the problem is that all these jobs tend to be very seasonal, and they require a great deal of investment in time, oxen and equipment in order to get the jobs done. On the other hand, ox use for transport is quite constant during the year.

Another large job for oxen is likely to be the levelling of termite mounds using scoops. With irrigation, the soil can be made suitably soft throughout the year, and the farm has enough mounds to keep several teams working every day for many years.

108 "Improving animal traction technology"

Tied-ridging tobacco on New Venture Farm using an ox-drawn implement developed by Bruce Danckwerts

Tobacco field with tied-ridges or "pot-holes" made by draft animals on New Venture Farm, Zambia

Economic considerations

Farm analyses show that a large proportion (40%) of farm fuel is used on transport. In 1991, the farm spent 3045 labour days on ox use (mainly for transport) which at about 80 Kwacha per labour day came to 243 600 Kwacha (US$ 1 ≈ 90 Kwacha in 1991).

A team of oxen saves the farm at least 10 litres of diesel fuel per day. For example, at harvest the teams each carry four 3-tonne loads of tobacco a day. They travel 7 km laden and 7 km empty. Most tractors would use at least 10 litres for such haulage work. At 70 Kwacha per litre saved (costed by the farm at double purchase price to cover wear and tear on tractors) farm fuel savings of 10 litres per team work day add up to just over one million Kwacha a year. As two people are used per team day, this represents about 800 000 Kwacha net savings.

Productivity is quite high as the ox team workers are more prepared to assist with cart loading than are tractor drivers. They also cause less equipment wear and tear and damage (unlike tractors and pick-ups, ox carts generally stop when there is a flat tyre or other problem).

Furthermore, the oxen appreciate in value: old oxen that are retired have a resale value higher (in real terms) than they had when they started training.

Tied-ridging tobacco on New Venture Farm using an ox-drawn implement developed by Bruce Danckwerts

Oxen are easily available and require very little management. The farm would probably not gain a lot by improving the harnessing system (using simple yokes) or feeding system (which is basic grazing plus some molasses in the winter when the breeding cows are supplemented). Donkeys, mules and horses are not readily available in southern Zambia and it is unlikely to be worth the effort to breed animals specifically for draft purposes.

Conclusions

Oxen can and should play a part on most large-scale commercial farms in Africa. Transport is the easiest job to allocate to oxen as the tractor implements (four-wheel trailers) are easily adapted to oxen. Transport is also a job which does not require any auxiliary drives from a power source and is in fairly constant demand throughout the year. Ox-pulled carts are the nearest thing available to reliable, low-cost, low-management transport for commercial farmers in Zambia.

Many other jobs can be given to oxen but the implements would have to be specially bought (or made) and would have to be bought in sufficient quantities to allow the job to be done within the time available. Finding suitable equipment is a problem for commercial farmers: the ox plows most commonly available in Zambia would not be able to plow to the standard normally required for commercial tobacco production.

It is not realistic for a commercial farm to train and maintain oxen unless they can be used regularly during the year. It is not sufficient to identify one short-term cultivation operation a year that could be carried out by oxen: it is better to select several jobs that can keep the oxen occupied during much of the year. However, if oxen can be used mainly for transport, it may be possible to give them some additional short-duration jobs.

A note on the potential profitability of animal traction in Nakuru District, Kenya

by

Paul Mugo Maina

Managing Director, Farming Systems Kenya Ltd, PO Box 2816, Nakuru, Kenya

Abstract

Since Kenyan independence, farm sizes in Nakuru District have been gradually reduced, first as African land buying companies bought farms from white, large-scale farmers and split them into smallholdings, and later as parts of the smallholdings were passed on to family members or sold. The average smallholding in most parts of the district is now less than 1 ha.

How to make the most economic and efficient use of their land, in order to maximise production, is the problem now facing small-scale farmers. The use of tractors is not cost-effective on such small farms, and so many farmers are having to resort to using hand hoes. Hand hoeing is time-consuming, produces a poor seedbed, and cannot control weeds adequately, so crop yields are low. Animal traction could provide the answer to these problems, but this technology is not common in Nakuru. Donkeys may be the most suitable draft animals in this area, but their successful introduction will require socioeconomic studies, training of both the donkeys and the farmers and the design of efficient implements.

Introduction

At independence Nakuru District of Kenya was inhabited mainly by white, large-scale farmers. After independence the government encouraged Africans to buy farms from the white farmers. Land buying companies were formed, and the government facilitated the buying by providing loans. When the loans had been repaid, the companies subdivided the farms into smallholdings ranging in size from 0.2 to 4 ha depending on the size of the farm, the number of shareholders and the number of shares owned.

Over the past 10 years the farms have been further divided as parts of smallholdings have been passed on to family members or sold. In most areas of the district, the average holding is now below 1 ha.

The problem that the small-scale farmers are now facing is how to make the most economic and efficient use of their land in order to maximise agricultural production. Farming systems research and extension practitioners are working towards easing the situation by carrying out detailed socioeconomic surveys aimed at influencing land use patterns and agricultural policies.

Farm size and use

The population of Kenya is predominantly (85%) rural, and the country's economy is based on agriculture: the agricultural sector contributes 30% of Gross Domestic Product, and about 70% of the working population is employed directly or indirectly in agriculture.

An important challenge facing the agricultural sector is sustainability of production: major constraints include the unprecedented subdivision of the already small holdings, the high cost of farm inputs, marketing problems and high labour costs. The major concerns of most development agents are the training of farmers, provision of credit, better management of farmers' resources and the timeliness of agricultural operations, particularly land preparation because the quality of the seedbed largely determines crop yields.

A recent survey conducted by the Ministry of Agriculture in conjunction with Farming Systems Kenya Ltd revealed that the average farm size in Nakuru District is 0.8 ha, while the average family has eight children. Most farm families have subdivided their farms among one or two sons who are married and living on the farm. Buildings occupy about 12.5% of the farm; the rest is used for food production. Major food crops include maize, beans, potatoes, tomatoes and a variety of vegetables. Some farmers grow tea and coffee.

Mechanisation

On large farms (4 ha or more) tractors are commonly used for land preparation and other field operations. Use of tractors is not cost-effective on smaller farms: tractors are expensive to hire and work is slow (and a lot of time is wasted) because, on small areas, tractors are constantly having to make turns. In fact, most farmers with only 0.8 ha cannot afford to hire tractors unless they have off-farm income, and even then the high costs of other farm inputs inhibits this option. Small farmers are therefore having to revert to using hand hoes.

This, combined with less use of fertiliser, is resulting in declining crop yields per unit of land.

Attempts have been made to introduce small tractors, and testing has been going on for more than 10 years at the Ministry of Agriculture's Central Workshop in Nakuru and at other centres. As yet no small tractor has made any significant entry onto the market. The work at Nakuru has shown that the cost of buying a so-called small tractor is not within reach of most small-scale farmers; even if they could afford the tractor, they probably would not be able to buy the necessary implements. Thorough research is needed to justify the costs of mechanisation of small farms, particularly in the light of the continued subdivision of farm land.

Traditional farming

The reversion of small-scale farmers to the use of hand hoes can be attributed to a number of factors, such as the high cost of tractor operations and the fact that tractors are not readily available when needed. Hand hoeing has many disadvantages: it is time consuming; the quality of the seedbed is poor; and it encourages regrowth of weeds which are often not properly buried. However, animal traction is not a common practice in Nakuru, and so farmers feel they have no alternative at present.

Low crop yields resulting from poor land preparation are a major concern. Thus what is needed is an alternative technology, and animal traction could certainly make an important contribution to solving these problems.

Animal traction

Farmers' priorities in farming are first to grow food for themselves and their families, and second to generate some income to take care of their other basic needs. Farmers are very careful not to engage in activities that may to put their farms—their livelihood—at risk; for example, they will resist any assistance that presupposes the loss of their farms if they cannot pay back the loan. They are therefore very business conscious.

Hence, in considering the best option for mechanisation thorough socioeconomic studies will need to be undertaken. For instance, while ox plowing is the most common form of animal traction in Kenya, farmers in high potential areas opt to keep dairy cows for milk production, the immediate benefit being income accruing from the sale of milk. But land cannot be used for both food crops and grazing at the same time. As feed requirements for oxen and dairy cows can be broadly similar (FAO, 1972), the implication is that dairy cows have a comparative advantage over the oxen. It is therefore imperative that the decision on the species of animal to be used for draft be based on maximum economic returns per hour.

Donkeys have gained acceptance in Kenya as a means of transport and are particularly common in high potential regions. Our observation in Farming Systems Kenya Ltd is that the donkeys are grazed on the roadside and very little attention is paid to them, unlike the cows and oxen. If a donkey is to be used for traction work it must be well fed, although donkeys require less feed than horses or oxen (FAO, 1972). Baseline surveys and socioeconomic studies need to be carried out to determine the acceptability of the species. This is crucial in Nakuru District where land holdings are becoming smaller because of subdivision of the land.

At the same time implements will need to be assessed and redesigned so that, hopefully, single animals could be used. The Agricultural Engineering Department of Egerton University has initiated student projects to redesign animal traction implements, an area that will need serious follow-up.

Conclusion

The potential role of work animals, particularly donkeys, in Nakuru District, appears very great. One major challenge is training of both the donkeys and farmers, but economic analyses should also be carried out as the profitability of animal traction is of major concern. It is recommended that more studies be carried out in the following areas:

- selection of the most economical species
- acceptance of the selected species
- design of efficient and economical implements
- utilisation of different species and their opportunity cost compared with other species, tractors and hand hoes
- labour-saving aspects
- sources of feeds and the requirements for the number of animals to be deployed based on available land
- possibility of communal management and use of the animals.

Farm size is certainly dictating that alternative methods be sought because the current trend of using either hand hoes or tractors has drawbacks that are reflected in the profit margins of the farms.

Reference

FAO, 1972. *Manual on the employment of draught animals in agriculture*. Food and Agriculture Organization of the United Nations (FAO), Rome, Italy. 249p.

Improving profitability of weeding technology in maize and sorghum production in Northern Nigeria

by

J O Olukosi[1] and A O Ogungbile[2]

[1] *Interim Coordinator, West African Farming Systems Research Network*
[2] *Head, Farming Systems Research Programme*
Institute for Agricultural Research, Ahmadu Bello University, PMB 1044, Zaria, Nigeria

Abstract

Maize and sorghum crops grown on land prepared by hand hoeing or ox cultivation were weeded using a hoe or herbicide. For both crops, ox cultivated plots required less weeding labour and gave higher returns per hectare and per labour-hour than hoe cultivated plots. Labour requirements in the months of June–August (the period of the weeding labour bottleneck) were reduced by 40% in maize and 59% in sorghum as a result of oxen use, and by 36% in maize and 27% in sorghum due to herbicide use. Ox cultivation has been found to be a better alternative to improving profitability of weeding technology than herbicide use.

Introduction

For a long time sorghum has been the most important cereal crop in Nigeria, in terms of cultivated land area and per capita consumption. This is followed by millet which is usually grown in mixture with sorghum in the drier north, while maize is grown together with sorghum in the wetter areas. Maize ranked third behind sorghum and millet as a major cereal crop in Nigeria; however, within the past decade or so, maize cultivation has been increasing in the sorghum areas as a result of the introduction of fertiliser, to which maize responds better than sorghum.

Weeding has been identified as the most limiting operation under the traditional farming systems (Norman, 1972; Olukosi, 1986). Hoe weeding is the most labour consuming of the pre-harvest operations either in maize or sorghum production under improved and traditional technologies (Norman et al, 1976a; b). It is therefore necessary to examine ways of improving weeding technology in the production of both sorghum and maize. Any intervention that will reduce the drudgery of hand-hoe weeding and save labour during the June–August peak labour demand period would be welcomed. However, the reduction in labour use should not be achieved at the expense of profitability.

The objective of this investigation was to determine the requirements and distribution of labour under different modes of cultivation and weed control technologies in the production of maize and sorghum and to determine the profitability of each option.

Materials and methods

The experiments were conducted on farmers' fields at Nasarawa (11° 40' N, 7° 05' E) where maize or sorghum was the sole crop. The maize variety used was TZB while the sorghum variety was L.187. A total of 60 farmers were involved, 30 for maize and 30 for the sorghum trials. In each group of 30 farmers 15 owned and used ox-drawn implements for ridging and remoulding of ridges, while the remaining 15 used hand hoes. A 0.4 ha plot was marked out on each farmer's field and the plot was further split into two equal halves. One half was weeded by hand hoe while herbicide was applied on the other half.

For maize one sub-plot was treated with Primextra (atrazine and metolachlor in the ratio 1:2) at the rate of 2.0 kg/ha pre-emergence in about 12 litres spray liquid/ha using a controlled droplet low volume sprayer (Micron-Handy). Single superphosphate and calcium ammonium nitrate were applied at 100 kg N and 60 kg P_2O_5/ha to both the herbicide treated and hoe weeded plots two weeks after sowing.

For sorghum, one sub-plot was treated with Sorgoprim (propazine and atrazine mixture) at the rate of 1.8 kg/ha in 12 litres spray liquid/ha. The same Micron-Handy sprayer was used. Single superphosphate and calcium ammonium nitrate were applied at 65 kg N and 45 kg P_2O_5/ha as side dressing to both herbicide treated and hoe weeded sub-plots two weeks after sowing. Sprayers were calibrated by the researchers while the farmers mixed the chemicals and applied them to their fields. Supplementary hoe weeding was carried out on the herbicide treated plots as necessary.

Table 1: Labour requirements by operation for maize and sorghum with and without ox cultivation using hoe and herbicide for weeding (average of the two years 1989 and 1990)

	Maize				Sorghum			
	Hoe cultivation		Ox cultivation		Hoe cultivation		Ox cultivation	
Operation	Hoe weeding (hours/ha)	Herbicide weeding (hours/ha)	Hoe weeding (hours/ha)	Herbicide weeding (hours/ha)	Hoe weeding (hours/ha)	Herbicide weeding (hours/ha)	Hoe weeding (hours/ha)	Herbicide weeding (hours/ha)
Ridging	59	70	15	16	94	90	20	14
Weeding	102	23	72	19	139	61	112	30
Harvesting	145	215	250	240	189	211	84	122

The experiments were farmer managed while an enumerator stationed in the village throughout the growing period recorded the use of labour and other inputs. Information was recorded from each farmer at least once a week for the whole period. The yield estimates were obtained by weighing the total threshed grains from each plot.

The common species of weed found in the village farms were similar to those reported by Ogungbile and Lagoke (1986; 1989). The organic matter and clay contents of the soil were 0.5–1.3 and 7.2–18.5%, respectively.

Results and discussion

Weeding operations

For both sorghum and maize the highest value for weeding labour was recorded when land preparation and weeding were carried out using hoes while the lowest value was obtained when land was prepared using oxen and herbicides were used to control weeds. Ox prepared plots required less weeding labour than hoe prepared ones. As expected, the herbicide treated plots required less weeding labour. The result shows that ox cultivation enhances weed control and reduces weeding labour requirements (Table 1).

Monthly labour distribution

The peak period for weeding labour is from June to August (Norman et al, 1976a; b). The use of oxen for cultivation saved 40% of the total labour required for all operations during this peak for maize and 59% for sorghum under hoe weeding conditions. Herbicide use saved 21% of total labour required during this peak for maize and 56% for sorghum under hoe cultivation; 16% for maize, 22% for sorghum under ox cultivation. This implies that ox cultivation saves more labour at the peak period in sorghum than maize under hoe weeding conditions but this is reversed under herbicide use. Herbicide use, however, saves more labour at the peak period in sorghum than in maize and both hoe and ox cultivation conditions (Table 2).

Financial costs and returns

Tables 3 and 4 show the costs and returns involved in producing one hectare of sorghum and maize, respectively, under the different cultivation and weeding methods. Hired labour constituted between 46 and 58% of the total labour requirement for sorghum production and between 48 and 63% for maize production.

Table 2: Labour requirements for maize and sorghum production during critical monthly weeding periods (average of the two years 1989 and 1990)

	Maize				Sorghum			
	Hoe cultivation		Ox cultivation		Hoe cultivation		Ox cultivation	
	Hoe weeding (hours/ha)	Herbicide weeding (hours/ha)	Hoe weeding (hours/ha)	Herbicide weeding (hours/ha)	Hoe weeding (hours/ha)	Herbicide weeding (hours/ha)	Hoe weeding (hours/ha)	Herbicide weeding (hours/ha)
June	95	115	29	31	13	65	30	47
July	106	20	89	37	162	62	83	42
August	23	42	16	45	161	20	25	18
Total	**224**	**177**	**134**	**113**	**336**	**147**	**138**	**107**

Table 3: Costs and returns per hectare of sorghum, with and without ox cultivation, using hoe and herbicide for weeding (average of the two years 1989 and 1990)

Item	Hoe cultivation		Ox cultivation	
	Hoe weeding	Herbicide	Hoe weeding	Herbicide
Output kg/ha	1491	1596	1688	1658
Gross value (Naira)	2684	2873	3038	2984
Input costs (Naira)				
Seeds and seed dressing	86	86	86	86
Fertiliser	140	140	140	140
Herbicide	0	600	0	600
Depreciation	150	150	600	600
Labour (hired)	696	751	375	300
Labour (all)	1513	1295	723	613
Total cost (hired labour)	**1072**	**1727**	**1201**	**1726**
Total cost (all labour)	**1889**	**2271**	**1549**	**2039**
Returns (Naira)				
Hired labour	1612	1146	1837	1258
All labour	795	602	1489	945
	± 75	± 100	± 260	± 121
Returns per labour-hour				
Total labour	1.3	1.16	5.15	3.86
Family labour	2.4	2.16	10.72	7.56
June–August labour	2.4	4.19	10.80	8.80
Weeding labour	5.7	9.86	13.30	31.53
Yield required to cover cost (kg)	**1049**	**1262**	**861**	**1133**

Sorghum valued at 1.8 Naira/kg (1 Naira ≈ US$0.12; US$1 ≈ 8 Naira)

For both crops, yields were higher (P<0.05) under ox cultivation and hoe weeding than under hoe cultivation and hoe weeding. For maize, the yield was higher (P<0.05) under ox cultivation and herbicide than under hoe cultivation and herbicide.

For both crops, the net returns per hectare were higher (P<0.01) under ox cultivation and hoe weeding than under hoe cultivation and hoe weeding, and higher (P<0.05) under ox cultivation and herbicide than under hoe cultivation and herbicide.

When the labour inputs for the different systems were considered, the trends for both crops were similar. Generally, the systems gave a higher marginal return per hour than the marginal cost of labour. Viewed against the June–August peak period, the ox cultivated plots gave significantly higher returns (P<0.01) than the hoe cultivated ones suggesting that using oxen to prepare land for the two crops is more profitable. Once the land is ox mechanised the superiority of using herbicide over the hand hoe is not very clear, especially as one supplementary hoe weeding was needed to support the herbicide treatment.

Summary and conclusion

The returns per hectare for both crops followed the same trend. Ox cultivation and hand hoe weeding treatment gave higher returns per hectare than ox cultivation and herbicide treatment, while the two are superior to the two hoe cultivation treatments. This shows that oxen technology is a better alternative for increasing profitability of weeding technology than the use of herbicide.

References

Norman D W, 1972. *An economic survey of three villages in Zaria Province: input-output study.* Samaru Miscellaneous Paper 37. Institute for Agricultural Research, Zaria, Nigeria. pp. 46–55.

Norman D W, Beeden P, Kroeker W J, Pryor D H, Hays H M and Huizinga B, 1976a. *The feasibility of improved sole crop maize production technology for small scale farmers in the Northern Guinea Savanna Zone of Nigeria.* Samaru Miscellaneous Paper 59. Institute for Agricultural Research, Samaru, Nigeria. pp. 9–13.

Norman D W, Beeden P, Kroeker W J, Pryor D H, Huizinga B and Hays H M, 1976b. *The feasibility of sole crop sorghum production technology for small scale farmers in the Northern Guinea Savanna Zone of Nigeria.* Samaru Miscellaneous Paper 60. Institute for Agricultural Research, Samaru, Nigeria. pp. 8–12.

Table 4: Costs and returns per hectare of maize, with and without ox cultivation, using hoe and herbicide for weeding (average of the two years 1989 and 1990)

Item	Hoe cultivation		Ox cultivation	
	Hoe weeding	Herbicide	Hoe weeding	Herbicide
Output kg/ha	2400	2631	2729	2957
Gross value (Naira)	4320	4736	4912	5323
Input costs (Naira)				
Seeds and seed dressing	86	86	86	86
Fertiliser	225	225	225	225
Herbicide	0	750	0	750
Depreciation	150	150	600	600
Labour (hired)	717	539	517	414
Labour (all)	1138	1068	1017	870
Total cost (hired labour only)	**1178**	**1750**	**1428**	**2075**
Total cost (all labour)	**1599**	**2279**	**1928**	**2531**
Returns (Naira)				
Hired labour	3142	2986	3484	3248
All labour	2721	2457	2 984	2792
	± 230	± 250	± 270	± 261
Returns per labour-hour				
Total labour	5.98	5.76	7.33	8.02
Family labour	16.20	11.70	14.90	15.30
June–August labour	12.10	13.90	22.30	24.70
Weeding labour	26.68	106.70	41.40	146.90
Yield required to cover cost (kg)	**888**	**1266**	**1071**	**1406**

Maize valued at 1.8 Naira/kg (1 Naira ≈ US$0.12; US$1 ≈ 8 Naira)

Ogungbile A O and Lagoke S T, 1986. On-farm evaluation of the economics of chemical weed control in oxen-mechanised maize production in Nigeria Savanna. *Tropical Pest Management* 32(4):269–273.

Ogungbile A O and Lagoke S T, 1989. On-farm assessment of the potential for the use of herbicide in oxen-mechanised

sorghum production in the Nigerian Savanna. *Tropical Pest Management* 35(2):133–136.

Olukosi J O, 1986. *Income generation and distribution among farmers in two villages: the case of two villages in Kwara State.* Samaru Miscellaneous Paper 114. Institute for Agricultural Research, Samaru, Nigeria. pp. 59–69.

Increasing agricultural production by using animal traction: a rural development puzzle

by

Jacques de Graaf *

Animal Draft Power Development and Training Officer
Palabana Animal Draft Power Project, Private Bag 173, Woodlands, Lusaka, Zambia

Abstract

This paper deals with animal traction development in Zambia's rural economy. It discusses some economic issues, animal traction in peasant households and the influence of the broader economic and institutional environment on animal traction adoption. Some implications for development projects are discussed, and suggestions are made for improving animal traction development interventions.

Introduction

Using work animals to increase agricultural production has been recognised, by both the Zambian Government and donor agencies, as an appropriate alternative to motorised technologies. In an recent report it was estimated that approximately 200 000 oxen are used as draft animals in Zambia (Starkey, Dibbits and Mwenya, 1990). In certain regions cows and donkeys are being employed.

This paper presents a brief outline of the role of animal traction in the rural economy, and of obstacles hindering animal traction development. Several policy options for reducing these obstacles and for increasing the use of animals in agricultural production are discussed. Also, some suggestions are made for improving project interventions.

Economic considerations

In several provinces in Zambia (eg, Western, Southern) draft animals are part of the traditional mixed livestock and crop farming system; in others (eg, Luapula) animals have rarely been kept and have less economic importance. Despite these regional differences it is generally appreciated that cattle perform several economic and social functions in the society (Beerling, 1986; Tembo and Rajeswaran, 1986). These include:

○ draft power
○ food supply (milk, meat)
○ manure
○ byproducts (hides, etc)
○ social and cultural
○ investment.

These multiple functions of cattle make it difficult to provide economic assessments of draft cattle as such, because the other costs and benefits involved in cattle keeping cannot be separated. However, as an individual farm operation, animal traction should reduce the costs of production (by increasing labour productivity), thus making it a viable power source for peasant farmers. This means that when the costs of oxen and implements are spread over a given period and given land area, the return to labour should be higher with the use of oxen than without oxen; animal traction is considered a labour saving technology.

In Zambia, animals (oxen) have mainly been employed in primary soil tillage (plowing), leading to an expansion of the cultivated area. Because of this phenomenon, animal traction has mainly functioned as a labour *shifting* technology rather than as a labour *saving* one, because labour peaks in planting, weeding and harvesting were not alleviated. In some areas labour peaks have even increased due to the expanded area under cultivation (Francis, 1988; Agrisystems, 1990). The increased workload especially affected women, as they are often involved in planting, weeding and harvesting.

The major gains from using animal traction arose from the increase in area under cultivation. Several studies indicated that when farm operations were diversified and animals were used for off-farm labour (eg, transport), animal traction became potentially more attractive (Corbel, 1986; Francis, 1988; Huybens, 1988; Rauch et al, 1988; Agrisystems, 1990). It is argued that the degree of labour saving will thus be related to the intensity, diversity and level of use throughout the agricultural production process. Enhancing animal traction development will therefore require progressive changes in farming systems, such as new secondary tillage techniques, agronomic adaptations, improved

Subsequent address:
Jacques de Graaf (Maputo, Mozambique)
c/o Ministry of Foreign Affairs
PO Box 20061, 2500EB Den Haag, The Netherlands

animal husbandry practices, etc. In order to allow for such complex adaptations in farming systems, and to justify investments in animal traction technology, input and output prices, among others factors, will play a crucial role.

Animal traction in a peasant economy

It is well known that national agricultural production must be increased, and the standard of living of people living in the rural and urban areas must be improved, if peasants are to be integrated into the broader economy. This integration may take place when farmers have reasons and incentives to do so. Unfortunately, farming in Zambia (with or without animal traction) has been marginal, and the overall economic environment did not allow a sustained integration of peasant farmers in the economy. Zambian peasants are only partially integrated in the broader economy: while they often rely on family labour and produce to satisfy their needs, they also make use of the broader economic system for their input requirements and for sales of their, often limited, surplus produce. Peasant farmers are not necessarily interested in maximising their profits. In many cases they prefer to optimise their output and to avoid risks in farming, as their ultimate aim is household survival (Ellis, 1988).

Farmers' decisions on adopting or enhancing the use of animals on their farms are not necessarily based on financial profitability. Tangible social and cultural benefits also play a significant role in the adoption process. Zambia's rural economy is complicated and dynamic, and there are important differences within the peasant communities concerning sizes of farms, household structures, labour allocation, etc. These differences should be understood before advising farmers to invest in animal traction technology. Nonetheless, to allow animal traction to be adopted or enhanced requires that the risks of farming be reduced. Therefore, from an economic viewpoint, it is argued that when markets become more reliable and the farming essentials (input supply, credit, marketing, etc) are being reliably taken care of, the use of animals in farming will become more attractive, and peasants will become more likely to accept changes and integrate animal traction in their farming systems.

Obstacles to animal traction development

Several institutional and economic development obstacles have major influences on the adoption of animal traction and other agricultural innovations by small-scale farmers. These include:

- ○ lack of marketing
- ○ lack of institutional development
- ○ lack of private entrepreneurship and market development
- ○ lack of grassroots constituencies and participation
- ○ lack of capital
- ○ lack of market value prices.

Lack of marketing

Zambia's economy is highly unstable and unreliable. The inadequacy of Zambia's marketing infrastructure is indicated by the fact that farmers are often not paid until months after their produce has been collected. In some districts the marketing organisation does not collect all the produce.

The reasons for the parastatal's poor performance are well known:

- ○ it is a large organisation with a monopolistic status which is characterised by large diseconomies of scale, exacerbated by relatively scattered and remote farming communities
- ○ it lacks the individual and institutional capacity to manage its affairs
- ○ it lacks accountability and responsibility.

Lack of institutional development

Most Zambian institutions involved in agriculture, and hence directly or indirectly with animal traction, are heavily "top-down" organised. Bureaucracy is the rule rather than the exception. These large bureaucratic institutions are difficult to manage and rarely create animal traction development opportunities.

Lack of private entrepreneurship and market development

The previous government did not create an economic environment in which private entrepreneurship and local markets could flourish. Lack of such initiatives and markets resulted, for example, in shortages of rural craftsmen and artisans and of implements and spare parts, and a lack of private investments and markets.

Lack of grassroots constituencies and participation

Rural Zambia has few small-scale farmers' organisations. Individual peasants, living isolated and scattered, lack the power to make claims on institutions.

One of the reasons why many primary cooperative societies have failed to become successful in helping farmers to obtain ox-drawn equipment and other inputs is that a centre-down policy has prevailed over participatory, bottom-up, approaches.

Lack of capital

Many small-scale farmers lack financial resources to invest in animal traction technologies.

Lack of market value prices

Prices for agricultural outputs do not reflect their true economic scarcity value. Government pricing policies on both farm inputs and outputs are not appropriate (Harvey, 1988).

Improvement of animal draft power

The full benefits of animal traction cannot be realised unless support systems are created that provide the necessary incentives (such as prices), economic opportunities (markets) and access to resources and inputs to enable peasants to increase their agricultural production in a sustainable way. Therefore, animal traction development inherently requires institutional reform, the paying of market value prices to farmers, market development, rural transport (oxen), feeder road development and rural industrialisation (support services).

Marketing

There is an urgent need to improve the marketing system in Zambia in order to increase the impact of, and sustain, animal traction development initiatives. The present and previous governments have directed their policies to market liberalisation (prices) and privatisation in order to get the marketing "right". It is believed that privatisation could contribute to:

o an increase in competition between private buyers and parastatals, urging the parastatals to reorganise into a more efficient institution

o the creation of a diverse and innovative trading and processing community

o price differentiation and development of trade and local markets.

But there are also arguments against privatisation of marketing institutions and allowing private entrepreneurs to compete on the market:

o food security is a national matter

o private traders may exploit unknowledgeable farmers

o multiple trading channels undermine the so-called "stop order credit recovery system".

The discussion concerning privatisation and liberalisation entails much more than is covered in this paper. Privatisation and liberalisation require careful and in-depth analysis. Without care and sensitivity in promoting market liberalisation, there could be a risk of repeating such experiences as previously occurred in Zambia.

Institutional development

Agricultural institutions will continue to play an important role in agricultural development. It is therefore important to address the issue of institutional development. This issue can be interpreted in different ways. Accepting the debate concerning institutional development in this paper, it refers to strengthening the management and organisation of public sector institutions involved in the agricultural sector (the extension service, credit organisations, etc), to improve their efficiency and effectiveness. For example, if credit is properly managed it could be of great importance to animal traction development in Zambia. Some of the prerequisites of institutional improvement are financial sustainability, motivation of staff and accountability.

Private entrepreneurship

Private entrepreneurship and initiatives in local communities may form a basis for sustainable animal traction development. For example, private businessman could be involved in input supply, development and maintenance of ox-drawn implements and carts and distribution of spare parts, provided such involvement is profitable. Such a bottom-up approach to development should be supported by top-down assistance. Local markets and trade could stimulate farmers to sell their surplus produce for direct payments.

Farmers' organisations

Project sustainability analyses (Cernea, 1987) have suggested that farmers' organisations, founded in local organisational patterns and with a high degree of interest among members, have contributed to the success of development interventions. In some cases the concept of generating funds for the organisation has contributed to its success. Where countervailing power is created, farmers might be more prepared to demand realistic prices for their produce in an open competitive market, and thus may avoid exploitation by private traders. The local farming community must participate actively in the development process to sustain animal traction development. One complicating factor in organising peasant farmers is the low population density in the rural areas.

Improvement of project interventions

Variations in, and the complex nature of, peasant households (resources, culture, etc) within an unreliable economic environment ensure that the outcome of animal traction development projects remains uncertain. However, within this complex and unpredictable environment, animal traction development projects will continue with their interventions in the rural economy.

Development projects and programmes should mainly address institutional, organisational and managerial dilemmas if animal traction is to be enhanced. However, significant attention should also be given to technical aspects, because the introduction or enhancement of animal traction requires progressive changes in the farming systems, such as new tillage techniques, agronomic adaptations, improved animal husbandry practices, etc. Because each of the constraints discussed above has a different importance in each district or development area, no generally applicable solutions can be provided. The following suggestions for improving the use of animals in farming are therefore considered a basis for discussion rather than blueprints or panaceas.

Project identification

Animal draft power development projects are seldom initiated by the beneficiary community; most current animal traction development projects are part of a national development strategy. Future animal traction projects should be formulated on the basis of the needs of the beneficiaries (identified through baseline studies, providing socio-economic and infrastructural data), and the beneficiaries should participate in project identification.

There is a role to play here for a national coordination body which should, whenever possible, involve the local community in project identification.

Planning

Because animal draft power development initiatives can still be considered as "puzzling" rural development efforts which take place in an unreliable environment, the costs and outcomes are difficult to predict. Consequently, planning of animal traction projects should be flexible and should result in an evolutionary project design. Representative examples are the District Development Support Programme in Mpika, which allows planning within a learning process approach, and the Animal Draft Power Development Programme in Western Province. Learning by doing, combined with research and experience, allows the "provincial plan" to develop into a more viable "district plan".

Some general characteristics of the planning process will include (de Graaf, 1989):

○ an emphasis on action oriented training among staff and beneficiaries
○ a monitoring system
○ a concern for participatory decision making

○ a redesign orientation, allowing periodic revision of project organisation, project objectives and job descriptions for project personnel
○ a management and planning focus on the type of resources needed to continue the flow of animal traction benefits after the end of project funding, and the institutionalisation of the capacity to provide them
○ planning and implementation reinforcing each other.

Project implementation

Project implementation is the stage in which the planned animal traction strategies are tested in the harsh light of reality. Because circumstances change, learning proceeds and experience accumulates over time, a flexible approach to management, which allows for adjustments if required, is suggested.

Emphasis should change from isolated short-lived projects to longer-term initiatives of developing institutional and individual capacity within institutions, thus allowing sustainable animal traction development. Projects could, for example, function as intermediate organisations, with the aim of linking small-scale farmers with the broader economy (such as external markets) and with government agricultural agencies and private or non-governmental organisations. These links will imply that projects should emphasise assistance to agricultural agencies and entrepreneurs and to the organisation of small-scale farmers into constituencies.

Projects should use their expertise to contribute to the design of policies and strategies to support the creation of farmer organisations. There is a clear need for viable local organisations and for strategies to create them. At present, trying to make farmers and other "actors" in development aware of their own responsibilities in the process is a huge task for projects. Projects should assess the possibilities of involving and stimulating local entrepreneurs, such as artisans, marketers and other businessmen in the development process.

In general, emphasis should shift away from attention to the projects' own cycle, towards the post-project achievements and the ability of different organisations to use these achievements as the basis for further initiatives.

Monitoring and evaluation

The national coordination body could assist in developing monitoring and evaluation procedures. These guidelines should be circulated to all projects dealing with animal traction development. The collected and processed data should be evaluated and the results could form the basis of an "early warning system".

Conclusions

Animal traction has functioned as a labour shifting technology rather than as a labour saving one because labour peaks in planting, weeding and harvesting were not alleviated; indeed they were sometimes increased due to larger areas under cultivation. The major gains from using animal traction arose from increases in area under cultivation. Making animal traction a more attractive individual farm operation requires that animals are used throughout the agricultural production process. Enhancing animal traction development will therefore require progressive changes in the farming systems, such as new techniques, agronomic adaptations, improved animal husbandry practices, etc. In order to justify animal traction investments and allow for changes in farming systems, input and output prices will play a crucial role. Thus government policies (for example, on producer prices) will play an important part in enhancing and sustaining the use of work animals. Animal traction development takes place in a changing economy which is characterised by high degree of instability and unreliability. This, coupled with the complexity of peasant households and decision-making structures, means that animal traction development remains a puzzling rural development issue. Outcomes of project intervention are not predictable.

However, improving animal traction technology inherently requires that the essentials (input supply, credit, marketing, etc) are taken care of. Projects should pay attention to general issues such as marketing, animal traction technology, institutional development, provision of capital to small farmers, farmers' organisations and participation. Projects should adopt the role of intermediate organisations and should aim to avoid bypassing institutions and other "local actors in development".

References

Note: all these publications are available at Palabana ADP Training Project, Box 31905, Lusaka, Zambia

Agrisystems, 1990. *The mid-evaluation: Luapula Rural Development Programme mission report.* Agrisystems (Nordic) AB, Uppsala, Sweden.

Beerling M-L E J, 1986. *Acquisition and alienation of cattle in the Western Province.* Department of Veterinary and Tsetse Control Services, Mongu, Western Province, Zambia. pp. 1–50.

Cernea M, 1987. Farmers organizations and institution building for sustainable development. In: Davis T and Schirmer A (eds), *Sustainability issues in agricultural development.* Proceedings of the seventh agricultural sector symposium. World Bank, Washington DC, USA.

Corbel H, 1986. The economics of animal power in Koinadugu district, Sierra Leone: a case study of the work oxen introduction and credit programme. pp. 299–311 in: Starkey P and Ndiamé (eds), *Animal power in farming systems.* Proceedings of the second West African Animal Traction networkshop held 17–26 September 1986 in Freetown, Sierra Leone. Vieweg for German Appropriate Technology Exchange, Deutsche Gesellschaft für Technische Zusammenarbeit (GTZ), Eschborn, Germany.

Ellis F, 1988. *Peasant economics, farm households and agrarian development.* Wye Studies in Agricultural and Rural Development. Cambridge University Press, Cambridge, UK. pp. 3–11.

Francis P A, 1988. Ox draught power and agricultural transformation in Northern Zambia. *Agricultural Systems* 27:35–49.

de Graaf P J, 1989. *Sustainability aspects of rural development intervention in Third World countries.* MSc Dissertation. Department of Agricultural Economics and Management, University of Reading, Reading, UK. pp. 48–62.

Harvey C, 1988. *Agricultural pricing policy in Africa.* MacMillan, London, UK. Chapter 2.

Huybens E, 1988. La rentabilité du labour attelé dans la sous-préfecture de Bangouya, Guinée. pp. 168-173 in: Starkey P and Faye A (eds), *Animal traction for agricultural development.* Technical Centre for Agricultural and Rural Development (CTA), Ede-Wageningen, The Netherlands. 475p.

Rauch T, Dantz K, Lengemann A, Mayer S, Michalik S, Siebert M and Suhlrie D, 1988. *The sustainability of the impact of the integrated rural development programme (IRDP) Zambia N/W Province.* Centre for Advanced Training in Agricultural Development, Technische Universität Berlin, Berlin, Germany. pp. 1–20 and 120–138.

Starkey P, Dibbits H and Mwenya E, 1990. *Animal traction in Zambia: status, progress and trends.* Ministry of Agriculture, Lusaka, Zambia, in association with IMAG, Wageningen, The Netherlands. 115p.

Tembo G and Rajeswaran K, 1986. *Animal draught power in Southern Province: an assessment.* Agricultural Engineering Section, Ministry of Agriculture and Cooperatives, Lusaka, Zambia. 88p.

Photograph opposite
Women with donkey cart collecting forage for their donkeys and stall-fed animals, Tanga, Tanzania

Improving animal traction technology

The management
of draft animals

Improving draft animal management

by

R Anne Pearson and A J Smith

Centre for Tropical Veterinary Medicine, Easter Bush, Roslin, Edinburgh EH25 9RG, Midlothian, Scotland

Abstract

In some areas of the world draft animal power is traditional; in others it is a relatively new technology. When thinking about improving management of draft animals it is important to be aware of these two categories.

Some aspects of management, including training, feeding, consequences of using draft cows and the need to maintain healthy animals, are discussed in this paper. In some cases strategies to influence and improve management are available, largely as a result of research; in others, more information is required.

Introduction

Animal power is used in virtually every environment and on every continent in the world. Although the location, type of animal and role they play may vary, many of the goals of management remain the same: the provision of adequate feed, housing, disease protection and training. The aim is to ensure that animals are capable of expressing their full potential for work, given the resources that are available.

Resource availability is often the deciding factor. In practice, management often means management of resources rather than of the animals themselves. If feed is in short supply it is difficult to provide the required level of feeding. If vaccines or drugs to protect against disease are too expensive or not available, disease must be controlled using local medicines and good management practices. Good management and husbandry are often a matter of compromise because of the various constraints in a system. For example, using cows to provide draft power makes heavy demands on management skills; requirements for work and the availability of feed are often seasonal, and cannot be changed, and so the aim of good management is to ensure that these requirements can be met without jeopardising reproduction and lactation performance.

In this paper some important issues in managing draft animals are considered. Although this discussion concentrates on livestock issues, animal power also encompasses agronomic, engineering and socioeconomic issues—and these can have a significant effect on animal management decisions.

Patterns of draft animal use

Management of draft animals is greatly influenced by the importance placed on them in a farming system. Animals are used alongside mechanical and manual power. There are many factors that can influence the relative proportions of these power sources that are used in any particular area. For example, where high population pressure leads to expansion of arable land at the expense of grazing land, animal power can become less available and farmers may have to resort to greater use of manual labour. Tembo (1989) stated that shortages of animal power in the communal lands in Zimbabwe are a major constraint to increased productivity of these areas.

A shortage of animal power is often made worse by drought and disease outbreaks which reduce the populations of all animals, including those used for draft. Following good harvests mechanised power is more available as farmers can afford to hire tractors.

It is important to remember that although the "technology" of animal (and mechanical) power may be available within an area, other factors can restrict its use. Changing economic factors may dictate that farmers switch between power sources. The priority a farmer gives to management of draft animals may be constantly changing.

Farmer experience of animal power

In areas of the world where draft animals are part of the traditional way of cultivating the land, for example, in Ethiopia, India, Indonesia, Nepal, North Africa and most of Latin America, people are accustomed to keeping, training and managing their draft animals. Implements are readily available locally, usually made from local materials, and there is a local system for repairing and replacing them. Decisions on whether to own, or to hire or borrow, draft animals are mainly influenced by farm size and family structure.

In the Koshi hills of Nepal, where 85% of farmers keep adult male oxen, mainly for draft purposes, hiring or lending is common (Gurung et al, 1989). A survey carried out in 1989 found that 72% of farmers had hired or borrowed oxen and that

Table 1: Energy expenditure of draft animals under various production systems compared with beef and dairy animals

Type of animal	Function	Estimated energy expenditure as a multiple of maintenance
250 kg draft ox	5 hours plowing small hill terraces as a pair in Nepal	1.30–1.38
400 kg draft buffalo	5–6 hours pulling loads over level tracks as a pair in Nepal	1.76–1.79
620 kg draft ox	5.5 hours cultivating large fields as a pair in Costa Rica	1.42–1.67
650 kg draft horse	8 hours pulling a loaded cart singly in Chile	1.86–2.35
300 kg dairy cow	producing 3 litres of milk per day	1.4[1]
500 kg dairy cow	producing 10 litres of milk per day	2.0[1]
400 kg beef steer	gaining 0.20 kg per day	1.2[1]
500 kg beef steer	gaining 0.75 kg per day	1.7[1]

[1] *Theoretical calculations from MAFF (1984)*

lending and borrowing was often a reciprocal arrangement (Gatenby, Pearson and Limbu, 1990). In Tanjungwangi village near Subang in west Java, Indonesia, only 7.5% of draft animal "rearers" use their animals solely to prepare their own crops, over 50% also rent them out and 30% both rent out and use their animals for shared work where they join forces with other farmers and cultivate together to speed up operations. One such example of this is the plowing of flooded rice fields when water is too scarce to allow flooding of all fields at the same time (Santoso et al, 1987): this communal use of draft animals could be considered as an example of management of draft power at its best. Preparation of land by trampling using groups of cattle (over 100 head have been recorded in some places), a relatively common practice in Timor, is another example of communal management. Farmers pool their animals and work on their fields in turn until "cultivation" is completed.

In areas of the world where draft animal power is a relatively new technology, for example, in many parts of eastern and southern Africa, the infrastructure necessary to train and manage animals or produce and repair appropriate implements is often not available locally. As a result, management of animals in these areas can be considerably different to that in the traditional areas. Training animals is often a problem, and it is not uncommon to see two or three people working a pair of oxen; this is a rare sight in traditional areas of animal use. A further complication in the "newer areas" of animal traction is the cost of obtaining the draft animals and implements. This can restrict the amount of additional money that farmers may be able or willing to spend on animal management.

Feeding

Probably the key issue farmers are faced with when keeping draft animals is the provision of sufficient (quantity and quality) feed at the time when the animals are required to do the most work. Most of the food eaten by draft animals is used to provide energy; their requirements for protein, vitamins and minerals, other than for maintenance, are negligible, unless they are growing or are pregnant or lactating. Expressed as a multiple of maintenance, the extra costs for work are relatively low. Even under conditions of optimum feeding and management oxen rarely expend more than 1.8 times maintenance in a working day (Lawrence, 1985; Pearson, Lawrence and Ghimire, 1989; Pearson, 1989a) which is similar to that seen in beef or dairy cattle (Table 1).

Information gathered on oxen and buffalo at the Centre for Tropical Veterinary Medicine, Edinburgh, UK, and elsewhere has been used by Lawrence (1990) to produce tables predicting total energy requirements, food intake and changes in liveweight of draft oxen, taking into account liveweight, quality of diet normally fed to draft ruminants, the decrease in energy expenditure over the working day and the effect of work on resting metabolic rate. The tables can be universally applied where quality and availability of feed for draft animals are known, so helping to improve the management of the feed resources available, to benefit not only draft animals but also other farm animals. Similar information is not readily available for equines. Information on requirements of donkeys and small horses for work, particularly in tropical areas, is largely anecdotal.

The start of the cultivation season is usually the time when feed stocks are at their lowest, particularly in areas where the dry season is long. In many areas the quality of food is so low that

Table 2: Mean daily work output of single oxen in Mali, according to liveweight and condition score

	Mean work output (MJ/day)		
Condition score	310 kg liveweight	360 kg liveweight	Mean
Medium (M+)	0.95	3.49	2.22
Lean (L+)	2.55	3.44	2.94

The work involved walking around a flat circuit for up to 10 km pulling a loaded sledge with an average draft of 374 N
Conditions scores followed the classification of Nicholson and Butterworth (1986)
Differences between liveweights and between condition scores and the interaction between liveweight and condition score were significant (P<0.001)
Source: ILCA (1988a)

animals can only just maintain their liveweight, even when they are not working. When working, they lose weight.

There is some evidence that horses increase their intake of moderate roughage diets when working for short periods (Orton, Hume and Leng, 1985). However, when oxen (Lawrence, 1985; Pearson, 1990), buffaloes (Wanapat and Wachirapakorn, 1987; Bamualim and Ffoulkes, 1988) and donkeys (Pearson and Merritt, 1991) receive high roughage diets they do not increase their feed intake to match their increased energy demands. When work occupies more than five to six hours a day intake may even decrease, as less time is available for eating (Pearson, 1990). Only by increasing the quality of the diet can both work and liveweight be sustained. Where the quality of feed is very poor it is often better to have two animals doing what little they can, rather than one large animal.

Management of weight and body condition prior to work

As many animals lose weight when working, particularly over a long season when the feed is of low quality, it is not surprising that liveweight and body condition are important in determining the optimum management of draft animals. The amount of work an animal can do is proportional to its liveweight—the larger the animal the higher the draft force it can generate. This means that the larger the animal (irrespective of body condition) the easier it will be able to carry out a particular task and the less stressed it will be doing this than a smaller animal. A large-framed animal may also be better able to respond to an increasing supply of food over a rainy season than a smaller, fatter one. However, animals in good condition have "fuel" in reserve, which may be mobilised to compensate for any shortages in feed which may occur at the start of the cultivation season. Thin animals do not have this reserve. Kartiarso, Martin and Teleni (1989), in

a study of the pattern of utilisation of free fatty acids by working cattle and buffalo of different body conditions, suggested that in a short working period (30–50 days) animals in good condition can be worked on their fat reserves with minimal nutritional input, whereas thin animals would do best on a diet of high glucogenic potential.

Despite the apparent benefits of having heavy animals in good condition at the start of work, studies in which animals have been supplemented over the dry season have not always shown any significant benefit in work output or crop yields. Studies by Bartholomew in villages in Mali and on-station showed that supplementation of work oxen during the dry season increased their body weight and condition, but that heavier weights and better condition were not associated with the highest work outputs (Table 2; ILCA, 1988a; Bartholomew, 1989). Since dry season weight gain did not seem to improve subsequent work output, Bartholomew (1989) suggested that there may be little benefit to be gained by dry season supplementation of draft oxen in these areas. The implication would seem to be that feeding during work has a greater impact on performance. In the village studies in Mali, animals had an average weight gain of 17% from the start of field work to the end of the rainy season work, presumably due to the improvement in feed supply.

Clearly the economics of dry season feeding vary with location. In areas where animal working periods are short (20–30 days), supplementary feeding in the dry season may not be cost-effective, but in areas where animals work for longer periods, or spend considerable time transporting loads during the drier parts of the year, the economic return of such a practice may be considerable.

Feeding and management during work periods

The level of feeding and management during the working season has a marked effect on work

Table 3: Optimal model solutions obtained by linear programming for representative farms in the Ethiopian highlands using traditional (two ox), single ox and cow traction for power

Item	*Optimal model obtained by linear programming*		
	Traditional two ox	*Single ox*	*Cow traction*
Net farm income (birr)	848.7	438.5	2535.0
Total arable land (ha)	2.55	2.55	2.55
Area cropped (ha)			
Teff	0.68	0.68	2.28
Wheat	1.66	0.27	0.27
Faba bean	0.21	1.42	–
Area left fallow	–	0.18	–
Total labour use (labour hours)	**1098.8**	**981.4**	**1881.0**
Productivity			
Land (birr/ha)	332.8	172.0	994.1
Labour (birr per hour of family labour)	0.77	0.45	1.35

Conversion: 2 Ethiopian birr = US$ 1
Source: ILCA (1988b)

achieved. Unless body condition score is high at the start of work, weight loss during work is almost always associated with a fall in work output and in willingness to work regularly, whereas increases in nutrient intake, liveweight and body condition produce increased work output. For example, Lawrence (1985) observed that under conditions of moderate feeding three pairs of oxen doing regular work in Costa Rica maintained weight and used energy equivalent to 1.51 times maintenance when working a 5.5-hour day: the same oxen on a poorer diet, such that they lost substantial amounts of weight, only used energy equivalent to 1.42 times maintenance. This response was more evident in inexperienced animals. In Nepal, improvements in work rate of buffalo carting loads regularly over a three-month period were associated with good feeding and improved body condition (Pearson, 1989a). When feed is in short supply some farmers prefer to supplement their draft oxen at the expense of other livestock to ensure that the animals can work regularly enough to meet cultivation requirements (Tennakoon, 1986).

Management of draft cows

Cows are becoming more widely used as draft animals. In places where pressure on land is high and the ratio of pasture to cultivated land is decreasing, the use of cows for draft purposes is one way of reducing the numbers of animals kept. A linear programming model was used to show that cow traction was more efficient in terms of resource use and productivity than traditional (two ox) or

single ox traction in the Ethiopian highlands (Table 3; ILCA, 1988b).

Although cows can be used for animal traction, this is not without a cost. If a cow is to work as well as produce a calf and a good supply of milk it needs good quality feed. In a study in Costa Rica, cows in mid-lactation needed to be fed food energy equivalent to 2.2 times maintenance to work and maintain milk production (Lawrence, 1985). To achieve this energy intake the basal diet must normally be supplemented with considerable amounts of concentrates. Because these are not always available, or are too expensive, most farmers have to accept that milk production is unlikely to be maintained if cows are also required to work.

Reports in the literature show different effects of work on milk production. Jabbar (1983) in Bangladesh found that milk yield fell when cows were used for draft. Goe (1983) reported that on work days, cows can show a 10–20% decrease in milk yield. Similarly, Matthewman (1989), in experiments with Hereford x Friesian cows, found that milk yields (as well as yields of lactose and protein) fell during exercise, but recovered following two days of rest; yield of milk fat was not affected by exercise. When supplements based on barley, fishmeal or sugarbeet (glucogenic, aminogenic or lipogenic) were fed with straw diets, the nature of the dietary supplement did not seem to have any significant effect on the impact of exercise on lactational performance. Rizwan-ul-Muqtadir, Ahmad and Ahmad (1975) in Pakistan found no reduction in daily milk production during work. In Ethiopia, Zerbini found no marked effect on milk

Photo: Anne Pearson

Fulani oxen with muzzles transporting plow in Kufana, northern Nigeria

production in crossbred dairy cows worked for 90 days (four hours a day pulling sledges at an average draft force of 400 N for four days a week), starting two weeks after calving (ILCA, 1991). However, he noted that work had a dramatic effect on cow weight: three months after giving birth, working cows had lost an average of 26 kg, whereas non-working cows had lost less than 11 kg. Supplementary feeding with noug (*Guizotia abyssinica*) cake, wheat millings, salt and bone meal did not eliminate these weight losses. These differences in response may well be a reflection of differences in availability of nutrients and competition for these nutrients between the mammary gland and muscle. Any situation which results in an increase in this competition (such as a sudden increase in work done) is likely to result in a reduction in milk production and/or liveweight, since muscle contraction is a basic tax on the nutrient economy of the animal (Teleni and Hogan, 1989).

In some areas where draft cows have been used for a considerable time, even if work during the later stages of pregnancy and lactation is avoided, there is evidence that calving intervals are getting longer (Robinson, 1977; Petheram et al, 1982) and there is a danger that the supply of replacement milk and draft animals will not match demand in the future. It

was reported that oestrus occurred on fewer occasions in working cows than in non-working ones during a trial in Ethiopia (ILCA, 1991). Although supplementary feeding increased oestrous activity, some of the supplemented working cows cycled during their resting period, but none of the unsupplemented ones did so. Similarly in Indonesia, Bamualim, Ffoulkes and Fletcher (1987) reported reduced ovarian activity in working buffalo cows compared with non-working animals. Even if working cows do show oestrus, they may miss the chance of service by a chosen bull because of their work.

Again the emphasis is on good management so that productivity is not jeopardised too much by the use the cows for work. Matthewman, Dijkman and Zerbini (1993) drew up an annual management calendar for draft cows in areas where food supply is seasonal, to help ensure that requirements for work, pregnancy and lactation could be met with minimum supplementation of the basal diet.

Health care of draft animals

There is some evidence and much conjecture in the literature that sub-clinical diseases reduce work output and, equally, that the additional stress of work can predispose draft animals to disease (Hoffmann and Dalgliesh, 1985; Wells, 1986).

Draft oxen weeding with an Arara *cultivator in Niger*

Pearson (1989b) suggested the reduced power output and inability to work of otherwise well-fed and apparently healthy buffaloes may have been due to chronic fasciolosis. Payne et al (1991) observed that although exercise did not appear to exacerbate the effect of *Trypanosoma evansi* infection in buffaloes, the infection had a marked effect on body temperature and blood packed cell volume (PCV) profiles of infected buffaloes, both of which could adversely affect an infected animal's work output and heat tolerance.

Helminth parasites are thought to be a major cause of unthriftiness and low life expectancy of working donkeys. In Morocco (Khallaayoune, 1991) and Greece (Bliss et al, 1985), for example, anthelmintic treatments resulted in healthier and stronger donkeys. The study by Samui and Hugh-Jones (1990) is one of the few to attempt to quantify the financial and production losses due to a disease in draft animals. They conservatively estimated that the cost of draft oxen being affected by bovine dermatophilosis in Zambia was 428 Kwacha (US$ 193) per affected ox. This was based on loss due to reduction in area of land plowed and lowered income from hire of the animals.

A dead draft animal cannot work and so land cultivation and crop production suffer. In places where a farmer relies on a single animal this can have serious consequences. Even where a pair of animals is used, the loss of one of the pair, especially just before or during the working season, can be critical. Some efforts to prevent acute diseases in an area would seem to be economically justified by a farmer who keeps draft animals, whether it be by management, local medicines or purchased drugs.

The sub-clinical diseases are more difficult to cope with than the acute diseases; they may not kill the animal, but they can severely reduce its productivity. Systematic studies are now underway in West Africa and Indonesia to investigate the consequences of sub-clinical diseases on work and, conversely, work on disease. In both these areas trypanosomiasis is the first disease to be studied in this context. The basic questions that need to be answered are: what are the risks involved in not treating draft animals to prevent disease; and is there an increase in work output and farm income that justifies the expense involved in treatment? The results of these studies should provide information that can be used to assist farmers in such areas in planning the management of their animals to ensure that they remain healthy and are fit to work when required.

Management of draft power

This paper has concentrated on highlighting some of the main issues in the management of draft animals—training, feeding and health care. However, management of draft animals is not only a matter of good husbandry; it should also involve efficient management of the power itself, both when it is required in seasonal tasks (management as a communal use, referred to above, is one such example) and over the rest of the year so that the resource of animal power is not wasted.

One way of optimising the use of animal power is to encourage other uses for draft animals. In areas where the draft animal is unlikely to be replaced on farms, there is considerable potential for this. Reducing the number of idle days in the year is a relatively easy way to increase efficiency of animal power on a farm. Water-lifting, milling, and other stationary power devices have been designed and built throughout the world incorporating animal power, some more elaborate than others. Earthmoving and road building are less conventional uses which have application in some places.

It is usually the simplest idea or design that is the most successful as it is the one that can be most easily adopted. When improvements in management of draft animals are being considered this aspect should not be overlooked.

With the increases in population pressure in many areas, and problems of dwindling feed resources for animals as pressure on grazing land and fodder supplies increases, the management of the resource of animal power is likely to become an even more important issue than it is at present.

Future developments

While much is known about the training, feeding and health care of draft animals, particularly in areas where they have been traditionally used and

research has gone some way towards identifying the consequences that particular management strategies can have, in some areas it is apparent that more information is required. There is scope for research into the role and management of draft equines, particularly donkeys, in tropical agriculture. The donkey is often the first source of power the least wealthy farmer can afford, other than family labour. In the past donkeys have had a relatively low social status and have largely been ignored by agriculturalists.

Investigation of the effects of liveweight, body condition and nutrient intake of draft animals would seem to be of high priority in areas where seasonal fluctuations in feed quality and supply are considerable. In these areas feed strategies need to consider the number and frequency of working days required of the draft animals. It is in these areas that draft animal power is often being encouraged as a new technology to increase farm productivity, and positive guidelines on feed allocation are needed, perhaps more so than in areas where farmers have traditionally kept working animals.

The use of cows for draft is likely to become increasingly common on many farms. The partition of feed energy between maintenance, body reserves, milk production, work and pregnancy is clearly one aspect which requires greater understanding if cows are to be successfully used for work at minimum cost to their other functions on the farm. The productive and economic consequences of disease and the interaction with nutrition have until recently been largely neglected and would benefit from further study. In short, there is much that can still be done to provide information to assist in the improvement of management practices such that draft animal power is used to its maximum effect on farms in tropical and sub-tropical areas.

References

Bamualim A and Ffoulkes D, 1988. Effect of work and level of feed intake on nutritional parameters and body weight change of swamp buffalo cows. *DAP Project Bulletin* 7:2–8. Draught Animal Power Project, James Cook University, Townsville, Australia.

Bamualim A, Ffoulkes D and Fletcher I C, 1987. Preliminary observations on the effect of work on intake, digestibility, growth and various activity of swamp buffalo cows. *DAP Project Bulletin* 3:6–10. Draught Animal Power Project, James Cook University, Townsville, Australia.

Bartholomew P, 1989. Feeding strategies for draft animals: feed supplementation and work output of oxen. pp. 69–70 in: *ILCA Annual Report 1989*. International Livestock Centre for Africa (ILCA), Addis Ababa, Ethiopia.

Bliss D H, Svendsen E D, Georgoulakis I E, Grossmanidis S, Taylor F and Jordan W J, 1985. Strategic use of anthelmintics in working donkeys in Mediterranean climatic conditions. *Veterinary Record* 117:613–614.

Gatenby R M, Pearson R A and Limbu T B, 1990. *A survey of local and Jersey crossbred draft oxen in the hills of East*

Donkey cart in southern Niger

Photo: Anne Pearson

Nepal. Technical Paper 128. Pakhribas Agricultural Centre, PO Box 106, Kathmandu, Nepal. 17p.

Goe M R, 1983. Current status of research on animal traction. *World Animal Review* 45:2–17.

Gurung H B, Gatenby R M, Neopane S P, Shrestha N P and Chemjong P B, 1989. *Numbers of animals on farms in the Koshi Hills*. Technical Paper 109. Pakhribas Agricultural Centre, PO Box 106, Kathmandu, Nepal. 20p.

Hoffmann D and Dalgliesh R J, 1985. A multidisciplinary approach to health and disease in draft ruminants. pp. 134–139 in: Copland J W (ed), *Draught animal power for production*. ACIAR Proceedings Series 10. Australian Centre for International Agricultural Research (ACIAR), Canberra, Australia. 170p.

ILCA, 1988a. Feeding strategies for draft animals: effect of body weight and condition of oxen on their work capacity. pp. 67–68 in: *ILCA Annual Report 1988*. International Livestock Centre for Africa (ILCA), Addis Ababa, Ethiopia.

ILCA, 1988b. Alternative sources of draught power: economic analysis of animal traction innovations in the highlands of Ethiopia. pp. 68–71 in: *ILCA Annual Report 1988*. International Livestock Centre for Africa (ILCA), Addis Ababa, Ethiopia.

ILCA, 1991. Cow traction—what about milk and calves? *ILCA Newsletter* 10(1):5. International Livestock Centre for Africa (ILCA), Addis Ababa, Ethiopia.

Jabbar M A, 1983. Effect of draft use of cows on fertility, milk production and consumption. pp. 71–85 in: Davis C H, Preston T R, Haque M and Saadullah M (eds), *Maximum livestock production from minimum land*. Proceedings of seminar held 2–4 May 1983. Bangladesh Agricultural University, Mymensingh, Bangladesh.

Kartiarso, Martin D and Teleni E, 1989. The pattern of utilisation of body fat reserves by working cattle and buffalo. *DAP Project Bulletin* 8:7–8. Draught Animal Power Project, James Cook University, Townsville, Australia.

Khallaayoune K, 1991. Benefit of a strategic deworming programme in working donkeys in Morocco. pp. 174–180 in: Fielding D and Pearson R A (eds), *Donkeys, mules and horses in tropical agricultural development*. Centre for Tropical Veterinary Medicine, University of Edinburgh, Edinburgh, UK. 336p.

Lawrence P R, 1985. A review of the nutrient requirements of draft oxen. pp. 59–68 in: Copland J W (ed), *Draught animal power for production*. ACIAR Proceedings Series 10. Australian Centre for International Agricultural Research (ACIAR), Canberra, Australia. 170p.

Lawrence P R, 1990. Food energy requirements of draft oxen. pp. 7–27 in Cockrill W R (ed): *Working animals international*. Proceedings of inaugural meeting of World Association for Transport Animal Welfare Studies (TAWS), held 12 December 1989, Oxford, UK. TAWS, Department of Physiology, Oxford, UK. 78p.

Matthewman R W, 1989. The effects of exercise on lactational performance. PhD Thesis. University of Edinburgh, Edinburgh, UK. 294p.

Matthewman R W, Dijkman J T and Zerbini E, 1993. The management and husbandry of male and female draught animals: research achievements and needs. pp 125–136 in Lawrence P R, Lawrence K, Dijkman J T and Starkey P H (eds), *Research for development of animal traction in West Africa*. Proceedings of fourth workshop of West Africa Animal Traction Network held 9–13 July, 1990, Kano, Nigeria. Published on behalf of the West Africa Animal Traction Network by International Livestock Centre for Africa (ILCA), Addis Ababa, Ethiopia. 322p.

MAFF, 1984. *Energy allowances and feeding systems for ruminants*. Ministry of Agriculture, Fisheries and Food (MAFF) Reference Book 433. Her Majesty's Stationery Office (HMSO), London, UK. 85p.

Nicholson M J and Butterworth M H, 1986. *Guide to condition scoring of cattle*. International Livestock Centre for Africa (ILCA), Addis Ababa, Ethiopia. 29p.

Orton R K, Hume I D and Leng R A, 1985. Effects of dietary protein and exercise on growth rates of horses. *Equine Veterinary Journal* 17:381–385.

Payne R C, Djauhari D, Partoutomo S, Jones T W and Pearson R A, 1991. *Trypanosoma evansi* infection in worked and unworked buffaloes (*Bubalus bubalis*) in Indonesia. *Veterinary Parasitology* 40:197–206.

Pearson R A, 1989a. A comparison of draft cattle (*Bos indicus*) and buffaloes (*Bubalus bubalis*) carting loads in hot conditions. *Animal Production* 49:355–363.

Pearson R A, 1989b. Reduced work output of well fed buffaloes pulling carts on the terai in East Nepal. *Tropical Animal Health and Production* 21:273–276.

Pearson R A, 1990. A note on liveweight and intake and digestibility of food by draft cattle after supplementation of rice straw with the fodder tree *Ficus auriculata*. *Animal Production* 51:635–638.

Pearson R A and Merritt J B, 1991. Intake, digestion and gastrointestinal transit time in resting donkeys and ponies and exercised donkeys given *ad libitum* hay and straw diets. *Equine Veterinary Journal* 23:339–343.

Pearson R A, Lawrence P R and Ghimire C, 1989. Factors influencing the work done by draft oxen: a study in the eastern hills of Nepal. *Animal Production* 49:345–353.

Petheram R J, Liem C, Yayat Priyatna and Mathuridi, 1982. *Village buffalo fertility study*. Serang District of West Java Report 1. Research Institute for Animal Production, Bogor, Indonesia. 36p.

Rizwan-ul-Maqtadir R A G, Ahmad M and Ahmad Z, 1975. Draft power and its effect on milk yield and milk composition in lactating buffaloes during winter season. *Pakistan Journal of Agricultural Science* 12:93–98.

Robinson D W, 1977. *Preliminary observations on the productivity of working buffalo in Indonesia*. Centre Report 2 (Bogor). Centre for Animal Research and Development, Bogor, Indonesia. 32p.

Samui K L and Hugh-Jones M E, 1990. The financial and production impacts of bovine dermatophilosis in Zambia. *Veterinary Research Communications* 14:357–365.

Santoso, Sumanto, Perkins J and Petheram R J, 1987. An agroeconomic profile of Tanjungwangi village, Subang, with emphasis on draft animal rearing. *DAP Project Bulletin* 2:4–28. Draught Animal Power Project, James Cook University, Townsville, Australia.

Teleni E and Hogan J P, 1989. Nutrition of draft animals. pp. 118–133 in: Hoffmann D, Nari J and Petheram R J (eds), *Draught animals in rural development*. ACIAR Proceedings Series 27. Australian Centre for International Agricultural Research (ACIAR), Canberra, Australia. 347p.

Tembo S, 1989. Draft animal power research in Zimbabwe: current constraints and research opportunities. pp. 61–68 in: Hoffmann D, Nari J and Petheram R J (eds), *Draught animals in rural development*. ACIAR Proceedings Series 27. Australian Centre for International Agricultural Research (ACIAR), Canberra, Australia. 347p.

Tennakoon M U A, 1986. *Drought hazard and rural development*. Dissertation. Central Bank of Sri Lanka, Colombo, Sri Lanka. 168p.

Wanapat M and Wachirapakorn C, 1987. Effect of walking on feed intake and digestibility of rice straw by water buffaloes. p. 332 in: *Proceedings of the 4th Animal Science Congress of the Asian-Australian Association of Animal Production*. Hamilton, New Zealand.

Wells E A, 1986. Health in working animals. pp. 50–60 in: Falvey J L (ed), *An introduction to working animals*. MPW, Melbourne, Australia. 198p.

Effect of draft work on lactation of F_1 crossbred dairy cows

by

E Zerbini[1], Takele Gemeda[2], Alemu Gebre Wold[3] and Abiye Astatke[4]

[1] Animal Scientist, International Livestock Centre for Africa, PO Box 5689, Addis Ababa, Ethiopia
[2] Research Officer, Institute of Agricultural Research, PO Box 2003, Addis Ababa, Ethiopia
[3] Head, Animal Science Department, Institute of Agricultural Research, PO Box 2003, Addis Ababa, Ethiopia
[4] Agricultural Engineer, International Livestock Centre for Africa, PO Box 5689, Addis Ababa, Ethiopia

Abstract

In Ethiopia, the use of crossbred cows for traction could improve total on-farm production by decreasing the need to maintain draft oxen year-round and a follower herd to supply replacement oxen, provided that lactation and reproduction are kept at levels comparable to non-working cows.

In a study to estimate the effect of draft work on milk production and reproduction, 40 F_1 crossbred dairy cows were assigned to four treatments (non-working non-supplemented, non-working supplemented, working non-supplemented, working supplemented). Working cows consumed more dry matter compared to non-working cows and supplemented cows more than non-supplemented cows. Milk production was greater in supplemented cows, but was similar in working and non-working cows. Body weight loss was greater for non-supplemented cows. Work considerably decreased reproductive ability of non-supplemented cows but only delayed onset of oestrus and conception in supplemented cows. Results indicate that feeding had a greater effect than work on milk yield and reproductive performance. Feeding strategies for draft cows are proposed.

Introduction

In Ethiopia, oxen are only worked for short periods of time, primarily for land cultivation and threshing. The opportunity costs for farms supporting them are considerable. The use of cows for traction would be of obvious benefit to total animal production from the farms by alleviating the need to maintain draft oxen year-round and a follower herd to supply replacement oxen. However, a prerequisite is that lactation and reproduction are kept at levels comparable to non-working cows (Jabbar, 1983; Barton, 1991; Matthewman, Dijkman and Zerbini, 1993). The use of cows, instead of oxen, might be particularly beneficial in areas where major inputs of exotic blood have been made for dairy development schemes in smallholder farming.

An available supply of crossbred cows is one of the most important factors for their adoption as draft animals in Ethiopia. Yet farmers in remote rural areas may not accept the risks of a reduction of herd size and of disease and injury—factors which would limit land cultivation capabilities. On the other hand, around urban areas where crossbreeding programmes and milk collection schemes are implemented, the introduction of cows for the dual purposes of draft and milk production could be feasible. Farmers in areas with profitable milk prices and available feed supplements and veterinary services would more readily accept the introduction of crossbred cows for draft (Gryssels and Goe, 1984).

A study conducted by the International Livestock Centre for Africa (ILCA) on the effect of work on productive and reproductive performance of crossbred dairy cows in the Ethiopian highlands indicated that work had no significant effect on milk production, lactation length, days open, calving interval and services per conception (Agyemang et al, 1992). Cows worked only 84 and 140 hours in the first and second lactation, respectively. These working times were sufficient to cultivate 2.5 ha of land, but are lower than normal working hours for farm oxen. In addition, all cows were supplemented with an average of 3.5 kg concentrate per day during lactation, although such supplements may not be available to smallholders. The study suggested that, with adequate feeding and low work levels, dairy cows could be used for draft with minimal effect on production performance.

Results from an on-farm trial with farmers using crossbred cows for land cultivation in the Debre Zeit area indicated that work had only a minimal effect on lactation. However, a necessary condition was the availability to farmers of sufficient forage, concentrate and adequate management (Gryssels and Anderson, 1985).

An ILCA study relating the effect of lactation and work on feed intake (Lambourne and Zelleka Getahun, 1989), using lactating F_1 Friesian x zebu cows and zebu oxen, would suggest that feed intake has greater influence on lactation than does plowing.

The objective of this on-going study is to investigate in detail the functional relationship between milk production, reproduction, feed utilisation and draft work in *Bos taurus* x *Bos indicus* crossbred dairy cows in the Ethiopian highlands.

Materials and methods

The cow traction study is part of a collaborative project between the Ethiopian Institute of Agricultural Research (IAR) and ILCA (Zerbini and Takele Gemeda, 1991). It is carried out at Holetta IAR Research Centre, 50 km west of Addis Ababa.

Animals

Forty F_1 crossbred dairy cows (20 Boran x Friesian and 20 Boran x Simmenthal), each with 3–5 completed lactations, are being used for the study.

Treatments and measurements

In a 2 x 2 factorial experiment, pregnant cows were stratified, according to previous milk production, number of lactations completed, crossbred type, body weight and previous reproductive efficiency, into four treatment groups (10 animals each):

- non-working, non-supplemented
- non-working, supplemented
- working, non-supplemented
- working, supplemented.

All animals are fed natural pasture hay *ad libitum* providing about 7 MJ of metabolisable energy (ME) per kg dry matter (DM). Supplemented animals are also offered concentrate providing 25% crude protein and 11 MJ ME/kg DM. Working animals spend four hours a day, four days a week pulling sleds with a draft force of 350–450 N at a speed of 0.4–0.6 m/s.

Work starts two weeks after parturition; each cow is worked 100 days a year, in two periods of 50 days each, separated by a three-month rest period. The daily working schedule is three hours work, followed by one hour rest then one hour work.

Cows are individually fed in a stanchion barn at 0700, 1200 and 1700 hours, and are milked twice a day at 0500 and 1530 hours. For each cow, the total experiment will cover two consecutive lactations or four working periods over two years.

The measurements taken during the trials include:

- walking speed, distance and force during work
- heart rate, respiration rate and body temperature before, during and after work
- body weight and condition score
- milk yield and composition
- feed quality, feed intake and utilisation
- onset of oestrus, days open, conception rate and calving interval
- plasma progesterone.

Results

Preliminary results reported here concern intake of feed dry matter (DM), milk production, and body weight change over one year after parturition, including two complete working periods of 50 days. Average results are reported for the different working and resting periods.

Daily hay DM intake was greater for working cows during working periods and rest between work periods (Table 1). Total intake (hay + concentrate) of working cows, as well as for supplemented cows was also greater than non-working and non-supplemented cows, respectively (Table 2). Total hay intake was greater for working cows than non-working cows (3118 *vs* 2777 kg). Supplemented

Table 1: Effects of draft work and diet supplementation on average daily hay dry matter intake of crossbred dairy cows during work and rest periods over one year after parturition

			Average daily hay dry matter intake (kg)			
	Days after calving	0–14	15–89	90–179	180–269	270–359
Treatment		Rest	Work	Rest	Work	Rest
Non-working	Non-supplemented	7.8	7.9	6.5	6.5	6.3
	Supplemented	8.5	8.5	8.5	7.5	7.5
Working	Non-supplemented	9.0	9.4	7.2	7.6	7.5
	Supplemented	8.3	8.5	7.7	7.3	7.1
	Standard error	0.4	0.5	0.3	0.5	0.6
Friesian x Boran		8.3	8.5	7.7	7.3	7.1
Simmenthal x Boran		8.6	9.0	8.0	7.8	7.8
	Standard error	0.2	0.4	0.2	0.4	0.5
F-test probabilities	Work	NS	P < 0.05	P < 0.05	P < 0.05	NS
	Supplement	NS	NS	P < 0.001	P < 0.05	NS

Table 2: Effects of draft work and diet supplementation on average daily total dry matter intake of crossbred dairy cows during work and rest periods over one year after parturition

		Average daily total matter intake (kg)				
	Days after calving	0–14	15–89	90–179	180–269	270–359
Treatment		Rest	Work	Rest	Work	Rest
Non-working	Non-supplemented	7.8	7.9	6.5	6.5	6.3
	Supplemented	10.6	11.1	11.0	9.6	9.2
Working	Non-supplemented	9.0	9.4	7.2	7.6	7.5
	Supplemented	10.4	11.8	11.9	11.4	10.3
Standard error		0.3	0.5	0.3	0.5	0.7
Boran x Friesian		9.4	9.8	9.0	8.5	8.0
Boran x Simmenthal		9.6	10.3	9.3	9.0	8.8
Standard error		0.2	0.4	0.2	0.4	0.5
F-test probabilities	Work	NS	P < 0.05	P < 0.05	P < 0.05	NS
	Supplement	P < 0.001	P < 0.001	P < 0.001	P < 0.001	P < 0.001

cows consumed more than non-supplemented cows (3082 *vs* 2813 kg) (Table 3). Total intake (DM) followed a similar pattern: 3179 *vs* 3585 kg for non-working and working cows and 2813 *vs* 3950 kg for non-supplemented and supplemented cows, respectively. The effect of work on average daily milk yield was not significant even though milk yield was affected by work during the first working period (90 days) (Table 4). Daily milk yield was greater for supplemented cows during both working and rest periods. Total milk production in one year postpartum was similar for working and non-working cows (1288 *vs* 1321 kg) (Table 5). However, supplemented cows produced significantly more milk than non-supplemented cows (1781 *vs* 828 kg). In addition, Friesian x Boran cows

Table 3: Effect of work and diet supplement on total dry matter intake of crossbred dairy cows in one year after parturition

		Dry matter intake	
Treatment		Hay (kg)	Total (kg)
Non-working	Non-supplemented	2598.8	2598.8
	Supplemented	2955.0	3756.5
Working	Non-supplemented	3027.2	3027.2
	Supplemented	3209.2	4142.4
Standard error		132.4	140.7
Friesian x Boran		2867.7	3310.0
Simmenthal x Boran x		3027.4	3453.6
Standard error		93.6	99.5
F-test probabilities	Work	P < 0.01	P < 0.01
	Supplement	P < 0.05	P < 0.001

Table 4: Effect of draft work and diet supplementation on average daily milk production of crossbred dairy cows during work and rest periods over one year after parturition

		Average daily milk production (kg)				
	Days after calving	0–14	15–89	90–179	180–269	270–359
Treatment		Rest	Work	Rest	Work	Rest
Non-working	Non-supplemented	6.1	3.5	1.8	1.7	1.7
	Supplemented	8.1	6.1	5.3	4.5	4.8
Working	Non-supplemented	6.6	3.2	1.5	1.1	0.7
	Supplemented	8.3	4.9	5.0	4.3	3.8
Standard error		0.7	0.4	0.4	0.4	0.6
Friesian x Boran		8.2	4.9	3.4	3.3	3.0
Simmenthal x Boran		6.4	4.0	3.4	2.5	2.6
Standard error		0.5	0.4	0.3	0.3	0.4
F-test probabilities	Work	NS	NS	NS	NS	NS
	Supplement	P < 0.05	P < 0.001	P < 0.001	P < 0.001	P < 0.001
	Breed	P < 0.05	NS	NS	P < 0.1	NS

Table 5: Effect of work and diet supplementation on total milk production of crossbred dairy cows in one year after parturition

Treatment		Total milk yield (kg)
Non-working	Non-supplemented	848.8
	Supplemented	1792.6
Working	Non-supplemented	806.7
	Supplemented	1769.9
Standard error		152.2
Boran x Friesian		1458.5
Boran x Simmenthal		1150.5
Standard error		107.6
F-test probabilities	Work	NS
	Supplement	P < 0.001
	Breed	P < 0.05

produced more milk (P < 0.1) than Simmenthal x Boran cows.

Non-supplemented cows lost body weight throughout the year, while supplemented cows, except for working cows during the first working period (90 days), maintained or gained body weight (Table 6). Total body weight losses were similar for working and non-working cows (–14.6 vs –19.5 kg). Total body weight change in non-supplemented cows was significantly different (P < 0.001) from that of supplemented cows (–60.6 vs 26.4 kg). Rate of body weight change during work and rest periods for Boran x Friesian crosses tended to be greater than for Boran x Simmenthal. This was also the case for total body weight loss over two working periods.

Within the timeframe adopted (360 days postpartum for all cows), reproduction parameters could be summarised as follows:

○ all supplemented non-working cows were bred and pregnant
○ all supplemented working cows were bred but 90% were pregnant
○ 60% of non-supplemented non-working cows were bred and pregnant
○ 20% of non-supplemented working cows were bred and pregnant.

Work delayed onset of oestrus by 108 days in supplemented cows, indicating that there was an effect of work on reproduction even when nutrition was adequate. However, diet supplementation had a much greater effect on onset of oestrus than work.

Discussion

Results indicate that the greater feed (DM) intake of working, compared to non-working, cows was utilised partly to sustain milk production and/or support energy expenditure for work. Assuming that average daily energy expenditure for work was 31.8 MJ metabolisable energy (ME) (work = 4 hours, work rate = 250 watts, body weight = 450 kg), the increase in hay intake to meet that energy demand should have been 4 kg per working day. Low hay digestibility limited intake and at 90 days postpartum, the increase in hay intake was only 1.6 kg/day for working non-supplemented cows (equivalent to 12 MJ ME). This was associated with a body weight loss of 0.39 kg/day (equivalent to 14.4 MJ ME). Energy equivalents of hay intake and body weight loss would account for a total of 26.4 MJ ME per day of extra energy supply for work and milk production.

Table 6: Effect of draft work and diet supplementation on cumulative body weight change (kg) of crossbred dairy cows during work and rest periods over one year after parturition

	Days after calving	0–14	15–89	90–179	180–269	270–359
Treatment		Rest	Work	Rest	Work	Rest
Non-working	Non-supplemented	–3.3	–29.0	–45.8	–41.9	–59.6
	Supplemented	–2.9	4.4	17.8	22.7	20.5
Working	Non-supplemented	–11.3	–34.8	–46.2	–52.9	–61.6
	Supplemented	–12.4	–22.5	15.7	4.9	32.3
Standard error		2.8	4.8	7.9	9.8	13.1
Friesian x Boran		–9.4	25.9	–23.2	–25.9	–22.5
Simmenthal x Boran		–5.6	–15.0	–11.1	–7.7	–11.7
Standard error		2.0	3.4	5.6	7.0	9.1
F-test probabilities	Work	NS	P < 0.01	NS	NS	NS
	Supplement	NS	P < 0.01	P < 0.001	P < 0.001	P < 0.0001

Body weight change from parturition (kg)

Compared to the calculated requirement of 31.8 MJ ME/day, this indicates a deficit of 5.4 MJ/day, which would affect milk yield and additional body weight loss if work output remained constant (Table 7).

As shown in Table 5, milk yield over a one-year period was similar for working and non-working non-supplemented cows. This suggests that either energy requirements for work were lower, or energy content of hay was greater than estimated.

Feeding concentrate supplied sufficient energy for work with minimal loss of body weight and reduction of milk production. Protein supplementation not only increased total feed intake but also tended to increase hay intake, perhaps by increasing its digestibility. Weight loss of supplemented cows was lower and milk yield was higher compared to non-supplemented working cows. However, concentrate may not be readily available on local markets and its inclusion in the diet may not be feasible throughout the year.

While inadequate feeding may not affect work output, high rates of body weight loss lead to decreased milk production and reproductive ability. Body weight losses greater than 15% have been reported to impair ovarian activity in buffaloes (Teleni et al, 1989). Our results suggest that reducing body weight loss from 0.39 to 0.25 kg/day with supplementary feeding could improve reproductive performance by about 65%. However, work carried out in early lactation delayed onset of oestrus by more than 108 days, indicating that work, partially independent from nutrition, might have an effect on reproduction.

Complete analysis of reproduction parameters will be carried out at the end of two lactations and the two-year working periods. This will allow for a comprehensive evaluation of the efficiency of cows used for draft. Future work would include a more detailed study of reproductive parameters of working cows and testing cow traction technology within the farming system.

In view of these preliminary results, two possible feeding solutions may be recommended where crossbred cows are used for draft.

Production and feeding of improved forages (grasses + legumes, legumes, or other fodder) would increase digestibility of forages and energy intake of cows to levels which would allow them to support milk production, reproduction and work with an acceptable level of physiological body weight loss.

Production and feeding of well-managed natural pasture hays and improved quality crop residues

Table 7: Effect of draft work on energy balance for work of draft crossbred dairy cows fed natural pasture hay *ad libitum*

	90 days postpartum	
Hay dry matter intake (non-working cows)	8.0	kg/day
Hay dry matter intake (working cows)	9.6	kg/day
Hay dry matter intake increase	1.6	kg/day
ME available from extra hay intake	12.0	MJ/day
Body mass loss	0.39	kg/day
ME available from body reserves (after CSIRO, 1990)	14.4	MJ/day
Total ME available for work	26.4	MJ/day
Total ME required for work	31.8	MJ/day
Balance	–5.4	MJ/day

associated with concentrate feeding during early lactation would be appropriate, especially if cows are due to work during that period. Application of new techniques and research findings for better conservation of the natural forage during particular periods of the year needs particular attention.

Conclusions

As indicated above, the Ethiopian highlands are increasingly unable to maintain a large cattle population. Therefore it will become more difficult for farmers to maintain the breeding stock required for replacement and draft. Reduction of herd size by using crossbred cows for traction will depend primarily on the available supply of crossbred animals. Increased risk associated with decreased animal numbers needs to be considered. Farmer access to suitable feeds and veterinary services should also be examined. Farmers in peri-urban areas characterised by scarcity of land could find the technology most attractive, given a profitable market for milk and calves. Evidence from this study would suggest that if cows are fed adequately, the effect of draft work on lactation is minimal.

Crossbred cows could play an important role as dual-purpose animals in the highland farming systems. In particular, their preference over oxen could contribute to a better utilisation of already scarce feed resources. Additional research should be carried out on the management and nutritional requirements of the lactating draft cow and possible ways to meet its nutrient needs—especially in early lactation when the high energy demand for lactation is associated with work energy needs.

References

Agyemang K, Abiye Astatke, Anderson F M and Woldeab Wolde Mariam, 1992. A study on the effect of work on reproductive and productive performance of crossbred dairy cows in the Ethiopian highlands. *Tropical Animal Health and Production* 23:241–248.

Barton D, 1991. The use of cows for draught in Bangladesh. *Draught Animal Bulletin* 1:14–25. James Cook University of North Queensland, Townsville, Australia.

CSIRO, 1990. *Feeding standards for Australian livestock: ruminants.* Australian Agricultural Council Ruminants Subcommittee and Commonwealth Scientific and Industrial Research Organisation (CSIRO), Melbourne, Australia. 266p.

Gryssels G and Anderson F M, 1985. Use of crossbred dairy cows as draft animals: Experiences from the Ethiopian highlands. pp. 237–258 in: *Research methodology for livestock on farm trials.* Proceedings of a workshop held March 25–28 at Aleppo, Syria. International Development Research Centre (IDRC), Ottawa, Canada.

Gryssels G and Goe M R, 1984. Energy flows on smallholder farms in the Ethiopian highlands. *ILCA Bulletin* 17:2–9. International Livestock Centre for Africa (ILCA), Addis Ababa, Ethiopia.

Jabbar M A, 1983. Effects of draft use of cows on fertility, milk production and consumption. pp. 71–83 in: Davis C H, Preston T R, Haque M and Saadullah M (eds), *Maximum livestock production from minimum land.* James Cook University, Townsville, Australia.

Lambourne and Zelleka Getahun, 1989. Relative effects of lactation and work on feed intake of crossbred cattle. pp. 195–200 in: *Proceedings of Second National Livestock Improvement Conference held 24–26 February 1988, Addis Ababa, Ethiopia.* Institute of Agricultural Research, Addis Ababa, Ethiopia.

Matthewman R W, Dijkman J T and Zerbini E, 1993. The management and husbandry of male and female draught animals: research achievements and needs. pp 125–136 in Lawrence P R, Lawrence K, Dijkman J T and Starkey P H (eds), *Research for development of animal traction in West Africa.* Proceedings of fourth workshop of West Africa Animal Traction Network held 9–13 July, 1990, Kano, Nigeria. Published on behalf of the West Africa Animal Traction Network by International Livestock Centre for Africa (ILCA), Addis Ababa, Ethiopia. 322p.

Teleni E, Boniface A N, Sutherland S and Entwistle K W, 1989. The effect of depletion of body reserve nutrients on reproduction in *Bos indicus* cattle. *DAP Project Bulletin* 8:10. Draught Animal Power Project, James Cook University of North Queensland, Townsville, Australia.

Zerbini E and Takele Gemeda, 1991. Use of crossbred dairy cows for traction. *Draught Animal Bulletin* 1:26–29. James Cook University of North Queensland, Townsville, Australia.

Animal traction use in Tabora Region, Tanzania

by

A P B Luziga, S Nyakalo and T E Simalenga

Sokoine University of Agriculture, PO Box 3004, Morogoro, Tanzania

Abstract

This study was conducted to examine problems affecting the use of draft power in the semi-arid areas of Tabora Region, Tanzania. Inadequate nutrition during the dry season was found to be among the major reasons why draft animals are physically weak, and hence cannot perform well, at the onset of the rainy season.

Introduction

Little research on the use of draft animal power has been done in Tanzania, and it is only recently that serious attempts have been made to test the suitability of various animal-drawn implements and to conduct cultivation trials at the Centre for Agricultural Mechanisation and Rural Technology (Camartec), the Uyole Agricultural Centre and the Mbeya Oxenisation Project (Camartec, 1988; Lutende, Shetto and Kwiligwa, 1989; Mkomwa and Loewen-Rudgers, 1992).

In the semi-arid areas especially, working animals lose body weight towards the end of the dry season because the supply of pasture is inadequate. Body weight loss may restrict the period of work (Preston, 1986)

Tabora is one of the semi-arid regions in the west central part of Tanzania (Figure 1). The region covers about 76 120 km^2 and is divided into four administrative districts: Igunga, Nzega, Tabora and Urambo. The region has about 2.4 million ha of arable land, but only 500 000 ha are used for agriculture and only about 30 000 ha are cultivated using animal power (Kivuruga, 1989).

Tabora Region is divided into two main agroclimatic zones. The north-east zone, which covers Igunga and Nzega Districts, receives an annual rainfall of 600–850 mm. This zone is susceptible to frequent drought, leading to crop and pasture failure in some years (Kivuruga, 1989). About 84% of the total cattle population of the region is found in this zone (MALD, 1984). The southern zone, which covers Tabora and Urambo Districts, receives more rain (850–1000 mm per year), but expansion of the use of animal power in this zone is limited by the presence of tsetse flies.

Due to high labour costs for tractors, draft animal power will remain the only alternative for expansion of agriculture in Tabora Region. The purpose of this paper, therefore, is to discuss the nutritional problems affecting draft animals in the region, and to suggest measures to solve them in order to maintain a constant draft power output throughout the year.

Materials and methods

Data were collected from the Tabora Regional Mechanisation Office, using their Annual Reports on power utilisation in cultivation (tractor and draft animal) from 1983/84 to 1990/91.

Results and discussion

The population of draft animals in Tabora Region has decreased from about 111 000 in 1986 to about 60 000 in 1991, mainly due to lack of adequate nutrition, particularly during the dry spell in 1987 and 1988. About 16% of the working animals are donkeys (see Table 1).

Most farmers use the Tanzanian short-horned zebu (average body weight 200–250 kg) for draft power.

Figure 1: Administrative boundaries of Tanzania showing Tabora Region

Table 1: Approximate numbers of draft animals in Tabora Region

	1986/87	1987/88	1988/89	1989/90	1990/91
Oxen	80 900	80 100	66 600	62 700	50 200
Donkeys	30 400	30 200	9 700	9 700	9 700
Total	111 300	110 300	76 300	72 400	59 900

Crosses of these with large zebu such as Boran and Brahman are found only on the National Tobacco seed multiplication farm in Urambo District. The use of these large oxen has been very successful as land preparation is done during the dry season.

The distribution of implements in Tabora Region by type and district is shown in Table 2. Draft animals are used mainly for dry-land cultivation, and most farmers only own plows. Animals are also used for transport and, to a lesser extent, for harrowing and ridging. Main crops grown include cash crops such as cotton, tobacco and sunflowers, and staple crops such as maize, sorghum, groundnuts and cowpeas. Draft animal cultivation also dominates in the wet lowlands (known as "Mbugas") where rice is grown.

Ox carts are used to carry harvested cash crops from the field to the house and to market and, during the dry season, to ferry firewood, charcoal and water (especially in the drier parts of Igunga District). In Igunga and Nzega Districts oxen pulling carts can walk an average of 40 km per day. During the dry season most semi-nomadic pastoralists in Igunga District use ox carts to transport essential items such as grain when moving their animals across to the south Usangu plains of Mbeya in search of pasture.

Problems hindering use of draft animals

The work performed by a pair of draft oxen depends on animal type, design of implements, soil type, and level of training of the animals (Mrema and Hatibu, 1989). Nutrition and disease are the major obstacles hindering the efficient use of draft animals.

In the north-east part of Tabora Region the major problem leading to inefficient utilisation of animal power is scarcity of animal feeds. Draft animals are weak and emaciated at the start of the rainy season,

and so cultivation of the land is difficult. Peasants use up to three pairs of oxen in black cotton soils to alleviate this problem.

Inadequate pasture during the dry season leads to severe loss of weight, which reduces the draft force and draft power output of draft animals, and may restrict the period of work (Preston, 1986). There is a great need, therefore, to prevent this weight loss during the dry season through improved nutrition.

Options for improving animal traction

Crop residues which can form an important feed component in the dry season are not fully exploited in Tabora Region at present (Kabatange and Kitalyi, 1989). Their use as feed for oxen does not constitute competition for food with humans or monogastric animals (Preston and Leng, 1987). Crop residues can easily be collected from the field using ox carts, and stored for use as required.

Whenever possible crop residues could be supplemented with protein-rich oil cakes or surplus cotton seeds. Manonga cotton ginnery, on the border between Igunga and Nzega Districts, could supply oil cake byproducts to farmers in the villages of the north-east zone.

Farmers in the north-east part of Tabora Region could be educated, and encouraged, to establish fodder banks which can be used to feed draft animals towards the start of the rainy season when natural pasture is inadequate. In the south, where rainfall is good, shrub legumes such as *Leucaena leucocephala* and drought-resistant legumes such as *Macroptilium* (Siratro), *Trifolium* and *Stylosanthes* spp could be grown (Kabatange and Kitalyi, 1989). *Leucaena* could supply oxen with green foliage throughout the year: it is very palatable, one hectare

Table 2: Distribution of animals and implements in Tabora Region in 1990/91

	Igunga	Nzega	Tabora	Urambo	Total
Ox plows	12 299	7 440	5 160	2 000	26 899
Ox harrows	53	30	50	30	163
Ox ridgers	9	30	48	20	107
Ox carts	1 627	807	650	78	3 162
Oxen	28 975	14 858	5 436	889	50 158
Donkeys	2 887	6 400	348	98	9 733

can supply enough dry matter (5500 kg) to feed two oxen per season, and it gives long-lasting stands when first established compared to other dry season supplementary feeds such as hay and silage.

However, in the districts which receive adequate rainfall (Tabora and Urambo) and in some parts of Nzega Districts, farmers could be advised to select areas where they can keep standing hay (commonly known as "Ngitile") that can be grazed when natural pasture is scarce.

With the help of government leaders and livestock experts a specific ranch area could be set aside for grazing draft animals from the north-east parts of the region. These could be grazed throughout the dry season when pasture is scarce and returned to their home areas after the start of the rainy season.

Recommendation

A nationally coordinated research programme involving agricultural engineers and animal nutritionists is required to study the relationship between draft power output, level of feeding and management of draft animals.

References

Camartec, 1988. *Annual report 1988*. Centre for Agricultural Mechanisation and Rural Technology (Camartec), Arusha, Tanzania.

Kabatange M A and Kitalyi A J, 1989. Constraints to cereal crop residue utilization in central Tanzania. pp. 232–238 in: Said A N and Dzowela B H, *Overcoming constraints to the efficient utilization of agricultural by-products as animal feed*. Proceedings of the Fourth Annual Workshop held 20–27 October 1987, Institute of Animal Research, Mankon Station, Bamenda, Cameroun. African Research Network for Agricultural By-products (ARNAB), International Livestock Centre for Africa (ILCA), Addis Ababa, Ethiopia.

Kivuruga J A, 1989. Utilization of animal and tractor power in Tabora Region. pp. 56–59 in: *The role of agricultural engineering research in national development*. Proceedings of the Tanzania Society of Agricultural Engineers. Volume 2

Lutende D D K, Shetto R M and Kwiligwa E M B, 1989. Agricultural engineering research highlights at Uyole Agricultural Centre. pp. 18–30 in: *The role of agricultural engineering research in national development*. Proceedings of the Tanzania Society of Agricultural Engineers. Volume 2

MALD, 1984. *National livestock count: final results*. Preliminary release. Ministry of Agriculture and Livestock Development (MALD), Dar es Salaam, Tanzania. 50p.

Mkomwa S S and Loewen-Rudgers L, 1992. Experience in promotion of animal traction amongst smallholder farmers in Mbeya, Tanzania. pp.141–151 in: den Hertog G and van Huis J A (eds), *The role of draught animal technology in rural development*. Proceedings international seminar held 2–12 April 1990, Centre for Tropical Veterinary Medicine, University of Edinburgh, Scotland. Pudoc, Wageningen, The Netherlands. 233p.

Mrema G C and Hatibu N, 1989. Draft animal power and agricultural production: an engineering view point. pp. 53–66 in: *Proceedings of the 7th Tanzania Veterinary Association Annual Scientific Conference held 4–8 December 1989, Arusha, Tanzania*. Volume 7. Sokoine University of Agriculture, Morogoro, Tanzania.

Preston T R, 1986. *Better utilization of crop residues and byproducts in animal feeding: research guidelines. A practical manual for research workers*. FAO Animal Production and Health Paper 50/2. Food and Agriculture Organization of the United Nations (FAO), Rome, Italy. 154p.

Preston T R and Leng R A, 1987. *Matching ruminant production systems with available resources in the tropics and sub-tropics*. Penambul Books, Armidale, NSW, Australia. 245p.

Care and management of work oxen in Tanzania: initial survey results

by

G J M Mgaya, T E Simalenga and N Hatibu

Department of Agricultural Engineering, Sokoine University of Agriculture, PO Box 3003, Morogoro, Tanzania

Abstract

Results of a preliminary survey on use and management of work oxen in Tanzania are presented. A total of 100 oxen-using farmers in seven regions of the country were interviewed.

All respondents used indigenous male animals for work. Average number of work animals per household was seven (range 2–18). All respondents used animals for cultivation/plowing: 85% of respondents also used animals for transportation, 16% used them for planting and 5% used them for weeding. Animals were worked for an average of five hours/day (range 3–7 hours/day). Average productive life span was 8.5 years (range 5–12 years).

Most respondents (85%) reported that animals lost condition during the working period, while 9% claimed that their animals gained weight (although even they admitted that their animals lost condition at the beginning of the work period). Only 34% of respondents supplemented their working animals with crop residues and byproducts during the working period.

The majority of respondents (62%) said they would continue using draft animals even if a tractor were available; the rest said they were prefer to use a tractor if the opportunity arose.

Introduction

Mainland Tanzania has about 12 million cattle, concentrated in the north and north-east (Figure 1). In 1984 there were estimated to be just over one million working animals of which about 840 000 were cattle, 220 000 were donkeys and 2000 were horses (Table 1). The working animals are mainly concentrated in those areas with higher cattle populations.

The development and expansion of ox plowing has been associated with a particular type of land use—the fairly extensive grass-fallow cultivation system found in the cool southern and northern highlands, in the warmer, semi-arid north-western area of the central plateau and in the more humid south-eastern part of the Lake Victoria plateau (Kjærby, 1983).

The main limitations to the wider adoption of ox plowing are tsetse infestation and the lack of a

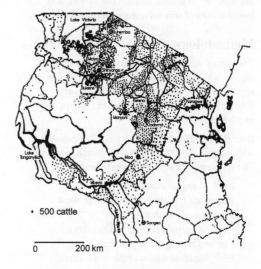

Figure 1: Distribution of cattle in Tanzania

tradition of animal ownership. But efforts are being made to introduce draft animals into new areas, together with appropriate technical packages to help villages look after them and get the maximum output from them (MALD, 1983).

Experience from other countries has shown that a pair of draft oxen is capable of working 4 ha per season (Giles, 1975; Starkey, 1981). On this basis, the 0.8 million draft oxen in Tanzania should be able to work about 1.6 million ha. However, only minimal use is currently being made of this resource (Hatibu and Simalenga, 1992). The main reasons for this, as reported by MALD (1983), are:

° low efficiency of power utilisation

° the small size of the Tanzanian zebu cattle

° lack of appropriate equipment and harnesses

° management and feeding problems which leave oxen in poor condition at start of the working period.

To promote the use of draft animals in Tanzania, the Ministry of Agriculture and Livestock Development

(MALD, 1983) proposed the following goals for Tanzania's livestock policy:

○ improvement of extension and veterinary services

○ adequate seasonal feeding of draft animals

○ efficient draft animal husbandry during periods of high work demand

○ production of appropriate implements for use with draft animals.

In 1991 Sokoine University of Agriculture carried out a survey of animal traction use in Tanzania. Initial results of this survey are presented here.

Methodology

The survey was carried out during the cropping season in the seven regions of the country with the highest number of working animals, namely Shinyanga, Singida, Mara, Mwanza, Tabora, Mbeya and Iringa.

Data were obtained through a guided questionnaire administered to 100 farmers who owned work oxen. The following parameters were studied:

○ types of animals used

○ operations for which animals were used

○ area plowed per day

○ working period per year and per day

○ care and management practices

○ feed supplementation of the work animals.

Results and discussion

All farmers interviewed use indigenous male animals for work because they have a good temperament, are strong and can be used throughout the year. As animals are in a poor state at the start of the work period, many farmers work their animals in pairs, or even larger teams, to increase work efficiency.

The majority of farmers (64%) bought all of their work animals; 26% inherited them or obtained them through dowries; and 10% acquired them by a combination of purchasing and inheritance/dowries. Average number of animals per household was seven (range 2–18).

Use of animals

The use of animals for different agricultural and household operations is shown in Figure 2. Animals are usually fit to start work when they are between two and five years of age (Figure 3), depending mainly on the adequacy (quality and quantity) of their feeding. Animals reared under harsh conditions start working later. Most animals continue to work for up to 10 years (Figure 4), after which they are

Table: 1: Working animals in Tanzania in 1984

Region	Working cattle	Horses	Donkeys
Arusha	67 556	309	107 768
Coast	15	20	383
Dar es Salaam	0	67	23
Dodoma	18 182	74	30 268
Iringa	53 322	322	3 847
Kagera	863	47	96
Kigoma	201	31	2
Kilimanjaro	3 491	162	6 477
Lindi	22	7	2
Mara	107 949	71	5 519
Mbeya	44 045	238	4 695
Morogoro	651	72	1 827
Mtwara	10	10	3
Mwanza	103 729	77	6 051
Rukwa	45 481	6	3 825
Ruvuma	93	74	40
Shinyanga	247 078	181	11 281
Singida	72 480	40	22 759
Tabora	71 032	107	8 166
Tanga	172	134	4 244
Total	**836 373**	**2048**	**217 276**

Source: MALD (1984)

usually sold: working animals are not slaughtered and consumed by the household owning them because they are regarded almost as members of the family.

Work rates of work oxen

The area a pair of oxen cultivate a day is very small (Figure 5). Poor nutrition, inadequate training (of both animals and operators) and inefficient utilisation are the main reasons for the low work rate.

Poor nutrition is a particular problem. Draft bulls and oxen need feed supplementation if they are to do the work expected of them (Mohamed-Saleem and Von Kaufmann, 1989), but only 34% of the households surveyed supplement their working animals with crop residues and byproducts (maize and rice straw and, to a lesser extent, sorghum straw, hay and maize bran). Work animals are usually grazed separately after working but because pastures are poor in terms of both quality and quantity animals are undernourished.

Work periods

On average, animals work for about five hours a day (Figure 6), depending on conditions; when there is moonlight work can start as early as 0300 hours and go on until 2200 hours.

The length of the annual working period can vary widely (Figure 7) because in some areas animals are

% of respondents

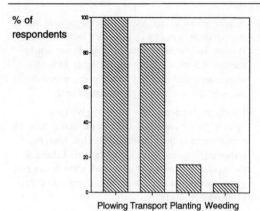

Figure 2: Use of animals for different operations

% of respondents

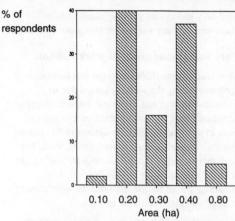

Figure 5: Area plowed/cultivated per day per pair
Range: 0.10–0.80 ha/day. Mean: 0.36 ha/day

% of respondents

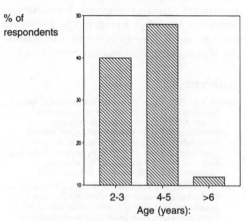

Figure 3: Age at which animals start working

% of respondents

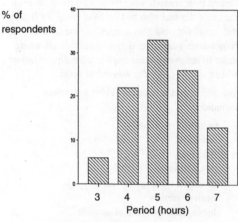

Figure 6: Working period per day
Range: 3–7 hours/day. Mean: 5 hours/day

% of respondents

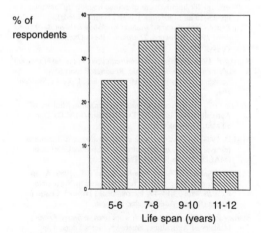

Figure 4: Productive life span of working animals
Range: 5–12 years. Mean 8.5 years

% of respondents

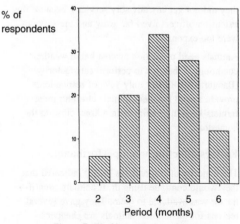

Figure 7: Working period per year
Range: 2–6 months/year. Mean: 4 months/year

used only during one growing season while elsewhere they are worked for two growing seasons.

Care and management of work animals

Most respondents (85%) reported that animals lose condition during the working period due to undernourishment and overwork. Farmers therefore sometimes have to team up three or four pairs of oxen to pull one plow. Some farmers (9%) claimed that their animals gained weight during work, but even they admitted that the animals do lose weight at the beginning of the working period. The remaining 6% of farmers reported no weight change in their animals in response to work.

Most respondents dipped their animals frequently (Figure 8): if a cattle dip was not available they used hand sprays. The few respondents who rarely dipped their animals were those who lived far from the cattle dip and who had no hand spray (or if they did, could not obtain an acaricide). The 24% of respondents who never dipped their animals where those living even farther from a cattle dip, or those whose village cattle dip was out of order.

The advice and services provided to farmers included:

o treatment of diseases

o castration

o .dehorning

o vaccination

o advice on training animals

o feeding animals

o dipping and spraying of animals.

Sixty-six per cent of respondents received such services, the same number who dipped their animals at the recommended frequency. The remainder said they did not get any advisory services, because the extension officers lived far away and the services were too expensive.

Animals need protection against harsh weather conditions if they are to perform satisfactorily (Bangura, 1988). But only 14% of respondents provide a shed for their animals at night; most farmers keep their animals in a kraal close to the homestead.

Factors affecting work performance

The majority of respondents (62%) indicated that they would continue using draft animals even if a tractor was available to them. They gave several reasons for this choice: animals are cheaper to

acquire than a tractor; using a tractor requires skilled management; a tractor cannot work in areas with stumps; and the sizes of their farms do not justify the use of a tractor. However, the other 38% of respondents said that they would prefer a tractor because they could then plow a larger area.

Finally, respondents were asked to give their opinion on the importance of several factors to work performance of their animals. It is clear from the responses (Figures 9 to 13) that farmers believe that the work performance of their draft animals can be greatly improved through proper nutrition and other management practices.

Conclusions

This study has shown that care and management of work oxen should be an area of concern for both research and extension programmes. The viability of animal draft technology depends to a great extent on the improvement of animal husbandry, management and efficient utilisation of available power.

References

Bangura A B, 1988. The utilisation and management of draft animals at farm level. pp. 293–298 in: Starkey P and Ndiamé F (eds), *Animal power in farming systems.* Proceedings of Second West African Animal Traction Networkshop, held 17–26 September 1986, in Freetown, Sierra Leone. Vieweg for German Appropriate Technology Exchange, Deutsche Gesellschaft für Technische Zusammenarbeit (GTZ), Eschborn, Germany. 363p.

Giles G W, 1975. The reorientation of agricultural mechanization for developing countries: policies and attitudes for action programmes. pp. 71–90 in: *Proceedings of meeting of FAO/OECD expert panel on effects of mechanization on production and employment.* Food and Agriculture Organization of the United Nations (FAO), Rome, Italy.

Hatibu N and Simalenga T E, 1992. Research and development strategy for improvement of animal traction in Tanzania. pp. 23–26 in: Simalenga T E and Hatibu N (eds), *Proceedings of animal traction workshop held on 8–10 April 1991, Morogoro, Tanzania.* Mbeya Oxenization Project, Mbeya, Tanzania. 57p.

Kjærby F, 1983. *Problems and contradictions in the development of ox-cultivation in Tanzania.* Research Report 66. Scandinavian Institute of African Studies, Uppsala, Sweden. 164p.

MALD, 1983. *The agricultural policy of Tanzania.* Ministry of Agriculture and Livestock Development (MALD), Dar es Salaam, Tanzania. 19p.

MALD, 1984. *National livestock count: final results.* Preliminary release. Ministry of Agriculture and Livestock Development (MALD), Dar es Salaam, Tanzania. 50p.

Mohamed-Saleem M A and Von Kaufmann R R, 1989. A rapid survey of feeding regimes for draft cattle in Niger state. *ILCA Bulletin* 33:14–17. International Livestock Centre for Africa (ILCA), Addis Ababa, Ethiopia.

Starkey P H, 1981. *Farming with work oxen in Sierra Leone.* Ministry of Agriculture, Freetown, Sierra Leone. 88p.

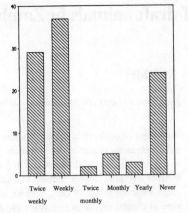

Figure 8: Dipping frequency

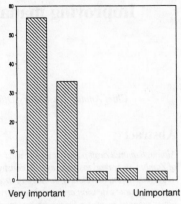

Figure 11: Importance of equipment type on work performance of draft animals

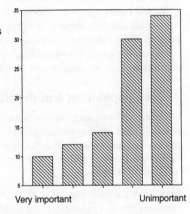

Figure 9: Importance of equipment type on work performance of draft animals

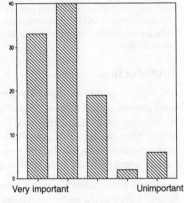

Figure 12: Importance of animal nutrition on work performance of draft animals

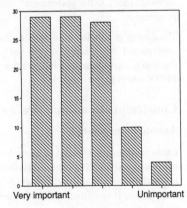

Figure 10: Importance of animal health on work performance of draft animals

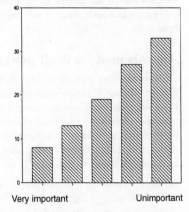

Figure 13: Importance of soil type on work performance of draft animals

Improving management of draft animals in Zambia

by

Gervazio B M Phiri

Chief Animal Husbandry Officer, Ministry of Agriculture, PO Box 50291, Lusaka, Zambia

Abstract

Although animal draft power is widely used in some areas of Zambia, its spread to other areas is constrained by poor management and nutrition, a shortage of draft animals, and inadequate extension and veterinary services. This paper suggests measures for the expansion of the use of animal traction, especially in non-cattle-keeping areas. Proposals include reviewing the communal land tenure system to facilitate the adoption of improved husbandry methods, strengthening extension and veterinary services, using cows as draft animals, giving farmers access to credit to procure animals and the inputs necessary for good management, and providing training facilities for farmers and animals.

Introduction

The use of oxen for cultivation was introduced into parts of Southern and Eastern Provinces of Zambia 60–70 years ago by missionaries and European settlers. Over the years it has spread slowly to the central, western and north-western areas of the country where cattle are traditionally kept.

In the mid-1970s, when fuel prices increased, it became clear that the use of mechanical power for smallholders was generally uneconomic. Thus, in recent years, draft animals have become increasingly important in Zambian agriculture, particularly in the southern part of the country. In the north, where cattle are scarce, cultivation is still largely done with hand tools.

Animals used for draft power

Oxen are the main animals used for draft power in Zambia. The use of female cattle for draft purposes is not yet widespread, perhaps due to a general belief that oxen are the only sort of cattle which can be worked. It is, however, becoming increasingly common to see female cattle being used, especially for transportation in rural areas.

Donkeys are used for transport in some southern and western parts of Zambia. There is little experience in the management of donkeys in the country, although they are generally known to be hardier than cattle. Extension services have yet to develop extension packages for donkey husbandry suitable for use in Zambia. In 1967, after noting the usefulness of donkeys in the smallholder agriculture of neighbouring countries, the government decided to import a number of donkeys and to distribute them as free gifts to poor farmers in areas where cattle were not normally kept. Nothing was heard or seen of the donkeys after two years. However, from the experience gained from other parts of the country, it is evident that donkeys can play a vital role in supplementing the use of oxen in the rural areas, and a more systematic approach to importation and distribution of donkeys is being planned. The breeding of mules may also be attempted. Horses are mainly used for sporting activities by European commercial farmers.

Animal population and distribution

Cattle are predominantly indigenous local breeds—Tonga and Barotse (Sanga type) and Ngoni (zebu)—and are concentrated in Southern, Western, Central and Eastern Provinces, with isolated "pockets" in Northern Province.

Since 1964, the cattle population has been increasing steadily, especially in the traditional sector. In 1964, there were 1 069 000 cattle in this sector: by 1971 there were 1 444 000 and by now there may be about 2.2 million. This increase can be attributed partly to the government's animal health programmes.

The donkey population is not very high and is concentrated in Southern, Western and Central Provinces. Latest estimates indicate that there are 1400 donkeys in the country.

Constraints to animal draft expansion

Animal management

Cattle management is based on commercial and traditional systems. The commercial sector's system is based on modern husbandry methods and management is consistent with commercial means of production.

Major constraints are experienced in the traditional sector where rearing is done communally and proper management cannot always be ensured. There is a lack of systematic breeding and inbreeding can be a problem. The breeding season is generally not restricted and unproductive animals are not systematically culled, mainly because herds tend to be owned by several different people.

The traditional sector also suffers from inadequate health services. Despite efforts by government animal health services, it is difficult to extend veterinary supervision to every corner of the country. Moreover, the existence of tsetse flies in almost one third of the country, reduces the area where cattle can be reared successfully. In Eastern and Southern Provinces, tick-borne East Coast Fever and Corridor disease, respectively, play a major role in reducing cattle productivity.

The traditional sector is characterised by poor animal nutrition. In the dry season, grazing becomes increasingly scarce and poor, a situation made worse by overgrazing and indiscriminate bush fires that reduce the natural grazing areas.

Shortage of draft animals

In areas where cattle are traditionally kept people attach a high value to young work oxen and are reluctant to sell them. It is therefore difficult to rely on these areas as sources of draft animals, and non-cattle owners have to depend on other sources such as commercial and state farms. However, the state farms are failing to meet the demand, and commercial farms charge prices that are prohibitive for small-scale farmers. Even cattle rearing areas are experiencing a shortage of oxen, and already recourse is being made to the use of donkeys.

Inadequate extension services

Experience has shown that extension workers from the Department of Agriculture generally spend more time on crop extension than on the livestock sector. Perhaps this is because the extension workers get greater support to perform crop extension functions,

but whatever the reason, the livestock sector is not receiving an adequate extension service.

Measures toward improvements

Good management is a prerequisite for the better performance of draft animals. Draft cattle can generally be managed like other cattle, but special attention should be paid to ensuring that the animals are in good condition just before the growing season.

The adoption of improved methods of cattle husbandry is usually difficult under communal grazing systems. It is important that the land tenure system be reviewed to facilitate changes.

Particular efforts should be put into introducing animal draft power into cattle-deficient areas in the north of the country. Such efforts might include:

o strengthening extension services to upgrade farmers' knowledge of breeding, nutrition and disease prevention

o encouraging farmers in non-cattle-keeping areas to breed their own cattle instead of repeatedly purchasing replacement draft animals or relying on government agencies to procure them

o encouraging farmers to use female cattle as draft animals so the same animal can provide traction power, reproduction, milk and beef. This would help to alleviate the animal supply problem but considerably improved management and adequate nutrition will be necessary if cows are to perform all their functions satisfactorily

o giving farmers access to credit facilities to enable them acquire animals and the inputs necessary to ensure satisfactory management

o facilitating the supply of veterinary drugs and services

o providing facilities for training of farmers and animals.

Characteristics and uses of donkeys in Botswana

by

A A Aganga and K Maphorisa

Department of Animal Health and Production
Botswana College of Agriculture, Private Bag 0027, Gaborone, Botswana

Abstract

Donkey traction is an accepted form of technology in Botswana. Donkeys are friendly, quiet and intelligent. A survey was carried out on donkeys in Kweneng and Kgatleng Districts. Average body weight of mature male and female donkeys (4 years old) was found to be 140 and 139 kg respectively (range 105–182 kg for both males and females). Average body length was 97.4 cm (range 85–115 cm) for males and 100.0 cm (range 80–115 cm) for females. Average height at withers was 112.9 cm (range 80–123 cm) for males and 109.4 cm (range 98–122 cm) for females. Chest girth of the donkeys surveyed averaged 114.6 cm (range 88–128 cm) for males and 114.3 cm (range 84–128 cm) for females. Aspects of donkey use, management and nutrition are discussed.

Introduction

The donkey is an important animal in rural Botswana. It is used traditionally as a transport animal for riding, packing and pulling carts. It is also important as a draft animal. Donkeys are usually harnessed in pairs or in larger teams of up to eight for agricultural work. Donkeys provide valuable work for the rural dwellers as the animals have great patience and are highly dependable; because of these attributes they can be controlled by women and children. Botswana has the largest number of donkeys per person in Africa (Jones, 1991) and no special breeds are yet being preserved.

A study was carried out to investigate the body characteristics, feeds and feeding, management and uses of donkeys in Kweneng and Kgatleng Districts in Botswana.

Donkeys in Botswana

The donkey population in Botswana was about 148 000 in 1988 (MoA, 1988). Table 1 shows the distribution of donkeys by district and region. Table 2 shows donkey numbers per farm in relation to herd size. The number of donkeys on traditional farms varied from two to more than 16. For the whole country, including commercial farms, the average donkey herd was 5.5 animals (MoA, 1988).

Donkey survey

A sample of 120 mature (about four years old) male and female donkeys (jacks and jennies) in Kweneng and Kgatleng Districts were measured for body weight, body length, height at withers and chest girth. The animals were visually appraised for coat colour and hair texture. Information on the animals' feeds, feeding, management and uses was collected.

Body and behavioural characteristics

Coat colour varied from cream and light brown through brownish grey and grey to dark grey. The hair was normally fine, short and smooth but untidy

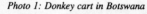

Photo 1: Donkey cart in Botswana

Photo: Paul Starkey

"Improving animal traction technology"

Table 1: Donkeys: farms, animals and average herd sizes by district and region

Region and districts	Donkey farms		Total donkeys		Average herd
	Number	Percentage	Number (000s)	Percentage	(Donkeys/farm)
Traditional farms					
Southern Region					
Barolong	500	1.8	2.5	1.7	5.0
Ngwaketse South	1 900	7.0	12.2	8.2	6.4
Ngwaketse North	2 100	7.8	10.0	6.8	4.8
Total	**4 500**	**16.6**	**24.7**	**16.7**	**5.5**
Gaborone Region					
Bamalete	300	1.1	2.0	1.4	6.7
Kweneng South	2 600	9.6	11.7	7.9	4.5
Kweneng North	1 000	3.7	4.7	3.2	4.7
Kgatleng	1 100	4.1	7.5	5.1	6.8
Total	**5 000**	**18.5**	**25.9**	**17.5**	**5.2**
Central Region					
Mahalapye East	1 400	5.2	8.9	6.0	6.4
Mahalphe West	900	3.3	7.5	5.1	8.3
Palapye	2 000	7.4	11.4	7.7	5.7
Serowe	2 100	7.8	10.5	7.1	5.0
Bobonong	3 300	12.2	21.7	14.7	6.5
Total	**9 700**	**35.8**	**80.0**	**40.6**	**6.2**
Francistown Region					
Tati	1 200	4.4	6.1	4.1	5.1
Tutume	1 300	4.8	5.4	3.7	4.2
Total	**2 500**	**9.2**	**11.5**	**7.8**	**4.6**
Maun Region					
Ngamiland West	1 800	6.7	7.4	5.0	4.1
Ngamiland East	1 500	5.5	7.8	5.3	5.2
Chobe	100	0.4	0.5	0.3	5.0
Total	**3 400**	**12.6**	**15.7**	**10.5**	**4.6**
Western Region					
Ghanzi	700	2.6	3.2	2.2	4.6
Kgalagadi	1 100	4.1	4.9	3.3	4.5
Total	**1 800**	**6.7**	**8.1**	**5.5**	**4.5**
Total traditional	**26 900**	**99.4**	**145.9**	**98.6**	**5.4**
Total commercial					
(all regions)	160	0.5	2.0	1.4	12.4
Botswana total	**27 060**	**100.0**	**147.9**	**100.0**	**5.5**

coats were observed in poorly kept animals. Legs were straight and well-muscled, when viewed from the side, front and back. The feet were concave and well-angled. The line of the backbone of the donkey was straight, especially between the shoulders and the rump. The chests of most donkeys evaluated were deep and wide. The means and ranges of the various body dimensions measured are given in Table 3.

The donkeys were generally calm, quiet and obedient. They were very easy to handle for work and transport, and appeared to learn quickly.

Feeding systems

When they are not working, donkeys are traditionally left to graze freely on the range, throughout the year. There is a wide range of grasses in the veld, depending on location and

Table 2: Donkey numbers in Botswana in relation to herd size

	Donkey farms		Total donkeys		Average herd size
Herd size	Number	Percentage	Number (000s)	Percentage	(Donkeys/farm)
1–5	17 700	65.8	54.9	37.6	3.1
6–10	7 000	26.0	52.5	36.0	7.5
11–15	1 600	5.9	20.4	14.0	12.8
16+	600	2.2	18.1	12.4	30.2
Total	26 900	100.0	145.9	100.0	5.4

Source: MoA (1988)

season of the year, including *Panicum maximum*, *Brachiaria nigropedata*, *Digitaria eriantha* and *Eragrostis porosa*.

During the dry season, when grasses are scarce and their quality and crude protein contents are low, some farmers give their donkeys crop residues such as sorghum, maize and millet stovers and brans, cow pea husks and water melon fruits. Some farmers supplement their donkeys with fermented sorghum residue known as *chibuku*, and a few farmers give the donkeys salt licks. Donkeys may need about 10–20 litres of water a day.

Management

Traditionally donkeys are not provided with roofed shelter. They often spend the night on the ranges although at times they stay in paddocks or roofless enclosures (*kraals*), made from branches, close to the farm.

Donkeys are very hardy animals; they are usually fit and strong and rarely experience health problems. Occasionally, cases of dourine, pneumonia and internal worms are reported to veterinary clinics.

Semi-arid Botswana provides a healthy climate for donkeys, who do not like wet environments. Even during the rainy season (October to February) there are long breaks between rain showers when the hot sun quickly dries up the rainwater.

Uses

Donkeys are widely used for agricultural work on Botswanan farms. A donkey's ability to draw

agricultural implements is limited because of its low body weight (average about 140 kg). Consequently, donkeys are usually harnessed in pairs or in larger teams for farm operations. A donkey is said to be able to pull about 250 N, the equivalent of 16–20% of its weight, at a speed of 2.5–2.8 km per hour for 3 to 3.5 hours a day (Jones, 1991).

Donkeys are commonly used in rural Botswana for carrying people and loads, such as firewood. Normally a pack donkey's back is protected with a sack or an old blanket. Donkeys are commonly ridden by children and small people.

Donkeys are widely used to pull carts (Photos 1–3), both on roads and across flat, but uneven, land. Usually the donkeys are harnessed in teams to pull carts. Firewood and drums of water are often carried in donkey carts in rural areas (Photo 3). Donkey hire services are available in rural communities. The charges vary between districts, but a fee of 12 Pula (equivalent to about US$ 6) might be charged to move household materials and goods over a distance of about 12 km.

Although both donkey milk and meat are edible, neither is popular as human food in Botswana. Donkey skin can be used for leather.

Constraints to donkey power

There are several constraints on the use of donkey power in Botswana. These include:

o low numbers of donkeys per household or farm among poor farmers

Table 3: Body characteristics of donkeys

	Male			Female		
Characteristic	Average	Range	Standard error	Average	Range	Standard error
Body weight (kg)	140.1	105–182	2.61	139.2	105–182	2.28
Body length (cm)	97.4	85–115	0.87	100.0	80–115	0.93
Height at withers (cm)	112.9	80–123	0.81	109.4	98–122	0.67
Chest girth (cm)	114.6	88–128	1.20	114.3	84–128	1.11

Photo 2: Donkey cart crossing river in Botswana

o   poor nutrition and management of donkeys, so that the animals cannot exercise their potential tractive power

o   reproductive behaviour. Male donkeys normally search out females in oestrus and neglect their work when nearby females are "on heat". This problem can be solved by castrating male work donkeys

o   pregnancy in a female donkey which may reduce her tractive power. Pregnant animals are less likely to be used for traction in the last trimester of gestation

o   diseases and poor health, which will reduce donkeys' tractive power. This problem can easily be overcome by giving the animals prompt veterinary care

o   lack of suitable donkey implements, which impairs the animals' effectiveness in farming.

o   the preference of some farmers for oxen; such farmers do not like to use donkeys at all for draft

o   lost animals. Some donkeys are lost as a result of extensive roaming when grazing. Although some have identification marks which allow them to be rapidly returned to their owners, others may be missing throughout the crucial plowing period.

Prospects for donkey power

There has been a considerable increase in the use of donkeys for traction in Botswana over recent years. There are good prospects for donkey power for traction and for transport in rural areas. National development and credit programmes like ALDEP (Arable Lands Development Programme) encourage farmers to use donkeys for traction.

Donkeys are very cheap compared to work oxen. A donkey costs about 100 Pula (US\$ 50) while an ox costs about 800 Pula (US\$ 400). This implies that more peasant farmers will be able to afford donkeys than oxen. Good, well-trained donkeys can be kept

Photo 3: Donkey cart carrying water in Botswana

for many years. Since donkeys are not popular meat animals, they are kept until they become unserviceable.

Conclusions and recommendations

Donkey power has been called an "accepted yet neglected technology" (Spore, 1990). This is certainly the case in Botswana. Farmers are very aware of the uses of donkey power and donkeys play prominent roles in the lives of rural people. Donkeys need to be given more serious attention by those concerned with rural development. Research is required on the nutritional requirements of donkeys in Botswana.

Acknowledgement

The authors are grateful to Mr J M Madimabe for his technical assistance and to Botswana College of Agriculture for permission to publish this paper.

References

Jones P A, 1991. *Training course manual on the use of donkeys in agriculture in Zimbabwe*. Agritex Institute of Agricultural Engineering, Borrowdale, Harare, Zimbabwe. 81p.

MoA, 1988. *Botswana agricultural statistics*. Planning and Statistics Division, Ministry of Agriculture (MoA), Gaborone, Botswana.

Spore, 1990. Donkey power: an accepted yet neglected technology. *Spore* 30:5. Technical Centre for Agricultural and Rural Cooperation (CTA), Ede-Wageningen, The Netherlands.

Donkey power for appropriate mechanisation and transport for women in Zambezi Valley, Zimbabwe

Project Manager, Project Entrepreneurship amongst Rural Women, Ministry of Community and Cooperative
Development, St Andrews House, Samora Michel Avenue, Harare, Zimbabwe

Abstract

The marginal communal areas of Zimbabwe are suffering from a shortage of draft power for agriculture and transport. It has been argued that tractors are the only solution to this problem. However, buying and maintaining sufficient tractors to cultivate the marginal areas would cost enormous sums, mostly in foreign exchange, and the increased yields due to improved land preparation would be marginal in comparison. Also, hiring tractors makes no economic sense for the farmer.

Animal traction is the main source of draft power in the communal areas. Cattle ownership per household has been declining, for several reasons—human population growth not matched by increased livestock numbers, environmental degradation leading to shortage of grazing land, drought, disease and the need for households to sell cattle to provide cash income. Donkeys could provide an alternative source of draft power. They are cheap, easily trained, hard working, thrive in arid conditions, can survive in tsetse areas, are not affected by bovine diseases and would not be used for food. As well as being suitable for cultivation work, they could be used by women to reduce their heavy workload. A donkey traction project is being established in the Zambezi Valley, one of the poorest areas of Zimbabwe in terms of rainfall, soil type and general infrastructural development; it plans to set up donkey traction groups, with a bias towards assisting women, and to produce donkey equipment using existing knowledge and local resources.

Introduction

Since time immemorial, animals have supplemented the power of human limbs by providing power to till the soil and to transport farm produce, even to distant towns. The type of animal used has been, and still is, varied, ranging from small donkeys to large Indian elephants. Draft animal power is used today on a large scale in many parts of the world (Starkey, 1988).

The choice between draft animal power and the tractor or truck will depend on many factors,

including the land being tilled and the terrain over which goods have to be carried. The availability of fuel, spare parts and maintenance will also effect whether motorised power is appropriate. Unlike oil, which in many cases has to be imported, draft animal power is a renewable resource. Draft animals can be bred where they are needed for work and can provide fertiliser and fuel for the farmer (Bodet, 1987). Draft animals can assure the timely movement of agricultural inputs, seeds, fertiliser and manure, and such timeliness is important in areas of low rainfall. Work animals can also undertake efficient transport of harvested crops.

The Zimbabwean economy is heavily dependent on agriculture which accounts for over 11% of the Gross Domestic Product. Agriculture in Zimbabwe can be broadly divided into four farming sectors:

○ communal farming
○ resettlement
○ small-scale commercial
○ large-scale commercial

The large- and small-scale commercial farms are owned by individuals while in the communal areas the land is owned by the community: arable land is allocated to families to cultivate, and grazing land is communally used. The resettlement schemes are part of the government's land redistribution efforts, and settlers have use rights to the land.

Over 60% of the population of Zimbabwe lives in the communal areas, where 70% of the inhabitants are children and women. Zimbabwe is classified into five agro-ecological regions, based on soil type, rainfall and other climatic factors. Classification is in the order of decreasing agricultural potential. Over 75% of the communal farms are located in marginal regions 4 and 5. It is against this background that the issue of availability of animal or mechanical power to till and transport produce becomes crucial to most of the country's population.

This paper shares the ideas of an agricultural development initiative which is soon to be implemented in the one of the marginal areas of the

[*] Subsequent address:
Zero Regional Network of Environmental Experts,
44 Edmonds Avenue, Belvedere, Harare, Zimbabwe

"Improving animal traction technology"

country, the Zambezi Valley. This has a special focus on the needs of women and includes a donkey traction project.

Mechanisation in communal areas

Prospects for tractor power

Rusike (1986) estimated that there were 2900 tractors in the communal areas. Estimates of other authorities put the figure as low as 600. Most of these tractors have depreciated beyond their efficient working life and are only used on the owner's farm and for transport.

The government also runs a tractor tillage unit through the District Development Fund (DDF). This unit was initially set up to plow the land of farmers who had been resettled. The unit consists of 260 tractors and from the limited information available it is understood that these tractors each plow roughly 60 ha/year. DDF also runs 1000 additional tractors used for road grading. It is understood that these are also used for three months of the year for plowing, using plows borrowed from the commercial sector. Even if the tractors also work at a rate of 60 ha/year, the total tractor-plowed area is insignificant, at less than 2.4% of the total cultivated communal land (Elliot, 1989).

The government-run scheme appears to make very inefficient use of capital resources. This is in line with findings from other countries on the inability of government tillage units to operate on a financially sound basis.

Arguments have been made that because of the rising population, the increasing area under cultivation and hence the reduction of grazing lands, tractors are the only solution to the draft power shortage. However, a brief look at the costs involved dispels this notion. The total area under cultivation in the communal areas is now roughly three million hectares. Assuming a high operational efficiency of seven hours/ha including travelling, an eight-hour working day and an eight-month plowing period, each tractor should have a potential to plow 200 ha/year. To plow three million ha each year would thus require 15 000 tractors. At a price of 65 000 Zimbabwe dollars (Z$) for a 75 kW tractor this amounts to Z$ 975 million (US$ 1 ≈ Z$ 6 in 1992). Assuming a 10% replacement rate, this would amount to Z$ 97 million per year with both amounts being in foreign currency. Fuel costs, also primarily in foreign exchange, would amount to roughly Z$ 54 million per year excluding travel between fields (200 ha x 30 litres/ha x Z$ 0.6/litre x 15 000 tractors). The costs of maintenance and repair can be estimated at 10% of initial cost, or Z$ 97 million per year. Thus, based on these figures, which provide extremely low estimates of the actual costs, using tractors to overcome the draft power shortage would require an initial outlay of Z$ 975 million and annual costs of around Z$ 250 million, most of which would be in foreign exchange.

This annual figure amounts to almost exactly the total crop sales of Z$ 220 million to the marketing boards by the communal farming sector in 1986. The increased yields due to improved land preparation would be marginal compared to the costs (Elliot, 1989). The exact figures are complicated by the rate of inflation which was above 150% in early 1992, and by fuel prices which have almost doubled over the past two years. Nevertheless, it should be clear that it is unrealistic to view mechanical traction as an immediate or viable solution to the draft power and transport problems in marginal communal areas. (The situation in the high potential agro-ecological areas is different and tractors may prove appropriate there.)

Animal traction in Zimbabwe

In the communal areas of Zimbabwe, animal traction is the predominant source of draft power. Oxen and cows are the main draft animals. There are over three million cattle in the communal areas and over 20% of these are used for work. Over the past five years there has been a dramatic decrease in the number of cattle owned per family. The factors that have contributed to the decline include:

○ the rapid increase of population (3.5% annually, dropping to 2.8% recently) which has not been matched by a similar increase in livestock numbers

○ rapid environmental degradation which has reduced the carrying capacity of the land and has resulted in an acute shortage of grazing. This shortage will get worse unless alternatives are found, and so many households may have to live without cattle. For example, the recommended stocking rate in agro-ecological region 5 is one livestock unit per 20 ha. If this carrying capacity were to be strictly applied in the communal areas, families having the average land holding of 2.5 ha would not even be able to keep one beast at home

○ drought and diseases which have resulted in the loss of thousands of cattle

○ the increasing importance of the cash economy, with the result that more households have faced cash shortages and so have been forced to sell their cattle for slaughter, so reducing the number of cattle owned by families.

Table 1: Some advantages and disadvantages of donkeys

Advantages	Disadvantages
Friendly towards humans	Suffer from being alone
Willing to work	Friends not easily separated
Can turn in a small space	Need shelter from cold and damp
Easy to train	Meat not eaten (in Zimbabwe)
Need little supervision in work	Mature slowly
Can utilise poor feed well	Comparatively small in size
Not affected much by external parasites	Breed slowly
Need little water	Manure is fibrous
Can survive in tsetse areas	
Comparatively cheap to buy	
Strong relative to size	
Live/work more years in good care than other animals	
Milk good for humans	

Source: after Jones (1991)

These factors are not a temporary feature but will continue unless solutions are found. One option might be a different draft animal species, one which might not require the same amounts of grazing, water and management, and which would not be slaughtered for meat or kept for purposes other than traction. One such animal, that has been used for centuries in parts of Africa and is widely available in Zimbabwe, is the donkey.

Donkey power for semi-arid areas

The donkey is the most numerous domesticated African equine (67% of equines kept in Africa are donkeys) and more than 30% of the world donkey population is found in Africa. Donkeys are mainly found in drier ecological regions, where drought has been widespread in recent years, and it has been speculated that donkeys could be used to prevent the recurrence of famine and starvation.

Before discussing in detail how donkeys can be supported it is necessary to look at the advantages and disadvantages of domesticating donkeys (see Table 1). The following material comes mainly from a training manual on the use of donkeys in agriculture in Zimbabwe (Jones, 1991). This was recently produced by the Institute of Agricultural Engineering under the Department of Agriculture, Technical and Extension Services in collaboration with the German Agency for Technical Cooperation (GTZ).

The donkey is said to be one of the most rewarding animals to train and once trained it can be trusted to do many tasks without human supervision. A donkey will learn quickly both from other donkeys

and from humans, and it has a remarkable memory, especially for paths and routes.

A donkey can work for up to four hours, pulling forces of about 250 N. Donkeys are smaller than cattle, at 120–300 kg, but can often undertake much of the work that cattle can do: this has given rise to the suggestion that donkeys produce more work than cattle per kilogram liveweight. Well-trained donkeys need only one person to work with them. Donkeys like to walk in straight lines and can recognise and follow furrows easily, and quickly learn where to turn.

Donkeys can be used for plowing where soils are light and sandy. They may also be used for ridging, weeding and threshing. For cultivation and carting, they may be worked singly, in pairs or in larger teams. On level terrain, a donkey can pull a cart with a 450 kg load. In many parts of the world where there are no roads, the main work of donkeys is as pack animals. Pack donkeys enable people in remote areas to sell and buy goods in urban markets and keep in touch with development. There is practically nowhere a donkey cannot go; with four feet it can often manage steep rocky paths better than a human can.

Although donkeys have many attributes, their adoption depends on the judgement and attitudes of farmers. In general donkeys are regarded as low status animals. If this continues to be the case, donkeys might have limited future significance in African development. However, if Africa is to develop through its own devices there is a need to mobilise all available resources for sustainable development. Development strategies based mainly on external resources will not solve the current problems on the continent. It would therefore be unjustified and wasteful to neglect donkeys as an available, sustainable and valuable resource.

In light of this, the Ministry of Community and Cooperative Development in Zimbabwe intends to introduce donkey traction in the Zambezi Valley area, as a pilot on-farm research trial. This will be done in the context of a project entitled "Entrepreneurship development amongst farmers with a special focus on the needs of women".

Farming in the Zambezi Valley

The Zambezi Valley is one of the poorest areas of Zimbabwe in terms of rainfall, soil type and general infrastructural development. The area is still characterised by a presence of tsetse flies and wildlife which have been responsible for a number of deaths of domestic animals. Communication from one area to another is very difficult because of the poor infrastructure. The rains are so erratic that even obtaining water for home consumption can be difficult. Women often walk tens of kilometres through thick bush infested with dangerous, wild animals to fetch water, which is transported by head. Even though the area is marginal for crop production, people try to cultivate drought-tolerant crops like sorghum and millet for survival. Table 2 shows the low crop yields obtained.

At present most households cultivate their farms by hand hoeing. Some farmers hire the District Development Fund tractors to plow their land at a cost of Z$ 70 per hectare, often using the meagre cash which they have received as remittances from their working relatives in town.

Given the low yields recorded in Table 2, basic arithmetic suggests that it makes no economic sense to promote tractors in such marginal areas. For example, in 1984 the producer price of maize was Z$ 140 per tonne and average yields of maize in and around the Zambezi Valley were 146 kg/ha (Agritex, 1985). Thus in monetary terms the average farmer

obtained about Z$ 20 per hectare, whilst to hire a tractor for plowing cost Z$ 55 per hectare.

In 1988/89 the producer price of maize increased to Z$ 210 per tonne and the plowing fee was Z$ 70 per hectare. The average maize yield in the area in 1988/89 was 360 kg/ha. With this yield, the gross income per hectare was Z$ 75, which allowed those hiring tractors just Z$ 5 "profit", less all other production costs (labour, seeds and other inputs).

It seems clear that there is no logic in employing mechanical traction in such a low-yielding environment. Furthermore, many farmers' fields are not suitable for tractor tilling because of steep slopes, the small size of the farms and the large distances between farms which necessitates much road travel. As the Zambezi Valley is remote, tractors are often idle due to lack of fuel and spare parts. It is therefore surprising that government agencies continue to encourage tractor plowing at the expense of animal traction.

Need for animal traction

Given this background the only realistic option for alleviating transport and draft problems is the use of animal traction. In most parts of the country cattle are normally used for this type of work, but cattle cannot be kept in the Zambezi Valley because of the presence of tsetse flies and wildlife. The presence of buffalo, which can carry foot and mouth disease, strongly mitigates against the introduction of cattle. (Zimbabwe exports meat and on a number of occasions much foreign currency has been lost due to outbreaks of foot and mouth disease.)

As an equine, the donkey is not affected by bovine diseases such as rinderpest and foot and mouth disease, and is relatively tolerant to trypanosomiasis. It is cheap to buy (about Z$ 150) and thus if attacked by wildlife its loss is not as drastic as would be that of an ox or cow (costing Z$ 500). Thus the donkey has been selected as the most suitable draft animal for the Zambezi Valley.

Table 2: Crop yields in Manjolo communal area, Zambezi Valley, 1984–89

Crop		1984/85	1985/86	1986/87	1987/88	1988/89
Maize	Yield (kg/ha)	146	165	68	273	360
	Area (ha)	770	385	392	411	345
White sorghum	Yield (kg/ha)	180	209	90	300	270
	Area (ha)	10	1670	1700	1790	300
Millet	Yield (kg/ha)	270	315	136	364	270
	Area (ha)	1760	2 034	2074	2180	405

Source: Agritex Crop Production Branch Databank 1984–1989

Donkeys for women

For a long time the heavy workload of women has been highlighted, but no practical solutions have been found. Their work involves transporting fuelwood, water and food grains over large distances. Experience has shown that donkeys can be employed to do these tasks, as in other parts of Africa and to a lesser extent elsewhere in Zimbabwe. Also, as a way of supplementing household food needs, women normally work on vegetable gardens, which need regular watering. Simple, donkey-pulled carts with water drums could go a long way toward in reducing women's workloads in transporting the water. Distances to grinding mills can be so great that women travel a whole morning to reach the mill, carrying the grain on their heads. More grain could be carried using donkeys, thus reducing the number of trips women make to the mill.

Donkey traction project

The Ministry of Community and Cooperative Development has expressed interest in establishing a donkey traction project in conjunction with the Intermediate Technology Development Group, the Institute of Agricultural Engineering and the Kulima Mboluni Training Centre. It plans to set up donkey traction groups, with a bias towards assisting women. The women will identify the type of equipment to be used with the donkeys to lessen their daily workload.

As this is a pilot project it will aim at producing the necessary donkey equipment at grassroots level, using already existing knowledge and local resources. This pilot scheme will therefore require close cooperation with the Animal Traction Network for Eastern and Southern Africa (ATNESA) for the purposes of information exchange.

Conclusions

It is well-known that changes in farmers' practices are gradual. This implies that short-term projects are unlikely to have any impact and that any attempt to promote a technological change will require a long-term commitment.

The perceived social status of any initiative is a crucial factor. In this context, draft animals and donkeys are sometimes viewed with suspicion in certain quarters where they may be considered a feature of the past. Such attitudes are understandable and logical arguments alone may not be sufficient to overcome them. If, in countries where there is a significant number of donkeys, leaders could give encouragement and promote scientific examination of donkey use, this would prepare the way for an objective technical discussion of an area of crucial importance to overall national development. Scientists could be encouraged to look at the possibilities of crossbreeding stronger equines, by crossing good horse breeds with donkey breeds to produce hardy and powerful mules. The potential for breeding a productive and adapted equine animal seems higher, now that horses and zebra have been successfully crossed.

In 1992 there were reports in the press informing the public that the rural areas of Zimbabwe had once more experienced disaster in the form of a drought. In one province, 7000 cattle died in one month, and many others were likely to die of starvation, despite all the efforts of farmers to save them. Donkeys were said to be coping with the drought better then cattle, and seemed able to survive on the small amounts of plant material that remained. This suggests that donkeys are particularly appropriate to the drought-prone environment of Zimbabwe.

References

Agritex, 1985. *Agritex crop production branch databank.* Ministry of Agriculture, Harare, Zimbabwe.

Bodet P, 1987. Animal energy: an introductory review. *World Animal Review* 63:2–6.

Elliot K M, 1989. The draught power shortage in the small-scale farming sectors of Zimbabwe. pp. 1–22 in: *Proceedings of a workshop on animal draught power and tractor use in the small-scale farming sector of Zimbabwe, held 25–28 September 1989.* Agritex Institute of Agricultural Engineering, Borrowdale, Harare, Zimbabwe. 194p.

Rusike J, 1986. *Agricultural mechanization in communal farming systems: a case study of the Chiweshe Tractor Mechanization and Cooperative Project.* University of Zimbabwe, Harare, Zimbabwe.

Jones P A, 1991. *Training course manual on the use of donkeys in agriculture in Zimbabwe.* Agritex Institute of Agricultural Engineering, Borrowdale, Harare, Zimbabwe. 81p.

Starkey P, 1988. The introduction, intensification and diversification of the use of animal power in West African farming systems: implications at farm level. pp 97–115 in: Starkey P and Ndiamé F (eds), *Animal power in farming systems.* Proceedings of networkshop held 17–26 September 1986 in Freetown, Sierra Leone. Vieweg for German Appropriate Technology Exchange, GTZ, Eschborn, Germany. 363p.

Improving draft animal management with strategic chemoprophylactic control of trypanosomiasis

R J Connor*

*Regional Tsetse and Trypanosomiasis Control Programme of Malawi, Mozambique, Zambia and Zimbabwe,
PO Box A560, Avondale, Harare, Zimbabwe*

Abstract

Food production in Africa must increase if the continent's rapidly growing human population is to be adequately fed. One factor in achieving this is to improve and expand the use of animal traction for crop production. Vast tracts of sub-Saharan Africa are infested with tsetse flies which transmit the disease trypanosomiasis to both man and animals. The anaemia associated with trypanosomiasis causes weakness, lethargy and a lack of stamina, which reduce the efficiency of working animals. Thus, control of this disease is a prerequisite for sustainable agricultural development in this region.

In the past, trypanocides were freely available from government veterinary personnel. With the introduction of cost recovery schemes, farmers will be required to pay for treatment of their animals. Thus, poor farmers may treat individual animals only, rather than their whole herds.

A strategy is proposed for the chemoprophylactic treatment of work oxen before the start of the plowing season. The strategy should be affordable and acceptable to farmers, and close cooperation between animal husbandry and veterinary personnel is essential for its success. A similar approach to the control of other diseases to improve animal traction should also be considered.

Introduction

Sub-Saharan Africa is poor and becoming poorer. It is affected more severely than many other parts of the world by the two closely linked crises of high human population growth rates and environmental degradation. Food shortages are estimated to affect one quarter of the population of sub-Saharan Africa, excluding South Africa and Namibia (World Bank, 1989). To overcome these shortages, to feed the growing population (reckoned to double over the next 20 years) and to reduce dependence on food imports, food production must be increased by 4% annually. Suitable policies need to be put into practice, and improved, appropriate technologies must be adopted to achieve this increase. Of crucial

Subsequent address:
Professor R J Connor, Department of Veterinary Tropical Diseases, University of Pretoria, Private Bag X04 0110, Onderstepoort, South Africa

importance is the greater use of improved animal traction, to enable increased cultivation and to provide transport in rural areas for crops, fertiliser and other goods.

A unique problem faced by sub-Saharan Africa is that of tsetse-transmitted trypanosomiasis, a disease complex that affects man and animals. Tsetse flies infest 10 million square kilometres. Their presence is a serious constraint on rural development since susceptible livestock cannot be kept where tsetse numbers are high. Even in areas of lower tsetse population density trypanosomiasis poses a serious threat to animal health, and heavy losses occur. The control of tsetse and trypanosomiasis is thus an essential element in the expansion of animal traction and hence sustainable rural development.

Control of trypanosomiasis

The control of African animal trypanosomiasis can be achieved by removal of the tsetse fly, removal (with drugs) of the trypanosomes responsible for causing the disease or rearing breeds of livestock tolerant of trypanosomes. Modifications to management, such as improved nutrition and reduced production stress, can also mitigate the severity of trypanosomiasis. No vaccine against trypanosomiasis exists and none is likely to be available before the year 2000.

Tsetse control can be achieved by several different methods which have to be used on a large scale to be successful against the widely dispersed savanna species of fly common in southern Africa. Consequently, the means to alleviate trypanosomiasis by controlling tsetse lie beyond the resources of an individual farmer, or even of a group of farmers. This is in contrast to other parts of Africa where inexpensive bait methods used by a group of livestock owners can reduce the impact of trypanosomiasis to manageable levels. Neither can farmers in southern Africa exploit trypanotolerant breeds of livestock; these breeds are not available in the region.

Pending large-scale tsetse control the main approach to trypanosomiasis control continues to be the use of trypanocidal drugs, either to treat infected animals or to protect healthy stock. Historically in southern Africa, trypanocides have been administered by government veterinary staff, often through mass inoculation campaigns. Trypanocides also provide the individual farmer with a way to control the disease.

The rational use of trypanocides is determined by the local epidemiology of the disease. This is always complex and results from the interaction of tsetse flies, livestock, wild animal hosts and management practices. These aspects are all dominated by climate and season. The unimodal rainfall in this region results in the seasonal dispersal of tsetse flies soon after the rains begin, followed by a rise in the incidence of trypanosomal infections.

In addition to this seasonal increase in the risk of trypanosomiasis, the movement of livestock into tsetse habitats or the gradual advance of tsetse into previously uninfested areas also places livestock at risk. Tsetse-transmitted trypanosomiasis is thus a highly dynamic problem, and the timing of trypanocidal treatments should reflect local variations in the risk of disease.

The Pan-African Rinderpest Campaign (PARC) of the Organisation of African Unity has as a major objective the revitalisation of veterinary services. One of the principles promoted by PARC is that of cost recovery. Farmers will therefore be required to pay for treatments their animals receive. This policy is about to be implemented in many countries of southern Africa.

In tsetse-infested farming areas, livestock owners are unlikely to be willing or able to pay for the continued prophylactic inoculation of entire herds of cattle, even through treatment of individual sick animals may not adequately contain the trypanosomiasis problem.

Trypanosomiasis as a threat

The widespread use of the curative drug diminazene ("Berenil", Hoechst) by farmers to treat undiagnosed cases of 'tsetse fly disease' obscures the true picture in many parts of the region. Consequently, the prevalence of trypanosomiasis is always underestimated. Recent investigations in western Zambia and in the Eastern Caprivi District of Namibia have shown that bovine trypanosomiasis is a serious problem threatening work oxen in particular (Connor, 1991).

The most sensitive direct parasitological method for the diagnosis of animal trypanosomiasis entails examination of the buffy coat of centrifuged blood (Murray et al, 1983). A major advantage of this method is that the haematocrit, or packed red blood cell volume (PCV), can be measured. The PCV is a good indicator of anaemia—the most common pathological sign of trypanosomiasis. Anaemia reduces the blood's oxygen carrying capacity, causing weakness, lethargy and lack of stamina in infected animals.

Although no studies have been reported of the direct effect of trypanosomiasis on animal traction, anecdotal evidence obtained from farmers is convincing. Affected animals are reported to be "lazy to work" and are goaded by being whipped and beaten. More severely affected animals collapse soon after they are yoked. The PCVs of such animals commonly indicate severe anaemia: some individuals have lost half of their red blood cells.

An assessment of trypanosomiasis in work oxen was made in north-west Zimbabwe, the Caprivi District of Namibia and in western Zambia (Connor, 1991). No animal had a PCV lower than 25% and no evidence of the disease was found in north-west Zimbabwe. Of the oxen sampled in Caprivi, 25% were markedly anaemic whereas in the sample from western Zambia 65 out of 95 oxen were anaemic (Figure 1). These findings were made at the beginning of the rainy season when draft animals are in peak demand. The general condition of cattle at the end of the dry season is often poor, and this increases the severity of trypanosomiasis.

A strategy is required to enable farmers to ensure that their draft animals are in good health when they are needed most. The problem of trypanosomiasis must therefore be addressed in tsetse areas.

Strategic chemoprophylactic control

Few livestock owners will be able or prepared to pay for chemoprophylactic treatment of their whole herd when the cost recovery scheme becomes effective, and so tactical chemoprophylaxis has been advocated (FAO, 1991). This tactical approach involves the treatment of selected categories of animals perceived by the farmer to be of greatest economic value. Draft animals are one such category.

The requirements of strategic chemoprophylactic control of trypanosomiasis are that it must be:

○ affordable to the farmers
○ acceptable to them (they must perceive a tangible benefit)
○ economically sustainable

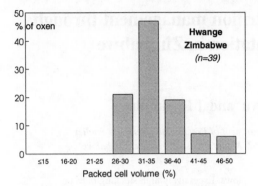

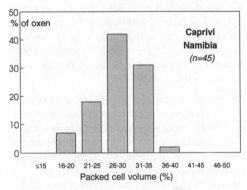

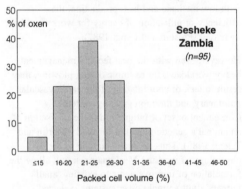

Figure 1: Frequency distributions (%) of packed cell volumes (percentage of blood volume) of oxen sampled in Zimbabwe, Namibia and Zambia in November 1991

The selective treatment of work oxen with the prophylactic trypanocide isometamidium ("Samorin", RMB Ltd) before the end of the dry season has been recommended. This may have to be preceded by curative treatment of sick animals. Isometamidium should be injected deeply into the muscles of the rump two weeks before the animal is worked, to allow the tissue reaction at the injection site to subside. Treatment may need to be repeated after 8 to 12 weeks to maintain protection. The strategic use of trypanocides in this manner would offer protection to the "work force" at a critical time

of the year. Diagnostic surveillance would be necessary to enable the regimen to be modified to suit local epidemiological conditions.

Discussion

To improve the condition of work oxen at the end of the dry season supplementary feeding has been advocated, in the belief that animals in better condition will have a higher work output. Recent findings indicate that this practice gives little benefit to the farmer (ILCA, 1991). Irrespective of their condition score, work oxen used in the trials fulfilled the tasks demanded of them by the farmer. However, it is important to distinguish between physical condition and physiological condition. The anaemia associated with trypanosomiasis, or for that matter other diseases, impairs oxygen uptake and work output, and affected animals are also often in poor condition. It is necessary to recognise trypanosomiasis and to adopt strategic chemoprophylaxis.

To implement the strategy on a wide scale will require close collaboration between animal husbandry specialists and veterinary staff. Arrangements to ensure the simultaneous availability of drugs, needles, syringes, transport and trained personnel will have to be made. It would also be essential to inform farmers of the objectives and anticipated benefits of the strategy before its implementation, in order to secure their participation on a cost recovery basis.

This proposal considers only the strategic control of trypanosomiasis in draft animals. However, the same arguments apply to the control of liver fluke, foot and mouth disease and other major diseases. There is a need to link disease control in general more closely with sustainable animal production.

References

Connor R J, 1991. *Mission report 77/RTE/91. Zimbabwe, Namibia and Zambia. 16 December 1991.* Regional Tsetse and Trypanosomiasis Control Programme, PO Box A560, Avondale, Harare, Zimbabwe. 15p.

FAO, 1991. *Trypanosomiasis control as an element of sustainable agricultural development.* Report on a meeting of the FAO panel of experts on technical and ecological aspects of the programme for the control of African animal trypanosomiasis and related development. Harare, Zimbabwe, 24–26 June 1991. Food and Agriculture Organization of the United Nations (FAO), Rome, Italy. 22p.

ILCA, 1991. *ILCA 1990: annual report and programme highlights.* International Livestock Centre for Africa (ILCA), Addis Ababa, Ethiopia. pp. 15–24.

Murray M, Trail J C M, Turner D A and Wissocq Y, 1983. *Livestock productivity and trypanotolerance.* Network Training Manual. International Livestock Centre for Africa (ILCA), Addis Ababa, Ethiopia. 198p.

World Bank, 1989. *Sub-Saharan Africa. From crisis to sustainable growth. A long-term perspective study.* World Bank, Washington, DC, USA. 300p.

Improving draft animal nutrition management through strategic supplementation in Zimbabwe

by

J Francis[1], L R Ndlovu[1] and J R Nkuuhe[2]

[1]*Department of Animal Science and* [2]*Department of Preclinical Veterinary Studies*
University of Zimbabwe, PO Box MP167, Mount Pleasant, Harare, Zimbabwe

Abstract

Four pairs of Mashona oxen (3.5 years old, average weight 328 kg (SD=35)) were used in a cross-over design to determine the effect of time of supplementary feeding on work output and concentrations of plasma lactate, pyruvate and free fatty acids in draft animals. Work consisted of pulling a mouldboard plow from 0600 to 1000 hours for four successive days. Plows were set to penetrate 13–16 cm deep into red clay soils. When not working, animals were allowed access to maize stover on arable lands. They were also fed crushed maize grain (500 g/head per day) as supplementary feed either immediately before or 12–14 hours before working. Lactate, pyruvate and free fatty acid levels in plasma, and body weight, of all oxen were monitored. Draft force, distance covered and work output of each span were recorded daily.

Ten minutes after work lactate, pyruvate and free fatty acid concentrations were, respectively, 50–350, 20–130 and 120–580% higher than pre-work levels. Accumulation of lactate during work caused fatigue, particularly in the smallest team with a mean animal weight of 290 kg. Signs of overstress (increased drooling of saliva, heavy panting, sluggish walking, reluctance to work and laying down) became evident after 2–2.5 hours of work in this team. (Such stress reactions would represent a serious problem if plowing was urgently required for timely planting.) All teams worked erratically in the last hour of work. Strategically timing the feeding of crushed maize grain failed to stop the mobilisation of free fatty acids from fat depots to fuel work. Smaller oxen lost a greater proportion of their weight than heavier ones.

Body weight of oxen strongly influenced work performance. Heavier spans outperformed lighter ones in terms of mean distance covered and work output. Daily draft forces varied slightly.

Introduction

Of all the uses of Mashona cattle in Zimbabwe's small-scale agricultural sector, manure and draft power constitute critical crop production inputs. Farmers generally consider that four oxen are needed to provide adequate draft power, and 30–40% of the 650 000–850 000 communal area households own four or more oxen (Shumba, 1984). For tillage operations, such as plowing, two or more animals are harnessed together to pull mouldboard plows. Excessively high stocking rates on communally-grazed pasture and crop residues result in low availability of feed biomass, particularly during the long dry season. Huge weight losses are therefore inevitable. The animals are made to work soon after the first rains, even though they are least fit to do so at that time.

It would be expected that supplementing these cattle with crushed maize grain would increase glucose availability during work by supplying bypass starch. This would improve the rumen ecosystem leading to increased microbial growth, and promote propionate production relative to other volatile fatty acids. Because feeding crushed maize grain is associated with low methane and heat production, the efficiency of utilisation of energy for work would be increased (Preston and Leng, 1987).

However, even with the best feeding management, heavy workloads, for example during plowing, may result in lack of coordination of the cardiovascular, pulmonary and thermoregulatory systems. Consequent onset of fatigue limits the realisation of an animal's genetic potential for work (Martin and Teleni, 1988). Thus an understanding of the physiology of working Mashona oxen will allow the formulation of improvements to existing small farmers' draft animal power systems. Selected physiological parameters were studied and are reported here.

Materials and methods

Eight fairly well-trained Mashona oxen aged three to five years, in good condition and with a mean liveweight of 328 kg (SD=35), were teamed in pairs according to weight and compatibility. They were harnessed using double withers yokes and pulled mouldboard plows set to penetrate 13–16 cm into dry red clay soils. The normal communal area practice of winter plowing for four hours a day (0600–1000 hours) in June was followed. In a cross-over design, each team worked for four successive days, then rested for 14 days before working again. A plowman worked with the same team while another individual led the animals.

Basal diet consisted chiefly of crop residues which were grazed freely by the animals when not working or penned at night. Each ox was fed 500 g of crushed maize grain (CMG) per day irrespective of its weight, immediately (Treatment 1) or 12–14 hours (Treatment 2) before work. Water was provided *ad libitum* except when the animals were working.

Blood was sampled by jugular venipuncture on the fourth day of work, 5–10 minutes before and after work. Plasma lactate, pyruvate and free fatty acids were determined as outlined in the modified methods of Noll (1974), Czok and Lamprecht (1974) and Hron and Menahan (1981), respectively.

Animals were weighed to the nearest 5 kg at 1000 hours (after work) on the first and fourth days. Distance covered and working time were recorded during work using a tape measure and stopwatch. A hydraulic dynamometer was used to monitor the force transmitted in the draft chain as the oxen worked. As the dynamometer readings varied continuously, a subjective assessment of the mean reading was made every 10 minutes and averaged each half hour.

Draft forces were then obtained using the formula of Matthews (1987):

$$Actual\ draft\ force\ (kN) = \frac{RF \times \sqrt{L^2 - (H - h)^2}}{L}$$

where
RF = Recorded draft force (kN)
H = Height of attachment to the yoke (m)
h = Load working height (m)
L = Length between the load and yoke (m)

These records were later used to calculate work done. The magnitudes of changes in lactate, pyruvate and free fatty acids were calculated for individual oxen before making comparisons between animals. Comparisons were also made between the two feeding treatments for individual teams of oxen, before comparing ox teams with each other. In this way, each ox or team acted as its own control for all parameters monitored. In-depth statistical analysis has yet to be carried out on these data. Preliminary findings only are reported in this paper.

Results

Ten minutes after completion of work, raised levels were recorded for plasma lactate (up 50–350%), pyruvate (up 20–130%) and free fatty acids (up 120–580%), as shown in Figures 1, 2 and 3. Lactate and free fatty acid concentrations were slightly higher when crushed maize grain was fed 12–14 hours before work than when it was fed immediately before work. No consistent pattern of change in pyruvate concentration was apparent under these two treatments.

Lighter oxen lost a greater proportion of their initial weights during work than heavier ones (Figure 4), but weight losses under the two feeding treatments were almost the same. All oxen regained weight during the 14-day rest period.

Draft forces varied little throughout the study. For all spans, mean daily work output was highest on the first and least on the fourth working days. Mean hourly draft performance fell from the first to the last hours of work (Figure 5). Heavier spans outperformed lighter ones.

Discussion

Pyruvate and lactate levels rose with work, showing that anaerobic pathways of energy supply operated. Singh, Nangia and Dwaraknath (1980) reported that changes in blood lactate were proportional to work done. Accumulation of lactate leads to fatigue in draft cattle (Martin and Teleni, 1988) and shows severity of workloads (Pearson and Archibald, 1989). Drooling of saliva, continuous panting, increased reluctance to work, and laying down were most marked in the lightest team (span 2, with mean animal weight of 290 kg) after 2–2.5 hours of work. Unexpected work stoppages became more frequent thereafter, which indicated that the intensity of work stress was highest in this team. It was, however, more difficult to control all work teams in the last hours of work when performance, especially by lighter members of these spans, became erratic.

The increases in plasma free fatty acid concentrations observed in this study are consistent with their increased role in energy supply to skeletal muscles during heavy exercise (Pethick, 1984).

The fact that all oxen lost weight when they worked, but managed to regain it during the 14-day rest period, implies that the oxen could not meet their high energy requirements by raising voluntary feed intake. This agrees with Soller, Reed and Butterworth (1986). It also suggests that 500 g per head of crushed maize grain, strategically fed before work, fails to provide the extra energy required for work. Lighter animals lost more weight than heavier ones, probably due to a more intense work stress which resulted in heavier mobilisation of stored body energy sources.

Mobilising reserves of glycogen or glucose to provide ready energy for work cannot be sustained

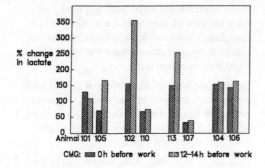

Figure 1: Percentage changes in blood lactate levels in oxen fed maize 0 or 12–14 hours before work

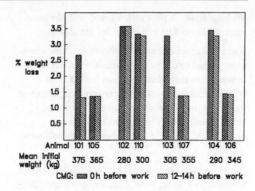

Figure 4: Percentage changes in body weight of oxen fed maize 0 or 12–14 hours before work

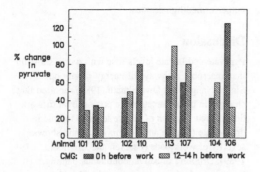

Figure 2: Percentage changes in blood pyruvate levels in oxen fed maize 0 or 12–14 hours before work

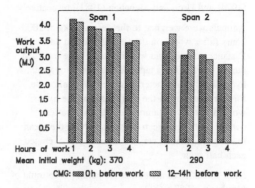

Figure 5: Mean hourly work done during four-hour period of oxen fed maize 0 or 12–14 hours before work

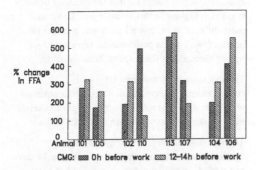

Figure 3: Percentage changes in free fatty acid levels in oxen fed maize 0 or 12–14 hours before work

for long since they are soon depleted and work performance drops (McMiken, 1983). Maybe this is why mean hourly work performance per day declined gradually in this study. Pearson (1989) also reported a decline in speed and other work performance indices due to onset of fatigue as work progressed. The results reported here show that Mashona oxen used in this study were overworked,

culminating in fatigue. Overstressing the oxen on successive days may also explain the observed continuous fall in draft output from the first to the fourth day.

Conclusion

This study has demonstrated that work animals should be rested when signs of overstress become evident. If this is not done, the rate of draft work may suffer. Strategic timing of feeding crushed maize grain to supply energy for work could not stop the animals from mobilising body fat depots. Communal area farmers should aim to have their animals in good condition before using them for plowing for protracted periods.

Acknowledgement

The authors appreciated the active support given by staff at Thornpark Estates and technical staff in the Department of Animal Science, University of Zimbabwe. The financial support and cooperation of the Rockefeller Foundation and the University of Zimbabwe Research Board are gratefully acknowledged.

References

Czok R and Lamprecht W, 1974. Pyruvate, phosphoenol pyruvate and D-glycerate-2-phosphate. p. 1446 in: Bergmeyer H-U (ed), *Methods of enzymatic analysis*. Second edition. Academic Press, London, UK

Hron W T and Menahan L A, 1981. A sensitive method for determination of FFA in plasma. *Journal of Lipid Research* 22:377–381.

Martin D and Teleni E, 1988. Fatigue in buffaloes on different workloads. *DAP Project Bulletin* 8:2–6. Draught Animal Power Project, James Cook University, Townsville, Queensland, Australia.

Matthews M D P, 1987. Measuring draught animal power of carabaos crossed with exotic buffaloes (The Philippines). *World Animal Review* 63:15–19.

McMiken D F, 1983. An energetic basis of equine performance. *Equine Veterinary Journal* 15:123.

Noll F, 1974. Lactate: determination with LDH, GPT and NAD. p. 1475 in: Bergmeyer H-U (ed), *Methods of enzymatic analysis*. Second edition. Academic Press, London, UK.

Pearson R A, 1989. A comparison of draught cattle (*Bos indicus*) and buffaloes (*Bubalus bubalis*) carting loads in hot conditions. *Animal Production* 49:355–363.

Pearson R A and Archibald R F, 1989. Biochemical and haematological changes associated with short periods of work in draught oxen. *Animal Production* 48:375–384.

Pethick D W, 1984. Energy metabolism in skeletal muscle. pp. 277–287 in: Baker S K, Gawthorne J M, MacIntosh J B and Purser D B (eds), *Ruminant physiology: concepts and consequences*. University of Western Australia, Perth, Australia.

Preston T R and Leng R A, 1987. *Matching ruminant production systems with available resources in the tropics and sub-tropics*. Penambul Books, Armidale, NSW, Australia. pp. 65–66.

Shumba E M, 1984. Animals and cropping systems in communal areas of Zimbabwe. *Zimbabwe Science News* 18:7–8.

Singh N, Nangia O P and Dwaraknath P K, 1980. Effect of exercise on biochemical constituents of blood in entire, castrated and vasectomised buffalo males. *Indian Journal of Dairy Science* 33:3.

Soller H, Reed J D and Butterworth M H, 1986. Intake and utilisation of feed by work oxen. *ILCA Newsletter* 5(2):5–7. International Livestock Centre for Africa (ILCA), Addis Ababa, Ethiopia.

Improving the management of feed resources for draft animals in Mangwende, Zimbabwe

by

S Chikura

Farming Systems Research Unit
Department of Research and Specialist Services, PO Box 8108, Causeway, Harare, Zimbabwe

Abstract

Poor body condition of draft animals at the onset of the rainy season prevents farmers from undertaking operations at optimal times. This leads to poor yields. This paper presents the results of on-farm trials in which draft cattle were supplemented during the plowing period. There were no significant differences between the weight gains of supplemented and non-supplemented animals, nor in the rate of use of the animals by farmers. This suggests that farmers are more concerned with timely land preparation than with the condition of their oxen. The farmers claimed it was important to cultivate rapidly with whatever animals were available, knowing that the animals would gain condition later in the season.

Introduction

The Farming Systems Research Unit (FSRU) of the Department of Research and Specialist Services, Zimbabwe, was established in 1984 to study communal area farming systems. One of the areas chosen for detailed study was Mangwende: with 800–1000 mm annual rainfall, this area is representative of the high potential communal areas of Zimbabwe.

Lack of adequate draft power during the time of land preparation is one of the main constraints to the farming systems in this area (FSRU, 1985; Shumba, 1985). At the onset of the rains, when draft cattle are needed for land preparation, the animals tend to be in very poor condition because during the dry season feed resources are limited and the feeds that are available—dry forage and crop residues—are of poor quality. The animals are therefore only capable of working small areas each day, so land preparation may be delayed, and resulting crop yields may be low (Scoones, 1990). Farmers may use spans of four animals, instead of just two, to reduce stress on their animals, but this effectively reduces the number of draft animals available for work.

One way of increasing draft power availability would be to improve the condition of draft cattle during land preparation. Animals in better condition should be able to work faster and for more hours each day, and could also be used in spans of two,

rather than four, thus making more teams available from the existing cattle population.

As maize stover is one of the main feeds available during the dry season, one way of improving animal condition at the end of the dry season would be to improve the management of this feed resource. Traditionally some farmers in the communal areas just leave stover in the field to be grazed *in situ* by the animals soon after harvesting (Mombeshora, Agyemang and Wilson, 1985). Other farmers collect their stover after harvesting and store it at the homesteads. However, during the late dry season, the stored stover is simply piled into the night pen (kraal) and so is available to all animals, working ones and others (GFA, 1987). Under an improved management system, the stored stover could be used to supplement working animals. A trial was therefore undertaken to investigate the possible benefits of such a system.

Materials and methods

Farmers selected for the trial owned at least two draft oxen, and were willing to harvest and store maize stover and feed it separately to their work oxen. Those farmers who were willing to harvest and store stover, but who could not do so because of labour constraints, were assisted by the researchers. Farmers were visited individually to ascertain whether their maize stover was adequate and whether they had separate feeding facilities.

Scales provided by the researchers were used to estimate the bulk of stover that was approximately equivalent to 6 kg, which was the calculated quantity for daily maintenance of each animal. The animals were fed after their release from work before they joined the rest of their herd. A block lick containing 24% crude protein and 5% urea (Rumivite Economy) was placed in the feeding stall of each ox and the animals were allowed about one hour per day to lick and feed on the crop residues. The intake of the block lick was estimated weekly by weighing. The oxen were weighed once a month for three months. The control group of animals

Table 1: Average daily liveweight changes of draft oxen and plowing performance

	Group A (no supplement)	Group B (supplemented)
Number of animals	26	26
Average daily liveweight change (kg)	+0.17	+0.20
Average plowing time per day (hours)	3.9	4.2
Duration of plowing (days)	15–21	10–22

grazed normally but had neither maize stover nor block lick. The feeding trial lasted for 90 days starting in mid-November 1984.

Results and discussion

Table 1 shows the average weight changes of the draft animals, and the average time spent plowing, during the study period of November, December and January.

Contrary to expectations, animals in both groups gained weight and there was no significant difference in the rate of gain between the supplemented and unsupplemented animals. One pair of oxen in the control group lost weight during the period, but none of the supplemented animals did so.

The figures in Table 1 for average plowing time per day do not give a clear impression; early in the plowing season animals worked up to seven hours a day, but plowing hours were much reduced as the season progressed. However, on average, neither the time spent plowing each day, nor the number of days spent plowing, differed between the groups.

There may have been differences in the area plowed per unit time, and in the total area plowed. However, it is not possible to give figures for these, because the total area plowed per household, as measured by the research staff, did not agree with the totals calculated from daily estimates recorded by the farmers. The problem may have been due to inaccurate farmer estimates of area of land worked in a given time. In any case, these differences

illustrate one of the problems of managing and recording this type of farmer-managed, on-farm trial.

The results appear to suggest that the amount of work farmers obtain from their draft oxen is not greatly influenced by the presence or absence of supplementary feeding. Informal discussions with some farmers revealed that they were mainly interested in plowing their fields as early as possible, and would do so whatever the condition of the oxen and whatever their apparent stress. Farmers knew the animals would recover later in the season, and they did not seem very concerned about the condition of their animals in the short term. It is not clear whether such attitudes would prevail in areas of lower potential or in more severe years. It is also possible that farmer attitudes would be different if animals were supplemented throughout the dry season and were in good condition at the start of the plowing season.

Acknowledgement

The author acknowledges the FSRU field teams that collected the data, P Jeranyama for help with data analysis and P G Mombeshora (Head, FSRU) and M Mudhara for correcting the draft scripts.

References

FSRU, 1985. *Annual report 1983–1984.* Farming Systems Research Unit (FSRU), Department of Research and Specialist Services, Ministry of Agriculture, Harare, Zimbabwe. pp. 33–56.

GFA, 1987. *Study on the economic and social determinants of livestock production in the communal areas of Zimbabwe.* Gesellschaft für Agrarprojekte mbH (GFA), Hamburg, Germany. pp. 79–80.

Mombeshora B, Agyemang K and Wilson R T, 1985. *Livestock ownership and management in Chivi and Mangwende communal areas of Zimbabwe.* Farming Systems Research Unit (FSRU), Department of Research and Specialist Services, Ministry of Agriculture, Harare, Zimbabwe.

Scoones I, 1990. *Livestock and the household economy: a case study from Southern Zimbabwe.* PhD Thesis. University of London, London, UK.

Shumba E M, 1985. On-farm research priorities resulting from a diagnosis of the farming systems of Mangwende, a high potential area in Zimbabwe. *Zimbabwe Agriculture Journal Special Report* 5:38–44.

Feeding crop residues for improved draft power

by

V L Prasad[1], C T Khombe[2] and P Nyathi[3]

[1] *Chief Research Officer, Makoholi Experimental Station, Private Bag 9182, Masvingo, Zimbabwe*
[2] *Research Officer, Makoholi Experimental Station, Private Bag 9182, Masvingo, Zimbabwe*
[3] *Assistant Director, Department of Research, Ministry of Agriculture, Harare, Zimbabwe*

Abstract

A short-term feeding trial was conducted to study the effect of crop residues as diet supplements for draft animals. Twenty-four 35-month-old Mashona steers (average weight 275 kg) were allocated to three feeding treatments (eight animals each). All animals were grazed during the day at a set stocking rate of one livestock unit (500 kg) to 2.5 ha and fed at night in pens. Group 1 steers received 2 kg maize stover per animal. Steers in group 2 received 1.5 kg maize stover plus 0.5 kg groundnut haulms per steer. Group 3 steers were not fed any supplement. Body weight changes at the end of a 90-day feeding period were –12.6, –5.6 and –16.9 kg for groups 1, 2 and 3, respectively. During a one-hour plowing test, the walking speed, area plowed and work done by a span of four animals were higher for the two supplemented groups than for the control group. It is concluded that regular dry season supplementation with crop residues is appropriate.

Introduction

Communal farmers in Zimbabwe keep cattle mainly for the draft power use (Shumba, 1984; Eckert and Mombeshora, 1989). The critical role of cattle as an input for crop productivity was illustrated by survey results comparing farmers who were cattle owners with those who did not own cattle (Shumba, 1985). Cattle owners were shown to have relatively larger arable holdings and better and more timely seedbed preparation and weed control than non-cattle-owners. They also applied more manure and achieved higher yields.

The five- to eight-month dry season which precedes the crop cultivation season leaves animals weak, and farmers are faced with the problem of having inadequate draft power (Mombeshora, Agyemang and Wilson, 1985; Shumba and Whingwiri, 1988). The dry season is characterised by a decline in the quality of grazing. Crude protein content of grasses declines from 15% in November and December to 3% by the end of May (Elliot, 1967). The grazing situation is exacerbated by the high density of cattle, with stocking rates of four times the recommended levels being reported in certain areas (Christensen and Zindi, 1991). The end of the dry season is the critical time of underfeeding, but also the time when animals need to be in good condition to pull the plow (Soller, Reed and Butterworth, 1986).

Most farmers feed crop residues, mostly maize and sorghum stover and groundnut haulms, to ameliorate the nutritional stress during this period (Mombeshora, Agyemang and Wilson, 1985; Sibanda, 1986). This paper reports on a study of the effect of dry season supplementation on the liveweight and draft output of steers.

Materials and methods

Twenty four 35-month-old Mashona steers (oxen) with an average weight of 275 kg were used for a period of 90 days during the late dry season of 1988. All steers were grazed during the day at a set stocking rate of one livestock unit (500 kg) to 2.5 ha. The animals were penned in three different feeding groups between 1630 and 0700 hours. Each group had eight animals.

The feeding treatments were:

○ group 1: 2 kg maize stover per steer per day
○ group 2: 1.5 kg maize stover plus 0.5 kg groundnut haulms per steer per day
○ group 3: No supplementary feeding (control).

The maize stover was milled through a 25 mm screen and the groundnut haulms were fed whole. Individual feed intake was monitored.

Starved liveweight (taken after 24 hours fasting with the last 12 hours without water) was measured at the beginning of the feeding period and after 90 days.

At the end of 90 days the animals were put to a one-hour plowing test. A uniform piece of land with granite-derived sandy soil was divided into 15 plots of 70 x 30 m. Animals from each feeding group were used in spans of four with one span per feeding group used each day. By interchanging animals within the groups, five spans per group were used. Implement draft was measured using a spring dynamometer. Five draft readings per team were taken during the first 15 minutes and five during the last 15 minutes of the test. The distance travelled and area plowed were measured using

Table 1: Liveweight changes of steers from each experimental group

	Group 1 (maize)	Group 2 (maize/groundnut)	Group 3 (control)
Initial liveweight (kg)	276 ± 20	275 ± 19	276 ± 28
Final liveweight (kg)	263 ± 21	270 ± 19	259 ± 26
Change in liveweight (kg)	−12.6 ± 9.2	−5.62 ± 4.4	−16.9 ± 7.4
Change in liveweight (g/day)	−140 ± 102	−62.4 ± 49	−188 ± 82

All figures are means ± standard deviation

Table 2: Plowing performance of spans of four steers across treatment groups

	Group 1 (maize)	Group 2 (maize/groundnut)	Group 3 (control)
Area plowed (m²)	1090 ± 16	1180 ± 210	841 ± 85
Rate of plowing (m/s)	1.18 ± 0.19	1.28 ± 0.21	0.916 ± 0.16
Distance covered (m)	2198 ± 380	3066 ± 500	1828 ± 460
Draft (N)	1465 ± 85	1480 ± 81	1400 ± 80

All figures are means ± standard deviation

tapes. From the measurements of time, distance, area and draft, the work output and power generated were calculated.

Results

The liveweight changes of steers during the 90-day feeding period are presented in Table 1. The control group lost more body weight (P<0.05) than the group supplemented with maize stover and groundnut haulms (188 versus 62 grams per day). Steers supplemented with maize stover alone lost 140 grams per day.

The area plowed in one hour was significantly (P<0.05) greater for the supplemented groups than for the control group (Table 2). Similarly steers from groups 1 and 2 plowed faster and covered a greater distance (P<0.05) than steers from the control group. Across groups, the recorded draft was approximately 14% of liveweight and did not differ significantly (P>0.05) between treatments. Figure 1 shows the calculated work and power outputs per span of the three groups of steers.

Discussion

The results seem to support the general proposition that feeding crop residues may improve the draft power output in communal areas. However, the data obtained in the present study should be treated with some caution as the experimental animals were only subjected to a one-hour test. The main difference between the groups was the speed of walking, and

this is reflected in the calculated work and power outputs, which were higher for the supplemented animals. The differences may have been due to the feeding regimes, but the effect of the operators on animal speed and implement draft cannot be ruled out.

In the present study the supplementation was restricted to 2 kg per steer because it is unlikely that communal farmers would be able to feed more than that amount. Feeding a limited amount of crop residues throughout the dry season seems to be a more sound nutritional proposition than feeding a large amount in the late dry season. The efficiency of utilisation of low quality feeds (such as crop residues) is higher for maintaining a particular liveweight than for growth (Pearson, 1986).

Further comparative studies on supplemented animals, with more comprehensive traction tests, are underway.

Figure 1: Work and power output of experimental teams

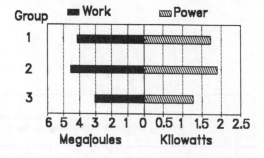

References

Christensen C and Zindi C, 1991. *Patterns of livestock ownership and distribution in Zimbabwe's communal areas.* Working Paper 4/91. Department of Agricultural Economics and Extension, University of Zimbabwe, Harare, Zimbabwe. pp 4–6.

Eckert M V and Mombeshora B, 1989. Farmer objectives and livestock functions. pp. 213–252 in: Cousins B (ed), *People, land and livestock.* Proceedings of a workshop on the socio-economic dimensions of livestock production in communal lands of Zimbabwe, held 12–14 September 1988, Masvingo, Zimbabwe. Centre for Applied Social Science, Harare, Zimbabwe.

Elliot H C, 1967. Voluntary intake of low protein diets by ruminants: intake of food by cattle. *Journal of Agricultural Science, Cambridge* 69:375–383.

Mombeshora B, Agyemang K and Wilson R T, 1985. *Livestock ownership and management in Chibi and Mangwande communal areas of Zimbabwe.* Small Ruminant and Camel Group Document 2. International Livestock Centre For Africa (ILCA), Addis Ababa, Ethiopia. 14p.

Pearson A. 1986, Feeding and management of draught animals. *Indian Journal of Animal Production* 2:48–69.

Shumba E M, 1984. Animals and croping system in communal areas of Zimbabwe. *Zimbabwe Science News* 18:7–8.

Shumba E M, 1985. On-farm research priorities resulting from a diagnosis of the farming systems in Mangwande, a high potential area in Zimbabwe. *Zimbabwe Agricultural Journal* 5:38–59.

Shumba E M and Whingwiri E E, 1988. Prospects for increased livestock production in communal areas: an agronomist's perspective. pp. 134–138 in: McLaren G G (ed), *Committee for on-farm research and extension.* Proceedings of a workshop on livestock research and extension for communal area farming systems held 16–18 February 1988 at Henderson Research Station, Mazowe, Zimbabwe. Ministry of Lands, Agriculture and Rural Resettlement, Harare, Zimbabwe.

Sibanda S, 1986. The use of crop residues in livestock production systems in the communal areas of Zimbabwe. pp. 140–144 in: Preston T R and Nuwanyakpa M Y (eds), *Towards optimal feeding of agricultural byproducts to livestock in Africa.* Proceedings of a workshop held at University of Alexandria, Egypt, October 1985. African Research Network for Agricultural Byproducts (ARNAB). International Livestock Centre for Africa (ILCA), Addis Ababa, Ethiopia.

Soller H, Reed J D and Butterworth H M, 1986. Intake and utilisation of feed by work oxen. *ILCA Newsletter* 5(2):5. International Livestock Centre for Africa (ILCA), Addis Ababa, Ethiopia.

Photograph opposite
Weeding maize with oxen at Magoye, Zambia, during the ATNESA workshop field visits

Photo: Lotta Sylwander

Animal-powered tillage and weeding technology

Improving animal-powered tillage systems and weeding technology

by

Piet A Stevens

Agricultural Engineer, Palabana Animal Draft Power Research and Development Programme
c/o Royal Netherlands Embassy, PO Box 31905, Lusaka, Zambia *

Abstract

Tillage is discussed in relation to soil erosion and water management. Conservation tillage, primarily aimed at improving soil structure and organic matter content, is unlikely to be a practical answer for most smallholder farmers in Africa. In order to become successful, improved tillage systems should address the problems of farmers' direct labour capacity and of soil degradation at the same time. Alternatives to plowing are reviewed. The potential of ridging is highlighted and some practical aspects discussed. Ridging should be encouraged on fairly even land in subhumid areas and on heavy soils in semi-arid areas. Ties between ridges should be recommended. Ripping has great potential on sandy soils in semi-arid areas. However, further adaptive research is still required to investigate the practical implications of both ridging and ripping and to see how they can be tuned to farmer needs and preferences. Weed control will be a major bottleneck, but the specific management problems of preventing the risk of increased erosion and run-off should also be given attention. Although weeding remains a major problem on farms, labour-saving solutions do exist and further research is not a primary requirement at present. Farmers should be given access to information about weeding using animal traction, and to appropriate implements. Different existing weeding techniques are considered. In particular, weeding methods that reduce the need for additional hand labour should be promoted. The availability and quality of most weeding implements must be improved.

Introduction

The three major factors that influence crop production are soil condition, climate (rainfall) and farmers' skills (management). Because tillage influences yield only indirectly (Vogel, 1991), it is difficult to improve yields by tilling the soil in a different ("improved") way (Palabana, 1991). This is not serious, since improved tillage serves other immediate objectives: it alters soil conditions and affects farm management requirements.

Improving tillage can mean the introduction of draft animals where only hand labour was used before. In

___
* A subsequent address of the programme (formerly the Animal Draught Power Research and Development Project) is P/Bag 173, Woodlands, Lusaka, Zambia

many cases, however, it refers to finding suitable alternatives for conventional plowing, or it means diversification and intensification of tillage practices.

Improving weed control within the context of animal traction generally implies using animal-drawn weeding implements instead of a hand hoe. Reducing weed infestations plays a role in farmers' decisions almost the whole year round, starting with land preparation.

A number of topics on the above themes are dealt with in this paper. They are only a few, but the predominant, facets of the problem of improving smallholder farming under different conditions using animal traction technology. The information and views presented here are based partly on personal experience in Zambia, Zimbabwe, Niger and Indonesia, and very much on the experience of others working on the same problems. The topics covered are:

o tillage and conservation
o ridging and tie-ridging systems
o tine tillage and ripping
o comparison of weed control methods and implements.

Tillage and conservation

According to Lal (1988), widespread soil degradation is an important factor responsible for the continuing food shortage in sub-Saharan Africa. People try to escape the degradation of their fields by extending them, or by moving to nearby fields, and finally by migrating to other areas, leaving behind land unsuitable for cultivation, thus creating more pressure on the land still available, and spreading the problem (Stocking, 1988).

Soil degradation is an extremely complex problem, of which soil erosion is a major part. Soil tillage plays a vital role in the analysis of its causes and the formulation of solutions. Sheet erosion, caused by raindrop impact on bare soil, is the root of all erosion (Elwell, 1986). Tillage techniques for improved soil and water management are helpless against rill and gully erosion once started, but are aimed at counteracting sheet erosion, and hence at preventing the advancement of those two more visible and devastating offspring of sheet erosion.

Soil structure and organic matter

Reduced tillage, minimum tillage, zero tillage, mulch or residue farming and conservation tillage are all different techniques but with the same aim—to provide better control of soil erosion and water and nutrient run-off than the so-called conventional techniques of plowing and harrowing. This is best indicated by the word *conservation*; soil, water and nutrients must be maintained to secure agricultural production. The other terms imply that less tillage is a prerequisite for this; seedbed preparation and weed control should take place with less energy being applied to the soil. A key element is soil structure, which is believed to be generally poor after years of cultivation. Conventional mouldboard plowing is a technique imported from European temperate zones, where its damaging impact is much less profound than in tropical hot and dry climates, unless irrigation is applied (Elwell, 1989). However, by considerably reducing the soil disturbing actions of tillage operations, the soil structure would rejuvenate to pre-cultivation levels. Tillage loosens the soil, but only temporarily: ultimately it leads to more compact soils (Foth, 1984). However, restoring or maintaining a good soil structure under minimal tillage can take place only if the organic matter content of the soil increases considerably.

Conservation tillage

Vowles (1989) defines conservation tillage as any tillage practice which leaves at least a 30% crop residue cover on the soil surface after planting. The crop residues serve two main purposes: to build up organic content in the soil, and to protect the soil surface from erosion, run-off and extreme temperatures. The resulting intensive biological activity has a loosening action on the soil, and this replaces tillage.

Conservation tillage is currently receiving a lot of attention in Zimbabwe within the commercial farming community, initially probably more because of the reduced tractor running costs and time-saving in land preparation than because of reduced soil erosion and the long-term effect of improved soil structure. Oldreive (1989), a large-scale farmer in Zimbabwe who practises conservation tillage with great success, is convinced of its potential for smallholder farmers also, depending on the availability of animal draft power and hand labour. However, most African smallholder farmers live in remote areas characterised by poor soils and climatic conditions, high population pressure and poverty. One major problem is that often not enough crop residues are available to serve as soil cover and to improve soil condition; the little that are produced are required for many other purposes. Another problem is that conservation tillage is not without risk; if it is not properly managed, weeds, pests and diseases become insurmountable problems. Large-scale commercial farmers in the USA, who have been applying conservation tillage techniques successfully for decades, use herbicides and other chemicals to overcome these problems, but such a solution is generally not available to small-scale farmers in Africa: although economic analyses show the profitability of herbicides (eg, Tembo, 1989), these inputs are usually too costly.

Farmers' goals

The primary goal of improvements in agriculture is increased production—higher outputs. The conservation approach, however, focuses on economising on inputs, with the aim of helping to make production levels sustainable rather than maximal. The scarcity of all the factors involved in the production system is emphasised.

In this sense, conservation tillage techniques can help smallholder farmers who have access to animal traction to overcome some of their most urgent problems. A major goal of farmers is to increase labour productivity at maintained or increased production levels (in weight and money terms). Farmers want to increase production, but if they have to rely on hand labour for land preparation, and especially weeding, they can only cultivate a limited area. Sensible use of oxen, donkeys or cows, or even camels, with suitable implements, provides them with the potential for increasing their labour capacity. Hence they can extend their cropped area, intensify soil and crop management, achieve timely planting and fast weeding, and grow more cash crops. Although most farmers recognise the general problem of erosion and water loss in the many areas where this occurs, and acknowledge the fact that this affects their farm as well, the labour capacity problem is more urgent to them. Stocking (1988) goes further by stating that: "Soil conservation and the prevention of land degradation are never seen as ends in themselves by farmers". If improved tillage systems are to be successful in the long term, they should address both the labour capacity problem and the erosion problem at the same time.

Plowing

Plowing is, for good reasons, still the tillage practice that is most recommended. Indeed, in many areas the plow is the only implement available to farmers who use draft animals. Where other implements are available, these are generally of secondary importance.

The essential feature of plowing is that soil inversion is carried out over the whole surface. Plowing must be deep enough to achieve this—in Zimbabwe the recommended depth is 20–25 cm (Smith, 1989)—and so the operation is quite an intensive soil treatment, in terms of both time and energy.

Plowing normally takes place at the beginning of the season, at a time when draft animals are not in their best condition (they have been weakened by the dry season and often require some retraining). Farmers need to plant as early as possible, but in many years too little rain, or even drought, at the beginning of the season delays land preparation. Many farmers have to hire or borrow draft animals, and so have to wait until the owners of the animals have finished their own work. Probably, in view of the time constraint, farmers tend to plow too wide, with the result that stretches of the soil surface between the furrow lines are not worked at all, but are covered only with some soil sliding off the mouldboard. Shallow plowing, which some farmers have to resort to as a way to offset the problem of draft power shortage, restricts water infiltration and is likely to induce run-off and soil loss (Norton, 1987). The Animal Draft Power Research and Development Programme in Zambia has demonstrated that "proper" plowing—plowing with a well-set and maintained or new plow (rather than a worn one)—results in greater plowing depth and cutting width, and leads to higher crop yields and fewer weeds (Meijer, Chanda and Hoogmoed, 1990). Still, for many farmers "proper" plowing seems to be unnecessary or even inappropriate. Besides, there are better options.

Ridging and tie-ridging

Ridging results in better soil and water management than plowing. Ridging determines the slope along which water can run off. Thus ridging can effectively reduce the slope of a field, from, say, 4% (the actual slope of the field) to, say, 1% (the slope of the ridges and furrows). With correct ridging that reduces the effective slope, water cannot run down the field at a high and destructive speed. Excess water should be able to flow away through the furrows. If the ridges are laid out exactly along the contour, during heavy storms water will fill up the furrows. It will then spill over the ridges and run straight down the hill, making rills or small gullies

on its way and thereby increasing the streaming water mass. This would be a more devastating situation than run-off on flatly plowed fields where water continuously and evenly spread over the surface can flow in a more gentle manner, a situation, however, that is prone to sheet erosion.

For Zimbabwe, Gotora (1991) advises that ridges be laid out on fairly even land and at a maximum slope of 1%. Ridges should not be laid out on stony fields or fields with many rock outcrops or termite heaps; and uneven land resulting from rill erosion or bad plowing should be smoothed (Elwell and Norton, 1988). Laying out ridges is a complicated task, especially on fields with steep slopes or slopes in more than one direction. Meijer (1992) warns of the danger of increased erosion under these circumstances. The risk of run-off from higher land must be taken into account when planning to ridge a field. Even if ridges are properly designed, severe erosion can result if they are not adequately maintained (Unger, 1984). During the season, ridges should be rebuilt when necessary, particularly after heavy storms, to bring washed-away soil back onto the ridges. This operation also helps to control weeds.

Cross-ties keep the water in small pools so that it can slowly infiltrate the soil and become available to the crop. They are therefore very useful in dry areas and during dry spells in more humid areas. Gotora (1991) suggests that ties be constructed only half to two-thirds as high as the ridges, so that water will flow over the ties and remain in the furrow instead of streaming over the ridges and running downhill. Under very wet conditions, or when the soil profile is saturated, ties should not be constructed, or should be broken down (Elwell and Norton, 1988) if the water itself has not already washed them away (Gotora, 1991).

Tie-ridging

In the USA, tie-ridging as a water conservation method for subhumid and semi-arid areas appears not to reduce crop yields in wet years, and probably leads to increased yields in dry years, if properly applied (Harris and Krishna, 1989). Considerable increases in cereal yields from ridging and tie-ridging have been reported from research in Burkina Faso and Mali (van der Ploeg and Reddy, 1988).

In Niger, van der Ploeg and Reddy (1988) studied the effects of ridging and tie-ridging as water conservation techniques for sorghum on clay soils, compared to flat cultivation. Usually these soils are plowed late, after the millet has already been planted on the upland sandy fields. Labour is

Table 1: Comparison of tillage systems for sorghum on clay soils in Kolo, Niger

Tillage system	Grain yield (t/ha)			Stover yield (t/ha)		
	1985	1986	1987	1985	1986	1987
Flat	1.0	0.5	0.4	5.3	2.1	3.4
Ridged	1.2	0.7	0.7	5.3	2.8	5.2
Tie-ridged	1.6	0.8	0.7	7.1	3.3	5.7

Source: van der Ploeg and Reddy (1988)

somewhat less of a limiting factor at that time, although weeding of the upland crops may demand attention then. Table 1 shows harvest results for Kolo, in the valley of the Niger near Niamey. Ridging increased yields considerably compared to flat cultivation (plowing): on plots where ties were made, yields were even higher. Straw production is very important in a country where biomass is a scarce product; it is used for animal feed during the long dry season, as building material or fuel, or for making mats.

Table 2 illustrates the beneficial effect of establishing the ridges before planting instead of afterwards during weeding (which is the normal farming practice); seed germinated more vigorously, and plants grew higher and bigger and produced more grain and stover. A probable reason is that the plants can develop a bigger root system, which makes the crop less vulnerable in dry spells, reduces seepage losses (van der Ploeg and Reddy, 1988), and is favourable for good soil structure and fertility. However, it was expected that farmers would have a major problem with establishing the ridges and the ties during land preparation, in view of the weakness of the draft animals at the beginning of the season, and because of the limited labour available (van der Ploeg and Reddy, 1988). This does not necessarily imply that farmers do not already know the advantages of ridging before planting: it is very likely that most farmers are just not in a position to adopt the "best" system, because of time constraints and lack of available farm power. The benefits of that "best system" are apparently not big enough to persuade farmers to take a risk.

Vogel (1991) reported rapid water percolation below root depth on coarse-grained soils in unsaturated conditions, which destroyed the water harvesting effect. On the other hand, ridging prevented crops planted on the ridges from becoming waterlogged in more humid areas: this is also important in dry areas for crops, such as millet, that are very sensitive to waterlogging and suffer after only a short time (some days). Ridging to control temporary excess of water in the field is a traditional technique known to farmers; loose (and comparatively fertile) topsoil is brought together in ridges on undisturbed strips of soil by hand hoe, thus combining better water management with relatively fast land preparation (Meijer, 1992). When the move to animal traction is made the plow and flat cultivation take over. However, later in the season (when the soil becomes saturated) many farmers use their plow, or a ridger, to earth-up the crop rows and weed at the same time. Apparently, making ridges after plowing but before planting is not always practical; it requires extra time in a period in which no time should be lost for planting. Recently-plowed soil can still cope with the rains at the beginning of the season.

From point of view of erosion control, and in order to catch more water for the crop so that it is better able to withstand dry spells, (tied) ridges should be laid out at the start of the season. Two approaches to facilitate this are being reviewed: direct ridging, as is being studied by the Animal Draft Power Research and Development Programme in Zambia; and the so-called "no-till tie-ridging" system developed by the Institute of Agricultural Engineering in Zimbabwe.

Table 2: Comparison of establishing ridges before and after planting sorghum on clay soils in Niger

	Germination (plants/m^2)	Plant height (cm)	Plant weight (g)	Grain yield (t/ha)
Ridging before planting	27	11	0.5	0.8
Ridging after planting	15	4	0.2	0.5

Source: van der Ploeg and Reddy (1988)

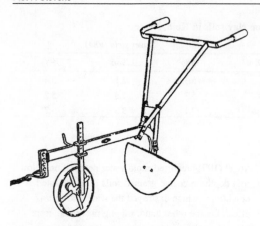

Figure 1: A simple ridge-tier

"No-till tie-ridging"

"No-till tie-ridging" aims to combine the advantages of minimum tillage and tie-ridging in one system that is practical for farmers. It is a permanent or semi-permanent system of ridges.

In the first year of construction of the ridges, good plowing is recommended to produce enough loose soil to build large ridges—about 25 cm high before consolidation (Gotora, 1991). Plowing is probably good also because it keeps weeds under control from the beginning, thus enabling a good start for the system. Ridging is done with a mouldboard plow, and great care is taken to set out the first "master" ridge at an acceptable slope. Ties are made with a hand hoe or a simple ridge-tier made out of scrap material; this consists of a mouldboard or a (half) disc of a disc harrow or plow fitted on an implement frame (Figure 1) or a wooden pole. Planting is done on top of the ridges, as early as possible, but only when the ridges are wet throughout (Elwell and Norton, 1988). Earthing-up during the season, and supplementary weeding (additional to hand weeding) on the top of the ridges, are done with the plow.

In subsequent years the ridges of the previous season are merely re-ridged for the next season (thus the system is actually "reduced till" rather than "no-till"). It is also foreseen that in "no-till tie-ridging" the land should be plowed afresh once every few years (for example, to incorporate manure or to loosen the soil). The length of the tillage cycle is not yet known, but will probably be at least four years for sandy soils and more than 10 years for clay soils. As a result the system as a whole would require less time and energy input than annual plowing (Elwell and Norton, 1988).

It is claimed that if the ties are properly put in and maintained, soil losses will decrease to less than 2 t/ha per year (from 50–100 t/ha per year under conventional tillage) and that run-off losses will drop from 30–40% of the seasonal rainfall to 10%, with minimal nutrient losses (Elwell and Norton, 1988). Vogel (1991) suggests that 5 t/ha per year is the critical level of acceptable soil erosion.

On-station results from three years of "no-till tie-ridging" in Zimbabwe, in a subhumid region (Harare) and a semi-arid region (Masvingo), are shown in Table 3. Vogel (1991) recommends tie-ridging as a most promising technique for the higher rainfall areas of Zimbabwe, because of the consistently good yields resulting from improved protection against waterlogging in combination with little soil loss. This is consistent with findings from on-farm trials in different agro-ecological zones in Zimbabwe (Stevens, 1989). The poor yields for "no-till tie-ridging" in the much drier area of Masvingo are attributed to drought in combination with inadequate management (planting when ridges are not yet moist enough, untimely first weeding) which leads to poor emergence on the still dry ridges (Vogel, 1991). Complementary to the on-station trials, adaptive on-farm trials have been established in Zimbabwean Communal Areas from 1989/90 onwards (Gotora, 1991); conclusive results from these trials are not yet available.

Table 3: Comparison of tillage systems for maize on sandy soils in Zimbabwe

	Subhumid zone			Semi-arid zone		
	1988/89	1989/90	1990/91	1988/89	1989/90	1990/91
Grain yield (t/ha)						
Conventional tillage	3.8	2.8	3.1	2.8	6.5	1.9
"No-till tie-ridging"	5.0	4.6	4.6	2.3	5.4	1.0
Sheet erosion (t/ha)						
Conventional tillage	1.7	9.5	1.1	0.7	1.3	5.7
"No-till tie-ridging"	0.2	2.2	0.3	n/a	0.1	0.1

Source: Vogel (1991)

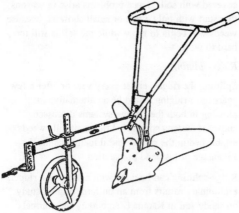

Figure 2: West African type of ridger (made by Lenco, Lusaka)

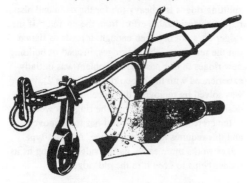

Figure 3: "Safim-type" ridger

Direct ridging

The Animal Draft Power Research and Development Programme in Magoye, Zambia, has been studying direct ridging since 1988 (Meijer, 1992). An animal-drawn ridger is used to make ridges at the beginning of the season without any prior tillage operation. Among the ridgers used was one manufactured in Lusaka by Lenco, which was based on a design that is widely used in francophone West Africa (Figure 2). Once installed, the ridges are re-ridged at the beginning of subsequent seasons. Meijer (1992) reports time savings of more than 50% as compared to plowing, and 70% when compared to ridging after plowing, while draft force requirements on moist sandy loam were found to be comparable (slightly lower) to those for plowing. However, ridges on direct-ridged plots tend to be smaller than those made on plowed plots.

Draft force requirement and ridge size vary with the type of ridger used. The most common ridgers in eastern and southern Africa are commonly known as the "Safim-type" (Figure 3). Although various manufacturers make these ridgers and they differ in

various ways, they are all similar to the ridgers that used to be made by the Safim company of South Africa. In most parts of the region, Safim-type ridgers are the only ones available. They are big, heavy implements with large triangular shares, rudders and long curved wings that can turn inward and outward on hinges. Their draft force requirement is generally high and they are heavy to operate. Production of this rather complicated design is often of low quality resulting in ridgers which may be difficult to control and adjust. Unlike the ridger used in francophone West Africa, the Safim-type ridger consists of many bits and pieces. Its frog which holds the soil working parts is moulded and tends to break if it hits a stump. Because of its high draft force requirement it is considered unsuitable for direct ridging. In tests at the Institute of Agricultural Engineering in Harare Safim-type ridgers were rejected (because of their high draft force requirement) in favour of locally-made prototypes based on the West African design (Chatizwa, Nazare and Norton, 1988; Chatizwa and Norton, 1989). However, attempts to interest local manufacturers in producing these have so far been unsuccessful.

In a three year on-station trial at Magoye Regional Research Station, Zambia (Meijer, 1992), higher weed pressure and greater soil compaction in the ridges of directly-ridged plots became apparent in the third year; crop development was clearly impeded and yields (of cotton) were only two-thirds of those on plowed and ridged plots. These observations led to the rather radical assumption that annual re-ridging should not be recommended; it would instead be better to alternate each year of direct ridging with a year of plowing. The advantages of ridging as a primary tillage method would then apply only half of the time. A practical objection (from a farmer's point of view) to alternating ridging and plowing every year could be the more difficult plowing of the undulating fields that were ridged during the previous year. Consequently, farmers might consider it better to forget about ridging altogether, and to continue annual plowing.

"No-till tie-ridging" versus direct ridging

One essential difference between "no-till tie-ridging" and direct ridging occurs in the first year. The extra effort required for the initial plowing in the first year of "no-till tie-ridging" will certainly discourage farmers. Another important difference is the much greater care needed in the "no-till tie-ridging" system to lay out the ridges properly, in view of potential erosion hazards. Originally, "no-till tie-ridging" was supposed to be an extension to the "contour layout". This consists of grass waterways, storm drains and contour ridges to protect arable land from rill and gully erosion and is a very common feature in the better farming areas of Zimbabwe. The new ridging system should take care of the sheet erosion that hitherto could not be controlled (Elwell and Norton, 1988). This scrupulous concern for land protection is understandable: "no-till tie-ridging" is developed in a country with much sloping land and a grave erosion problem. Genuine soil conservationists in Zimbabwe even regard the "no-till tie-ridging" system merely as a practical compromise for smallholder farmers without enough crop residues to practise true conservation tillage (Elwell and Norton, 1988). Two other, but not crucial, differences between "no-till tie-ridging" and direct ridging are the use of a plow instead of a ridger, and the making of ties; both features could easily be interchanged between the systems without changing them basically. Making ridge-ties should be seen as an extra operation to improve any ridging system.

The obvious advantage of using a plow for (re-)ridging is that (apart from a simple ridge-tier) only one implement, the most common one, is required; it is assumed that a plow will remain indispensable on the farm, even when a ridger is available. Another practical advantage is that farmers only need a plow yoke, and not a second, longer (weeding) yoke for making and weeding ridges with a ridger; a span of oxen on a long yoke is relatively difficult to handle. However, plowing is not nearly as fast as ridging.

Re-ridging

Elwell and Norton (1988) envisage that soil structure will be improved as a result of the slight soil disturbance of re-ridging, although the results from the Magoye trial (Meijer, 1992) seem to contradict this. Re-ridging in subsequent years may not destroy (cover) weeds on the sides and tops of the ridges satisfactorily, as experienced in Magoye while using a ridger (Meijer, 1992). A plow brings more soil onto the ridge, but if it is not properly set it can easily cut away part of the ridge base. In general, more care must be taken than in annual plowing to keep weeds under control, also during the late season and even after harvest. It is very important that weeds are prevented from producing seed; occasional hand pulling of the biggest weeds should be an effective means of ensuring this. Timely ridging at the beginning of the season is vital; in particular, weeds in the future crop lines must not be so high that they cannot be fully

covered with soil. Hence problems arise in seasons that start with only a few or small showers, because weeds will begin to grow while the soil is still too hard to work.

Ridge-splitting

Splitting the ridges, either every year or after a few years of re-ridging, could be an alternative to plowing in both the ridging systems discussed above; it loosens compacted ridges, it kills weeds established in the ridges, and it maintains the advantage of fast land preparation.

Ridge-splitting can be done with a plow or a ridger. Preliminary results from an on-farm ridging study on sandy soil in Kaoma (Zambia) by the Animal Draft Power Research and Development Programme indicate that, with the ridgers currently available, splitting ridges is a heavy job for the oxen and also requires considerable effort from the operator. If the ridger does not dig deep enough, it tends to flatten out the remains of the old ridges, instead of building new ridges in one pass. This problem was initially experienced with the Lenco ridger (Figure 2), but was solved by removing the wheel to reach the desired working depth. When the ridger is working at the correct depth a lot of soil has to be moved and this requires a high draft force. A Safim-type ridger works more easily during ridge-splitting as its rudder helps to keep it in the old ridge.

Ridge-splitting must be done with a plow yoke. One ox is forced to walk in a furrow in which a new half ridge has already been built during the foregoing pass.

Ridging and planting

Planting on ridged land requires different techniques to planting on flat, plowed land.

Several planting methods are available for plowed land, and the farmer can choose the one most appropriate to the crop and to the time and labour available. A very common method is planting behind the plow, whereby seeds are dropped by hand in a furrow and covered with soil by the next pass of the plow. This method is only as fast as the plowing itself, but planting can begin as soon as the land is ready for plowing. A much faster method, but one that can begin only when plowing is completed, is hand planting into a small furrow made with a plow or ripper. Seed placement is more regular and not necessarily as deep as with planting behind the plow. Broadcasting seed, followed by harrowing, can be used with small-grained crops like millet. Planting in regular lines marked out with a rope is a time-consuming process. Some farmers, particularly those with a considerable area of cash

Figure 4: Cross-section of ridges with sharp crest (left) and flat crown.

crops, use a planter. The most common planter, and probably the only available one in most countries in eastern and southern Africa, is the "Safim-type" planter, with either chain or Pitman drive.

A method similar to planting behind the plow can be used on land that is being ridged; seeds are placed on the first half of the ridge and covered with soil when the ridge is finished at the second pass. This method, although fast, is not recommended because seed placement is too deep and irregular, and seeds may fall from the ridges. A planter suitable for planting on ridges does exist, but is not available in the region (Bordet, 1988). The Institute of Agricultural Engineering in Harare is studying the use of an animal-drawn tine to open a plant line on top of the ridges.

The method generally recommended for planting on ridges is to hand plant in holes made using a hoe or a stick, and then to close the hole and cover the seed using the feet. This method is labour-intensive and therefore might mitigate against the acceptance of ridging as a land-preparation system. A variation of this method, but one which avoids the need to make holes by hand, involves changing the way in which the ridges are constructed. If, during the second pass of the ridger, the implement is kept a little further away from the first half ridge, then it will gently deposit soil against the side of the first half ridge, rather than push soil partly over it. The result will be a massive, strong ridge with a broad base and a flat crown instead of a sharp crest (see Figure 4). Hand planting can then take place immediately; seeds can be dropped in the small depression on top of the ridge and covered by the action of walking over it. Experience with this planting system for millet (on-station) and cowpeas was gained in Niger

with direct ridging on sandy soil after the first shower (15–20 mm) had moistened the soil enough for planting (Stevens, 1988). Planting cowpeas on ridges using this method was found to be faster than traditional planting in hand-made holes on flat land (Table 4).

The crop is normally planted on top of the ridge, to prevent it from becoming waterlogged and to permit mechanised weeding. In the dry south of Zimbabwe, ridging for water harvesting is being studied on Vertisols in Chiredzi with different crops planted in the furrow bottom; crop growth and yields are significantly higher than for crops on flat land, but weeding is a major problem (Jones, 1990).

Tine tillage and ripping

Tined implements such as cultivators (Figures 5–9) can be used as primary tillage implements on light soils to loosen the soil with little turning or incorporation of surface residues.

In dry areas with sandy soils, on which a crust forms after showers, a shallow cultivation to break the crust enhances water infiltration considerably, and can result in increased crop yields (Stevens, 1988). The disadvantage of full-surface cultivation, however, is that draft force requirements are likely to be high under relatively dry soil conditions, while in moist conditions too fine a tilth may be obtained, hence increasing the risk of water and wind erosion and accelerated formation of a new crust. Furthermore, multi-tined implements tend to sweep surface residues off the field when these get stuck between the tines and the tines are then unable to penetrate very deeply. Besides, quite strong and durable cultivators are required, with rigid tines that are well fixed to the frame.

Ripping is working the soil in a narrow strip. It requires relatively low draft force. Implements used should combine strength and durability with simplicity, ease of operation and low production costs (Figure 10). Rippers can be used for opening a line in which to hand-plant directly afterwards.

Table 4: Labour requirements for direct ridging plus hand planting and traditional hand planting on flat untilled land for cowpeas on sandy soil in Niger

Operation	Direct ridging and planting (hours/ha)	Traditional planting on untilled land (hours/ha)
Ridging (4 hour/ha for a team with 2 operators)	8	n/a
Making holes with planting hoe	n/a	9
Hand planting	9	12
Total	17	21

Source: Stevens (1988)

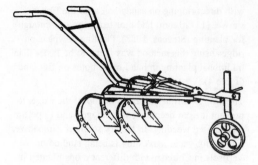

Figure 5: Houe Manga *cultivator*

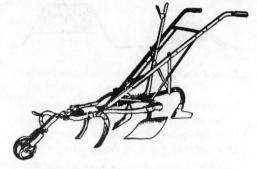

Figure 8: Adjustable cultivator with hiller blades

Figure 6: Adjustable cultivator with chisel tines

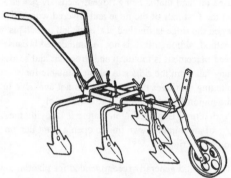

Figure 9: Cultivator on multipurpose toolbar

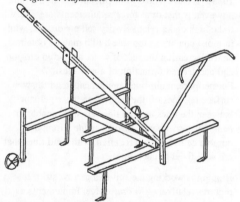

Figure 7: Mbeya Oxenization Project over-the-row cultivator (Source: Shetto and Kwiligwa, 1989)

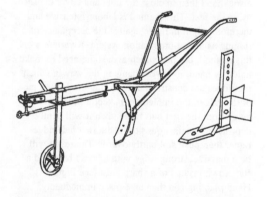

Figure 10: Plow beam fitted with ripper tine (left) and Konni ripper tine (Source: Kruit, 1991)

Ripping enhances water infiltration and favours crop growth and yield compared with direct planting on untilled land (Stevens, 1988). It is a good technique to bring degraded and abandoned fields back into cultivation (Kruit, 1991). It is fast and does not delay planting, compared with hand planting in untilled land (Stevens, 1988). It even enables earlier planting than can be obtained with plowing.

A big disadvantage of ripping is the poor weed control between crop lines at the beginning of the season. A cultivator could control early weeds, but the soil may still be too hard. The weed problem is less serious in more arid areas where weeds cannot grow abundantly because of drought. Another disadvantage is the increased risk of soil erosion by water on sloping land, especially on crust forming soils. In Zimbabwe, ripping is recommended only on fields having a good mulch cover. However, in the semi-arid area near Masvingo, Vogel (1991) reported that sheet erosion losses on ripped plots without mulch were only moderate (less than the critical level of 5 t/ha), while yields were slightly higher than on tied-ridged plots but slightly lower than on plowed plots. In more humid areas ripping should only be applied on soil protected by mulch. During wet periods, low soil temperature and poorer aeration may stunt crop growth. Ripping is not recommended on heavier soils because of water infiltration and weed problems.

Comparison of weed control methods

Shortage of labour capacity

Most farmers weed by hand, using a variety of well-developed traditional hand hoes (Raulin, 1984). Weeding is widely recognised as a serious bottleneck in crop production: in many cases the farm labour available for weeding determines the final area that can be harvested. It is quite common for the workforce to be unable to cope with the weeds on all the fields, so parts of the crops become overgrown and have to be written off: even on fields that have not been abandoned, yields are considerably reduced by inadequate weeding. In a literature review on weeding research, Shetto and Kwiligwa (1989) describe the decisive impact that proper weed control has on crop yields and total production. The answer to the weeding problem of many households in an increase in labour capacity, which can be provided by draft animals.

Weeding with animal traction

All too often the development of animal traction technology in an area seems to halt after plows and carts have been introduced. Animals are rarely used for weeding in Africa, even in areas where plowing has been practised for generations. Planters and weeding implements are used in some areas, but sales of such implements are only a fraction of those of plows. Several factors may account for this low interest in planters and weeders. Perhaps development programmes have given too much emphasis to plowing. Perhaps it is the men in farming households who generally take major decisions but they themselves are not very involved in weeding operations. Perhaps it is just too costly to invest in more than one implement. Probably the answer is a combination of such factors. Nevertheless, draft animals do provide a clear opportunity to alleviate the problem of labour shortage for weeding.

One study of maize weeding in the southern highlands of Tanzania compared different weed control systems involving combinations of hand labour and animal draft power (Kwiligwa, Shetto and Rees, 1994). Table 5 highlights the main results of this study. The labour requirement for weeding was reduced tremendously when weeding was

Table 5: Comparison of weeding systems for maize in the southern highlands of Tanzania, 1989/90

Weeding system	Weed dry weight 70 days after planting (t/ha)	Maize yield gain[1] (t/ha)	Weeding labour input (hours/ha)	Weeding labour productivity (kg/hour)	Variable weeding costs[2] (TSh/ha)	Overall net profit[3] (TSh/ha)
1 Hand} 2 Hand} = farmers' practice 3 None}	6.4	3.1	184	17	22 000	31 000
1 Hand} 2 Hand} = recommended practice 3 Hand}	3.8	3.5	227	15	32 000	25 000
1 Cultivator 2 Cultivator 3 Ridger	8.7	1.4	42	33	9 000	26 000
1 Cultivator (early) 2 Cultivator (early) 3 Cultivator (early)	8.0	1.1	49	22	9 000	23 000
1 Cultivator + hand (intra-row) 2 Cultivator + hand (intra-row) 3 Ridger	4.6	3.3	120	28	16 000	38 000
LSD (5%)	2.0	1.5	10			

[1] Maize yield gain over yield of unweeded control plots which was 1.9 t/ha
[2] Cost calculations based on open market prices and costs for 1989/90 season. Figures in Tanzanian shillings (Tsh)
[3] Based on maize price of Tsh 13 200 per tonne (US$ 1 ≈ TSh 150)
Source: Kwiligwa, Shetto and Rees (1994)

entirely with animal draft implements instead of hand hoes. However, in these circumstances yields dropped as well, as a result of poor weed control within the crop rows. Weeding earlier (at maize heights of 5, 25 and 45 cm instead of 10–15, 45 and 90 cm) did not improve this situation. With additional hand labour for within-row weeding, yields were again back at normal level. This was of course at the expense of some of the gained reduction in labour input. Nevertheless the system of animal traction weeding with additional hand labour led to a 65% increase in labour productivity, and a 23% higher net benefit, compared with farmers' practice of hand weeding twice. It is interesting to note that the recommended practice of weeding three times instead of twice gave only a slightly higher yield, but in financial terms led to a 19% decrease of the overall net benefit.

In other trials by the same research team in Tanzania, herbicides were found to reduce labour requirements even more than using animal traction. Herbicides led to yields comparable with the best manual and animal traction techniques, and therefore resulted in enormous labour productivity. Nevertheless the high cost of herbicides meant that the overall profitability of the herbicide treatment was no greater than some other weeding treatments (Shetto and Kwiligwa, 1989).

Reducing additional hand labour

A farmer with animal traction and much land but with little labour could simply cultivate all the land quickly with animal power. The farmer could accept the loss in yield caused by the within-row weeds as total production and net benefit would probably be higher than that when hiring additional hand labour.

It would seem that improved implements and working methods could dramatically reduce the need for additional hand weeding (or the use of herbicides) without reducing yields.

In the weeding comparison study in the southern highlands of Tanzania, mentioned above, an over-the-row cultivator, developed by the Mbeya Oxenization Project (Figure 7), was compared with the more common adjustable inter-row cultivator (Figure 6). No remarkable improvements were observed for the prototype over-the-row cultivator, although the short yoke that goes with any over-the-row cultivator seemed to improve the teamwork of the oxen, as compared to the long yoke used with inter-row cultivators (Kwiligwa, Shetto and Rees, 1994).

Cultivators

The use of cultivators for weeding is most appropriate for early weed control on smooth, clean fields. Weeding with cultivators becomes troublesome on land heavily infested with weeds, particularly when the implement has many short tine shanks; clods of soil and uprooted weeds get stuck between the tines and the cultivator starts acting like a rake, not penetrating the soil any more, but just sweeping the gathered ball of soil and weed mass forward. The same problem occurs in fields with high levels of crop residues (which are desirable in conservation tillage systems). Another disadvantage of the cultivator is the rather complex design, as compared to ridgers and plows. In practice this results in bulky tools which are often poorly assembled and which generally cannot be set as specified.

Adjustable cultivators

The most common cultivators in eastern and southern Africa are all more or less successful versions of the well-performing Safim design (see examples in Figures 6 and 8). All are meant to be adjustable in working width during operation without the need to stop. A serious disadvantage of most cultivators found in the region is their poor durability; moulded shanks break easily, tines made of mild steel wear and bend after a short period of use, and the frames are not strong enough for most of the conditions under which they are used.

Cultivators on multipurpose toolbars

In francophone West Africa cultivators are usually attached to multipurpose toolbars (Figure 9). The durability and performance of these implements are mostly good, but they are not easily adjustable during operation. The overall working width and the distance between the tines must therefore be set before weeding begins. Hence, for maximum working efficiency inter-crop row distances should be as regular as possible; if crop row distances are irregular, fewer tines can be used, or a narrower working width must be set and two passes are needed along each row. On some types of multipurpose toolbars the tine shanks are attached to the frames with clamps. This system avoids the need for spanners to adjust the tines, but there are two serious disadvantages: the clamps add to the weight of the implement and, if not perfectly produced, their grip tends to loosen during use. It is very common for tines to fall out unexpectedly, even though they were carefully tightened a moment earlier.

The *Houe Manga*, developed in Burkina Faso (Figure 5), seems to offer a compromise between the above mentioned disadvantages of cultivators on toolbars and the complexity of Safim adjustable cultivators.

Hiller blades

A pair of hiller blades attached to an adjustable cultivator (Figure 8) can be used to cover weeds within crop rows. It performs excellently when used under the proper conditions for cultivators, leaving an almost completely weed-free field. If any tall weeds remain, they can be rapidly pulled out by hand. This adjustable cultivator with hiller blades is widely used and appreciated by farmers in Zimbabwe. The Animal Draft Power Research and Development Programme in Zambia has also found such cultivators are also easily accepted by farmers once they have seen them working.

Ridging

Ridging is a fast and simple weeding method which, like plowing, can cope with crop residues, big weeds and relatively high weed densities. Ridgers and plows are reasonably easy to use on fields with tree stumps and shrub remains. Ridging covers weeds within the crop rows, but ridging early in the season runs the risk of covering seedlings as well as weeds. It would require good management to use a ridger or a plow effectively for first weeding on flat land; weeding must be done early enough to prevent unacceptable yield reduction and build-up of weeds, but not so early that the crop may be damaged. When the crop is planted on ridges this might be less of a problem. Hence ridging is particularly recommended as a technique for the second weeding.

As noted in a previous section relating to direct ridging, there are two main types of ridgers—the type used in francophone West Africa (Figure 2) and the Safim-type (Figure 3). During weeding demonstrations organized by the Animal Draft Power Research and Development Programme in

Figure 11: Sweep tine (left) and Konni donkey hoe (Source: Kruit, 1991)

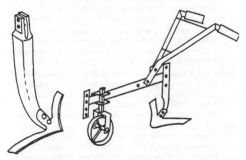

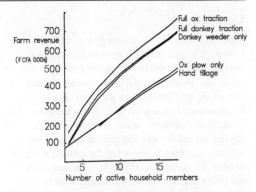

Figure 12: Increases in farm revenue with animal traction for different farm sizes in Burkina Faso. Source: Sanders (1985) after W Jeager (1984)

Zambia two weeding implements proved popular—the West African ridger and the adjustable Safim cultivator fitted with hillers.

The West African ridger's simplicity and ease of handling are quite remarkable. It does a proper weeding job with good coverage within the plant lines for crop row distances of up to about 90 cm. However, if the soil is hard and dry, penetration, and hence effective working width, are reduced. The ridger cuts a clearly edged furrow which some farmers dislike. The wings can be easily adjusted; each one pivots around a bolt turning simultaneously either outwards and downwards, or inwards and upwards. This enables effective (re-)ridging at different inter-ridge distances and prevents damage to the ridges by the wings during re-ridging at small inter-ridge distances. This is unlike the Safim ridger (Figure 3) with its horizontally turning wings on hinges. Nevertheless, the Safim type ridger, although heavy to pull and handle, suppresses weeds effectively, leaving behind a flat, large furrow with no edge at the ridge base.

Weeding with donkeys

Weeding with donkeys has great potential on light soils in semi-arid areas, and should be encouraged further. In many of these areas crops are rapidly hand planted in untilled land as early as possible. The limiting labour bottleneck occurs at the first weeding (Sanders, 1985). Kruit (1991) recommends the introduction of donkey weeding with a relatively cheap and simple sweep tine of 35 cm width, originally intended for groundnut lifting, mounted on a toolbar (Figure 11). The graph in Figure 12, from an economic study in Burkina Faso, reported by Sanders (1985), clearly illustrates how attractive donkey weeding can be.

Conclusions

Improving tillage involves changing complete systems. Changes in tillage necessitate changes in working methods and in subsequent farming operations (planting, weeding, harvesting). It may take a long time before there are observable improvements in soil properties, yields and costs. Practical and simple solutions are required, with appropriate and durable implements and easy and well-proven methods. However, the systems must be flexible, for farmers benefit most when they adapt and refine implements and techniques to their particular, ever-changing conditions.

Ridging, and especially tie-ridging, has good potential for soil and water management, particularly in subhumid regions and on heavier soils in semi-arid areas. Ridges reduce waterlogging and soil loss and facilitate drought survival. In semi-arid regions, ridging on sandy soils reduces wind erosion problems but may lead to crop failure if ridges dry out before roots reach ground water.

Ripping is very fast and improves water infiltration in semi-arid areas, but may not control weeds adequately. Both ridging and ripping require less labour than plowing (and less than direct hand planting on untilled land). Nevertheless further adaptive research is necessary to develop ridging and ripping systems well adapted to the farmers' needs.

Weeding with animal traction is much faster than hand weeding and is physically lighter (benefiting all people including women, children and the elderly). Animal power makes the timely weeding of all fields possible, with benefits for labour productivity and production. Animal-drawn weeding techniques are more cost-effective than herbicides and are more likely to be available to smallholder farmers. Animal-drawn weeding techniques should eradicate weeds within crop rows at an early stage to reduce the need for additional hand-weeding. Cultivators with hiller blades are useful tools for this. It is not essential to have a cultivator that can be adjusted while weeding, although this can be useful where rows are irregular. Excessive vegetation or crop residues can cause problems for cultivators which tend to act as rakes. This is less of a problem for ridgers, which ideally combine ease of use with reliability and durability. However, ridgers cannot be used easily when the crop is still small. Ridgers are ideal weeding implements on both flat and ridged fields, but are less effective in dry conditions, and where crops are widely spaced (80–90 cm). Rapid progress in weed control in the region is more likely to come from familiarising farmers with existing methods of animal-powered weed control rather than from further research programmes.

References

Bordet D, 1988. *From research on animal-drawn implements to farmers appropriation: successes and failures of development experience in Senegal.* Paper 88–384 for presentation at AG ENG 88, Agricultural Engineering International Conference, Paris, March 2–5 1988. International Journal of Agricultural Engineering, London, UK.

Chatizwa I and Norton A J, 1989. *Evaluation of two pre-production prototype ridges.* Institute of Agricultural Engineering, Department of Agricultural Technical and Extension Services (Agritex), Harare, Zimbabwe.

Chatizwa I, Nazare R M and Norton A J, 1988. *Report on evaluation of ox-drawn ridgers.* Institute of Agricultural Engineering, Department of Agricultural Technical and Extension Services (Agritex), Harare, Zimbabwe.

Elwell H A, 1986. *Soil conservation.* The College Press, Harare, Zimbabwe.

Elwell H A 1989. Personal communication. Institute of Agricultural Engineering, PO Box 330, Borrowdale, Harare, Zimbabwe.

Elwell H A and Norton A J, 1988. *No-till tied-ridging, a recommended sustained crop production system.* Institute of Agricultural Engineering, Department of Agricultural Technical and Extension Services (Agritex), Harare, Zimbabwe.

Foth H D, 1984. *Fundamentals of soil science.* 7th edition. John Wiley & Sons, New York, USA.

Gotora P, 1991. Adaptive no-till tied ridging trials in small-scale farming areas of Zimbabwe. pp. 410–416 in: *Soil tillage and agricultural sustainability.* Proceedings of the 12th International Conference of the International Soil Tillage Research Organisation (ISTRO), held July 1991, Ibadan, Nigeria. Ohio State University, Colombus, Ohio, USA.

Harris B L and Krishna J H, 1989. Furrow diking to conserve moisture. *Journal of Soil and Water Conservation* July–August 1989: 271–273.

Jones E, 1990. Personal communication. Department of Research and Specialist Services, Harare, Zimbabwe.

Kruit F, 1991. *La culture attelée au Niger.* Récherche 1989 et 1990, Départements de Tahoua et Maradi, Institut National de Recherches Agronomiques du Niger (INRAN), Niamey, Niger.

Kwiligwa E M, Shetto R M and Rees D, 1994. The use of animal-drawn cultivators for maize production in the southern highlands of Tanzania. pp. 170–178 in Starkey P, Mwenya E and Stares J (eds), *Improving animal traction technology.* Proceedings of first workshop of the Animal Traction Network for Eastern and Southern Africa (ATNESA) held 18–23 January, 1992, Lusaka, Zambia. Technical Centre for Agriculture and Rural Cooperation, Ede-Wageningen, The Netherlands. 480p.

Lal R, 1988. Soil degradation and the future of agriculture in sub-Saharan Africa. *Journal of Soil and Water Conservation,* November–December 1988, pp. 444–451.

Meijer R A, 1992. *Ridging as a primary tillage practice, compiled results of three years of applied research.* Palabana Animal Draft Power Research and Development Programme, Department of Agriculture, Lusaka, Zambia.

Meijer R A, Chanda B and Hoogmoed W B, 1990. *Report on the tillage experiments by the Animal Draft Power Research and Development Project, season 1989–1990.* Palabana Animal Draft Power Research and Development Programme, Department of Agriculture, Lusaka, Zambia.

Norton A J, 1987. *Conservation tillage: what works?* Paper presented at Natural Resources Board workshop on conservation tillage at the Institute of Agricultural Engineering, Department of Agricultural Technical and

Extension Services (Agritex), Harare, Zimbabwe, 19 June 1987

Oldreive B, 1989. Conservation tillage in action. Chapter 3, pp. 19–31 in: *Conservation tillage: a handbook for commercial farmers in Zimbabwe*. Commercial Grain Producers' Association, Harare, Zimbabwe.

Palabana, 1991. *Course on regional demonstrations*. Palabana, September 11–13, 1991. Palabana Animal Draft Power Research and Development Programme, Department of Agriculture, Lusaka, Zambia.

van der Ploeg J and Reddy C K, 1988. *Water conservation techniques for sandy and clayey soils of Niger*. Paper presented at International Conference on Dryland Farming, August 15–19, 1988. United States Department of Agriculture (USDA) Conservation and Production Research Laboratory, Bushland, Texas, USA.

Raulin H, 1984. Techniques agraires et instruments aratoires au sud du Sahara. In: *Les instruments aratoires en Afrique Tropicale, la fonction et la signe*. Cahiers Orstom, Série Science humaines, Vol XX, no 3–4, Orstom, France.

Sanders J H, 1985. *Profitability of animal traction: field study in Burkina Faso*. Paper presented at Workshop on Technologies Appropriate for Farmers in Semi-Arid West Africa, Ouagadougou, Burkina Faso, 2–5 April 1985. [Summary of PhD thesis by W Jeager: "Agricultural Mechanization: The Economics of Animal Traction in Burkina Faso", Stanford University, 1984]

Shetto R M and Kwiligwa E M, 1989. *Weed control systems in maize based on animal drawn cultivation*. Research Report. Uyole Agricultural Centre, Mbeya, Tanzania.

Smith R D, 1989. *Tillage trials in Zimbabwe 1957 to 1988*. Institute of Agricultural Engineering, Department of

Agricultural, Technical and Extension Services (Agritex), Harare, Zimbabwe.

Stevens P A, 1988. *Rapport de recherche: techniques de préparation de sol, systèmes de semis, sarco-binage à la culture attelée sur sols sableux avec l'accent sur mil dans le Département de Tahoua*. Institut National de Recherches Agronomiques du Niger (INRAN), Niamey, Niger.

Stevens P A, 1989. *Observational tillage trials: final report*. Institute of Agricultural Engineering, Department of Agricultural Technical and Extension Services (Agritex), Harare, Zimbabwe.

Stocking M, 1988. Socio-economics of soil conservation in developing countries. *Journal of Soil and Water Conservation*, September–October 1988, pp. 381–385.

Tembo E, 1989. *Procedures in deriving a workable recommendation for small farmers (CIMMYT findings)*. Interesting Information No 5/89, Reference B/333/3. Department of Agricultural Technical and Extension Services (Agritex), Harare, Zimbabwe.

Unger P W, 1984. *Tillage systems for soil and water conservation*. FAO Soils Bulletin 54. Food and Agriculture Organization of the United Nations (FAO), Rome, Italy.

Vogel H, 1991. *Conservation tillage for sustainable crop production systems*. Project Research Report 2. Deutsche Gesellschaft für Technische Zusammenarbeit (GTZ) GmbH, Institute of Agricultural Engineering, Department of Agricultural Technical and Extension Services (Agritex), Harare, Zimbabwe.

Vowles M, 1989. Introduction. Chapter 1, pp. 7–10, in: *Conservation tillage: a handbook for commercial farmers in Zimbabwe*. Commercial Grain Producers' Association, Harare, Zimbabwe.

The use of animal-drawn cultivators for maize production in the southern highlands of Tanzania

E M Kwiligwa[1], R M Shetto[1] and D J Rees[2]

[1]Agricultural Engineers and [2]Adaptive Research Adviser
Uyole Agricultural Centre, PO Box 400, Mbeya, Tanzania

Abstract

Experiments on weed management techniques for maize production were carried out at the Uyole Agricultural Centre and on farmers' fields in Mbozi District, Tanzania. The treatments involved hand weeding and the use of the Cossul inter-row cultivator and of the over-the-row cultivator developed by the Mbeya Oxenization Project.

There were no marked differences in field capacities between the two cultivators, although the over-the-row cultivator tended to have slightly higher capacities. Field capacities tended to be higher when the maize was 45 cm high.

The use of cultivators alone reduced labour inputs for weeding by up to 80%, and the use of cultivators combined with hand weeding reduced labour inputs by 40%, compared to manual weeding alone.

Manual weeding, and a combination of manual and cultivator weeding, gave the best control of weeds, and similar high yields (5 t/ha compared to 2 t/ha with no weeding). The use of cultivators alone gave significantly poorer weed control and reduced yield advantages (3.3 t/ha).

The results emphasise the importance of weeding for high maize yields in the southern highlands of Tanzania. Farmers who cannot afford, or do not have access to, ox-drawn systems can obtain high yields by manual weeding alone, but at the cost of high labour inputs, representing high levels of family drudgery or high labour hiring costs. Those farmers who have access to ox-drawn systems are advised to do additional within-row manual weeding to ensure high yields. Ox-drawn cultivation alone for weeding is suitable only where labour is scarce.

Introduction

Weeds are unwanted and undesirable plants which interfere with the utilisation of land and water resources, adversely affecting human welfare (Rao, 1983). Their vegetative habits and demand for resources are usually similar to those of desirable plants, and so there is competition for nutrients, water, space and sunlight. There is also growing evidence for allelopathic effects of some weeds which exude chemical compounds harmful to crops, human beings and livestock (Rice, 1984). The overall effect of weeds is reduced yields of desirable plants.

Estimates of yield losses due to weeds vary greatly depending on the magnitude of the weed population, the weed species and the fertility level of the soil. It is accepted that about 10% loss of agricultural production in the world can be attributed to the competitive effect of weeds. In 1975 it was estimated that the loss of food due to weeds worldwide was 287 million tonnes, or 11.5% of total food production (Parker and Fryer, 1975).

Mani, Gautam and Chakraborty (1968) reported maize yield reductions due to weeds of about 30–74%. At Morogoro, Mugabe, Sinje and Sibuga (1980) have shown that yields of maize, sorghum, soya beans and greengram were, respectively, about 61, 96, 97 and 97% lower in unweeded fields compared with weed-free ones. At Uyole it was reported that if weeds grow unchecked maize yields can be reduced by over 70% (UAC, 1989). In The Gambia early control of weeds by either hand hoeing or hand application of low rates of *atrazine* or *propazine* increased maize yields by more than 50% in 1985 and by more than 30% in 1986, compared with farmers' normal practice (Carson, 1987).

Weed control is therefore one of the main factors determining crop production by smallholder farmers. Improved weed control often leads to substantial yield increases, even in the absence of other improvements in farming practices (Armitage and Brook, 1976). Indeed, improvements such as the introduction of improved varieties and increased fertilisation rarely increase yields if weed control is not also improved (Croon, Deutsch and Temu, 1984; Matthews, 1984).

According to Acland (1971) and Terry (1984), maize should be kept free of weeds for the first month after emergence and weeding should be done three times—when the maize is 5–10, 45 and 90 cm high. Moreover, if maize growth is checked by weeds shortly after emergence it never fully recovers. Croon, Deutsch and Temu (1984), in their experiments in the southern highlands of Tanzania, found that one weeding of maize at 10 cm resulted in an average yield of 4.2 t/ha compared to 2.3 t/ha in unweeded plots. They concluded that poor weeding of maize is the biggest constraint to maize production in this area. They went on to suggest that timely weeding was itself more important than the use of improved varieties, fertilisers or insecticides, or timely planting. In a survey of 320 farmers in 20 villages in Mbeya Region, late weeding was identified as one of the many constraints to crop production (Loewen-Rudgers et al, 1990).

In the whole cropping cycle, weed control is often the operation with the highest labour demand. The amount of land a farmer can plant is often restricted to the area that can be kept free of weeds. Improved and efficient weed control may therefore enable a farmer to cultivate more land and hence increase total yield. In addition, the time the farmer gains from improved weed control may be devoted to the cultivation of additional crops or to more profitable off-farm employment (Lewis and Watson, 1972).

Although animal-drawn weeders are available in most African countries, only 5% of farmers who use animal traction for plowing also use the weeders on row crops (Starkey, 1986; 1988). The figures vary from almost zero in Botswana, Mozambique, Tanzania, Uganda and Zambia to between 10 and 20% in Cameroon and Mali and to as much as 40% in South Africa and Zimbabwe (Kjærby, 1983; ILO, 1987). Rain (1984) identified the lack of good animal-drawn weeders as the main constraint to crop production by those farmers who plowed with animals.

Because of the benefit of timely weeding through the use of animal traction, it is important to develop appropriate animal-drawn weeders for small-scale farmers in Tanzania. The overall objective of this research was to develop effective and economical mechanical weed control methods based on animal-drawn implements.

Materials and methods

Location

The study was carried out in 1988 and 1989 at five locations in Mbeya Region, Tanzania—Uyole in Mbeya District, and Wassa, Iyula, Isangu and Igunda villages in Mbozi District.

Soils at Uyole are young, volcanic and of Tertiary to Recent origin, with top soils consisting of haplic phaeozem overlying pumice gravel. Those at Iyula and Wassa are gravelly, moderately deep cambisols while those at Isangu and Igunda are deep granular ferralsols (Rombulow-Pearse and Kamasho, 1981).

Mbeya Region is located between latitudes 7 and 9° S and longitudes 32 and 35° E. Rainfall ranges

between 600 mm in the lowlands and 3600 mm in the highlands. The rainfall pattern is monomodal, with the rainy season between November and May. The altitude of Mbeya Region ranges between 400 and 2700 m above sea level: Uyole is 1800 m above sea level. The agricultural production potential of Mbeya Region is high with maize, wheat, beans, rice, coffee, tea, cotton, pyrethrum and tobacco as the major food and cash crops.

Although Mbeya Region has a high cattle population, with over 900 000 head, including 33 000 oxen, hand labour is still the major source of farm power (Shetto and Kwiligwa, 1988). However, in Kyela and Mbozi Districts draft animals are extensively used for plowing and for pulling sledges.

Implements and experimental design

Two animal-drawn cultivators were used. The over-the-row cultivator designed and fabricated by the Mbeya Oxenization Project (MOP) consists of a long pole attached to a rigid frame (Figure 1). Shanks are attached to the rigid frame by clamps so that the width of operation can be adjusted by simply sliding them on the frame. Several soil engaging parts, ranging from simple tines to duck-foot sweeps, can be attached to the shanks. The two wheels on the cultivator enable the depth to be adjusted on either side of a crop row so that an ordinary length yoke can be used (Mkomwa, 1992).

The Cossul inter-row cultivator (Figure 2a), designed in India by Cossul Company, consists of a flexible frame on which shanks are permanently fixed. The cultivator is hitched to the yoke through a trek chain. The wheel on the cultivator is used to adjust depth, and the width of cut is controlled by a

Figure 1: Prototype over-the-row cultivator, developed by Mbeya Oxenization Projet (MOP)

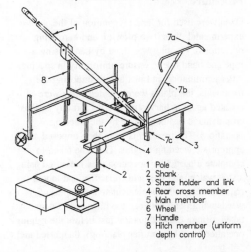

1 Pole
2 Shank
3 Share holder and link
4 Rear cross member
5 Main member
6 Wheel
7 Handle
8 Hitch member (uniform depth control)

lever. It is designed to weed between the crop rows, so a long yoke is required. The Cossul ridger used in some treatments is a large and heavy implement (Figure 2b).

The experimental design was a randomised complete block with three replications. The plot size was 20 x 3 m. Hybrid maize H6302 was used with a spacing of 75 x 30 cm. Fertiliser and insecticide were used as recommended.

Treatments

The study investigated the following weeding systems:

1. Hand hoe weeding at 10–15, 45 and 90 cm maize height (the recommended practice).
2. Weeding with the MOP over-the-row cultivator at 5, 25 and 45 cm maize height.
3. Weeding with the MOP over-the-row cultivator at 10–15 and 45 cm maize height and ridging at 90 cm maize height.
4. Weeding with the MOP over-the-row cultivator, followed immediately by hand hoe weeding, at 10–15 cm and again at 45 cm maize height, and finally ridging at 90 cm maize height.
5. Weeding with the Cossul inter-row cultivator at 5, 25 and 45 cm maize height.
6. Weeding with the Cossul inter-row cultivator at 10–15 and 45 cm maize height and ridging at 90 cm maize height.
7. Weeding with a Cossul inter-row cultivator, followed immediately by hand hoe weeding, at 10–15 cm and again at 45 cm, and finally ridging at 90 cm maize height.
8. Hand hoe weeding at 30–40 and 90 cm maize height (normal farmer practice).
9. No weeding.

Procedure

Oxen were used for land preparation of the experimental plots (two plowing and harrowing operations). Planting was done by hand, using a rope and hand hoe to ensure uniformity in spacing. After germination and just before imposing the treatments, the plants were counted (they were counted again at harvesting to check if any serious crop damage had been done by the weeding operation). The treatments were then imposed at the appropriate weeding heights. The time taken to complete a particular operation was measured using a stop watch, and the field capacities and labour requirements were then calculated. Samples of weeds within and between the maize rows were taken using a 0.25 m quadrat just before the ridging operation (at 70 days after planting), then dried and

Figure 2a: Cossul inter-row cultivator

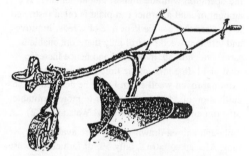

Figure 2b: Cossul ridger

weighed. The most common weeds at each site were identified. The middle three rows of each treatment were harvested and the yield recorded. After statistical analysis of the data, partial budget, return to labour and marginal analysis calculations were performed (Perrin et al, 1979: CIMMYT, 1988).

Results and discussion

The common weed species at each experimental site are shown in Table 1. Chinese lantern (*Nicandra physalodes*) was very vigorous at Uyole, Iyula and Igunda whereas *Commelina benghalensis* was common at Wassa, Igunda and Uyole. Grasses were not very common at any site, probably because the fields chosen for the experiments were those cultivated annually.

Table 2 shows the effective field capacities of the animal-drawn cultivators. No marked differences in field capacities were observed between the two cultivators, although the MOP over-the-row cultivator tended to have higher capacities. The long yoke used for the Cossul inter-row cultivator may have decreased the oxen pair's "spirit of teamwork" leading to slightly lower field capacities. There was a tendency for the field capacities to increase as the maize height increased. This is probably due to the fact that the animals could easily move between the clear maize rows.

The use of animal-drawn cultivators reduced the labour input by between 50 and 80%. When

Table 1: The most common weeds on the experimental sites

Weed	Uyole	Wassa	Iyula	Isangu	Igunda
Galinsoga parviflora	yes	yes	yes	yes	yes
Nicandra physalodes	yes	yes	yes	no	yes
Commelina benghalensis	yes	yes	no	no	yes
Eleusine indica[1]	yes	no	yes	no	yes
Bidens pilosa	no	no	yes	no	yes
Digitaria milanjiana[1]	yes	no	no	no	no
Cyperus spp[1]	no	no	yes	no	no
Leucaus spp	no	no	no	yes	no
Setaria spp	no	no	no	yes	no

[1] *These are considered to be among the "top ten worst weeds in the world" by Holm et al (1977)*

Table 2: Effective field capacities of animal-drawn cultivators at different maize heights

Effective field capacities (ha/hour)

Maize height (cm)	Uyole		Wassa		Iyula		Isangu		Igunda		Mean and standard error			
	IC	OC	IC	OC	IC	OC	IC	OC	IC	OC	— IC —		— OC —	
5	0.11	0.12	0.11	0.10	0.12	0.13	0.12	0.11	0.09	0.08	0.11	0.010	0.11	0.019
10–15	0.11	0.14	0.13	0.12	0.13	0.15	0.10	0.14	0.08	0.09	0.11	0.021	0.13	0.024
25	0.14	0.12	0.13	0.12	0.12	0.16	0.18	0.13	0.13	0.13	0.14	0.023	0.13	0.017
45	0.18	0.16	0.14	0.14	0.24	0.24	0.16	0.14	0.12	0.14	0.17	0.046	0.16	0.044

IC: Inter-row cultivator; OC: Over-the-row cultivator

Table 3: Labour input for the various weeding systems at different experimental sites

Labour input (hours/ha)

Treatment	Uyole	Wassa	Iyula	Isangu	Igunda	Mean
1	281.2	213.4	159.9	230.9	288.4	226.7
2	46.1	51.8	40.0	57.5	38.2	49.9
3	50.1	51.2	31.0	55.0	55.4	47.9
4	181.9	128.0	111.6	129.3	125.7	135.4
5	46.4	48.5	39.1	48.7	64.8	49.2
6	26.1	47.9	41.5	41.1	59.8	41.8
7	136.4	117.8	106.4	112.8	134.5	119.6
8	241.2	218.3	141.7	130.3	203.0	184.1
9	0	0	0	0	0	0
Mean	126.2	109.6	83.9	100.7	121.2	106.8
LSD (0.05)	19.7	17.7	20.3	25.4	18.4	10.2
CV%	8.9	9.2	13.8	14.4	7.2	13.7

animal-drawn cultivators were supplemented by hand hoe the labour input reduction was about 40% (Table 3).

The weed dry weights for the different weeding systems at different sites are shown in Table 4 and Figure 3. Despite the good land preparation at all sites, Wassa, Igunda and Uyole had highest weed infestations. High overall weed intensity was associated with the presence of *Nicandra* and *Commelina* species. Results indicate that using animal-drawn cultivators alone (treatments 2, 3, 5 and 6) was not effective in controlling weeds within the maize rows. Supplementing animal-drawn cultivators with the hand hoe effectively controlled weeds both between and within the maize rows (treatments 4 and 7). This trend was the same within and across sites. The differences in weed dry weight between treatments 4 and 7 were not significant.

Table 4: Total weed dry weight (g/0.25 m²) for different weeding systems at each site

Weed dry weight (g/0.25 m²)

Treatment	Uyole	Wassa	Iyula	Isangu	Igunda	Mean
1	82.5	112.2	62.2	108.6	107.8	94.7
2	170.0	365.2	153.7	154.2	336.1	235.9
3	184.9	372.7	142.8	161.0	314.2	235.1
4	95.3	256.0	95.7	121.0	118.3	137.3
5	164.4	295.5	182.1	137.0	221.3	200.1
6	233.3	238.9	189.4	190.5	235.5	217.5
7	90.3	166.5	99.5	97.6	120.1	114.8
8	150.4	221.7	135.0	149.8	146.8	161.1
9	443.2	474.3	295.5	240.4	391.4	369.0
Mean	179.6	278.1	150.7	151.1	221.3	196.2
LSD (0.05)	84.1	161.5	123.0	40.1	88.7	49.1
CV%	27.1	33.5	47.2	15.3	23.2	34.5

A) Uyole

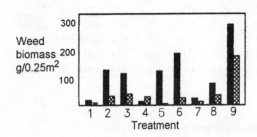

D) Isangu

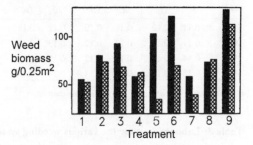

B) Wassa

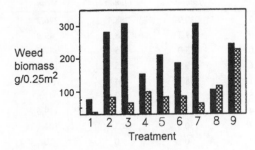

E) Igunda

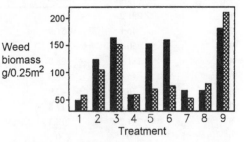

C) Iyula

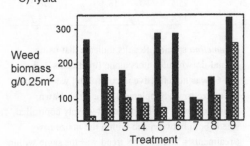

F) Across all locations

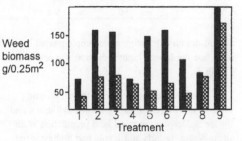

▨ Between maize rows
■ Within maize rows

Figure 3: Weed biomass at the different sites and across locations

"Improving animal traction technology"

Table 5: Effect of weeding systems on maize yields at each site

| | Yield (tonnes/ha) | | | | | |
Treatment	Uyole	Wassa	Iyula	Isangu	Igunda	Mean
1	6.0	4.2	5.8	6.6	5.2	5.4
2	2.5	3.7	4.8	5.7	2.0	3.6
3	3.2	3.3	4.5	5.3	2.1	3.6
4	5.5	3.8	5.1	5.8	4.5	4.9
5	1.9	2.8	3.3	4.6	2.3	3.0
6	3.0	2.9	3.7	5.5	1.4	3.3
7	5.3	4.1	5.1	7.5	3.9	5.2
8	5.8	2.8	6.1	6.2	4.2	5.0
9	1.3	1.4	2.5	3.9	0.1	1.9
Mean	3.9	3.2	4.4	5.7	2.9	4.0
LSD (0.05)	1.3	1.0	1.7	1.6	1.4	0.6
CV%	19.6	18.5	22.9	16.5	28.5	21.2

This shows that animal-drawn cultivators when supplemented with a hand hoe can control weeds effectively. Moreover, both the MOP over-the-row and Cossul inter-row cultivators performed equally well in controlling weeds.

Weeding with a hand hoe three times, and using cultivators supplemented with hand hoe (treatments 1, 4 and 7) effectively controlled weeds both between and within the maize rows in all sites. The consistency of these weeding systems in different environments allows the techniques to be recommended to farmers with some confidence.

Some weeding techniques, especially those involving animal-drawn cultivators, did not control weeds effectively at Wassa and Igunda. The dominant weed species at these sites are stoloniferous types which are difficult to control.

The plant stand was good at all sites and ranged between 37 000 and 45 000 plants per hectare. Table 5 shows the maize yields for different weeding systems at different sites. Weeding by hand hoe and by cultivators supplemented with a hand hoe (treatments 1, 4, 7 and 8) gave the highest yields. This supports the effectiveness of these treatments on weed control, as shown by the correlations in Figure 4. Generally there was a good negative correlation between yields and weed dry weight within the maize rows (the correlation coefficient is –0.757). This shows that weeds within the maize rows affect crop production more than those between. Hence the importance of supplementing animal-drawn cultivators with the hand hoe.

Table 6 summarises the costs and benefits of the different weeding systems. Hand weeding three times gave the highest yields, but at a considerable

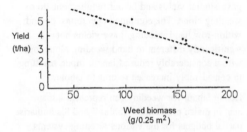

Figure 4a: Yield versus weed biomass within rows

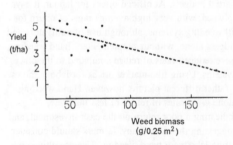

Figure 4b: Yield versus weed biomass between rows

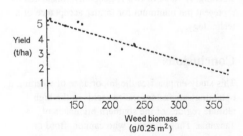

Figure 4c: Yield versus total weed biomass

Table 6: Partial budget and returns to labour of averaged data for the weeding system trial

Treatment	1	2	3	4	5	6	7	8	9
Labour (hours/ha)	227	50	48	135	49	42	120	184	0
Yield (t/ha)	5.4	3.6	3.6	4.9	3.0	3.3	5.2	5.0	1.9
Gross profit (TSh/ha)[1]	57 024	37 594	38 650	51 955	31 469	34 848	54 701	53 011	19 536
Implement costs (TSh/ha)[1]	62	279	289	299	300	273	309	55	0
Net profit (TSh/ha)[1]	56 962	37 315	38 361	51 656	31 169	34 575	54 392	52 956	19 536
Net benefit (TSh/ha)[1]	37 426	17 779	18 825	32 120	11 633	15 039	34 856	33 420	–
Return to labour (TSh/hour)[1]	165	356	392	238	237	358	290	182	–

[1]The figures are given in Tanzanian shillings (Tsh) which have changed greatly in international value in recent years. In 1991 US$ 1 ≈ Tsh 100, but in this and other tables, comparision of treatments is more important than the absolute values

cost in labour requirement, while ox weeding gave the lowest yields, but with much reduced labour requirements. Ox weeding, with a ridging operation replacing the third weeding (treatments 3 and 6), gave similar yields and labour requirements to ox weeding alone. The combined operations, ox and within-row hand weeding, gave yields not significantly different to hand weeding alone, but with a considerably reduced labour input, resulting in considerably increased returns to labour.

Hiring labour for weeding can represent a major cost in maize production. Tables 7 and 8 summarise partial budgets for the various weeding systems, including costs of hiring labour for weeding, using both official and open-market prices and costs. Table 9 presents a rate of return analysis of the partial budgets. At official prices for labour, it pays to weed, with very high average rates of return for all weeding systems, although use of cultivators and ridgers alone, without supplementary hand weeding, gave reduced rates of return compared to the other systems. Using free-market prices for labour shows a rather different picture, however. Hand weeding alone gives rates of return of less than one, indicating a poor return on the cash investment, and suggesting that few, if any, farmers should consider hiring labour for hand weeding. Use of cultivators and ridgers gave an average rate of return of one, as did the use of cultivator plus supplementary hand weeding. A value of two is generally considered to represent the minimum for farmer acceptance of a technology.

Conclusions

This study emphasises the importance of weeding in obtaining satisfactory maize yields in the high altitude regions of the southern highlands of Tanzania. Those farmers who cannot afford or obtain ox plowing and weeding equipment can still achieve high yields if they can arrange the high labour inputs for manual weeding, but this would be at a disadvantageously high cost if the labour has to be hired rather than supplied from within the farm family. Those farmers who can afford/obtain ox plowing and weeding equipment can only obtain high yields if they can arrange manual inter-row weeding to supplement ox cultivator weeding. In the context of smallholder farming in the southern highlands of Tanzania, where maize is an important staple for home consumption, as well as a cash crop, and where most labour inputs are supplied from within the family, ox weeding, combined with manual within-row weeding, offers a significant reduction in drudgery, while maintaining high yields for food security and cash production. In the context of those farmers able to hire labour, this system offers one of the better rates of return to weeding.

Acknowledgements

The authors wish to thank the Uyole Agricultural Centre, the Finnish International Development Agency, the Mbeya Oxenization Project and the Cilca Project for their material and financial support. Thanks are also due to the Agricultural Engineering Support Staff, the Chemical Laboratory Staff and the Computer Unit Staff of the Uyole Agricultural Centre. Grateful acknowledgement is also due to all the village government leaders in the villages where the research trials were carried out for their good cooperation, and also to the farmers who occasionally loaned their oxen during critical periods.

References

Acland J D, 1971. *East Africa crops.* Longman, London, UK.

Armitage M S and Brook C E, 1976. The case of weed control to spearhead improvements in maize and cotton husbandry in Swaziland. pp. 165–172 in: *Proceedings, 13th British Weed Control Conference, Vol 1.* British Crop Protection Council, London, UK.

Carson A G, 1987. Improving weed management in the draft cattle based production of early pearl millet in The Gambia. *Tropical Pest Management* 33(4):359–363.

CIMMYT, 1988. *Introduction to economic analysis of on farm experiments: draft workbook.* Centro Internacional de Mejoramiento de Maíz y Trigo (CIMMYT), Londres, Mexico.

Croon I, Deutsch J and Temu A E M, 1984. *Maize production in Tanzania's Southern Highlands: current status and*

Table 7: Partial budget of averaged data from the weeding system trial (information based on government official prices and costs)

Treatment	1	2	3	4	5	6	7	8	9
Yield (kg/ha)	5 400	3 560	3 660	4920	2 980	3 300	5 180	5 020	1 850
Adjusted yield[1] (kg/ha)	4 320	2 848	2 928	3 936	2 384	2 640	4 144	4 016	1 480
Gross field benefit[2] (TSh/ha)	57 024	37 594	38 650	51 955	31 469	34 848	54 701	53 011	19 536
Labour for weeding[3] (TSh/ha)	2 028	992	976	1 642	1 025	902	1 589	1 810	0
Implement costs (TSh/ha)	62	279	289	299	3 00	273	309	55	0
Total variable cost (TSh/ha)	2 089	1 272	1 265	1 941	1325	1 175	1 895	1 865	0
Net benefit (TSh/ha)	54 935	36 321	37 385	50 014	30 144	33 673	52 805	51 146	19 536

[1] Adjusted by 20% (10% for the low management level of farmer and 10% for the small plot size)
[2] Official price: 15 TSh/kg less 1 TSh/kg for harvesting, 0.5 TSh/kg for transport and 0.3 TSh/kg for shelling and bagging
[3] Ox operator cost at 20.5 TSh/hour and hand hoeing at 9.0 TSh/hour (official government figures)

Table 8: Partial budget of averaged data from the weeding system trial (information based on open market prices and costs)

Treatment	1	2	3	4	5	6	7	8	9
Yield (kg/ha)	5 400	3 560	3 660	4 920	2 980	3 300	5 180	5 020	1 850
Adjusted yield (20%) (kg/ha)	4 320	2 848	2 928	3 936	2 384	2 640	4 144	4 016	1 480
Gross field benefit (TSh/ha)	57 024	37 594	38 650	51 955	31 469	34 848	54 701	53 011	19 536
Variable costs[1] (TSh/ha)	32 400	8 640	8 640	17 086	8 640	8 640	16 265	21 600	0
Net benefit (TSh/ha)	24 624	28 954	30 010	34 870	22 830	26 208	38 436	31 411	19 536

[1] Labour hiring average 10 000 TSh/ha in weeding and 30–39% of this cost when hand hoe supplements cultivator
Cost of hiring oxen with cultivator/ridger plus two operators is 2600 TSh/ha

Table 9: Rate of return analysis of the various weeding systems

Treatment	Costs	Net benefit	Additional costs	Additional net benefit	Average rate of return
Official prices and costs					
No weeding (9)	0	19 536	0	0	–
Two hand weedings (8)	1 865	51 146	1 865	31 610	16.9
Three hand weedings (1)	2 089	54 935	2 089	35 399	16.9
Cultivator (2/5)	1 299	33 233	1 299	13 697	10.5
Cultivator/ridger (3/6)	1 220	35 529	1 220	15 993	13.1
Cultivator/hand (4/7)	1 918	51 410	1 918	31 874	16.6
Free market figures and costs					
No weeding (9)	0	19 536	0	0	–
2 hand weeding (8)	21 600	31 411	21 600	11 875	0.5
3 hand weeding (1)	32 400	24 624	32 400	5 088	0.2
Cultivator (2/5)	8 640	25 892	8 640	6 356	0.7
Cultivator/ridger (3/6)	8 640	28 109	8 640	8 573	1.0
Cultivator/hand (4/7)	16 676	36 653	16 676	17 117	1.0

recommendations for the future. Centro Internacional de Mejoramiento de Maíz y Trigo (CIMMYT), Londres, Mexico.

Fletcher W W, 1983. *Recent advances in weed research.* Commonwealth Agricultural Bureaux. Unwin Brothers, The Gresham Press, Old Woking, Surrey, UK.

Holm L, Plucknett L D, Puncho V J and Herberger P J, 1977. *The world's worst weeds: distribution and biology.* University Press of Hawaii, Honolulu, Hawaii, USA.

ILO, 1987. *In quest of agricultural mechanisation policy and strategies in the United Republic of Tanzania.* Proceedings of national workshop on farm tools and equipment technology: basic needs and employment, held 8–10 October 1985, Dar es Salaam, Tanzania. International Labour Organisation (ILO), Geneva, Switzerland. 69p.

Kjærby F, 1983. *Problems and contradictions in the development of ox-cultivation in Tanzania.* Research Report 66. Scandinavian Institute of African Studies, Uppsala, Sweden and Centre for Development Research, Copenhagen, Denmark. 164p.

Lewis C J and Watson G A, 1972. Extension work with herbicides in the small scale tropical farm situation. pp. 107–133 in: *Proceedings, 11th British Weed Control Conference.* British Crop Protection Council, London, UK.

Loewen-Rudgers L, Rempel E, Harder J and Klassen Harder K, 1990. Constraints to the adoption of animal traction weeding technology in the Mbeya Region of Tanzania. pp. 460–471 in: Starkey P H and Faye A (eds), *Animal traction for agricultural development.* Proceedings of the third workshop of the West Africa Animal Traction Network held 7–12 July 1988, Saly, Senegal. Technical Centre for Agriculture and Rural Cooperation, Ede-Wageningen, The Netherlands. 475p.

Mani V S, Gautam K C and Chakroborty T K, 1968. Losses in crop yield in India due to weed growth. *Pans* 14:142–158.

Matthews L J, 1984. Improving weed management at the small farm level. *FAO Plant Protection Bulletin* 32(4):129–137.

Mkomwa S, 1992. Research and development experiences of the Mbeya Oxenization Project in animal draft technologies. pp. 31–33 in: Simalenga T E and Hatibu N (eds). *Proceedings of an animal traction workshop* held 8–10 April 1991, Morogoro, Tanzania. Mbeya Oxenization Project, Mbeya, Tanzania. 57p.

Mugabe N R, Sinje M E and Sibuga K P, 1980. A study of crop weed competition in intercropping. pp. 96–111 in: Keswani C L and Ndunguru B J (eds), *Intercropping.* Proceedings of the 2nd Symposium on Cropping in Semi-arid Areas, held 4–7 August 1980, Morogoro, Tanzania. Sokoine University of Agriculture, Morogoro, Tanzania.

Parker C and Fryer J O, 1975. Weed control problems causing major reductions in world food supplies. *FAO Plant Protection Bulletin* 23:83–95.

Perrin R K, Winkelmann D L, Muscardi E R and Anderson J R, 1979. *From agronomic data to farmers recommendation: an economic training manual.* Information Bulletin 27, Centro Internacional de Mejoramiento de Maíz y Trigo (CIMMYT), Londres, Mexico.

Rain D K, 1984. *The constraints to smallholder peasant agricultural production in Mbeya and Mbozi Districts, Mbeya Region.* Report to Canadian International Development Agency, Hull, Quebec, Canada.

Rao V S, 1983. *Principles of weed science.* IBH Publishing Company, Oxford, UK.

Rice E L, 1984. *Allelopathy.* Academic Press, New York, USA. 542p.

Rombulow-Pearse C W and Kamasho J A M, 1981. *Land resources of Mbeya Region: a provisional reconnaissance assessment.* Working Paper 19. Uyole Agricultural Centre, Mbeya, Tanzania.

Shetto R M and Kwiligwa E M, 1988. *Survey of oxcart production and use in Mbeya Region.* Mbeya Oxenization Project, Mbeya, Tanzania. 69p.

Starkey P H, 1986. *Draft animal power in Africa: priorities for development, research and liaison.* Networking Paper 14. Farming Systems Support Project, University of Florida, Gainsville, Florida, USA. 40p.

Starkey P H, 1988. *Animal traction directory: Africa.* Vieweg for German Appropriate Technology Exchange, GTZ, Eschborn, Germany. 151p.

Terry P J, 1984. *The guide to weed control in East African crops.* Kenya Literature Bureau, Nairobi, Kenya.

UAC, 1989. *Annual Report, 1989. Agricultural Engineering Research Progress Report.* Uyole Agricultural Centre (UAC), Mbeya, Tanzania.

Techniques and implements for weeding with draft animals in Tanzania

by

A K Kayumbo

Agricultural Officer (Mechanisation), Ministry of Agriculture, PO Box 9071, Dar es Salaam, Tanzania

Abstract

Small-scale farming generally relies on the use of hand tools for seedbed preparation, planting and weeding. Weeding using hand tools is a slow and tedious task, because a person is only capable of generating limited power output. Most weeding operations can be carried out more efficiently using animal power, supplemented by hand weeding only where necessary. This paper discusses techniques for weeding with draft animals in crops planted on ridges or on flat fields. Good soil preparation helps to control weeds. Implement options reviewed include tine cultivators (with points, sweeps and/or hillers) and plow beams fitted with large sweeps or earthing-up bodies.

Introduction

Weeding with a hand hoe involves scraping the soil to cut the roots of weeds just below the soil surface and shaking the soil off the roots to prevent regrowth. When hand weeding a crop that has been planted on ridges, the ridges need to be rebuilt at the same time, by scraping the soil upward from the furrows. In both cases the operation is slow and tedious.

All crops can be weeded using oxen or donkeys provided the inter-row spacings allow passage of the implement without causing damage to the roots and stems of the crop plants. Oxen and donkeys can also be used to weed along and across rows of fruit trees and plantation crops such as citrus, bananas, coffee, tea, sugar cane and vines. This paper outlines how animal power can be applied to weeding in Tanzania and so relieve the farmers of drudgery.

Plowing, harrowing and planting

The secret of successful and effective weeding using draft animals lies in adequate preparation, both of the animals and of the crop.

To make the crop easy to weed, it should be planted in parallel rows at least 45 cm apart. This can be achieved by planting behind the plow; by hand planting with jab planters, punch planters, etc, ensuring row spacing by using row markers or by estimating through experience; or by using a five-tine cultivator fitted with furrow openers, a seed covering device and a row marker. The farmer can also use hillers to construct half ridges along which seed and fertiliser can be dropped and covered as the ridge is completed on the following run.

Plowing, harrowing and planting should be arranged and timed such that the crop germinates before the weeds, so that at weeding time the crop plants are taller than the weeds. If the land is plowed immediately after the onset of the rains, the farmer should allow three to five days for the first weed population to germinate before harrowing and killing the weeds using suitable implements

An alternative approach is to kill the first and second weed populations before planting. In this case, plowing is delayed until after the first weed population has germinated, about four days after the onset of the rains. After the first plowing, three to five days should be allowed for a second weed population to germinate before harrowing and killing the weeds.

In either case, the crop should be planted on the same day the field is harrowed. Post-emergence weeding should begin two to three weeks after the crop germinates.

Weeding in flat cultivation systems

For weeding crops planted on the flat a two stage approach is necessary. First the farmer has to cut the weed roots just below the ground surface in between the rows of the growing crop. The second operation is to bury the weeds by earthing-up using a hiller, the plow or the tie ridger/weeder blade (Kayumbo, Chitopela and Mnyau, 1987).

The animals must be adequately trained, and are best led from the front during the weeding operation. It is easier to weed with a single animal than with two, but if two animals are used the farmer should use a 240 cm yoke or evener. The farmer could also take precautions against the animals grazing the crop, by using muzzles or halters.

Photo 1: Cultivator with reversible teeth and rear sweeps for inter-row weeding

Photo 3: Five-tine cultivator with reversible teeth

Photo 4: Hiller fitted on a ridger beam. This arrangement is used for weeding by earthing-up

Cutting weed roots between crop rows

Several implements can be used to cut the roots of weeds between crop rows:

º a cultivator fitted with two (or four) reversible teeth in the front and three 20 cm sweeps on the hind tines (Photo 1)

º a five-tine cultivator fitted with two reversible teeth in the front and a sweep on the rear tine, the size of which depends on the inter-row spacing

º a sweep, the size of which depends on inter-row spacing, fixed on the beam of a plow or ridger by means of a bracket (Photo 2).

The five-tine cultivator, fitted with reversible teeth on all tines (Photo 3), can be used to disintegrate the soil to expose the roots of weeds to the sun for desiccation after the weeding implements have been used.

Earthing-up to bury weeds

Hillers are used following sweeps. They can be attached to the steel beam of a plow or ridger (Photo 4) or to the rear of a cultivator, with or without the other tines on the frame (Photo 5).

In the absence of the hiller the farmer can use an ordinary plow for earthing-up.

Photo 2: Sweep fitted to a ridger beam for inter-row weeding

Similarly the tie ridger/weeder blade can be used for weeding when used in the tilted position, where necessary making use of the bracket on the plow beam, the standard on the ridger steel beam or the rear tine of the five-tine cultivator, with or without the other tines on the frame.

Cutting weed roots and earthing-up in one operation

A five-tine cultivator fitted with two reversible teeth in the front, a pair of 20 cm sweeps in the centre and a hiller on the rear tine is a complete implement

Photo 5: Hillers fitted to a cultivator for earthing-up (sweeps are also fitted)

Photo: A K Kayumbo

Photo 6: Cultivator fitted with reversible front tines, hiller blades and rear sweep

Photo: A K Kayumbo

Photo 8: Tie-ridger/weeder blade fitted on the frame of a five-tine cultivator

Weeding in ridged cultivation systems

Land preparation for ridged cultivation involves the construction of 70–90 cm ridges using an ox ridger or a mouldboard plow adjusted to cut at maximum width and depth. Crops are then planted on the ridges.

Ridged cultivation systems can be weeded using a tie ridger/weeder (Photo 7). Farmers can make a blade for this implement by cutting a 55–60 cm diameter used plow disc in half and drilling two holes vertically at the centre of one of the half discs. The blade can be fitted on a plow beam, on the standard of a ridger steel beam (after the ridger body has been removed) or on the rear tine of a cultivator, with or without the other tines removed (Photo 8). The implement can then be used for weeding between the ridges and for tying the ridges, all in one operation.

As the implement is pulled between the ridges by one or two animals it cuts all the weeds growing on the sides the ridges and on the bottom of the furrow. By lifting the implement every few paces soil is deposited in the furrow, thus tying the ridges.

However, this implement cannot be used to weed the tops of the ridges; this operation must therefore be done using hand tools.

suitable for inter-row weeding and earthing-up to bury the weeds along the row of crop plants. The implement can be adjusted to give a shallow or deep cut. A similar combination with front points and side hillers is shown in Photo 6.

Alternatively the tie ridger/weeder blade can be fixed on the rear tine of the cultivator instead of the hiller for inter-row weeding and earthing-up, when used together with sweeps and or reversible teeth.

The farmer can also use the ordinary mouldboard plow for inter-row weeding and earthing-up along the growing crop during weeding.

Reference

Kayumbo A K, Chitopela A T and Mnyau W, 1987. *Draught animal power.* Teacher's manual. Ministry of Agriculture and Livestock Development, Dar es Salaam, Tanzania.

Photo 7: Tie-ridger/weeder fitted to ridger beam

Photo: A K Kayumbo

Improving animal-powered tillage systems in Tanzania

by

A K Kayumbo

Agricultural Officer (Mechanisation), Ministry of Agriculture, PO Box 9071, Dar es Salaam, Tanzania

Abstract

In many developing countries agriculture is still largely based on hand tool technologies, with animal traction and tractors playing minor roles. Agriculture could be made more efficient and successful if this situation were reversed, with animal traction being the major source of farm power, supplemented by hand tools and engine-powered technologies where required.

Unfortunately animal traction is still regarded as no more than the use of ox plows on the farm. Ox plows are important in any tillage system as a means of relieving the farmer from the drudgery of hand tool cultivation, but unless other animal-powered implements, for example for harrowing, planting, weeding and even harvesting, are used in conjunction with plows, the full benefits of using ox plows may not be realised. Indeed, exclusive use of ox plows without such other implements could put an additional workload on the farmer.

This paper discusses the use of a wide range of animal-powered agricultural implements that could be used to improve the efficiency of agriculture in Tanzania.

Background

A major benefit of using ox plows is that a given area of land can be cultivated in a much shorter time than it can using hand hoes. But this increased efficiency can also have its drawbacks. For example, weeds can be growing over an entire field within a few days, and if the household relies only on hand tools for weeding, and if hired labour is not available, this can cause a serious labour bottleneck. If weeding is excessively delayed, there is a risk that the farmer may even lose a portion of the crop. If the farmer capitalises on the use of ox plows by increasing the area under cultivation, while still relying on hand tool technologies for other agricultural operations, the labour constraints become even more serious.

A solution to this dilemma is to complement the use of ox plows with more efficient methods and implements for other farm activities—harrowing, planting, weeding and even harvesting—also using animals as the source of power. Unfortunately, many farmers lack the technical know-how to use animals for these other agricultural tasks, largely because suitable effective and durable implements are not available.

This paper describes some animal-powered implements that could be used to increase agricultural efficiency in Tanzania.

Plows

In many countries, including Tanzania, the most commonly used plows are the 25 cm mouldboard types on short steel beams (Photo 1). Several other types of plow, are available, for example:

° ripping plows including the Ethiopian *maresha* and the ripper tine
° 15 cm single mouldboard plows on wooden or steel beams which can be short or long
° 25 cm reversible plows
° 25 cm single mouldboard plows on steel and wooden beams or toolbars and toolcarriers
° 25 cm double mouldboard plows on steel frames or toolcarriers.

A potential hazard with the extensive use of ox plows is the possibility of accelerated soil erosion, particularly in areas where farmers do not observe soil conservation measures. Thus while the plow may be introduced to improve primary and secondary tillage operations the overall benefits may be negative if soil degradation occurs over the plowed land in subsequent years (Elwell, 1990).

The plow should therefore be used in conjunction with proper tillage systems such as contour plowing using appropriate plowing patterns, reversible plowing, plowing between contour grass strips and trash bunds, plowing between terraces, etc.

Photo 1: Mouldboard plow commonly used in Tanzania

Photo: A K Kayumbo

The plow steel beam can also function as a simple toolbar: various attachments for weeding, furrow opening for planting purposes, ripping and earthing-up can be fixed to it with a bracket (Starkey, 1988).

Harrows

Farmers in upland farming systems rarely harrow after plowing, mainly because harrowing with hand tools is such a tedious operation. Farmers in these areas generally carry out a second plowing to kill weeds immediately before planting, but harrowing would be a quicker and much more efficient way to prepare a fine seedbed free from weeds, if a suitable and effective implement were available.

Many of the harrows currently available on the market are too light to be effective in breaking up soil clumps and killing weeds (Figure 1).

Five-tine cultivators can be used as harrows in a two-stage process. First, the cultivator is fitted with two reversible teeth in the front and three 20 cm sweeps (or one 70 cm sweep) on the hind tines, to cut the weed roots just below ground level. Second, reversible teeth are fitted on all five tines of the cultivator (Photo 2) to disintegrate the soil, thus shaking the soil from the weed roots to expose them to the sun for desiccation. Alternatively the two operations can be combined in one by fitting a 70 cm sweep in the rear and four reversible teeth in the front.

Planters

Planting is also a very tedious and time-consuming operation, particularly when the inter-row and within-row spacings are small. Many farmers tend either to broadcast the seeds or to plant them in hills with two or more seeds per hill.

Row planting is equally difficult to achieve with hand planting methods and most farmers prefer to plant behind the first or second plowing operation, dropping seed every two or three furrow slices behind the plow (Kjærby, 1983).

Photo 2: Cultivator fitted with five reversible tines for harrrowing

The main problem with using planters is the need to use graded seed. The seed must be graded both in size and shape and appropriate seed plates used (Kayumbo, 1987). Vertical seed metering devices tend to be more effective than horizontal seed plates.

Most animal-powered planters on the market are single row planters. Donkeys are best used to pull such single row planters as planting can be cumbersome with two oxen. The use of multiple row planters may have potential. Initially very simple ox-drawn multiple row seeders should be introduced. Such seeders are basically to be provided with furrow openers with which to open shallow furrows along which seed and fertiliser can be dropped and covered.

Having this idea in mind it is possible to adapt and convert some implements for seeders. A simple tine can be attached to the beam of a mouldboard plow to make a simple furrow opener (Photo 3). The five tine cultivator can be converted to operate as a simple ox-drawn multiple row hand seeder by fitting furrow openers, seed tubes and simple fertiliser and seed hoppers. A seed covering device and a row marker can be added but seed and fertiliser can be dropped or metered by hand behind the implement.

Alternatively, a farmer can opt to open half ridges using a hiller and then drop seed along the top and fertiliser along the bottom of the half ridge by hand; these are covered as the ridge is completed on the return pass. The hiller can be fitted on the rear tine of a five-tine cultivator or on the steel beam of the plow and ridger.

Ridge cultivation systems

It is interesting to see a farmer constructing a 90 cm ridge using a hoe. The farmer first cuts a half ridge piling three slices of soil at a time with the first slice neatly turned under to bury the weeds as the half ridge is formed. Similarly, when completing the ridge the farmer does the same, ending with a well-formed and weed-free ridge.

Figure 1: Zig zag harrow

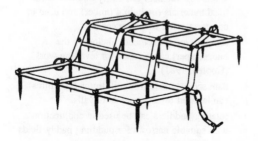

Photo 3: Furrow opener for planting

In order to form a good, weed-free ridge using the ox ridger the farmer has to observe the following:

- ideally, the land is plowed and the first weed population allowed to germinate before ridging

- young weeds are best killed using effective weeding implements leaving unweeded strips along which the ridges are built. By following this procedure ridges will be well formed and free from weeds

- in light soils, such as sandy loams, it may be possible to split old ridges with the ox ridger without plowing by allowing the first generation of weeds to germinate and then cleaning the ridges of all weeds before constructing new ridges

- to clean the weeds on the old ridges using oxen, a tie ridger/weeder blade fitted on the plow or ridger steel beams or fitted on the hind tine of the cultivator can be used. The blade is used in the tilted position if necessary

- when the plow is used to construct new ridges, old ridges are best cleaned of weeds using the tie ridger/weeder

- the tie ridger/weeder blade is also a suitable implement for weeding between 70–90 cm ridges and tying them in one pass to conserve soil and water.

Minimum tillage

In semi-arid areas, shifting cultivation is still a common practice. Shifting cultivation consists of slashing bush followed by burning and direct seeding in the first year. In subsequent years, however, the farmer has to clean the field of all crop residues before burning and planting. Here the farmer may plant the seed after the first showers of rain or dry plant just before the rains start. This means the weeds germinate ahead of the crop, or together with the crop, and the farmer must start hand weeding immediately the weeds start germinating or just after planting if the field was already infested with weeds at the time of planting.

If herbicides are not available, this system of cultivation can be improved through the use of the ripper tine in combination with sweeps as follows:

- the first generation of weeds is allowed to germinate for three days after the onset of the rains

- the young weeds are killed using sweeps

- the ripper tine is used to break the soil in rows at the recommended inter-row spacing

- the seed can then be planted immediately along the loosened row, preferably using a jab planter.

Subsequent weeding operations are possible using sweeps and hillers.

Alternatively the ripper tine can be used just before the onset of the rains, but planting is then delayed until the first young population of weeds has germinated and been killed using sweeps.

Irrigation farming

Although animals are rarely used in irrigation farming in Tanzania, here are several interesting possibilities for the use of various ox-powered implements and farm equipment (Starkey, 1989):

- furrowers can be used in collaboration with plows to construct irrigation furrows

- wooden bund formers (Figure 2) can be made locally and used for the basin irrigation system

- single row ditchers can easily be made from local materials (including timber) and used to construct water transport canals

- scraper type implements (including the buckscraper) can be used for levelling work (Hopfen, 1981)

- dam scoops made from oil drums (200 litres) can be used to construct dam walls.

- rotating puddlers can be used in conjunction with suitable harrows for puddling paddy fields.

Figure 2: Wooden bund former

Terraced cultivation systems

As mentioned above, the farmer has to use the ox plow together with proper soil conservation measures, particularly the use of terraces.

Although little is known in Tanzania about animal-powered implements that can be used for the construction of terraces, the following possibilities exist:

- different types of plows and ripper tines can be used to loosen the soil so that earth-moving implements can be used

- dam scoops can be used to move the loosened soil and level the terrace
- similarly, scraper blades can be used with the dam scoop for better levelling and quicker results.

References

Elwell H A, 1990. *A review of current erosion research at the Institute of Agricultural Engineering (IAE), Harare, Zimbabwe*. Institute of Agricultural Engineering, Harare, Zimbabwe.

Hopfen H J, 1981. *Farm implements for arid and tropical regions*. (Revised edition). FAO Agricultural Development Paper 91. Food and Agriculture Organization of the United Nations (FAO), Rome, Italy. 159p.

Kjærby F, 1983. *Problems and contradictions in the development of ox-cultivation in Tanzania*. Research Report 66. Scandinavian Institute of African Studies, Uppsala, Sweden. 164p.

Kayumbo A K, 1987. Constraints to the wider use of farm equipment in the rural areas. pp. 35–39 in: *In quest of agricultural mechanisation policy and strategies in the United Republic of Tanzania*. Proceedings of national workshop on farm tools and equipment technology: basic needs and employment, held 8–10 October 1985, Dar es Salaam, Tanzania. International Labour Organisation (ILO), Geneva, Switzerland. 69p.

Starkey P, 1988. *Perfected yet rejected: animal-drawn wheeled toolcarriers*. Vieweg for German Appropriate Technology Exchange. GTZ, Eschborn, Germany. 161p.

Starkey P, 1989. *Harnessing and implements for animal traction*. Vieweg for German Appropriate Technology Exchange, GTZ, Eschborn, Germany. 244p.

Development of an animal-drawn disc ridger for a tied ridging system of conservation tillage

by

Jürgen Hagmann

GTZ Conservation Tillage Project, PO Box 790, Masvingo, Zimbabwe

Abstract

Draft power and labour constraints in the communal areas of Zimbabwe make it difficult to implement tied ridging using the local winged ridger or mouldboard plow. In response to these problems an animal-drawn disc ridger was developed. Using this implement, draft and work time requirements were reduced by 45 and 40%, respectively. Although the implement is quite heavy, it contributes to an easier and less labour-intensive management of tied ridging. Its use is not limited to tied ridging as it can also be operated as a ridger for other ridging systems.

Introduction

A recent erosion survey in Zimbabwe showed that 27% of the total communal land could be classified as seriously or very seriously eroded (Whitlow, 1988). This fact demonstrates that protective measures taken against soil erosion during the past 50 years have not been effective. During this period, emphasis was given to preventing rill and gully erosion by contour layouts (storm drains, waterways and contour ridges). No measures have been taken against sheet erosion. However, a substantial part of the degradation in communal lands is due to arable sheet erosion between the contour ridges. Conservation tillage systems are therefore being developed to help prevent sheet erosion and so facilitate sustainable crop production.

A major constraint for tillage in communal areas is draft power. Droughts during the past decade have reduced the number of cattle and made them too expensive for many farmers. The existing animals are generally in a poor condition. Draft constraints are so severe that tillage operations such as plowing for planting are often much delayed at peak times, and such delays can contribute to complete crop failures. Therefore, conservation tillage systems are most likely to be successful if they require low draft power.

Tied ridging system

One conservation tillage system developed in Zimbabwe is known locally as "no-till tied ridging" (Elwell and Norton, 1988). Further research on

conservation tillage is presently being carried out by the Department of Agricultural, Technical and Extension Services (Agritex), assisted by the German Agency for Technical Cooperation (GTZ), in the Conservation Tillage for Sustainable Crop Production Systems Project, also known as "ConTil".

The conservation tillage system is based on the conventional tied ridging system (Prestt, 1986) which is a type of basin tillage. Ridges and cross-dams (ties) in the furrows form basins which reduce surface runoff and thus conserve soil and water. In the conventional tied ridging system these ridges are plowed every year. In the "no-till" system the ridges are semi-permanent. Draft power requirements are less because, after the first year, only ridge maintenance and weeding have to be carried out.

In the first year the land is plowed to the recommended depth of 230 mm. Ridges about 900 mm wide and a minimum of 250 mm high are constructed either by an animal-drawn ridger or with a single furrow mouldboard plow (Elwell and Norton, 1988). Ridges are laid out at a grade of 1:250 to 1:100. Cross-ties, one-half to two-thirds of the height of the ridge, are made by hoe or low-cost tie-maker at intervals of about 1.5 m. In wet years, or in soils prone to waterlogging, the ties can be removed or allowed to break during storms in order to drain away excess water. Planting is carried out on top of the ridge once the ridge is moist throughout. Early weeding is achieved through re-ridging. After harvest, re-ridging is carried out in order to eliminate late weeds.

Problems of animal-powered tied-ridging

Tied ridging has performed well on research sites (Vogel, 1991) especially in terms of soil conservation. However, implementation of tied ridging using a conventional (high-wing) ox-drawn ridger proved to be draft-intensive. It was less draft-intensive but much more time-consuming if a plow was used. Other problems encountered during the preceding observational tillage trials (Stevens,

1989) and during the continuing adaptive on-farm trials (Gotora, 1991) were that:

- ridge tying requires another operation with draft animals provided a low-cost tie-maker is available. If not, ties must be built up by hoe which is extremely labour-intensive. In this regard it is understandable that some farmers with few resources, stopped ridge tying, although this operation is essential to the conservation objectives of this system
- timeliness of all operations suffers due to the time-consuming procedures involved. Untimely weeding is particularly serious, since late ox-powered weeding may fail, resulting either in high weed infestation or in investment in time-consuming manual weeding
- planting on ridges can be a problem: one labour-intensive procedure involves holing-out using a hoe. Making a planting furrow on the ridge using draft animals is less time-consuming, but is difficult, depending on the shape of the ridges.

Against this background it was clear that tied ridging was a new system that required more development if it was to be accepted by farmers in communal areas. Optimal animal-drawn implements were not yet available. Using the existing animal-drawn implements or manual operations, the system required more labour and draft power than most farmers have available.

Development of a disc ridger

In response to the problems mentioned, notably the high draft of the conventional (high-wing) ridger and long time requirement with a plow, it was decided to develop an animal-drawn disc ridger. This was intended to reduce both draft power and time requirements. In addition, the disc ridger was expected to fulfil the following criteria:

- ridge shape and size must be adequate: ridges must have a width of 900 mm, a height of at least 250 mm and a flat crest (like an inverted W)
- work efficiency in ridging, re-ridging and tying must be very much higher than with the present equipment. Re-ridging and tying ideally should be achieved in one operation. This would guarantee more timely operations
- weeding performance must be satisfactory
- the ridger should be easy to handle, to facilitate its use by the many old farmers now operating in communal areas
- design should be simple and robust

- the ridger should require very little maintenance (wear and tear should be at a minimum)
- the ridger must be affordable for communal farmers
- the ridger must be capable of being manufactured with locally available materials without the need for foreign currency
- where practicable, further attributes, such as self-cleaning, should be built into the ridger design.

With the above requirements in mind, a first prototype was designed and built. As soon as a prototype was found to perform well on-station, ridgers were given to farmers participating in on-farm trials. Ways of improving the implement according to the needs of potential users were intensively discussed with farmers, and appropriate changes were included in the next version. The present implement is a result of this step-by-step procedure which will continue in the future.

Technical design

The main difference between the disc ridger and a high-wing plow-ridger is the use of revolving discs for moving the soil. These reduce frictional resistance and draft power. The disc ridger consists of a main beam and a central crossed beam to which two adjustable discs are attached. A duckfoot tine is mounted in front, and behind is a tie-maker attached to a handle that can be lifted and dropped by the operator (see Figure 1). The disc ridger is pulled by a wooden draw bar which allows good control of the implement. All adjustments can be set without spanners. Bolts with handles or bolts pushed by spring mechanisms are used. The ridger can be operated in two different ways: ridging and re-ridging. Furthermore, the discs can be put to a transport position.

Figure 1: Components of the disc ridger
1: beam with draw bar attachment; 2: handle;
3: tie-maker; 4: attachments for distance between discs
and disc angle; 5: king pins with disc shafts; 6: discs;
7: duckfoot-tine; 8: draw bar

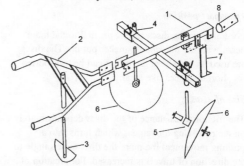

Photo: Jürgen Hagmann

Photo 1: Disc ridger in ridging mode

Photo: Jürgen Hagmann

Photo 2: Disc ridger in re-ridging and ridge-tying mode

Ridging mode

For an initial installation of ridges the "ridging mode" is used (see Photo 1). The revolving discs scrape the pre-plowed soil into a ridge between the discs. The width and the height of the ridge can be varied by adjusting the disc angle and the distance between the discs. The handle is in a fixed position. If required, a ripper tine can be mounted on the tie-maker and can be used for ripping an additional line on top of the ridge (eg, for a planting furrow). The duckfoot tine in front can be adjusted to loosen the soil if required, or it can be left idle.

Re-ridging and tying

For re-ridging in the furrow (eg, for weeding or rebuilding an existing ridge), including tying, the "re-ridging mode" is applied (see Photo 2). In this position the revolving discs move soil from the furrow bottom to the flanks and, depending on the adjustment, on to the top of the ridge. The tine pulls in and loosens the soil in the furrow. Simultaneously the handle with the attached tie-maker is pressed down and lifted up every three steps. By doing so, soil in the furrow is pushed to form ties at a spacing of approximately 1.5 m. Re-ridging and tying are achieved in one operation. The same position can be applied for installing ridges, but for this purpose handling is less stable than with the ridging mode.

Transport position

For transport the discs are set parallel to the main beam with the tine and tie-maker put up. The discs are used as wheels so the ridger can be transported for short distances like a cart.

Size of discs

The frictional resistance of the discs depends mainly on the revolving movement which turns into a pushing movement the more the disc angle (angle to the direction of travel) is increased. For creation of 900 mm wide ridges, larger diameter discs need a narrow disc angle (leading to lower frictional resistance and lower draft requirement than smaller discs). The main disadvantage of big discs is their weight. The price difference between small and large discs is small. A suitable compromise for tied ridging was found to be a diameter of about 60 cm, available locally as "26 inch" discs for tractor plows.

Tilt angle

The tilt angle (disc inclination angle) which determines the slope of the ridge shoulder has experimentally been found to have its optimum at 28° for both positions (ridging and re-ridging). This angle was fixed in order to make manufacturing easier and to avoid the necessity for many adjustments.

Weight

Due to the poor quality of available steel, the weight of the implement is 81 kg. Using high quality steel (not currently available in Zimbabwe), the weight could be reduced by about 30% without loss of strength. As a comparison, the high-wing ridger weighs 43 kg, while the conventional plow weighs 41 kg.

Practical experience

Handling and operational performance

A comparative test of the disc ridger along the lines recommended by Nazare and Norton (1988) for plow ridgers has not yet been carried out. The experience of the use of the disc ridger recorded in this paper is based on the feedback given by 16 farmers who participated in on-farm trials. From these trials and the on-station experience the following conclusions can be drawn so far.

Table 1: Comparison of draft and work requirements for ridging with different implements

	Ridging		Tying[1]		Ridging and tying	Re-ridging		Re-ridging and tying
	Mean draft (kN)	Time (hours/ha)	Mean draft (kN)	Time (hours/ha)	Time (hours/ha)	Mean draft (kN)	Time (hours/ha)	Time (hours/ha)
Disc ridger	0.96	4.7	0.53	3.2	7.9	1.24	5.2	5.2[2]
High-wing ridger	1.73	5.8	0.53	3.2	9.0	1.76	5.5	8.7
Inkunzi plow	1.37	11.0	0.53	3.2	14.2	1.46	11.8	15.0

[1] Using low cost tiemaker
[2] Simultaneous re-ridging and tying

Ridging

Ridge shape and size fully correspond to the required specifications. Ridge height mainly depends on depth of previous plowing. However, even on shallow plowed fields satisfactory results could be obtained. Ridge formation was very precise and homogeneous ridges and spacings were obtained, especially with the ridging mode. Handling during operation proved to be very good. Old farmers as well as women could operate it easily. A disadvantage of this mode is that an extra operation is needed for tying.

Re-ridging and tying

With proper adjustment (depending on crusting of soil) re-ridging results were found to be good. Simultaneous tying by lifting the tie-maker up and down gave good results as well. Handling during this operation requires a stronger control than in the ridging mode. Initially, farmers found it difficult to simultaneously re-ridge and tie. When they had more experience (each of them found their own best technique) they classified the operation as easy. Improperly trained oxen caused the major problem. The disc ridger, being mainly controlled through the draw bar, should only be operated with well-trained oxen.

Maintenance and wear

The bearings of the disc shafts should be lubricated once or twice a season depending on the size of the

Table 2: Average prices for animal-drawn farm implements in Zimbabwe, November 1991

	Z$	US$
Disc ridger	750	150
High-wing ridger	445	89
Inkunzi plow	214	43
Cultivator	345	69
Planter	920	184
Animal-drawn cart	2196	440

tilled area. Wear is spread over the entire circumference of the discs and is relatively light.

Draft power and work time requirement

Draft power requirements were quantified on-station. Farmers' experience supported the on-station results as they considered the ridger to be a "light" implement to use. Farmers accustomed to using donkeys as draft animals used donkeys for ridging and re-ridging. Both operations could be well managed by one pair of donkeys. Results of a draft power test are shown in Table 1.

For ridging, draft power required for the disc ridger was 45% less than for the high-wing ridger and 30% less than for the plow. For re-ridging, the disc ridger with the attached tie-maker reduced draft power by 30% compared to the high-wing ridger and by 15% compared to the plow. Work time requirements for re-ridging and tying could be cut down by 40% compared to the high-wing ridger and by 65% compared to the plow. These results show that the disc ridger has a high potential for conditions with low draft power.

Cost efficiency

So far, the disc ridger has not been manufactured commercially. A tentative estimate for end-user price following serial manufacture in Zimbabwe was 750 Zimbabwe dollars (Z$) or US$ 150 (November 1991 prices). For comparison, prices for the most common animal-drawn farm implements are shown in Table 2.

The disc ridger is 68% more expensive than the high-wing ridger. For resource-poor communal farmers it will definitely be a big investment considering the prices they actually get for their products. Therefore, farmers who have already experienced the advantages and benefits of tied ridging will be the potential buyers.

In the long term the disc ridger should be financially rewarding. Savings in draft power and labour (which often must be hired) and yield benefits due to timely operations could contribute to a reasonable amortisation of the ridger. Farmers are often willing to invest after good seasons when they have buying power. For example, many farmers bought new animal-drawn carts after high yields in the 1989/90 season.

It will mainly be those progressive farmers with some resources and who perceive the advantages of tied ridging who would be potential buyers of the disc ridger. Some small-scale commercial farmers who saw the implement were very interested in buying it.

Conclusion

The disc ridger contributes to an easier and less labour-intensive management of tied ridging. While a conclusive comparative test of the disc ridger has yet to be carried out, practical experience indicates that it satisfies most of the identified requirements with respect to ease and timeliness of operations.

The most important advantage is the reduction in time required for ridging and for re-ridging and tying. This will enable farmers to cope with cultivation of their land in a much shorter period of time. As a result, other farming activities can also be carried out with greater timeliness. Other implements which reduce time and labour must also be developed in order to make the conservation tillage system attractive to farmers.

The second essential advantage is the greatly reduced draft power required for this ridger compared to the high-wing ridger. This is particularly important for drought prone areas where draft power is very limited. In these areas, numerous donkeys are available and cheap, whereas oxen are often too expensive for farmers. Therefore implements must be light enough to be pulled by donkeys. The disc ridger fulfils this condition. However, while donkeys are widely used to pull

carts, their use for tillage purposes has yet to be widely adopted.

The use of this disc ridger is not limited to tied ridging. It is possible to set the disc ridger for different dimensions of ridges. Therefore, this implement might be of interest not only for communal farmers but also for small-scale commercial farmers. It could also be used as an animal-drawn tobacco ridger.

Acknowledgements

The development of the disc ridger was greatly assisted by the dedicated work of Mr Gloss (Masvingo) whose technical competence contributed greatly to the present design. In addition, the support of farmers in Zaka and Chivi Districts and of the ConTil team is gratefully acknowledged.

References

Elwell H A and Norton A, 1988. *No-till tied-ridging: a recommended sustained crop production system.* Institute of Agricultural Engineering, Department of Agricultural, Technical and Extension Services (Agritex), Harare, Zimbabwe. 39p.

Gotora P, 1991. Adaptive no-till tied ridging trials in small-scale farming areas of Zimbabwe. pp. 410–416 in: *Soil tillage and agricultural sustainability.* Proceedings of the 12th International Conference of the International Soil Tillage Research Organisation (ISTRO), held July 1991, Ibadan, Nigeria. Ohio State University, Colombos, Ohio, USA.

Nazare R M and Norton A J, 1988. *Evaluation of ox-drawn ridgers.* Institute of Agricultural Engineering, Department of Agricultural, Technical and Extension Services (Agritex), Harare, Zimbabwe. 12p.

Prestt A J, 1986. Basin tillage: a review. *Zimbabwean Agricultural Journal* 83(1).

Stevens P A, 1989. *Observational tillage trials.* Paper presented at the Agritex Technical Conference, 16–20 October 1989, Nyanga, Zimbabwe. [Available from the Institute of Agricultural Engineering, Department of Agricultural, Technical and Extension Services (Agritex), Harare, Zimbabwe]

Vogel H, 1991. *Conservation tillage for sustainable crop production systems.* Project Research Report 2. Institute of Agricultural Engineering, Department of Agricultural, Technical and Extension Services (Agritex), Harare, Zimbabwe. 38p.

Whitlow R, 1988. *Land degradation in Zimbabwe: a geographical study.* Report prepared on behalf of the Department of Natural Resources, Harare, Zimbabwe. 62p.

Improving animal-powered reduced tillage systems in Zimbabwe

by

S Chikura

Farming Systems Research Unit
Department of Research and Specialist Services, PO Box 8108, Causeway, Harare, Zimbabwe

Abstract

Low cattle numbers and poor cattle condition at the start of the rainy season increase the time taken for land preparation, resulting in delayed maize establishment. This has contributed to low yields, particularly for farmers who do not own cattle and therefore must wait for other farmers' cattle to become available. On-farm trials were undertaken to try to alleviate the problem. Using an animal-drawn ripper tine in combination with a herbicide increased maize yields in the Mangwende Communal Area of Zimbabwe. The system appeared economically appropriate, mainly due to a decrease in labour requirements at planting and weeding. Labour is a critical limiting factor during these periods.

Introduction

The Farming Systems Research Unit (FSRU) of the Department of Research and Specialist Services, Zimbabwe, was established in 1984 to study communal area farming systems.

According to a survey by FSRU in these areas, low cattle numbers and poor cattle condition at the start of the rainy season result in insufficient draft power (FSRU, 1985; Shumba, 1985). This has contributed to low maize yields particularly for non-cattle owners (GFA, 1987). The same survey also established that there were labour bottlenecks during planting and weeding periods. Some farmers were found to be "winter plowing" in March to May soon after harvesting and when moisture is still available.

Trials and methods

In order to capitalise on the existing "winter plowing" practices, a trial was initiated in the 1983/84 season using a ripper tine. In this trial a ripper tine was compared to the conventional use of plowing before planting. The use of a herbicide compared to hand weeding was superimposed on this trial. In the first season, 1983/84, the trial was conducted on eight sites that were divided into three groups according to rainfall pattern (Table 1).

Results

The results from this trial are shown in Table 2. The amount and distribution of rainfall received in January had a strong influence on overall crop performance. The January period coincided with the tasselling and silking period since the crop was planted in the second half of November at most sites. January rainfall also influenced the effects of individual treatments on yield.

The tine treatment significantly out-yielded the conventional tillage treatment in rainfall group 1. The yield increase was not significant in rainfall groups 2 and 3.

Since the ripper tine was associated with deeper penetration and basal fertiliser application at planting it might have resulted in deeper root penetration. This might have allowed the crop to cope better with the dry January period. Planting for both the tine and conventional plow was done on the same day at two sites in group 1, so that the increase in yield could not be attributed to differences in planting date.

Herbicide use significantly increased yield at the sites in rainfall groups 2 and 3. At one of the sites in group 1 it failed to work because it was applied

Table 1: Rainfall distribution in three grouped trial sites in Mangwende during the 1983/84 season

Sites	October	November	December	January	February	March	Total
	Average rainfall (mm)						
Group 1 (3 Sites)	28.3	55.0	126.6	40.0	123.3	100.8	**474.0**
Group 2 (2 Sites)	12.5	47.5	97.5	58.7	178.5	160.0	**554.7**
Group 3 (3 Sites)	18.5	52.5	119.5	109.2	156.2	98.5	**554.4**

Source: FSRU (1985)

under dry conditions (this explains the site by treatment interaction).

Economic implications

An economic analysis of the pooled data from this trial was carried out and the results are presented in Table 3. They show the highest net returns to labour for the treatment involving the ripper tine and herbicide. The lowest returns were for the treatment with ripper tine cultivation plus hand weeding.

Based on these results it might be appropriate for farmers to adopt the tine and herbicide technology. This will require less labour and draft power. Based on these results the trial was continued in the subsequent seasons, with farmers taking an active role in the management of the trial.

Follow-up trials and implications

After running the trial for six seasons, a survey was carried out in Mangwende in 1990 to see how the farmers were taking the ripper tine and herbicide technology (FSRU, 1991). It was established that farmers were very interested in the tine and saw no particular problems in using it.

Some farmers noted that they might have problems in using the herbicide. Cash problems for buying sprayers and the herbicide were associated with the technology. Some farmers expressed the wish to have credit to buy the sprayer and the herbicide.

To overcome the problems of herbicide use, farmers could profitably combine the tine with the use of an ox-drawn cultivator to control weeds. This would

Table 2: Main effects of tillage and weed control methods on maize yield in Mangwende, 1983/84

	Mean yields (t/ha) and significance at each site		
	Group 1	Group 2	Group 3
Tillage			
Conventional plow	1.23	3.07	5.40
Ripper tine	1.73	3.25	5.76
Significance of treatment	P<0.01	NS	NS
Significance of site and treatment	NS	NS	P<0.01
Weed control			
Oxen/hand	1.51	2.82	5.25
Herbicide	1.45	3.50	5.92
Significance of treatment	NS	P<0.01	P<0.05
Significance of site and treatment	P<0.05	NS	NS

NS = not significant
Source: FSRU (1985)

reduce the labour required for weeding and could enable more farmers to adopt the technology.

In the 1990/91 season, a trial was run to compare the use of a herbicide with an animal-drawn cultivator. Two weeding regimes were employed:

○ weeding at emergence, and emergence + 30 days

○ weeding at emergence + 14 days and at emergence + 30 days.

The results of this trial are shown in Table 4. They show that there were no significant yield differences

Table 3: Economic analysis of maize tillage and weed control methods in Mangwende, 1983/84 season: pooled for all sites

	Conventional plowing		Ripper tine	
Criteria	Hand weeding	Herbicide	Hand weeding	Herbicide
Average yield of maize (t/ha)	4.65	4.78	4.03	5.20
Value of grain production (Z$)[1]	501.74	515.74	434.84	563.24
Treament cash cost (Z$)[2]	0.00	25.03	2.41	27.44
Non-treatment cash costs (Z$)[3]	192.50	192.50	192.50	192.50
Total labour cost (Z$)	85.77	57.72	98.31	50.98
(Total labour cost (hours))	(393)	(282)	(439)	(266)
Net benefit (Z$)	223.47	240.49	141.62	292.32
Net returns to labour (Z$/hour)[4]	0.57	0.85	0.32	1.10

[1] Yields were reduced by 10% to reflect the difference between experimental yields and farmers' expected yields
[2] Costs included Z$16 for herbicide, fixed costs of tine and sprayer and opportunity cost on capital
[3] Costs included Z$169 for 600 kg fertilizer, Z$7.5 for 5 kg Dipterex and Z$16 for 20 kg hybrid seed
[4] Returns calculated from (value of grain production – total costs)/labour hours
US$1 ≈ Z$3 (1984)
Source: FSRU (1985)

Table 4: Main effects of weed control methods on maize grain yield in Mangwende, 1990/91

Treatment	Yield at location (t/ha)			
	Zihute	Musami	Muchinjike	Mean
Herbicide (Atrazine)	4.40	5.06	3.23	4.23
Cultivator at emergence and 30 days later	5.55	3.80	3.27	4.20
Cultivator at 14 and 30 days after emergence	5.43	4.55	3.63	4.55
Significance (NS = not significant)	NS	NS	NS	
CV%	15.7	12.6	13.7	

between the treatments. This suggests farmers could use either method depending on the most important limiting factor for them. Thus cattle owners could easily use the tine and animal-drawn cultivator technology. Other farmers could use herbicides, and the least cost analysis suggested that farmers can benefit from using the tine and herbicide combination. The results of the economic analysis are shown in Table 5.

The 1990 survey identified that ripper tines were not available in the local shops, making it difficult for farmers to purchase them. To test the potential adoption rate of the technology, some tines were distributed to extension workers in Mangwende. The

results will be assessed before encouraging the manufacturer to produce more tines.

References

FSRU, 1985. *Annual report 1983–1984*. Farming Systems Research Unit (FSRU), Department of Research and Specialist Services, Ministry of Agriculture, Harare, Zimbabwe. pp. 33–56.

FSRU, 1991. *Annual report 1990–1991*. Farming Systems Research Unit (FSRU), Department of Research and Specialist Services, Ministry of Agriculture, Harare, Zimbabwe.

GFA, 1987. *Study on the economic and social determinants of livestock production in the communal areas of Zimbabwe*. Gesellschaft für Agrarprojekte mbH (GFA), Hamburg, Germany. pp. 83–90.

Shumba E M, 1985. On-farm research priorities resulting from a diagnosis of the farming systems of Mangwende, a high potential area in Zimbabwe. *Zimbabwe Agriculture Journal Special Report* 5:38–44.

Table 5: Economic analysis of the three weeding methods after ripper tine cultivation

Criteria	Herbicide	Ox weeding 0 and 30 days	Ox weeding 14 and 30 days
Yield of maize grain (kg/ha)	4228	4202	4553
Variable costs (Z$)			
Cost of herbicide (2.5 litres/ha) (Z$)	49.13	–	–
Labour for applying herbicide (Z$)	2.25	–	–
Cost of hiring sprayer (Z$)	5.00	–	–
Cost of ox cultivating (Z$)	–	154.00	154.00
Cost of hand weeding (after cultivating) (Z$)	–	16.88	33.75
Total variable costs (Z$)	**56.38**	**170.88**	**187.75**

The prices used to compile the partial budget were as follows: Cost of Atrazine = Z$19.65/litre
Labour for applying the herbicide = Z$5/day; Time for herbicide application = half day/ha
Hiring sprayer = Z$5/day; Cost of cultivating = Z$77/ha; Weeding (after cultivating) = Z$16/ha
US$1 ≈ Z$5 (1991)

Design innovations to simplify the regulation of animal-drawn mouldboard plows in Zambia

by

Hans Helsloot[*]

*Farm Implements and Tools (FIT) Section, TOOL Consultancy Department
Sarphatistraat 650, 1018 AV Amsterdam, The Netherlands*

Abstract

Many problems with the use of the ox-drawn mouldboard plow are caused by improperly adjusted regulators: farmers often do not understand how to set up this rather complex mechanism. Therefore, a regulator has been developed according to the design principle "form follows function". With the new design there is only one way to adjust plowing depth and this does not require tools. Thus plows are more likely to be properly adjusted, resulting in improved tillage and a lower energy requirement.

Introduction

Ox-drawn mouldboard plows are the most important farming implements after hand hoes in the Eastern Province of Zambia. However, operation of these plows is often problematic. The regulator of such a plow is rather a complex mechanism, and the most common reason for failure is that farmers do not understand how to use it correctly. Indeed, none of the farmers visited in Eastern Province used the regulator: it was either dismantled, or broken and not repaired. Instead, farmers use the wheel as a depth regulator, to push the plow out of the ground to the desired working depth. This causes overloading of the bearing unit (which is often poorly designed anyway), and excessive wear on the wheel axle so that the wheel can fall off. Another common problem is missing bolts and nuts. Many farmers do not tighten the bolts regularly, and often find it difficult to acquire new bolts or nuts to replace lost ones.

A new regulator has been designed according to the design principle "form follows function". In the new design, there is only one way to adjust plowing depth, and tools are not required to do so. Thus, plows are more likely to be properly adjusted, resulting in:

---

[*]*Subsequent address:*
Havensingel 70, 5211 TZ Den Bosch, The Netherlands

○ a substantially decreased pulling force, thus reducing the burden on the oxen and increasing the area that can be plowed in a given time
○ improved soil inversion and plowing quality
○ decreased wear and tear of soil touching parts, leading to lower repair and maintenance costs
○ easy handling of the plow for the plow operator.

Evaluation of the problem

Regulator

The main cause of regulator malfunction is a consequence of how plows are transported. Many farmers drag their plow to the field, without using a sledge or cart. The regulator, and other parts, are damaged by being scraped along the ground.

The regulator is not replaced when it is worn out. Some farmers remove the regulator altogether because they do not understand its function. They hitch the chain direct to the beam because they think that depth adjustment should be done with the wheel (Photo 1).

On the *Rhino* plow ("Safim type", manufactured by Northland Engineering), depth and width are adjusted with just one bolt (Figure 1). But farmers often do not know how to operate the regulator (and many of them do not even own spanners), and there is no indication on the plow itself of how this should be done. As a result, when the bolt is

Figure 1: Safim type Rhino *plow showing regulator*

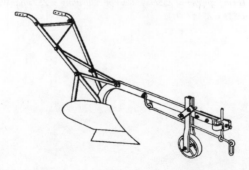

Photo 1: Farmer plowing in Zambia with the regulator of the Safim type plow removed and the chain attached directly to the beam

loosened, half the regulator falls apart. The design of the Lenco regulator is much better. Its width and depth are independently adjustable without tools. Its design indicates by its form that a vertical and a horizontal adjustment can be made.

Compared with the depth regulator, the horizontal width regulator is more easy to understand. When walking behind the plow, the operator can see what happens when the hitch point is moved sideways.

Ergonomic "incompatibility"

Adjustment of the plowing depth should be done with the depth regulator. Before that, however, the steadying wheel should be raised to its highest point. Then a short furrow should be plowed and its depth observed. If the furrow is too deep, the position of the regulator should be lowered slightly. Then another few metres must be plowed and the depth observed again. This procedure is repeated until the desired plowing depth is achieved. The steadying wheel is then lowered again until it just touches the soil surface.

None of the farmers or agricultural extension workers interviewed in Eastern Province knew anything about this procedure. It was generally thought that adjustment should be done by raising or lowering the steadying wheel. The functioning of the regulator is completely unknown. As mentioned above, many farmers simply hitch the draw chain directly to the plow beam. Even when the regulator performs well, the draw bar is set parallel to the beam, so the plow is set for deep plowing and the wheel is, wrongly, used to correct this.

Two ergonomic problems have been mentioned here, causing inefficient plowing.

○ it is not clear to the farmers or the agricultural extension workers that the steadying wheel should be fully raised while setting plowing depth with the depth regulator

○ the process by which depth should be adjusted with the regulator is unclear. In ergonomics language, its use is "incompatible" with its function: to plow deeper, the regulator must be moved up. It would seem to be more "common sense" to lower something in order to make the plow work deeper.

Solutions

The combination of the two ergonomic problems mentioned above provides the basic idea for a simplification of the regulator design. The steadying wheel and the regulator are integrated to make the depth adjustment device compatible with its function.

Although moving up the regulator does not look obvious, moving up the wheel is generally done by the farmers to increase the working depth. This is explained by the fact that, in our perception, the regulator refers to the plow, which has to go down, whereas the wheel refers to the distance between soil surface and the plow beam.

In the theoretically ideal case, as indicated in Figure 2, the depth adjustment bar has a curved shape. As a result, the wheel and the hitch point will describe a circle when being adjusted. The hitch point is located closer to the centre of the circle than the wheel. Thus, its height will change less than that of the wheel when the plow is adjusted. A more elaborate explanation of the functioning of the integrated regulator is given in Helsloot (1987).

The five holes in the adjustment bar allow the plow to work at five different depths (5, 7.5, 10, 12.5 and 15 cm). Minimum workable plowing depth is 5 cm and most farmers plow between 8 and 12 cm. Plowing deeper than 15 cm is too heavy for oxen.

As oxen pairs differ in size, it must be possible to change the height of the hitch point without moving

Figure 2: Initial concept of the new regulator

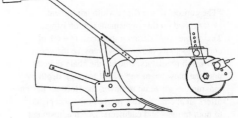

Key:
a - grips
b - handles
c - beam
d - frog
e - mouldboard
f - share
g - landside
h - landside heel
i - horizontal regulator and hitch point
j - vertical regulator and wheel arm
k - hitch arm
l - wheel
m- axle and brush

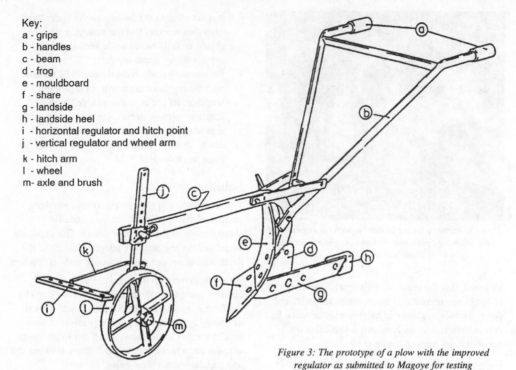

Figure 3: The prototype of a plow with the improved
regulator as submitted to Magoye for testing

the wheel bar. The three holes in front of the wheel
are the hitch points relating to the different ox sizes.
It can be seen that some parts have been eliminated,
making the plow somewhat lighter and cheaper.

Test results

Some work has been done to simplify production of
the regulator. The intention was to build the
regulator out of parts readily available in many
countries. Therefore, a prototype has been made
with a straight wheel arm (see Figures 3 and 4). The
wheel arm extension was screwed on, instead of
cutting the whole arm out of one piece. By making
the extension plate rotate, the width adjustment
could be welded on.

A prototype of the implement described has been
made by Rumptstad. This was subjected to tests by
the Animal Draft Power Research and Development
Project in Magoye, Zambia. The project concluded
(Meijer and Simuyemba, 1991) that:

"The concept of the depth/width adjustment
system used on this implement is promising.
Taking into consideration that most owners of
conventional ox-drawn plows remove the depth
and width regulators, connect the chain directly
onto the plow beam and adjust working depth by
moving the wheel up or down, the Helsloot design
offers an alternative that might prove acceptable
to both farmers and engineers. Depth adjustment

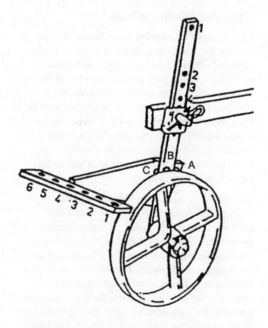

Figure 4: Detail of the prototype regulator
as submitted to Magoye for testing

can be done in the simple way most farmers are used to, by raising or lowering the wheel, while this action will simultaneously raise or lower the hitch point. As a result, depth adjustment can be easily explained and easily remembered. The implement's unconventional appearance, however, will for many farmers take time to get used to."

It was also mentioned that:

"Handling the plow is easy and it is light to lift. ... Setting the working depth by means of the wheel arm is, like width adjustment, easy and requires no tools. ... Position B of the hitch arm [see Figure 4] seems to offer the combination of best depth range, lowest draft requirements and fair stability."

Conclusions

The main improvement of this new regulator is that there is only one way to change the plowing depth because the depth regulation mechanism and the

steadying wheel have been combined. The way farmers are used to adjusting the plow, which until now was wrong, has become the right and only way to adjust it. For that reason, someone who has never plowed before will also adjust the plow properly.

If a hitch point is chosen that does not accord to the size of the oxen, everyone will notice that something is wrong. Either the wheel will not touch the ground, or the plow will not enter the soil.

References

Helsloot H, 1987. *Design of small-scale farm equipment for rural Zambia.* MSc Thesis. Department of Industrial Design Engineering, Delft University of Technology, Delft, The Netherlands. 158p.

Meijer R A and Simuyemba J, 1991. *Results of tests conducted with the Helsloot/Rumptstad prototype ox drawn mouldboard plow.* Animal Draft Power Research and Development Programme, PO Box 11, Magoye, Zambia. 15p.

Improving the *Hata* donkey-drawn weeder in Niger: experiences and results

F Emhardt

Institute for Agricultural Engineering, University of Hohenheim (440)
Postfach 700572, 70593 Stuttgart 70, Germany

Abstract

The labour burden of traditional farmers in the semi-arid tropics of West Africa can be considerably reduced through mechanisation of weeding by donkey-drawn Hatas *(houe à traction asine). The* Hata *prototype has completed its first working season under on-farm conditions. Some drawbacks have been discovered and these, together with experiences gained during 1991, will be used to develop a new 1992 model, which will be disseminated in the Republic of Niger in collaboration with several development projects.*

Weeding with the Hata *can take less than half the time of manual weeding (17.9 vs 41.1 hours/ha). Weeding efficiency of the* Hata *approaches that of manual weeding; double-pass measurements on* Hata *operations showed efficiency values of 76% for zero-tilled fields and 85% for ridged fields, compared with 96 and 91%, respectively, for manual weeding.*

Future investigations will focus on the suitability of the Hata *for different soil conditions. Other applications of the* Hata, *such as scarifying, will also be studied. The objective of this research is to enable poor small-scale farmers in rural areas of other African countries to use the* Hata *in their farming activities.*

Introduction

Weeds are a constant problem in agriculture: they compete with crops for nutrients, water and light, and hence reduce crop yields. It is estimated that about one-third of harvest losses worldwide can be attributed to weeds (Strobel, 1991).

In the semi-arid tropics of West Africa weeding is primarily done by hand. This can cause labour bottlenecks because the first weeding is necessary while sowing is still in progress.

The Institute for Agricultural Engineering at the University of Hohenheim, Germany, is developing animal drawn implements to improve traditional agriculture in the Sahelian zone in general and in the Republic of Niger in particular. One such implement is a donkey-drawn hoe, the *Hata* (houe à traction asine), for mechanised weeding on sandy soils.

From research prototype to on-farm implement

The design criteria for the *Hata* were (and still are) that the implement should:

° be light enough for donkey traction, as donkeys are the most common draft animals in Niger

° be understood, manufactured, repaired and maintained by local village blacksmiths; hence, forging and riveting were the chosen fabrication and fitting techniques

° cost less than 10 000 CFA francs (about US$ 40), so that as many farmers as possible can afford to buy it.

The first *Hata* prototype was presented at the West African Animal Traction Networkshop in Kano in 1990 (Betker, 1993). This prototype was tested on-farm during the 1991 rainy season and, based on the experience gained from these trials, an improved implement was constructed (Figure 1).

Structural improvements of the *Hata*

The first *Hata* prototype consisted principally of a flat iron triangle to which three traditional hand tool blades were fastened. To increase the rigidity, a U-profile was attached to the triangle's axis of symmetry. The model was completed by fixing a handle in the U-profile.

The current model of the *Hata* (Photos 1 and 2) incorporates several improvements: a depth control system; a better position of the hook for draft beam attachment; different shaped blades; and a redesigned handlebar.

Depth control and rigidity

During weeding on sandy soils the front blade often penetrated too deeply. The operator had to press down on the handle to adjust the working depth back to 3–5 cm. Inexperienced farmers often overcompensated, so that the blade came out of the soil. Not only was this inefficient, because parts of the fields remained unweeded, but the work became

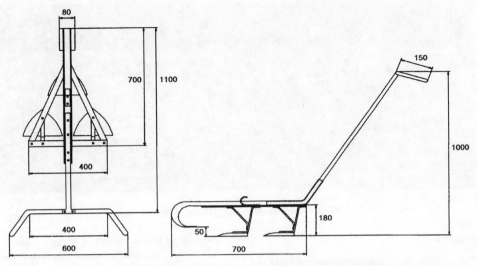

Figure 1: Improved Hata *(houe à traction asine). All dimensions in millimetres*

unnecessarily exhausting for both the farmer and the animals.

This problem was solved by fitting an additional skid at the front of the *Hata*. A supporting wheel would have had a lower frictional resistance, but the skid is cheaper and easier to make; it can be forged out of the central U-profile.

The U-profile is the backbone of the implement and guarantees sufficient robustness. To enable the skid to be forged, the U-profile had to be extended by 200 mm. At the rear end, the U-profile is extended by 150 mm in order to increase the rigidity of the connection between the handle and the main body of the *Hata*.

With the new depth control mechanism the flow of materials has been improved, ie, crop residues and other materials can easily be turned aside, without clogging the implement.

Hook position for draft beam attachment

Farmers like to be as close as possible to the donkey when working, in order to exercise better control. In general it is easier to steer the animals using a short draft rope or chain. However, this results in an undesirable increment in the angle of the line of draft force; the front blade might leave the soil due to the increased vertical draft force component. Unfortunately it is not obvious to most farmers that the implement works better the smaller the angle of the draft force.

Therefore, the hook for draft beam attachment was repositioned: it is now fitted further back on the U-profile by means of two rivets. The back rivet is also used to attach the front blade mounting.

The new hook position also simplifies manipulation of the working depth, as the operator can easily tip the implement around this joint point.

Blade design

Initially the blade of the traditional hand tool, the *Hiler*, was chosen for the donkey-drawn implement. It was thought that this would facilitate acceptance of the *Hata* by farmers in Niger.

However, the *Hiler* blades are not strong enough for animal traction use. The ends were often distorted and the two close rivets which adjust the blades on their bases sometimes could not withstand the torques which occurred while weeding. Also, the *Hiler* blade is used for pulling and pushing whereas the *Hata* blades are only pulled. Thus the rear of the *Hata* blade does not need to have the special shape of the *Hiler* blade.

For optimal results it is necessary that the tool cuts as it is drawn. Therefore the new blades are characterised by a more pointed shape. In addition, stronger material was used. The compact design allowed a wider spacing between the rivets for even greater strength. Figure 2 shows both traditional *Hiler* blade and the innovative *Hata* blade.

Figure 2: Traditional Hiler *(left) and innovative* Hata *blade design*

Photo 1: Farmers tilling with a Hata cultivator in Niger

Handlebar

The handlebar is the interface between the user and the implement. It should allow easy steering and effective control, especially when the implement hits stones or roots. Ergonomics was an important factor in the design. The height, width and winding can be adjusted to suit the farmer (Göhlich, 1987). The handlebar design is shown in Figure 1.

Field studies with the improved *Hata*

The *Hata* was compared to the traditional hand tool, the *Hiler*, in terms of labour time requirement and weeding efficiency. Field studies were carried out with and without depth control on either zero-tilled or ridged fields. Two passes were made per measurement.

Labour time

Using the manual *Hiler*, both inter-row and in-row weeding are carried out at the same time. Single pass animal-drawn weeding works only between the rows; in-row weeding would then require supplementary time-consuming manual work. However, on-farm mechanised double-pass weeding is possible because of the large spacing between the pockets. The first pass takes care of in-row weeding and the second weeds the inter-pocket spaces.

Table 1: Demand for labour time

	Total time (hours/ha)	
	Zero-tillage	Ridges
Hata without depth control (two passes)	20.3	20.0
Hata with depth control (two passes)	17.9	19.0
Hiler	41.1	28.4

Total labour time is the sum of working time, turning time, preparation time and supplementary time, as applicable.

The calculation of total labour time for both *Hata* models takes account of the fact that two persons, an adult and a child, are usually involved in on-farm weeding operations: the farmer steers the implement and the child controls the donkey.

Weeding with the *Hata* was found to be considerably faster than manual weeding with the *Hiler* (Table 1).

Weeding efficiency

Weeding efficiency is a measure of the working quality of an implement. It is determined as amount (in kg dry matter) of weeds cut or lifted by the weeding operation, expressed as a percentage of the total weeds in the field before treatment.

Two types of weeding efficiencies can be calculated. In the first, the efficiency is given in relation to the working width of the implement. In the second, the weeding efficiency is calculated in terms of the area between the rows. The latter option was used to obtain the values presented in Figure 3. Clearly the efficiency of the improved *Hata* approaches that of the traditional hand tool.

Weeding efficiency was higher on ridged fields because the ridges helped in steering the animal and implement. On the other hand, the total amount of weeds on ridged fields was lower, because ridging helps to control weed infestation.

Summary and recommendations

On-farm application and testing of the donkey-drawn hoe *Hata* has been realised in cooperation with several development projects in the south-western areas of the Republic of Niger. The

Photo 2: One person working with a donkey-pulled Hata *cultivator in Niger*

practical experiences gained during the 1991 rainy season have helped tremendously in the on-going improvement of the implement.

On-farm experiments with the *Hata* show a remarkable decrease in labour time compared with traditional hand tool weeding. The efficiency of mechanised weed control approaches that of manual weeding and could be enhanced.

The *Hata* can be made and maintained in the country's rural areas. However, the fabrication of a durable model depends strongly on the abilities of village blacksmiths. Therefore, an overall strategy of mechanisation must incorporate sound and thorough training of local blacksmiths.

Farmers also need training on how to use the implement and how to dress the animals properly. Better education of farmers would help to involve more donkeys in farming activities; at present, of

the estimated 500 000 donkeys in Niger (FAO, 1987), only about 10 000 are used for work (Starkey, 1988).

The *Hata* is designed for use on sandy soils, and was sometimes damaged when used on heavier soils. In such cases farmers did not rely on the blacksmiths to repair the hoe, but continued their work manually. Research is therefore underway to develop the *Hata* for use on heavier soils. A stronger *Hata* could then be used for other purposes such as scarifying. Such technically improved *Hatas* might be also socially and economically viable in other African countries.

Acknowledgements

The author would like to thank the farmers in the Republic of Niger, and the scientific staff of ICRISAT Sahelian Centre, Sador, Republic of Niger, and of the University of Hohenheim, for their collaboration and support.

References

Betker J, 1993. Research on the mechanisation of weeding with animal-drawn implements. pp. 99–103 in: Lawrence P R, Lawrence K, Dijkman J T and Starkey P H (eds), *Research for development of animal traction in West Africa.* Proceedings of the fourth workshop of the West Africa Animal Traction Network held 9-13 July 1990, Kano, Nigeria. International Livestock Centre for Africa (ILCA), Addis Ababa, Ethiopia. 322p.

FAO, 1987. *FAO Yearbook.* Vol 41. Food and Agriculture Organization of the United Nations (FAO), Rome, Italy.

Göhlich H, 1987. *Mensch und Maschine.* Verlag Paul Parey, Hamburg and Berlin, Germany.

Starkey P, 1988. *Animal traction directory: Africa.* Friedr. Vieweg Braunschweig/Wiesbaden for German Appropriate Technology Exchange, GTZ, Eschborn, Germany. 151p.

Strobel G A, 1991. Unkrautbekmpfung nach dem Vorbild der Natur. Spektrum der Wissenschaft 9/91. Spektrum-Verlag, Heidelberg, Germany.

Figure 3: A comparison of weeding efficiencies

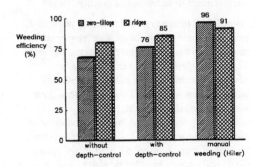

Animal draft tillage systems: the need for an integrated approach

by

Frank M Inns

Consultant Agricultural and Mechanical Engineer, 53 Alameda Road, Ampthill, Bedford MK45 2LA, UK

Abstract

The animal draft tillage system comprises the draft animal(s), the harness, the implement, the operator and the soil. In order to flourish the system must optimise its own inherent efficiency, it must compete with systems using alternative power sources and it must integrate beneficially with the agricultural production system and other systems within a broad national framework.

The animal draft tillage system has been brought to its present state by empirical development. Theoretical studies in draft animal ergonomics and animal/implement interaction are now needed to ensure further progress. Animal power is essentially complementary to human and engine power. Each farming operation has its own characteristics which will integrate best with a particular power source. Operational control of the power source by the farmer is of major importance in achieving timeliness in farming operations.

Integration of draft animal power into the national framework depends on farmer demand. Imposition of new implements and techniques is unlikely to succeed, however benevolent the intentions. Government policies often provide economic incentives which favour tractor power, making it difficult for draft animal power to compete on a fair basis.

Introduction

The animal draft tillage system has five essential components: the draft animal(s), the harness, the implement, the operator and the soil whose changed condition is the primary purpose of the system. The effectiveness of the system is often judged solely on its own internal performance, but a true assessment must also take account of its external relationships with the agricultural production system which it serves. Also, it must be judged within the prevailing social, industrial, economic and political factors at national and international levels. Figure 1 shows some of the factors which may interact with the animal draft tillage system, often exerting a strong influence on its viability.

The performance, and possible improvements, of animal draft tillage systems may conveniently be examined under three broad headings:

○   performance in isolation from other systems

○   performance in comparison with systems using other power sources

○   performance as part of a wider system

Animal draft tillage systems in isolation

The best performance of any system depends upon the characteristics of each individual component and how the components interact. Interaction involves compromise in the interests of the system as a whole, not domination of the system by any particular component. For example, the performance of tillage implements, in terms of working depth and area rate of work, must be restricted to a level at which their draft requirement is matched to the sustained draft capability of the work animals.

Technological development generally proceeds through three phases. The first phase is empirical: advances in technology are achieved by trial and error combined with experience and shrewd insight. The second phase is theoretical: the experimental technology is reinforced by scientific (frequently mathematical) analysis, often involving idealised assumptions to simplify the theory. The third phase is one of accelerated practical development in which theoretical analysis facilitates rapid and significant improvements to technological practice.

Animal draft tillage systems are mainly at the first, empirical, phase of technological development. This phase, which has lasted some 5000 years, has led to some highly developed and technologically advanced systems, notably Indian and Pakistani tillage systems which use a traditional plow (*desi hal*). The second, theoretical, phase has unfortunately been diverted, by the introduction of tractors, to the analysis of tractor-powered systems. Equivalent attention to animal draft tillage systems would undoubtedly have led by now to a much better understanding of the technology, with consequential improvements. The theoretical phase is only now starting to make an impact.

Scientific studies into animal health, nutrition and work output are well advanced. They should be

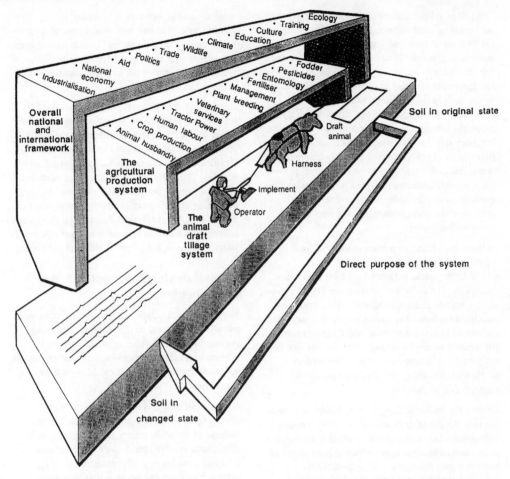

Ecology
Training
Culture
Education
Climate
Trade
Wildlife
Politics
Aid
National economy
Industrialisation

Fodder
Pesticides
Entomology
Fertiliser
Management
Plant breeding
Veterinary services
Tractor Power
Human labour
Crop production
Animal husbandry

Overall national and international framework

The agricultural production system

The animal draft tillage system

Draft animal

Harness

Implement

Operator

Soil in original state

Direct purpose of the system

Soil in changed state

Figure. 1: The animal draft system, showing some factors which interact internally and externally

complemented by "draft animal ergonomics" as a new subject area which would include an investigation of muscular and skeletal interactions ("postural mechanics"?) as a contribution to harness design.

The theoretical study of soil/implement interactions is well established for tractor-pulled implements and the same principles are directly applicable to conventional animal draft implements.

Theoretical studies of animal/implement interactions have been made by Devnani (1981) and Inns (1990; 1991). These interactions influence the design and operational adjustment of both harnesses and implements, the development of which is still proceeding mainly on an empirical basis. These studies, together with theoretical studies in draft animal ergonomics, implement design and operator ergonomics, will provide a comprehensive basis for the accelerated practical development of draft

animal technology, leading to the optimisation of animal draft systems.

Animal draft tillage systems and other power sources

In many areas draft animal systems have been long established, and their form and performance have changed little over many centuries. The introduction of tractor power during the past half century has upset this established equilibrium or near-equilibrium. Many of today's farmers have the freedom to choose between animal- or tractor-powered tillage systems, available under various ownership or hire arrangements, or to continue to use human-powered systems. Faced with this choice farmers will want to examine individual operations within the animal draft tillage system, to identify the most suitable power source for each.

The tillage system comprises operations aimed at land clearing and breaking, primary cultivation, seedbed preparation, ridging, sowing seed or transplanting seedlings and intercultivating for weed control and/or to improve soil condition by aeration, etc. Each operation has its own distinctive character. Some, such as land breaking and primary cultivation, demand high power inputs. Others, such as intercultivation for weed control, need less power but more skill and judgement in their application. Binswanger (1988) identified the "power intensive" operations as the first ones to be taken over by new, more powerful, sources of power when they became available, while the older power sources will continue to be used, advantageously, for "skill intensive" operations.

In these circumstances it is completely rational and valid for farmers to use tractor power, when available, for some, but not all, of their cultivation operations. The criteria of Binswanger (1988) can be used, with due caution, to identify those operations which are best suited to tractor power. Primary cultivation is the first of these while intercultivation for weeding would be among those less suitable for early tractor mechanisation. Current interest in single-animal working for weeding operations supports this proposition.

At the other end of the spectrum it will be unwise to promote the use of draft animal power for primary cultivation when tractor power is reliably available as an alternative. Operations which require teams of more than two animals would be particularly vulnerable to takeover by tractors. Efforts to develop big-team working are probably justified only in exceptional circumstances, and when tractor power is very uncompetitive.

For the individual farmer the move from animal power to tractor power is not solely a question of economic advantage. Smallholder farmers have very meagre (if any) cash reserves, so certainty in their cropping, and hence in the family's food supply, is of overwhelming importance. They are aware that prompt planting at the start of the rains generally leads to more reliable cropping and higher yields. The best guarantee of prompt action at critical times is given by operational control over power and machinery inputs, which is best achieved through ownership. For many farmers ownership of a draft animal team and implements is more desirable than tractor hire and more feasible than tractor ownership.

From the farmers' viewpoint the most profitable crop production system may well be one using a mixture of power sources—human, animal and engine. Each operation would be undertaken by the most suitable power source as judged by effectiveness, cost and operational control, to give an "integrated mechanisation" system having many advantages over the "comprehensive tractorisation" systems which attract the attention and support of many authorities.

Animal draft practitioners should be sensitive to both the advantages and the limitations of animal power applied to individual tillage operations, concentrating on those operations which offer significant technical, economic and operational benefits. The comparative advantage of animal-powered tillage operations will vary with locality, depending on the extent to which tractor power is available to the smallholder farmer. The comparative advantage is likely to be greater in those operations which require higher levels of skill and judgement.

Animal draft tillage systems in a broad context

The animal draft tillage system must be efficient in its own right, it must be competitive with tillage systems powered by other sources and it must interact with other systems—agricultural production, industrial, commercial, political, etc—to their mutual benefit.

Animal draft tillage systems cannot develop effectively in isolation from external influences. Because of the wide variety and complexity of the interactions involved there can be few common solutions. And because of constantly changing relationships there can be no definitive answer. A questioning, flexible and imaginative approach is a constant necessity.

Farmers should not be expected to change their agricultural production systems to suit draft animal technology. It is the animal draft tillage system which must serve the needs, including development, of the agricultural production system which is in use, not *vice versa*. According to Starkey (1988)

> ". . . research and development programmes should start with a humble approach and an understanding of local farming systems derived from discussion with farmers. Programmers should work closely with farmers and jointly identify and evaluate methods of improving farm productivity and incomes".

The successful introduction of new equipment is a consequence of demand by the farmer, not of a "solution" imposed from above.

Most developing countries have by now reached a stage where animal draft equipment can be manufactured locally, with consequent benefits to the development of local artisanal and managerial skills. Experiences with local manufacture have been mixed. It has flourished in countries such as India, Pakistan and Thailand, where relatively small-scale manufacturers are in close contact with local farmers and respond to their expressed demands. In other countries, however, most of the factories set up by government or aid agencies to supply animal draft equipment have failed to operate profitably despite subsidised distribution and sale of the manufactured goods. Unsold stocks bear testimony to a failure to consult the farmers, primarily on what they want but also, to a lesser degree, on what they can afford. Production has been "supply led" rather than "demand led".

Commercial sector involvement with animal draft systems is weak in many countries. The import, manufacture, distribution and supply of animal draft equipment and replacement parts, and loans for the purchase of such equipment, are often undertaken by government and quasi-governmental agencies. In most cases farmers would be better served by commercial agencies, which respond more quickly and positively to their needs.

Political support for draft animal power is patchy. A number of countries have adopted a deliberate policy of concentrating attention on tractorised agriculture to the virtual exclusion of animal-powered systems. Even when priority promotion of draft animal power is an expressed policy, tractor power often receives disproportionate advantages, such as lower import duties, subsidised local production, subsidised fuel prices, acceptance and distribution of tractors through "aid" programmes and an emphasis on tractor power for government-run farms (military, prison and "commercial"). The work of research and testing institutions is often directed exclusively to tractor-powered equipment.

It may be difficult politically to smooth out economic and administrative distortions which interfere with power selection on a rational basis, but this must be done if a country is to benefit from a proper economic balance between alternative power sources on the farm. Sound progress in agricultural development depends upon a level playing field.

Conclusions

Within the animal draft tillage system attention should be given to building up a theoretical base in draft animal ergonomics and animal/implement interactions to accelerate improvements in harness design, which is seen as a critical factor in system efficiency.

Draft animal power, engine (tractor) power and human power should be seen as complementary power sources for agricultural production, not as mutually exclusive ones. The optimum mix will depend upon the requirements of each individual farming operation. It will vary from country to country and will change with time according to the viability of alternative power sources.

Farmers should have operational control over their power inputs if they are to start and complete farming operations on schedule. Ownership of draft animals gives a better opportunity for operational control than tractor hire.

The introduction of draft animal power in new areas, and of "improved" or new implements, should be a consequence of farmer demand, not a policy imposed from the top, however benevolent the intentions might be.

The relationships between farmers, manufacturers and commercial organisations should be allowed to develop symbiotically without undue interference.

Governments should provide a "level playing field" for human, animal and engine power through an even-handed approach to import duties, taxes, subsidies, "aid" programmes and support for research, development and extension.

Animal draft development activities should be pursued as integrated programmes, taking account of interactions with agricultural production, industrial, commercial, political, social and other relevant systems.

References

Binswanger H P, 1988. *Agricultural mechanization: a comparative historical perspective,*World Bank Working Paper 673, The World Bank, Washington DC, USA. 88p.

Devnani R S, 1981. *Design considerations for harnesses and yokes for draught animals.* Central Institute of Agricultural Engineering, Bhopal, India. 67p.

Inns F M, 1990. The mechanics of animal draught cultivation implements. Part 1. Chain-pulled implements. *The Agricultural Engineer* 45(1):13–17.

Inns F M, 1991. The mechanics of animal draught cultivation implements. Part 2. Beam-pulled implements. *The Agricultural Engineer* 46(1):18–21.

Starkey P, 1988. *Perfected yet rejected: animal-drawn wheeled tool carriers.* Vieweg for German Appropriate Technology Exchange, Deutsche Gesellschaft für Technische Zusammenarbeit (GTZ), Eschborn, Germany. 161p.

Development of an animal-drawn puddler for rice production on the Usangu Plains of Tanzania

by

M L Lecca, I A Kinyaga and J B Bunyinyiga

Usangu Village Irrigation Project, PO Box 336, Mbeya, Tanzania

Abstract

Where rice is grown under irrigation, puddling—churning soil with water to achieve suitable conditions for transplanting rice seedlings—is a difficult and time-consuming operation. A survey of farmers on the Usangu Plains of Tanzania found that this work requires between 350 and 700 hours/ha using hand hoes.

The Usangu Village Irrigation Project has designed and fabricated an animal-drawn rotating puddler. Tests of this puddler in the Majengo Scheme showed that the implement had an effective field capacity of 0.047 ha/hour using a pair of oxen, and a labour requirement of 43 hours/ha. Farmers were pleased with both the rate and the quality of work. A labour bottleneck might be considerably reduced if this implement were adopted. The cost of the implement in 1991 was about 20 000 Tanzanian shillings (US$ 87).

Introduction

In many developing countries, the human population is growing faster than agricultural production. Most agriculture is in the hands of small farmers, who are generally poor and depend mainly on hand-hoe technology. Thus farms are small and production is low; most small farmers produce just enough for household consumption, with very little, if any, surplus. To overcome this constraint, small farmers need to intensify the use of animal power technology.

In Tanzania, draft animals are used mainly for land preparation, notably primary tillage. Although they could be used for many other farm operations, such as harrowing, levelling, puddling, sowing, threshing and transport, this is not common practice.

The Usangu Plains, located in Mbeya Region, cover an area of about 15 500 km^2, of which 7900 km^2 have potential for rice production. Swamp rice is grown in lowland areas by smallholder farmers. After plowing, suitable conditions for transplanting rice seedlings are created by puddling—churning soil in the presence of excess water. Puddling reduces leaching of water, kills weeds and makes the soil softer and ready for transplanting. However, as this work is generally done manually using hand hoes, it takes a very long time. A sample survey of farmers in the area of study indicated a labour requirement of 350–700 hours/ha (Bunyinyiga, 1989).

In order to speed up land preparation and reduce the burden on the farmer, a simple animal-drawn rotating puddler has been designed, fabricated, tested and demonstrated to farmers (Photo 1).

Photo 1: The animal-drawn rotating puddler in use

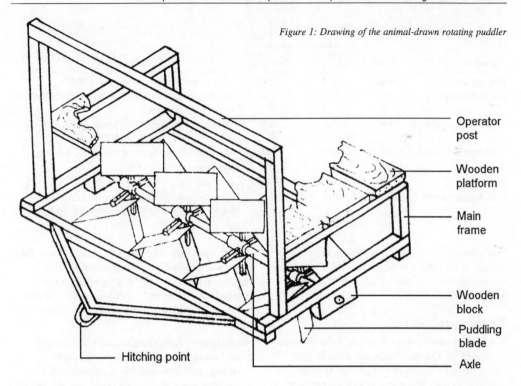

Figure 1: Drawing of the animal-drawn rotating puddler

Operator post

Wooden platform

Main frame

Wooden block

Puddling blade

Axle

Hitching point

Description and operation of puddler

The puddler frame has three parts: an operating blade axle support, a hitching point and an operator post (Figure 1). Most parts are welded to the frame.

The operating blade axle is similar to the device used in Indian puddlers. It consists of four equidistant hubs with four perpendicular blade-supporting fingers welded to it (Photo 2). The blade axle rotates on two wooden bearings which are fixed to the frame by bolts. The operating blades are fixed to the fingers by bolts. Both the bearings and the blades can be easily and cheaply replaced when they wear out. Two bushes are fixed on both sides of the blade axle to keep it well centred on the frame.

The frame of the implement is made of hollow rectangular steel sections. Four supporting crossed-finger bladed hubs were fabricated in the nearby workshop of the Mbeya Oxenization Project. The materials used are summarised in Table 1. The cost of the implement in late 1991 was about 20 000 Tanzanian shillings (US$ 87).

The rotating puddler is pulled by draft animals guided by an operator. The blades sink and roll in the flooded plowed soil, breaking the clods and making a layer of mud. The blades also cut weeds, roots, straw and stubble and submerge them in the

Table 1: Materials used in puddler construction

Materials	Quantity
Hollow rectangular steel section for frame (25 x 50 mm) by mm	8040
Arc welding rods (2.5 mm) by kg	1
Timber for platform (pieces 25 x 150 x 1100 mm)	4
Bolts and nuts for fixing timber to frame (10 x 40 mm)	8
Bolts and nuts for fixing wooden bearing to frame (10 x 75 mm)	4
Wooden block axle bearing (50 x 150 x 70 mm)	2
Metal plates for wooden bearings (3 x 50 x 150 mm)	2
Hollow round steel for hubs (68 mm external diameter, 29 mm internal, 79 mm long)	4
Solid steel square bar (25 x 25 x 80 mm or 30 x 30 x 80 mm) for blade finger support	16
Steel plates (3 x 130 x 240 mm)	16
Bolts and nuts [or rivets] (10 x 40 mm) for fixing blades on fingers	32
Rivets for fixing bladed hub on the operating axle (10 x 50 mm)	1
Axle bush (46 mm external, 30 mm internal, 120 mm long)	1
Axle bush (46 mm external, 30 mm internal, 70 mm long)	1
Axle galvanised pipe (29 mm external diameter, 1100 mm long)	1

Table 2: Results of field trials with puddlers

Parameter	Units	Recorded values		Remarks
		Buffalo pair	Oxen pair	
Field capacity	ha/hour	0.154	0.047	Oxen frequently sank in the flooded plots
Field efficiency	%	74	34	Achieved efficiencies were low due to both animal and operator inexperience
Effective working width	mm	900	500	Measured as average of four passes. The overlap was excessive when using the ox team
Implement draft (force)	N	900	800	Measured with spring dynamometer
Working speed	m/s	0.55	0.25	Measured at different times
Puddling depth	mm	100–150	100–150	Estimates only
Labour requirement	hours/ha	11	18	Water buffaloes performed better than oxen. Labour using only hand hoe is about 350 hours/ha

mud where they can decompose. When there is a lot of grass in the field, a comb harrow should be used before puddling. The harrow can also be pulled by a pair of animals.

Testing procedures

The rotating puddler was first tested in the Majengo Scheme of the Usangu Village Irrigation Project, during the rainy season of 1990. Seven farmers' plots and one plot in the Project's experimental field were used for the tests. The rectangular plots were about 200 m², ranging from 8 x 25 m to 10 x 20 m. All the plots were plowed before flooding with ox-drawn mouldboard plows. Each plot was flooded with water one week before plowing with animal-drawn mouldboard plows. A layer of water 50–100 mm deep was maintained. One of each

Photo 2: View of the puddler from underneath

Photo: I A Kinyaga

farmer's plots was puddled with a pair of oxen, the other was puddled using a pair of buffalo. The animals worked only in the morning. Two people worked with the animals: a driver, usually standing on the draft implement, and an assistant encouraging the animals.

Measurements were taken of area worked, time taken, working speed, working width, depth of puddling, draft force and labour requirement. In calculating field capacity (area cultivated per unit of time), turning time at the headlands was included, but stops of more than two minutes (for any reason) were not included. The effective field capacity (working rate while actually moving) was calculated for one passage of the implement.

Field efficiency (actual rate of work as a proportion of theoretical rate) was calculated according to the test code of the Regional Network for Agricultural Mechanization (RNAM, 1983). Average working speed was calculated by measuring the time required to puddle a distance of 15 m. Force was measured twice in each plot, at different times, using a spring dynamometer. The effective width was taken as the average of the working widths of four implement passages. Precise measurement of puddling depth was difficult, and so only estimates could be made.

Results

The puddler performed well in fields with a layer of water of about 100 mm. A single passage of the implement churned the soil sufficiently to provide reasonably good conditions for transplanting paddy seedlings. The trial results are summarised in Table 2.

Working speed, effective field capacity and field efficiency were all higher with water buffaloes than with oxen. Oxen seemed reluctant to work in flooded plots and usually stopped when they sank more than 300 mm into the mud. The theoretical working width of the implement is 1000 mm; the differences in effective working width were due to greater overlap using oxen (50%) than using buffaloes (10%). The depth of puddling was similar for both oxen and water buffaloes, as it was based on the vertical length of the blades on the rotating axle. The recorded implement draft (force) was 900 N when pulled by a pair of water buffaloes and 800 N when pulled by oxen. The difference between the forces was thought to be due to the increased pulling angle for buffaloes since they were taller than the oxen. This might have also affected implement depth.

Some recommendations

Construction of the hub assembly and blades required a special tool, made by the Mbeya Oxenization Project. A simpler method of construction would be desirable. The hitching point should be higher for the implement to remain horizontal when operating, otherwise the puddler tilts backward and begins to collect debris behind it. However, this modification must not complicate the frame. Since bolts and nuts are expensive in the area, they should be replaced by rivets which can be made locally from scrap round bars.

In order to reduce wear on the blades and wooden bearings, the puddler should be transported to the field on a sledge pulled by draft animals.

Field efficiency could be increased by more and better training of both the operator and the animals. Improving the skill of the operator in simultaneously guiding the animals and the implement should increase the effective working width by reducing the overlap.

In order to gain further feedback and information on the potential for using these rotating puddlers, more prototype implements should be fabricated and made available for use by smallholder farmers.

References

Bunyinyiga J B, 1989. Mechanization level in the Usangu Plains. *Proceedings of the Tanzanian Society of Agricultural Engineers*, 2:119.

RNAM 1983. *Test codes and procedures for farm machinery*. Technical series No. 12. Regional Network for Agricultural Machinery (RNAM), Pasay City, Philippines. 33p.

Tillage and weed control on medium potential lands in Kenya

by

J M Kahumbura

National Agricultural Research Centre, Muguga, PO Box 30148, Nairobi, Kenya

Abstract

Kenya has a high diversity of physical relief, climate and soil types that influence the types of crops that can be grown and the tillage systems that are feasible. This paper analyses factors which influence the low rate of adoption of animal-powered and tractor tillage. Human concentration on small pockets of land is a major constraint to the introduction of mechanised tillage. Low produce prices reduce the ability of farmers to increase farm income and invest in tillage implements. Some of the tillage implements introduced have been inappropriate, and this has discouraged subsequent acquisition of new implements. Low levels of education affect awareness of new tillage options. Cropping seasons are short and create labour bottlenecks which increase monetary costs. Herbicide use is constrained by high costs. There is an urgent need to improve animal draft power packages for tillage, and research will continue to play a vital role in this.

Introduction

Kenya is a small country in East Africa covering an area of about 582 000 km^2. Over 75% of the land surface is classified as arid and semi-arid, with very low agricultural production potential. The present human population is estimated to be about 23 million; 65% of the population is concentrated in areas of higher agricultural production potential, and so some good agricultural areas are net food importers.

Agriculture is mainly rainfed and the agro-ecological classification is based on rainfall probability, evaporation and the physical relief. The areas of medium agricultural production potential occur in small pockets in boundary regions between high rainfall and semi-arid areas.

These areas of medium agricultural potential experience bimodal rainfall patterns with a long rainy season between March and May and a short rainy season in October and November. The distribution of the available rain over two seasons reduces the effectiveness of the total rainfall for crop production and the drought occurring between the seasons causes soil moisture stress that inhibits crop development and reduces potential biomass production. Thus the only crops that can be grown successfully are short season ones with low biomass yields.

Crop production in Kenya is mainly done by smallholder peasant farmers using hand tools. Information on farm mechanisation has been generally available for more than 40 years. However, data from district surveys indicate that only about 20% of the farmlands (about 600 000 ha) are fully mechanised (tractorised); of the remainder, about 200 000 ha are farmed with animal-drawn implements and about 1.8 million ha are farmed manually.

Industrial farm equipment and implements are very expensive in Kenya and are becoming more so. Maintenance and servicing of farm equipment are also very expensive, and repair facilities are often not within easy reach: vital work days may therefore be lost when the equipment is unserviceable.

Manual tillage systems

Most of the smallholder farmers in Kenya are mixed farmers. Many of them have migrated from areas of higher to areas of lower agricultural production potential, but they continue to apply farming practices which have been handed down through the generations, even though they may not be appropriate in the new settlements. The result is many operational problems and poor crop yields.

In general, crop farming is underdeveloped. Initial bush clearance and land preparation are often done using low-work-output hand tools: the main implements for bush clearance are still the axe and the *panga* slashing knife. In the high tropical surface air temperatures manual workers get tired quickly and can only work effectively for a few hours each day. Initial land clearance work therefore requires many labour-days per hectare. The reduction of effective working labour-hours inflates the real costs of land preparation and tillage. In many instances labour costs may be beyond the reach of poor peasant farmers, who are then forced to use destructive methods of land preparation such as bush burning, which leave the surface layer baked by heat and prone to severe wind and water erosion.

Poor peasant farmers have very few financial resources for investing in good agricultural practices. Even where "improved" tools are available such farmers continue to use the low performance hand tools, notably the *jembe* and *forked jembe* hoes and the *panga*, which are are available in different sizes and shapes in the local markets at prices which the farmers can afford. As long as smallholder farmers' crop production margins remain very low they will continue to use these inefficient tools.

The physical characteristics of the soils force the farmer to delay land preparation until after the onset of the rains. This practice reduces the length of the crop growing season and, because the rainy seasons are short for cereal production, any reduction of the growing season leads to severely reduced yields.

The time available for land tillage is often critical and sets the farmers in a state of panic. Labour is scarce at this time and the cost of daily labour increases, severely affecting the crop production costs. In this working environment where labour is in short supply, the quality of land tillage is reduced, resulting in substandard seedbed preparation and early infestations of noxious weeds while the crop seedlings are still at the critical juvenile growth stage.

On old land the *jembe* achieves very good weed control, the only limitation being the rate of work output. However, tillage with the *jembe* is generally shallow, so that in places and soil types where deep cutting is desirable in order to increase the level of rainwater infiltration, the *jembe* is not suitable; its use will lead to a low level of soil water storage and the soils will quickly dry out to the extent that the plant extractable soil moisture will be below the rooting zone. In this case the crop will not achieve its yield potential.

Tillage using draft animals

Some farmers do achieve a higher level of farming income and are able to hire or own draft animals and animal-drawn implements.

The most important aspect of any power unit is its source of energy. The energy of a draft animal comes from its feed. Therefore the feeding and management of the draft animal is very important in order to efficiently tap the animal's power. The animal's energy is in high demand when the heavy duty operations are at the peak; this normally occurs during the dry season when fodder and pasture are in short supply. Management of the draft animal therefore requires the provision of storage facilities for animal feed for dry season feeding and for water.

In Kenya, the widely used animal-drawn tillage equipment is the Victory mouldboard plow. It is generally manufactured locally and when made from good quality steel it is light and popular with farmers. It is used for land preparation, ridging, furrow opening for seed planting, inter-row weeding, soil spreading and harrowing. The implement requires high draft power, particularly when the soils are dry and hard. Thus the farmer may be forced to use as many as three pairs of working oxen which may make the tillage operations expensive and uneconomical for the low value food crop production.

With the conventional mouldboard plow, animal energy is used in turning over the soil: ripper tines require less energy for turning and shifting soil and can therefore cut deeper into the hard soil crusts in order to facilitate better rainwater infiltration. In the hot temperatures of the tropics overturning the soils layers exposes the moist soil layer to increased, faster drying, thus worsening the plant seed growth environment. Exposure of lower soil layers to high surface temperatures also speeds up volatilisation of plant nutrients from the soil. The soils become degraded and corrective measures are often needed after successful cropping. In the higher plateaux where temperatures are cooler and the rainy season is longer, overturning the soil layers and burying the young weeds is still considered an effective means of weed control.

Research and development programmes have continued to acquire "improved" animal-drawn implements suitable for tillage both in the high rainfall mountain ranges and low rainfall savannah. The Bukara toolbar was recently designed to operate with a single pair of working oxen. The equipment is light and sturdy and the design allows easy adjustments. The toolframe can be fitted with a one- or two-furrow plow, cultivator tines, furrow openers, two-furrow ridger, seed planter and blade cultivators. The equipment and tools are still undergoing field experiments and evaluation.

Reduced tillage and herbicides

A large part (over 50%) of farm inputs is associated with tillage operations. Reducing the level of tillage without significantly reducing crop production could play a major role in increasing profitability.

Although reduced tillage is practised in the high rainfall areas, it is rare in medium potential areas as the majority of smallholder farmers lack the appropriate technical knowledge.

However, in a few scattered river basins, where irrigation schemes allow high value crops such as fruits, onions and flowers to be grown, limited integrated weed control is commonly practised.

Herbicides are applied using small pressure knapsack sprayers before transplanting the seedlings. Later the plots are weeded using hand tools to control the second generation of weeds.

Financial resources are major constraints limiting the adoption of any expensive farming technology. In Kenya herbicides are quite expensive, which contributes to the low rate of adoption. Herbicides also require large amounts of water for dilution before spraying. Fetching water, and transporting it to the fields where all the operation are carried out manually, requires a lot of labour and may also contribute to the low rate of adoption.

Many of the weeds found in the farms produce large quantities of seed with varying degrees of dormancy. When a flush of newly germinated weeds is controlled with a herbicide a new generation of weeds later emerges from a reservoir of dormant seeds and could easily reduce the effectiveness of the initial herbicide application. Several of the weeds are hardy and difficult to eradicate using the

available herbicides. As a result farmers often combine chemical weeding with mechanical weeding and often cannot quantify the role played by each practice.

Most smallholder farmers are poorly educated. This may pose problems of understanding the recommended quantities and methods of applying the herbicides. Reduced tillage systems will depend on extensive farmer orientation and product information transfer through the agricultural extension services and the chemical firms' technical field officers.

Conclusion

Draft animal power is expected to continue to occupy a significant place in tillage practices in the medium potential areas of Kenya. Its development and improvement in all aspects including animal production for draft animal provision and animal-drawn implements will continue to be priority areas for applied agricultural research.

Photograph opposite
Stockpile of plows at the Lenco factory, Zambia

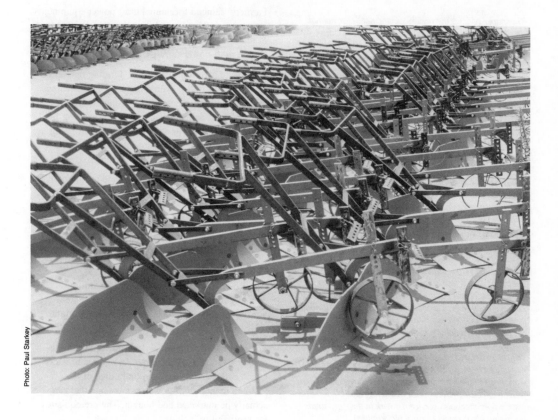

Photo: Paul Starkey

The supply and distribution of implements

Supply and distribution of implements for animal traction: an overview with region-specific scenarios

by

Aalbert A Wanders

Department of Development Cooperation, Institute of Agricultural Engineering (IMAG-DLO)
Mansholtlaan 10–12, Postbus 43, 6700 AA Wageningen, The Netherlands

Abstract

This paper reviews the region-specific needs for animal draft power implements, and the existing animal draft power supply and distribution systems, in West Africa and Zambia. The process of local development, manufacture and introduction of animal draft power in West Africa is highlighted, emphasising the need for local adaptation and diversification of the range of implements, in accordance with the type of draft animals available, the prevailing soil and agro-ecological conditions and the cropping and farming systems practised. The West African experience is considered highly relevant for Zambia (and other countries in eastern and southern Africa) where the lack of local adaptation and diversification of animal draft power equipment is a result of long-standing importation (mainly of plows, of various origins) and centralised (government/cooperative union) distribution.

A review of animal draft power implement supply and distribution scenarios illustrates the general failure of the centralised, top-down approaches followed by large-scale manufacturers and (parastatal) distribution agencies in both West Africa and Zambia. Present constraints on further development of animal draft power (particularly in Zambia) include poor profitability of small-scale farming, poor marketing and distribution and severe logistic and rural communication problems. The need for farmer-oriented, and thus area-specific, supply and distribution systems is stressed: these should include competitive local manufacture (including establishment of assembly workshops in the main animal draft power regions), linked with an effective private-sector marketing and distribution/after-sales service network in the rural areas (including involvement of rural blacksmiths).

Introduction

Animal draft power is recognised as the most viable technology for the development of the smallholder farm sector in most regions in Africa. In order to develop this technology successfully, a balance must be achieved between the farmers' needs (**demand**) and the **supply** of animal draft power equipment. This requires a **region-specific** approach which takes into account the diverse and changing agro-ecological and economic conditions.

Demand

Farmers' demand for animal draft power equipment reflects both the practical farm power requirements of the local environment, and the profitability of animal draft power farming.

In order to carry out the various farming operations using animal draft power, a range of implements is needed: the implements must be suitable for the types of draft animals available, the prevailing field and soil conditions and the farming and cropping systems practised. Successful introduction and use of animal draft power therefore requires:

○ farmer awareness of existing and/or alternative animal draft power systems, implement designs and quality

○ adequate communication with the supply side, in terms of effective feedback from the field on farmers' needs and on the acceptability of implements.

Applied research and development institutions, animal draft power extension services and area development programmes will all play important roles in meeting these requirements.

The profitability of animal draft power farming is mainly a function of economic and logistic factors which determine the number and range of the required animal draft power implements that can actually be marketed and bought. The prerequisites for profitability include:

○ adequate agricultural product marketing and pricing policies (and credit facilities) which offer real incentives to produce food-crop surpluses and/or to incorporate cash crops into the cropping system

○ timely availability of animal draft power equipment (and other production inputs) at affordable prices in the rural areas.

Supply

In the African context, local manufacture of animal draft power equipment is, to a large extent, based on the selection and adaptation of designs and products originating from other regions with similar conditions. Adaptation of existing implements to meet the needs of local farmers requires adequate engineering knowledge and skills within the country. In particular, local manufacturers must be capable of undertaking design and construction adaptations and of initiating implement diversification. In some cases the establishment of local assembly or manufacturing facilities may require external assistance in the initial phase.

Local manufacture or assembly of animal draft power equipment must be competitive (implements must be of acceptable quality, and must be available when they are needed at prices which farmers can afford) and must be accompanied by adequate local supply and distribution systems and after-sales services, particularly for spare parts. Prerequisites for this include:

º government commitment and policy measures: tax and import duty system, foreign currency regulations in support of local manufacture

º a sound economic setting (adequate marketing and price policies) and stable markets (profitable small-scale farming).

Comparison of animal power demand in West Africa and Zambia

In many ways, the experience gained during 30 years of animal draft power development and related implement supply in West Africa appears relevant to the situation in Zambia (and other countries in eastern and southern Africa). Some of the similarities and differences in the conditions in which animal draft power is used in the two regions are outlined below.

Similarities

Small-scale farming in the areas of West Africa and Zambia that have 700–1200 mm of annual rainfall is characterised by highly variable environmental and soil conditions which require the supply of region-specific animal draft power equipment.

In both these 700–1200 mm rainfall areas, similar breeds and types of traditional draft cattle are used and cropping systems are dominated by upland cereals, such as maize, sorghum/millets, with groundnuts, wetland rice (in certain regions) and, to a varying degree, cash crops such as cotton.

Regional/integrated rural development programmes and societies play important catalytic or supporting roles in the development of animal draft power (particularly in new introduction areas with external

assistance). A number of West African animal draft power regions benefit from pronounced support from cotton marketing agencies.

Differences

Zambia (with only 50–60% of its population living in the rural areas) can be characterised by its "empty countryside", with severe infrastructural, marketing, distribution, logistic and communication constraints. Comparable agro-ecological regions in West Africa (80–85% rural population) are more densely populated and have more roads, with cheap public/private transport services operating between the many villages.

In the drier areas of West Africa donkeys/horses are predominantly used, whereas the use of donkeys in similar dry areas in Zambia is only just emerging. In Zambia the use of two to three pairs of oxen pulling one plow is common, whereas in West Africa oxen are used only in single pairs.

In comparison with West African farm holdings, most Zambian rural areas appear to face more serious seasonal labour shortages as a result of smaller family sizes and of a larger proportion of households being female-headed.

With the present economic crisis, profitability of food crop production by small farmers in Zambia is under heavy pressure (low producer prices, difficult marketing, high inflation, limited credit availability). Zambia's animal draft power manufacturing and trading sector is facing serious raw material and hard currency constraints. Comparable agro-ecological regions in West Africa benefit in general from a more stable and favourable economic setting and a liberalised marketing and trading system (with, in some regions, cash crops such as cotton generating considerable revenues). Weekly markets exist in almost all villages in West Africa, and animal draft power is widely used for both on- and off-farm transport.

Animal draft power in West Africa

Equipment diversity in relation to animals used (with reference to Senegal)

In Senegal, the use of animal traction for field operations was introduced in the Groundnut Basin (see Figure 1a) as early as the 1930s. In this 500–800 mm rainfall area, where minimum tillage is the traditional practice, the use of imported one-row seeders, drawn by horses or donkeys, allowed timely and quick planting of groundnuts and traditional cereals.

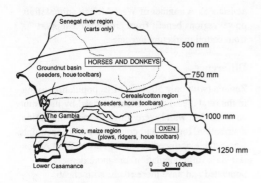

Figure 1a: Agricultural regions, annual rainfall zones and animal draft power systems in Senegal

In the 1960s a massive rural development programme was implemented in this region. Foreign financial and technical assistance was provided for research and development of animal draft power equipment, for training and extension and for supply/distribution of agricultural inputs. In addition, seasonal and medium-term credit systems were set up, and local manufacture of implements was started with the establishment of the Siscoma factory in 1963.

This "crash" programme resulted in the local manufacture and introduction of large numbers of implements—20 000 to 30 000 units/year, enough for almost the entire horse/donkey population (Bordet et al, 1988). The *Super-Eco* one-row seeders, supplemented by light toolbars (*Houe Occidentale* and the heavier, more versatile *Houe Sine*) fitted with cultivator tines, weeding and groundnut-lifting devices proved to be perfectly adapted to the draft animals available.

In spite of considerable research and development efforts in the 1960s and 1970s, which resulted in a wide range and variety of implements, including those suitable for use with oxen, the introduction of animal traction in the more humid southern regions of Senegal proceeded at a much slower pace. Reasons for this included availability and costs of the oxen as well as animal husbandry and health considerations.

With the increased draft power of the oxen, plows and/or ridgers are used to an increasing extent in these 800–1200 mm rainfall areas, either as single-purpose implements or as part of the *Sine* and *Arara* toolbars.

In the 1960s a large variety of multipurpose implements were developed and manufactured in Senegal (Bordet et al, 1988).

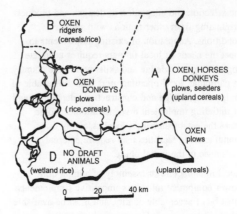

Agricultural zone	Percentage of farmers owning		
	Oxen	Horses	Donkeys
A	68	18	8
B	17	–	2
C	10	–	9
D	1	–	–
E	12	–	–

Figure 1b: Area-specific animal draft power systems in Lower Casamance, Senegal (Source: Ndiamé, 1988)

The more complete, heavier and expensive wheeled toolcarriers (*Polyculteur* and *Tropiculteur*) and the Ariana type toolframes (basic frame supported by small wheels) did not receive spontaneous or widespread farmer acceptance. Although these implements are of high quality and are versatile and easy to use, their introduction remained limited to specific areas and intensive extension programmes only. This was due to:

○ high investment costs

○ multi-row cultivation techniques not being easily mastered by farmers (or animals)

○ the requirement for properly cleared fields and strong animals

○ in practice, incompatible timing of the use of different components (eg, plowing and ridging are overlapping operations).

The lighter and cheaper *Houe Sine* toolbars ("multiculteurs") with their range of cultivating, weeding, ridging and groundnut-lifting devices were, however, widely accepted in different West African regions because they were better adapted to less optimal field conditions, and suitable for a wider range of draft animals.

The example of the Lower Casamance region in southern Senegal (Figure 1b) shows that, even within a small region, introduction and use of animal power varies enormously, being dictated by

Table 1a: Typical animal draft power use in Lower Casamance, Senegal

	Cattle	Horse/donkey
Average yearly use (days)	32	22
Average yearly use (hours)	154	62
Percentage of time spent on:		
Ridging	32%	0%
Plowing	21%	0%
Seeding	21%	64%
Weeding	0%	23%
Transport	0%	13%
Renting out	26%	0%

Table 1b: Additional uses of experienced animals (after 3 years) in Lower Casamance

Animal type	Young animals	Experienced animals
Cattle	plowing/seeding	also ridging
Horse/donkey	mainly transport	also seeding/weeding

Source: Sonko (1985)

type and availability of draft animals and cropping and farming systems practised.

Table 1 illustrates that the types of field operations carried out in this region vary according to:

○ the draft animals available: primary tillage operations, such as plowing or ridging, are done by oxen, and seeding and weeding operations by horses/donkeys

○ the experience/age of the animals: row cultivation (seeding, ridging and weeding) requires trained animals.

As well as field operations, horses and donkeys (and to a lesser extent oxen) are widely used for on- and off-farm transport all over Senegal (see Figure 2). Locally manufactured simple high-platform carts, based on imported conventional roller bearing/axle assemblies, are used in large numbers.

Figure 2 also illustrates that the termination of the massive rural development programmes around 1980 (resulting in suspension of the parastatal supply and credit structure and closing of the Siscoma factory), had an important impact on the further expansion of animal draft power in Senegal.

Towards the end of the 1980s, the use of animal draft power in Senegal stabilised at the level of some 200 000 horses, 200 000 donkeys and 140 000 oxen (Havard and Faye, 1988).

Diversity of equipment in relation to farming systems (with reference to Mali)

The pattern of the introduction of animal draft power in Mali was different from that in Senegal (see Figures 2 and 3). One reason for this is the difference in availability of draft animals: because there is a long-standing tradition of cattle holding in Mali, oxen are predominantly used for farm operations there. By 1957, 40 000 work oxen were already being used in Mali, compared with only 2000 in Senegal (Bordet et al, 1988). Use of donkeys in Mali is mainly limited to transport and to seeding/weeding operations in the groundnut region.

Another reason is that important integrated rural development programmes have been implemented in the different agro-ecological regions of Mali (see Figure 4a). With foreign (French and later multi-donor) assistance, two rural development societies played, and still play, an important role in the development of region-specific animal draft power-based farming-systems in Mali. One is the Office du Niger which, since 1957 (when tractorised tillage ceased), has introduced oxen for plowing and harrowing in a 50 000 ha area of wetland rice production. The other is CMDT (Compagnie Malienne pour le Développement des Textiles), the cotton development authority in southern Mali, which supports the development of cotton-based

Figure 2: Evolution of the use of animal draft power implements in Senegal (Harvard and Faye, 1988)

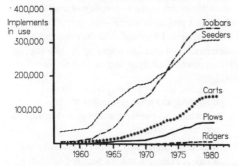

Figure 3: Evolution of use of animal draft power implements in Mali (Source: Zerbo and Kantao, 1988)

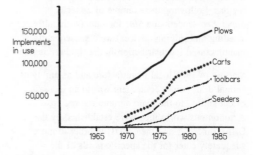

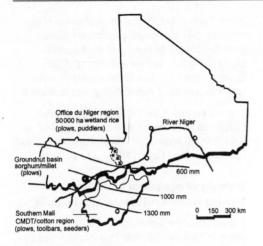

Figure 4a: Agricultural regions and animal draft power
introduction in Mali

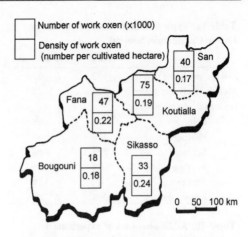

Figure 4b: Animal draft power in southern Mali

farming systems. The cotton marketing structure of CMDT has an important influence on the profitability of animal draft power based smallholder farming. By providing support for, research, training and extension programmes, input supply and distribution systems, including seasonal and medium-term credit for production inputs (such as animal draft power equipment), rural blacksmith programmes (training and implementation), marketing and processing systems, and regional assembly workshops (since 1986), these autonomous parastatal societies achieved the introduction of a range of region-specific animal draft power implements.

Categories and sources of animal power equipment

The supply of animal draft power implements was initially based on importation of different makes of plow from France. After the establishment of the parastatal Smecma factory in Bamako in 1974, one make of plow (the relatively lightweight *Bajac TM* plow, originally designed for use in the uplands) continued to dominate the market, supported by government directives for standardisation (Bordet et al, 1988). Until 1985 this same plow model was also most common in the heavy clay rice-growing regions. Following the example of Senegal, *Super-Eco* seeders and *Sine* toolbars (with cultivator, weeding and ridging devices) were subsequently manufactured for distribution in the southern region.

Starting in 1986 local manufacture and assembly of animal draft power equipment was to an increasing extent shifted to the main agricultural regions. Autonomous workshops were established by the Office du Niger and the CMDT, in order to more adequately cater for the specific needs of the

farmers in these regions. This has resulted in new designs of plows and harrows, better adapted to the heavier soils in the rice-growing area of the Office du Niger. More recently, in answer to the large-scale adoption of rice transplanting practices, animal-drawn puddlers and levelling boards for wetland tillage have also been developed and manufactured locally. Another aim of the workshops was to assist in the further development of rural blacksmiths in these regions. The blacksmiths participate in spare-part supply and distribution, offer repair services to the farmers and are involved in village level local manufacturing initiatives.

Large numbers of carts have also been introduced in all areas of Mali. Mainly designed to be pulled by donkeys, they are simple platform carts based on conventional roller bearing/axle assemblies. They are manufactured locally, not only by Smecma, but also, to an increasing extent, by rural and urban workshops in the regions.

Importance of cash crops for animal draft power

Experience with the introduction of animal draft power in Senegal, Mali and other countries in West Africa demonstrates the importance of cash crops in achieving a profitable animal draft power based farming system. Integrated rural development programmes and societies operating in such regions play an essential catalytic and supporting role through:

○ marketing and price guarantees by the concerned development societies and marketing and trading partners

○ infrastructural support and services, including training, extension and the supply and distribution of various essential production inputs (seed, fertiliser, etc)

○ regular supply (recently based on on-the-spot manufacture and assembly) and distribution of animal draft power implements (with or without medium-term credit), including after-sales service provisions (spare-part supply, rural blacksmith programmes).

Figure 4b shows that the density of animal draft power use varies among the different districts in southern Mali. In this region cotton cultivation increased from 40 000 ha in 1958 to 140 000 ha in 1986, average cotton yields being 200 and 1200 kg/ha respectively (Bordet et al, 1988).

The percentage of farms that have adopted animal power for their field operations varies from roughly 80% ("nearing saturation") in the more advanced areas, such as parts of Koutilla and Sikasso (Sangaré et al, 1988), to between 33 and 57% in the more recently supported Bougouni region.

Undeniably, the availability of medium-term credit for purchasing work oxen and implements plays an essential catalytic role, particularly in new animal draft power development areas. However, farmer initiatives and cash purchases still remain the most important method of acquiring oxen and implements, also in the traditional CMDT supported regions.

Table 2 shows that, for an "old" CMDT area in Sikasso district, most of the "traditional" implements (plows, harrows and carts) have been acquired by cash purchase. Credit support proved especially important for the "second phase" diversification of animal draft power, with about 50% of the toolbars and seeders being obtained on credit (Whitney, 1981).

Similar observations can be made for Bougouni region, where support has been provided more recently by CMDT. In three years of support so far, only 11% of the farms have had access to credit:

96% of the plows in use have been purchased on a cash basis, but about 20% of the work oxen and toolbars in use were more recently obtained on credit.

In general, cultivation of a cash crop, such as cotton, requires more attention and is more labour intensive than the growing of traditional cereal crops (millet, sorghum and maize). Incorporation of cotton in a cropping pattern in this region therefore provides an additional incentive to diversify and intensify the use of animal draft power on a farm, in order to be able to extend the cultivated area: as well as plowing and ridging, oxen are used more for weeding and seeding operations.

Table 3 illustrates this more intensive and diversified use of animal draft power implements in the case of cotton growing.

Implement diversification according to soil conditions, farm size and cropping systems

Plowing versus reduced tillage practices

In many regions in West Africa, animal draft power based tillage systems (and related implements) are to a large extent determined by the prevailing soil and climatological conditions.

The customary zero and minimum tillage practices applied in the 700–1000 mm rainfall regions (such as in Senegal, with direct seeding and direct ridging of the lighter soils) reflect the prime importance of **timely** and quick interventions at the start of the short rainy season. The more time-consuming full-field plowing is hardly practised at all, in spite of extensive research and extension efforts in these regions (and in spite of proof that better water conservation and deeper rooting of the crops leads to increased yields). For the same reasons of timeliness and speed of crop establishment, direct or split ridging is the most common primary tillage technique in the main animal draft power region of Togo, as shown in Table 4 (Sabi, 1990)

Table 2: Method of acquisition of animal draft power implements (case study of Bambadougou villages, Sikasso, 1978)

Implement	Cash purchase	Government credit
Plows	80%	20%
Toolbar (ridger/weeder)	50%	50%
Harrow	100%	0%
One-row seeder	43%	57%
Ox cart	63%	37%
General average	65%	35%

Table 3: Animal draft power use in relation to crops cultivated, CMDT region, Mali

	Percentage of farmers using implements		
Implement	Cotton	Millet/ sorghum	Maize
Plows	89	50	35
Seeders	50	18	16
Toolbar (weeding)	86	33	27
Toolbar (ridging)	58	17	19

Table 4: Typical animal draft power operations in Togo in 1987

	Savanna Region	Central Region
Average farm size (ha)	8	34
Area of cash crops	30%	23–34%
Principal crops (ha)		
Maize	–	1.65
Cotton	1.0	0.60
Sorghum/millet	5.0	0.50
Groundnut	1.5	–
Field operations (% of farmers)		
Plowing	3	96
Ridging	97	4
Weeding	67	30

Source: Sabi (1990)

The same applies to many other 700–1200 mm rainfall areas in West Africa (including parts of Mali) where, as well as ridgers, standard plows are also used to split old ridges or to form back furrows (leaving 50% of the land untouched). In Nigeria the *Emcot* ridger has been widely accepted by farmers since the 1940s because of its simple and durable construction and its multipurpose use for direct ridging, split-ridging, re-ridging, weeding and even groundnut-lifting (Gwani, 1990).

More time-consuming full-field plowing, enabling complete inversion of the arable layer, appears only justified, from the farmers' point of view, in heavier soils and higher rainfall areas because of the need to bury abundant weed infestations: a well designed plow is, without doubt, the most effective implement for controlling weed growth.

Animal draft power supplementing family labour

It is widely accepted that the introduction of animal draft power enables farmers to extend their cultivated area. Generally, adoption of animal draft power follows a step-by-step approach, whereby the need for a more diversified range of animal draft power equipment seems directly linked with the amount of family labour available on the farm. Animal draft power is merely supplementing the available human labour force, in the first instance by alleviating labour/time constraints for the primary tillage operations. Extension of the "plowed" area, however, will soon be limited by labour constraints for the subsequent weeding and other crop husbandry operations. In a second phase, the need for a more diversified and intensive use of the available draft animals will grow with a gradual adoption of seeding, ridging and/or weeding implements.

Experience demonstrates that farmers are seldom able to acquire the whole package of animal draft power implements in one go (even if adequate credit is available), so credit schemes should consider gradual, step-by-step introduction as the most viable approach.

The interaction between larger family sizes and more intensive and diversified use of animal draft power with a related range of implements is clearly demonstrated by a case study in southern Mali (Whitney, 1981). Table 5 illustrates that the introduction of a more or less diversified range of animal draft power implements is merely supplementing the existing labour force. The use of plows (80% purchased on a cash basis) for primary tillage increased not only the cultivated area per farm but also the area per active worker available. However, further increase in the cultivated area (including the incorporation of more labour-intensive cash crops in the cropping pattern) appears possible only if the use of a more diversified package of animal draft power implements (average 50% purchased on a credit basis) can be matched by an increased availability of family labour.

A similar relationship between the size and wealth of a farm and the number and range of animal draft power implements used (and area of cash crops

Table 5: Animal draft power equipment in relation to available family labour and cultivated area (case study of Bambadougou villages, Sikasso, 1978)

Categories of farmers	Cultivated area per family (ha)	Active workers per family (persons)	Area per active worker (ha/person)
Non-equipped farmers	2.8	5.4	0.51
Farmers owning one plow	4.9	7.2	0.78
Farmers owning complete package[1]	13.0	16.5	0.73
Average	5.8	9.6	0.64

[1] *Package includes plow, toolbar, seeder, harrow and ox cart*

Table 6: Average cultivated area of crops on large and medium farms in Gladié village, southern Mali

Categories of farmers and animal power use	Average cultivated area per farm (ha)			
	Cotton	Millet/maize	Sorghum	Total
Large farms using 5 pairs of oxen with 2 plows, 1 toolbar, 1–3 one-row seeders, 1–2 harrows and 1 ox cart	9.0	7.7	5.7	**22.4**
Medium farms using 1–2 pairs oxen with 1 plow and 1 toolbar, no seeder, no harrow and no ox cart	2.9	2.3	9.0	**14.2**

Table 7: Cropping pattern in relation to farm size and animal draft power equipment available (case study of Bambadougou villages, Mali)

Categories of farmers	Family food[1] (ha/family)	Cash crops[2] (ha/family)	Personal[3] (ha/family)	Total (ha)
Non-equipped	2.14 (77%)	0.22 (8%)	0.42 (15%)	**2.78**
Plow only	3.69 (75%)	0.44 (9%)	0.78 (15%)	**4.91**
Well equipped	8.63 (66%)	1.78 (14%)	2.62 (20%)	**13.03**
Average	4.12 (71%)	0.65 (11%)	1.04 (18%)	**5.81**

[1] Millet/sorghum, maize and rice
[2] Cotton, sesame, sweet potatoes and tree crops
[3] Women's rice fields and vegetable gardens

cultivated) was demonstrated by another case study in southern Mali (see Table 6).

These and other studies reveal that an increase in cultivated area cannot simply be considered as the effect of the introduction of animal draft power as such. Instead they indicate that the need for (and the ability to correctly manage) additional ranges of animal draft power implements is to a large extent determined by traditional differences in general "wealth" among farmers within a particular area. "Wealth" is here expressed in terms of number of cattle owned, access to more and better permanent land and the size of the family, particularly number of women and older children present.

Effect of animal draft power on cropping systems

Table 7 illustrates, for the same categories of farmers in southern Mali, that those with larger and better-equipped farms are able to attach relatively more importance to cash crops. The more intensive use of draft animals with a more diversified range of implements helps to alleviate the peak labour bottlenecks in the weeding season, allowing the

women to extend their personal rice area and vegetable gardens (Whitney, 1981).

The same study reveals that there is a marked impact of the more diversified use of animal draft power on the applied tillage and cropping systems and field size. Table 8 shows that:

o farmers equipped with animal draft power cultivate larger fields and more fields; they are able to carry out the field operations with greater speed and efficiency

o farmers who only own plows continue to practise the traditional intercropping systems (millet/sorghum intercropped with maize, beans, groundnuts) in which the cereals are planted on the ridges made by the plow (cotton and rice being cultivated in pure stands)

o farmers who also own seeders and toolbars practise more monocropping (even of the traditional millet/sorghum crop) because they own weeding/ridging implements.

In general, the well-equipped farmers benefit also from better timeliness of cultivation (planting and

Table 8: Effects of animal draft power equipment use on cropping pattern and field size (case study of Bambadougou villages, Mali)

Categories	Number of fields per farm	Average field size (ha)	Percentage pure stand all crops	Percentage pure stand of millet and sorghum
Non-equipped	4.8	0.58	51	26
Plow only	6.6	0.74	57	20
Well-equipped	14.5	0.90	84	67

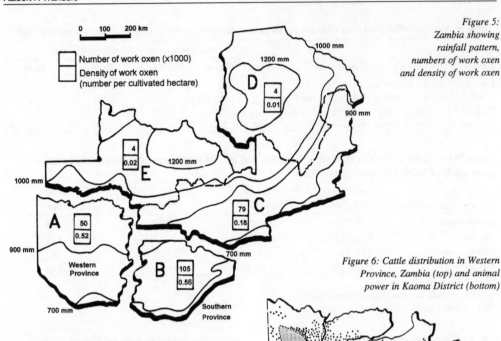

Figure 5:
Zambia showing
rainfall pattern,
numbers of work oxen
and density of work oxen

weeding) and easier transport by carts of their farm
inputs (including manure) and produce.

Animal draft power introduction in Zambia: current trends and needs

Regional introduction of animal draft power

The use of animal draft power in Zambia has always
been (and still is) largely confined to those regions
having a long-standing tradition of cattle holding, in
particular the Western and Southern Provinces (see
Figure 5). These two provinces have the highest
densities of work oxen per cultivated hectare (MoA,
1985; Starkey, Dibbits and Mwenya, 1991),
although within them the distribution of work oxen
is very uneven.

Distribution of work oxen is largely determined by
the traditional availability of cattle and region-
specific animal health constraints. Figure 6
illustrates the low density of work oxen in the
relatively new settlement areas of Kaoma District in
Western Province (0.13 per hectare, compared with
0.52 per hectare for the whole of the province).
Considering its high potential for increased food
crop production (and export to the urban regions),
supply and distribution of both work animals and
implements has a particularly high priority in this
district.

This uneven distribution and ownership of cattle
resulted in an important need for ox hiring in most
regions of Zambia, 20–30% of farmers relying on

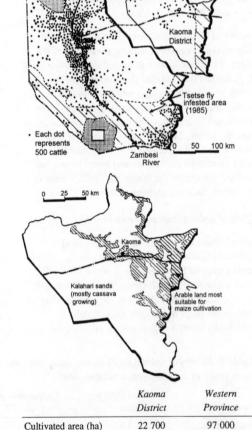

Figure 6: Cattle distribution in Western
Province, Zambia (top) and animal
power in Kaoma District (bottom)

	Kaoma District	Western Province
Cultivated area (ha)	22 700	97 000
Trained oxen	2 900	50 000
Trained oxen per ha	0.13	0.52

hiring of oxen for, often delayed, plowing (Tembo and Rajeswaran, 1989).

Table 9 illustrates that, in Kabwe region, farmers relying on ox hiring are in a much weaker position than ox owners, in terms of both cultivated area and available cattle and labour force (Baker and White, 1983).

In most other provinces of Zambia there is little or no tradition of cattle keeping. Introduction of animal draft power is thus a slow and difficult process which requires considerable investment and development efforts in the areas of animal husbandry and health, general extension and training, marketing and distribution and credit.

As in West Africa, regional integrated rural development programmes (with foreign financial and technical assistance) have to play an important initiating role in the development of animal draft power in new introduction regions of Zambia. Compared to West Africa, however, the development of animal draft power (and of smallholder farming in general) in Zambia appears severely constrained by a number of socio-economic and logistic conditions (particularly at the present time).

First, farming is not very profitable: producer prices for maize and other food crops are low, and in most regions there is no real cash crop. Figure 7 illustrates the high relative investment costs of work oxen and implements in Zambia (expressed in kg maize equivalent) compared with some other African countries.

Second, high inflation and price/marketing policies make it impossible to implement realistic credit schemes.

Third, low rural population densities result in seasonal labour shortages in the rural areas (characterised by a relatively high percentage of female-headed households).

Fourth, poor rural communications in the "empty" countryside result in logistic and economic constraints in terms of marketing and distribution of production inputs (including animal draft power equipment) and of provision of adequate after-sales

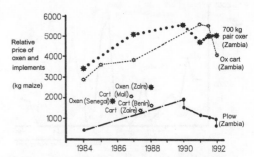

Figure 7: Relative animal draft power investment costs in Zambia, with some comparisons from other countries (Comparison sources: Kabeya, 1990; Kokoye, 1990)

service support (including supply constraints of rural workshops and blacksmiths).

Sources and diversity of animal draft power equipment

Compared to the situation in most West African regions, the introduction of animal draft power equipment in Zambia can be characterised by a lack of diversification of animal draft power tillage practices (and related implements). Essentially one type of plow is being used all over Zambia, and introduction of ridgers and cultivators has been limited. The use of ox carts for transport is also poorly developed.

This lack of diversity has arisen as the result of long-standing importation (even after the establishment of the first local manufacturer in 1978) of batches of implements of various origins, supplied and distributed through government and parastatal trading and distribution agencies (see Figure 8).

In the central planning, "top-down" approach followed, little attention is given to adequately assessing region-specific requirements of the farmers, nor are private-sector trading and manufacturing initiatives being promoted in the different regions in order to develop equipment (adapt imported implements) and to establish a proper distribution and after-sales service network.

In Zambia, as in West Africa, a certain degree of diversification in the use of animal draft power (and related equipment) appears called for, taking into account the diverse soil conditions and different farming systems practised throughout the country.

Primary tillage operations

In many regions of Zambia conventional full-field plowing is, without doubt, the most appropriate technique for controlling the abundant weed growth

Table 9: Case study of ox hirers and ox owners in Kabwe region in 1981

	Ox hirers	Ox owners
Active workers per household (aged 15–55 years)	2.9	3.9
Average cultivated area (ha)	2.7	3.7
Average number of cattle	1.6	17.0

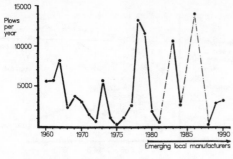

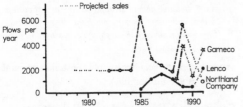

Figure 8: Annual plow inports (top) and local plow production and sales (bottom) in Zambia

at the start of the rainy season. It is questionable whether one single plow design is equally appropriate for all the different conditions of use throughout the country: considering the enormous variety in soil type (from light/sandy soils to heavy and often not properly cleared soils) and draft power availability (from one to three pairs of oxen used in plowing), there appears to be room for several different plow designs in Zambia. On the other hand, the need for better timeliness and speed of crop establishment, especially in the drier regions which have lighter soils, may, as in similar agro-climatological regions in West Africa, provide a real incentive for farmers to investigate the use of alternative tillage practices, such as direct ridging and/or split ridging techniques, which are better adapted to the conditions and hence less time-consuming.

Other animal draft power field operations and rural transport

In most rural regions in Zambia, there appears to be an important need to supplement the limited family labour available, particularly for weeding. Table 9 shows that family sizes in Kabwe region are very small—only three or four active workers per household. An animal draft power survey in Southern Province (Tembo and Rajeswaran, 1989) revealed an important variation in family size and in the number of active workers available on the farm. Families have, on average, seven workers, of which at least two-thirds are female; only a few younger men are available.

Under these circumstances a serious labour shortage occurs during the peak weeding season, and so there is an important need for weeding/ridging implements to help to alleviate this bottleneck. Similar needs are also evident in other regions of Zambia, such as the new settlement areas in Kaoma District. In the past, however, only a limited number of weeding and ridging implements have been imported or manufactured locally. Moreover, most cultivators and ridgers offered to the farmers in the past were heavy and expensive (especially when compared to the designs common in West Africa). In addition, some of these implements, depending on their origin, show more or less serious design shortcomings and construction compromises.

Where transport is concerned, there is an obvious need (and market) for locally made ox carts, particularly considering the recently more liberalised marketing, trading and local processing initiatives in the rural areas. Some alternative axle/bearing and wheel designs may continue to be of relevance for small-scale manufacture of ox carts in specific areas in Zambia (in relation to technical assistance and manufacturing skill available). On the whole there appears to be a big demand for conventional axle/roller bearing assemblies and pneumatic tyres, to be fitted locally with wooden bodies. Farmers' preferences in this direction are evident (as they are in the rest of Africa), and the unavoidable tyre punctures are not considered a major constraint.

Animal draft power supply and distribution: West Africa and Zambia

Relevance of West African experience

As far as the development, manufacture, supply and introduction of adapted animal draft power equipment is concerned, many West African regions have a lead of some 15 years of relevant experience over Zambia. Already in the 1950s and 1960s important animal draft power research, development and extension efforts in Senegal resulted in a wide range of region-specific implement designs. Over the years, small-scale farmers and manufacturers in other West African regions have subsequently chosen, adopted and fully accepted some of the equipment designs proposed. For comparable agro-ecological regions in Zambia, local adaptation/manufacture of relevant West African designs may constitute a valuable starting point to effectively initiate a more diversified use of animal draft power.

In West Africa, large-scale local manufacture by central (parastatal) companies started as early as

1963 (Senegal) and 1974 (Mali). Raw materials and implement components were supplied from France, with a varying but often low locally added value (eg, Smecma in Mali). Because of declining markets and a distinct over-capacity of manufacturing facilities established in the region on the whole, these centralised manufacturers started to face serious financial problems in the 1980s, resulting in suspension of production. This situation was the result of several factors:

○ the "saturation effect" after the initial "crash" programmes of large-scale introduction in the 1970s

○ the breaking-down of the (parastatal) supply, distribution and credit system

○ increased competition from more effective and better placed regional/rural workshops, including blacksmiths' manufacturing initiatives.

In other West African countries (such as Burkina Faso, Niger and Togo) smaller (both private and parastatal) workshops have been established closer to the main animal draft power regions. These workshops took advantage of earlier experience of implement development and manufacture from Senegal by selecting and adapting existing designs to suit local conditions of use. In line with government policies to implement rural development "from the bottom up" and to promote private sector initiatives (instead of previous central planning and "top-down" approaches), regional assembly and manufacturing workshops were established in the 1980s in the heart of the main agricultural regions in Mali. These autonomous regional workshops are in the position to assure a timely supply and distribution of a range of implements specifically adapted to the regions concerned, involving and supporting rural blacksmith workshops.

Along with local manufacture, blacksmith training and support programmes have been implemented since the 1970s in most West African countries. Relatively dense networks of rural blacksmiths (in Mali: associations) are to an increasing extent able to serve farmers' needs in terms of implement repair and manufacture and supply of spare parts. In more advanced regions, blacksmiths' workshops are able to supply local farmers with complete (simple) implements; the quality is moderate to poor, but the prices are distinctly lower.

Scenario A: Supply relying on importation

Recent experience in Zambia represents a supply scenario biased towards imports. Following a "top-down", central planning approach involving

mainly parastatal agencies and international tenders, bulk supplies of implements of different origins and varying designs and quality are obtained. This is illustrated schematically in Figure 9.

Constraints to relying on imports to satisfy demand for animal draft power implements arise from the risks that:

○ implements supplied to farmers will be, at best, poorly adapted to local conditions, and farmers will have no choice of implements

○ few efforts are made to take account of region-specific farmers' needs or to diversify the use of animal draft power

○ limited (or no) attention is given to the need to develop an adequate after-sales service organisation (poor standardisation of production and neglected spare-part supply/distribution).

Scenario B: Centralised local manufacture

In a number of African countries, such as Mali, Senegal and Zambia, centralised production is (or has been) realised by just one (often parastatal) manufacturer. In such monopoly situations, an essentially "top down" approach is being followed

Figure 9: Schematic representation of recent supply and distribution in Zambia

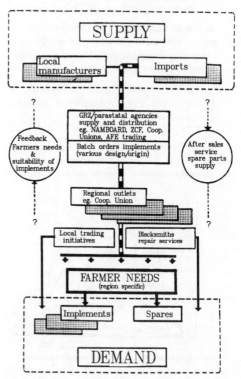

as far as the supply and distribution of often a limited range of implements is concerned.

In retrospect, it can be observed that the central production facilities that were established were often too large: for example, in Senegal, and to a lesser extent in Mali, factory capacities were based on the initial (artificially) high production rates, which were aimed at exports to other countries in the region as well as at domestic consumption. This resulted in limited diversification and flexibility of production. It also resulted in heavy dependence on sometimes inadequately functioning (parastatal) trading and distribution agencies, and hence reliance on the economic survival of such agencies, with limited possibility to fall back on private sector marketing and distribution systems if parastatal animal draft power supply/credit programmes should be reduced or suspended. Figure 10 illustrates the highly variable manufacture and supply of animal draft power implements by Siscoma in Senegal, with the non-sustainable high production figures in the 1970s.

The disadvantages of relying on a single local manufacturer of animal draft power implements are that:

o little, if any, attention is given to developing or adapting implement design in accordance with diverse region-specific needs (limited choice)

o there is limited incentive to diversify the product range, and a tendency toward design and quality compromises in case of monopoly situations (poor standardisation)

o there is limited possibility and incentive to develop an effective distribution and after-sales service network.

Figure 10: Annual introductions of animal draft power implements in Senegal, showing effects of two rural development programmes (after Havard and Faye, 1988)

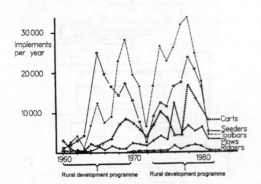

Where local manufacture is realised by a number of medium- to small-scale central manufacturers, both private and parastatal (as is the present tendency in Zambia), an element of competition is introduced, which allows the alleviation of some of the above constraints. In order to develop its market, each manufacturer will be forced to invest in agricultural engineering and design know-how, maintain and improve design and quality standards, and act upon actual farmers' needs, thus introducing a range of implements, and an after-sales service and spare-part supply and distribution network into the rural areas.

This does not solve all of the problems, however, because it will still be difficult to adjust manufacture to the diverse, region-specific farmers' needs, in terms of types and diversification of implements and spare parts; this difficulty is exacerbated by poor communication with, and feedback from, the regions. There will still be a need to invest in the establishment of an adequate (private sector) animal draft power marketing and distribution system in the regions, possibly involving assembly workshops and consequently subsidiaries in the main regions.

Scenario C: Decentralised manufacture

In many African countries (such as Burkina Faso, Mali and Togo) the region-specific needs of the rural sector would be best served by decentralised manufacture/assembly of implements. Regional workshops would ensure a more timely supply and distribution of a well-adapted range of implements and would facilitate the organisation of an effective after-sales service and spare-parts distribution network in which rural blacksmiths, for example, could participate (see Figure 11).

Basically equipped regional workshops could operate in liaison with (as subsidiaries of) a central manufacturer, which would supply raw materials and key components, and carry out special machining and heat treatment operations.

Alternatively, regional workshops could operate independently to manufacture or assemble a region-specific range of implements. Because the start-up of such workshops would require external assistance, an autonomous regional integrated development programme could be involved to help in providing investment capital, raw materials and management capacity. In time, however, once a regional workshop has assured its autonomous status with adequate capital resources, and established links with its own commercial suppliers of materials and components, external assistance could gradually be phased out, and decentralised manufacture or assembly could become a sustainable activity.

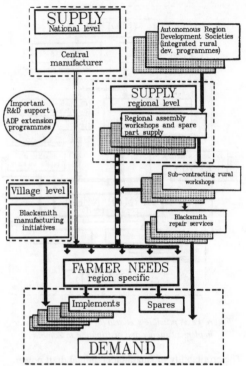

Figure 11: Schematic representation of a decentralised system of supply and distribution of animal draft power implements based on West African experiences

Lessons from the different scenarios

Some positive points and limitations of the three animal draft power supply scenarios that have been outlined are summarised in Table 10.

In practice, centrally planned, top-down implement supply scenarios (types A and B) that relied heavily

on government or parastatal manufacturing, trading or distribution institutions have suffered from institutional weaknesses. Various constraints (economic, logistic or operational) have tended to result in partial or complete suspension of the animal draft implement supply and distribution system in a country. There have been examples of this in Mali, Senegal and Zambia. Furthermore, experience has shown that establishment of centralised large-scale implement manufacturing facilities has often been based on unrealistic local demand forecasts and export potential. Diminishing markets and vanishing exports, together with competition from more flexible or better placed smaller workshops, have resulted in suspension of a number of such large-scale production units, such as Siscoma in Senegal.

As far as the quality and local adaptation of animal draft power equipment is concerned, a monopoly situation with centralised manufacture and supply may result in design and construction decisions and compromises which are not in the interest of the actual users. Relatively small-scale, more flexible private sector manufacture and distribution facilities may be better able to serve the rural community needs. Government involvement (and animal draft power policy measures) should aim to create the conditions required for such farmer-oriented private sector initiatives. Experience from West Africa suggests that external financial support and technical cooperation may be required. This is likely to be most important in the initial phases of animal power development, both at the level of the manufacturers (transfer of design and manufacturing skills) and in the rural areas (support to rural development programmes with animal draft power components).

Table 10: Positive and negative aspects of the three implement supply scenarios

	A	B	C
		Central	Decentralised
	Importation	workshops	workshops
Communication with rural sector			
Feedback on farmers' needs and implement acceptability	−	−/+	+
Farmers' choice of type of implement (diversification potential)	−	−/+	+
Spare-part supply service	−	−/+	+
Supply and distribution			
Possibility to adapt design according to regions	−	−/+	+
Local components/added value	−	+	+
Effective supply/production planning (reacting to seasonal demand)	−	−/+	+
Timely distribution to the rural sector	−	−/+	+
Possibility of effective after-sales network for spare parts	−	−/+	+
Liaison with and support to rural blacksmiths (repair services and sub-contracting manufacture/assembly)	−	−/+	+

Prospects for Zambia

The parastatal animal draft power implement supply and distribution system in Zambia recently came near to breakdown. This, and the national reorientation toward a liberalised marketing system with private sector involvement, may lead to a more effective farmer-oriented approach to local manufacture, marketing and distribution of adapted implements and spare parts (see Figure 12).

The recent establishment of some small-scale assembly and manufacturing facilities may, through competition, result in a more adapted range of higher quality implements being marketed in the rural regions. This may lead to increased involvement of small assembly workshops in the main rural regions. Ideally the system will evolve to reflect the actual demand, choice and preferences of farmers, and provide an effective after-sales service and spare-part supply organisation.

A crucial prerequisite is the revival of the economy in Zambia in general, and an increased profitability of animal draft power farming in particular.

Zambia suffers from difficult communications with the rather isolated and "empty" rural regions and this has resulted in poor feedback. In view of the high investment costs required to establish a farmer-oriented marketing and distribution system and spare part supply, rural development programmes had important liaison and supporting roles, especially in regions where animal power is being introduced. Both in new and more traditional animal traction areas, animal draft power research and extension institutions (such the Magoye–Palabana on-farm testing programme) may help to bridge the gap between the supply side and the users. They may do this by creating and improving farmers' awareness of both existing and recently adapted animal draft power technologies through on-farm trials and demonstrations. This should help assure adequate feedback, from the different regions to the supply system, concerning the needs of farmers and the acceptability of implements.

Implementation constraints

Local manufacturers of a wide range of adapted animal draft power equipment in Zambia require greater support (this has already been suggested by recent changes in tax and import duty regulations). The problems of raw material supply and foreign currency constraints need to be addressed to enable the private sector to invest in the required marketing and after-sales service system.

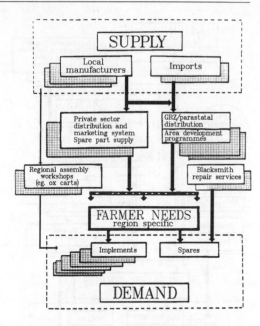

Figure 12: A possible scenario for animal draft power implement supply and distribution in Zambia

The profitability of smallholder animal draft power farming is under heavy pressure and access to credit is almost nonexistent. Nevertheless, recent developments indicate that there is an important demand for animal power equipment. There is a real interest in ox carts, ridging/weeding implements and spare parts in general. On-farm animal power trials and demonstrations of different tillage and weeding systems have provided clear indications that:

○ farmers have poor awareness of existing and new implement designs and qualities

○ once farmers are offered a choice of implements, their "tolerance" of design/construction shortcomings will rapidly change into a more critical selection of implements adapted to the local requirements

○ implements and spare parts must be available for sale in rural areas: in particular, adoption of weeding/ridging implements does not depend only on economic or credit factors, but is mainly dictated by whether or not distribution and sales outlets are available close to farmers.

In the past manufacturers paid little attention to initiating private-sector distribution/marketing of implements and spares through retail stores and rural blacksmiths. With the exception of parts of Eastern Province (where blacksmith support programmes were in operation), the involvement of blacksmiths in the local manufacture of animal

Table 11: A comparison of southern Mali and the Western and Southern Provinces of Zambia

	Southern Mali	Westerm Province, Zambia	Southern Province, Zambia
Total area (ha)	10 000 000	13 000 000	8 500 000
Cultivated area (ha)	1 087 000	97 000	190 000
Percentage cultivated	11	0.7	2.2
Number of inhabitants	2 300 000	607 000	n/a
Number of inhabitants per km^2	25	5	n/a
Number of inhabitants per cultivated ha	2	6	n/a
Number of villages	4 000	n/a	n/a
Implement distribution points	130	6 district cooperatives	6 district cooperatives and some retail stores
Manufacturing	1 provincial workshop 25 assembly workshops	None	None
Implement repair services by rural blacksmiths	2500 blacksmiths including 130 well-equipped and 70 fully equipped with welding facilities	Few	Few

power spares and the repair of implements is poorly developed in Zambia.

Many rural areas are "littered" with plows in need of spare parts. This is a result of the long-standing importation of various designs of plows requiring different spares, together with the lack of spares distribution to the regions and limited means of rural blacksmiths. Some sources have estimated that only 60% of introduced plows are actually in use.

Regional marketing and logistical constraints

The urgently-needed private animal power marketing and distribution system will face important constraints for its development.

Communications in the rural areas are much worse than those in similar agro-ecological zones in West Africa. Establishment of sales outlets in the main rural areas (through hardware stores, blacksmiths or other regional workshops) will require logistic and financial support from the manufacturers.

Table 11 illustrates the enormous rural communication differences existing between southern Mali and the traditional animal draft power regions in Zambia (Southern and Western Provinces).

The "emptiness" and poor communication of the Zambian countryside is even more clearly shown in Figure 13, which depicts the situation in the new animal power introduction areas in Zambia and Mali.

Figure 13:Comparison of Bougouni District (Mali) and Kaoma District (Zambia) showing roads and infrastructure

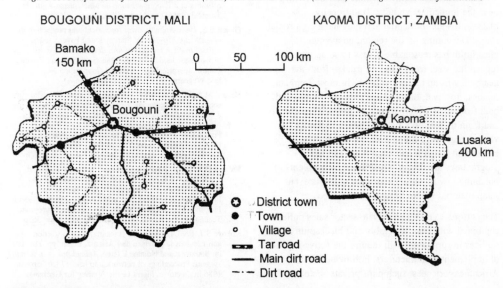

Table 12: Summary of reported surveys relating to rural blacksmiths in West Africa and Zambia

	Mali		Senegal		Togo	Zambia
	Southern Mali	Office du Niger	Nioro and Fatick	Lower Casamance	North Central	Southern Province
Total number of blacksmiths	2500	150	207	85	93	320
Number of well-equipped blacksmiths	130	20	–	–	–	–
Number of fully-equipped blacksmiths	70	8	–	–	–	–
Cultivated area (000s ha)	1087	50	232	–	–	190
Cultivated area per blacksmith (ha)	400	300	1100	–	–	600
Number of farm holdings (000s)	125	10	37	–	–	97
Number of farm holdings per blacksmith	50	67	180	–	–	300
Number of work animals (000s)	212	20	–	–	14	96
Pairs of animals per blacksmith	42	67	–	–	78	150
Number of villages	4000	150	810	60	–	–
Number of blacksmiths per village	0.6	1.0	0.3	1.4	–	–
Total area (000s km^2)	100	–	5	7	–	85
Area per blacksmith (km^2)	40	–	25	85	–	265

Zambia has a very low rural population density, combined with a low and highly dispersed land-use pattern. Consequently there are few villages, poor connections, no public or private transport inside the rural areas, and no weekly markets. In order to obtain their supplies, farmers and blacksmiths alike must make enormous efforts to reach the district towns, and even then have no guarantee that implements, spares or raw materials are available.

Rural blacksmith constraints

Table 12 gives a summary of the blacksmith situation in some surveyed areas in Mali, Senegal, Togo and Zambia. In Mali and Senegal, blacksmiths are able to service farmers within their own villages or in the immediate vicinity. Traditionally, blacksmiths are influential and may have high social status. Depending on the region, an average blacksmith has reasonable access to scrap material (eg, spring steel from cars and trucks) from the nearby towns and larger villages. In most Zambian regions, however, blacksmiths appear very isolated, both from their widely dispersed potential customers and from their supply possibilities. Experience in various regions in Zambia shows that rural blacksmith training and equipment support programmes are severely restrained by problems of obtaining raw materials and spare parts, as even scrap material is rare in remote rural areas.

Thus efforts to establish private sector sales outlets combined with basic assembly and blacksmith repair services in rural areas will require the active support of implement manufacturers. Following West African experiences, such pilot private-sector rural

workshop initiatives may lead to the sustainable development of rural blacksmiths in areas of high market potential. For example, in the Southern Province alone, a large proportion of some 25 000 unused plows could be usefully overhauled once spare parts and repair services became available.

References

Baker R and White P, 1983. *An evaluation of policy toward agricultural technology choice for power in Zambia*. Discussion Paper 121. School of Development Studies, University of East Anglia, Norwich, UK. 24p.

Bordet D, Lhoste P, le Moigne M and le Thiec G, 1988. *Draft animal power technology in French-speaking Africa: state of the art*. Report prepared for Food and Agriculture Organization of the United Nations (FAO) by Centre d'Etudes et d'Expérimentation du Machinisme Agricole Tropical (CEEMAT), Montpellier, France. 195p.

Gwani E S, 1990. Animal power for agricultural production in Nigeria. pp. 376–380 in: Starkey P and Faye A (eds), *Animal traction for agricultural development*. Proceedings of workshop held 7–12 July 1988, Saly, Senegal. Technical Centre for Agriculture and Rural Cooperation, Ede-Wageningen, The Netherlands. 475p.

Havard M and Faye A, 1988. Eléments d'analyse de la situation actuelle de la culture attelée au Sénégal: perspectives d'études et de recherches. pp. 241–252 in: Starkey P and Ndiamé F (eds), *Animal power in farming systems*. Proceedings of networkshop held 17–26 September 1986 in Freetown, Sierra Leone. Vieweg for German Appropriate Technology Exchange, GTZ, Eschborn, Germany. 363p.

Kabeya D S, 1990. Expériences en traction bovine du Projet Rural Diocésain, Zaire. pp. 435–441 in: Starkey P and Ndiamé F (eds), *Animal power in farming systems*. Proceedings of networkshop held 17–26 September 1986 in Freetown, Sierra Leone. Vieweg for German Appropriate Technology Exchange, GTZ, Eschborn, Germany. 363p.

Kokoye S J, 1990. Impact socio-économique de la traction animale dans la province de l'Atacora, Bénin: pp. 186–191 in: Starkey P and Ndiamé F (eds), *Animal power in farming systems*. Proceedings of networkshop held 17–26 September 1986 in Freetown, Sierra Leone. Vieweg for German

Appropriate Technology Exchange, GTZ, Eschborn, Germany. 363p.

MoA, 1985. *Animal draught power*. Investment Plan Task Force, Planning Division. Ministry of Agriculture and Water Development (MoA), Lusaka, Zambia. 159p.

Ndiamé F, 1988. Animal traction in Lower Casamance: technical aspects and socio-economic implications. pp. 253–262 in: Starkey P and Ndiamé F (eds), *Animal power in farming systems*. Proceedings of networkshop held 17–26 September 1986 in Freetown, Sierra Leone. Vieweg for German Appropriate Technology Exchange, GTZ, Eschborn, Germany. 363p.

Sabi I, 1990. La culture attelée au Togo: données statistiques. pp. 344–347 in: Starkey P and Faye A (eds), *Animal traction for agricultural development*. Proceedings of workshop held 7–12 July 1988, Saly, Senegal. Technical Centre for Agriculture and Rural Cooperation, Ede-Wageningen, The Netherlands. 475p.

Sangaré M I, Ladrette C, Mungroop R R and Berthé A, 1988. Contraintes et améliorations de la traction animale en Mali-sud: l'expérience de la DRSPR. pp. 191–211 in: Starkey P and Ndiamé F (eds) *Animal power in farming*

systems. Proceedings of networkshop held 17–26 September 1986 in Freetown, Sierra Leone. Vieweg for German Appropriate Technology Exchange, GTZ, Eschborn, Germany. 363p.

Starkey P H, Dibbits H J and Mwenya E, 1991. *Animal traction in Zambia: status, progress and trends*. Ministry of Agriculture, Lusaka in association with IMAG-DLO, Wageningen, The Netherlands. 105p.

Tembo G and Rajeswaran K, 1989. *Animal draught power in Southern Province, Zambia: an assessment*. Agricultural Engineering Section, Ministry of Agriculture and Cooperatives, Lusaka, Zambia. 88p.

Whitney T R, 1981. *Changing patterns of labor utilisation, productivity and income: the effects of draft animal technology on small farms in southeastern Mali*. MS Thesis, Purdue University, USA.

Zerbo D and Kantao A, 1988. Traction animale au Mali. pp. 175–181 in: Starkey P and Ndiamé F (eds), *Animal power in farming systems*. Proceedings of networkshop held 17–26 September 1986 in Freetown, Sierra Leone. Vieweg for German Appropriate Technology Exchange, GTZ, Eschborn, Germany. 363p.

Improving the supply and distribution of farm implements in Ethiopia: some experiences and constraints

by

Hans Zaugg

Technician of Selam Vocational Training and Farm Implements Production Centre
PO Box 8075, Addis Ababa, Ethiopia

Abstract

Agriculture in Ethiopia is in a transition phase. Previous government policy was oriented toward highly mechanised collective farming, but today's policy starts from the assumption that the peasant sector will be most important for several decades to come. Present policy provides room for private and commercial enterprises to take part in the technology development and promotion process oriented toward the peasant sector. This paper outlines government efforts to guide this process, and describes some views and steps taken by a small private farm implement and tool manufacturing enterprise. Major problems are inadequate transport, communication, maintenance and repair facilities. Joint government and private efforts, and links with relevant international networks, may provide effective and efficient solutions.

Introduction

The previous Government of Ethiopia followed a socialist policy for agriculture: the aim was that all farming would be carried out on mechanised collective or state farms. But lack of infrastructure and industrial skills hampered the introduction of large-scale mechanised farming. Today it is recognised that the peasant sector will be most important for several decades to come, and with this in mind, new agricultural policies and strategies are being developed. Important elements are increasing private sector involvement and participation of the peasant sector in developing new agricultural technologies, including farm mechanisation technologies.

This paper gives a brief outline of the approach and activities of a small private production workshop for farm implements. It begins by describing the various institutions involved in agricultural implement development and distribution, and their modes of collaboration; the way farm mechanisation has been taken up in Ethiopia in recent years; and some of the main bottlenecks encountered.

Institutions involved in implement development and promotion

A major institution involved with farm mechanisation in Ethiopia is the Rural Technology Promotion Department (RTPD). This department was created in 1985 to coordinate and give impetus to the development and transfer of rural technologies, including farm tools and implements. Before that time, several other government institutions and projects were involved in this work, but with unsatisfactory results.

RTPD has established seven rural technology promotion centres (RTPC) throughout the country. These have several functions, including adaptive research, initial production and extension, and they support a network of about 200 cooperative-based Farmer Technical Service Stations (FTSS). The FTSS provide a wide range of services, including blacksmithing and welding services, as well as rental services for seasonally used machinery such as threshers. The collective and semi-commercial nature of these workshops, however, has important drawbacks. This is why RTPD became increasingly oriented toward commercially viable and privately run enterprises.

RTPD can be seen as one component of a "technology development system". Other components comprise projects, government institutions and private enterprises, such as the Institute of Agricultural Research (IAR), the Agricultural Implements Research and Improvement Centre (AIRIC), the Farming Systems Research Department of IAR, the International Livestock Centre for Africa (ILCA) and the Agricultural Extension Department (AED). In this system, all the component institutions and enterprises have important complementary technology development and promotion functions. The Ministry of Industry would mass produce those implements which have been proven to be acceptable to the farmers.

Main elements and bottlenecks of the mechanisation programme

A farm implements and tools industry cannot fully mature in only six years—certainly not through efforts of independently operating institutions. It is mainly due to the difficult and adverse circumstances the country has experienced that effective linkages between the various relevant institutions have not developed.

In order to meet an apparent urgent demand for small implements on the one hand, and in response to pressure from above for quick and visible results on the other, RTPD itself was forced to assume a number of essential functions and tasks of the technology development and promotion process.

RTPD started its programme by importing advanced and promising equipment from such countries as China, India and North Korea, as well as France, Germany and The Netherlands. The aim was that, through its RTPCs, RTPD would gradually allow for the local manufacture of most, if not all, parts of the implements which were acceptable to farmers. However, lack of raw materials and adequately trained workshop technicians were among the factors responsible for limited performance at this level.

RTPD faces serious difficulties in reaching farmers and involving them in adaptive trials. The Agricultural Extension Department (AED), which seems a natural partner for such activities, is confronted with resource constraints of its own. In this situation AED gives priority to extension related activities on crops and livestock rather than to tools and implements. It is the experience of RTPD, moreover, that extensionists lack the knowledge and skills to properly guide the adaptive research stages of implement and tool development. However, RTPD cannot mobilise enough experienced people of its own. The department is also confronted with inadequate means of transport. Investment in facilities for communication and transport is urgently needed if implements are to be successfully introduced and sustained in the peasant sector.

Repair and maintenance services are also crucial for the viability of the new technologies. Initially the idea was that the FTSS would perform these functions. Experience has shown, however, that such functions cannot be performed properly by collectively run institutions. The FTSS were but one component of rural cooperatives managed by a central board. Important management problems arose and the FTSS were found to be out of touch with the economics of using equipment. It is now considered that the technical facilities of the FTSS may be used by some sort of "loose network" of private blacksmiths who are currently returning to the scene. Obviously this will be a long-term process in which RTPD and collaborating institutions may have important organising and training roles.

The question of how to remove these and other bottlenecks in the development and transfer of farm mechanisation technologies is currently the subject of considerable debate within the RTPD. Clearly RTPD is becoming more "outward oriented", which has given private enterprises such as ours an opportunity to develop meaningful ties with the department.

Approach and activities of Selam

Our private production workshop for farm implements, which is about to begin operations, is part of a vocational training centre, which in turn is part of an orphanage (Selam) in Addis Ababa. Selam is financially supported by various international non-governmental organisations (NGOs).

In order to prepare pupils of Selam for a good future, the Selam board decided that teaching them to design and repair small farm implements and tools might be a very meaningful thing to do. Because it was felt that students would only pick up the required skills and management insights in a true machinery development and production environment, a commercially operating independent production workshop was established.

The first step being taken by Selam is similar to the first step taken by RTPD—importing promising equipment in knocked-down kits. There are several differences between Selam and RTPD—for example, the scale of operations and the type and size of the implements. Also, Selam is trying to introduce the implements on a purely commercial basis, right

Photo 1: Prototype broadbed maker with ducksfoot tines for the cultivation of vegetables

Photo: Hans Zaugg

Photo 2: Prototype implements made at Selam workshop. Based on Latin American designs, they fit onto a long wooden beam. From bottom left to right: mouldboard plow, chisel plow, ridger, cultivator, ridger and potato lifter

from the start. As a new enterprise, we do not have much experience of how this will work in practice.

Although we have encountered numerous types of small imported farm implements in this country, it is our experience that the international machinery industry has little to offer the peasant sector. They are keen to offer some of their prototypes but they do not invest much of their research and development capacity in follow-up activities, such as adaptive trials.

These and other considerations led us to conclude that before setting up a production unit with a significant capacity, it would be vital to collect more information and to take farmers' views and insights into account when designing our products. At the present state of farm mechanisation development in Ethiopia, distribution of small farm implements cannot be seen in isolation from intense on-farm testing; to our knowledge few, if any, newly introduced implements have already proven their viability over time.

With this in mind we are strengthening our ties with RTPD. We can offer, on a modest scale, expertise in production techniques. In fact, with help of the NGO community, we have been able to provide a training course in technical skills to some RTPC technicians. In its turn, RTPD offers us participation in the supply and on-farm testing and distribution network: although the present production at Selam is limited to a small multipurpose toolbar for tillage implements and animal-drawn carts, we are experiencing difficulties in having them distributed and assessed by end-users. Finally, because of our international contacts, we have access to promising types of machinery (Photos 1 and 2), and so can supplement the efforts of RTPD in importing technologies from foreign countries.

Participating in ATNESA workshops and activities is is another way in which Selam can collect information on promising implements used in conditions similar to those in Ethiopia. Through ATNESA contacts, Selam can also learn of on-farm testing approaches and methodologies which may be followed in the process of their adaptation.

Improving the supply and distribution of animal traction implements: the thoughts of an inventor

by

Jean Nolle[*]

Designer of animal traction implements and international consultant, Paris, France

Abstract

This paper is a brief overview of the philosophy and practice of animal traction development, as seen through the eyes of an inventor who, during a 58-year career, has invented more than 200 machines, tools or implements for agriculture. It discusses the two opposing concepts of development—that of industry, or the manufacturer, and that of agriculture, or the farmer. It also addresses issues such as the differences between engineers and inventors; the role of animal intelligence; the development of village workshops; and the part that animal traction can play in the emergence of a modern rural society. Some of the implements invented by the author are described. Many of these were manufactured by the author himself in the countries where they were to be used, his main reason being to show the people of these countries how to make their own tools. This, it is concluded, is the true engine of development: work, not words.

Introduction

"Improving animal traction technology" is the title of this workshop and "Improving the supply and distribution of animal traction implements" is the title of my paper. There is one important word common to both titles, *improving*. This word can mean several things, depending on the context: it does not necessarily mean the same thing for agriculture as it does for industry.

I think I am qualified to speak about both areas, as I have been involved in agriculture for 58 years, in industry for 48 and in tropical agriculture for 42. During that time I have invented more than 200 machines, tools or implements of every kind for agriculture. My career has been unusual, and so I will describe it briefly before developing the theme of my paper.

Personal background

I began my career as a farmer in 1934, when I was 15 years old. I had 120 ha of land which I plowed with 21 draft horses. I expected to remain a farmer

[*]Jean Nolle died in France on 30 September 1993 at the age of 74. He had proof-read and approved this edited version of his paper

all my life, but the advent of the Second World War forced me in another direction. There were many difficulties during the war, one of them being a shortage of labour. To overcome this I designed and built a big potato-digger that enabled me to harvest 10 ha on my own. But in 1945 I was obliged to leave my farm. So I started a new career, in industry. My first job was to improve, supply and distribute the potato harvester I had invented.

My harvester was a great success, so much so that in 1950 I was asked by the French Compagnie générale des oléagineux tropicaux (CGOT) and Secteur expérimental de modernisation agricole (SEMA) to invent another digger for use in Senegal. After the war the industrial revolution had been having an dramatic impact on agriculture in France, and our trusty draft animals were killed to make way for tractors. In Africa, also, CGOT and SEMA cultivated groundnuts using tractors, and displaced many farmers. After four years they realised the error of their ways; they threw out their costly tractors and rediscovered the farmers. It was then that they asked me to invent an agricultural implement for them. I invented a "bullock tractor"—the famous *Polyculteur*.

In 1958 I exhibited my *Polyculteur* with different attachments at the Bambey exhibition (Figure 1). I put a sign next to it that said "The *Polyculteur* affords freedom to African farmers, by enabling them to do their work by themselves". My sign was shocking, because it pointed to the fact that although France was giving African countries political *independence*, it was still trying to maintain African economic *dependence*, particularly by the process of industrialisation, including agricultural industrialisation. I was offering the African farmer an alternative, a means of economic *independence*.

Needless to say, the idea of giving African farmers improved animal-powered technology was immediately rejected by the French politicians. Now we can see the disastrous results of their blind faith in industrialised agriculture. That is why we are here at this workshop, to try to repair the damage that has been caused.

Development philosophies

This workshop is about development. But development of what? Development of agriculture, or development of industry? There is a dilemma here, because developments in industry do not necessarily lead to developments in agriculture. All too often, as industry becomes richer, agriculture becomes poorer; rural areas decline as urban areas expand and spread, often dangerously so. Animal traction can offer a solution to this dilemma. Animal traction technology can revitalise agriculture and the rural economy because it depends on *natural* energy instead of the *artificial* energy that the cities depend on. This is important because right now we are in the midst of the worst war the world has ever known: a war between two energies—artificial energy and natural energy. But I do not want to speak of war and destruction; I want to speak about improvement and development.

Any development project has two main phases:

○ fundamental and applied research, leading to *invention*

○ refinement of the invention for a specific purpose, followed by its supply, distribution and use.

The improvement process marks the transition between the two phases: then it continues throughout the life of any invention. The inventor, the first manufacturer, the manufacturer's agents—all have a role to play in the cycle of development. Each "actor" makes a different, but vital, contribution to modifying the usefulness and successful application of the original invention. This is as true in the field of animal traction technology as it is in any other human endeavour.

As already mentioned, there are two opposing concepts of development: the agricultural, or farmer's concept; and the industrial, or manufacturer's one.

For farmers, a new agricultural technology is a **means** to an end, the end being a better life, with less pain and drudgery as they go about the task of growing food. But the farmers' livelihood does not depend solely, or even primarily, on the technology itself; the importance of a new technology, machine or implement ranks at the end of a long list of other factors which influence a farmer's work, such as soil, climate, insects, diseases and the market. Farming is hazardous; farmers can never be certain of the results of their work because the forces of nature are involved. Because of this unpredictability, a farmer's thinking is *long-term oriented*.

For a manufacturer, a new agricultural technology is the **end** itself. A manufacturer's job is to make and sell as many products as possible, as quickly as possible and, most importantly, for as much profit as possible. Manufacturers are not concerned with the unpredictable, uncontrollable variables that affect a harvest, and they are the controllers of their own destiny. Because their work is predictable and controllable, their thinking is *short-term oriented*. This conception of life is dangerous as far as protection of life and the environment are concerned, but it makes sense to economists concerned with development, because it involves easily measurable units of productivity and profit.

For us, the simple-minded approach of measuring everything by how much profit can be made is dangerous, because we are concerned with the poorest people in the world—the small, forgotten farmers. How can they fit into such a scheme? How can the welfare of nature and the environment fit into such a scheme?

Figure 1: Artist's impression of the display of Polyculteurs with different attachments at Bambey, Senegal, in 1958

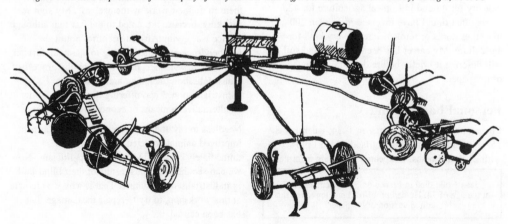

When inventors or first manufacturers are designing their prototypes they pay careful attention to the least detail, to make sure that their products will be accepted by their clients. But after a product has been developed and sold, and the inventor is no longer involved, the manufacturer becomes interested in a new aspect of the product—*"after-sales service"*. From this point, the term *improve* takes on a new significance. For example, manufacturers (or their agents) can make the implement more complicated: thus, while deluding their clients into thinking they are getting a better product, prices, and hence profits, can be increased. Alternatively, they can simplify the implement in order to undercut the competition. More products can be sold and so, again, profits can be increased, but the farmer, or the environment, may suffer.

When an implement is sold far away from the factory, the local government can ask the manufacturer, or agent, to demonstrate its use to farmers. Alternatively, the local government can use its own agents to make the demonstrations. In either case there is a risk that incompetent demonstrators will give farmers a wrong impression of the usefulness of the implement. Demonstrations should only be given by certified officials who understand the implement and its uses under normal and difficult conditions, and who care about their reputation and credibility.

When a local government wants to modify an old implement in order to create a new, improved model, it must be certain that the person it hires for the task is both competent to perform it and aware of the working conditions and practices of the farmers. The fact that such precautions are not always taken is one of the reasons why development is so slow in some countries.

Finally, improvements (in the industrial sense) often do not take into account the philosophy of the farmers. Manufacturers (and their agents) and governments are seduced by the novelty of a new invention because they consider routine hard work as drudgery, as a factor of stagnation in the lives of farmers and in the economy as a whole. But farmers understand that routine means security and they are wary about adopting a new technology and hence possibly jeopardising their security. They are patient, and prepared to wait until the benefits of a new technology have been proved. We, too, must have patience, and be aware of all the consequences of *improvement*, if we are to be successful in our quest to bring about sustainable development.

Animal issues

Implements are only one part of animal traction technology. Much more important are the animals used to pull or operate them. If farmers do not know how to work with animals, there is little point in buying plows or ridgers; the farmers will not pull them themselves! An animal traction development effort must therefore consider the improvement, supply and distribution of draft animals. In the animal context:

◦ **improve** means training the animals better, working them better, harnessing them better and developing better methods to use them in the fields

◦ **supply** means providing food for the animals, including storing forage or making silage for use during times of feed scarcity

◦ **distribute** means providing someone with a draft animal, or establishing breeding programmes to produce animals better suited for work.

How can animals be trained and worked more effectively? Traditional farmers do not know how to do this, and the people who come from developed countries to help them are even less well informed. It is, indeed, a great skill; a person who can control an animal, and make the animal understand what it is expected to do, is extremely clever. It is not my purpose at this workshop to teach animal training. I can, however, relate some anecdotes from my own experience, which may give a taste of working with animals.

In Ecuador I asked farmers: "Who is the most intelligent of the three workers in the field? The plow? The bullocks? Or the farmer?" "The farmer", they replied. When I asked them if they were sure, they did not understand what I meant. So I asked them: "Why do your bullocks raise their heads when pulling your wooden ard plow (*arado de palo*)?" Nobody could answer, so I answered my question myself: "It is because your bullocks are more intelligent than you." "I do not believe that," said Don Modesto. In order to make my point, I held out my hand, horizontally, with my middle and index fingers extended. "Imagine that my middle finger is the pole of your plow and my index finger is the spike," I said. "The angle between them is constant, as with your arado. So, when I raise my middle finger—the pole—the spike rises too, and the plow cuts less deeply. Your bullocks have detected the *effect* and understand the "cause". They know what they are doing. But do you?"

In Senegal, the bullocks lower their heads when pulling the plow. They do so for the same reason, to reduce their pain. But in Senegal the plow is fitted to the Polyculteur, behind the wheels, so when the bullocks lower their heads the plow rises.

Another day I asked the farmers: "Do you know why the bullocks walk straight when they are attached to the same pole?" No-one knew. The answer is that bullocks have hairs along their bodies and these hairs detect the pole, just like a cat's whiskers can detect a mouse.

When you watch animals for a long time you can see how intelligent they are. In Lesotho I saw a bullock taking another bullock to feed. He had taken his companion's rope in his mouth and was pulling him towards a plot of grass, just like his master did for him with his hands. Curious, isn't it?

Of course, all animals are perfectly conscious of their environment, more so than we are. Their ears are more acute than ours. A horse knows when a hare is passing around him in a field. Most animals are very sensitive to sound, which is why it is very important to accustom a draft animal (horse or bullock) to the voice of its controller: for example, in the early morning, when rubbing them while they are eating their oats. The voice is an important means for the animal to recognise its controller. When animals hear their controllers, they work hard to please them.

Animal traction and civilisation

Animal traction technology has existed for about 4000 years, and has hardly changed in all that time. My impetus for attempting to introduce a new concept in animal traction technology came when I was in Senegal, in 1954, when CGOT and SEMA realised their mistake in relying on tractors and threw them away. I wrote about that in my book *L'accident de civilization* (Nolle, 1989).

Figure 2: Tropiculteur *toolcarrier invented as a development and improvement of the original* Polyculteur

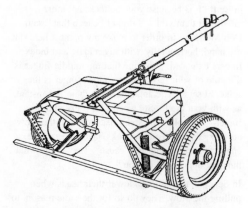

I do not claim to have revived interest in animal traction, which has continued to provide an important means of producing food crops, with or without my participation. I claim only to have adapted the technology to modern circumstances. All the people who have copied my machines or implements are not thieves but my associates, since they are also working for a new civilisation—a modern rural society.

Only agriculture and animals can save our civilisation, by giving us true self-sufficiency. The tractor is useless for tropical agriculture; it has many more disadvantages than advantages. But it has given me a valuable technological example in my work of designing improved tools for animal traction.

Implement development

As I have explained in my books, of the several hundred implements that I have designed in 38 years, I am especially proud of four. Two are pulled with a chain (*Houe Sine* and *Ariana*) and the other two with a shaft or pole. One implement with a shaft is my *Polynol* which derives from my earlier *Polyculteur* and *Tropiculteur* (Figure 2)

I named my other major invention pulled with a pole the *Kanol*—K as in *Kolba* (an Afghan wooden ard plow) and Nol as part of my name. I chose this name after a thief had copied my *Houe Sine* and named it after himself!

Figure 3: Invention of the Kanol
The Houe Sine *toolbar (A) was combined with the long pole of an ard (B) to form a prototype long-pole toolbar (C). Attachments developed included a plow (D), subsoiler (E) and weeding tines (F). Source: after Nolle (1986)*

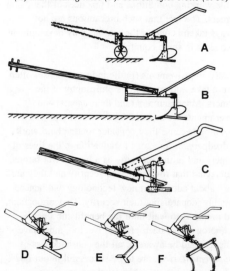

Photo: Jean Nolle

Photo 1: Kanol with "vibrocultor" being tested in Tchad

I invented the Kanol in 1974 when I was in Nicaragua (Figure 3). Since 1985 I have been improving it, little by little, as a result of my experiences in Tunisia, Sumatra, Ecuador and Chad. By working out the improvements myself, I could be sure of the quality of the changes.

The new Kanol is both similar and different to the original design. Similar, because the central part of the toolbar, the *module*, is still an adjustable triangle. Different, because it is quicker and easier to fit numerous tools to the device called the *crochaxe*; this is now made as an "open hole" through which sand and dirt can escape, so that the "peg" easily be fitted or removed by hand, while a specially shaped hook keeps the peg in place. The weight of the central module, including the pole but without tools, is less than 10 kg, so it can easily be carried on the shoulder, even over rough ground. There is no wheel to control the depth, as the adjustable triangle makes it unnecessary

I manufactured the main tools myself on site in various countries (in Chad, for example). I had three main reasons for wanting to manufacture locally:

○ to see if it was possible to invent something in various countries
○ to improve the implements and adapt them to specific local conditions
○ to give an example to the people who lived in the countries. If an old European man is able to produce some metal tools in the tropics, why

cannot the young local people do the same themselves. This is the true engine of development: work, not words.

The new implements I made were improved almost immediately. The original plow is now reduced to its body (share and mouldboard). The support is limited to a peg, with a nail on the upper part which can be hooked on the *crochaxe*; all the tools have such a nail, and so can be very quickly fitted onto the adjustable triangle.

I made six implements on location. The people who watched me work can now design and make other new tools themselves.

Implement attachments

In addition to my modifications to the plow, I also adapted the ridger, with the same support, keeping only its share and mouldboard. These are carried by a simple straight body, provided with the standard peg on the top to fix it to the *crochaxe*.

I manufactured a "vibrocultor", a type of cultivator equipped with five special spring tines fitted on the frame—two on the front bar and three on the rear one (Photo 1). Because of the rigid pole, this equipment is perfectly stable; it does not twist when in use. If the central rear tine is removed, the tool can be used as a hoe, the operator straddling the row while working.

For the cultivation of sorghum, millet, cotton or groundnuts, I produced an earthing-up device. This straddles a crop row, and two half ridgers, one on either side, lift the soil around the plants. Earthing-up kills weeds, by burying them (easier than digging them up), and also enables water in the damp soil between the rows to reach the crop roots. Henceforth, the traditional method of hoeing between two rows can be replaced by "hoe-straddling", which is possible whether or not the rows are perfectly parallel.

Subsoilers are well known, but my own design is rather different; it is based on an old broken spring from an abandoned car or lorry, and it can be easily produced by a village blacksmith. The tine is made from a flat spring of 50 x 6 mm or more, and at its lower extremity has a spike that can be made in various sizes, according to the soil conditions. In the future I plan to add two lateral wings to make the implement into a ridger.

I devised a special attachment to enable a donkey to pull a small bicycle trailer. I plan, sometime, to make a bigger one, to be pulled by two bullocks, for transporting manure or compost.

Finally, I invented a special "leveller" that can be used as a harrow or a clod-crusher. It can also be fitted with two or three adjustable fingers under the main blade, and used as a marker for hand-planting various seeds in straight, parallel lines.

Village workshops

While I was working on improving tools, I was also helping village workshops to improve their capabilities, by giving a lot of advice to their managers on how they could face challenges in the future. It will be some time before these village workshops are able to manufacture the hardened steel components of various implements, such as shares, mouldboards, blades, springs, tines, etc. They can produce the frames and various supports for these wearing parts, and they can act as suppliers and distributors of imported parts.

Research and development

After research comes invention. Who invents the machines and their technologies—engineers or inventors? Do not confuse them: engineers and inventors are different, even when their work looks similar.

Engineers are "mercenaries" who work for money or pride. They belongs to the industrial system which is pirating everything—people, animals, forests, soil, water, minerals, even human blood and life itself.

Inventors are "volunteers" who work for their ideas, and consequently do not follow the dictates or values of industry. Invention is a *vocation*, not a *profession*. Inventors, therefore, respect moral values, since they are intuitively in touch with the forces of nature, and are not seduced by money or pride. They feel that real development must be diversified, not selective.

The first people are dangerous to civilisation, howling with the industrial wolves. The second are practically defenceless before such industrial powers, as they are generally alone and nonviolent. The two types represent two forces which are at work in the world: one, driven by greed, attempts to exploit the earth through ruthless industrialism; the other creative in a gentle way that seeks to live in harmony with creation. What will be the outcome of this conflict?

Concluding thoughts

○ It is almost incredible that tropical countries still exist, considering their poverty or indebtedness

○ It is an incredible fact that the developed countries, too, are sinking into poverty and chaos, despite their outward appearance of opulence and pride

○ It is an incredible reality that farmers in the developed countries, having killed all their draft animals, are now sentenced to death by their own economy!

○ It is an incredible observation that the developing countries are consequently being led to discover, at last, the value of animal traction to their survival

○ But do not over-improve your animal traction technology. Remember that *perfected* is often *rejected* by the proud

○ Finally, animal traction technology is now a *job* for you and a *chance* for the future of the world. Do not spoil it. Be serious. Follow your conscience.

References

Nolle J, 1986. *Machines modernes à traction animale: itinéraire d'un inventeur au service des petits paysans*. Editions L'Harmattan, Paris, France. 478p.

Nolle J, 1989. *L'accident de civilization*. Boutique des arts, Besancon, France. 44p.

Jean Nolle, 1918–1993

Jean Nolle, the famous French agricultural engineer, died on 30 September 1993, one day before his 75th birthday.

He had been actively involved in the design of animal traction equipment since the 1950s, and developed an implement design philosophy based on simplicity, multipurpose uses and standardisation of components. He was a visionary and an influential advocate of animal traction technology, even in the 1950s and 1960s when it was often considered unfashionable. He stressed the needs of smallholder farmers for well-designed and well-manufactured animal traction implements. Among his more famous implements have been the *Houe Sine* toolbar and the heavier *Ariana* multipurpose toolframe. He was the "father of the wheeled toolcarrier", inventing his first *Polyculteur* in 1955 and going on to develop the *Tropiculteur* and *Polynol*. With the assistance of the International Crops Research Institute for the Semi-Arid Tropics (ICRISAT), Nolle's *Tropiculteur* became the world market leader in wheeled toolcarriers, and it was bought by development projects in many countries. His *Kanol* long-beamed multipurpose toolbar is also innovative and has recently been tested in several countries.

Jean Nolle never became rich from his work in designing such implements. Only his *Houe Sine* was sold in large numbers (about half a million of these, and its derivatives, are now used in West Africa). This implement, and other Nolle designs, have often been copied without credit to the inventor. With the publication of his semi-autobiographical book *Machines modernes à traction animale*, many of his plans and ideas were given to the public domain. His animal-drawn wheeled toolcarriers did not receive the widespread adoption which he had expected. He joked that he accepted just half of the

Jean Nolle at the ATNESA workshop in Lusaka with the Kanol toolbar he brought and donated to the Zambian Animal Draft Power Research and Development Programme

book *Perfected yet rejected* about these implements, he agreed that his toolcarriers had indeed been perfected, but he could not accept that they had ever been rejected by farmers. He blamed their limited adoption on inadequate promotion by projects and he maintained a "conspiracy theory" suggesting that manufacturers and distributors refused to manufacture or promote his products lest the success of Nolle implements reduce their other markets.

In recent years, Jean Nolle acted as an international consultant and helped small manufacturing workshops in many countries in Africa, Asia and Latin America to manufacture his implements. The patience and skill with which he imparted his expertise earned him devoted friends in many countries, although the frankness with which he put forward his ideas and criticisms seldom ingratiated him to formal development organisations. In later years, he became very concerned with the wider issues of ecological sustainability and human development, and his mission reports and publications (notably *L'accident de civilisation*) became increasingly philosophical. He became a valuable member of the African animal traction networks, attending meetings in several countries in Africa at considerable cost to himself, particularly when he carried and donated samples of his equipment. His films always proved popular at network meetings, as did his jibes at the lack of realism of certain research techniques.

With the death of Jean Nolle, animal traction has lost a good designer, a patient teacher and a colourful personality. Luckily many of his ideas and designs have already been passed on to the next generation, and they are presently benefiting the smallholder farmers for whom he worked. His achievements will influence us for many years to come.

Paul Starkey, Reading, 1993

A note on improving the supply and distribution of animal-drawn implements in Zambia

by

E A Sakala

Agricultural Engineering Department
Natural Resources Development College (NRDC), PO Box 310099, Lusaka, Zambia

Abstract

Animal draft implements are manufactured in considerable numbers in Zambia, but their actual use in rural areas is limited. Lack of availability of implements in rural areas, poor quality and high cost of the implements, and the lack of credit facilities for farmers to buy equipment, are some of the reasons why animal traction is not more widespread. This paper discusses these factors, and offers some solutions.

Introduction

Zambia has a number of companies producing a wide range of animal-drawn agricultural implements. Despite this, the demand for these implements by Zambian farmers is not being met.

Farmers cite several reasons for their low level of use of animal draft implements:

- poor availability of implements in rural areas
- poor quality of implements
- high cost of implements
- lack of credit facilities.

Availability

Although manufacturers' warehouses are full of implements, spot-checks in the countryside show few implements being used in the fields in many areas. The problem is mainly one of a lack of aggressive marketing by the manufacturers: there seems to be no organised infrastructure for marketing—no networks of distribution or sales agents catering for the needs of the rural areas.

One solution would be for manufacturers to open sales outlets in all parts of the country and to make their products available through local merchants, farmers' groups, cooperative unions, etc.

Another solution would be for the implements to be manufactured in the rural areas, by local artisans (blacksmiths) who would be able to obtain raw materials from central sources. Donor agencies could play an important role here, by facilitating technology transfer and by supporting training of local craftsmen.

Quality

Poor quality of implements is largely a result of appropriate raw materials not being available on the local market. The Steel Board is the major importer of steel, and so this organisation should be encouraged to import the right quality and quantity of steel, and to make it available to manufacturers and local artisans. The government also needs to play its part in this process, by making foreign exchange available to the Steel Board.

Another problem is lack of quality control on the manufacture of implements. Some implements have been sold in the country without proper certification, largely because not all manufacturers can afford to carry out their own research, development and testing programmes. However, Magoye Research Station has the capacity and the equipment to carry out implement testing, and it is proposed that implement manufacturing companies should not be allowed to market any implements without certification from Magoye Research Station.

Price

One reason that prices of implements are high is that manufacturers are not able to sell sufficient of their products to enjoy the benefits of economies of scale. This, in turn, is largely due to the lack of an organised marketing infrastructure; even though the quality of the implements manufactured in Zambia is poor, farmers would still buy them if they were readily available.

Once an adequate marketing system is in place, several steps could be taken to increase the demand even further (which might, possibly, lead to further price reductions). For example, extension services could be encouraged to promote the use of animal traction technology by giving demonstrations, providing training and organising plowing competitions.

Credit facilities

Even if implements are readily available, at a reasonable price, many farmers may not have the resources to buy them. The provision of credit facilities is therefore an important factor in the increased use of animal traction. But providing financial assistance to farmers for the purchase of agricultural equipment is not always straightforward. For example, small-scale farmers are not always enthusiastic about taking out loans from the credit institutions because of past experience and because of the conditions that underline the loan facilities: many farmers get loans without fully understanding the terms and the consequences of failure to repay them. Also, loan officers are often not able to reach people in the countryside because of their own logistical problems. Furthermore, loans may not easily be utilised by farmers in remote rural areas if farm equipment outlets are located only in the towns.

Some suggested ways of overcoming these problems are for:

○ loan officers to explain fully the terms of the loans to the farmers, including the method of paying back

○ financial institutions to work through NGOs and local organisations in order to reach the farmers

○ financial institutions and manufacturing companies to work together to facilitate the spread of farm mechanisation.

Other important considerations are that loan interest rates should be made favourable to the farmers, and that women farmers, who play such an important role in agricultural production, should be encouraged to use credit facilities.

Other observations

Two other factors are worth mentioning in the context of the spread of animal traction technology in Zambia.

First, even when credit facilities are available, farmers must be confident that they will be able to repay their loans, and hence must have a secure source of income. The present marketing system for agricultural produce in Zambia suffers from late payments to farmers, which obviously prevent farmers from being able to plan ahead financially. This system therefore needs to be reorganised.

Second, the successful use of animal-drawn implements depends on availability of well-trained and healthy work oxen. Efforts to spread animal traction technology therefore need to include such measures as making animals available to interested farmers, providing training facilities for farmers and animals, and supporting veterinary services.

Improving the distribution of animal traction implements in Mbeya Region, Tanzania

by

J Y Jumbe

Mbeya Oxenization Project, PO Box 2904, Mbeya, Tanzania

Abstract

Mbeya Region is a maize-producing area in the southern highlands of Tanzania. Many farmers in the region use hand hoes. A few use animal-drawn implements, but the supply of these implements in villages is a problem: they accumulate in towns where nobody buys them. The distribution problem is caused by the main manufacturer, importer and supplier, the parastatal Ubungo Farm Implements (UFI), based in Dar es Salaam, 800 km from Mbeya. UFI supplies implements to parastatal intermediaries in urban centres, but these intermediaries do not have outlets in the villages.

Mbeya Oxenization Project (MOP) was established in 1987 to develop animal traction in the region. MOP is trying to improve the distribution of implements through a network of village-based agents. The agents obtain implements on credit and receive a commission on sales. There are positive signs but the exercise will be fruitless unless the existing marketing channels and village-based agents adopt the distribution system themselves and become independent of MOP. The cooperative movement in Mbeya Region also has potential to improve the distribution of animal-drawn implements because it already has village depots.

Introduction

Mbeya Region is situated in the southern highlands of Tanzania, adjacent to Malawi and Zambia. The main crops in the region are maize, rice, coffee and cotton. Farming is mainly at the subsistence level. The main farming tool is the hand hoe, although a few farmers, especially in Mbozi District, use animal-drawn implements. In Tanzania 10–15% of tillage is carried out using draft animals: a similar figure applies in Mbeya Region. The number of farmers using animals for agricultural production has been increasing in Mbeya Region, especially since the commencement of the Mbeya Oxenization Project (MOP) in 1987. Farmers in the region use animal-drawn implements mainly for plowing and, to a lesser degree, for transport. MOP wants farmers in the region to use animals for weeding and transport as well as plowing, and some farmers have started adopting these technologies.

MOP is now planning phase two of its programme, which will run from January 1993 to December 1996. During the first five years of the project it became apparent that poor distribution of animal traction implements to farmers in Mbeya Region was one of the critical problems constraining the increased adoption of animal power technology.

Distribution problem defined

In marketing terms, distribution can be defined as planning, implementing and controlling the physical flow of goods and materials from points of origin to points of use, to meet customer needs at a profit. The main objective of distribution should be getting the right goods to the right places at the right time for the least cost. Uncoordinated distribution results in high costs while improved distribution can stimulate demand and attract additional customers by offering better services or lower prices.

It is unfortunate that, in Tanzania, distribution in general, and distribution of animal-drawn implements in particular, seldom involves such a marketing approach. Vander Ende (1991) writes that, within the Tanzanian context, the principle of marketing is almost exclusively associated only with the selling of goods. Okoso-Amaa (1989) states that poor infrastructure, inadequate marketing channels and the poor financial position of some of the channel members results in ineffective outlets. In the Tanzanian experience, centralised marketing infrastructure has tended to place the distribution and equipment services too far away from the farmer. Poor transport systems make it difficult for some farmers to reach distribution points when the need arises.

Implement supply in Tanzania

The main source of animal-drawn implements in Tanzania is Ubungo Farm Implements (UFI), located in Dar es Salaam, some 800 km from Mbeya. UFI, a public parastatal organisation, manufactures and imports animal-drawn implements for the whole of the country: it is the starting point of the distribution network and also the main distributor of animal traction implements in Tanzania. Distribution should involve marketing channels that ensure a flow of goods from the source point to consumers.

Unfortunately, the distribution and marketing system for animal-drawn implements does not reach the end-user farmers in the villages in Mbeya Region. It starts at UFI in Dar es Salaam and often ends in the regional capitals, occasionally reaching district centres. In the case of Mbeya Region, the marketing channel ends at the towns of Mbeya, Kyela and Mbozi. This still leaves the implement market a considerable distance from the farmers, who may have to travel for two days by bus to purchase an implement or spare.

The marketing channel system for animal-drawn equipments consists of UFI as the producer/supplier, the wholesalers (agriculture-related public institutions) and retailers (a few interested private businessmen). Wholesalers in Mbeya Region include Mbeya Regional Trading Company (RTC), Agricultural and Industrial Supplies Company (AISCO) and Tanganyika Farmers' Association (TFA). These wholesalers, which sometimes also act as retailers, are not really interested in selling animal-drawn implements: they see sales of these implements as seasonal, consequently tying up their capital. As these institutions are under the control of government, which is interested in serving its farmers, they are instructed to sell animal-drawn implements. Such pressure from the government implicitly results in partial distribution, subsidised prices and distribution points ending in larger urban areas. Animal-drawn implements accumulate in towns where nobody buys them, while farmers are looking for them in the villages.

The government apparently realised this serious distribution weakness in a major maize-producing region of the country. It therefore established a second agricultural implement factory in Mbeya town. This "Zana Za Kilimo" factory is not actually very interested in making animal-drawn implements. Its own distribution system for farm implements (mainly hand hoes) also ends in towns, despite the fact that it regularly advertises on the national radio that it offers "door to door" sales services.

The main cause of these inefficient and ineffective distribution systems for animal-drawn implements in Mbeya Region is lack of proper planning, implementation and control of the physical flow of implements by UFI and its intermediaries (RTC, AISCO, TFA, the cooperatives, etc). None of these marketing institutions appears to practise marketing management. They do not seem to know their market segments and niches, or the demand for animal-drawn implements in Mbeya Region. This failure leads to an inefficient, money-losing

distribution system for animal-drawn implements in Mbeya Region.

Vander Ende (1991) reported that, in recent years, the Government of Tanzania, donors and other local organisations have carried out five independent studies on the demand for animal-drawn implements for Tanzania. All the studies came up with different figures. This resulted in the government ordering 100 000 plows, many of which stayed for years in warehouses in Dar es Salaam. It is government policy to develop animal traction technology and make implements available to farmers in villages. Unfortunately nobody seems to have made a serious attempt to implement this policy.

Mbeya Oxenization Project

The purpose of MOP is to promote smallholder agricultural development in Mbeya Region of Tanzania, through the development, production, marketing and extension of animal traction technologies appropriate to smallholder farming systems. The marketing objectives of MOP are to:

- distribute relevant and appropriate animal-drawn implements to farmers in Mbeya Region
- in cooperation with MOP Engineering, promote the use of village workshops where farmers can obtain spare parts, have repairs done, or even purchase complete animal draft implements
- establish a reliable and permanent distribution system for animal-drawn implements.

These three objectives all relate to ensuring the availability of animal-drawn implements in the villages of Mbeya Region. The problem was how to achieve this in view of resource constraints and the lack of interest of existing marketing institutions in the distribution of animal-drawn implements.

The main distribution task for MOP was to extend the marketing network for animal-drawn implements from towns to villages. This involved using two approaches:

- direct selling of implements to farmers in the villages by MOP itself
- selling to farmers in the villages through village-based sales agents.

The direct selling approach was started as a short-term strategy, aimed at making the farmers aware of the project. The second approach of using village-based sales agents is the long-term strategy. MOP currently has 16 sales agents in different villages of Mbeya Region and plans to have a total of 45 village-based agents by phase two of the project. Most agents are employees of cooperative societies, trading companies, agricultural extension officers or private businessmen.

Implements sent by MOP to the agents are charged to the agents' credit accounts which have a ceiling. Agents receive a commission of 10% of their cash sales in each quarter. MOP visits the agents regularly to take orders and collect cash from sales. MOP also arranges seminars for the agents and teaches them elements of marketing and book-keeping. The MOP Extension and Marketing sections are training farmers in the use of other types of implement to help stimulate additional demand.

The aim of the MOP approach is to convince the village-based agents that the business of animal-drawn implements is profitable and that there is demand for implements in the villages. It is hoped that some agents will continue the business on their own after MOP has completed its term. It is encouraging to report that some agents have shown much interest in the scheme and plan to open their own outlets for selling animal-drawn implements.

MOP hopes that its approach can be a "model" that can be copied by the current official marketing institutions. This may occur in different ways. One way is through pressure by employees (who are MOP agents) on their organisations. Another is through pressure by farmers (who have enjoyed the MOP distribution service) on their local village cooperative societies or private shops. The cooperative movements have village depots which sell some agricultural inputs such as fertilisers, seeds and insecticides, but not animal-drawn implements.

The MOP marketing approach is not ideal. One weakness is that it is expensive on transport. In future, distributors will be encouraged to sell implements at higher prices to recover transport costs. However, this is not seen as a serious limitation as farmers in the villages are paying higher prices for animal-drawn implements sold by petty traders in village auctions. MOP strongly supports farmers buying implements at realistic market prices.

Conclusion

Distribution of animal-drawn implements in Mbeya Region has been very inefficient, as the marketing network initiated by UFI has not reached the villages. The implements are simply not in the right place and the right time. With highly seasonal sales and low profits, intermediaries in the distribution network have not had incentives to sell animal-drawn implements. The attempt of MOP to extend marketing channels into the villages has been effective in the short term. It will only work in the long term if the government and parastatal organisations adopt the system. The cooperative movement in Mbeya Region could help by supplying animal-drawn implements through its village depots which already sell other farm inputs.

References

Vander Ende S, 1991. *Bridging a paradigm shift. Marketing at the grassroots in Mbeya Tanzania: MEDA's experience.* Mennonite Economic Development Associates (MEDA), Mbeya, Tanzania. 5p.

Okoso-Amaa K, 1989. *Creating farmer awareness and preferences for new products (with references to the Mkombozi plow).* Department of Marketing, University of Dar es Salaam, Tanzania. pp. 9–11.

Photograph opposite
A woman and an ox at an on-farm demonstration, Tanga, Tanzania

---

Improving animal traction technology

Women and animal traction technology

Women and animal traction technology

by

Lotta Sylwander

*Socioeconomist, Agricultural Operations Technology for Small Holders
in East and Southern Africa (AGROTEC), PO Box BW540, Borrowdale, Harare, Zimbabwe*

Abstract

This paper gives a broad introduction to the most important issues and experiences concerning women and animal traction technology in eastern and southern Africa.

Animal traction should be gender-neutral: it should be accessible and adaptable to both men and women. However, experiences from the region show that women are generally not users of animal traction and that they do not have access to this technology. Women are mainly cultivating by hoe to produce subsistence food crops for the family. Men, on the other hand, are engaged more in cash crop production and often have access to improved technology like animal traction.

There is a need to increase agricultural production in Africa. This can only be done if the majority of farmers (ie, women) are provided with an opportunity to use improved technologies that enhance agricultural production. Women can clearly benefit from animal traction. Their tasks in agricultural production and their domestic workload (including transport of fuel and water) can be considerably reduced using animal power.

It is argued that the commonly held belief that women cannot use animal draft power is only a cultural notion based on certain gender roles and division of work within communities. Given proper access to cash/credit, extension services, information, training, land, animals and implements, there is no reason why women cannot use animal traction technology effectively.

Introduction

In the best of worlds it would not be necessary to write specifically about women and animal traction. Unfortunately, women and animal traction technology has become a *problem* that needs special attention. This paper gives the background to the present day situation and the causes of the problem. It also points to possible solutions for further discussion.

A user perspective is generally lacking among organisations working with animal traction. A gender-neutral user perspective is especially uncommon, as is one that gives special attention to the needs, options and constraints for women in relation to animal traction. Animal traction as a technology should be gender-neutral in the sense that it should be accessible and adaptable to both men and women. However, animal traction is not presently a *neutral technology* because it is not accessible to and used by both sexes.

Women and men have different gender roles and needs which have led to a differentiation in the use and adoption of animal traction technology. There are historical, socio-cultural, economic, structural, institutional and other reasons for this which are touched upon in this paper.

To facilitate a broad discussion, the paper has been written with a holistic perspective. The position and role of women in the community and in the economy at large, as the main food producers in the region, are analysed with special reference to animal traction technology. Overall improvement of animal traction technology can only be accomplished if gender issues are addressed in the process of development. It should be a development ambition to solve the *problem* of women and animal traction in order to increase agricultural production.

Historical background

Animal traction is not new in the history of agriculture but has only relatively recently been introduced into eastern and southern Africa. The first attempts to use and transfer animal draft power in agriculture in sub-Saharan Africa were carried out by the white colonialists and their extension apparatus, at the beginning of this century.

Sub-Saharan Africa was, and to a certain extent still is, a sparsely populated continent dominated by shifting cultivation and pastoralism. Shifting cultivation is a very extensive farming system with few external inputs, long fallow periods and simple technology, such as hoes and sticks.

Even in the early stages of agricultural development there is some division of labour, the main criteria being gender and age. In shifting cultivation or hoe cultivation the work is mainly done by women. The European colonialists and extension agents tended to interpret the division of labour among African shifting cultivators as "lazy African farming", where men did little or nothing.

Unintentionally the colonists managed to modify this distribution of labour between the sexes to some extent. This was done through the introduction of a monetary system and cash crops. With these the colonisers tried to induce the underemployed male villagers to cultivate commercial crops for export to Europe. Poll taxes and other colonial measures were used to stimulate more intensive agricultural production. To enhance agricultural intensification and the production of cash crops, male villagers were introduced to new technologies, such as animal draft power for field operations (Boserup, 1970; Kjærby, 1983; Starkey, 1991). Animal draft power was, until then, an unknown technology in sub-Saharan African agriculture, and it only slowly made progress through the continent. The transition from shifting cultivation to plow cultivation was also due to other factors, including population increase, land pressure and informal technology diffusion (Pingali, Bigot and Binswanger, 1987).

Female and male farming systems

Shifting cultivation or hoe cultivation has been labelled as a "female farming system" (Boserup, 1970). In so-called female farming systems, men are responsible for activities at the fringes of the production system (like clearing land, building and herding) but women do most of the actual agricultural work. As women are the main producers of food, they hold crucial positions in their communities, influencing both production and reproduction.

Due largely to the colonial intervention in agriculture, cash crops and mechanised agriculture were, from an early stage, in the hands of men. This still remains a major feature of agricultural systems worldwide, and in Africa in particular. The general rule appears to be that when agriculture becomes more mechanised, women continue to perform the simple, labour-demanding, manual tasks while men operate more efficient technology operated by animals or mechanical power. Consequently the type of farming system, using animal draft power for cash crop production, has been labelled as a "male farming system". Today, both systems can be found side by side, even in the same family, with specific gender division of labour.

The tremendous population increase in eastern and southern Africa over the past decades has led to an intensification as well as an extensification of agricultural production. Unfortunately there is nothing to suggest that agricultural production per head has increased in sub-Saharan Africa. Animal traction, however, is often associated with increased

production for the particular household, and with a change from traditional, multi-species intercropping to systems where single crops are grown in large areas (Starkey, 1987). In countries like Kenya, Lesotho and Malawi, the pressure on available agricultural land has stimulated intensified production, often using animal power for plowing.

Majority of farmers are women

Even though women constitute the main agricultural labour force in the region (70%), men cultivate a larger area, and may produce more, due to their access to improved technology. Starkey (1991) suggests that animal traction can increase total production not only by the direct effects of tillage, but also by the improved timeliness of field operations. Women cannot achieve the timeliness necessary for optimal production due to lack of appropriate power and implements, ie, animal traction technology. Consequently, although women spend more time on agricultural production, they cultivate less land and produce less.

It has been argued by many people (eg, Boserup, 1970; Rogers, 1980) that intensification of agriculture through the use of animal draft power can separate women from agricultural life, thereby *domesticating* women (in the sense of making them spend more time in the home or homestead). This does not seem to be the normal case in eastern and southern Africa, where interdependent and complementary female and male farming systems exist alongside each other. Women have active roles to play in the production systems. The simple facts that the majority of farmers in the region are women and that generally 70% of agricultural work in the region is done by women contradict the argument that women are becoming domesticated and isolated from agricultural production through animal traction.

It can be legitimately argued, though, that women become isolated from production of *cash crops* with the introduction of draft animals (Boserup, 1970; Zweier, 1986). Male farmers are more involved in producing cash crops such as tobacco and hybrid maize using animal traction. Family food consumption is still largely dependent on female (hoe-based) farming systems.

Women and animal traction use

In regions of Africa where women are engaged in cash crop production, such as The Gambia, there is some evidence that when (male-owned) draft animals are introduced to assist women-managed cash crops, the women may lose the right to grow the cash crop on their own behalf (Jones, 1988).

There is also evidence from Cameroon that women can be reduced to "helpers" with the introduction of animal traction (Zweier, 1986).

In most communities in eastern and southern Africa, women do not themselves use draft animals for field operations. Nevertheless, women are still very much involved in the production cycle and, for example, they will manually weed fields that have been plowed by animals (Rwelamira, 1990; Hocking, 1991; 1994; Marshall and Sizya, 1994).

Although the regional pattern is that women do not use animal draft power, there are exceptions to the rule. In communal areas in Zimbabwe, such as Lower Gweru, women are well accustomed to plowing and weeding with draft animals. They have been receiving special attention from the extension service in terms of training and advice. Women can also be seen plowing in Kenya, Tanzania and Zambia, but it is more of an exception to the general (male) rule.

In some parts of the region women use donkeys as pack animals. Donkeys are often identified as "female" animals, while cattle tend to be "male" animals.

Some development projects have successfully introduced women to the use of oxen for plowing in Zambia (Hocking, 1994), Cameroon (Walker, 1990) and in the Mbeya Oxenization Project of Tanzania (Marshall and Sizya, 1994). Special project methodologies have been tried and developed in order to address gender issues. These success stories are still few but there are some important and useful lessons to be learned from them.

Benefits and uses

The use of animal traction often leads to larger total areas being cultivated, but an increase in (male-dominated) cash crop production does not imply any reduced production of food crops. Women can therefore face even heavier workloads when animal traction is introduced as their food production is kept to the same level, but they are also expected to assist with manual operations relating to the cash crop. Although animal traction can actually increase the workload for women, there are conspicuously few references in the literature to this subject and the topic should be elaborated further (Kjærby, 1983).

Animal traction is usually only used for purposes and tasks that are identified as male tasks and men sometimes do not even see the possibility of using animal traction for women's tasks (Marshall and Sizya, 1994).

Women plowing, Lower Gweru, Zimbabwe

Women, as has been stressed, have a key role in crop production, notably hoeing, planting, weeding and harvesting (activities often described as women's "productive" tasks. Women's work in eastern and southern Africa typically also includes fetching water, collecting firewood and different types of food processing (activities known as "reproductive" tasks). Women suffer from drudgery in all these tasks and have few advanced technical solutions at their service.

Most of the female tasks mentioned could be done with the help of animal power. Water and firewood could be transported using pack donkeys or donkey carts, although this is still relatively rare. Transporting crops to a mill using work animals could save women much time and effort: more grain could be processed at one time and women would be relieved from the drudgery of head-load porterage. In small communities with limited access to infrastructure, animal-powered mills might be a viable solution (Nelson-Fyle and Sandhu, 1990). Weeding is often considered the most labour-consuming and dreaded task by women, but rarely do women use animal-drawn cultivators. Hand weeding is preferred.

Socio-cultural environment

In many communities in eastern and southern Africa there are strong socio-cultural objections to women using draft animals. Cattle are, by tradition, owned by men, kept by men and handled by men. Cattle are used for the acquisition of wives, lobola or bridewealth and the exchange of cattle has a social value sometimes beyond economic reason.

Even if there are direct economic benefits of allowing women to use draft animals, most men seem reluctant to let them do so. All communities are unique and have their own reasons why this is so. Although it is not possible to review the diverse explanations here, it seems reasonable to generalise and say that communities in eastern and southern Africa have the common socio-cultural notion that cattle are male property. Cattle, it is felt, should be handled by males and their use for traction purposes is a male responsibility and task. Thus, it seems that the use of animal traction is an inherently male activity, and most communities would identify animal traction as male work according to the gender division of work.

In countries such as Lesotho such cultural obstacles are stopping women from plowing even when the economic necessity is there (Rwelamira, 1990). Men are absent most of the time and many households are female-headed. Although land is scarce and timeliness of field operations is crucial, women are culturally inhibited from taking on the responsibility of animal traction.

The Lesotho example shows that socio-cultural reasons can sometimes be stronger than economic rationale. This is particularly true for activities that are not purely productive but rather reproductive (eg, food preparation and water and fuel collection). These activities seldom have an attached measured value, although they can be a heavy work burden for women.

It is important to note here that the absence of women users of animal traction is a clear gender issue and has nothing to do with women's capacity or capability to handle draft animals (Zweier, 1986; Marshall and Sizya, 1994). Given proper training and opportunities, women are perfectly able to use draft animals. The cultural notion of animal traction as something strictly for men is therefore just that—a culturally determined idea as part of the system of concepts and rules that underlie, and are expressed in, the way communities live and organise their lives.

Trying to modify and change an organised system of gender roles can be difficult as communities feel that such a change is too radical and a threat to their cultural identity (Marshall and Sizya, 1994). A sensitive and participatory approach in project and programme design and implementation is therefore crucial.

Resource access

Animal traction use involves access to such resources as land, cash, credit and implements. By traditional law, land is often allocated to, or owned by, men. Women often till land controlled by their husbands, and generally the man has the deciding power over production, consumption and marketing. In most eastern and southern African countries women have the legal right to own land, but they rarely do so. In strict legal terms, women generally have equal status to men, but in rural areas

customary laws prevail, and women are often only acknowledged as minors. The right to own land is often determined by traditional community leaders, such as tribal chiefs, and land is allocated to male family members even if the household is, in practice, female-headed (Rwelamira, 1990).

In a few cultures women can inherit and own their own cattle, but in most cases women have to acquire cattle and draft animals on the open market. This is quite difficult for female-headed households, with little cash income. Credit is normally needed in order to finance the buying of implements, draft animals and other inputs such as fertiliser. As women rarely have any collateral, such as land, it is difficult for them to obtain institutional credit and hence is difficult, or even impossible, to obtain draft animals and implements (Rwelamira, 1990; Marshall and Sizya, 1994). In places where a woman can get credit it is common that her husband has to sign any loan papers before credit is granted to the woman. Alas, no husband, no loan.

In some development projects, such as the Mbeya Oxenization Project, this problem has been addressed by creating credit facilities to allow women's groups to purchase oxen (Marshall and Sizya, 1994).

At present, most female-headed farm households that do make use of animal draft power in the region have to hire labour, implements and animals. Such households may receive remittances from one or more family members earning wages, and in this way they may obtain enough cash to hire (or even purchase) draft animals. If reliable access through hiring is possible, this may be most appropriate to the limited resources of women. Unfortunately, women (and men) hiring animals have to wait until they have finished working for their owners (usually men), and so timeliness, and production, are seldom ideal.

Many female-headed households in the region do not receive cash remittances and are dependent on the income they can generate from their own production. Since such households generally do not own draft animals, and cannot afford to hire them, they have difficulty in achieving surplus production. Thus their incomes remain low, and they remain unable to afford animal draft power. This vicious circle needs to be addressed in development and technology transfer programmes.

In the prevailing socioeconomic conditions, where women's resources are limited and hard to obtain, animal traction may sometimes appear too risky in economic terms. Ownership of small numbers of work animals (which can become sick, injured or stolen) can be a major risk. A crucial issue is therefore whether women want, or need, complete ownership and *control* over animal traction or whether *access* to the technology through hiring of oxen is acceptable.

Information, extension and training

As stated earlier, the extension service of the colonial powers in sub-Saharan Africa was directed towards men. Sadly, little has changed since that time, and men are still the main targets for modern extension services. Few agricultural extension officers are women, and even fewer are aware that women or gender issues have to be addressed specifically. Very few female extension workers are trained in animal traction technology, and consequently have little knowledge of the subject to communicate to women farmers.

If one takes even a quick look at extension materials, it is apparent that farmers are considered to be men. Drawings depict men conducting different farm operations, particularly when it comes to animal traction and implements. Women can sometimes be seen doing manual weeding.

Extension services, in general, do not address the farmers as farming families. They tend to direct their information towards individual male farmers. This misdirection has been noted by some countries in the region and female farmers have now (officially) been given special attention in national plans. In practice, at the grassroots level, things remain the same. It has been noted by several researchers concerned with women and animal traction that unless training and extension programmes include a well-planned, active women's component, information and technology transfer is unlikely to reach female farmers (Zweier, 1986; Walker, 1990; Hocking, 1994; Marshall and Sizya, 1994).

Research

A great deal of agricultural engineering research and development relating to animal draft power technology has been undertaken in eastern and southern Africa. This work appears to have been entirely directed towards male users. The available literature and reports give no indication as to whether research relating specifically to women's needs in this area has been undertaken, or even whether such research is needed.

While much of the research in animal traction technologies has come from agricultural engineers and technology-oriented persons, there is a clear need for increased research in animal traction by

Girl and women plowing in Zimbabwe using an ox and a cow

social scientists. This should identify possibilities, constraints and methodologies for the possible introduction of animal traction use to women. Kjærby (1983) suggested that research into the actual benefits to women of animal traction (for example, reduced workload) should be seriously considered.

In short, it is clear that much more research into women and animal traction needs to be conducted in eastern and southern Africa and elsewhere.

Conclusion

Animal traction technology offers Africa's growing population a means of increasing labour productivity and agricultural production while simultaneously reducing human drudgery. Full benefits can only be achieved from the technology if women, who are the majority of farmers in the region, are able to make use of draft animals. With the prevailing regional trend of male labour migration to the urban centres, women are likely to constitute the main agricultural labour force for the foreseeable future. Animal traction should allow women to produce more. The technology appears to have particular potential to reduce the drudgery and labour bottleneck of weeding. Animal transport should also lead to considerable savings for women in work time and drudgery. Since women normally have an excessive workload, these direct benefits will also indirectly benefit many other aspects of family and community life.

Animal traction has historically been used only within male farming systems. Women themselves ought to have direct access to animal traction: it should be available and affordable to them, through ownership or hire, and technical skills should be imparted if necessary.

Information, transfer of technology, extension services and credit facilities have been aimed at men, but should be available to both female and male farmers. At present men control most of the resources associated with animal traction, including land, animals and income from farm sales. To comprehensively involve women in animal traction diffusion, the support of men has to be gained. Animal traction programmes clearly need to involve all concerned in farming, that is, the whole farming family.

Research in animal traction has almost completely neglected its use by women. Agricultural engineers should ensure that the available technology is optimised for use by women. All animal traction researchers should become aware of gender issues in animal traction, and ensure that research relating to animals, management systems and cropping systems addresses the needs of the women farmers.

Questions for consideration

Many questions remain to be answered on the subject of women and animal traction technology. The following questions have been touched upon in this paper, but need further elaboration.

○ How can women best benefit from developments and improvements in animal traction technology?

○ Do women want or need *access to* or *control of* animal traction technology?

○ Is it more crucial to introduce animal traction for women for *productive activities* or *reproductive activities* (including domestic work and household transport)?

○ How can women's access to training and information dissemination on animal traction be improved?

○ Can cultural and social constraints against women's use of draft animals be used to advantage or overcome?

○ How can the possible disadvantages of animal traction for women, such as increased manual weeding, be avoided?

○ How do we formulate innovative extension programming to reach women farmers?

○ Can any methodologies be identified in animal traction project and programme implementation that will ensure women's participation?

○ How can women be assured access to credit and the availability of financial facilities for investment in animal traction technology?

○ Is there a need for specific research in animal traction technology for women?

○ Is there a need for specific animal traction equipment and implements for women?

○ How can governments increase training of female extension workers in animal traction?

○ How can national technology and mechanisation programmes address gender issues?

Acknowledgement

This paper was prepared with much reference to the papers written by J Rwelamira (1990) and K Marshall and M Sizya (1994). It was initially intended that this should have been a joint, coauthored paper by Sylwander, Rwelamira, Marshall and Sizya. Regrettably, time constraints made this impractical, but the author would like to warmly thank these people for their cooperation.

References

Boserup E, 1970. *Woman's role in economic development.* Earthscan Publications, London, UK. 283p.

Hocking C, 1991. *The impact of mobile ox-ploughing courses for women: a study in Kaoma East and in areas surrounding the Lui river valley, Western Province, Zambia.* MSc Thesis, University of Newcastle-upon-Tyne, UK. 53p.

Hocking C, 1994. The impact of mobile ox plowing courses for women in the Western Province of Zambia. In: Starkey P, Mwenya E and Stares J (eds), *Improving animal traction technology.* Proceedings of Animal Traction Network for Eastern and Southern Africa (ATNESA) workshop held 18–23 January 1992, Lusaka, Zambia.

Jones A, 1988. Socio-economic constraints to the use of animal traction for rainfed rice production in The Gambia. pp. 310–314 in: Starkey P and Faye A (eds), *Animal traction for agricultural development.* Third Regional Workshop of the West Africa Animal Traction Network, held 7–12 July 1988, Saly, Senegal. Technical Centre for Agricultural and Rural Cooperation (CTA), Ede-Wageningen, The Netherlands. 475p.

Kjærby F, 1983. *Problems and contradictions in the development of ox-cultivation in Tanzania.* Research Report 66. Scandinavian Institute of African Studies, Uppsala, Sweden, and Centre for Development Research, Copenhagen, Denmark. 163p.

Marshall K and Sizya M, 1994. Women and animal traction in Mbeya Region of Tanzania: a gender and development approach. In: Starkey P, Mwenya E and Stares J (eds), *Improving animal traction technology.* Proceedings of Animal Traction Network for Eastern and Southern Africa (ATNESA) workshop held 18–23 January 1992, Lusaka, Zambia.

Nelson-Fyle M R and Sandhu R, 1990. The impact of animal traction on women. pp. 153–155 in: Starkey P H and Faye A (eds), *Animal traction for agricultural development.* Third Regional Workshop of the West Africa Animal Traction Network, held 7–12 July 1988, Saly, Senegal. Technical Centre for Agricultural and Rural Cooperation (CTA), Ede-Wageningen, The Netherlands. 475p.

Pingali P, Bigot Y and Binswanger H, 1987. *Agricultural mechanization and the evolution of farming systems in sub-Saharan Africa.* World Bank, Washington DC, in association with Johns Hopkins Press, Baltimore, MD, USA.

Rogers B, 1980. *The domestication of women: discrimination in developing societies.* Tavistock, London, UK. 200p.

Rwelamira J K, 1990. *The social and economic aspects of animal traction in agricultural production amongst female-headed households of Lesotho and Swaziland.* Faculty of Agriculture, University of Swaziland, Luyengo, Swaziland. 11p.

Starkey P, 1987. Animal power in development: some implications for communities. *Community Development Journal* 22(3):219–227.

Starkey P, 1991. Animal traction: constraints and impact among African households. pp. 77–90 in: Haswell M and Hunt D (eds), *Rural households in emerging societies.* Berg, Oxford, UK. 261p.

Walker S T, 1990.*Innovative agricultural extension for women: a case study in Cameroon.* Working Papers, Population and Human Resources Department, World Bank, Washington DC, USA. 53p.

Zweier K, 1986. Women can handle draught oxen, too. *GATE* 4:17–19. German Appropriate Technology Exchange (GATE), GTZ, Eschborn, Germany.

Women and animal traction in Mbeya Region of Tanzania: a gender and development approach

K Marshall*and M Sizya

Mbeya Oxenization Project, PO Box 2094, Mbeya, Tanzania

Abstract

Agricultural technologies are not value-neutral. They have associated with them certain assumptions and choices which can greatly alter the existing social structures into which they are being introduced. The promotion of a technology thus requires an understanding not only of the technology but also of cultural issues. This paper outlines the attempts of a development project in Tanzania—the Mbeya Oxenization Project—to promote the use of animal traction in a "gender sensitive" way. Challenged with the reality that animal traction is considered a male activity, and that gender issues are often perceived as a threat, the project designed strategies to ensure that female farmers are effective participants in, and beneficiaries from, project activities. By fitting the Mbeya Oxenization Project's experience into a "gender and development" approach, a useful framework evolves which could be used by other animal traction projects in their efforts to integrate gender concerns.

Background

The successful introduction of a technology into a culture involves an understanding of both the culture and the technology—how they fit, or do not fit, together. All too often a technology is considered value neutral, meaning that only its physical attributes are considered. But experience has shown that all technologies have associated with them certain assumptions and choices which have implications when the technologies are introduced to the public. Technologies reflect relationships between people and machines. And culture is not static; cultures, or patterns of interaction between people, develop as a result of various environmental, economic, social and political influences, and are in a continual state of flux. Without careful prior investigation, the introduction of a technology into a culture can have unexpected and often unintended results (Sylwander, 1990).

This is not a new idea. People have recognised this fact for some time, but have not understood its impact on the change process; indeed, it has often been ignored or overlooked in development projects.

*Subsequent address:
28 Hearn Avenue, Guelph, Ontario N1H 5Y4, Canada

This paper discusses the experience of the Mbeya Oxenization Project—an animal traction project based in Mbeya, Tanzania—and its attempt to involve both male and female farmers as effective participants in animal traction technology. By placing the project's experience within a developmental framework—a gender and development approach—some lessons are identified which may assist others in their attempts to integrate "gender issues" into an animal traction project.

Project context

The Mbeya Oxenization Project (MOP), located in the southern highlands of Tanzania, was initiated in 1987 as a joint venture between the Government of Tanzania and the Canadian International Development Agency. Its primary objective was to promote agricultural development by encouraging smallholder farmers to use animal traction technologies to increase production, and alleviate drudgery, in a way that "contributes to growth with equity among smallholder farmers" (MEDA, 1986). Although the project planners intended that both men and women would be effective participants and beneficiaries, no strategies to implement this intention were identified in the planning documents. Early in the project, MOP staff found themselves using a passive approach, which resulted in them working only with men; they were frustrated by being given little direction on how to involve the main farmers of the area, the women.

A year after MOP began, an effort was made to solve this problem by creating a Gender Issues Section within the project. The mandate of this section was to develop a programme which did not just assume that women would benefit from the use of animal draft technologies, but which listened to, and worked with, women, as farmers and agents of change. With little support and no blueprint to follow, this section was given the task of developing and implementing guidelines to ensure that women's needs, opportunities or constraints would be considered at all levels, and in all activities, of the project.

Misconceptions about women and animal traction

It did not take long for the gender issue staff to realise that in order to develop a methodology for integrating the so-called women's concerns, two major issues had to be recognised and dealt with. The most visible of these was the fact that in most peoples' minds, and throughout the literature, animal traction is regarded as a male-oriented/dominated activity. For example, posters and brochures promoting the use of animal traction rarely mention women as farmers who could use this technology. Also part of this perception are the ideas that women are too weak and afraid to handle oxen, that women will destroy the equipment because they are not capable of understanding it, that women have no interest in learning to use draft animal technologies, that there is no need for women to use oxen, etc. Decision-makers from regional government to village levels were not aware, or were not willing to acknowledge, that women have any meaningful role to play in an animal traction project.

The second major issue is that many people working in development do not understand what gender issues really mean. For many, gender issues translate into the threat of radical change, where culture and traditions are disregarded as women take control over men. Fear of this anticipated change immediately raises barriers to communication.

Such misconceptions are likely to be present in any project which is promoting change—whether it be animal traction or any other activity—and if they are to be overcome they must be discussed by men and women together. It needs to be understood that being culturally sensitive is not necessarily the same as being gender-sensitive.

Both these issues had to be considered in formulating MOP's methodology.

Strategies for integrating women in animal traction

As relationships with rural women developed through frequent interaction it became obvious that it was only men who had misconceptions about women and animal traction. Women were indeed interested in using oxen, but they felt powerless to try. In Mbeya Region, only men own oxen and they exercise complete control over them, giving women little access to their use or benefits. It therefore seemed crucial that MOP facilitate a process whereby women could at least have access to this resource, even if not control over it.

Women hand weeding, Njelenje, Mbeya District

MOP approached this goal in two ways. At the household level, an awareness campaign was started among contact farmers. Discussions were initiated with both men and women, to raise awareness of who benefits, and who could benefit, from the use of draft animal technologies. These discussions covered such questions as which members of the household were responsible for what cropping and other activities. It was emphasised, for example, that ox carts could be used to carry water for domestic use (women's responsibility) as well as for brick making (men's work); or that an ox-drawn ridger could be used for ridging a woman's bean field as well as a man's maize field (Wekwe and Marshall, 1991). Training seminars and exchanges were organised, where husband and wife had to attend together. Gradually a new perspective was seen to be developing within households. Men became more aware of the potential benefits of animal traction for the whole family—for agricultural activities and for domestic use. Women gained skills and confidence, not to mention relief from some of their responsibilities. It seems that positive change can be brought about, albeit slowly, by promoting this kind of awareness.

A second approach was to help women actually to have access to and control over draft animal technology. The strategy used was to organise women into groups. By providing women's groups with loans to purchase oxen and equipment, and to manage an income-generating project based on animal traction, the perceived barriers to women using oxen were again shattered. In the "group" context women felt that they were strong enough to counter family, community and cultural constraints. As individuals they may never have had the courage to plow a field with oxen, but when they had the support of other women of like mind they were enthusiastic students of draft animal use. Many are seeking creative ways in which animal traction could enable the group to meet its objectives (such as hiring out their oxen and equipment). In some groups, individual members saw this as an opportunity to reduce their personal workload. Working with groups allowed MOP the opportunity to train many women at one time, stressing animal traction and project management skills, as well as encouraging women to be more self-confident and aware of their role in development.

These "village based" activities are not enough. Although there is much talk these days of "women in development", "gender issues", etc, it is not always clear what these terms mean, particularly in the context of an animal traction project. There is a considerable and expanding theoretical base concerning "gender", but there is little practical knowledge with which to guide a project.

An example will illustrate how MOP handled this situation. A concern of the Gender Issues Section was that if MOP staff themselves do not understand (or even agree!) why they are trying to involve women, what message will they send to the people in the villages, or will the message they are sending be consistent? To address this issue, a "gender sensitisation" process was initiated within the project. Using some basic organisational tools, all project staff went through a process of recognising their fears or ideas surrounding women's issues; discussed what gender issues are for development workers; and the implications for an animal traction project. It became clear that it would be necessary to deal with comments such as "I am afraid about what will happen if women are equal", as well as to raise awareness on issues of gender, before a gender-sensitive animal traction programme could be designed. This does not happen spontaneously! Gender issues must be understood as a development issue, rather than an equality issue, in order to objectively, and constructively, plan and analyse activities. It should be mentioned that the participation of MOP staff has been active and honest, and recommendations emphasised the need to continue this awareness process.

Farmers' group at weeding demonstraion, Njelenje, Mbeya District

Photo: Sam Vander Ende

Gender and development approach: MOP's experience

The following discussion outlines some of MOP's attempts to ensure gender "equity" within the project. However, it must be stressed that the programme has developed through trial and error. As there is no single way to address gender concerns that will be appropriate for all situations, MOP's methodology should be considered as one of many possible alternatives.

If MOP's experiences are fitted into a theoretical framework, a pattern, or guideline for activities, emerges which may be helpful when analysing other animal traction projects. An appropriate perspective to ensure that women are equal participants in the development process seems to be the "gender and development" approach, as defined by Young (1988) and Rathgeber (1989), among others. This approach is not concerned with women *per se*, but with the socially defined and defended *gender* relations between men and women (Young, 1988). In other words, what women do, or do not do, is related to what men do, or do not do.

One way that gender relations are evidenced in a society is through the sexual division of labour, which is based on a set of ideas about what men's and women's capacities are, and what is appropriate for them to do. The sexual division of labour in any society includes both a set of ideas and a set of material practices, all of which are specific to a particular culture and time. Although the sexual division of labour can be seen as a structure of division between men and women, it should also be seen as forming the basis of social connection, as men and women become interdependent in their combined efforts to meet household survival needs.

Applied to an animal traction project, this approach would emphasis the need to examine the division of labour between men and women for productive, as well as domestic, activities, and to try to predict how a change in one activity will affect others. MOP experience indicates that the introduction of animal traction into a household can affect the labour allocations of the whole household, and for many cropping activities (Vander Ende, 1990; 1991). For example, data collected over the entire cropping season from some 20 farming households who own oxen and 20 who do not show that overall labour requirements increase for those households which own oxen, compared to non-owners. This is not surprising, as ox owners cultivate nearly twice as much land (for the three main crops) as non-owners. However, the extent to which the labour inputs of

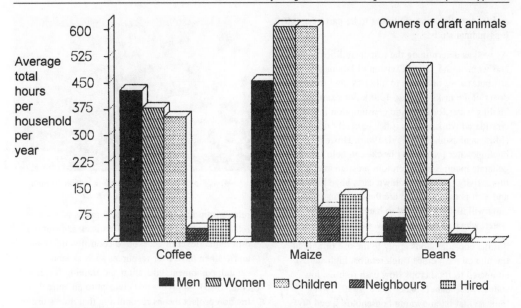

Figure 1: Household labour allocation for animal traction owners. Data collected in three villages of Mbozi District. Based on average areas of 2.4 ha coffee, 2.5 ha maize and 1.0 ha beans (two crops). Household composition of 6.25 persons actively involved in cropping activities. Source: Adapted from Vander Ende (1990; 1991)

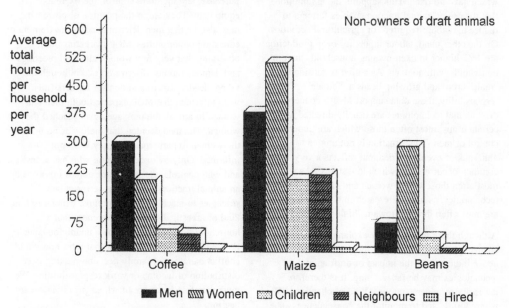

Figure 2: Household labour allocation for non-owners of animal traction. Data collected in three villages of Mbozi District. Based on average areas of 0.6 ha coffee, 1.6 ha maize and 0.7 ha beans (two crops). Household composition of 3.5 persons actively involved in cropping activities. Source: Adapted from Vander Ende (1990; 1991)

different members of the household increase varies considerably: for the three main crops, males in oxen-owning households invest 26% more time in cropping activities, females 54% more and children 338% more than their counterparts in households which do not own oxen (see Figures 1 and 2).

Although it is true that households with oxen are larger (more wives and more children) than those without, it is not clear whether they are larger simply because of the higher labour requirement. The cause and/or effect response to draft animal technology adoption/ownership and labour patterns and labour allocation continues to be part of an MOP longitudinal study.

As well as determining the responsibilities of men and women, the sexual division of labour also attributes a set of values to all tasks, and to the doers of the tasks (Young, 1988). For example, hauling water for domestic consumption is hardly considered work, and so it has basically no status (Mascarenhas and Mbilinyi, 1983). However, hauling water for making bricks can help to generate income, and therefore prestige attaches to this activity. As animal-drawn carts have high status, and as it is the men who are the decision-makers, carts will usually be used to haul bricks rather than water, which is considered "women's work".

Similar considerations apply to the use of animal traction on cash crops (high returns, high status) compared to food crops (low cash returns, low status). MOP data (Vander Ende, 1990; 1991) indicate that oxen-owning households spend 46% less time per unit area (total time of all household members) on coffee production than households which have no oxen. This supports the assumption that the use of animal traction enables farmers to reduce the labour required for agricultural activities. On the other hand, labour inputs for bean production are 16% higher in oxen-owning households than in households with no oxen. As coffee is considered a "male" crop, and growing beans a "female" responsibility, these data support MOP's concern that draft animal technologies are usually directed at certain crops, most often those which are under the control of men. This situation is not unique to Tanzania, or even to Africa, but reflects a very common occurrence in which low status jobs are most often those which women and children do, and technologies, as well as research into technologies, are most often directed towards high status activities.

Although there may be many explanations of these changes in labour allocation, the data referred to above indicate that the impact of draft animal technologies may be far reaching. It is therefore necessary to understand what kind of changes MOP is promoting, and to monitor the consequences. The gender and development approach provides a framework for reminding us of the many aspects which must be considered. The implications for an animal traction project are clear: if we want to give women a real chance to have access to and to benefit from such technology, we will have to challenge the typical path that most technological development follows.

Equally (perhaps more) important is the fact that gender relations reflect power relations. The

Women participating in a weeding demonstration, Njelenje, Mbeya District

relationship between males and females is not a relationship between equals. This is clear from the differential level of access and control which men and women have over resources such as land, capital, equipment, education and training (Overholt et al, 1985). Applying this concept to an animal traction project means recognising that men's use of animal traction, to the exclusion of women, can be based simply on the fact that men have the capital to purchase, and therefore control, the oxen and equipment. They are in the position of power. It may also be that men determine access to training or education opportunities. MOP marketing staff, observing that very few women attended meetings and demonstrations, discovered that although the village leaders (men) and contact farmers (men) were informed that MOP expected both men and women to attend, the message never reached the women. The men decided that there was no need for the women to participate, so they were not informed. Only by understanding who has access to, and who controls, the various resources involved in an animal traction project can we formulate strategies to reach our target groups. Crucial to this kind of investigation is the awareness that a household decision may not be a unanimous one. Folbre (1986) makes the point that intra-household conflict can arise in family decision-making over distribution of income or work responsibilities. We must therefore be aware of whose priorities we are hearing.

It is important to acknowledge, when doing such analyses, that culture plays a major role in determining who does what, and with what technology. However, development projects often find that certain activities cannot be done because of cultural restrictions or constraints. Although the local culture provides a pattern for interaction, the pattern is not set in stone. It may be a convenient excuse to blame culture, when in fact the real problem is our inability to understand the

Women's group weeding, Iyula, Mbozi District

social/cultural environment (Prindiville, 1991). Only by recognising the positive and dynamic nature of culture, and identifying opportunities and openings, can we develop strategies for change within the parameters of the culture. For example, MOP was often told that for male extension workers to talk to women, with no men around, was inappropriate within the local cultural context. However, MOP identified an opening: by organising women into groups, it was quite acceptable for male staff to talk with women, even when no men were around. The culture was respected and in a small way change is being promoted.

Conclusion

The experience of MOP has clearly shown that assumptions that all household members benefit equally from the use of draft animal technologies are not valid. We have also seen that by using a gender and development framework we can be systematic in our analysis, and better able to design activities to meet our objectives. By analysing the local situation—for example, who is responsible for what work (domestic as well as productive activities), with what technologies, what skills are needed for this work, and what are related activities—and bringing this to the attention of the household, we are better prepared to understand how all these aspects could be influenced by the introduction of a new technology into the household. It is also important to scrutinise existing power relations, such as who has control over which resources. Are we content to work within these structures, or do we want to try to change them?

By promoting animal traction for women's crops and activities, we may indeed be challenging traditional attitudes and values on many fronts. First, domestic activities (eg, carrying water and firewood, milling maize) have to be considered as real work, not just "the things that women do". Second, we

need to convince decision-makers, farmers, researchers, producers, leaders and politicians, all usually men, that there is reason to direct "high status technologies" to "low-status work and workers". We need to go beyond merely teaching women to plow with oxen, to actually addressing the structures which keep women in their secondary position. Animal traction is an ideal vehicle to promote such change.

A review of most animal draft technology projects shows a consistent association between men and animal traction. In this paper we have challenged some traditionally held perceptions as to why this is so. It is suggested that it may be a reflection of the shortcomings of development projects and the way they are planned, rather than direction dictated by culture. The challenge for all of us is to stop accepting the "same old reasons" and to explore other issues, and listen to alternative priorities. By adapting a gender and development framework, planners and implementers can begin the journey towards truly "gender-sensitive" development.

References

Folbre N, 1986. Cleaning house: new perspectives on households and economic development. *Journal of Development Economics* 22:5–40.

Mascarenhas O and Mbilinyi M, 1983. *Women in Tanzania: an analytical bibliography*. Scandinavian Institute of African Studies, Uppsala, Sweden. 256p.

MEDA, 1986. *Oxenization: an appropriate technology for smallholder farmers of Mbeya Region, Tanzania. Project design and plan of operation*. Mennonite Economic Development Associates (MEDA). Canadian International Development Agency, Hull, Quebec, Canada.

Overholt C, Anderson M B, Cloud K and Austin J E (eds), 1985. *A case book: gender roles in development projects*. Kumerian Press, Connecticut, USA. 326p.

Prindiville J, 1991. *Social sustainability: a background paper for CIDA*. Canadian International Development Agency (CIDA), Hull, Quebec, Canada. 18p.

Rathgeber E M. 1989. *WID, WAD, GAD: trends in research and practice*. International Development Research Centre (IDRC), Ottawa, Canada. 26p.

Sylwander A-C. 1990. *Socio-economic aspects of animal draught power*. Agrotec, Harare, Zimbabwe. 5p.

Vander Ende S. 1990. *Analysis and reports of labour studies and the use of animal draught technology in villages near Mbozi Maize Farms (State Farm) and Magamba Village, Chunya District*. Internal Report for Monitoring and Evaluation. Mbeya Oxenization Project, Mbeya, Tanzania. 20p.

Vander Ende S, 1991. *Analysis and reports of labour studies and the use of animal draught technology in Msanyila and Igunda Village of Mbozi District*. Internal Report for Monitoring and Evaluation. Mbeya Oxenization Project, Mbeya, Tanzania. 41p.

Wekwe J and Marshall K, 1991. *Gender sensitivity within agricultural engineering: an experience of animal draught technologies in Mbeya Region*. Paper presented at Agricultural Engineering Conference, Arusha, Tanzania, 17–20 September 1991. 7p. [Available from Mbeya Oxenization Project, Mbeya, Tanzania]

Young K, 1988. *Gender and development: a relational approach*. Institute of Development Studies, University of Sussex, Brighton, UK. 11p.

Transportation by women, and their access to animal-drawn carts in Zimbabwe

by

J Doran[*]

UNIFEM (United Nations Development Fund for Women), PO Box 4775, Harare, Zimbabwe

Abstract

The magnitude of rural household transport activities, particularly by women, is highlighted. One way to alleviate women's transport tasks is by increasing their access to more efficient means of transport, such as animal-drawn carts.

Some findings from research on gender aspects of ownership and use of livestock and animal-drawn carts in Zimbabwe are presented and analysed. Female-headed households are much less likely to own livestock than female-managed or male-headed households. Cart ownership is much more common among male-headed households. Many female-managed households own livestock and these are considered a target group for assistance in cart acquisition.

Within households, women are generally at a disadvantage in terms of access to carts, but cart ownership is, on balance, beneficial to women. Carts can allow some of women's transport tasks, such as firewood collection, to be delegated to young men and boys. Households owning carts and large drums often delegate water collection to boys.

Introduction

The transport element of rural household activities is frequently not made explicit. Once transport is perceived as the movement of people and goods, irrespective of the mode of transport employed, it becomes a much more important aspect of development. In considering transport activities at the rural household level, one of the main findings from recent surveys is the extent to which transport is undertaken within the village compared with travel outside the village. When this hitherto largely unmeasured element of transport activity was recorded, the very considerable amounts of time and energy being expended on transport activities came to light. Of particular note is the high proportion of the time and effort of women expended in transport activities. This is high both in absolute terms and relative to the transport work of other household members.

---

[*] *Subsequent address:*
Rural Transport Adviser, ITDG Kenya
PO Box 39493, Nairobi, Kenya

Surveys in Ghana and Tanzania

Transport

Several surveys have been carried out by Intermediate Technology Transport (IT Transport, UK) to determine the characteristics of transport in rural households in Africa. Figures from studies in Tanzania (Barwell and Malmberg-Calvo, 1988) and in Ghana (Howe and Zille, 1988) indicate the magnitude of household time and effort spent on transport. The "tonne-km"—the effort involved in moving a one-tonne load over a distance of one kilometre—was used as a measure of effort.

In Ghana, the average household spent about 4800 hours in time and 2600 tonne-km in effort per year. In Makete, Tanzania, the corresponding figures were nearly 2600 hours and about 90 tonne-km. The much higher figures for the Ghana survey were partly attributable to the larger household size in Ghana (more than twice that found in the Tanzanian survey) and to the greater cultivation and marketing of cash crops. A remarkably high proportion of time and effort (about three-quarters of the total) was expended on transport tasks within the village.

Most rural transport involves the movement of small loads over short distances. In the Tanzanian study, the three domestic activities of water and firewood collection and taking maize to the grinding mill accounted for almost 90% of the tonne-km transported by the household. They represent nearly 50% of the total household time spent in transport activities. Water accounted for 70% of the tonnage carried. Seasonal activities, such as the transportation of harvested crops, may also require significant household effort.

Women as load bearers

The IT Transport surveys (Barwell and Malmberg-Calvo, 1988; Howe and Zille, 1988) also analysed the transport activities carried out by different members of households. The Tanzanian study showed that women undertake the major proportion of rural transport, particularly the load-bearing. In terms of time they are responsible for nearly 70% of for nearly 70% of transport and in terms of effort nearly 85%. An average female in Makete spends nearly 1600 hours a year (averaging over four hours a day) on transport alone. In the Ghana study the average female spent about 1000 hours a year on transport. Figure 1 gives the daily transport workload of household members in the study in Makete, Tanzania.

Women perform other transport activities and express a need for closer and easier access to such facilities as health centres. However, the largest proportion of their annual time and effort spent in transport activities is involved in water and firewood collection, and taking maize to the grinding mill. In the Makete survey these tasks were all done by headloading. Spending an average of more than four hours a day on transport tasks which involve the equivalent of carrying approximately 180 kg a distance of 1 km is a significant use of time and energy. This might well constrain women from using their labour more productively and improving their welfare and that of their households. The physical strain of headloading might also have a detrimental effect on women's health. There is therefore a strong case for trying to alleviate the transport burden of women (Doran, 1989) and one way is through improved forms of transport.

UNIFEM survey in Zimbabwe

The United Nations Development Fund for Women (UNIFEM) perceives the lack of access to efficient means of transport to be a major constraint for African rural women. This constraint prevents them from realising their economic potential and being released from labour-intensive tasks that have poor remuneration.

UNIFEM commissioned a study to determine the gender aspects of ownership, use and hire of transport devices, particularly animal-drawn carts, in rural Zimbabwe (Gaidzanwa, 1990). This study focused on households in communal and "model A" resettlement schemes. It covered all five agro-ecological zones (designated within Zimbabwe

Women's group benefiting from cart transport

as zones 1–5, with zone 5 having the least rainfall). Respondents from 129 households in 12 villages were interviewed. Households were categorised in three ways:

Female-headed households were those which were run and represented by a widow or a divorced or single woman without the mediation of a husband, father or male relative in the routine, day-to-day activities of that household.

Female-managed households were those which were managed on a day-to-day basis by a woman on behalf of a labour migrant who was the final decision maker on important issues pertaining to that household.

Male-headed households were those where a man was present and was the final decision maker in the important issues pertaining to the household.

Respondents were asked, among other details, about their transportation assets, their transportation tasks on and off the farm and their livestock used for transportation purposes. The ownership of cattle and donkeys was also analysed since it was one of the factors which might affect the acquisition of animal-drawn carts and other animal power transport technologies.

Women and livestock ownership

The UNIFEM survey (Gaidzanwa, 1990) indicated that most (83%) of the households surveyed owned large livestock (Table 1). In the drier areas (zones 4 and 5), households tended to own donkeys rather than oxen and cows. Donkeys are cheaper than cattle and are hardier in areas of low rainfall.

As might be expected, the majority of livestock-owning households were male-headed. Among the livestock-owning households run by women, a much higher proportion of female-managed households than female-headed ones owned livestock. This difference might be explained by such factors as wage remittances to female-managed households and their higher general level of access to resources.

Figure 1: Daily transport workload of household members in Makete, Tanzania
Source: Barwell and Malmberg-Calvo (1988)

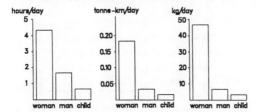

Table 1: Household types in relation to ownership of large livestock

Agro-ecological zone	Households without livestock				Households with livestock			
	Female-headed	Female-managed	Male-headed	Total	Female-headed	Female-managed	Male-headed	Total
1	1	–	–	1	–	6	–	6
2	2	2	3	7	4	11	8	23
3	1	–	1	2	1	3	34	38
4	1	–	–	1	7	4	5	16
5	2	1	8	11	3	4	17	24
Total	7	3	12	22	15	28	64	107

Livestock ownership, or lack of ownership, is not necessarily an indicator of a household's animal transport capability. Some households which own livestock may not be able to use them for work if the animals are too young or too old, or if they are cows near the date of calving. Some households which own livestock might have only one cow or ox in which case they would still need to borrow or hire one or more animals from neighbours or relatives. On the other hand, households which do not own large livestock may still have access to such animals. Such households are likely to invest in livestock for plowing and transport purposes before investing in a cart, particularly since cattle are seen as a symbol of wealth.

Cart ownership

Ownership of animal-drawn carts was also analysed according to type of household (Table 2). Almost 45% of households owned carts, ownership being heavily skewed towards male-headed households. Cart ownership was highest in households headed by elderly men who were, or had been, involved in wage labour. The wages of such people were often used to purchase carts. With both livestock and cart ownership it is generally the households of widows and younger households which tended to be more disadvantaged.

The two aspects of livestock and cart ownership are brought together in Table 3. While most of the male-headed, livestock-owning households also owned carts, very few female-headed or female-managed households did. The disparity between female-managed and female-headed households was again apparent. Some households owning animals but not carts had access to hired or borrowed carts. However, their access was probably not total; they would not have had first call on the carts at periods of high demand, such as harvest.

Transport scarcity

A number of other observations of the survey can be highlighted. In the drier agro-ecological zones, the transport tasks of water and firewood collection are more onerous since the sources are further away. In the higher rainfall zones, greater amounts of agricultural produce need to be transported.

Motor vehicles are the preferred means of transporting crop surpluses to depots and markets. Because of the scarcity of lorries and other motor transport, animal-drawn carts are often used to transport produce beyond what is considered their normal range. This may have an adverse effect on the animals, and carts that are deployed away from

Table 2: Ownership of animal-drawn carts by household type and agro-ecological zone

Agro-ecological zone	Total households	Households without carts			Households with carts		
		Female-headed	Female-managed	Male-headed	Female-headed	Female-managed	Male-headed
1	7	1	6	–	–	–	–
2	29	6	12	–	–	–	11
3	40	2	–	15	1	3	19
4	17	8	3	–	–	1	5
5	36	4	5	9	1	–	17
Total	129	21	26	24	2	4	52

Source: Gaidzanwa (1990)

Table 3: Ownership of large livestock and animal-drawn carts by household type

| Type of household | Percentage of total | Percentage of type of household owning | | Percentage of livestock-owning households also owning carts |
		Livestock	Cart(s)	
Female-headed	18	67	9	13
Female-managed	23	92	13	14
Male-headed	59	84	68	81
All types	100	83	45	54

Source: Gaidzanwa (1990)

households are not available for tasks such as firewood and water collection.

Women's access to carts

Women are in a disadvantaged position in using carts for transport tasks for which they have responsibility. This is because the carts are generally seen as male property and their use is dependent on access to animals which are generally owned by men. In the survey, it was noted that households having fewer than five oxen or donkeys were less willing to use the animals for water or firewood collection, even if a cart was owned. Households had to choose between conserving the energy of their animals or that of their women; in many cases the choice favoured the animals. Similarly, during peak agricultural seasons, women often resort to headloading water, firewood and maize as the carts are being used by men to carry manure or produce.

Some implications

One important observation of the survey was that cart ownership can lead to delegation of duties

Use of donkey carts and drums has allowed children to assist with water collection in north-east Zimbabwe

Photo: Paul Starkey

within households. In households which own carts, women's traditional transport tasks and load carrying may be done by some other household members. In households owning carts, older women tended to delegate the tasks of water and firewood collection to young men and boys, especially if the household also owned large drums for water collection and storage. Factors such as water drums, animal ownership and the presence of boys or young men in the household should be noted when promoting or analysing cart use and ownership.

Carts are most likely to be acquired by households owning suitable animals. Two-thirds of the female-headed households already own large livestock, as do the great majority of female-managed households. These groups seem most likely to want to purchase carts, and would make a suitable target group for organisations wishing to promote animal-drawn carts. Credit availability for such women should be addressed.

In some cases, carts can have a detrimental impact on women. For example, women may lose control of certain income if men use carts to transport produce that was formerly headloaded to market by women. However, almost all the women interviewed in the UNIFEM survey felt that, on balance, animal-drawn carts were of benefit to them.

References

Barwell I and Malmberg-Calvo C, 1988. *Makete Integrated Rural Transport Project. Household travel demand in Makete District: findings from village-level transport survey.* Archive 192. Intermediate Technology Transport, Ardington, Oxon, UK. 127p.

Doran J, 1989. *A moving issue for women: is low cost transport an appropriate intervention to alleviate women's burden in Southern Africa?* Gender Analysis in Development Subseries 1. School of Development Studies, University of East Anglia, Norwich, UK. 83p.

Gaidzanwa R, 1990. *Consultancy report on low cost rural transport in Zimbabwe.* United Nations Development Fund for Women (UNIFEM), Harare, Zimbabwe. 29p.

Howe J and Zille P, 1988. *The transport demands of small-farm households in Africa: a synthesis of IT Transport research.* Archive 169. Intermediate Technology Transport, Ardington, Oxon, UK. 36p.

Women and animal traction technology: experiences of the Tanga Draft Animal Project, Tanzania

by

Andrew C Makwanda

Counterpart Project Manager, Tanga Draft Animal Project, PO Box 228, Korogwe, Tanga, Tanzania

Abstract

Tanzanian national policies recognise that society cannot develop fully without actively involving women. Women are much more involved in agricultural production and in domestic activities than men, but at present they do not enjoy equal status with men. In particular, they do not have the same opportunities as men to acquire skills in new technologies, such as animal traction. One of the main constraints is women's lack of access to investment capital or loans to purchase draft animals and implements: available loan schemes require securities which women cannot provide. Also, social and cultural factors mitigate against women using animal traction.

In contrast to many development projects, which only pay "lip service" to women's issues, the Draft Animal Project in Tanga Region is involved in several programmes specifically designed to help give women access to investment capital through unsecured loans, and hence to involve them fully in the development and use of animal draft technologies. Key issues for the future include the provision of specialised training opportunities based on the use of women trainers to overcome cultural barriers.

Background

Agriculture is the main occupation of the people in Tanzania: this sector employs more than 80% of the country's population of about 24.5 million people, and contributes around 61% of Gross Domestic Product and 75% of foreign earnings. Tanzania's agriculture is mainly based on smallholdings, and only 14% of the land is cultivated by larger enterprises.

Tanga region, in the extreme north-east of Tanzania, covers an area of 2800 km^2, of which almost 18% (480 500 ha) is cultivated, and about 3% is used for grazing and pasture. The rest of the land is covered by bush, forests and swamps.

With annual rainfall ranging from 600 to 2000 mm, most areas in the region appear to get sufficient rain to sustain rainfed agriculture. But the unreliability of rainy seasons and the relatively low probability of minimum precipitation are major problems for agriculture. Average temperatures range from 5 to 32°C.

The present population is 1.32 million, 86% of which live in rural areas. The average population density for the whole region is 49 people/km^2. The annual population growth rate (1978 to 1988) is 2.1%, which is slightly less than the national average of 2.8%. Children (0–14 years old) comprise 46.7% of the population, the middle-aged group (15–54 years) 44.9% and the aged group (over 55 years) the remaining 8.4%. The active labour force comprises 41.6% of the total population; 39.4% are engaged in agriculture and 2.2% in industry, including part-time craftsmen.

By 1990 Tanga region had a total of 866 000 cattle and some 3800 donkeys: 160 of the donkeys were imported into the region from neighbouring areas through the efforts of the Tanga Draft Animal Project

Animal traction promotion

By December 1991 the Tanga Draft Animal Project had promoted animal traction to a total of 300 farmers in 120 villages spread over the region; a further 60 farmers had started using the technology, but had stopped, for various reasons, since 1981. Of the existing active farmers, 32 are women (24 as individuals and the rest in organised groups). Active working animals and implements in the region comprise about 450 oxen, 240 donkeys, 270 plows, 170 carts, 25 ridgers, 35 cultivators and 30 harrows. A total of 16 farmers' clubs (self-help "savings and credit" societies) have been organised and supported to assure sustainability of the technology.

A total of 21 demonstration plots are operated and maintained as a means to disseminate suitable crop husbandry practices to farmers. Some 131 local village extensionists have been trained on the technology and are fully involved in providing extension services to farmers. These complement the efforts of 11 seconded extensionists (one being a woman) and 12 animal trainers (two being women) stationed at the project to serve farmers in rural areas.

Position of women in Tanzania

Tanzanian national policies emphasise the need to give adequate attention to the development of women in society. It is recognised that society cannot develop fully without actively involving, and tapping the potential of, the greater portion of the community—the women. Women do almost all the domestic work and play a major role in agricultural production. But they own hardly any land (they thus find it difficult to get loans and are overlooked by agricultural advisors and projects) and are concentrated in the lowest paid occupations.

Women are dramatically under-represented in decision-making bodies (from household level up) because of their poorer education, lack of confidence and greater work load. In addition, male "chauvinism" very often tends to overshadow women's initiatives and efforts, and poses a threat to further initiatives.

Although the household appears to operate on a team-work basis with regard to family-oriented activities, women and children are generally regarded as "helpers" in achieving goals set by men. Household members' rights and obligations to each other are determined by their relative positions in a male-dominated age–gender hierarchy. The responsibility for ensuring that households are able to meet their survival needs rests with the household head, who allocates resources such as land, draft animals and equipment and provides purchased inputs for agricultural production.

Because women are not property owners, it is difficult for them to have full control over the use of family resources, especially when their ideas or interests are in conflict with those of the male household head.

The rate of adoption of animal power for farm operations could have been faster if a more appropriate approach had been taken to recognising women as farmers in their own right, independent from men. One major problem is that there has been little progress with regard to women's access to capital for draft animal investment. Although women are encouraged to apply for loans, banks and other financial institutions have very strict and tough regulations on loans (for example, on compulsory securities) which many women cannot meet.

Many women's programmes do little more than pay "lip service", for propaganda reasons, to women's issues: although projects may decide to include women as a priority, this is often just to be able to meet their own ends rather than to help women to solve their social and economic problems. Worse still, most women in rural areas are not aware of the facilities offered by financial institutions in urban areas. How can one expect them to make full use of such services?

Women and animal traction in Tanga

The Draft Animal Project in Tanga Region initially followed the traditional approach of supporting household heads (in most cases men), the

Women learning to plow during a demonstration arranged by the Tanga Draft Animal Project

Photo: Paul Starkey

assumption being that they would disseminate the acquired skills to all the other members of their families. This approach, however, reached only a few women, and the impact on them was negligible. By 1987 it was, in the main, only male household members who had access to the technology, and worked with draft animals and implements.

There are several reasons why the men have not involved the women in animal traction. For example:

Physical factors. Draft animals are regarded as wild animals, to be confronted by men who are deemed to be somehow stronger and more courageous than women.

Cultural barriers. Along the coastal belt (which is mainly Muslim), women cannot stay away from the house for long periods without the prior consent of their parents or husbands. Because using animal traction technology would keep them away, it contradicts the cultural norms and values.

Status. Women have no power of disposition over the household's resources and means of production (land, capital, labour, know-how, etc).

Something needs to be done to boost the social and economic position of this disadvantaged group in society.

Since 1988 the Draft Animal Project has been striving, through publicity meetings, demonstrations, open discussions and interventions during extension work, to encourage women to make full use of this technology. Women are now convinced that draft animals can relieve their day-to-day burden of supporting their families. Female members of farming families, women household heads and women's groups are approached actively and shown how they can benefit socially and economically. Some examples of the success of this approach are presented below.

Since November 1990 two women's groups and two individual women farmers have been working on a road regravelling scheme run by the Norwegian sponsored rural roads maintenance programme (RRM), in cooperation with the Draft Animal Project. RRM finances the procurement of the required draft animals and implements. It does this in cooperation with the special fund for promoting self-help activities, sponsored by the Norwegian Agency for International Development (NORAD). The sponsored farmers are contracted by RRM and are obliged to work for a reasonable time while servicing the loan. No security is required from the women, and loan recovery is effected through monthly deductions from their wages. The women do all the work themselves, from excavating the gravel to spreading it on the road. This arrangement not only gives the women gainful employment (albeit seasonal), but also helps them to acquire investment capital. The scheme has also attracted more farmers to draft animal technology.

The Draft Animal Project has created a small "revolving fund" from its own resources to help needy women farmers who are in a position to repay extended short-term loans. The women enter into a contract with the project and a loan recovery schedule is mutually agreed between the two parties. Five women's groups and 22 individual women farmers have been assisted by this programme.

Other organisations have also started to show an interest in assisting women farmers in the region, in cooperation with the Draft Animal Project. For example, the GTZ-supported Village Development Programme has assisted one women's group by financing the purchase of draft animals and implements. The United Nations Development Fund for Women (UNIFEM) has just become active in the country, concentrating mainly on small projects. It has already shown interest in exploring ways of assisting women farmers in the region. Existing farmers' clubs, organised as self-help "credit and savings" societies, are a potential source of initial investment as well as the working capital. As women are active members of these clubs, they can share this advantage with their fellow male members.

The Draft Animal Project's efforts have shown that good progress can be made towards extending the use of draft animal power if women have access to capital for initial investment.

Some key issues

Strategies for development of women

Without proper strategies the move to accelerate the involvement of women in development, by giving them easy access to initial investment capital (at least for their mini-projects), will never materialise. Most programmes seem to be initiated in the name of "female emancipation" by people who do not want to be seen to be unaffected by the propaganda and pressure surrounding the International Decade for Women. Because there are no appropriate strategies directed at women, these "propagandist" programmes mainly end up benefiting men (as usual).

If we are to be serious about the development of women, women should be approached and fully involved as a group independent from men: women's particular social and economic characteristics must be considered and, if possible, incorporated into the planning and implementation of the programmes. For example, because women are not sole property owners at household level, asking them to provide securities for bank loans is both pointless and an obstacle to full utilisation of what are sometimes known as "soft bank loans for women development".

Sustainability

If the use of animal traction is to be sustained and expanded among women, the sociological aspects of animal traction need to be addressed at least as much as the technical and economic issues.

Status of animal traction

Some planners and policy-makers discourage the promotion of animal traction technology; they perceive it as merely an archaic technology to be used only as a "hobby" or as a last resort, even when it is demonstrably appropriate under prevailing social and economic conditions. This deprives women of opportunities to engage in income-saving and income-generating activities through, for example, the use of draft animals for contract work on rural road regravelling, plowing and transport.

Training

When planning training in animal traction technology, thought should be given to the particular needs of women. For example, women might feel more confident about learning to use animal traction if they were taught by women trainers. Also, many husbands and parents are hesitant to allow their wives or daughters to stay away from the farm or home during training with male trainers, and the use of women trainers might alleviate this problem.

Conclusion

Experience of development projects has proved that projects that are not gender-specific do not treat women and men equally. On the contrary, women are often not given the same opportunities as men, even though they are much more involved in agricultural production and domestic activities. It is therefore justified to pay specific attention, and give explicit support, to women to enable them to use draft animal technology efficiently.

The major constraint to the full involvement of women in draft animal use is lack of access to draft animals and implements, due to the lack of investment capital and to male "chauvinism". Specific measures must be designed and implemented to address these problems and to involve women fully in this technology. Women need to be trained in the use of animal traction either by including them in existing programmes or by designing specific women's programmes. The prevailing social and economic situation in most of our societies confirms the impression that animal traction is a useful and appropriate technology, with many advantages to women; if properly utilised, this technology could lead to important increases in women's incomes and to improved nutrition for their household members.

A woman farmer, who was trained by the Tanga Draft Animal Project, using donkeys for weeding

Women's access to animal traction technology: case studies from Darfur, Sudan, and Turkana, Kenya

by

Simon Croxton

Intermediate Technology Development Group, Myson House, Railway Terrace, Rugby CV21 3HT, UK

Abstract

This paper compares and contrasts the experiences of two projects—one in Sudan and the other in Kenya—which have, as part of a wider work programme, attempted to introduce animal traction technology. In both cases there has been an explicit attempt to ensure that women, who are traditionally responsible for the majority of cultivation tasks, are provided with the necessary skills and knowledge to access this new technology. Project successes and failures are described and discussed. The paper concludes that local culture and the context in which innovation takes place are crucial factors that need to be addressed if, in patriarchal societies, women are to gain access to animal traction technology. The importance of understanding technological innovation as a social process is stressed.

Introduction

This paper examines the experience of two development projects which have, as part of wider programmes of work, attempted to ensure that women have access to animal traction technology. Although these two projects—one in Sudan and the other in Kenya—were in very different cultural settings, there are many similarities between them. The projects' experiences are compared and contrasted to draw lessons that may be applicable to other projects. The paper briefly examines each project's approach to draft animal technology and looks specifically at their experience of attempting to that ensure women have access to this.

In both projects there was, on paper, a firm commitment to ensuring that women cultivators had equal access to project extension messages. Both projects worked through local institutions as a means of ensuring community participation in decision making and of working towards long-term sustainability. In both cultures most cultivation work is done by women. Both are patriarchal societies, where men are far more likely to take the lead in any new initiative. Men will also take the lead in any interchange with people from outside the community. In both cases the use of animal draft for cultivating was an innovative practice.

Kebkabiya, Darfur, Sudan

Kebkabiya Area Council lies in a remote part of Sudan's western state of Darfur. The majority of the population practise rainfed subsistence agriculture, with millet being the major crop. The Oxfam funded Kebkabiya Smallholders' Project works mainly with rainfed cultivators.

Project work started in 1986, developing out of a relief initiative following the famine of 1984/85. In its early days the project concentrated on establishing seed banks in a number of central villages as a means of increasing food security. However, the project soon became involved in providing a small level of agricultural extension.

To facilitate the operation of the seed banks and, later, other activities, the project worked through local committees in several villages that were natural centres of rural life. These committees consisted of elected members representing the central village and outlying hamlets.

In some of the areas the women formed separate committees, as they felt that they were unable to make their voices heard at meetings where men were present. In other centres the committees comprised both men and women. The project did not have a fixed policy on this, but rather preferred to allow women to make up their own minds on the institutional structure that they felt was most appropriate and would best serve their needs.

Despite men's tendency to dominate relationships with project staff, they have never objected to the formation of women's committees or to the project's attempts to target women specifically.

The committees were able to articulate farmers' priorities to project staff and, as the project expanded, it began to try to address a number of these. Assistance with introducing draft animal power was one of these priorities.

The majority of farmers had never used draft animals in their fields. A few of the wealthier families had used camels for plowing, but most farmers could not afford to use these expensive animals. Donkeys, which are widely used as beasts of burden, were chosen as an alternative draft animal. Nearly all households own at least one donkey.

Donkey plows

Early work with draft animal technology concentrated on identifying and developing suitable tillage equipment. Because of the combination of low household cash incomes and very poor communications with the remainder of the country, it was felt important to develop equipment that could be made by local village blacksmiths.

Experiments with various designs were initially carried out on the project's three demonstration plots. Farmers were also encouraged to try plows in their own fields and their experiences were fed into the design process. Training courses in plow maintenance, cultivation techniques, donkey training, husbandry and harnessing were held throughout the project.

By the end of 1988 the project had identified two possible alternative plow designs, which were being manufactured by blacksmiths and sold to farmers. The demand was very high and the project could not ensure that enough plows were manufactured to meet it. Despite the considerable support provided by the project, a survey in 1989 indicated that very few women had any knowledge of plows or had seen them in operation at the demonstration sites. It was clear that the plows were being used predominantly by men, and hardly any women used or owned plows. This is despite the fact that women traditionally do the majority of cultivating.

Involvement of women

The project was explicit in its determination to understand and take account of the particular situation facing women. However, this proved to be far easier to state on paper than to put into practice.

Merely talking to women proved difficult. It was easy to sit and talk with men, who dominated all contacts with outsiders (eg, project staff). Even when women were specifically addressed by female project staff, progress was slow. Although Arabic is used as a general language, many women do not speak it, but use their own language. To complicate matters further, there are various ethnic groups living in the project area, each with their own language. Women's lack of fluency in Arabic reflects their culturally determined role. Women travel about far less than men, and women are far less likely to receive formal education than men (and formal education is limited for both sexes). Female project staff who initially worked on the

project came from other parts of Darfur. This reflected the original policy of the project to employ staff with formal educational backgrounds (nearly all were graduates). The female project officers identified their own lack of local language skills as a major constraint to progress with the women's groups in general. This general difficulty was reflected in the lack of success in reaching women with the project's animal traction programme.

Female extension staff

In an attempt to overcome this constraint, two local women were recruited as "women's project officers". Although neither of these were graduates, they did speak *Fur* (the local language of one of the larger ethnic groups in the project area); in the light of experience, this was felt to be more important than formal qualifications. However, their own lack of training and experience in either community development or agriculture slowed the pace of work.

Employing new female staff members did not immediately improve the situation. The new female staff initially suffered from another form of prejudice on the part of some project staff. The problem was not so much that they were women, but that they did not have formal training.

The overall thrust of project policy was not to push for radical change in the cultural make-up of the communities with which it worked, but merely to ensure that women had equal access to any extension messages or other services offered by the project. To do this adequately, it was necessary for the female project officers to understand all aspects of project work. The agricultural extension messages were simple, being based around improving crop rotations, contour cultivation and using draft animals for cultivating. However, there was resistance from some staff members to providing this basic knowledge to the newly appointed female staff. It was claimed at first that, because these two women had no formal training in (for example) agriculture, they could not possibly be rapidly trained.

These problems were raised during routine project management meetings and, over time, were resolved through discussion. This has resulted in greatly improved relationships among the project staff and should enable the female staff to work more effectively in future.

Unfortunately, drought has caused major crop failures during the past two seasons and this has disrupted the project's programme of work. It still remains to be seen if the project is any closer to providing women cultivators with greater access to draft animal technology.

Lokitaung, Turkana, Kenya

Lokitaung Division is in the north-east corner of Kenya's remote Turkana District. The Turkana people are pastoralists who supplement their diet with cereals: some have traditionally cultivated sorghum in the wet seasons.

The Lokitaung Pastoral Development Project (LPDP: formerly the Lokitaung Water Harvesting Project) has been active since the early 1980s. Animal draft had been mentioned in the original project proposals and has been an important component of project work since 1985.

As in Kebkabiya, work at LPDP developed out of relief initiatives after widespread livestock epidemics in 1979–81 devastated the Turkana's pastoral economy. Following the famine a major relief effort was launched and, as part of this, Food for Work (FFW) was used in a widespread way throughout Turkana. The construction of bunds to capture run-off was a common form of "work" that was used on various projects. During its early days, when the LPDP was concentrating on improving sorghum gardens by incorporating bunds, the project also used FFW.

Earth-moving with oxen-drawn scoops

Considerable earth movement is necessary to construct bunds and level the gardens. The heavy workload imposed on people, especially women, in carrying loads of earth on their heads in *karias* (metal bowls), prompted project staff to introduce draft animals for earth-moving.

Although the Turkana own many animals, they had never used cattle or donkeys for draft before. They would not, initially, use their own animals and so the project purchased oxen, and also provided scoops and scraper boards.

Although the "new" technology was adopted fairly rapidly, it soon became clear that the draft animals were being monopolised by the men, while the women continued to have to move earth on their heads.

By this time, project staff were increasingly concerned about the effect of FFW on people's perceptions of the job they were undertaking. It appeared that people were alienated from the purpose of garden construction, feeling they had little control over decisions and were working merely for food payments. However, with so much FFW being offered by neighbouring projects, it was difficult for the project to move away from FFW

completely. People had expectations of receiving food for any activity. (The negative effect of FFW on project activities, and attempts to overcome these by moving away from it, are not discussed in this paper.)

The project then changed the way in which FFW payments were made. First, FFW rates were lowered. Then, instead of FFW payments being calculated on the amount of earth moved, individual contracts were made with garden owners. Food payments were made once a garden was completed. Although this change was made in an attempt to overcome some of the negative effects of FFW, it had an unintended effect on the use of draft animals. Gradually, the men stopped monopolising the draft animals and women were able to use them as well.

It appears that a change in perception of the usefulness of draft animals was triggered by the change in the way the work was organised. While there were relatively large payments of food for moving relatively small amounts of earth, there was no real incentive to use animal draft. As FFW rates dropped, more interest was shown in animal draft. However, there was still little incentive for men to share the draft animals with women. Although the removal of drudgery from the work was appreciated by men, they had used their dominant position in their society to keep the technology for themselves. The fact that the women had to work very hard was not regarded by the men, who controlled decision making, as a sufficiently serious problem to justify widening access to the "new" technology. However, once contracts with individual gardeners were made, it became worthwhile for everybody to work in the most efficient way to ensure that garden construction took the minimum length of time. This meant that as many people as possible should use animal draft power for rapid earth-moving. It was then that women's access to draft animal technology increased.

Project work on draft animal technology continued, identifying and developing suitable implements and training local blacksmiths to manufacture them. Animal draft was introduced for cultivating as well as for earth-moving, as it was felt that the use of draft animals merely for earth-moving was unlikely to be a sustainable practice. As no one was prepared to use their own oxen, the emphasis moved towards the use of donkeys as draft animals. Turkana women traditionally control the use of donkeys as pack animals.

Anthropological study

At the same time, an anthropologist was working with project staff on a study of women's roles in

Turkana society. The anthropologist was able to feed results from this study directly into project policy through informal conversations with the project coordinator as well as through more formal written reports. It is also possible, although untested, that the anthropologist increased the women's self-confidence merely by treating many of their concerns as valid areas for attention and possible change.

One of the major impacts of the anthropological study was the use of women as extensionists in garden cultivation. Acknowledging women as the people who traditionally did most of the cultivating, the project relied on specially trained women to show others how to use draft animals. Using extensionists who have a good understanding of the traditional role of women in gardening, and who are sympathetic to their needs, has resulted in a situation where a high proportion of women have at least some experience of using draft animal technology.

The anthropological study also resulted in elected women representatives sitting on the local Management Board that nowadays runs the project. This ensures that the voice of women is heard at the senior decision-making level and this in turn reinforces their access to all activities promoted by the project, including animal traction technology. The animal draft component of the project was the first activity that women became involved in and it served a valuable secondary role in providing a mechanism for empowering women and has resulted in their active participation in other project activities.

Very recently, the FFW component of garden construction has ceased. This will allow the project to develop more responsive initiatives to traditional gardeners in the area. The real test of the value of the project's approach to draft animals will be to see if the new technology can "escape" the confines of the project and its members and become available to the women who tend the traditional sorghum gardens.

Conclusion

What lessons can be learned from these two case studies? First, it is clear that local culture needs to be taken into account when introducing a new technology. In both cases, the patriarchal nature of the society required special attention to be given to the situation facing women. One means of addressing this problem is by ensuring that the

project is able to interact with women in a suitable fashion, for example by having staff that speak the local language (as in Kebkabiya), employing female extensionists (as in Lokitaung) and by having women represented in the decision-making forum (as is done on both projects). The experience in Kebkabiya also draws attention to the need for all project staff to be supportive to this process, even when it challenges entrenched ideas of professionalism.

It is worth noting that in neither of the examples have men objected to the project targeting women in specific situations. The problem of ensuring equitable access to a new technology stems instead from the general status of women in these patriarchal societies, where men dominate decision making.

Second, the context in which a new technology is introduced may also have a great bearing on the manner of its adoption. The LPDP experience, of the increased access of women to draft power following a change in the way FFW rates were calculated, is an example of this. It also provides an illustration of how, when the relative returns to labour change, new practices become attractive.

While progress at Kebkabiya would appear to be slower than at Lokitaung, it must be realised that there have been considerable disruptions to work on this project over the years. These disruptions have been due to factors beyond the project's control, such as inter-tribal fighting, widespread banditry, and successive droughts and the resultant harvest failures. It is fair to say that in both projects there is still considerable room for improving women's access to draft animal technology.

The underlying message in these case studies is that technological innovation is a social process. It is not merely a matter of providing technically suitable solutions to a given technical problem. While it is important to get the technical side right (plows that do not work well or are difficult to maintain are unlikely to be adopted), it must not be forgotten that technical innovations come about as a response to on-going social processes. Projects attempting to introduce new technologies must ensure that they are taking these social factors into account. In both examples, the issue of women's access to draft animal technology had little to do with the design of implements, but a great deal to do with the approaches adopted to promote the new technology.

The importance of women's participation in animal traction in Zambia

by

Margaret Lombe[1], Christine Sikanyika[2] and Annie N Tembo[3]

[1] Deputy Animal Draft Power Coordinator, Department of Agriculture (Northern Province)
PO Box 410018, Kasama, Zambia
[2] Senior Agricultural Supervisor, [3] Senior Female Extension Officer
Female Extension Section, Department of Agriculture, PO Box 50291, Lusaka, Zambia

Abstract

Although animal traction technology may be said to increase the workload of women, because the use of animal power allows larger areas to be cultivated, it can also provide many benefits, especially if women can own their own draft animals and animal-drawn implements. Increased agricultural production will improve the nutrition and general standard of living of rural women and their families.

The development of animal traction technology should be appropriate to suit the conditions under which women operate. Thus women should be fully involved in the development process, they should be consulted on the design of animal-drawn implements and equipment, they should be properly trained in the handling and care of draft animals, and they should be given access to credit facilities for purchasing animals and implements.

Introduction

In recent years efforts have been made both by the international community and in Zambia as a whole to integrate women in all aspects of agriculture and rural development. Yet development experts have often tended to introduce technologies and activities that cut women off from critical resources.

It is generally assumed that developing countries will not be able to produce enough food to sustain their predicted populations if traditional methods of farming continue to be used. There have been a number of donor-supported programmes aimed at introducing improved technologies into agriculture and food production. Although improved agricultural technologies can provide rural women with the means to perform their traditional tasks more efficiently, rural women in general lack both access to improved technology and the education necessary to increase their productivity.

This paper discusses some of Zambia's stated objectives for the agricultural sector and the implications and impact of women's access to animal traction technology. The majority of Zambia's rural population depend on agriculture for their livelihood, and although women make up 53% of this group, their participation in animal traction activities has been minimal. The paper makes suggestions for more and better integration of women in animal traction technology.

Why the emphasis on women?

Research shows that women play a very important role in agriculture, and the need to integrate women in development is now widely recognised.

This recognition has further been backed up by the inclusion in Zambia's Fourth National Development Plan of some objectives that relate to the issues of women and development of the agricultural sector. These objectives state that, during the period of the plan, the agricultural sector is expected to:

o   achieve a satisfactory level of self-sufficiency at household, community and national levels in the production of staple foods

o   promote the use of animal draft power, with emphasis on oxenisation

o   improve rural employment and incomes

o   ensure that rural women and the youth are active participants in, and beneficiaries of, agricultural and rural development activities.

These objectives can only be achieved by giving preferential treatment to traditional and small-scale farmers, the majority of whom are women.

In Zambia's rural population there are, on average, 85 men to every 100 women, and up to one-third of rural households are headed by women. These figures vary by province, and in Northern Province about 16% of households are female-headed.

Constraints to women's productivity

Women carry out the major part of the workload on subsistence food crops: they plant, apply fertiliser, weed, harvest, market and process for consumption. They are also fully involved in the preparation of this food for their families. Although women are expected to perform all these tasks, they lack access to production services and resources. The problem stems from the fact that rural women are not perceived as "real farmers" by development officers, especially field extension workers.

A major constraint to increased crop production by women is the lack of labour resources, especially during the peak of the agricultural season. Therefore women cannot grow labour-intensive crops (they thus concentrate on subsistence crops) and they are unable to cultivate large areas of land. The introduction of labour-saving technologies such as ox-drawn equipment could greatly improve women's food crop productivity.

Rural women's lack of access to farm tools and equipment is common in much of Zambia. Even simple tools such as hoes, axes and rakes are normally unavailable. Most agricultural equipment and implements introduced to Africans in the colonial days only benefited men. Today the situation has hardly changed: despite the increase in the use of ox-drawn plows and other equipment, very few women possess farm equipment. A recent study in Mazabuka and Mumbwa Districts found that women in these areas have to hire most of the equipment, such as tractors, plows, farm trucks and cultivators for their field operations (Milimo, 1985).

In a needs assessment survey carried out in Chadiza District in Eastern Province, only 16% of the women interviewed actually owned work oxen and only 11% owned major ox-drawn implements, such as ox plows. Half of those interviewed had access to work oxen through harrowing.

A survey by the Ministry of Agriculture in six provinces where a women's project was being implemented showed that a major problem faced by women was late planting, mainly caused by lack of labour to finish plowing ready for timely planting. This problem was said to be due to the lack of ownership by women of oxen and ox plows. Lack of credit to buy implements and animals was a major problem facing women, most of whom could not afford the prices of implements and animals.

Implications of animal traction on women's food productivity

Most rural women are traditional farmers who cultivate smallholdings of up to 2 ha, growing mainly subsistence crops such as cassava, finger millet, sorghum, beans, groundnuts and various types of local vegetables. Such farmers hardly ever use expensive farm technology such as tractors. They depend largely on family labour and they mainly use simple hand tools such as the hoe, axe

and rake, not because of preference but because they are resource-poor and have no other choice. However, in those areas where they keep cattle, oxen are used to provide draft power and manure.

This animal draft power can be of great use to rural women for plowing and cultivating their fields. Plowing is less tedious than hand hoeing, and enables more land to be cultivated (Beerling, 1986). Animal-drawn carts can be used for haulage of farm produce from the field to storage and to market. Carts can also carry water and firewood and can be a source of income when hired out to transport fellow villagers and their goods.

Although animal traction technology may sometimes increase the workload of women in the field (because of the increased area cultivated) it has many more benefits than disadvantages, especially if women own their draft animals and animal-drawn equipment. Appropriately designed animal traction equipment can greatly reduce the excessive burden of tedious work faced by most rural women. Time and labour saved can be used for other household tasks such as taking care of children.

The development of animal traction technology must be appropriate to suit the conditions under which women operate. Women need to be fully involved and consulted about the design of animal-drawn implements and equipment and they should receive proper training in how to handle and care for the animals, and how to use the implements.

Oxenisation programmes in Northern Province

Cattle have been used as draft animals in Northern Province since the late 1970s. Some animal power schemes have been operating in the area, but they have experienced considerable difficulties with the introduction of oxen, largely because of:

o   lack of familiarity in keeping cattle
o   problems in obtaining steers
o   problems in obtaining implements and spares
o   inadequate veterinary facilities
o   lack of skilled artisans for repairing and maintaining implements.

In 1992 the Department of Agriculture took over the oxenisation programme from the Village Agricultural Programme (VAP) and the Integrated Rural Development Programme (IRDP) funded by SIDA (Swedish International Development Agency). The programme is now under the Extension Training Support Programme (ETSP) funded by NORAD (Norwegian Agency for International Development).

Programme activities to be carried out include:

○ purchase and supply of oxen

○ teaching farmers to train and use oxen

○ supply of implements and ox carts

○ liaison with the Provincial Animal Draft Power Steering Committee

Constraints causing women to shun the use of animal draft power

In the Northern Province about 16% of households are headed by females but the area cultivated by these households is only 9% of the farmed area, and their use of animal traction is very limited (Table 1).

Table 1: Some characteristics of farm households in the Northern Province, 1990/91

District	Method of cultivation	Number of households	Female-headed households (number)	Female-headed households (%)	Total cultivated area (ha)	Area cultivated by female-headed households (ha)
Kasama	Hand	299	48		517	45
	Oxen	6	0		19	0
	Tractor	0	0		0	0
	Sub-total	**305**	**48**	**16**	**536**	**45**
Mbala	Hand	204	48		400	51
	Oxen	44	5		187	11
	Tractor	0	0		0	0
	Sub-total	**248**	**53**	**21**	**587**	**62**
Isoka	Hand	258	50		614	61
	Oxen	1	1		11	2
	Tractor	2	0		102	0
	Sub-total	**261**	**51**	**20**	**727**	**63**
Chinsali	Hand	239	29		389	27
	Oxen	4	0		7	0
	Tractor	0	0		0	0
	Sub-total	**243**	**29**	**12**	**396**	**27**
Mpika	Hand	244	33		334	40
	Oxen	8	5		19	10
	Tractor	0	0		0	0
	Sub-total	**252**	**38**	**15**	**353**	**50**
Luwingu/Chilubi	Hand	190	25		199	18
	Oxen	1	0		3	0
	Tractor	0	0		0	0
	Sub-total	**191**	**25**	**13**	**202**	**18**
Mporokoso	Hand	187	32		274	19
	Oxen	0	0		0	0
	Tractor	0	0		0	0
	Sub-total	**187**	**32**	**17**	**274**	**19**
Kaputa	Hand	185	20		219	13
	Oxen	0	0		0	0
	Tractor	0	0		0	0
	Sub-total	**185**	**20**	**11**	**219**	**13**
Totals	Hand	1806	285		2945	274
	Oxen	64	11		246	24
	Tractor	2	0		102	0
Grand total		**1872**	**296**	**16**	**3294**	**298**

Source: Central Statistical Office, Kasama, Zambia

Among the reasons for lack of use of animal traction by women may be:

○ shortage of female ox-trainers to encourage women to take up the challenge of animal traction technology

○ male extension staff, who are in the majority, seem to favour the male farmers when it comes to procuring steers

○ most female-headed households cultivate very small areas (less than 2 ha) and so do not qualify for oxen loans from lending institutions

○ draft animals are not included in the loan package by funding agencies who support women's food-producing programmes (eg, UNICEF in Mungwi and Kasama East)

○ most animal-powered schemes are only carried out in specific areas, thus limiting widespread participation

○ trained oxen are rather too big for women who are not accustomed to handling cattle

○ lending institutions need some form of security or contribution from loanees, which the women are unable to provide. A married women would have to produce a letter of consent from her husband before she could be considered for a loan

○ steers are too expensive: the 1992 price of steers was 77 Kwacha (about US$ 0.80) per kg liveweight

○ ranches where steers are sold are out of reach

○ steers are scarce in the western part of the province (Mporokoso, Luwingu, Chilubi Districts)

We would like to stress that since the Department of Agriculture has taken over the running of the oxenisation programme the female-headed households should be given first priority in the securing of steers and implements.

Suggestions for more integration of women in animal traction technology

In order to involve more women in animal traction technology, women should continue to be considered a special target group, because of their multiple and diverse responsibilities. We suggest the following:

○ more research should be carried out on women, using farming systems research. This can be done using case studies on animal traction technology. In order to facilitate the research, we suggest the use of rapid rural appraisal which can be carried out by interviewing a sample of women from different farming systems. Some problems identified can be solved quickly while others will require more research. Before recommendations are made, on-farm research should be carried out to see whether the solutions proposed will actually work

○ a credit package in the form of a pair of trained oxen and appropriate equipment/implements should be given either to individual women or to women's groups

○ more female extension workers should be trained in handling ox-drawn implements.

References

Beerling M-L E J, 1986. *Ten thousand kraals: cattle ownership in Western Province*. Animal Disease Control Project, Department of Veterinary and Tsetse Control Services, Mongu, Zambia. 58p.

Milimo J T, 1985. *Oxen cultivation in Zambia*. Research Report 23. Rural Development Studies Bureau, University of Zambia, Lusaka, Zambia. 77p.

The impact of mobile ox plowing courses for women in the Western Province of Zambia

by

Cara Hocking[*]

Research Student, Western Province Animal Draft Power Project, PO Box 910067, Mongu, Zambia

Abstract

In the Western Province of Zambia, the Animal Draft Power Project has conducted training courses for both men and women. Courses for mixed groupd concentrated on how to improve the efficiency and effectiveness of using draft animal power. Courses targeted specifically at women aimed to teach women how to plow and make use of draft animal power. All the courses lasted one week, and covered plowing, yoking, parts of the plow and how to adjust it—in both theoretical and practical sessions.

A study was undertaken to assess the impact of the courses for women. The results of the study show that ox plowing courses for women are definitely beneficial. The overall number of women plowing has increased. It is apparent that women derive social benefits simply from knowing how to plow. The progression from benefiting from knowing how to plow, to benefiting from applying the skills, is strongly influenced by access to oxen. If oxen are owned by the household, then women who have had training tend to use them. Where the household has to borrow or hire oxen, the impact of the training is less beneficial from an economic point of view, but is still beneficial in social terms.

Animal Draft Power Project

In the Western Province of Zambia, the Animal Draft Power Project of the Department of Agriculture aims to promote and develop the use of animal traction. Recent emphasis has been in the Lui River Valley and Kaoma East District. The project receives Dutch technical assistance through the private sector company, RDP Livestock Services.

The Lui River Valley was selected by the Animal Draft Power Project because it has been identified as an area suitable for rice growing. At present only a small area of the potentially suitable land is under rice cultivation. The limiting factors that appear to be common to many farmers (Bastiaansen, 1990) are:

o lack of funds with which to purchase the inputs (fertiliser, implements, oxen) essential for the initial establishment of rice cultivation

o a shortage of the power (both human and animal) needed to increase the area cultivated,

and limited availability of animal draft power at the optimum time for farming operations

o limited availability and access to implements and spare parts

o poor marketing and infrastructure which provide few incentives for farmers to grow rice as a cash crop.

Kaoma East was selected by the Animal Draft Power Project because of the initial success of farmers in moving from traditional to commercially-oriented farming practices, such as growing maize for sale. However, several factors are limiting further development (Muwamba and Kalonge, 1989), the main ones being:

o shortage of animal draft power for land preparation and weeding operations

o shortage of resources and capital for purchasing commercial crop technology

o limited extension services for the transfer of knowledge to farmers converting from traditional to commercial crops

o poor infrastructure for transport and marketing of crops.

Training in draft power animal

In both project areas, the potential for animal draft power as a means by which farmers can improve their standards of farming and of living justified the promotion of this technology. The training of farmers in animal draft power, and support for the increased use of animal draft power, would provide farmers with the opportunity to:

o diversify from traditional crops to ones with more potential for commercialisation, particularly rice in the Lui River Valley and maize in Kaoma East

o increase the total input of power into the farming system

o improve the timely establishment of the required or planned crop activities.

Targeting women farmers

Women are largely responsible for the production of food for consumption, men for the production of

---

[*] *Subsequent address:*
Thrushes, Stroud Lane, Steep
Petersfield, Hants GU32 1AL, UK

"Improving animal traction technology"

crops for sale. Some women also have their own field separate from their husbands, over which they have sole responsibility and control. Women farmers are restricted in the development of their farming practices mainly by their ignorance about handling a plow and other animal-drawn implements.

Women were targeted by the Animal Draft Power Project for the following reasons:

○   to overcome cultural practices which largely restrict the use of animal draft power to men. By giving both women and men the opportunity to learn about animal draft power, the benefits of this technology are spread more equitably

○   to increase the effective use of animal draft power, by teaching women how to plow. With animal draft power, the potential for commercialisation can be better realised.

Ox-plowing courses have been run for mixed groups of both men and women farmers, as well as for women only. It was assumed that male farmers know how to plow, and so the courses concentrated on how to improve efficiency and the effectiveness of using animal draft power. Courses targeted specifically at women were organised to teach them how to plow and make use of animal draft power.

All courses lasted one week and included both theoretical and practical parts. The four main topics were plowing, yoking, parts of the plow and how to adjust the plow.

A research project was undertaken to assess the impact of the Animal Draft Power Project ox-plowing courses for women. This paper outlines the results of that study which was undertaken while the author was studying at the University of Newcastle-upon-Tyne, UK (Hocking, 1991).

The research project

Study design

The study compared the opinions and activities of women who had attended an animal draft power course with those of farmers (men and women) who had not. The information was collected using a flexible "questionnaire" and informal discussions. Impacts and benefits were identified from the responses. Using a "framework of questions", rather than a rigid questionnaire, gave flexibility to record and explore inevitable variations in the background of the respondents and gather additional information. Each question was used as an entry point into a topic and not merely as a specific enquiry with an expected answer.

The informal interviews, lasting approximately two hours, were held at the home or on the farm of the respondent. Direct observations were also made to verify information given and to provide insights into those activities undertaken by women but not discussed during the interviews.

Sampling

An area was selected within each Animal Draft Power Project area where animal draft power courses had been run in one or several villages, and individuals met by chance while travelling through the sample areas were invited to participate in the study. The information from the respondents was taken to be representative of the farmers of the area, but it may not be applicable to the population outside the selected areas. One week was allocated for data collection in each sample area, and information was collected from 52 respondents. Respondents were categorised as follows:

○   single women who had attended a course
○   married women who had attended a course
○   single women who had not attended a course
○   married women who had not attended a course
○   single men
○   married men.

Results and discussion

Information on the numbers and backgrounds of the respondents in each category is summarised Table 1.

Course implementation

Some women attendants said they avoided practical participation in the course, particularly in yoking. They were able to do this because males on the course yoked the oxen for them. Women also said that the teaching of the initial stages of plowing was too rapid. This could be due to the attendance of men on the course. Instructors apparently adapt the programme towards training in efficiency and effectiveness rather than in actually how to plow.

Benefits to women and their households from animal draft power

There is a distinction between the benefit felt from knowing how to plow, and the benefit from actually applying the skills.

In the Lui River Valley, those who did not apply their skills (attendants and non-attendants) expressed the benefits in social terms, such as independence, assurance and decision making. Those who applied their skills benefited from increased production, made possible by the expansion of their field area and by the increased speed and timeliness of land preparation by animal draft power.

Some respondents pointed out that learning how to plow, and applying this skill, can have negative

Table 1: Background of respondents

| | Women | | | | Men | | |
| | Attendants | | Non-attendants | | Non-attendants | | |
	Single	Married	Single	Married	Single	Married	Total
Lui River Valley							
Number of respondents	4	10	1	4	1	3	23
Number of households using animal draft power	4	10	1	4	1	3	23
Respondents with trained oxen owned and kept in own village	1	5	0	3	1	2	12
Respondents with trained oxen owned and kept in another village	0	1	0	0	0	0	1
Use borrowed oxen only	2	4	1	1	0	0	8
Use hired oxen only	1	0	0	0	0	1	2
Member of group	0	1	0	1	0	0	2
Know how to plow	4	10	0	1	1	3	19
Women who apply plowing skills	2	7	0	1	–	–	10
Men who apply plowing skills	–	–	–	–	1	2	3
Women who used oxen before attending course	2	4	–	–	–	–	6
Kaoma East							
Number of respondents	4	4	8	7	1	5	29
Number of households using animal draft power	4	3	5	6	0	4	22
Number of households using hand hoe only	0	1	3	1	1	1	7
Respondents with trained oxen owned and kept in own village	3	0	2	3	0	0	8
Respondents with trained oxen owned and kept in another village	0	2	2	0	0	0	4
Use borrowed oxen only	0	1	0	0	0	2	3
Use hired oxen only	1	0	1	3	0	2	7
Member of group	2	4	4	5	0	1	16
Know how to plow	4	4	2	1	1	5	17
Women who apply plowing skills	4	3	2	1	–	–	10
Men who apply plowing skills	–	–	–	–	0	3	3
Women who used oxen before attending course	2	0	–	–	–	–	2

impacts, such as an increased workload. In general, however, the benefits of increased production outweighed the disadvantages.

Factors limiting the application of skills

The main factor in determining whether or not women applied their skills was access to oxen. In the Lui River Valley, most of the women who benefited from applying their plowing skills had access to oxen belonging to the households in which they lived. In Kaoma East there is a shortage of oxen, both for hire and for purchase. Women with access to oxen belonging to their own households benefited both socially and economically; those hiring or borrowing oxen only benefited socially.

Another constraint on the application of skills was women's lack of confidence in their ability to plow.

Factors limiting the benefits of animal draft power

In the Lui River Valley the main factors limiting the benefits from animal draft power are poor marketing infrastructure—lack of transport to depots and late returns from sale of crops. The availability of spare parts is also a constraint where animal draft power is virtually a necessity for the cropping of rice.

In Kaoma East, marketing and weeding were identified as the main limiting factors to benefiting from animal draft power. The ability to expand field size using animal draft power leads to problems at weeding times, as the area is too big for farmers to cover and casual labour is scarce. In some areas there are also problems in the supply of fodder.

Course improvements

The most commonly suggested improvement to the course was that it should last longer. This must be assessed carefully. The reason attendants wanted a longer course may have been because their course had been adjusted primarily to the needs of latecomers rather than of those who came at the start.

In the Lui River Valley, management of oxen was suggested as an additional training topic. During discussions several respondents said they appreciated that not owning oxen limited the benefits of animal draft power. Most of the women respondents were hesitant about their abilities to own and manage oxen and thus be able to have direct control. For women, particularly single women and women in tribes that are not traditionally cattle keepers, the problems associated with the management of the oxen negate some of the beneficial impacts of animal draft power. The costs incurred in employing a manager, and of veterinary expenses, need to be considered.

Conclusions

Conclusions relating to both study areas
o   Animal draft power courses for women increased the overall number of women plowing.
o   The total input of power into the farming systems was increased by the additional input of women using animal draft power.
o   By using animal draft power farmers can extend the area cultivated, as animal draft power is faster and easier than hand hoeing.
o   Animal draft power courses provided the opportunity for women as well as men to benefit from this technology.
o   Women with access to oxen within their households are the largest group able to apply the skills learned.
o   Women applying the skills themselves benefit in social terms and indirectly through the economic benefits to the households.
o   Women who did not actually apply the skills benefited in various social ways.

Conclusions relating to the Lui River Valley
o   As animal draft power is almost always used for growing rice, increased use of animal draft power is increasing rice production.
o   Women are limited in applying their skills primarily because they do not have access to oxen owned within their households. Lack of confidence in yoking also inhibits them.

Conclusions relating to Kaoma East
o   The increased use of animal draft power in Kaoma East is providing the opportunity for farmers to commercialise crop production.
o   Shortage of oxen is the main factor limiting the application of skills learned on the course.

Recommendations

Involvement of Animal Draft Power Project
o   Integrate future developments with projects aimed at improving the marketing infrastructure, and the supply of oxen, particularly in Kaoma East.
o   Increase oxen ownership, particularly among single women. Income generated through small-scale group enterprises by women could be put towards the purchase of oxen.
o   Organise, together with extension programmes, follow-up practical courses in plowing and yoking. Women without access to oxen in their own households would then be able to practise skills and build up confidence.

Course structure and content
o   There is a need for a more structured system for advertising the courses being run. Such improvements should reduce the need to increase the length of the course or to repeat parts of the course to cater for latecomers.
o   Introductory meetings should make it clear that attendance is open, and that farmers do not have to be selected before they can attend.
o   Promotion of the courses should continue to be targeted at women. However, men, particularly husbands, should also be involved in the promotional meetings to avoid misconceptions.
o   Ox-plowing courses for women only should run concurrently with courses for men. This would ensure that the course would be suited to the needs of women rather than to those of men.
o   The main subject to be emphasised is yoking. The use of the cultivator or ridger could also be included for more advanced participants. Cultivators would be of direct advantage to women as it reduces the labour of weeding.
o   Including management of cattle in the course would be of advantage, particularly to single women who may be supervising others to manage their cattle.

References

Bastiaansen C, 1990. *Resources for rice cultivation in the Lui River Valley*. Land and Water Management Project, Department of Agriculture, Mongu, Zambia.

Hocking C, 1991. *The impact of mobile ox-plowing courses for women*. MSc Thesis. Department of Agriculture and Environmental Science, University of Newcastle-upon-Tyne, UK. 53p.

Muwamba J M and Kalonge S M, 1989. *Draft power supply and its implications on the improvement of the commercial farming systems of Kaoma District*. Department of Agriculture, Adaptive Research Planning Team, Mongu, Zambia. 9p.

A note on women and animal traction technology in Ethiopia

by

Oumer Taha

Agricultural Engineer, Rural Technology Promotion Centre, PO Box 6, Asela, Ethiopia

Abstract

Women must be integrated in the development process of any country if economic and social growth are to be achieved. Development requires the use of material and human resources. As the productive use of male and female human resources is a key factor in development, more attention should be given to the role women play, and could be playing in Ethiopia. Use of animal-drawn implements such as plows, harrows and carts, could enable women to be more productive, but shortages of implements, poor extension services, and lack of purchasing power limit their adoption. Development agencies should work towards solving these problems.

Introduction

Women comprise about 50% of the rural work force in Ethiopia. They work much longer each day than men because they are involved in both agricultural and household tasks. Women's agricultural tasks include clearing fields, weeding, harvesting, threshing and transport of crops from the fields to the homestead and markets. Household activities include transporting water and firewood, preparing food and looking after children. Yet these activities tend to be undervalued, and women's economic contributions to the household are not appreciated.

One way to raise the status of women, and to enable them to play a role in the development of the country, would be to provide them with labour-saving animal-drawn implements.

Animal traction implements

Several private and governmental organisations in Ethiopia are involved in the development, import and manufacture of animal-drawn implements. Among these the Arsi Rural Development Unit (ARDU), the Institute of Agricultural Research (IAR) and the Rural Technology Promotion Department (RTPD) have undertaken extensive programmes to develop and test different types of mouldboard plows, harrows and animal-drawn carts. The plows were produced by metal-working factories; the harrows and carts by local workshops.

Promotion of these implements mainly involves giving demonstrations and training to farmers and extension agents. Uptake has been low, with farmer interest in the new seedbed preparation implements only being significant in areas with light soils.

In addition to reducing the time needed to plow and prepare a seedbed, the mouldboard plow buries weeds and the spike tooth harrow drags weeds to the edges of the field. Both implements reduce the women's tasks of land clearing and weeding.

Animal-drawn carts

Women traditionally transport seed, fertiliser, farm tools, agricultural produce, water, firewood, etc, on their heads, backs or shoulders. Animal-drawn carts not only reduce the effort of transport, but also enable larger quantities to be transported in a given time. Use of a donkey and cart can increase a woman's transport efficiency more than 20-fold.

Factors limiting adoption

The main technical and socioeconomic factors that limit the development, manufacture and wide adoption of improved animal-drawn implements are:

○ shortage of implements due to underproduction
○ lack of coordination between ministries and other organisations engaged in development, manufacture, marketing and promotion
○ limited purchasing power of smallholders
○ lack of technical skilled manpower
○ shortage of transport, and hence limited opportunities to visit farmers' fields to demonstrate or give training on implement use.

Conclusion

The full integration of women in development will take place only when the human resources that women represent are no longer wasted. In developing countries such as Ethiopia, most women work from dawn to midnight. Introduction of improved animal-drawn implements can dramatically increase women's productivity in agricultural and transport tasks. This should be considered in government and NGO policies.

A note on the use of animal traction by women in North Western Province, Zambia

by

Ivor Mukuka

Agricultural Engineer, Department of Agriculture, North Western Province, PO Box 110041, Solwezi, Zambia

Abstract

The use of animal traction can lessen the burden of women involved in subsistence and semi-commercial farming. Draft animals can assist with land cultivation, planting, weeding, harvesting, carrying water from wells and transporting grain to hammer mills.

In North Western Province of Zambia, as in other parts of the country, women do not normally own animals and have no say over their use, because such decisions are traditionally considered to be in the male domain. Women are therefore deprived of the advantages and profits that arise from animal traction use.

Recently there have been limited changes in the use of animal traction by women in North Western Province. More needs to be done to integrate women farmers in the use of animal power. Women need to be targeted for extension advice and information about loans. Training should be made appropriate to women. The use of women trainers and the holding of plowing competitions for women would help overcome fears and prejudices

Introduction

North Western Province is the third largest province in Zambia. Two agricultural development projects are working in this area: in the northern region the International Fund for Agricultural Development (IFAD) covers Kasempa, Mwinilunga and Solwezi Districts, while the southern region is catered for by GTZ (the German Agency for Technical Cooperation) which covers Kabompo, Mufumbwe and Zambezi Districts.

Cattle owning is traditional in the southern region, but not in the north. The approach to the introduction and promotion of animal traction among female farmers has therefore been different in the two regions, much greater progress having been made in the south. For instance, in the GTZ supported southern area, 4177 out of 14 366 women farmers (30%) were involved in cash crop farming during the 1989/90 season, and of these, 20% had access to plowing services. Participation of women farmers in the work oxen programme has slightly improved with time. For example, the number of ox loans to women increased from six in 1988/89 to 29 in 1989/90, this increase being partly due to the

experience that people have gained in animal handling, but largely as a result of an intervention programme by GTZ, through the Integrated Rural Development Project (IRDP), directed toward women farmers. The IRDP has since established a women's section to promote women's activities.

In the northern region only 10% of oxen users are women. Farmers are generally unfamiliar with oxen because cattle are not generally available in this area.

Advantages of animal traction use among women

Animal traction technology can help to reduce the drudgery of women. For instance, it can make the transport of harvested produce for commercial purposes much easier (and thus help women to earn much needed income), and can also ease the burden of transporting wood and water.

Labour is a major constraint to crop production in the province. Women farmers contribute 59% of the total labour input, so the use of oxen considerably reduces the labour burden among those women farmers. For instance, in sorghum and maize production it is estimated that the average time spent on hand hoeing, ridging, planting and weeding amounts to 1071 hours/ha; use of oxen reduces this time by 56%, to 467 hours/ha.

As a result of the animal husbandry skills shown by the few individual women or groups who have oxen, deliberate efforts have been made to encourage women, either as individuals or in groups, to obtain loans from lending institutions in the province to purchase their own animals.

Constraints on animal traction use

Although the use of animal traction may seem to have been a success for some women, many factors have prevented it from being widely and effectively adopted. It is still difficult for a woman to have access to a pair of oxen in non-cattle-keeping areas such as Solwezi and Kasempa Districts. Here women are generally afraid to handle a pair of oxen.

It will take some time for women to build up their knowledge and confidence.

Among female-headed households, the extra labour involved in managing animals (for herding, for example) has discouraged some from owning oxen.

Incomplete mechanisation of farm operations using animal traction can present problems for women. The use of oxen for plowing can considerably increase the area cultivated, but this also causes an increase in the workload on non-mechanised operations such as planting, weeding and harvesting, which are mainly done by the same women. At peak periods for these operations, women therefore have much less time to devote to looking after their families.

Where oxen are owned jointly by a group of women, plowing is still often late because a large area must be plowed in a short time. This leads to late planting, reduced yields and, ultimately, less income from cash crops and a decrease in the quantity and quality of food crops available to the women's families.

Extension services as a whole are still biased towards men. So are the processes of selecting farmers to qualify for loans and credit. For instance, in 1989/90 only 29 out of 500 ox loans (6%) were given to women. In addition, women do not seem to be given proper information about the possibility of owning oxen.

Training in the use of animals does not take into account the social, cultural and economic conditions of women handling oxen for the first time. Sometimes women cannot join a training course because they are too busy taking care of children and performing other household duties, especially where they have no relatives nearby to help them.

Recommendations

Several steps should be taken to promote ox ownership among women. For example:

○ special efforts should be made to inform women about loans, and suitable women should be given priority in selection procedures for loans and credit

○ training courses for future ox owners should consider the specific fears of women; if married male ox owners participated in training with their wives, these women would become familiar with animals

○ recruitment of female ox trainers would help reduce women's fears and prejudices

○ plowing competitions among women should be encouraged.

Photograph opposite
Women learning to plow during a demonstration organised by the Tanga Draft Animal Project, Tanzania

---

The transfer of
animal traction technology

Transfer of animal traction technology: lessons from project experiences in Zimbabwe, Cameroon and Tanzania

by

René Fischer[*]

Project Manager, Tanga Draft Animal Project, PO Box 228, Korogwe, Tanzania

Abstract

Transfer of animal traction technology is defined as dissemination of knowledge and skills to people and includes extension or training.

Analysis of the extension and training approaches of three different projects suggests the following recommendations: farmers must be interested in what is taught; farmers must be able to use the new technology immediately after training, ie, they must have their own animals and implements; and training is ideally done with the farmers' own animals and implements and on their own fields.

Farmers must take over training and extension activities themselves (within families or from farmer to farmer) as soon as possible because the use of extensionists is costly and transport-intensive. Furthermore, extension staff often find animal traction technology relatively unattractive. Without intensive supervision, the quality of extension and training services deteriorates rapidly. Training of staff must always be accompanied by financial and logistical support and supervision as they work on the farms.

Animal traction technology must be introduced gradually, in a certain sequence, and not all at once. The technology must be profitable. Farmers are first interested in power-intensive operations such as plowing and carting. Later they adopt control-intensive operations such as planting and weeding.

When introducing animal traction to a new area, training and extension is quite straightforward: the main problems relate to economics, supply of animals and implements and animal health. When attempting to improve existing animal traction systems, the choice of extension topics and the upgrading and management of staff pose major difficulties.

Introduction

Transfer of animal traction technology has two main meanings. It can refer to the transfer of ideas, techniques or implements from one area, where they have worked effectively, to another; for example, transfer from industrialised countries to developing countries. This type of transfer is important in order to save unnecessary research and development work. It helps us to avoid reinventing the wheel.

In a narrower sense, transfer of animal traction technology can refer to the dissemination of knowledge or skills—transferring or communicating ideas and techniques to the people. Transfer, in this sense, involves basic extension and training.

This paper concentrates on the latter aspect of technology transfer—on agricultural training and extension. It briefly describes three projects on which the author has worked; these differ considerably and cover a range of extension and training approaches. It then discusses some general conditions which facilitate transfer of animal traction technology, and some obstacles frequently encountered.

WADA oxen project, Cameroon

The Wum Area Development Authority (WADA) oxen project was based in Bamenda, North-West Province of Cameroon. It later became the Project for Promotion of Permanent Farming Systems based on Animal Traction (PAFSAT). The project started with a one-year residential course for new farmers. It rapidly changed to a system involving four-week training courses in temporary training centres. This allowed participant farmers to sleep in their homes, and was much more successful. Credit was provided for oxen and implements, initially from the project, and later from an independent institution. Project extension workers provided follow-up services, including the project's animal health programme.

Later, the character of the project changed from a mechanisation or oxenisation project to a farming systems development project, also advising hand-hoe farmers.

Recently, marketing of crops was identified as one of the major bottlenecks for the farmers, and the project is trying to assist by transporting and selling crops.

This sequence of changes in the main focus of this project reflects two basic findings about agricultural development. First, that mechanisation, and particularly animal draft technology, is an integral part of the farming system. If the intensity of

---
[*]*Subsequent address:*
René Fischer, PO Box 5047, Tanga, Tanzania

agricultural production and the labour situation call for mechanisation, it can be introduced very rapidly. If not, even the best training and extension system will not establish the technology permanently. The second key point is that a farmer's choice of technology is very much influenced by economics.

The effects of these two conditions are very difficult to observe, particularly during the initial phase of a project when there is a temptation to introduce some additional incentives such as free services and soft loans to attract the first farmers who take on additional risks.

In the Cameroon project, when project progress was not as expected reasons were mainly sought in the training and extension approach and messages. In practice, the real causes of slow transfer were the inappropriate farming system and doubtful economics from the beginning.

Agricultural Engineering Training Centre, Zimbabwe

The Agricultural Engineering Training Centre (AETC) in Harare (Photo 1) is mainly an in-service training centre for the agricultural extension service Agritex. Its training manuals on topics such as ox training and plowing are now used in several other countries (AETC, 1986a; AETC, 1986b; AETC, 1987).

Animal draft power has been well introduced on smaller farms in Zimbabwe for a long time. General agricultural extension workers, who are working in areas where draft animals are used, go to the AETC for one-week courses to upgrade their knowledge and skills in mechanisation. Five one-week courses

on subjects related to animal draft power are on offer.

Apart from giving solid basic knowledge and skills in the use of oxen and their implements, special emphasis is given to easier control of oxen through the use of reins, to conservation plowing and to inter-row cultivation.

Considerable time and effort was spent on curriculum development, training of trainers and production of training aids and materials. The centre is well equipped with competent instructors and all the necessary training facilities. Courses are general and not too specific with regard to soils or climate. Once a year, animal traction courses are also run for participants from neighbouring countries.

When the author's four-years assignment with AETC ended, the centre had only just started to assess the impact of the training courses in the field. Some feedback was obtained from participants when they returned for another course, but there was no direct and immediate link to farmers.

Tanga Draft Animal Project, Tanzania

The Tanga Draft Animal Project in the north-east corner of Tanzania is introducing the use of draft animals to an area where this technology had practically no tradition. On the smallholder farms in the area, almost all operations are carried out manually.

Although cattle and donkeys are kept in Tanga Region they were never used for work, apart from using donkeys as pack animals and some short-lived

Ox cart in front of the mural on the workshop of the Agricultural Engineering Training Centre, Zimbabwe

Photo: René Fischer

Photo: René Fischer

Plowing competition organised by the Tanga Draft Animal Project, Tanzania

attempts to introduce oxenisation in the 1970s. Reasons for the absence of draft animals may be:

○ prevalence of many cattle diseases

○ traditional and religious taboos

○ advances in agromechanisation mainly took place on the big sisal, tea and coconut estates

○ investments for annual crops are considered risky due to unreliable rains.

There is need to promote the use of draft animals in the region because:

○ infrastructure and size of land holdings allow only limited economical use of tractors

○ labour is not sufficient to cultivate all land

○ suitable animals are kept in Tanga Region anyway

○ promotion of draft animal use is a national policy.

Project organisation and activities

The Draft Animal Project is run by the Tanzanian Ministry of Agriculture, supported by the German aid agency, GTZ. The project has one regional coordinator, six zonal extension coordinators, subject matter specialists (one of whom is a woman), 12 ox trainers (two women), one technician and three administrative staff, plus helpers and one expatriate adviser. These provide the following services to the farming community:

○ selection of suitable implements and animals, and recommendations for their use and maintenance

○ publicity campaigns to attract and select new farmers

○ assistance in procuring oxen, donkeys, implements and, where necessary, credit

○ training courses for extension and veterinary staff and farmers

○ follow-up services for active draft animal farmers: regular visits, demonstrations, field days, competitions (Photo 2)

○ maintenance of the Korogwe Animal Draft Centre: animals, implements and crops for training and demonstrations.

New project approach

The agro-ecological environment is very delicate, both where animal health and agricultural production are concerned. Since the beginning, when the project was promoting oxen, adoption has been slow. Diseases and animal losses were the major problems at that stage. Considerable improvements in adoption rates by farmers were achieved by making changes in the project's approach, namely:

○ switching to using local oxen

○ including donkeys as draft animals

○ introducing a suitable donkey cart

○ using animal-drawn carts for gravel haulage on a contract basis.

Substantial animal losses caused by various diseases (East Coast Fever, anaplasmosis, trypanosomiasis) seriously threatened the viability of the new technology. The exclusive use of farmers' own animals or cattle purchased in the farmers' villages reduced animal losses to an acceptable level and improved the viability of the technology. Previously, animals had been bought from ranches and then distributed to farmers living in a very different environment, and the rapid change of environment and management was often too much for an animal's delicate health. Further, by selecting cattle keepers, use could be made of farmers' existing experience in animal husbandry.

Donkeys became a very interesting alternative to cattle, particularly for farmers who did not have cattle or experience in cattle keeping and where animal draft was exclusively used for transport. Donkeys are more hardy than cattle and seem to be able to withstand local conditions with less intensive care. Adoption rates for donkeys did not increase substantially before a suitable design of donkey cart was found and produced locally.

An example of a problem

A women's group in Kabuku village in Tanga had purchased a pair of donkeys and a cart, were trained, and were seen using their cart frequently on the road, carrying water; the animals and cart were always in good condition. Recently, however, the project received a letter from the Chairman of Kabuku village, stating "... you manager come quickly with medicine to castrate your donkeys because they are eating our goats. Come here, hand in hand with the members of the women group and we will have a meeting to deal with you and your donkeys". When visiting the village project staff found that one male donkey, which was not castrated, had developed an interest in goats, particularly during market days when female donkeys came to the village. There was, however, no evidence to suggest that the donkey had seriously harmed the goats, even less eaten them! The project came to the conclusion that the villagers' allegations were mainly fuelled by jealousy of the women's group who were obviously earning a good income through transport. In order to remedy the situation the notorious male donkey was replaced by a female, and it is hoped that the donkeys will not give any more cause for complaints and that, given time, the villagers will tolerate or even appreciate the new technology.

Different project approaches

The objectives, activities and, particularly, training and extension approaches of the three projects differ considerably. The Draft Animal Project in Tanzania and PAFSAT in Cameroon are similar projects in that they both operate in areas of introduction, where animal traction technology was previously nonexistent. In both these areas animals and experience in animal husbandry are available and from agronomic, economic and sociological points of view animal traction technology was considered feasible. (Incidentally, it would be interesting to learn of any comparable animal traction feasibility studies which did *not* recommend the start of a project, to compare subsequent experiences.)

The Tanga project in Tanzania differs from the Cameroon project in that it was part of a larger integrated project which allowed a much more comprehensive approach towards improving the living conditions of the rural population.

On the other hand Tanga Region is not exactly an easy area for the introduction of animal traction technology. Oxen are small and plagued by trypanosomiasis and East Coast Fever. The local population is not very business-oriented and has strong traditional beliefs against putting animals to work. Farming systems are very diversified and include permanent crops such as coconuts and cashew nuts. There are very few examples of commercial, well managed field crops in the region, which also means that this concept is not present in the farmers' memory. Farmers cannot get credits from banks or other lending institutions.

To reduce animal losses the project insists that farmers have their own animals or buy them. Animal trainers stay with the farmer family for about four weeks to train animals and people. Extension officers provide follow-up services to help overcome initial problems and the project organises one-week courses for groups of farmers in the villages to complement animal training. Due to lack of credit it is not possible to train groups of farmers with their animals in the same location. Some experienced farmers have also started to help fellow farmers to train their first animals.

Veterinary services are provided by local veterinary assistants. The project is still the sole distributor of implements and spares in the region.

In order to assist the project to establish a permanent infrastructure to support the technology, the project has encouraged the farmers to form clubs.

At the moment the technology is profitable where farmers can combine on-farm use on their crops with contract plowing or carting. The critical question for more widespread use is whether farmers will perceive animal draft power technology as a means to reduce the negative effects of the typically unpredictable rainfall.

Factors favouring technology transfer

To summarise, the following are considered the most important factors influencing the successful transfer of animal draft power technology.

○ Farmers must be interested in the topics that the extension workers want to teach them. Farmers must see a realistic chance that the new technology will allow them to earn more money or make their lives easier.

○ Farmers must use the new technology when they go home after training, ie, they must have their own animals and implements.

○ Farmers must take over training and extension activities themselves (within the family or from farmer to farmer) as soon as possible, because the large number of small farms per unit area makes the use of paid trainers and extensionists very costly and transport-intensive; and because, for employed staff, animal traction technology is less attractive and motivating than other technologies. Without intensive supervision and staff management the quality of extension and training services deteriorates rapidly.

○ There is need for continual follow-up because draft animal farmers have limited means of communication and transport.

○ Animal traction technology has to be introduced gradually, in a certain sequence, and not all at once.

○ There must be an economic basis to run the technology profitably (mechanisation does not develop agriculture!)

○ Farmers are firstly interested in power-intensive operations such as plowing and carting. Only later do they adopt control-intensive operations such as planting and weeding, which need specific skills and interact with agronomic practices.

○ Training is ideally done with the farmers' own animals and implements and on their own fields. Maintaining a training centre with all the facilities for practical training is very costly.

○ Training of staff must always be accompanied by financial and logistic support and supervision when they work in the villages with farmers.

○ When introducing animal traction to a new area, training and extension are quite standardised and predictable: the main problems lie in economics, supply of animal and implements and animal health.

○ When attempting to improve existing animal traction systems, the choice of training and extension topics, and upgrading and management of staff, pose major difficulties. Trainers and extension workers must be more flexible and highly trained to communicate and cooperate with the farmer. In a well developed system it is not easy to find standard messages which apply to the majority of farmers.

References

AETC, 1986a. *Selection, care and training of draft cattle for agricultural extension workers and extension supervisors.* Manual AP1. Agricultural Engineering Training Centre (AETC), Harare, Zimbabwe. 161p.

AETC, 1986b. *Ploughing with draft animals: course for agricultural extension workers and extension supervisors.* Manual AP2. Agricultural Engineering Training Centre (AETC), Harare, Zimbabwe. 100p.

AETC, 1987. *Crop establishment using draft animals: course for agricultural extension staff.* Manual AP3. Agricultural Engineering Training Centre (AETC), Harare, Zimbabwe. 100p.

Experiences with the use of a single ox for cultivation in the Ethiopian highlands

by

Abiye Astatke[1] and M A Mohammed-Saleem[2]

[1] *Agricultural Engineer and* [2] *Agronomist and Team Leader, Highlands Research Site*
International Livestock Centre for Africa (ILCA), PO Box 5689, Addis Ababa, Ethiopia

Abstract

Tests on the use of a single ox with a modified maresha *plow were carried out in Ethiopia at the International Livestock Centre for Africa (ILCA) Debre Berhan station, on farmers' fields at Debre Zeit, and on a test track at the Agricultural Implement Research and Improvement Centre (AIRIC) near Nazareth. The power developed by a single local zebu animal using the V-yoke was 0.3 kW under field conditions and varied between 0.15 and 0.19 kW on the test track; a pair of oxen is capable of producing 0.4 kW.*

In 1985 the ox/seed project was started in the Ankober and Seladengay Woredas of Northern Shoa Province to help drought victims. A total of 1800 farmers were each supplied with an ox, grain seed, a modified maresha *and a V-yoke. There were problems with disseminating the use of single oxen in these areas. Extension of the technology was made difficult by the physical environment (steep slopes, high percentage of stone cover and hard soils) and by the farmers' negative social attitude towards the technology. Also, the farmers were not given adequate training in the use of the single ox with the modified* maresha. *The adoption rate of the technology was therefore low.*

Introduction

Oxen pulling the traditional plow (*maresha*) provide the main draft power for tillage operations in Ethiopia. The oxen used for traction are indigenous zebu breeds weighing 270–330 kg (Goe, 1987). A typical farmer uses a pair of oxen for 450 hours a year for cultivation and threshing (Gryseels, 1983).

The major constraint to crop production in Ethiopia is the inadequate availability of draft power, a result of the unequal distribution of oxen among households (Gryseels et al, 1984). According to the Ministry of Agriculture (MoA, 1980) 29% of Ethiopian farmers have no oxen, 34% have one, 29% have two and 8% own three or more. As oxen are traditionally paired for work, more than 60% of farmers have to rent or borrow at least one animal for cultivation.

Ox ownership and cropping pattern

Surveys by the International Livestock Centre for Africa (ILCA) (Gryseels et al, 1984) have shown that the number of oxen owned by a farmer strongly influences both the area cultivated and the cropping patterns.

To ensure timely cultivation, farmers with less draft power till smaller areas rather than spread the available draft power over larger areas, which may result in lower yields. In the Debre Zeit area, where land is intensively cropped, the surveys found a linear relationship between the number of oxen owned and the area cultivated (Table 1).

Because crops vary in their cultivation requirements, the choice of crops is influenced by the availability of draft power. Land preparation for cereal crops is more labour intensive and requires more draft power than preparation for pulses. Thus only farmers with adequate draft power are able to concentrate on growing cereals (Table 1). Furthermore, because the market value of cereal crops is about twice that of pulses, farmers with less draft power have lower

Table 1: Impact of ox ownership on area cultivated and cropping pattern at Debre Zeit, Ethiopia, 1980

Number of oxen owned by farmers	Average area cropped per farm (ha)	Percentage of area sown to cereals	Percentage of area sown to pulses
None	1.2	54	46
One	1.9	44	56
Two	2.7	67	33
Three or more	3.6	92	8

Source: Gryseels et al (1984)

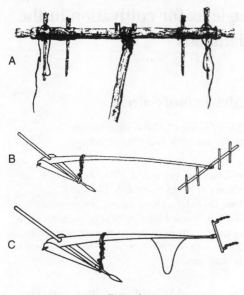

Figure 1:
A) Traditional Ethiopian double yoke (after Goe, 1987)
B) Yoke attached to traditional maresha *plow*
C) Skid and swingle-tree attached to traditional maresha
plow, to allow it to be used by a single animal

incomes than their counterparts with an adequate supply of draft power.

The availability of draft power is therefore a major factor affecting food production and income distribution.

Modified yoke and *maresha*

During 1983 ILCA developed a yoke and modified the traditional *maresha* to enable it to be used by a single ox. The traditional withers yoke used by a pair of oxen (Figure 1) was replaced by a V-yoke. The V-yoke is made of wood padded with processed animal skin (Photo 1); two hooks are bolted on each cross member of the V-yoke to tie the two trace ropes joining the swingle-tree. In the modified *maresha* a metal skid is attached under the shortened beam to overcome the tipping force in the absence of the counterbalancing force exerted by animals using the withers yoke.

On-station trials

On-station tests of the V-yoke and modified *maresha* (performed at Debre Berhan) revealed no technical problems (Photo 2). An adequately fed zebu ox could cultivate some 60–70% of the area plowed by a pair, although depth of cultivation was slightly shallower than with the traditional *maresha* (Gryseels, 1983). However, these trials were carried out on clay loam soils and on relatively flat fields with few stone outcroppings; these conditions are not typical of most of the farmers' fields in the area.

In 1983 a more detailed 23-week experiment was conducted by ILCA to determine the effect of diet restriction on work performance and body weight loss of crossbred (Friesian x Boran) and local zebu oxen. Animals were worked as singles with the V-yoke and modified *maresha* in farmers' fields in Debre Zeit. Cultivation started with the first plowing and continued until a proper seedbed had been prepared. The soils on all the fields were Vertisols. Ten local zebu and four crossbreds were divided into two groups to receive normal (control) and restricted diets. Average body weights were 450 kg for each crossbred ox and 300 kg for each local zebu ox. There were significant differences between breeds on depth of plowing, area plowed and cultivation rate (Table 2). However, diet did not have a significant effect on work performance.

The average force exerted by the local animals was 600 N with a power output of 0.30 kW; for the crossbreds the force averaged 680 N with a power output of 0.34 kW. Even though the force exerted by the crossbreds was significantly higher than that by the local zebu animals, power differences between the breeds were not significant. Power developed is a function of force and speed and the speed of animals varied considerably depending on the force and the ox handler. The large difference in the power developed between and within breeds could be attributed to the ox handlers' skills.

A more controlled test to compare the rigid withers yoke with the V-yoke, using a single animal, was carried out on a circular track at the Agricultural Implement Research and Improvement Centre (AIRIC) near Nazareth. The ox used weighed

Table 2: The effects of breed on depth of plowing, area cultivated and cultivation rate

Breed	Number of observations	Mean plowing depth (cm)	Area cultivated (m²/day)	Cultivation rate (m²/minute)
Friesian x Boran cross	256	14.6 a	998 a	4.04 a
Local zebu	613	13.9 b	920 b	3.67 b

Values in the same column followed by a different letter differ significantly (P<0.01)
Source: Abiye Astake, Reed and Butterworth (1986)

300 kg. A loading device fitted with a hydraulic brake mounted on a trolley across the top of the inner wall of the track enabled three levels of pull (300, 450 and 600 N) to be applied. Every day the animal worked for four hours in the morning followed by two hours rest and two hours work in the afternoon for three consecutive days for each yoke at each level of pull. The animal was rested for one day before the yoke was changed and for one week before the level of pull was changed. The type of yoke used and level of pull applied were determined at random.

Speed and power output obtained using the improved V-yoke were slightly higher than those obtained using the rigid withers yoke at all levels of pull (Table 3). For both yokes, the highest power output was obtained at 450 N pull.

The increase in physiological stress was greater during the four hours of work in the morning than during the two hours of work in the afternoon, for both yokes. However, working with the rigid withers yoke induced higher respiration rate, rectal temperature and pulse rate than working with the V-yoke. The modified version of the V-yoke was more effective because it provided a larger contact area for efficient utilisation of the animal's strength (Kebede and Kelemu, 1988). In another set of field trials using the V-yoke and the AIRIC single animal cart, an ox weighing 300 kg was able to pull up to 600 kg pay load on the dirt track for five hours a day without showing signs of fatigue.

Use of single ox on farm

During 1984 an extended drought in the lower altitude areas of the northern and central plateaux of the Ethiopian highlands caused acute food shortages

Photo 1: Skin-covered single yoke

Table 3: Speed and power output of a single ox using V-yoke and the rigid withers yoke

	V-yoke		Rigid withers yoke	
Draft force (N)	Speed (m/s)	Power (kW)	Speed (m/s)	Power (kW)
300	0.53	0.15	0.51	0.15
450	0.44	0.19	0.43	0.18
600	0.32	0.18	0.30	0.17

Source: adapted from Kebede and Kelemu (1988)

Photo 2: On-station demonstration of use of single ox at Debre Berhan

for millions of farmers. As food and seed grain stocks were depleted, livestock were selectively sold (first small stock such as sheep and goats, young cattle and equines, then cows and finally draft oxen) to provide cash to buy food grain (Gryseels and Jutzi, 1986). Cropping practices in the highlands rely heavily on draft animals so the loss of animals seriously jeopardised the ability of the farmer to cultivate sufficient land. To aid the drought victims, the ox/seed project was started in 1985 within the Ankober and Seladengay Woredas of Northern Shoa Province, 180 and 220 km north-east of Addis Ababa, respectively. A total of 1800 farmers received food aid and were also supplied with one ox each, sufficient seed grain, a single ox plow and the V-yoke on credit. Studying how drought-affected families re-establish agriculture and the role animals could play in post-drought recovery were some of the objectives of the ox/seed project (Gryseels and Jutzi, 1986).

The oxen used for traction in the project were mostly purchased in the drought-affected areas of the lowlands and were therefore generally in weak condition, weighing between 230 and 275 kg. Although they were given supplementary feed before being distributed to farmers, they still weighed less than the 300–350 kg that good draft oxen weigh under normal conditions. Gryseels and Jutzi (1986) observed that many farmers received oxen only in June, in the middle of the plowing season. Although the farmers had already started plowing using pairs of oxen under labour exchange agreements, they found the soils too hard, after the drought, to do the first plowing with a single ox. The farmlands of both Ankober and Seladengay were on steep slopes and were covered with stones. Kebede (1988), who also surveyed the project area, reported that the farmlands were heavily eroded and confirmed a good spread of rock outcrops in the fields. He also observed that on farms where the stone cover exceeded 50%, a single ox was ineffective and farmers resorted to pairs of oxen to pull the plow.

Of the 20 farmers monitored, 17 used the single ox plow in the first year, mainly after the third plowing and for planting and seed covering. Initial plowings were done with paired oxen. Because of the short period available for planting, farmers found the single ox useful because they could do the work without having to wait for neighbours' oxen to make up pairs. Comparison of the labour input for planting and seed covering indicates that single ox plowing required 33% more time than using a pair: a single ox needed 57 hours/ha for one pass against

43 hours/ha for a pair of oxen (Gryseels and Jutzi, 1986).

The single ox technology was introduced with the aim of coping with the low draft power at the disposal of farmers. But only less than half of the project farmers wanted to try the single ox technology because of low traction power (especially on stony fields), potential low farm income, and a bias against using a single ox (Kebede, 1988). The farmers' reluctance may also be attributed to inadequate training in the use of the single ox technology.

Problems encountered

Technical

There were several technical problems with the technology. The power that can be developed by a pair of local zebu oxen on hard strong soils after prolonged fallow is 0.4 kW at a working speed of 0.38 m/s (Goe, 1990) The power output of a single ox ranges from 0.2 to 0.3 kW and is therefore inadequate for deep plowing of the same hard soils. So more time is needed to plow with a single animal. But the major problem of using a single animal is that it is difficult to manoeuvre the implement on stony fields or sloping ground. Where a single ox was used for plowing, patches of ground were often left uncultivated; this problem did not arise when a pair of animals was used. These problems were not encountered in the on-station trials at Debre Berhan or during the tests on farmers' fields in Debre Zeit, as these were carried out on relatively moderate slopes (<10%) with no stone cover. On the heavy clay soils in Debre Zeit, plowing with the single animal was conducted during or after the small rains (March/April) when the soil was moist and soft and therefore required less draft power for cultivation.

The other problem was the farmers' unfamiliarity with controlling a single animal as opposed to a pair of oxen. Most farmers use vocal commands when working with pairs of animals, but the implement itself is also used to control the movement of the animals. If the animals move beyond the end of the field, the *maresha* is angled to penetrate the soil deeper to stop the animals. No reins are used in the traditional system for controlling animals. With the use of the single ox and the modified *maresha*, the implement could not be used to control the animal, and the expectations were that the animal would respond to the vocal commands. However, this was often not the case, and the farmers had problems controlling the animal. Also, the skid on the modified *maresha* bent frequently when used on a stony field and had to be changed for a stronger one.

Social

The attitudes of farmers towards a technology must be considered carefully if a high rate of adoption is to be achieved. Gryseels and Jutzi (1986) pointed out that even though the local farmers of the project area were friendly and hospitable, they had little contact with the outside world and were therefore extremely cautious about the introduction of new technologies. Many farmers expected that there were other, less noble, motives behind the project. Kebede (1988) also found that one of the causes of low adoption rates of the single ox technology in the project area was the existence of a cultural practice that goes against it. If these factors had been studied before the introduction of the technology, then decisions could have been made on whether or not to promote it.

Conclusion

The power developed by the single ox is, as expected, lower than that developed by a pair of oxen. For cultivation work, the single ox technology has to be used on lighter soils or on moist and workable Vertisols. Very steep slopes and stony ground should be avoided. Training of farmers in the proper use of the technology is an essential component of its dissemination.

Topographical and soil conditions in the project area were generally not suitable for the technology. Moreover, there was a traditional bias against using a single ox to pull the implement. Also, the project had a wide range of objectives, and it was difficult to concentrate just on the dissemination of the single

ox technology. Because of all these reasons, the adoption rate of the use of a single ox with the modified *maresha* was low.

Acknowledgements

We thank Drs J MaCann and E Zerbini and Ato Daniel Dauro for comments given on the earlier draft.

References

Abiye Astatke, Reed J D and Butterworth M H, 1986. Effect of diet restriction on work performance and weight loss of local zebu and Friesian x Boran crossbred oxen. *ILCA Bulletin* 23:11–14. International Livestock Centre for Africa (ILCA), Addis Ababa, Ethiopia.

Goe M R, 1987. *Animal traction on smallholder farms in the Ethiopian Highlands*. PhD thesis. Department of Animal Science, Cornell University, Ithaca, New York, USA. 280p. [also available from: UMI Dissertation Information Service, Ann Arbor, Michigan, USA.]

Goe M R, 1990. Tillage with the traditional maresha in the Ethiopian highlands. *Tools and tillage* 6(3):127–156.

Gryseels G, 1983. *On-farm animal traction research: experiences in Ethiopia with the introduction of the use of single oxen for crop cultivation*. Paper presented at the Third Farming Systems Symposium held 31 October–2 November, Kansas State University, Kansas, USA. 15p.

Gryseels G and Jutzi S, 1986. *Regenerating farming systems after drought: ILCA's ox/seed project, 1985 results*. Highlands Programme, International Livestock Centre for Africa (ILCA), Addis Ababa, Ethiopia. 46p.

Gryseels G, Abiye Astatke, Anderson F M and Assamenew G, 1984. The use of single oxen for crop cultivation in Ethiopia. *ILCA Bulletin* 18: 20–25. International Livestock Centre for Africa (ILCA), Addis Ababa, Ethiopia.

Kebede Y, 1988. *Economic evaluation of post drought recovery agricultural project: the case of Tegulet and Bulga District, Shoa province, Ethiopia*. MSc thesis. Department of Agricultural Economics, McGill University, Montreal, Quebec, Canada. 193p.

Kebede A and Kelemu F, 1988. *Performance evaluation of single animal harnesses*. Agricultural Implement Research and Improvement Centre, Melkassa, Ethiopia, and Institute of Agricultural Research, Addis Ababa, Ethiopia. 4p.

MoA, 1980. *Distribution of land and farm inputs among the farmers of Ethiopia with special reference to the distribution of traction power*. Ministry of Agriculture (MoA), Addis Ababa, Ethiopia. 52p.

The transfer of animal traction technology: some lessons from Sierra Leone

by

Paul Starkey

Animal Traction Development, Oxgate, 64 Northcourt Avenue, Reading RG2 7HQ, UK

Abstract

Animal traction was introduced in the West African country of Sierra Leone in the 1920s but it did not spread beyond the initial areas of introduction. In the 1950s, a successful animal traction scheme was abandoned due to lack of official interest in the technology. In the 1970s an attempt was made to transfer an Asian system of draft animal power without adapting it to local conditions. Uptake was minimal, partly because a subsidised tractor hire scheme was promoted simultaneously. Animal traction technology was revived in the 1980s by the Work Oxen Project (subsequently Programme) of the Ministry of Agriculture. Through various project initiatives numbers of working animals increased significantly from just 100 in 1980 to over 3000 in 1992. National animal power use is still low. N'Dama oxen are mainly employed in the north of the country for plowing for rice and groundnut cultivation. The use of weeders, ridgers and ox carts is very limited.

Low produce prices, limited farm profitability, weak rural infrastructure, crime, patronage, war, uncertain land tenure and project attitudes restrict many aspects of agricultural development. Specific constraints to draft animal adoption include unstumped farms, unfamiliarity with cattle husbandry, the high cost and low availability of oxen and disease risks. Two other important constraints, lack of suitable equipment and official scorn of the technology, have been largely overcome.

The on-station and village-level research and development activities of the Work Oxen Project provided many useful lessons. Comparative on-station field trials produced little scientific information but proved invaluable for obtaining support from national decision makers and aid agencies. Socioeconomic surveys based on mass data collection were found less valuable than more personal and subjective methods. Farmer testing of implements proved more useful than on-station evaluation, and changed the project's definitions of excellence. Local manufacture of implements posed many problems, and may not have been justified, particularly as the multipurpose toolbars have been used mainly as plows.

The overall approach of coordinated, multi-disciplinary, multi-donor, multi-organisation activities that have combined research, development and extension have provided a stable foundation for further animal traction development. External liaison has been valuable but there were problems in assessing the significance and worth of documents from other countries. The national plowing competitions proved important in making animal traction an accepted element of national development strategy.

Introduction

Objectives

The aim of this case history is to provide an overview of the efforts within one West African country to introduce draft animal power, and highlight features relating to the transfer of animal traction technology. Although some of the observations will inevitably be country-specific, it is hoped that some of the lessons learned in Sierra Leone will prove to be of interest to animal traction programmes in eastern and southern Africa.

This paper is not a comprehensive review of animal traction technology in Sierra Leone but more of an interpretive analysis relating primarily to *institutional* aspects of technology transfer. It therefore complements other published reports on the subject, including those of Starkey (1981; 1982), Allagnat and Koroma (1984), Corbel (1986), Starkey and Kanu (1986), Bangura (1988; 1990), Gboku (1988), Kanu (1988; 1990), Leaman (1988) and Bah (1990). Although the paper is intended to be objective, the presentation of material is inevitably influenced by the fact that the author worked in Sierra Leone from 1978 to 1985 during which time he was responsible for initiating the Work Oxen Project.

The agricultural context

Sierra Leone is a small West African country (73 000 km^2) with Guinea Savannah ecology in the north, where rainfall is 1800 mm, and rainforest in the south, where rainfall exceeds 2500 mm. The staple food of the population of four million people is rice. Upland rice dominates the rain fed intercropping of the traditional bush-fallow agricultural system which accounts for most of the cultivated area of the country. Swamp rice is also widely grown in numerous inland valleys.

The whole country is considered to be of medium trypanosomiasis risk, and the national herd of 333 000 cattle are all of the N'Dama trypanotolerant taurine type. Most (88%) of the cattle are found in the north of the country, where natural pasture is

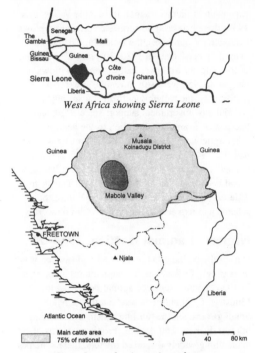

West Africa showing Sierra Leone

Sierra Leone showing main cattle area

available for most of the year, with dry season growth being stimulated by fire. Cattle ownership is concentrated in 5% of the farming population, notably within the Fula and Madingo ethnic groups. Cattle obtain all their feed from grazing natural pasture, but a traditional mineral supplement of leaves, salt and termite hill soil is provided two or three times a year. Cattle are the only important draft animal species: the few horses are seldom used, being maintained for reasons of social enhancement. Imported donkeys have not thrived.

The early years: 1928–1954

The first introduction

The use of animal power in Sierra Leone can be traced back to the 19th century when horses were used for both transport and recreation in Freetown, the capital city and major port. In 1856, a devastating outbreak of disease, now assumed to have been trypanosomiasis, eliminated most of the horses (Dorward and Payne, 1975). Since this time the presence of tsetse flies and trypanosomiasis has effectively prevented the use of horses for work in Sierra Leone. The indigenous trypanotolerant N'Dama cattle never replaced horses as a major source of urban transport, although in the 1920s oxen were used by the Department of Health to pull the Freetown refuse carts (Growcott, 1977).

The use of draft oxen for agricultural purposes dates from 1928. At this time the administration of the country made it illegal to continue a traditional practice of domestic slavery. The Madingo farmers most affected by this ruling complained that without their traditional labour force, they could no longer farm effectively. Tractors had not seemed a feasible option; the first tractor had been imported in 1922 and considerable problems had been experienced in keeping it in working order. However, reports had reached Sierra Leone that in neighbouring Guinea, a scheme had been started in 1919 to introduce draft animals for cotton production. The number of Guinean farmers using work oxen had increased from 24 in 1919 to over 4000 in 1928. Consequently, in an early example of regional cooperation, three Sierra Leoneans were sent to the farmer training school at Kankan in Guinea where 80 farmers each year were being trained.

The visit to Guinea was successful, and in 1928 oxen were trained in three areas of Sierra Leone, and were used to plow over 30 ha around Karina in the Mabole Valley. There followed five years of gradual expansion of use of work animals, and the assessment of British and French plows and harrows.

In 1933 an agricultural officer from Sierra Leone (who was British) was sent to southern India and Sri Lanka to study rice production systems and the use of draft animals. In a comprehensive report he recommended that long-beamed pole plows and triangular spike-tooth harrows be evaluated in Sierra Leone, and noted that although the Ransome *Victory* plow was of excellent quality, it was expensive, and a cheaper plow would be more appropriate for the small farmers (Granville, 1933). Few, if any, of the recommendations were acted on, and the official reports of the 1930s and 1940s contain the recurrent themes of lack of equipment, lack of spare parts, insufficient time for investigations and general economic stringencies. Fewer than 100 plows had been imported into Sierra Leone by 1945. The rate of expansion was in marked contrast to the more

Farmers in the Mabole Valley using Victory *plows bought in one of the early animal traction schemes. These plows have been been in use for over 30 years*

A survey in 1979 of farmers in Koinadugu that had continued to use work oxen since the 1950s although animal traction had officially "died out"

successful Guinean initiative that was stimulated by an export crop.

The Koinadugu and Mabole Valley schemes

In the 1950s there were two modest attempts to promote work oxen. In the Koinadugu District in the north of the country, 72 oxen were trained at the Musaia livestock station between 1950 and 1960, and farmers were able to purchase *Victory* plows. This initiative lasted about 10 years after which the numbers of plows in use slowly declined. The reason given by many farmers for stopping their use of animals was that their oxen, bought in the 1950s, had eventually died. The training had been entirely based at the official agricultural station. Farmers had never been taught how to train their own animals in their villages. A few had managed to train animals themselves, through contacts with farmers in Guinea, but many had simply stored their plows until the official training service reopened. This illustrates the danger of basing animal training in centres, rather than locating it in the villages.

In the north-central part of the country, the Mabole Valley Ox-plowing Scheme of 1950–53 had provided loans to 70 farmers for the purchase of plows and oxen. Although this scheme was abandoned by the government, it had a remarkable, long-term impact. While there had been no

Four people in the Mabole Valley in 1980 working with a 30-year-old Victory *plow for upland rice production*

expansion of animal traction in Mabole Valley after 1954 (there had been no further credit and no plows available for purchase), the technology had been extremely persistent. In 1980, 30 years after the end of the scheme, well over half the original plows bought in 1950 were still in regular use. Most importantly, the technology had been sustained without any government support since 1960, and had passed from one generation to the next. Few other agricultural projects in Sierra Leone have ever had such a long-term impact. The project had not "failed" for lack of farmer enthusiasm, but because it had been forgotten by the authorities. The clear difference between the official perception of the scheme and its value to farmers is very noteworthy.

Neglect of animal traction: 1954–74

During the period 1954 to 1974 animal traction was increasingly forgotten by the agricultural authorities. In 1954 "tractors replaced animal power" at the Ministry of Agriculture's headquarters at Njala. Small government tractor hire schemes were started in most districts, and despite chronic problems of maintaining widely dispersed tractors, these schemes were considered the backbone of the agricultural development strategies. Emphasis on tractorisation increased in the 1960s with independence providing great optimism that rapid agricultural development based on tractor power would be possible.

The establishment of Njala University College with assistance from the United States led to a whole generation of Sierra Leonean agricultural graduates being trained by lecturers who considered that animal traction was an outdated technology. Animal traction did not appear anywhere in the agricultural syllabuses of the university or of the schools.

By the early 1970s there was no official policy relating to animal traction. No one in a senior position within the Ministry of Agriculture, or the university, was aware that ox plowing was still in regular use in parts of the country. There was a general assumption that draft animals were of historical interest only. Even those people who recommended revitalising animal traction gave the impression that ox plowing had largely died out (Kamara, 1974; Growcott, 1977; Starkey, 1979).

Renewed interest: 1974–79

Chinese rice stations

In 1974 a network of rice production and extension centres was established in Sierra Leone, as a result of Chinese technical cooperation. It was envisaged that several technology options would be used and promoted: four-wheel tractors, power tillers, draft animals and hand cultivation. Chinese technicians trained oxen, bulls and cows to work in rice swamps. The animals were harnessed singly, with imported Chinese withers yokes, and pulled wooden plows with cast-iron shares. The equipment, techniques and even command language were those used with buffaloes and large breeds of cattle in China. There seems to have been no attempt to build on local experiences, for example using paired animals or a vernacular language for commands.

The plows were 25 cm wide and required a tractive effort of around 900 N, equivalent to 40% of the weight of a four-year-old N'Dama ox. There was no depth wheel, so that pitch control was difficult, and peak loads of 1.3 kN occurred (65% of the weight of a single ox). There was no attempt to modify the plows in order to reduce the draft to a level appropriate to the N'Dama breed.

The centres attempted to promote the use of draft animals in the same areas in which they were also providing highly subsidised plowing services with tractors and power tillers. Not surprisingly, farmers were not interested in investing in draft animals when they could obtain tractor plowing for a cost that only covered the fuel. By the time the tractors had all broken down, people had forgotten that there had ever been an animal traction component of the project. While animal traction and tractor power can be complementary rather than competitive, there seems little point in trying to transfer animal traction technology at the same time as providing subsidised mechanical cultivation services.

Proposals to develop animal traction

During the 1970s there were several proposals to develop animal traction in Sierra Leone. Kamara (1974) suggested that animal traction would be an ideal technology for the smaller farmers. A budget was included in the Koinadugu Integrated Agricultural Development Project in the north of the country to enable it to develop an ox training programme, and the Ministry of Agriculture accepted, in principle, a proposal to set up two ox training centres (Growcott, 1977).

In 1978, a pilot research programme was started at Njala University College (NUC), and a proposal was prepared for a project designed to investigate the feasibility of developing a national draft animal programme (Starkey, 1979). The project was intended to be a multidisciplinary study, based initially on equipment evaluation and replicated trials at NUC and the collection of documents and information from a wide variety of sources. It was envisaged that a well-documented research programme was justified even if it was decided that

animal traction was not a viable technology in Sierra Leone. Much of the project proposal was devoted to highlighting the probable constraints to the development of animal traction that would have to be addressed. Several academic staff of Njala University College considered animal traction a topic unworthy of research and criticised the programme as a "U-turn back to the stone age".

Sierra Leone Work Oxen Project

The Sierra Leone Work Oxen Project started in 1979 with a small budget provided by the Ministry of Agriculture. It was charged with promoting animal traction through adaptive research, extension and training. The project had its headquarters at Njala University College but initially there were no full-time staff and no budget for salaries. French and British volunteers were recruited to carry out programmes of experimental research, equipment evaluation and a socioeconomic survey on the potential use of draft animals. As funds became available to pay salaries, graduate research assistants were recruited locally, and after appropriate training they took over responsibility for the project.

All staff started their work by training a pair of animals themselves at Njala University College. Graduate staff expressed mild resentment of this at first, arguing they had not been recruited to work as ox handlers. However, the confidence that this experience gave them greatly assisted in their subsequent work. As the project developed this practice became standard, and although the *initial* resentment was always noticeable, project officers (Sierra Leonean, French and British) invariably concluded their experience had been invaluable.

On-station research at Njala University College

Initial work at NUC in 1979 included the training of animals, the testing of different equipment designs, and a study of the literature from past animal traction initiatives within Sierra Leone and

Use of a single ox to weed cowpeas during on-station trials at Njala University College

neighbouring countries. Field visits were made to find out the experiences of farmers who had used animal traction before, and at this point the strong persistence of the use of draft animals during previous decades became apparent. It was estimated that about 50 pairs of oxen were still in use in the country. Since farmers who had continued to use work oxen for many years were satisfied with their yoking system, head/horn yokes from the villages were copied for use at NUC.

In 1980 a series of comparative on-station field trials was undertaken to establish whether the use of draft animals was both technically and economically viable. Rice, maize, groundnuts and cowpeas were grown in replicated plots using hand cultivation, tractor cultivation and a range of different animal-drawn implements. Details were recorded of the labour inputs, the tractive efforts, the weed infestation and the eventual yields. These were analysed for statistical significance and the economic implications were discussed (Starkey and Verhaeghe, 1982; Starkey, 1981).

In retrospect these replicated trials conducted in a research station environment produced little scientific information of relevance to the farming systems of Sierra Leone. They established that good seedbed preparation with animal-drawn mouldboard plows could control weeds effectively, but this was already known to farmers both within and outside Sierra Leone. They also showed that while work oxen appeared economically attractive compared with either manual labour or tractors, crop farming in Sierra Leone was of very low profitability and any technological investments were hard to justify. Farmers knew this already.

Demonstration value of research plots

Despite their lack of realism, the experimental trials had important benefits for the animal traction programme in Sierra Leone. First, the trials built up the confidence of the project staff. Second, they provided comparative figures relating to the use of draft animals which, although derived from artificial farming systems, were essential for presenting the case to funding agencies for further work on the use of work oxen in Sierra Leone. Third, they provided valuable demonstrations to university staff and visitors that animal traction was a viable option.

At this time the most eloquent arguments in favour of developing animal traction could have been heard from the farmers of the Mabole Valley, but decision makers seldom, if ever, travelled there. Had the project spent all its efforts in the early years undertaking farming systems research in the villages of Koinadugu and the Mabole Valley, this would

have led to much greater understanding of the needs of small farmers. However, it is ironical that such understanding probably would not have changed national policies nearly as much as did the few unrealistic, on-station trials at the university.

The people with power to decide whether to support animal traction development in the country were senior ministry officials, heads of non-governmental organisations (NGOs), diplomats, representatives of donors and aid agency consultants. Such people spent most of their time in offices in the capital city, but occasionally they would visit Njala University College. Thus, in retrospect, the main value of the research plots had been to give animal traction crucial visibility and accessibility that stimulated discussion and enabled busy decision makers to quickly grasp a few points, that could later influence policies and budgets.

Attempts to make the formal trials more relevant by repeating them at several locations within the country overstretched the available staff. The large amount of variation produced within the multilocation trials meant that statistical analyses could not distinguish treatment effects from other variance. Replicated experimental trials were then dropped from the Work Oxen Project programme as requiring an unjustified amount of management time.

Instead more subjective comparative demonstrations were undertaken on farmers' fields. These were not sufficiently replicated to allow statistical analyses, and so, released from the need for uniformity, they could be modified during the course of a season in accordance with farmers' ideas. The results were not suitable for academic publication, but the lessons could immediately be discussed by the project and the farmers and by the farmers' neighbours. These trials paved the way for the more subjective, collaborative research and development that became an integral part of project strategy and philosophy.

On-farm demonstration of use of Pecotool *to weed upland rice in the Mabole Valley*

Photo: Paul Starkey

Search for information and contacts

From its inception, the Sierra Leone Work Oxen Project requested information concerning animal traction from several international, bilateral and NGO aid agencies. Many documents were received describing experiences in other countries, but in the early stages, it was very difficult to distinguish between hard experience and "nice ideas". Over half of the documents received had been produced by "appropriate technology" enthusiasts and had been published or disseminated by organisations such as the Intermediate Technology Development Group (ITDG) and Volunteers in Technical Assistance (VITA). Reports were almost invariably optimistic, yet there was no way of knowing whether the technologies had been successfully transferred to farmers, or rejected. For example, well-produced documents describing "successful" wheeled toolcarriers nearly diverted valuable project time to a technology that had never actually been accepted by farmers (Starkey, 1988a).

Several publications relating to a nearby country, The Gambia, strongly influenced project thinking during the next few years. These advocated the use of multipurpose toolbars that could be used for weeding as well as plowing (Matthews and Pullen, 1975; Mettrick, 1978). It is likely that these reports led the Work Oxen Project to place excessive emphasis on multipurpose implements; at that stage all the farmers wanted were cheap and simple plows.

As the Work Oxen Project developed its networking approach to information exchange, it participated in study visits and workshops in several neighbouring countries. Direct contact with other seasoned field workers and, more importantly, visits to farmers in other countries, provided the project with much experience and many insights to actual problems that could never have come from the optimistic literature received. In 1986, the project hosted an international workshop on Animal Power in Farming Systems (Starkey and Ndiamé, 1988).

Equipment evaluation

An early objective of the project had been to identify appropriate designs of animal-drawn implements. The only plows in the country were Chinese wooden ones which were insufficiently robust for upland soils and required excessive tractive effort in swamps. Several designs of multipurpose toolbar were imported including the *Houe Sine* from Senegal, and the *Anglebar* and *Pecotool* from the UK. Lightweight plows informally imported by traders from Guinea were also obtained.

On-station testing of a triangular harrow for swamp rice production at Njala University College

All proved satisfactory during on-station trials. They were then tested by farmers in 15 isolated villages around the country. Maintaining these implements in good condition throughout a plowing season provided unforgettable lessons for the project. A broken bolt, stripped thread or cracked weld that could have been repaired in minutes at the project headquarters, required a great deal of time and effort, including long motorcycle journeys hampered by the weight and bulk of replacement steel components. The project learned through uncomfortable experience and farmer reaction that reliability and ease of repair were generally more important than technical excellence. If equipment could be continuously used by farmers in remote villages in different parts of a country for at least one season it passed one major test relating to reliability and suitability.

At the end of the season, farmers were asked to return the equipment lent for evaluation. If it was readily returned, the equipment had probably failed the test of farmer acceptance (perhaps it had been difficult to use). When equipment had been really useful, the farmers would suggest numerous reasons why it should not be returned. Farmers who found equipment economically useful were generally ready to buy it for a realistic second-hand price.

Equipment production

An early objective of the project had been to have a facility for fabricating equipment. The main justification was not economic but was to allow standardisation and to allow designs to be rapidly changed in accordance with local demand. Various proposals were prepared and a donor agreed to fund a project to rehabilitate a Ministry of Agriculture workshop. An equipment designer from the UK worked with local staff to produce the jigs necessary to manufacture *Pecotool* multipurpose toolbars, using imported steel and components. Local manufacture posed many problems for the project, and the time and money spent trying to produce equipment locally may not have been justified.

The logo of the Work Oxen Project

Constraints to local production included the problems of maintaining isolated workshop services, obtaining spare parts for machines, theft and corruption, and obtaining a balance between excessive management supervision and ensuring quality control. There was also the problem of the parallel ("black") market. Goods, including steel or ready-manufactured implements, could be imported by the project at the low official exchange rate, and could be costed at this rate. On the other hand, most goods and services purchased in local currency, such as welding rods, diesel fuel and bottled gas, were based on prevailing black market prices. As a result it was cheaper (in terms of official exchange rates) to import fully manufactured implements than to make them locally. At the same time, inflation rose dramatically as the local currency was devalued by about 2000% in seven years. In such circumstances, the project should have started to increase its equipment prices frequently and charge on the basis of *replacement* costs (rather than actual purchase cost). However, in the interests of good relationships with farmers, implement prices were fixed every season. Thus a sustainable revolving fund could not be built up, and workshop funds were rapidly eroded by inflation.

Although the project invested its time, resources and reputation in selecting and fabricating a good quality multipurpose toolbar, single-purpose plows could have been made more strongly and more cheaply. Ready-manufactured plows could have been imported from Asia for a fraction of the cost. Had

Pecotool *toolbar manufactured in Sierra Leone*

Photo: Paul Starkey

there not been a local supply of plows, the various development projects in Sierra Leone would have had to order implements from other countries in accordance with the regulations of their supporting aid agency. This would have led to greater equipment diversity, but many more problems in providing spare parts and continuity of supply.

The project manufactured ox carts for sale, but relatively few have been sold. Two alternative designs were made. The first type used imported axles, with roller bearings and pneumatic tyres. This was considered of good quality but it was expensive and the tyres meant risk of punctures and theft (stolen for use on motor vehicles). The alternative "Wananchi" cart had metal wheels and wooden block bearings. This used locally-available materials but had a heavier weight and draft. Constraints to cart adoption included their high cost, hilly terrain and the very limited numbers of roads and wide tracks in rural areas.

Local blacksmiths have been instrumental in keeping plows working for over 30 years. The project tried to contact blacksmiths in all areas in which it has operated and identify their constraints. It has assisted blacksmiths with the supply of materials, tools and training (Kanu, 1990).

National coordination and catalytic role

To ensure adequate liaison, a national work oxen coordinating committee was established, comprising representatives of the Ministry of Agriculture, the university, all the main agricultural development projects with animal traction components, NGOs interested in animal traction and representatives of relevant aid agencies. The coordinating committee met twice a year and served several purposes: it allowed the sharing of ideas and experiences, restricted the unnecessary duplication of efforts, established communication channels and reduced jealousies and rivalries that might have existed (unofficially) between programmes.

From the outset the Work Oxen Project was designed to be catalytic, providing technical advice and training services to other agricultural development projects and organisations to enable them to develop their own animal traction components. The catalytic role was decided for pragmatic as well as methodological reasons: since the project had no significant funds of its own, its only option was to advise organisations that had resources to achieve the desired ends.

Had the Work Oxen Project been initiated in the form of a major project, co-funded by an aid agency, there would not have been the same need to cooperate with other projects. The project could have operated for the period of the external funding largely independent of other projects, possibly with a fleet of vehicles and project headquarters. At the end of the period of external funding, its activities and effectiveness would probably have collapsed. However, as a result of the multi-donor and catalytic approach, by 1986 more that 20 projects and organisations in Sierra Leone had their own draft animal programmes (Kanu, 1988). With such a range of programmes the "risks" were spread, and the outlook for animal traction development became far more stable than if activities were dependent on just one or two budgets influenced by the whims of key individuals within ministries or aid agencies.

Training and technology transfer

The project started from scratch, in a situation where almost no agricultural staff in the country (or in the project) had knowledge of animal traction. This may have been fortuitous, for the project was obliged to learn from experienced farmers and those few agricultural agents who had been involved in the schemes of the 1950s. With information gleaned from farmers, books and old annual reports, the project trained a small team of extension workers. The team gained practical experience in villages that already used animal traction, by assisting with equipment testing by farmers, situation analyses and data collection. The core team went on to train workers of other projects in areas selected for pilot introduction. From the outset, farmer training in areas of introduction was village-based and labour-intensive. Where possible, farmers were taken to see village-based demonstrations (such as plowing competitions) in areas of animal traction use. Demonstration sets of animals were maintained at cooperating institutions in several parts of the country, and these were taken to villages for demonstration purposes (and could be hired out for plowing and transport).

In the more favourable and cattle-rich areas, notably in the north, animal training became less of a problem, as farmers were encouraged to learn from other farmers. As knowledge and skill transfer became mainly farmer-to-farmer, the local projects concentrated more on issues of credit, implement supply and animal health. Elsewhere, particularly in new areas, basic knowledge of animal traction remained a limiting factor and extension agents were still required to demonstrate and teach animal traction skills. This remains the case in many parts of the country.

All staff of the Sierra Leone Work Oxen Project started by training a set of work oxen themselves

Publicity activities and plowing competitions

From the outset, the project placed high priority on publicity. It was a small and generally unknown project operating in a country where there was considerable scepticism on the practicality and desirability of using draft animals. The name "work oxen" was chosen as easier to understand than "draft animal". A project logo of animals plowing was developed and used to convey the objectives of the project. Wooden boards, shaped as silhouettes of oxen, were designed to catch the eye, and the project participated in agricultural shows, displaying equipment, oxen and exhibitions of photographs.

Such static exhibitions could be, and sometimes were, dismissed by planners and aid agency representatives as irrelevant enthusiasm for "appropriate technology". If such people went to the villages where farmers had used work oxen for generations and saw the farmers' own enthusiasm, they might be convinced that the technology was worth investigating. This led to the organisation of national plowing competitions at a village in the Mabole Valley to which senior ("air-conditioned") agriculturalists and decision makers were invited.

The farmers of the Mabole Valley responded with enthusiasm so that visitors saw 60 or more animals plowing at the same time. In addition, farmers came from far away, and the sight and sound of other farmers using draft oxen was far more convincing than any village extension demonstration by project staff could have been. The impact of these annual competitions on visitors was immense, for the spectacle was impressive and provided unique opportunities to see a widely dispersed technology in a concentrated form. As more ministry and university staff and aid agency representatives attended these competitions, the reputation of the project slowly changed. What had been a neglected and scorned technology became an accepted option

Invited guests, including the President of Sierra Leone, viewing an ox plowing competition

for the small farmers. In 1985, the President of Sierra Leone was the guest of honour at the village-based plowing competition.

Socioeconomic surveys

From the outset, the project was anxious to obtain as much information as possible concerning the realities of animal traction use in villages. A socioeconomic survey was planned in 1979 in accordance with the conventional wisdom prevailing at that time, when the large Integrated Agricultural Development Projects, and their supporting donors, favoured mass data-collection for baseline surveys. Enumerators were trained and assigned to each of nine villages in different parts of the country. They stayed in the villages throughout the cropping season, and details were recorded of areas cultivated each day by those farming with animals and those using hand labour. Information was collected on the daily use of the animals, and the time allocated for grazing them. Although some records were lost through sickness and absences, a filing cabinet full of data was built up, and partially analysed.

Unfortunately, the expatriate supervising the survey left prior to the final analysis, and this meant that even fewer lessons were learned from the difficult exercise than might have been the case. The data were never entered into a computer, and this may have been for the good, for statistical analysis may well have given a spurious authority to any conclusions. In practice, much information, including the "objective" measurements of times and areas, would have probably correlated mainly with the personalities and moods of the enumerators. The detailed data sheets and survey codings disguised the fact that the young men with secondary school qualifications seldom actually spent their days with a tape measure in a rice swamp or followed grazing animals with a stop watch. They were intelligent enough to produce imaginative estimates for the data sheets from the comfort of their lodgings.

Thus the first attempt at a socioeconomic survey provided useful (negative) lessons on the value of such exercises, and made the project realise that it did not really need data so much as a thorough understanding of the role that draft animals could play in the farming systems. This led to the development of a more subjective and personal approach to the socioeconomic impact of animal traction (Allagnat, 1984). Subsequent surveys were undertaken mainly by senior staff themselves, and rather than looking at daily work rates, the emphasis was placed on what was achieved during a season, and by whom. These surveys were stratified to allow various economic comparisons between ox-users and non-ox-users in villages where draft animals were maintained, and between ox-hirers and non-ox-hirers in villages where no work oxen were owned (Allagnat, 1984; Allagnat and Koroma, 1984).

Gender and age issues

At the outset the project tended to operate in a male-dominated environment: all project staff were men, as were most Ministry of Agriculture officials, aid donor representatives, traditional chiefs and cattle-owning farmers. Socioeconomic surveys indicated that women did obtain benefits from borrowing or hiring oxen, but at that stage most users of animal traction were men. While there seemed no evidence that women were marginalised by animal traction, it was noted that male children of oxen-owning families seemed slightly less likely to be sent to government-run schools (Allagnat and Koroma, 1984) although they benefited from traditional Islamic education.

In order to stimulate the interest of women in animal traction, the project provided training to members of a women's association near the Mabole Valley. In the short term, the association proved mutually beneficial in clearly demonstrating to organisations and local farmers that women could work with oxen as well as men (the winners of the 1985 national plowing competition were young women). However, almost as quickly as young

Members of a women's association plowing with oxen near the Mabole Valley

"Improving animal traction technology"

women were trained, they were married and became unavailable to the association. After some time, the women hired men to work with their animals. Women are involved with animal traction in several parts of the country, but the great majority of ox users are still men.

Present situation and constraints

In 1987, the Work Oxen Project lost its temporary "project" status, and became a programme of the Ministry of Agriculture and its staff were absorbed into the establishment. Animal traction had thus become a long-term element of national agricultural policy. Much of the programme work continued to be implemented through area-specific, donor-assisted projects that had appropriate resources.

By 1992, about 3000 N'Dama cattle were used for work in the country, mainly for plowing. Most implements in operation were single-purpose plows or multipurpose toolbars used only as plows. While some farmers used wooden or steel harrows, very few weeders, ridgers and ox carts were in operation. The numbers of farmers benefiting from the oxen were much greater than the numbers owning oxen, since ox owners almost invariably plowed for several other farmers in the area.

Two fundamental (institutional) constraints to the development of animal power during the period 1978–85 had been the people's attitudes towards the animal draft technology and the lack of equipment. As these two factors ceased to be limiting, the animal health constraint and overall economic conditions appeared increasingly important in many parts of the country.

Animal health

Animal traction had been well-proven by farmers in the north of the country, and animal power extension programmes could be recommended there with some confidence. Elsewhere, it appeared necessary to proceed with great caution. Pilot technology transfer programmes in the south, the east and the central part of the country had recorded heavy loss of animals due to health problems. The existing veterinary facilities and services had been inadequate to determine the causes of the mortality. Some locally-funded research had been undertaken on traditional means of ensuring the health and husbandry of the animals, and a revolving fund had been established to improve the supply of drugs in remote areas (McKinlay, 1990). Nevertheless, there appeared to be areas of the country where there seemed little point in trying to transfer animal traction technology, unless animal health constraints were also solved.

Economic, political and infrastuctural factors

A primary constraint to agricultural development in Sierra Leone in recent years has been low farm profitability. Low prices for farm produce have made it difficult to justify or encourage investment in agricultural technologies. As in many African countries, the influential urban population wants low food prices, and this encourages the government to import cheap food and accept "food aid". The requirement of farmers for assured and high produce prices is difficult to reconcile with this.

The long-standing economic problems have been compounded by more recent political problems, notably rebel incursions. Even outside the areas of unrest, the troubles have had a large psychological and economic impact. Thus, as in many other African countries, many constraints to transferring animal power technology in Sierra Leone have been economic and political rather than technical: large problems of technology transfer are small compared with the major economic and political problems.

Although the infrastructure of the rural areas is very weak, the ability of Sierra Leonean entrepreneurs to overcome such constraints has been convincingly demonstrated in recent years. Small-scale private-enterprise rural transport services (known as "podapodas") and private mining schemes in isolated areas have succeeded in keeping their machines running for prolonged periods despite chronic national shortages of fuel, spare parts and foreign exchange. The implication is that if farming in Sierra Leone was sufficiently profitable, the farmers and entrepreneurs would find ways of sustaining the necessary technologies.

Crime

Theft, corruption and patronage remain major sociological constraints to the development of agriculture in Sierra Leone. Animals can be easily stolen and disposed of as meat, equipment can disappear and crops can be stolen from the fields. Widespread corruption means that crime generally does pay. The combination of crime, corruption, uncertain land tenure and traditional and governmental patronage means that farmers face high risks. Farmers have been reluctant to put their time and money into long-term, high risk farming investments, such as animal traction, particularly when farm profitability has been low. Projects can do little to change such situations, but some interventions, such as the development of recognisable branding systems for work oxen, may increase confidence and/or reduce crime and improve the prospects for draft animals.

Project mentality

For the past thirty years, both the Ministry of Agriculture and the rural economy have been strongly influenced by donor-assisted projects, lasting between two and eight years. These have provided ministry staff with various "perks" and have temporarily provided subsidised services or inputs to farmers. Projects have been able to import equipment free from most of the problems and charges incurred by the private sector. A vicious circle has developed, and as projects have provided more subsidised products and services, the private sector has become less involved in the supply and distribution of comparable inputs. Even village blacksmiths have found it difficult to make a plow share from a car spring for less than the (subsidised) cost of an imported share.

While donors increasingly talk of privatisation of services and sustainable private sector initiatives, no one really expects the formal private sector to bother with something as difficult as animal traction (widely distributed market, high transport costs, seasonal sales and high price sensitivity). With the chronic shortage of steel and manufacturing capacity, any workshop that could make plows, could make more profit by making other items for the urban or transport markets. Thus all involved (government officials, private sector services and farmers) anticipate that if one project supplying inputs "fails", another donor-assisted initiative will follow. In such a situation, the prospects for long-term sustainability of local equipment supply seem poor, but prospects for village level persistence of the technology remain high.

Conclusions

Sierra Leone provides a fascinating case history relating to the transfer of animal traction technology. Despite various attempts at oxenisation and tractorisation, human energy remains the main power source in the dominant bush-fallow farming systems. Cattle are in short supply in much of the country. Apart from the north, the country appears only marginal for successful cattle raising (although climatic changes and increasing bush clearance have made it easier for draft animals to survive). Similar problems (but not identical conditions) relating to an apparently unfavourable combination of climate, disease, scarcity of animals and extensive farming systems based on shifting cultivation are found in many other West and Central African countries including Guinea, Guinea Bissau, Ghana, Togo, Benin, Nigeria, Cameroon, southern Tchad, Central African Republic and Zaire. They are also found in

several parts of eastern and southern Africa: including northern Zambia, north-east Tanzania, northern Mozambique and south-west Uganda. There have been some comparable pilot animal traction schemes within these countries and animal traction is slowly spreading in similar "unfavourable" humid and semi-humid areas.

In Sierra Leone, as in many other areas where animal traction has been largely unknown, lack of farmer knowledge of animal traction has been a limiting factor, requiring extension programmes. Often the whole of the support infrastructure needed for animal traction has been absent, and therefore needed to be supplied (on a temporary basis) from the introducing organisation (eg, provision of implements, spare parts, animals, veterinary services and credit). Once a critical mass of users has developed and the needs have been identified, such services can be provided by other organisations (private sector or governmental). The long-term sustainability of animal traction will depend on the development of such local support services.

Like several other countries in Africa, the economic environment in Sierra Leone has not been conducive to agricultural investment. Comparable problems of high inflation, foreign exchange shortages and/or corruption have been experienced by Angola, Ghana, Guinea, Mozambique, Nigeria, Tanzania, Uganda, Zaire and Zambia. In these and other countries, policies relating to the importation or pricing of staple foods have made profitable farming difficult. Such major macro-economic problems or distortions are likely to influence the success or failure of draft animal power far more than any "project" initiatives which might be suggested.

In common with many other countries in Africa, in Sierra Leone animal traction was scorned for a time, but has recently become an accepted element of national development strategy.

Interaction of the draft animal programmes in Sierra Leone with programmes elsewhere in Africa has been high. This, together with close-knit, inter-disciplinary research-development-extension teams and regular contact with farmers has helped keep morale high; the infectious enthusiasm of staff has probably been a factor in the relative success and durability of the programme. Collaboration between the various national institutions has been close and aid agencies' initiatives have generally complemented each other. Sierra Leone has managed to avoid some of the pitfalls of working in isolation, but in some cases, it may have suffered from giving more weight to ideas from other countries than to the wishes of the local farmers.

Animals have been used mainly for plowing, and early attempts to promote animal-powered weeding have been disappointing. This is similar to experience in other countries: weeding is often accepted several years after plowing. Furthermore, weeding technology is easier to transfer if the main crops are maize, cotton and groundnuts, rather than rice. The low use of animal-drawn carts appears surprising, and this seems an area for investigation.

The Sierra Leone experience should certainly not be taken as a model, but many programmes elsewhere in Africa could benefit from the many positive and negative lessons gained in attempting to transfer animal traction technology in a difficult environment.

Acknowledgement

This paper, prepared as a contribution to the ATNESA workshop theme of "transfer of animal traction technology", draws on an unpublished case history (Starkey, 1988b) prepared at the request of Silsoe Research Institute (then called AFRC-Engineering).

References

Allagnat P, 1984. *Methodology for an on-farm research: the case of a socio-economic survey of the use of ox traction in the Mabole Valley, Sierra Leone.* Sierra Leone Work Oxen Project and Association Français des Voluntaires du Progrès, Freetown, Sierra Leone. 128p.

Allagnat P and Koroma B, 1984. *Socio-economic survey of the use of ox traction in the Mabole Valley, Bombali District.* Sierra Leone Work Oxen Project and Association Français des Voluntaires du Progrès, Freetown, Sierra Leone. 119p.

Bah M S, 1990. Social constraints to the adoption and expansion of work oxen in Sierra Leone. pp. 337–341 in: Starkey P and Faye A (eds), *Animal traction for agricultural development.* Proceedings of workshop held 7–12 July 1988, Saly, Senegal. Technical Centre for Agriculture and Rural Cooperation, Ede-Wageningen, The Netherlands. 475p.

Bangura A B, 1988. The utilization and management of draft animals at farm level. pp. 293–298 in: Starkey P and Ndiamé F (eds), *Animal power in farming systems.* Proceedings of Second West African Animal Traction Networkshop, held 19–25 September 1986, in Freetown, Sierra Leone. Vieweg for German Appropriate Technology Exchange, GTZ, Eschborn, Germany. 363p.

Bangura A B, 1990. Constraints to the extension of draft animal technology in the farming systems of Sierra Leone. pp. 324–327 in: Starkey P and Faye A (eds), *Animal traction for agricultural development.* Proceedings of workshop held 7–12 July 1988, Saly, Senegal. Technical Centre for Agriculture and Rural Cooperation, Ede-Wageningen, The Netherlands. 475p.

Corbel H, 1986. The economics of animal power in Koinadugu District, Sierra Leone: a case study of the work oxen introduction and credit programme. pp. 299–310 in: Starkey P and Ndiamé F (eds), *Animal power in farming systems.* Proceedings of Second West African Animal Traction Networkshop, held 19–25 September 1986, in Freetown, Sierra Leone. Vieweg for German Appropriate Technology Exchange, GTZ, Eschborn, Germany. 363p.

Dorward D C and Payne A I, 1975. Deforestation, the decline of the horse and the spread of the tsetse fly and trypanosomiasis (Nagana) in nineteenth century Sierra Leone. *Journal of African History* 16(2):239–256.

Gboku M, 1988. Farmer social variables influencing the adoption of agricultural innovations in Sierra Leone. pp. 311–319 in: Starkey P and Ndiamé F (eds), *Animal power in farming*

systems. Proceedings of Second West African Animal Traction Networkshop, held 19–25 September 1986, in Freetown, Sierra Leone. Vieweg for German Appropriate Technology Exchange, GTZ, Eschborn, Germany. 363p.

Granville R R, 1933. *Rice cultivation: report of a visit to Ceylon and South India with proposals for Sierra Leone.* Department of Agriculture, Government Printer, Freetown, Sierra Leone. 30p.

Growcott L, 1977. *A project for the introduction of draught animals into Sierra Leone's agriculture.* Ministry of Agriculture and Natural Resources, Freetown, Sierra Leone. 10p.

Kamara J A, 1974. *Ox-ploughing in Sierra Leone.* Paper prepared for meeting of Agricultural Experts of the Mano River Union. Njala University College, Sierra Leone. 9p.

Kanu B H, 1988. Animal traction development strategies in Sierra Leone. pp. 277–287 in: Starkey P and Ndiamé F (eds), *Animal power in farming systems.* Proceedings of Second West African Animal Traction Networkshop, held 19–25 September 1986, in Freetown, Sierra Leone. Vieweg for German Appropriate Technology Exchange, GTZ, Eschborn, Germany. 363p.

Kanu B H, 1990. Village level engineering: the importance of the blacksmith in supporting animal traction and production. pp. 334–336 in: Starkey P and Faye A (eds), *Animal traction for agricultural development.* Proceedings of workshop held 7–12 July 1988, Saly, Senegal. Technical Centre for Agriculture and Rural Cooperation, Ede-Wageningen, The Netherlands. 475p.

Leaman S, 1988. The role of work oxen in swamp development in Sierra Leone. pp. 288–292 in: Starkey P and Ndiamé F (eds), *Animal power in farming systems.* Proceedings of Second West African Animal Traction Networkshop, held 19–25 September 1986, in Freetown, Sierra Leone. Vieweg for German Appropriate Technology Exchange, GTZ, Eschborn, Germany. 363p.

McKinlay W, 1990. Overcoming some animal health constraints to work oxen in Sierra Leone through a revolving fund. pp. 328–331 in: Starkey P and Faye A (eds), *Animal traction for agricultural development.* Proceedings of workshop held 7–12 July 1988, Saly, Senegal. Technical Centre for Agriculture and Rural Cooperation, Ede-Wageningen, The Netherlands. 475p.

Matthews M D P and Pullen D W M, 1975. *Cultivation trials with ox-drawn implements using N'Dama cattle in The Gambia.* Report Series, Overseas Department, National Institute of Agricultural Engineering, Silsoe, UK. 62p.

Mettrick H, 1978. *Oxenisation in The Gambia.* Ministry of Overseas Development, London. 68p.

Starkey P H, 1979. *Draught oxen project: background, proposals, progress.* Faculty of Agriculture, Njala University College, Sierra Leone. 15p.

Starkey P H, 1981. *Farming with work oxen in Sierra Leone.* Ministry of Agriculture, Freetown, Sierra Leone. 88p.

Starkey P H, 1982. N'Dama cattle as draught animals in Sierra Leone. *World Animal Revue* 42:19–26.

Starkey P, 1988a. *Perfected yet rejected: animal-drawn wheeled toolcarriers.* Vieweg for German Appropriate Technology Exchange (GATE), GTZ, Eschborn, Germany. 161p.

Starkey P, 1988b. *Draft animal power in Sierra Leone: a case history.* Report prepared by Animal Traction Development, Reading UK for AFRC-Engineering, Silsoe, UK. 15p.

Starkey P H and Kanu B H, 1986. Research and extension with draught oxen in Sierra Leone. *Draught Animal News* 5:11–12.

Starkey P and Ndiamé F (eds) 1988. *Animal power in farming systems.* Proceedings of workshop held 19–25 September 1986, Freetown, Sierra Leone. Vieweg for German Appropriate Technology Exchange (GATE), GTZ, Eschborn, Germany. 363p.

Starkey P and Verhaeghe H, 1982. Weed control in maize using draught animals. *Livestock International* 10(3):64–69.

Transfer of animal traction technology: cultural and social issues in Tarime District, Tanzania

by

Hussein Sosovele

Institute of Resource Assessment, University of Dar es Salaam, PO Box 35097, Dar es Salaam, Tanzania

Abstract

About 10–15% of farmers in Tanzania use animal traction implements in agricultural production. In Tarime District the use of ox plows began in the 1920s and by the late 1980s about 25% of the land was being cultivated by oxen. Although this technology is officially favoured by the government, little effort has been made to widen its use to cover all labour bottlenecks. The manner in which animal traction technology is transferred in Tanzania tends to change, but at the same time consolidate, social and cultural aspects of the division of labour in the households. The existing traditional divisions of labour and the socio-cultural tendencies that influence them can be changed through more appropriate ways of transferring this technology to the farmers. One of these ways might be a selective oxenisation approach which seeks to tackle known labour bottlenecks.

Introduction

It is now generally accepted that one of the benefits of using animal traction is a saving in labour use per unit of output (Pingali, Bigot and Binswanger, 1987; Spencer, 1988; Panin and de Haen, 1989). However, very often some important aspects of labour are not fully considered when attempts are made to transfer animal traction. For example, social costs need to be taken into account when attempting to introduce animal traction: the use of animals in cultivation alleviates the drudgery of the traditional cultivators (often men) but at the same time increases the social and economic costs of women and children who are often doing manual weeding and harvesting (Starkey, 1988).

This paper discusses the transfer of animal traction technology in Tarime District, Tanzania, and the extent to which it influences the organisation of labour. The manner in which animal traction technology is transferred in Tarime District appears to have dual effects; it causes changes in the social and cultural aspects of the organisation of labour, but at the same time it tends to perpetuate and to consolidate existing forms of the social division of labour. An attempt will be made to explain this paradox.

Animal traction in Tarime District

The use of animal drawn implements in Tarime District began in the 1920s. Animal traction was introduced into this area by enterprising Luo farmers (Iliffe, 1979; Tobisson, 1980; Kjærby, 1983) and by migrant labourers who learnt how to use it in Kenya.

The introduction of draft implements in this area coincided with an increasing demand for food and cash crops—the former being stimulated by population growth and the latter being a result of colonial economic policies. Farmers obtained cash from cultivating cotton and maize, and from selling their labour, and used this money to buy plows. By using plows for cultivation the farmers could alleviate the labour shortage problem which was partly caused by migration to gold mining areas in Tarime District.

There has been no particular programme or systematic project to transfer animal traction in Tarime District. By the late 1950s about 20% of households possessed a plow (Tobisson, 1980); by 1988, 30% of households did so (Sosovele, 1991). In 1988 there were about 40 000 oxen, 1660 donkeys and 14 000 plows in Tarime District and about 25% of the land in the district was cultivated using animal power. About 40% of the plow users do not have their own implements; they hire or borrow them, or participate in joint work teams (Sosovele, 1991).

Although the lack of specific animal traction programmes in Tarime District has not restricted the spread of this technology, it has influenced the nature of its transfer. Plows and sledges are the only animal traction implements used by the farmers in this area. Other implements are neither used nor known by the farmers and no attempt has been made to introduce them.

Technology transfer

Knowledge of how to use draft animal equipment and how to make harnesses, do simple repairs and train the animals has spread within the farming community of Tarime District through traditional

---

Photo: Paul Starkey

Women making ridges with mixed team of oxen and cows in Tarime District, Tanzania

social interactions. Farmers who know how to use draft equipment teach others; a father (or a male member of the community) teaches his male children (or other male members of the community), often by working with them. This pattern of transferring knowledge is based on gender and tends to consolidate the traditional division of work in the household in the form of gender specialisation.

This process is influenced by the traditional social system or ethics. Through traditional forms of socialisation and social control (such as various initiation rites, rituals and kinship relations) boys are taught to perform specific tasks which are different from those which the girls are taught and expected to perform in the community (Boserup, 1976). Under these conditions boys and girls are often taught separately, which tends to reinforce a sharp distinction between the males' and the females' tasks. This tendency is reflected in the transfer of knowledge about animal traction: male members of the community appear to have both operational and technical knowledge whereas women have only the operational knowledge.

Division of labour

Before ox plows were introduced in Tarime District, men used to clear the fields and, together with the women, do the first cultivation. Women were responsible for weeding, harvesting and transporting crops, and if manure was used it was the women who carried it and spread in on the fields. Some

men migrated to do wage labour after cultivation, but even those who stayed did not perform the other farming tasks because gender specialisation had been so deeply internalised among the farmers that they were unwilling to perform "women's" activities for fear of being ridiculed by the others.

The introduction of animal traction has partly changed the division of labour between the sexes. In households which have access to ox plows, cultivation is usually done by men and boys (13–15 years old): men guide the plows and the boys lead the animals. Women and girls (13–15 years old) do the planting, clear the weeds or lead the animals if boys are not around to do this work. Although women are usually no longer directly involved in cultivation, as they used to be when hand hoes were used, they may participate in cultivation if men are not around to do this work.

Transportation is the other activity where the introduction of animal traction has led to a change in the division of labour. Transportation is still regarded as a women's activity, but when ox sledges are available men do this work. Ox sledges are not common in Tarime District—less than 15% of the farmers who use ox plows also use sledges—but in households that do own them, men use them to transport not only farm inputs and produce and manure but also water and firewood.

But changes in farmers' attitudes about gender roles in agricultural and household activities have been limited, and the introduction of animal traction in Tarime District has not led to fundamental changes in the division of labour, for two main reasons. First, the transfer of this technology has not involved both sexes; male farmers have usually been the main contact group when "new technologies" have been introduced to the rural areas. Lack of formal training facilities has compounded this problem to the extent that training and transfer of knowledge has followed traditional patterns.

Second, the transfer of animal traction technology in Tarime District has not so far involved implements other than plows and sledges. So while changes in the division of labour have occurred in field activities that can be done by draft animals, for other activities traditional perceptions about gender roles are still dominant.

It can be argued that further changes might be brought about in other labour bottlenecks and difficult tasks if the transfer of animal traction technology can be improved. One possible area of improvement is a change in the approach to oxenisation; instead of transferring complete packages that include almost all the equipment, a better approach might be selective oxenisation, whereby farmers are introduced to specific equipment which will relieve them of drudgery and alleviate labour bottlenecks. Equipment for cultivation, weeding and transportation should be given top priority, and improvements in support institutions would also be needed. This form of oxenisation might possibly influence changes in the division of labour and social-cultural perceptions about farm work.

Conclusion

It is evident that social and cultural constraints on the division and organisation of labour in Tarime District are closely linked to the manner in which animal traction technology is transferred. A few changes in the organisation of labour have taken place, indicating that further changes are likely to occur if the transfer of animal traction can be improved to include both female and male farmers and also to focus particularly on known labour bottlenecks.

References

Boserup E, 1976. *Traditional division of work between sexes: a source of inequality. Women in the labour market.* Research Series 21. International Institute for Labour Studies, Geneva, Switzerland. pp. 1–8.

Iliffe J, 1979. *A modern history of Tanganyika.* Cambridge University Press, Cambridge, UK. 616p.

Kjærby F, 1983. *Problems and contradictions in the development of ox-cultivation in Tanzania.* Research Report 66. Scandinavian Institute of African Studies, Uppsala, Sweden. 164p.

Panin A and de Haen H, 1989. Economic evaluation of animal traction: a comparative analysis of hoe and bullock farming systems in Northern Ghana. *Quarterly Journal of International Agriculture* 28(1):6–20.

Pingali P, Bigot Y and Binswanger H, 1987. *Agricultural mechanisation and the evolution of farming systems in sub-Saharan Africa.* World Bank in association with Johns Hopkins Press, Baltimore, Maryland, USA. 216p.

Sosovele H, 1991. *The development of animal traction in Tanzania: 1900–1980s.* PhD Dissertation. University of Bremen, Germany. 352p.

Spencer D S C, 1988. Farming systems in West Africa from an animal traction perspective. pp. 91–96 in: Starkey P and Ndiamé F (eds), *Animal power in farming systems.* Proceedings of the Second West African Animal Traction Networkshop, held 19–26 September 1986, in Freetown, Sierra Leone. Vieweg for German Appropriate Technology Exchange, GTZ, Eschborn, Germany. 363p.

Starkey P H, 1988. The introduction, intensification and diversification of the use of animal power in West African farming systems: implications at farm level. pp. 97–115 in: Starkey P and Ndiamé F (eds), *Animal power in farming systems.* Proceedings of Second West African Animal Traction Networkshop, held 19–26 September 1986, in Freetown, Sierra Leone. Vieweg for German Appropriate Technology Exchange, GTZ, Eschborn, Germany. 363p.

Tobisson E, 1980. *Women, work, food and nutrition in Nyamwigura villages, Mara region, Tanzania.* Report 548. Tanzania Food and Nutrition Centre, Dar es Salaam, Tanzania. 135p.

Towards a sustainable system for animal traction technology transfer: experiences from Kilimanjaro Region, Tanzania

by

A Galema

*Agricultural Project Adviser, Mixed Farming Improvement Project (Mifipro)
PO Box 183, Mwanga, Kilimanjaro Region, Tanzania*

Abstract

The Mifipro (Mixed Farming Improvement Project) animal traction programme started in 1985. Within five years animal traction technology had been well adopted in an area where it was previously unknown. The programme embraces training of farmers and their oxen at village level, follow-up through farmers' groups, training of village ox trainers and government extension workers, and the provision of veterinary and maintenance services. Much emphasis is placed on the system for transferring animal traction technology, for example through integration with government extension services. However, the sustainability is very much determined by the extent to which farmers can manage the system themselves, and thus by the services available to them. To achieve sustainability, a farmers' network has been established with farmers' groups from the extension programme as its basic unit. This network is to play a coordinating role in introducing animal traction services to farmers.

Introduction

Animal traction has been used in Tanzania for several decades. According to Kjærby (1983), about 600 000 oxen are used for work and 15% of the crop land is cultivated by oxen. However, application of animal traction is mainly limited to distinct areas, such as the southern highlands, and initiated by settlers or special projects. Attempts to work towards a consistent development of animal traction technology are still in their early stages. The Mixed Farming Improvement Project (Mifipro) is one of the projects engaged on promoting animal traction technology. It is concerned mainly with introducing a systematic approach to the transfer of animal traction technology at farmer level, with a clear emphasis on its sustainability.

When Mifipro began in 1985, animal traction was an unknown phenomenon in the project's working area (the eastern lowlands of Mwanga District, Kilimanjaro Region). This area is classified as semi-arid, with an annual average rainfall of 600 mm distributed over two rainy seasons. However, irrigation from natural streams descending from the mountains enhances the opportunities for crop production.

From the perspective of crop production the area comprises six different agro-ecological zones distinguished by soil type (black clay, red loam–sand) and water availability (permanent irrigation, unreliable access to irrigation, solely rainfed). Most farmers have fields in several agro-ecological zones.

Agriculture is the basic source of livelihood for nearly everyone, sometimes supplemented by other sources of income such as government employment, fishing, livestock raising and small businesses. Consequently the availability of labour outside the family is very limited. Major crops are maize, beans, rice, cassava and, where permanent water sources are present, coconut palms and fruit trees. Important cash earners are livestock, fishing and rice.

A survey conducted in 1989 showed that roughly 60% of households own livestock. Most households have fewer than 20 head of cattle, although herds of more than 100 head do occur. Free grazing is the prevailing system, with little or no investment.

The area is relatively isolated, accessible by only two roads which are often impassable during the rainy seasons. Government services are poorly developed, as are marketing, input supply and repair facilities. The area experiences an increasing inflow of people from the highly populated mountain areas, in search of arable land. As a result, tension between crop and livestock activities is rising and farming intensity tends to increase.

The animal traction programme

Although commercialisation of agriculture never reached the stage where it could trigger the development of animal traction (in contrast to the case in several West African countries), and farmers were hesitant for cultural reasons to use animals for work, other conditions in the area were conducive to the introduction of animal traction. Therefore an oxenisation programme was started in 1985. The major elements of the programme are described briefly below.

Raising awareness

Although farmers acknowledged that labour was a main constraint, they were not aware that animal traction could be a solution. Cultural factors were denying the possibility of using animals for work. Demonstrations on-farm, and an initial individual approach, broke down the cultural obstacles reasonably quickly.

Training of farmers

On request, farmers and their oxen (in sessions of 7–14 pairs) are trained within their villages. Intervention by the project is kept to a minimum level. Farmers have to bring their own oxen, build a temporary shed for training, look after their own animals and provide an assistant during the time of the training. Implements and materials are supplied by the project on economic terms and veterinary services are provided by project staff. The training takes about five weeks during which project trainers live in the village. Until 1990 attention was focused on oxen. Recently the project has widened its scope to include donkeys.

Follow-up of trained farmers

After completion of training, farmers are asked to organise themselves into groups. Project technicians visit the groups on a regular basis (every one or two weeks) to give advice, check the animals and provide additional training. Normally these groups evolve from special animal traction groups into general agricultural groups where a broad spectrum of matters, such as crop production, soil conservation, livestock management, irrigation, etc, can be discussed. Through a participatory extension approach actual problems of farmers serve as a starting point for further training, during which attempts are made to achieve a synthesis between the farmers' knowledge and newly introduced ideas.

Training of village trainers

From each training group, one or two farmers, proposed by the others, are selected and brought to the project site to be given further training in animal traction technology. This training is usually given in two sessions of four to five days each. These farmers then have the task of assisting their fellow farmers to train their animals. This assistance is based on a financial agreement between the village trainer and the farmer.

Training of government extension workers

The project conducts regular training sessions for government extension workers and agro-mechanisation staff, to upgrade their knowledge and skills and to help them address farmers' animal traction problems. In addition, extension workers are trained in participatory extension skills to enhance an open dialogue with farmers.

Demonstrations at village level

In order to intensify the application of animal traction, especially for more complicated activities such as planting and weeding with oxen, demonstrations are organised within the villages, using the farmers' own oxen and potential alternative implements supplied by the project.

Support services

Apart from providing training and supplying implements (plows, ridgers, chains) at cost price, the project operates a modest workshop where, for example, ox carts are manufactured. Complete axles are obtained elsewhere while the bodies are built and assembled at the workshop. Repair facilities are also available. Recently a basic veterinary centre came into operation, facilitating proper diagnosis and treatment of animal diseases: these services are provided on economic terms.

General impact of the programme

A survey conducted in 1990–91 to evaluate the impact of the programme (Vanderschaeghe, 1991) showed that between 1985 and 1989 a total of 140 farmers were trained, 102 by the project and 38 (with their oxen) with the assistance of village trainers or neighbouring farmers. This represents about 7% of all families in the working area, or 9% of the families who own cattle.

Of the farmers who were trained during this period, 92% are still using their oxen for traction purposes, indicating a high level of continued adoption of animal traction technology. Of the farmers who have adopted animal traction, 7% had no cattle prior to the training; they obtained their oxen either by buying surplus animals from others or by inheriting them from their fathers "in advance". Some 32% of the farmers now have two or more pairs of oxen.

The fact that about a quarter of the trained farmers have trained their animals without direct assistance from the project indicates that the comprehensive approach in the training programme has resulted in a certain degree of self-reliance with regard to the adoption of animal traction technology. However, there seem to be differences in the application of animal traction depending on how the farmers were trained. Among the village trained farmers, relatively more use animal traction for transport purposes (95%), and fewer use this technology for field activities (24%) compared to their project trained counterparts (80 and 56%, respectively).

This partly reflects the fact that the use of animal traction for field activities requires a higher degree of skill and knowledge, both for the farmer and for the animals, compared to pulling carts. Apparently the spontaneous expansion of animal traction could not attain this quality aspect sufficiently.

Of all the 140 farmers trained, about 84% (118) use oxen for pulling carts. Fewer than half (66) use them for field activities and mainly for land preparation and planting; weeding with oxen is still poorly developed.

The introduction of animal traction for transport has definitely proved a success. This is especially true among women, who reported that ox carts substantially reduce their work burden for such tedious tasks as collecting water and firewood and ferrying the harvest from the fields to their home. Ox carts are also used for taking produce to the market and for various other, often income-generating, jobs. Incomes of 75 000–150 000 Tanzanian shillings per year (equivalent in 1991 to about US$ 750–1500) from renting out an ox cart have been recorded in villages with a low density of ox carts. As animals and equipment are mainly owned by men, men are also the main beneficiaries of this income.

Impact at farm level

All farm operations are carried out with single-purpose implements—mouldboard plows, ridgers and ox carts. (Tine cultivators are also used, but their numbers are very small and so their impact has not been evaluated.) The evaluation survey (Vanderschaeghe, 1991) showed that the labour input per hectare was considerably reduced by using animal traction. For example, for maize cultivation, doing all operations manually (from land preparation to transport of harvest) required a total of 16.6 workdays/ha (1 workday = 7 hours). Using a plow alone, a plow plus an ox cart, and a plow plus ridger reduced the labour requirement to 13, 12 and 9 workdays/ha, respectively.

This reduction of workload offered farmers several options for improving their farming. Some farmers chose to increase the area they cultivated, while others opted for a diversification of their income sources.

Another benefit of a reduced labour investment during land preparation is that farmers are better able to prepare fields located in different agro-ecological zones. At times of unfavourable rainfall (either too much or too little) they can easily shift their attention to the zone most suited to the current circumstances and by doing so increase their food security.

As the period between two consecutive rainy seasons is very short and rainfall is unpredictable, it is of vital importance to harvest the first crop as quickly as possible and to prepare the land again for the next rains. Animal traction increases the chance for timely execution of these field operations.

Reflections on the approach

The Mifipro animal traction programme has succeeded in introducing animal traction technology into an area where it was previously absent, and within a reasonably short period. This success can be attributed to the adoption of a comprehensive approach, comprising elements of training, follow-up and demonstrations, linking animal traction to general extension activities on crop production via farmers' groups, as well as the provision of veterinary, livestock and maintenance services—all of which are considered to be vital for successful animal traction projects (Pingali, Bigot and Binswanger, 1987).

On the other hand, several shortcomings were observed; some of these are related to operational elements of the programme, while others are of a more structural nature, taking into account the ability of farmers to sustain and regenerate the system of animal traction technology transfer.

Access to animal traction technology

Animal traction technology is mainly only within the reach of farmers who have achieved a certain level of wealth, in terms of both capital and, more importantly, cattle. The opportunities to reach resource-poor farmers with this technology, considering the relatively high initial investment, are few. It remains an argument for debate whether this should be accepted as a reality or whether special programmes (credit facilities) or approaches (group ownership of oxen and implements) should be launched in order to give resource-poor farmers access to this technology. The experience of the Mifipro project shows that group ownership of oxen and implements is often not a viable solution because of technical reasons (farmers need the oxen at the same time) and social factors (preference for individual ownership, little responsibility towards equipment). Credit facilities should be linked with a saving scheme, based on sound financial management, in order to create a more permanent credit scheme. Preferably these credit/saving schemes should have a wider scope that just animal traction to allow money to be invested in activities which have the highest return to capital.

In order to give women access to animal traction technology, use should be made of female ox trainers. However, as women can often be considered as resource-poor farmers, the above-mentioned concern about this group is also applicable here.

Selection and training of village ox trainers

It is recommended that candidate village ox trainers should be selected from among farmers who have reached a more or less settled stage in their lives. Youths are often mobile and move to other areas in search of work. Furthermore their position relative to older farmers is sometimes complicated by social factors.

Village trainers need continuing training opportunities in order to maintain and upgrade their knowledge and skills and to enable them to offer services aimed at full-scale mechanisation of field activities. Therefore close follow-up of these trainers is needed.

Implements

Within the context of Tanzania, development and production of basic animal traction implements should be left to central institutions which are well equipped to do this work. Local projects should not go beyond the tasks of maintenance, assembly and carpentry work.

Maintenance services

The establishment of a central, economically-viable workshop for production and maintenance services is probably difficult in remote areas. Once it has been decided precisely which services are vital for a successful animal traction programme, a better way might be to consider how local craftsmen can be helped to provide such services right from the start, outside the organisation of the project.

Towards a sustainable system of animal traction technology transfer

Experiences in many countries have shown that the introduction of animal traction is more complicated than is generally thought. It requires a long-term perspective. Moreover, animal traction projects should be well integrated in a more general service structure for farmers. This can ensure that animal traction recommendations are adequately supported by other extension messages. In addition, available extension staff can be used in the operation of the programme.

Apart from this, the participation of farmers is a crucial element in the effort to provide farmers with the services they need. In other words, farmers

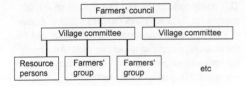

Figure 1: Present system of animal traction technology transfer in Kilimanjaro Region, Tanzania

should be in the position to obtain the services they need from respective institutions (whether government or others).

In order to realise these objectives, the Mifipro project has initiated the establishment of a farmers' network. As explained above, participants in ox-training courses organise themselves into a farmers' group after the training is completed in the village. Apart from these specific animal traction groups, other farmers' groups already exist and form the basis of the agricultural extension system. Extension workers, either from the project or from the government, visit these groups regularly. The group concept is useful not only because it can increase the efficiency of the extension services (wider reach) but also because adults seem to learn more easily when they are in a group. The element of empowerment of farmers comes from the union of the various groups. The present structure is outlined in Figure 1.

This structure consists solely of individual farmers; government structures are not involved. The farmers' groups are the units of the structure; at present about 40 groups exist. Leaders of the groups in one area (varying from three to five groups) are members of the Village Committees, of which there are presently 11 in the project area. Every committee elects its representative to the highest level, the Farmers' Council.

Various resources persons (such as nursery attendants engaged in production of tree seedlings for interested farmers, village ox trainers, etc) are available at village level. They are farmers who are trained by the project but who are coordinated by the Village Committees. The task of the Village Committees is to bring farmers and resource persons together when the former need any assistance from the latter. This offers several possibilities. The Committee can organise demonstrations or training for farmers who express interest in animal traction. If any assistance is needed from the project or from the extension service the Committee can address the issue to them. In case of structural problems the network allows for a flow of information to the highest level where solutions can be discussed. The

Farmers' Council can address the issue to any relevant institution. Presently the Council meets three times a year and it functions as an advisory body to the project. However, it could play this role to any other organisation. It is foreseen that the Farmers' Council could develop into a local legal institution representing the interest of the farmers.

Of course, such a network is not established overnight. The present network started to operate at the end of 1990 but a lot of work still has to be done to enable it to function effectively. All actors in the network have to be aware of their tasks and responsibilities and should have the skills to execute their tasks adequately. Here lies a challenging role for the project. Moreover, it requires a strong commitment by farmers at all levels towards the development of the area. This can only be retained if the system generates some clear benefits for the farmers, in the short as well as the long term.

In conclusion, the sustainability of the transfer of animal traction technology depends on many factors. An important factor which is often overlooked is the role farmers can play in managing the system. The experiences of Mifipro might contribute to the discussion on this aspect.

References

Kjærby F, 1983. *Problems and contradictions in the development of ox-cultivation in Tanzania.* Research Report 66. Scandinavian Institute of African Studies, Uppsala, Sweden. 164p.

Pingali P L, Bigot Y and Binswanger H P, 1987. *Agricultural mechanization and the evolution of farming systems in sub-Saharan Africa.* World Bank. Johns Hopkins Press, Baltimore, Maryland, USA. 216p.

Vanderschaeghe M, 1991. *Evaluation of the introduction of animal traction by Mifipro in the north of Tanzania.* Internal report. Mixed Farming Improvement Project (Mifipro), Mwanga, Tanzania. 52p.

A note on issues to be addressed in the transfer of animal traction technology in Tanzania

by

R L S Urasa

Rural Structures, Grain Processing and Transportation Project, PO Box 2199, Dodoma, Tanzania

Abstract

The problems that are being experienced in the exercise of technology transfer lie in farmers' attitudes and their reluctance to change agricultural practices which are dictated by social, economic and technical factors. For new technologies to be widely accepted they have to offer solutions to existing problems within traditional farming practices.

Technology transfer involves both imported and locally developed implements and equipment. Both may need modification to suit local conditions, and some examples are discussed briefly.

Introduction

The role of technology transfer in developing countries cannot be underestimated. A great deal of effort has been made by design engineers and manufacturing companies to make available various types of farm implements that will help farmers to improve labour productivity on their farm. However, there are various problems with introducing new technologies to small-scale farmers.

Choice of technology

The popularity of hand tools in agriculture is a result of long-term experience, highly influenced by social, economic and technical factors. Thus farmers who use traditional methods of seedbed preparation, planting, weeding and even harvesting, threshing and winnowing, need to be convinced that alternative methods are cheaper, more effective and easier to operate, and/or that they lead to a higher work output.

Animal traction, based on the use of simple animal-drawn implements, offers solutions to many agricultural problems. However, the change from hand tool farming to draft animal power technologies in a single step is not always appropriate—not only because of economic limitations but also because of low levels of technical know-how. Consequently the identification and selection of appropriate technology greatly depends on social, economic and technical factors.

Social factors

The technology transfer process must take account of the fact that rural women are major contributors to agricultural development. Thus a technology is not appropriate if rural women will not benefit from it. The labour distribution of members of a family must be identified as part of the process of selecting recipients of new technology.

Technology transfer depends on the willingness of farmers to accept new technologies. It is difficult to design implements or equipment to suit local farming practices, but farmers are also reluctant to change their ways of farming to suit new technologies.

Economic aspects

Most farmers in the developing world are poor. Thus any new machinery or equipment to be introduced into rural areas must be as simple and cheap as possible if it is to be widely adopted. High initial investment costs for a package of implements and farm equipment mean that only a few farmers will benefit from the new technology.

Technical aspects

A new technology will not be acceptable to the target group if it is not compatible with existing farming principles and cultivation practices. Thus farmers traditionally practising shifting slash-and-burn cultivation will find it difficult to use an ox plow unless they are first offered easier means of removing the bush and stumps. Similarly, farmers who traditionally practise flat cultivation may not readily accept the introduction of the ridger.

On the other hand, a new implement or technology may be readily acceptable if it is seen to solve a problem within the established farming practice. An important part of the technology transfer process, therefore, is identifying problems in the existing farming system for which new technologies or implements may offer solutions.

Most smallholder farmers have had only very limited education. It is therefore important that any new technology to be introduced is simple enough to be understood by the farmers.

The transfer of technology

Many developing countries continue to depend on imported technology, implements and machinery. Even when implements are manufactured locally, their design features may still reflect those of implements imported from developed countries where farming practices and conditions are often very different to those in developing countries. Thus even the best imported implements, or local products based on these implements, may not be entirely suitable to local conditions and modification of imported farm machinery and equipment designs is an important part of the technology transfer process. Some examples are given below.

Plows

The standard 25 cm plow demands high energy expenditure and two pairs of local African cattle are often needed to pull it. A smaller plow could reduce the initial investment costs in terms the number of oxen required to operate it.

Cultivators

The adjustable five-tine cultivator imported from Europe and Asia is used for weeding when fitted with three reversible teeth and a pair of hillers, and as a cultivator or harrow when fitted with reversible teeth on all five tines. The implement can also be used for two-stage weeding: on the first pass three 20 cm sweeps fitted on the hind tines cut the weeds just below ground level; and for the second pass the implement is fitted with the reversible teeth on all five tines to break up the soil and expose the roots for desiccation. On models currently available in Tanzania the swivel joints easily snap off, and improvements in the design are called for. With further modification, the cultivator could also be used as a furrow-opener for hand seeding.

Ridgers

The ridgers available in Tanzania are large and have poor penetration qualities. They must therefore be used in conjunction with ox plows in order to construct 90 cm ridges. For covering seeds and fertiliser at planting and/or for weeding purposes, a smaller ridger body would be better.

Seeders and planters

Most of the imported planters have plate type seed metering mechanisms which work well only with carefully graded seed. Consequently farmers who do not get graded seed would not use ox-drawn planters. Modifications to incorporate other types of metering mechanisms on planters would be highly desirable.

Simple toolbars

Promising designs for toolbars (already tested) are the *Unibar* and *Houe Sine*. With the help of a bracket on its beam, the plow manufactured in Tanzania by Ubungo Farm Implements (UFI) can be used for weeding when fitted with a sweep or hiller. It can also be used as a ripper tine when fitted with a reversible point.

Irrigation equipment

Very few designs of implements for ox-powered irrigation farming are available locally in Africa. Various designs can, however, be imported from Asia. These include the buck scraper, the levelling float, the dam scoop, the bund former and the single row ditchers. These implements can easily be made locally, modified as necessary to suit local conditions.

Farm carts

Although efforts are being made to manufacture some ox/donkey carts locally, there are still many problems with wheel bearings, wheels, the height of the drawbar and the types of harnesses and yokes used. Many of the ox cart designs impose excessive loads on the animals' necks, even when the cart is not loaded.

Ripper-tines

The ripper-tine is essentially a simple implement used to break the soil in rows ready for planting. The implement is most suitable for use in semi-arid areas just before the rains. Seed are planted along the loosened soil in the rows and herbicides are used to control weeds.

Sweeps

Sweeps are essentially weeder blades which cut the weeds just below ground level, leaving them to dry in the sun. When used together with herbicides, this implement can simulate zero tillage in which mulch is used to conserve soil and water in the field. However, if herbicide is not available, it would be better to use a ripper-tine together with the sweeps to replace hand-tool-dominated farming practices.

Transfer of animal traction technology in Mbozi District, Tanzania

by

Godfrey Mwakitwange

Agriculturalist, Mbozi Agricultural Development Programme, PO Box 204, Mbozi, Mbeya, Tanzania

Abstract

Transfer of animal traction technology by the Agricultural Development Programme in Mbozi, Tanzania, started immediately after farming systems research showed that poor soil fertility and labour shortages were the main constraints to food production in the working area. The project has operated by organising farmers into voluntary groups, at village level, and providing training in improved agricultural techniques, particularly the use of animal draft power for weeding, transport, incorporation of organic matter under ridges, etc. Organising farmers into groups enables the limited number of extension staff to provide a more efficient service, and also enables the farmers to build up their own organisations which can "pull down" the provided services as required.

Introduction

The Agricultural Development Programme, which started in Mbozi District, Mbeya Region, Tanzania in 1986, is an integrated agricultural project currently covering some 90 villages. Its aim is to increase food production of Mbozi smallholder farmers in a sustainable way. To this end, the smallholder farming system was analysed, and farmers were organised into groups and trained in various improved agricultural techniques. In order to achieve sustainability, strong emphasis was given to resource efficient agricultural methods (sometimes called low external input agriculture).

In order to help the farmers become more efficient, a mixed farming system is advocated, whereby the produce of the land is used to support the farmers' animals (through feeding crop residues and eventually through growing fodder crops), manure is used to improve soil fertility and animal draft power is used for various agricultural production activities.

The integrated approach means not only providing agricultural extension services but also supplying inputs, implements and other services at both village and divisional levels. At divisional level a so-called Farm Service Centre is available, where extension services are coordinated, training and demonstrations are held (in the training centre and at the trial and demonstration farm) and other services (such as building ox carts, wheelbarrows, etc, and sales of implements) are provided.

Organising farmers into groups enables the limited number of extension staff to reach them more efficiently, and also encourages them to build up their own farmers' organisations to a level where they can "pull down" the provided services and eventually take over the running of the Farm Service Centres.

Farming systems research

Farming systems research carried out in 1986/87 identified two main constraints to agricultural production in Mbozi District:

∘ decreasing soil fertility
∘ seasonal labour shortages (at planting and weeding times and during harvesting) because most farmers grow maize, beans (twice each season) and some coffee.

Use of draft animal power could alleviate these constraints, but although about 50% of farming households in Vwawa Division own cattle, only 15% use them for primary soil preparation and transport (using locally constructed sledges). The research identified several factors which limit the application of animal traction.

First, it appeared that the risks of owning cattle were quite high. There was a high death rate (about half of the calves died) attributable to several factors. Common diseases were East Coast Fever, Lumpy Skin Disease and Black Quarter. Veterinary services were relatively poor and medicines were either not available or were felt to be too expensive. The use of local medicines was limited. Witchcraft was also mentioned as a regular cause of death of animals. And poor housing and feeding of the animals also contributed to the high death rate.

Second, although cattle did have a high social and cultural value—for example, they were seen as a form of security for times of unexpected expenditure (serious illness in the family, a funeral, etc)—cows were preferred over oxen. Owning oxen was not seen as very economically attractive as they were mainly used for plowing and pulling sledges, whereas cows provide milk and offspring. Dowries had to be paid in cattle, but oxen could make up only a small part of the number of cattle requested. Also farmers had great respect for their cows and so were unwilling to use them for draft purposes because of the rough methods generally used in training.

Third, there was only limited cooperation among farmers in the use of their animals. Sharing animals was not very common. And animals from different families could not be brought together at one place for training because farmers feared negative influences from witchcraft which may kill their animals. However, farmers did frequently lend animals to other family members, and sometimes hired out their animals after they had plowed their own fields.

Finally, cattle were owned by men, and so it was the men who took care of the animals and worked with them. However, the culture is changing slowly and women are not completely excluded from handling oxen.

All the villages surveyed had some local ox trainers. The training offered was usually very basic (mainly getting animals accustomed to pulling a log and to obeying commands) and was carried out at the farm of the trainer. The actual plowing was done by the owner when he received his animals back.

Draft animal power policy

These findings, together with experience gained by the project in the working area, led to the formulation of an ox-mechanisation policy. The main elements of this policy are discussed below.

Soil fertility

The role of ox mechanisation should be defined in relation to all aspects of soil fertility:

- transport of organic matter to the fields
- incorporation of organic matter under ridges
- use of improved farmyard manure (stored in a pit or a heap) and compost.

Labour constraints

The role of ox mechanisation should be defined in relation to labour constraints, land availability and improvement of crop husbandry. The policy stresses three main aspects of this:

- timely and proper soil preparation, which includes plowing before the rains (either after the harvest or just before the onset of the rains), harrowing twice (the second time to kill

germinated weeds and prepare the seedbed for the maize), and planting with a plow or a cultivator

- the advantage of planting on ridges which, combined with the incorporation of organic matter, leads to higher yields
- the importance of weeding, as poor weeding is the biggest constraint to increased maize yields in the southern highlands of Tanzania. Because of labour shortages, only mechanised weeding can provide a solution to this problem.

Role of women

The role of women should be taken into account at all stages of the ox-mechanisation process. Women are the main actors in the food production cycle, and so would benefit most from the eventual reduction in workload.

Animal health care

Ox mechanisation and animal health care are topics in the general agricultural courses for link farmers and extension workers at the Farm Service Centre training centre. The fully ox-mechanised trial farm is used as a demonstration and training place during these courses.

Village organisation

The ox-mechanisation policy should be part of the general project village extension and organisation policy.

First, over a period of a year, link farmers attend three different seminars at which they are trained in general agricultural methods and resource-efficient agricultural techniques. The third seminar is devoted solely to ox mechanisation. Thereafter villages can enrol for on-site training, whereby five local ox trainers or ox users are selected for further training: at least one of these should be a woman. This further training covers the more advanced techniques of steering, weeding, planting, one-ox traction and the making of different types of yokes. The farmers who receive this further training then form an ox-mechanisation committee in their village, and are at the disposal of other farmers for demonstrations and training.

The village has to provide a training and demonstration plot as many people do not yet believe that it is possible to plant and weed with oxen. The training activities at the village are supported by an upgraded trainer from another village, and the village can borrow the necessary equipment from the project for a certain period.

After mastering all the techniques, the trained committee members also act as trainers in other villages, thereby reducing the role of the project to that of an intermediary, linking the people with the needs with those having the knowledge, and strengthening the links between villages.

Promotion and distribution of equipment

Equipment and implements are promoted and distributed through existing sales points and project shops, which are available in 48 villages at present. At the sales points equipment can only be ordered, while in the shops the different tools are available and specific promotion meetings are undertaken. As the availability of ox carts has been problematic in the past, these are now built at one Farm Service Centre workshop in collaboration with the Mbeya Oxenization Project which provides the axles.

Availability of equipment in the country is a bottleneck which the project cannot tackle. For example, appropriate cultivators and ridgers are still not available.

Results

The draft animal power component of the Mbozi Agricultural Development Programme was developed over a period of four to five years and was designed to fit within the general approach of the project using, as much as possible, existing local institutions and services such as the district agricultural extension staff and the Mbeya Oxenization Project.

In the initial years ox mechanisation was not given priority, as it was clear that only the larger farms

could benefit from it. A farmer needs a herd of at least five cattle (because sharing of animals is not common in the area), as well as cash to purchase implements.

Even so, between 1987 and 1991 the project managed to sell about 100 ox carts, 250 plows and a few cultivators and ridgers, despite the fact that in the first years availability of the implements was a major bottleneck.

In the past three years, three-day ox-mechanisation seminars have been held at the Farm Service Centre for 18 villages, and 450 link farmers have been trained in the basic skills of this technology. In the past two years ox-mechanisation committees have been trained in more advanced skills in 11 villages (about 55 people).

Expansion of these efforts is constrained by the number of staff available, and they are still only a limited activity within the general agricultural approach.

It is also clear that after all potential villages have had training, expansion can only come if the risk of cattle disease is reduced. The project has not entered this still difficult field—difficult because the supply of medicines in the country is insufficient, dipping is extremely difficult to organise, etc.

At the end of 1991, the project started an experiment with a women's group, in a very isolated area, engaged in maize grinding using an ox-driven maize mill. The mill has just been installed, so results are not yet available.

Improving animal traction technology in Uganda

by

Alphonse E Akou[*]

Head of Oxen Unit, Serere Research Station, Private Bag, PO Soroti, Uganda

Abstract

Ox cultivation has a great potential in Uganda where about 70% of the population are involved in agriculture. Until recently most farm operations in Uganda, apart from first plowing, were done by women because of a lack of appropriate animal-drawn implements. Imported implements were very expensive and supplies were irregular and subject to delays. Farmers lacked knowledge of ox training and of proper animal management. Now, however, efforts are being made to encourage local manufacture of animal-drawn implements (and spare parts) that are suitable for local soil conditions and available animals. Several Ugandan firms are producing ox plows, ox carts and spare parts, are planning to produce planters, weeders and a multipurpose toolbar, and are able to demonstrate these implements to farmers. Village blacksmiths can also play an important role in producing implements locally. Non-governmental organisations are promoting the use of oxen in rural areas; they aim to ensure a sufficient supply of implements and spares, and to providing training. The Ugandan Government, too, is encouraging the use of ox draft power in an effort to increase agricultural production and reduce drudgery for women.

Introduction

The economy of Uganda is greatly dependent on agricultural production, which accounts for 80% of foreign exchange earnings. About 70% of Ugandans are directly or indirectly involved in agriculture. Over the past few decades, efforts have been made to increase the agricultural production of the smallholder farmers in the north and east of Uganda through encouraging the use of oxen for cultivation. Farmers have increased their interest in the technology and, today, ox cultivation has a great potential in most areas of the country.

For a long time the use of oxen was confined to primary cultivation with a mouldboard plow. Sometimes oxen were used for a second plowing. All other farm operations, such as planting, weeding, harvesting and transport of crops, have been done by women, due to the lack of appropriate animal-drawn implements.

---

[*] *Subsequent address:*
A E Akou, Consultant, PO Box 99, Soroti, Uganda

In 1986 about 30–35% of households in Uganda were using oxen. Estimates of cattle populations and proportions of households using oxen are given in Table 1.

Ox-drawn equipment

The mouldboard plow continues to be the basic tillage implement. Most plows are imported from India by private firms and by the Agricultural Development Programme supported by the World Bank. The firms distribute the plows through farmer schemes and local banks. This recent arrangement is of great help to farmers who cannot afford to buy ox plows without credit.

Table 1: Estimates of the cattle population and percentage of households using oxen in the districts of Uganda

District	Cattle population (000s)	Households using oxen (%)
Soroti	1918.0	95
Kumi	317.6	90
Torore	334.9	90
Kitgum	248.7	85
Lira	155.1	80
Morote	244.4	75
Iganga	282.0	55
Gulu	128.8	50
Kotido	26.0	50
Mbale	89.0	45
Apac	183.7	40
Masindi	39.9	30
Kapchorwa	30.2	25
Jinja	14.6	20
Kamili	122.9	20
Hoima	32.0	15
Lwero	88.8	10
Nebbi	57.2	5
Arua	95.0	5
Kabarele	143.9	3
Moyo	16.0	3
Total	**4568.7**	

Source: MAAIF, 1987

The Indian plow weighs about 30 kg. This is relatively light for four small East African Zebu oxen to pull. Where soil is light, two oxen of reasonable size can pull the plow without much strain.

A major problem is that farmers often do not consider that proper animal management is important. As a result the animals are often underweight after drought periods and they are made to undertake work they cannot readily manage. Most farmers still lack knowledge of ox training and the proper maintenance of the implements.

Importation of ox plows and their spare parts is quite often irregular, and delays in the supply of spare parts means that agricultural production is retarded. Because of these outstanding problems, local parastatal and semi-parastatal bodies within the country are encouraged to make plow spare parts locally.

National effort to develop ox cultivation technology

The present efforts to encourage local firms to manufacture animal-drawn implements and spare parts is a result of past research at Serere Research Station. Most implements tested during the 1960s and 1970s were found to be unsuitable for local soil condition or were too heavy for the small local East African Zebu animals to pull. Some were too sophisticated for Ugandan conditions and very expensive in foreign exchange to import. The poor farmers could not afford them despite a heavy subsidy of 50% given by the government.

Soroti Agricultural Implement Machinery Manufacturing Company (Saimmco) is situated in the centre of Uganda. The company manufactures ox plows, spare parts and ox carts. It satisfies requirements for plow spares in eastern Uganda. For a long time 90% of the total land area in the east was cultivated with oxen, but animal draft has been considerably reduced in recent years by the political situation.

Saimmco plans to continue to make ox plows, shares and carts, in quantities that will be determined largely by the availability of raw materials, which depends on hard currency. The firm may look into the possibility of developing animal-drawn planters and weeders that would reduce human drudgery. One idea is to produce a relatively cheap multipurpose toolbar and ensure the availability of spare parts.

Saimmco has had one pair of oxen trained for use in testing the ox-drawn implements made by the firm, and to demonstrate their use to farmers. Land for this purpose has already been acquired at a nearby prison farm, and work should commence in April 1992.

In the far north of Uganda, West Acholi Cooperative Union Ltd (WACU) produces light ox plows and spare parts for the Indian type plows. They supply spares to the whole of northern Uganda, north-eastern Uganda (Karamoja) and parts of eastern Uganda. Their production capacity is high because they are able to import raw materials from abroad with the assistance of the non-governmental organisation, Acord.

WACU also manufactures ox plows with a rectangular hollow section beam, designed for lightness and strength. By July 1991, 100 ox plows were in stock together with several spares. This tool frame was tested at Serere during the early 1980s and was recommended for use by farmers. It is designed to be a simple but versatile toolbar that can be used for plowing, planting and weeding with cultivating tines. Although the toolbar is quite promising, it did not, unfortunately, achieve all these operations because tests and modifications were interrupted by the national political situation.

The informal sector of village blacksmiths is another source of implements and spares. However, currently this role is insignificant. Where individual attempts have been made, production has been of poor quality and the tools produced inefficient. For ox draft power to play a greater role in Uganda's economy, greater recognition and support must be accorded to traditional blacksmiths. This could, in the long run, improve the quality of their products and lead to a reliable supply of ox-drawn implements and spare parts.

While farmers in Uganda are to some extent satisfied with the ox plows, they still lack knowledge of ox training. This is the area of present concentration, especially as the technology is being re-introduced to the districts of north and east Uganda where the cattle population was considerably reduced by rustlers in the mid-1980s.

NGO efforts to improve ox technology

NGOs (non-governmental organisations—mainly church missionary societies from overseas and local church organisations) are playing an important role in promoting the use of oxen in rural areas of Uganda. Their efforts are concentrated in north-eastern Uganda (Karamoja), Soroti in eastern Uganda, and Mityana Diocese in southern Uganda.

They aim at ensuring a sufficient supply of ox implements and spare parts for the repair and reconditioning of implements currently in use. The NGOs have workshops for the repair of implements and also have ox units for demonstrating ox training and for running short courses for extension staff and farmers. The NGOs work closely with the ox cultivation experts of the Ministry of Agriculture, Animal Industry and Fisheries to keep them abreast of government policy regarding animal traction.

In Soroti, a church organisation has set up a cattle restocking programme to re-introduce ox cultivation into the area. The programme includes training of donkeys to supplement oxen wherever possible, especially for use as pack animals and for pulling carts. Three agricultural staff were sent from Uganda to Harare for a three-week training course. On their return they advocated the systematic method of ox training they had learnt about.

Problems remaining

There are several specific problems affecting efficient ox power that need to be tackled to reduce human drudgery and improve animal traction technology. These include:

○ poor management and feeding of working animals including, at times, inhumane use of animals at work

○ poor harnessing as a result of inadequate knowledge and training

○ lack of training

○ poor ox-drawn equipment and machinery

○ inadequate availability of equipment and spares when and where required

○ high prices of ox-drawn equipment and spares

○ lack of repair facilities including equipment for fabrication of spares by local blacksmiths

○ lack of equipment for fine seedbed preparation, row seeding, crop protection (spraying, etc) and harvesting groundnuts and tuber crops

○ farmer training and ox cultivation extension

○ quality of draft animals. The East African Zebu at 250–300 kg provides inadequate traction power, while the long-horned Ankole is considered unsuitable for work due to poor body conformation (long legs, weak shoulders, poor hind muscles, narrow chest and long neck).

Government policies

The present Uganda Government policy relating to ox draft power is to:

○ encourage first and second plowing with oxen

○ encourage row cropping using seeders so that inter-row cultivation with weeders is possible

○ integrate the use of oxen with tractors, by using animal-drawn transport for farm and household materials such as manure, farm produce, water, firewood and charcoal. This will be of particular benefit to housewives, relieving them of drudgery and giving them time for other useful work.

To work efficiently, oxen and the farmers must be well trained. The farmers must know about the parts, functions, basic adjustments and repair of plows and other available equipment. Positive efforts have in the past been made by the government, but in recent years many constraints have overwhelmed the technology. These have included budgetary constraints and inadequate funding of ox cultivation technology and inadequate training for ox cultivation extension staff and farmers.

Future developments

Training at a national level (when peace returns) will be conducted at the National Ox Cultivation Centre at Serere Research Station. At this level district extension agents and subject matter specialists will be trained in:

○ harnessing systems

○ care and maintenance of ox-drawn implements

○ training oxen

○ care and management of oxen

○ soil conservation using ox power

○ the philosophy of ox draft power.

The district subject matter specialists will then conduct similar training for extension agents in their respective District Farm Institutes. The trained agricultural agents in the districts will, in turn, conduct on-farm training of farmers and oxen. The success of the training programme will depend, in part, on the availability of oxen, of local breeds, in the districts.

Reference

MAAIF, 1987. *Agricultural survey for Dairy Development Committee*. Ministry of Agriculture, Animal Industry and Fisheries (MAAIF), Kampala, Uganda.

Developing extension programmes for transfer of animal traction technology in Uganda

by

J O Y Omoding

Assistant Commissioner for Agriculture
Ministry of Agriculture, Animal Industries and Fisheries, PO Box 102, Entebbe, Uganda

Abstract

The transfer of animal traction technology in Uganda has had varying degrees of success. The process is more advanced in the east and the north than in other parts of the country. This may have been due to differences in the availability of zebu cattle, soil and vegetation types and the attitudes and taboos of ethnic groups, but it is mainly due to differences in the success rates of ox cultivation extension programmes.

The success of extension programmes depends to a large extent on the planning effort that guides extension workers to establish objectives for measuring and evaluating progress. Successful programmes are characterised by a clear mission and philosophy, which is the driving force towards long-term development. They also have simple, flat and fluid administrative structures which allow for quick, independent decisions. Many successful programmes consider that situational analysis and motivation of staff and farmers are prerequisites for sustainable development of animal traction. In addition, involvement of clientele, extensionists, researchers and other groups enhances holistic development of farming systems where animal traction technology plays a major role.

Introduction

Ox cultivation, as an intermediate technology, was introduced to Uganda at the turn of this century. Its transfer was linked with the development of cotton growing, which followed the establishment of a road network and the extension northward of the railway system. The technology is now well accepted and adopted in eastern Uganda, particularly in Kumi, Pallisa and Soroti Districts, and moderately well adopted in northern Uganda, but its spread to other parts of the country has been slow. The variation in the degree of adoption of ox cultivation can be attributed to differences in availability of zebu cattle, soil and vegetation types and attitudes and taboos of the ethnic groups, as well as to the different approaches used to extend the technology.

The approaches used in Uganda to extend innovations, including animal traction, to farmers have included the use of traditional chiefs and rulers to implement extension programmes, colonial extension services, donor sponsored commodity extension services, holistic rural development, training and visits, farming systems support programmes and decentralised non-governmental efforts. The success of these approaches in transferring animal traction technology has varied considerably. For example, chiefs and rulers sometimes used coercion to implement the programmes, in order to please their masters, which probably accounted for unsustainable adoption of ox cultivation in some areas.

Technical and extension professionals can learn from one another's experiences and, through discussion, can get new ideas which can be applied in their own organisations. This paper features some personal experiences of developing extension programmes for animal traction technology in Uganda.

The need to develop extension for animal traction

Any transfer of knowledge, skill, technology or change involves the training of recipients and beneficiaries. The success of any training programme depends on planning for it to be progressive and forward looking. At all stages of animal traction technology transfer there is need to formulate a system of planning which encourages the transferring organisation to anticipate emerging issues and to develop responsive programmes.

Some basic reasons for planning extension programmes for technology transfer are to:

- ensure careful consideration of what is to be done, and why
- have a written statement for public use
- provide a guide against which to judge new proposals
- establish objectives for measuring and evaluating progress
- facilitate choosing between important and incidental problems, and between permanent and temporary changes
- prevent mistaking the means for the end

- ◦ develop both felt and unfelt needs
- ◦ aid in developing leadership
- ◦ promote efficiency and avoid waste of time and money
- ◦ help justify public budget appropriations.

Ingredients for an animal traction transfer programme

One of the reasons why some areas of Uganda have lagged behind others in adopting ox cultivation is that some extension programmes were more effective than others. What were the common characteristics of the successful programmes that the others lacked? Which types of programmes had the most positive effects in the community? The following are some characteristics of successful programmes for the transfer of animal traction technology in Uganda.

Philosophy and general mission

Ox cultivation programmes in Kumi, Pallisa and Soroti Districts at the turn of the century had a long-term commitment (by the British)—to produce cotton for the UK textile industry. The development of railways and a road network was fuelled by the same mission. Post-independence programmes have often lacked clear values, visions or long-range policies.

Similarly, the philosophy of programmes, especially regarding beliefs and attitudes towards clientele development, is often not clearly stated. A recent report on extension in Uganda sponsored by the World Bank (Bank of Uganda, 1990) states the philosophy that the only purpose of the extension service is to deliver educational programmes which "help people to solve problems for themselves". Boyle (1985) further states that programmes should improve the "health of the people and the community", by which he means improving the condition and situation of clientele. Euro-Action Acord, a non-governmental organisation (NGO), has emphasised overall economic development of farmers as its mission and philosophy in its programmes in Nebbi District in northern Uganda.

Organisation structure

Some organisations have a formal hierarchy with limited freedom to make independent decisions. These structures are a hangover from the colonial era: they may appear stable, complex and multipurpose, but they inhibit change. Simple, flat and fluid structures can respond quickly to changing conditions and opportunities. Government departments in Uganda often have structures which inhibit quick decision making. On the other hand,

organisations such as Acord and Action Aid, operating in Mityana Catholic Diocese, and the Lutheran World Federation, working in Moyo and Karamoja, have fairly simple structures, which accounts for their success in promoting ox cultivation in the areas where they operate, even though these areas are regarded as non-traditional with "hard soil" by the Department of Agriculture.

Situational analysis

The role of extension agents is to help effect desirable changes, such as increased knowledge, understanding, attitudes and skills in animal traction technology. Before animal traction technology is introduced the needs of the farmers should be identified and translated into goals and objectives. A need should be "felt". The need is a condition between what *is* and what *should be*, or between what *is* and what is *more desirable*. Needs should be determined systematically by collecting data and analysing them to discover priorities. Situational analysis encompasses the improvement of subject matter specialists, extension workers and the farmers themselves.

Motivation

Farmers and extension staff are motivated through fulfilling some of their needs. Many ox cultivation programmes run by NGOs attracted civil servants as staff or consultants. In some cases these people work for both the government and an NGO.

Staff and farmer training

Staff involved in animal traction work should be familiar with local farming and rural conditions. They should have training in the general type of agriculture needed in the community, and they should be familiar with, and able to use, the most effective teaching methods and equipment in an informal community setting. The type of staff is also important. Are they empathetic (in the shoes of farmers)? Are they highly motivated, or unrewarded and therefore apathetic? Do they participate regularly in staff development and training? The effectiveness of training farmers in animal traction is highly dependent on how staff themselves are trained.

Involvement

Clientele involvement in the programme development process was a major strength in the transfer of animal traction technology in eastern Uganda. Learning is most likely to change behaviour substantially when people try to improve situations that are relevant and important to them (Prawl, Medlin and Gross, 1984). Perhaps the success of programmes depends on a combined involvement of research specialists, teaching specialists, clientele with real felt needs, administrators and other stake holders.

Staff with different specialisations can complement one another when they work as a team. Communication and collaboration between different parties involved in transfer of animal traction technology might appear difficult at the beginning due to differing allegiances and interests, but later they enhance progress through the sharing of experiences and brain storming in solving common problems.

Many successful programmes have also used contact and contract farmers, unpaid professionals, volunteers and other local leaders.

However, programmes which are well integrated into the local political and social community network have a greater impact.

Decision making and judgement

Once data have been analysed and interpreted, decisions on programme priorities, goals and methods are normally made by top administrators in the hierarchy, without involving other staff and clientele. Such programmes tend to lack commitment from farmers and staff. The programmes are not theirs. Decentralisation of decision making stimulates the development of staff, who can then make their own judgements with confidence. Another consideration is whether judgements are made formally or informally. Rigidness in the organisation has often delayed the development of animal traction.

Research

Successful programmes have their directions, goals and methods based on up-to-date research, knowledge and technology. Research on the feasibility of carrying out the animal traction programme is very often ignored. Research, extension and close links with farmers are the prerequisites for successful transfer of animal traction technology. Research should be practical and adaptive (on-farm research), with work on experimental stations where necessary.

Objectives indicating the general direction towards which all the efforts in animal traction development are to be focused should be clearly and formally stated or written and then communicated to stake holders.

Planning of animal traction programmes can be divided into two parts:

- the long-range plan, sometimes called a programme of work or a strategic plan, is

normally broad in scope. It consists of a goal statement, a situation statement and long-range objectives which indicate the desired direction for the programme
- the annual plan of work sets out the objectives for the year, within the direction of the long-range plan. It must therefore be related to the long-range objectives and relevant to the situation statement.

The annual plan contains a list of activities to be carried out, for example:

- demonstrations to be given (numbers and types)
- meetings to be held (with dates)
- articles or leaflets to be prepared
- individuals to be met
- materials to be obtained.

The annual plan also has a provision for evaluating progress, achievements and failures.

Implementation

In Uganda NGOs carry out animal traction programmes according to set objectives: subject matter, teaching and learning principles, teaching strategies, audiences and levels of learning are all blended to achieve the desired outcomes. The Ministry of Agriculture, Animal Industries and Fisheries organises competitions in animal husbandry and ox cultivation techniques: attractive prizes arouse keen participation. Lack of finance often hinders the sustainability of these efforts. The most important component in the implementation plan is a monitoring system and feedback procedure at the completion of the programme so that appropriate revisions can be made to the plan of action.

Evaluation

Evaluating the programme is always a challenge. There are differing opinions on whether outsiders or people within the programmes, including farmers, should carry out this important exercise.

Evaluation is a scientific process to determine if objectives were, or are being, met, and if the animal traction programmes are suitable, effective and of high quality. It involves comparing evidence of the impact of the programme with criteria of "what the situation should be". Because it is an integral part of the planning process, evaluation is carried out continuously from the onset to the conclusion of the programme.

The evaluation plan should include details on how the indicators of impact should be collected, and who would collect them. Many animal traction programmes in Uganda have not been evaluated because care was not taken to collect the type of information needed at the time it could have been collected.

Budget and financing

The loss of some staff from government departments to NGOs may be due to inadequate budgets and problems with how they are determined and used. They may not provide for the necessary equipment, office work, travel and supplies needed to bring about change in rural community. Sometimes not enough staff are hired or retained.

Conclusion

Animal traction technology has not been transferred effectively to some parts of Uganda because the right programmes have not been used, or because there were not any viable programmes at all. This paper has attempted to outline some criteria, ideas or concepts for use in comparing and improving animal traction technology transfer programmes. They can be used to guide analyses of different programmes. The analyses, in turn, should help technicians and field workers identify shortcomings for further corrective action.

References

Boyle P, 1985. *Planning better programs*. McGraw Hill, New York, USA.

Prawl W, Medlin R and Gross J, 1984. *Adult and continuing education through co-operative service*. Missouri Cooperative Extension Service, Columbia, Missouri, USA. 73p.

Bank of Uganda, 1990. *Agriculture sector review*. Task Force Working Group 9B, Agricultural Secretarial Reports, Bank of Uganda, Kampala, Uganda. 15p.

A note on factors influencing the transfer of animal traction technology in Uganda

by

Emenyu Henry Smuts Ojirot

Project Coordinator, Animal Draft Power Training Programme, Animal Traction Development Organisation
PO Box 9112, Kampala, Uganda

Abstract

Many environmental, social, political and economic factors have limited the development, efficient use and spread of animal traction technology in Uganda. This paper lists some of the problems and describes efforts that are being made to develop the use of this technology in the country. Reference is made to the work of non-governmental organisations operating in Karamoja and other regions.

Some constraints to animal traction

Animal draft power was introduced in Uganda in 1909, but its potential has not been fully exploited. Many factors have limited the development and spread of animal traction technology in the country.

Environmental factors include steep, undulating topography in Kigezi and Bugisu; thick forests in Budongo and Budanga; tsetse infestations in the south-east and south-west.

Social factors incude migratory tendencies of pastoral communities such as the Bahima in western Uganda and Karamajong in north-eastern Uganda; inter-territorial raids or cattle rustling among various tribes; illiteracy; cultural and religious affiliations; large families; apathy and resistance to change and ideas that animal draft power is an out-dated technology compared to modern tractors.

Political factors include clashes between rebels and government troops leading to a dramatic decrease in the cattle population in affected areas of northern and eastern Uganda; mass exits of technical personnel during the military regime of the 1970s, and following economic difficulties in the country; policy variations as a result of changes in governments; attempts to satisfy the electorate during the post- independence era, such as massive investments in tractorisation schemes, at the expense of animal draft power technology—a result of politics overriding technical decisions.

Economic factors include poor infrastructure; lack of institutional support, scarcity of equipment; liquidity and capital limitations; foreign exchange constraints and keeping animals for prestige rather than for profit.

Karamoja programme

In Uganda, especially among the pastoral community of the Karamajong and Teaso, cattle keeping is a tradition. The work animals currently available include 38 000 pairs of oxen as well as some donkeys and camels. The need now is to provide institutional and infrastructural support to the farmers.

It is said that whatever the elders council "Akiriket Angi Kathikou" approves will be be adopted by the people. It is therefore a question of introducing the subject to elders to obtain their consent. For example, they might be convinced that the use of oxen could relieve the burden on the women of Karamoja who do much of the cultivation work and head porterage.

The oxenisation programmes in Karamoja are supported by several non-governmental organisations (NGOs), including the Lutheran World Federation, Inter-Aid, Action International contre la Faim and the Church of Uganda, all working under the coordination of Karamoja Development Agency within the policy framework of the Ministry of Agriculture, Animal Industry and Fisheries. For example, Inter-Aid provided inputs and implements at affordable prices and organises training workshops.

The Kangote Ox Training Unit was established in Bokara in 1988. The project involved volunteers selected through local authorities. Animals, volunteers and farmers were trained in practical workshops. The community identified problems and provided oxen, land and local materials for yoke making. They also paid for ox carts and equipment manufactured by the ox unit.

Some of the farmers who could not afford to pay the full price of an implement in one lump sum expressed the need for credit or hire purchase schemes. The government assisted by giving subsidies and reducing tax on agricultural inputs.

New developments

The newly initiated Animal Traction Development Organisation is an indigenous NGO that started from grassroots level in Kaabong. It has bases in Kaabong, Kotido, Namalu in Karamoja, Kasese in western Uganda, Mukono in central and Sebei in eastern Uganda.

The Dairy Industry Development Project implemented by the Food and Agriculture Organization of the United Nations (FAO) in conjunction with the Department of Animal Industry and Fisheries, launched a programme to promote use of animal power in dairy farming in Uganda. Training provided at Nakyesasa Livestock Station included basic training of field staff in ox handling, pasture establishment and the use of animal power. Buganda and western Uganda had not been using animal draft on a large scale. These areas often have thick elephant grass vegetation, and so land clearance and preparation is very important. Local people believed that oxen cannot work. Many observers came to watch the exercise with anxiety and interest, and realised that oxen can work just like a tractor. There is now a high demand for trained oxen, ox carts and implements in Buganda and the western region.

The recent fuel crisis and the high initial capital investment on tractors have increased interest in animal draft power. The fragmented land holdings are not economical for tractorisation and delays in land preparation are inevitable: oxen are more suitable and cheaper.

In Namulonge, heifers have been trained for traction. A collar harness system and an "improved" yoke have been tested by staff of the Ministry of Agriculture (supported by USAID). The NGO agency Acord has played a big role in Gulu and Kitgum Districts.

Concluding observations

There is urgent need to mobilise the fragmented resources and knowledge relating to animal traction in Uganda. This calls for a network for information exchange and dissemination, the production of audio-visual aids, and the monitoring and evaluation of the different programmes. This will lead to collaboration, cooperation among manufacturers, researchers, policy-makers and NGOs.

More use could be made of ox carts in order to alleviate the heavy transport burden of women.

Suitable animals are available in Uganda, but there is a need for improved supply in some areas.

Improving animal power utilisation in Malawi: the work of the Animal Power Utilisation Project

by

Wells Kumwenda[1] and Paul de Roover[2]

[1] Senior Agricultural Engineer, Chitezde Research Station, Box 158, Lilongwe, Malawi
[2] Chief Technical Advisor, Animal Power Utilisation Project, FAO, Box 30750, Lilongwe, Malawi

Abstract

Most countries in southern Africa have distinct wet and dry seasons, and optimum tillage time is limited to the first 23 days after the rains start if high yields are to be achieved. Timeliness in completing basic land preparation before planting is very critical on smallholder farms where labour bottlenecks occur because farm operations are done by hand. Farm size is therefore limited by how much land a farming family can till. It is difficult to mechanise small farms in Malawi using motorised equipment because of the cost, the size and location of fields and the farmers' lack of technical knowledge. The use of animal power on these farms seem more appropriate. This paper describes some project efforts to improve animal power utilisation. It includes details on training of staff, farmers and animals, testing of new equipment, organisation of revolving funds for supply of drugs and spare part distribution.

Introduction

Most Malawian farmers cannot use motorised equipment on their farms because of the high cost of the equipment and the lack of technical expertise and spares. Motorised mechanisation is also a major problem for the country as a whole because the import of equipment and oil causes a drain on foreign exchange. In a situation where agricultural operations are carried out by hand labour, animal traction technology offers a better alternative for increasing production.

Many advantages of using animal draft power in Malawi have been identified. For example:

- the cost is within the reach of most farmers because the animals and equipment are readily available in the country
- the technology fits very well into existing farming systems, allowing mixed cropping and involving all members of the farmer's family, including children
- the animals appreciate in value with time (except for donkeys), so the farmer can get many years' work from his animals and still sell them at a profit
- farmers can understand the technology, or can be trained to do so in a short time
- animal power is faster than hand labour
- animals and their equipment can be hired out, thus earning income for their owners
- working with animal power involves less drudgery than hand labour.

The common draft animals in Malawi are oxen and donkeys. They are used in agriculture and forestry for plowing, harrowing, ridging, carting and logging. There are several problems with using draft animals (Kumwenda, 1987), including:

- inadequate numbers and types of animals
- poor training of animals
- lack of trained personnel at grassroots level to encourage adoption and pass on skills and information to the users
- poor animal management
- pests, diseases and high mortality rates
- inadequate feed and water
- uncertain supply of equipment and spare parts
- lack of suitable equipment
- poor harnessing techniques
- shortage of land and poor terrain.

The Government of Malawi has recognised the need for farm mechanisation as a means of increasing agricultural production, and the important role that animal power can play in such a development. This recognition is reflected in the country's *Statement of Development Policies 1987–1996* (Government of Malawi, 1987), which states that the supply and training of work animals will be emphasised and that priority will be given to the training of farmers on how to use implements. It was as a result of these policies that the Animal Power Utilisation Project was established in 1986, with assistance from the Food and Agriculture Organization of the United Nations (FAO). The general objective of the project is to develop agricultural production and improve the living standards of rural people in Malawi through the enhanced and improved use of animal power, particularly for crop production and farm transport.

The specific objectives of the Animal Power Utilisation Project are to:

○ review current knowledge, understanding and extent of draft animal power utilisation in Malawi, as well as constraints to the development of this technology

○ strengthen the technical capacity of the Ministry of Agriculture, and other relevant organisations and institutions, to evaluate requirements for agricultural mechanisation through tractorisation or oxenisation, and to promote the use of animal power in the country where and when appropriate

○ assist the Ministry of Agriculture to establish an operational research capacity for the development of appropriate training and support for institutions and organisations engaged in the use of animal power in the country

○ promote liaison and communication within Malawi concerning all aspects of animal power utilisation

○ identify draft animal power equipment from other countries for production and use in Malawi

○ improve the availability of alternative draft animals in Malawi

○ establish an effective spare parts distribution system at the rural artisan level

○ establish an effective drug distribution system at the veterinary assistant level

○ train government and other staff, and farmers, in the use and maintenance of draft animal technology.

The primary beneficiaries of the Animal Power Utilisation Project are smallholder and estate farmers who can use animal power to intensify agricultural production and reduce tractor costs.

Rural communities will also benefit: ox cultivation will reduce the drudgery of hand hoeing, and animal-drawn transport will lessen the burden of headloading farm inputs and produce. Women in particular will enjoy the benefits of using appropriate farm and transport equipment.

Rural artisans will have an opportunity to increase their business by repairing animal-drawn implements and participating in spare part distribution networks.

The country in general will benefit through:

○ increased crop production resulting from improved timely tillage techniques and the use of animal manure, and leading to food self-sufficiency

○ reduced cost of tractor operated schemes in both agriculture and forestry. Tractors require imported spare parts and fuel, and the foreign exchange saved by their reduced use can be used to buy other commodities

○ reduced mortality rates of working animals through vaccinations against diseases

○ increased opportunity for individual investment in animal power equipment and spare part production and sales

○ reduced environmental degradation. Animal power is an ecologically appropriate technology.

Project achievements

Testing of alternative equipment

Several implements were obtained from abroad, for testing to see if they offered better alternatives to implements already manufactured in Malawi. The implements obtained were the Sebele planter from Botswana; wooden plows from the Philippines; a combined plow, ridger and toolframe from The Netherlands; a plow from Mozambique; and damscoops from Zimbabwe.

After testing, the Sebele planter was not recommended for use in Malawi because it could only plant on flat ground (it is recommended to plant on ridges in Malawi). Furthermore, it had no depth control and no marker, and the metering mechanism only worked with uniformly graded seed (large seeds blocked the metering mechanism and soft seeds, such as groundnuts, were damaged).

Wooden plows from the Philippines were unsuitable for upland work because they could not withstand the forces encountered in plowing such soils. There was also worry that wooden plows might encourage deforestation and the skill of making curved wooden frames was not available locally. It is now planned to have these made of iron, with a few modifications. It has also been decided that fast wearing parts be made detachable. Testing of these will continue on rice schemes.

The combined plow, ridger and toolframe made by Rumptstad of The Netherlands was made of very hard steel to resist wear. Testing showed that this implement could not be used in Malawi without modification, but even if its performance could be improved, Malawian farmers would not be able to buy the unit as its price is more than twice that of locally made implements.

The "Safim-type" plow from Mozambique is similar in every aspect to the ones made by Agrimal in Malawi. Damscoops were successfully used by farmers in the north and central fisheries project for making fish ponds.

Table 1: Numbers of work oxen and implements owned by farmers in the different Agricultural Development Divisions of Malawi in 1989

	Work oxen	Plows	Ridgers	Cultivators	Ox carts	Harrows	Toolbars
Karonga	20 750	3 317	438	24	372	4	–
Mzuzu	18 494	8 698	6 037	151	1 881	–	–
Salima	1 880	590	839	82	816	–	–
Kasungu	12 696	2 095	3 175	48	5 352	12	5
Lilongwe	16 041	1 740	1 507	191	8 883	9	5
Liwonde	788	641	430	74	561	–	9
Blantyre	414	148	126	22	239	–	–
Ngabu	1 260	458	189	16	631	–	–
Total	**72 323**	**18 047**	**12 741**	**608**	**18 735**	**25**	**19**

Alternative draft animals

Table 1 shows the numbers of draft animals and implements in Malawi. There are not enough draft animals in the country. Efforts have been made to produce steers on government farms and sell them to farmers, but the numbers produced have always fallen short of requirements.

An attempt was also made to increase the number of donkeys in Malawi by importing animals from Botswana (Kumwenda and Mateyo, 1991). But of the 250 donkeys ordered, only 42 had been imported by June 1991. The others, when given the Dourine test, were found to be seropositive, and they were kept in Botswana pending investigations of Dourine prevalence in Malawi. Tests on 73 Malawi donkeys showed that the disease does not exist in Malawi, and so the veterinary authorities have banned the import of the remaining Botswana donkeys.

In 1988 the Republic of China offered to send 10 water buffaloes to Malawi, for research at one of the Chinese assisted agricultural irrigation schemes. An expert would accompany the animals for a few years and would train local staff and farmers on all aspects of husbandry and draft utilisation. Study tours are foreseen for staff to go and learn about the use of water buffaloes in China. The importation has so far not materialised because the Department of Animal Health and Industry is afraid of importing new diseases.

Pest disease and animal management

Following the discovery that drugs and vaccines were in short supply in some parts of Malawi, drug revolving funds were created in those Agricultural Development Divisions (ADD) which were severely affected. These funds, which are controlled by the divisional veterinary officer at each ADD, are used to buy drugs and vaccines which are then sold to

farmers: the revenues from sales go back to divisional veterinary officer. The most common drugs purchased are antibiotics, wound healing drugs and dewormers.

Two ADDs, Karonga and Ngabu, both have a high cattle population and drugs were previously in short supply. Each of these ADDs has received drugs worth about 11 000 Kwacha (approximately US$ 2200). Despite problems at the start, Ngabu has managed to increase its revolving fund by 50% over a 10-month period, whereas Karonga has doubled its fund in just over eight months. A recent project evaluation mission recommended that similar drug revolving funds be set up in all the ADDs.

Distribution of spare parts

One of the reasons why spare parts are in short supply in rural areas is that most of the implement manufacturers are based in Blantyre in the Southern Region, and only a few have branches in the other two regions. Other reasons include the seasonality in demand for these spares, and the method of producing them. Large distributors are allowed to collect implements and spares on credit, while small ones are not yet allowed to do so. Yet the small distributors are the ones most suitably located for distribution. The Animal Power Utilisation Project investigated the possibility of establishing the revolving fund in all the ADDs but after detailed surveys it was concluded that such work would better be done by those institutions already in this business, such as Chipiku Stores, Peoples Trading Centre (PTC), Agricultural Development and Marketing Cooperation (Admarc) and individual entrepreneurs.

Review of knowledge and constraints

Detailed surveys have been carried out to examine some of the problems of animal draft technology in Malawi. For example Kasomekera and Mwinjilo (1989) investigated animal power utilisation in Malawi; Liuma (1989) studied the involvement of women in animal power utilisation; and Ashburner (1989) did a survey on local equipment produced within the country. A national workshop to discuss these findings was held for policy makers, manufacturers, researchers, distributors and extension personnel.

Phase I of the Animal Power Utilisation Project (August 1987 to February 1989) was, among other things, focused on staff training and on the identification, through national surveys, of problem areas in draft animal technology uptake. Special attention was given to the role of women in the uptake of the technology through a three-day national workshop held in Lilongwe in 1988. This was followed by a two-month consultancy on the involvement of women in animal power utilisation in Malawi (Liuma, 1989).

In Phase II of the project (March 1989 to April 1992), staff and farmer training, and research and development of appropriate types of implements and farm carts, have continued, and particular attention has been paid to the health and production of draft animals. Apart from training 3117 field extension staff and farmers in draft animal technology, the project has organised the following:

○ short courses in the UK and The Netherlands for six participants

○ a national seminar on "Mechanical and animal power strategy development"

○ one fellowship (which terminated in June 1991 due to the death of the fellow)

○ a study tour to India and the Philippines for two participants

○ a local study tour to Chikangawa for 96 ox trainers from all ADDs

○ training courses in ADDs

Future work

Although the Animal Power Utilisation Project has been successful in solving some of the farmers' problems, there is need to continue this work in future.

There is need to provide facilities for draft animal hire, both in the upland farms and on irrigation schemes. These would replace power tillers, which are difficult and expensive to run on irrigation schemes.

Training of animals and farmers should be a continuing process so that any new techniques, equipment or information can easily be relayed to the farmers.

There is a need to improve feeding and management of work animals by emphasising maintenance and supplementary feeding, good harnessing techniques and handling of animals.

Research and development is needed on new equipment, especially the weeder and planter which are not yet available to farmers.

Conclusion

Draft animal power is an intermediate technology that is cheap, technically easy and socially acceptable to many farmers. This technology can definitely increase the productivity of farms and ease the burden of carrying heavy things on the head and shoulders. If animal draft power is to be successful, continuous attention should be paid to animal health, feeding, ready availability of equipment and spare parts and providing farmers with credit to buy the package.

References

Ashburner J E, 1989. *Study on equipment manufacture, supply and distribution for DAP utilisation in Malawi*. Consultancy Report. Animal Power Utilisation Project, Ministry of Agriculture, Lilongwe, Malawi. 159p.

Government of Malawi, 1987. *Statement of development policies 1987–1996*. Office of the President and Cabinet, Department of Economic Planning and Development. Government Printer, Zomba, Malawi. 197p.

Kasomekera Z and Mwinjilo M, 1989. *Survey of animal power utilisation in Malawi*. Consultancy Report. Animal Power Utilisation Project, Ministry of Agriculture, Lilongwe Malawi. 55p.

Kumwenda W, 1987. Animal traction in Malawi: problems and potential solutions. In: Kumwenda W (ed), *Proceedings of the national farm machinery research and extension workshop held in January 1981 in Mangochi*. Chitedze Research Station, Lilongwe, Malawi. 71p.

Kumwenda W and Mateyo L, 1991. The potential and utilization of the donkey in Malawi. pp. 28–32 in: Fielding D and Pearson R A (eds), *Donkeys, mules and horses in tropical agricultural development*. Proceedings of a colloquium held 3–6 September 1990 at the Centre for Tropical Veterinary Medicine, University of Edinburgh, Scotland. Alexander Ritchie, Edinburgh, UK. 336p.

Liuma L, 1989. *The involvement of women in animal power utilization*. Consultancy Report. Animal Power Utilisation Project, Ministry of Agriculture, Lilongwe, Malawi. 30p.

Transfer of animal traction technology in Zambia: an historical perspective

by [*]

Adrian Wood [1] and John Milimo [2]

[1] Department of Geographical and Environmental Sciences, University of Huddersfield, Huddersfield, UK
[2] Rural Development Studies Bureau, University of Lusaka, PO Box 32379, Lusaka, Zambia

Abstract

Technological change is central to the development of traditional agriculture. Increased productivity of labour is necessary if farmers are to progress from subsistence levels of cultivation to production of regular surpluses for sale. In Zambia the development of small-scale, semi-commercial farming has been closely associated with the adoption of the plow and animal draft power. This paper reviews the evolution of animal traction technology in Zambia from its introduction in the last part of the 19th century to the present day. It identifies the factors which have facilitated the diffusion of this technology and the arguments which, in the past three decades, have surrounded its contribution to rural development.

Introduction

Animal traction is central to Zambia's agricultural development at present. Increased ox cultivation could lead to the increased involvement of small-scale producers in market-oriented agriculture, the expansion of agricultural output without increased foreign exchange costs, and the generation of attractive rural employment opportunities to encourage urban–rural migration and reduce urban unemployment. The adoption of animal draft power provides the economically viable method by which small-scale producers can overcome the labour constraint to increased output and thereby expand sales and raise their incomes. The productivity of rural labour can also be increased by the adoption of ox cultivation, and higher yields may be obtained because of more timely cultivation and better preparation of seedbeds. Increased use of ox carts could facilitate the growth of rural trade and marketing without dependence upon mechanised

[*]This paper draws on the work of several people. It was compiled and submitted by Henry Sichembe, Acting Head, Agricultural Engineering Section, Ministry of Agriculture, PO Box 50291, Lusaka, Zambia. The text is based on the report of Kimmage and Wood (1988) and the chapter by Milimo, Bussink and Jonsson in the book *The dynamics of agricultural policy and reform in Zambia*, edited by Wood, Kean, Milimo and Warren (1990). The main authors cited here fully acknowledge the contribution of their colleagues and collaborators

transport with its high foreign exchange costs, while the production of ox-drawn farm equipment could become a rural artisanal industry, provided suitable materials can be made available.

While many papers relating to animal traction in Zambia have concentrated on recent initiatives, this paper provides an historical overview of animal power in Zambia since the late 19th century. This is important in order to identify the circumstances which have facilitated the adoption of this technology, and to ensure that the lessons of past debates and analyses are taken into consideration in current and future activities in support of animal traction technology.

Origins of animal traction

Cattle keeping has been a tradition for many centuries in several parts Zambia, especially on the plateaux in the east and south and on the Zambezi floodplain and adjoining areas in the west. In much of the rest of the country, comprising over one-third of the land area, tsetse infestation has prevented the keeping of cattle. Over the centuries, considerable skills in cattle keeping have been built up by several ethnic groups, especially the Tonga, Lozi, Ngoni and Mambwe, but cattle were not used for draft power before the colonial period (Müller, 1986); instead they were kept for their production of milk, meat and leather, and as a store of wealth and a symbol of status. Consequently, in all the traditional farming systems cultivation was done by hand, using the hoe (Trapnell 1953; Trapnell and Clothier 1957), while trade and local transport of agricultural produce used either headloading or carrying poles and baskets.

The use of animal draft power was first seen in the 1870s when European traders and missionaries, such as Westbeech and Coillard in Barotseland, used mules and oxen for transport purposes (Huckabay, in press). By the turn of the century ox-drawn carts and wagons were widely used by traders and settlers trekking north into the newly opened-up territory. In Southern Province, where cattle and oxen were common, district commissioners used ox-drawn carts (Rangeley, 1965), while by 1900 several transport companies were operating services from Southern Rhodesia (Zimbabwe) into Southern Province using wagons drawn by 12 to 18 oxen (Murray, 1965).

Although the earliest use of animal draft power in Zambia was mainly for transport, oxen began to be used for cultivation during the first years of the 20th century as Europeans settled in the country. At that time ox cultivation was the most appropriate farm technology for the settler farmers and missionaries, who wanted to make the then Northern Rhodesia their home. European farmers, however, had no particular interest in transferring ox cultivation technology to the indigenous population. If anything, they would rather have prevented Africans from acquiring this technology because it was bound to make them unwelcome competitors in the agricultural produce market. As a result, settler farmers played only an indirect and passive role in the transmission of ox cultivation to the indigenous population through their advertisement of the value of the plow on their farms and through the employment of villagers as farm labourers (Dixon-Fyle, 1976).

Often African expatriates, such as Xhosa, Ndebele and Mfengu, who were employed as ox drivers on European farms because they were familiar with animal traction, were the main agents of diffusion, helping spread the techniques of ox plowing by training their Zambian work-mates (Vickery, 1978).

Diffusion of ox cultivation

The major role in the introduction of animal traction cultivation to African farmers in Southern Province should be credited to the Christian missionaries, the more far-sighted of whom made a conscious effort to improve the economic lot of their converts by actively promoting ox cultivation. Prominent among these was the Jesuit priest Father Joseph Moreau of Chikuni Mission in Monze (formerly Magoye) District. The plowing demonstrations he held at the mission in 1905 were immediately appreciated (Vickery, 1978), and he promoted ox plows by selling them through the mission (Dixon-Fyle, 1976). Moreau, who was popularly known as *Siabulembe* (the good gardener), is still lovingly remembered in the Chikuni area, 40 years after his death, as the man who brought about agricultural development in the area (Dixon-Fyle, 1976). Other missions assisted, to varying degrees, in introducing animal draft power among the Tonga of Southern Province so that this area became the earliest and

largest concentration of African ox-plow cultivation in the country.

The adoption of the plow in Southern Province was rapid and remarkable. While there were only three or four households with an ox plow in 1911, by 1916 every kraal in the neighbourhood of Chikuni had trained oxen and a plow (Vickery, 1978). Within Magoye District there were 200 plows by 1921, but following the introduction of the lighter Victory and Solomon plows in the 1920s (Müller, 1986), the rate of adoption increased so that by 1931 "plow cultivation had replaced hoe cultivation" (Vickery, 1978). Maize production from the Tonga plateau as a whole (of which Magoye was a part) almost quadrupled in 15 years from around 15 000 bags (1 bag = 90 kg) in the late 1910s to 55 000 bags by 1933 (Dixon-Fyle, 1976).

Labour migration also assisted, to some extent, the adoption of animal draft power. During their travels, particularly to the "south", migrants received further exposure to the use of oxen for draft power purposes, including plowing, as ox cultivation was more widespread in Southern Rhodesia and South Africa. Labour migration also provided some migrants with capital sums which they could use to buy oxen and plows.

The depression years of the 1930s and the Second World War slowed the process of oxenisation in Southern Province, and by 1945 farm implements in Tonga households were in a poor state (Allan, 1949; Colson, 1954). However, as the copper mining industry revived and the market for food increased, opportunities for expanding agricultural production grew. While agricultural marketing opportunities were the major stimuli to the wider adoption of ox cultivation, in the late 1940s the government introduced a number of measures to encourage the development of African agriculture.

In Southern and Central provinces the African Farm Improvement Scheme was inaugurated. This included subsidies on the purchase of ox-drawn equipment, aimed at increasing the number of plows, cultivators, wagons and scotch carts in use. This contributed to the growing importance of African agricultural production in this area (Anthony et al, 1979).

By independence Southern Province dominated in the process of oxenisation, with widespread African ownership of plows and ox carts (Hellen, 1965). Farmers in Eastern and Central Provinces, however, were also adopting animal draft power. Credit for farmers without plows, and in many cases without cattle, was provided in Eastern Province through the African Peasant Farming Scheme which, combined with the general growth of market-oriented agriculture in this area, led to a major expansion in the ownership of farm equipment. Whereas in 1936 Africans in Eastern Province owned only two plows, by 1965 there were 10 000 plows and more than 4000 scotch carts (Kay, 1965). In Central Province the progress was also later than in Southern Province, but rapid once it began. In Kabwe Rural, the most accessible district in Central Province, a threefold increase in plows occurred during the 1950s (Muntemba, 1977).

Elsewhere oxenisation progressed more slowly. Although Lewanika, the Lozi king, had tried to introduce ox-drawn equipment into Barotseland (Western Province) in the first two decades of the century, the adoption of the plow was less rapid in the province primarily because of the limited opportunities for marketed agricultural production (Kimmage and Wood, 1988). The cattle-keeping areas of Mbala and Isoka in Northern Province were other localities where some use of animal traction was adopted before independence. In addition, in the 1950s Shona settlers from Southern Rhodesia (Zimbabwe) introduced the plow into Ndola Rural District of Central Province (Müller, 1986).

In other parts of the country tsetse infestation and, to a lesser degree, limited agricultural marketing opportunities retarded the adoption of animal draft power, leaving much of the north of the country without this means for increasing production above subsistence level.

Tractor technology

In contrast to the growing adoption of animal traction by many African farmers after the Second World War, this form of farm technology was being abandoned by the European commercial farmers. In place of oxen the settler farmers were increasingly using tractors, and the number of these was seen by the government as one of the major indicators of agricultural change on the commercial farms during the 1950s. The colonial authorities encouraged the adoption of tractor farming as a way for the country to regain food self-sufficiency and for the settler farmers to remain viable and competitive against the growing number of market-oriented African producers.

Post-independence policies and strategies

In the years immediately following independence, concern for developing African agriculture to redress the imbalance favouring settler farmers led to a search for ways in which traditional agriculture could be most rapidly developed, mostly using technology adopted by the large-scale commercial farmers in the 1950s. Government thinking was influenced by the Seers Report (UNECA/FAO, 1964), which saw the wider use of tractors as a way to expand arable production and produce food more efficiently. The government was particularly concerned about maintaining food production for the towns after the departure of about half of the settler farmers. Western donors also encouraged tractor mechanisation by supporting a transformation approach to African agricultural development.

Various measures were introduced to encourage the use of tractors by some groups, especially cooperatives: for example, the direction of credit in favour of tractor farmers rather than ox cultivators; and the introduction of heavily subsidised units that were established in the latter half of the 1960s (Siddle, 1971). In the following years, the use of tractors was also favoured by other aspects of economic policy, especially the overvalued local currency, which made fuel and machinery imports unrealistically cheap.

Comparison of tractors and oxen

Despite the strong support for tractor mechanisation as part of the government's modernisation and transformation strategy for African agriculture, there was concern over the appropriateness of this form of mechanisation, given its capital intensive and labour replacing characteristics (see, for example, the speech by President Kaunda at Mulungushi in April 1968, quoted by Müller, 1986). In recognition of this problem and the potential role of animal traction, an animal training (ox cultivation) project was begun in 1968 (MAWD, 1985). Further doubts about the appropriateness of tractors for small-scale producers continued to grow through the 1970s. Problems were encountered in keeping the tractors in the government mechanisation units operational. The rising prices of oil and spare parts led to the services becoming highly subsidised (MAWD, 1984).

As foreign exchange became scarce from the mid-1970s, shortages of spare parts disrupted tractor plowing services, while the decline in government recurrent revenue made it clear by the early 1980s that the subsidy for tractor plowing services could not be maintained. The foreign exchange shortages and the rising prices of fuel and spare parts also affected individual farmers. Small-scale farmers found it increasingly difficult to replace their tractors because, with small areas in cultivation, they were not covering their depreciation costs. Even large-scale commercial farmers began to look for ways of reducing their reliance on tractors at this time, and while some reduced the arable area and hence mechanised operations on their farms, others began to use animal draft power for some tasks.

An analysis of the relative costs of oxen and tractor cultivation, undertaken in the early 1980s, confirmed the economic problems that small-scale farmers faced with the use of tractors (FAO, 1981). This showed that a yield of 50 bags of maize per hectare was needed to break even on a farm of 20 ha if tractor plowing was used: this is a very high yield for Zambian small-scale farmers. On the other hand, if oxen were used the break-even yield would be only 23 bags per hectare. Several other studies have confirmed this situation. Figures for Eastern Province in 1984–85 showed tractor cultivation to be between 2.3 and 10 times more expensive than oxen cultivation (de Toro, 1984), while a national estimate for the same time period suggested that tractors were 2.6 times more expensive on a 20 ha unit, and almost six times more expensive if labour costs were not included (Müller, 1986).

Full cost/benefit data would be needed for a definitive analysis, but these figures suggest that in the mid-1980s animal traction was much more attractive for a farmer; not only were capital investment costs lower, but profits could be realised with much lower yields and a smaller farm area. In subsequent years, the situation moved increasingly in favour of ox traction, due to the rapid devaluation of the Kwacha.

Animal draft power initiatives

While the need for increased use of oxen is clear financially and economically, and supports the rural development goal of involving more small-scale producers in market-oriented agricultural production, leaving the adoption of ox cultivation to the market forces of innovation diffusion might result in a decreasing rate of adoption of ox cultivation (MAWD, 1985). The most suitable areas for oxen already have quite high rates of ox use, and only the poorer households in these areas do not use animal traction (Kimmage and Wood, 1988). Further, logistical problems are now being faced in obtaining oxen and training them, especially in areas where oxen are not common, while there is also a serious shortage of basic ox-drawn implements and a lack of rural repair services.

Consequently, from the mid-1970s onwards there has been a growing emphasis upon oxenisation programmes. In 1978 a Work Oxen Supply Project was introduced in the Third National Development Plan to increase the availability of work oxen by some 41% in seven years. This project built on the previous Animal Training (Ox Cultivation) Project (which had provided staff to help farmers training oxen to plow), but now tried to introduce oxen use into areas where traditionally they had not been kept. Hence the supply of oxen and the training of farmers to care for cattle became elements of this new project. This initiative was supported by the promotion of ox cultivation in the extension services, especially those provided at the Farmers Training Centres, and by the importation and local production and repair of ox-drawn equipment (GRZ, 1979).

Because of widespread support of this initiative among most of the Western donors, many of the donor-funded Integrated Rural Development Projects and other major donor schemes have involved some oxenisation element. There have been three common characteristics of these activities. The first, and perhaps most common, feature is the training of oxen and their owners, usually undertaken at a residential training centre, although increasingly use has been made of mobile training units. A second feature is the supply of trained oxen, especially important in areas where cattle are not common. In areas where cattle are kept this supply of trained oxen has often been undertaken on an exchange basis. A third characteristic is the provision, sometimes by local manufacture, of ox-drawn implements, especially plows, harrows, cultivators and ox carts. The availability of a range of equipment is crucial if the adoption of draft power is to be made economically attractive for small-scale farmers. A range of equipment will permit farmers to use their oxen for a number of tasks, besides plowing, while an additional advantage is keeping both the farmer and the oxen familiar with draft power by using it not only in the plowing season but also during the rest of the year.

These oxenisation projects initiated by donor projects and the Work Oxen Supply Project have been undertaken in many parts of the country. Progress in some areas has been quite rapid although in those areas where tsetse infestation occurs it has been necessary to proceed with caution. Overall these initiatives have been effective in improving the availability of trained oxen for small-scale farmers; over the decade from 1976 to 1986 the number of such oxen is thought to have almost doubled from 90 000 to 179 000.

To date, because of the differences around the country in oxen availability, disease restriction, agricultural history, and social fabric, different programmes have evolved for promoting animal power in different provinces. Animal traction interventions have evolved in a semi-vacuum with the design and implementation taking place without any central direction and formal agricultural mechanisation structure, significantly reducing the effectiveness of animal draft power promotional efforts.

Consequently, in 1985 a national animal traction coordinating unit was established. It has coordinated a wide range of activities including input supplies, credit, local manufacture of equipment, blacksmith support and training. It has also coordinated the provincial animal traction programmes, working through the provincial agricultural engineers. The programme makes use of mobile training teams and emphasises the role of local blacksmiths' skills in constructing and repairing ox-drawn equipment.

Other relevant institutions involved in the national animal draft power programme include:

o   Palabana Animal Draft Power Training Project, established to organise the training of provincial and district staff involved in animal traction

o   Magoye Agricultural Engineering Centre, where animal traction equipment is tested and evaluated

o   University of Zambia, of which several departments (notably Agricultural Engineering) aim to undertake research relating to animal power.

The programme aimed to raise the number of Ministry of Agriculture ox trainers from 58 to 125 over the five years from 1986 to 1990 and increase the number of work oxen in the country from 180 000 to 260 000. It was predicted this might increase the area cultivated by oxen from 250 000 to 375 000 ha.

A recent assessment of how this programme has been implemented and what it has achieved is presented elsewhere in this volume (Mwenya, Mwenya and Dibbits, 1994)

Conclusion

The popularity of animal traction technology has varied over the decades, as has its adoption across the country. In recent years, the development of oxenisation components in development programmes for small-scale producers has helped re-establish the respectability of animal traction for farmers progressing to semi-commercial levels of production. However, there are still considerable

areas in the country where animal draft power is still little used, while many households in cattle-keeping parts of the country have little or no access to oxen. The challenge to meet the needs of these groups, to coordinate services to support animal traction use, and to ensure that the various aspects of agricultural policy remain favourable to oxenisation, is considerable.

References

Allan W, 1949. *Studies in African land usages in Northern Rhodesia*. Rhodes-Livingstone Papers 15. Oxford University Press, London, UK.

Anthony K R M, Johnson B F, Jones W O and Uchendu V C, 1979. *Agricultural change in tropical Africa*. Cornell University Press, Ithaca, New York, USA.

Colson E, 1954. The Tonga and the shortage of implements. *Rhodes-Livingstone Journal* 14:37–38.

Dixon-Fyle M S R, 1976. *Politics and agrarian change among the Plateau Tonga of Northern Rhodesia, c 1924–63*. PhD Thesis, University of London, London, UK.

FAO, 1981. *Agricultural mechanization in development: guidelines for strategy formulation*. Food and Agriculture Organization of the United Nations (FAO), Rome, Italy.

GRZ, 1979. *Third national development plan*. National Commission for Development and Planning. Government of the Republic of Zambia (GRZ), Lusaka, Zambia. pp. 155–157.

Hellen J A, 1965. *Rural economic development in Zambia, 1890–1964*. Afrika-Studien 32. Ifo-Institut für Wirtschaftsforschung München. Weltforum Verlag, Munich, Germany.

Huckabay J D, in press. The development of transport in Western Province. In: Wood A P (ed), *A development handbook to Western Province*. Zambia Geographical Association, Lusaka, Zambia.

Kay G, 1965. Resettlement and land use planning in Zambia: The Chipangali scheme. *Scottish Geographical Magazine* 81:163–177.

Kimmage K and Wood A, 1988. *Oxenisation in Mongu District, Western Province [Zambia]*. Report prepared for Department of Veterinary and Tsetse Control Services, Mongu, Zambia. 136p.

MAWD, 1984. *Analysts of tractor hire rates charged by land development services*. Planning Division Special Study Report 7. Planning Division, Ministry of Agriculture and Water Development (MAWD), Lusaka, Zambia.

MAWD, 1985. *Investment plan for agriculture, 1986–90*. Planning Division, Ministry of Agriculture and Water Development (MAWD), Lusaka, Zambia.

Milimo J T, Bussink M and Jonsson L-O, 1990. Animal draught power. pp. 523-540 in: Wood A P, Kean S A, Milimo J T and Warren D M (eds). *The dynamics of agricultural policy and reform in Zambia*. Iowa State University Press, Ames, Iowa, USA. 690p.

Müller H, 1986. *Ox power in Zambian agriculture and rural transport*. Edition Herodot Socioeconomic Studies in Rural Development 65. Rader Verlag, Aachen, Germany. 151p.

Muntemba M S, 1977. *Rural underdevelopment in Zambia: Kabwe Rural District, 1850–1977*. PhD thesis. University of California, Los Angeles, USA.

Murray F C, 1965. Zeederberg in Northern Rhodesia. *The Zambia (Northern Rhodesia) Journal* 6 (2):223–228.

Mwenya E, Mwenya W and Dibbits H, 1994. Animal draft power in Zambia: constraints to development and possibilities for improvements. pp 469–473 in Starkey P, Mwenya E and Stares J (eds): *Improving animal traction technology*. Proceedings of workshop held 18–23 January 1992, Lusaka, Zambia. Animal Traction Network for Eastern and Southern Africa (ATNESA) in cooperation with Technical Centre for Agriculture and Rural Development (CTA), Ede-Wageningen, The Netherlands.

Rangeley H, 1965. Memoirs. *The Zambia (Northern Rhodesia) Journal* 6(1).

Siddle D J, 1971. Co-operatives. pp. 61–65 in: Davis D H (ed), *Zambia in maps*. Hodder and Stoughton, London, UK.

de Toro A, 1984. *Evaluation of the mechanization systems of different groups of farmers in the Eastern Province of Zambia*. International Rural Development Centre, Swedish University of Agricultural Sciences, Uppsala, Sweden.

Trapnell C G, [1943] 1953. *The soils, vegetation and agriculture of North-Eastern Rhodesia*. Report of the ecological survey. Government Printer, Lusaka, Zambia.

Trapnell C G and Clothier J N, [1937] 1957. *The soils, vegetation and agriculture of North-Western Rhodesia*. Report of the ecological survey. Government Printer, Lusaka, Zambia.

UNECA/FAO, 1964. *Report of the UNECA/FAO economic survey mission on the economic development of Zambia. The Seers Report*. UNECA/FAO (United Nations Economic Commission for Africa/Food and Agriculture Organization of the United Nations). Falcon Press, Ndola, Zambia.

Vickery K P, 1978. *The making of a peasantry: imperialism and the Tonga plateau economy*. PhD Thesis. Yale University, New Haven, Connecticut, USA.

Wood A P, Kean S A, Milimo J T and Warren D M (eds), 1990. *The dynamics of agricultural policy and reform in Zambia*. Iowa State University Press, Ames, Iowa, USA. 690p.

Constraints and opportunities in the transfer of draft animal technologies in Zambia

by

Martin Bwalya

Head of Animal Draft Power Training Department, Palabana Animal Draft Power Training Project
PO Box 50199, Lusaka, Zambia

Abstract

Technological advancement proceeds in two stages: the technical and highly scientific design and construction or development of a technology; and the adoption and integration of that technology by the community or system for which it is meant. Different farmers react differently to new technological innovations, and promoters often have their own ideas of the value of innovations. This paper focuses on the adoption and integration stage. It broadly analyses and exposes various non-technical constraints and opportunities in the promotion (transfer) of agricultural technology in general, and animal draft technologies in particular, within the context of a Zambian smallholder subsistence farming system. Factors discussed include national agricultural policies, credit and marketing facilities, extension services and strategies, and support services, such as veterinary services.

Introduction

During the past decade there have been considerable changes in the orientation and priorities of Zambia's agricultural policies. One area where such policy changes have occurred is in the field of farm power and, hence, farm mechanisation. Agricultural engineering policies have drastically changed with regard to input innovations.

As a result of government policy on smallholder farmers' power sources, enormous human and financial resources have been mobilised, at various levels, to mount an integrated effort for the realisation of effective and efficient use of animal power in farm operations. In this pursuit, which has involved foreign and local funds channelled through government and non-governmental organisations, one important problem identified has been the actual transfer of the technology. Most of the strategies and methodologies employed to promote the sustainable transfer of the draft animal technology have been inappropriate.

Research work has mainly been directed towards design and manufacture of implements—perfecting the "technical element". In general, this effort has been successful. Unfortunately, the same cannot be said when appropriateness of such technologies to

intended beneficiaries is considered. Getting a technology appropriate and acceptable in a given farming system is an issue often taken for granted or simply overlooked. Often design and manufacturing of technology and designing and planning of developmental innovations have been based on vague and over-simplified views on what beneficiaries require.

Unlike technical design and construction work, the "laboratory" and field for transfer of an agricultural technology are highly complex, dynamic and quite unpredictable, with some factors, such as climate, being completely uncontrollable.

Farmers' reality

For many small-scale farmers the bottom line of their activities is survival. This means that their decisions on cropping patterns, implement choice, etc, are essentially based on risk avoidance. Because they have very little control over either their economic or natural environments, extremely limited alternatives exist for them.

Production strategies and situations are highly community oriented. It is a highly vulnerable community. Farmers' lack of reserves for coping with crop failure, the death of an animal, sudden input price increases, etc, only serves to perpetuate their poverty and misery. These are people whose economic decisions operate mainly within the concept of what some scholars have referred to as the "economics of affection". Farming and many other activities in these communities are family affairs. Most of these farmers are essentially agriculturalists, often with little or no incentive to grow more than for their own subsistence needs.

In Zambia, as in other Third World countries, the concept of a monetary economy is relatively new in the subsistence farming systems. The same applies to the use of commercial inputs, such as hybrid seed, inorganic fertilisers, etc.

There exist in these communities traditions and cultural practices to which their survival is attributed. So anything that threatens this "base" without offering immediate tangible benefits and/or opportunities is viewed with much suspicion which can only guarantee its rejection.

Most farming households in the southern part of Zambia are traditional cattle keepers. However, until very recently, for many of these farmers cattle have primarily been kept for reasons other than draft.

The northern half of the country is traditionally a non-cattle-keeping area. Therefore, promotion of animal power in this area also entails introducing cattle keeping to these people.

Over the years, smallholder and subsistence farmers have been subjected to many "development efforts". Unfortunately, most of these efforts have been designed and implemented without the local peoples' consent, even less their participation.

Focusing on the farmer, and not on the technology *per se*, this paper broadly analyses the various parameters (subjective as well as objective) that hinder or offer opportunities for effective and sustainable transfer (integration) of draft animal technology in a Zambian small-scale subsistence farming community.

Accessible technology

One area that has to be addressed in a discussion on planning for transfer of a technology is farmers' accessibility to that technology. There are two aspects to this issue:

- physical supply and distribution (availability of the technology)
- monetary accessibility (credit).

Physical availability means the supply of implements and cattle and all other support services needed, such as blacksmiths, veterinary services, marketing systems, etc.

For many of Zambia's smallholder subsistence farmers, especially those in the northern half of the country where cattle keeping is a new phenomenon, it is becoming increasingly difficult to find animals (steers). In Mpika district of Northern Province, close to 40% of the approved oxen loans in the 1990/91 season could not be taken up because of the scarcity of steers in the area.

The supply and distribution of animal-drawn implements has been highly chaotic to say the least. Some efforts have been made (mainly by non-governmental organisations and project institutions such as the Smallholder Development Projects in Kabwe and Mpongwe) to "provide" the farmer, not only with the steers, but also with veterinary services, drugs and implements. Where

veterinary services have been part of the oxenisation programme, mortality has been greatly reduced. However, the sustainability of these projects (in the reality and circumstances in which they are operating) has yet to be assessed.

A technology transfer programme should, as a prerequisite, ensure that essential facilities are available and some practices such as dipping of animals, implement supply and repair are integrated in that community's system.

Extension staff and farmer training

Another factor that any technology transfer programme should address is appropriate training for both farmers and extension workers. Although there is no alternative to experience, training still remains indispensable. Lack of, or inadequate, knowledge and skills in draft animal technology among extension workers has slowed down and sometimes misdirected efforts aimed at promoting the technology.

The training of extension staff in Zambia, especially at higher levels (diploma/degree), is divorced from reality, making graduates unable to appreciate and realistically analyse the farmers' environment, especially its non-technical elements. Training of extension workers seems to centre more on changing the farm; they learn about soil use, plant varieties, fertilisers and animal nutrition. The farmer is only another "object". Also, agricultural training is so segmented that the notion of analysing farmers' problems in a holistic multidisciplinary manner is defeated. For those already in the field it is hoped that in-service courses, such as that being offered by Palabana Animal Draft Power Training Project, will help to redress the situation.

Transfer of draft animal technology will demand a perception and treatment of the farmers' reality as one system with various technical and non-technical factors interacting in a complex and dynamic manner.

On the other hand, we want farmers with "local" initiative and participation to appreciate and define their problems—in this case, farm power related problems (farm power limitations, the role and demands of animal power, etc). In the end it is the farmers who have to decide. Therefore, farmers' training should be characterised by extensive awareness campaigns which aim to "place the farmers" in consciously critical confrontation with their reality, to make them the agents of their own advancement.

Whereas short intensive courses are sometimes adequate, it is important to develop a continuous learning process in the field, with the integration of the technology in the socio-cultural fabric of the people with their full involvement and participation.

The extension system

The Zambian agricultural extension system, with all the characteristics of a government public service organisation—huge size, confused priorities, bureaucratic red tape, unmotivated staff, etc—struggles more to sustain itself than to address farmers' issues. Zambia has mainly used the training and visit system. It becomes obvious, from the operation of this system, that, as a system, it only vaguely understands the farmer reality. A lot of the recommendations promoted are more technically oriented, with very little regard for the farmers' needs and aspirations and other internal and external factors that influence the farming system. Identification of farmers' needs is often heavily biased towards donor and/or implementer preferences.

Promotion of animal power will be more realistic and effective when all such factors are given due consideration, in an integrated manner. This also entails supervision and back-up support for field extension workers.

Human resource development is often ignored in agricultural extension. Human resource development (community development, institution building, leadership development, mobilisation, organisation, etc) focuses on developing people themselves and not "developing farms through people" (Roling, 1988). The extension agents, and indeed their recommendations, must be oriented primarily towards the farmers' perceived problems, and not towards agricultural technology.

The strategies and methodologies employed in promoting draft animal technology messages and recommendations should take into account the fact that one is not starting with a "blank" farmer; the target group already has certain ideas and practices that should be acknowledged and respected.

Agricultural credit and marketing

Transfer of animal power technologies in the Zambian system would require a sound credit scheme and a stable and adequate marketing infrastructure. As mentioned above, the main target group for the transfer of draft animal technology is farmers whose farming has predominantly been subsistence; the money economy is a relative new phenomenon, with survival as the bottom line for all

the farmers' activities and decisions. Financial (cash or material) assistance should then be taken as essential, especially in the initial acquisition of the technology (animals, implements, drugs, etc).

The important word here is "initial", because although huge sums of money have in the past gone into loans to smallholder/peasant farmers, the general impact of these loans has largely been insignificant: farmers become perpetually dependent on loans.

Sound design, planning and execution of a small-scale agricultural credit scheme are essential if such a scheme is to be effective and successful for both the farmer and the lender. Ill-conceived, hastily planned and poorly implemented credit programmes not only lead to their own collapse, but also reduce the farmers to a state of dependence associated with loss of integrity and confidence in themselves and their system.

An appropriate draft animal technology credit scheme, like any other agricultural credit scheme, should be productive, appropriate, accessible to as many farmers as possible, cheap, self-sustaining and capable of being managed in the long term on local resources.

One of the greatest constraints for smallholder/peasant farmers in Zambia in the adoption of draft animals is the lack of capital or credit to buy the animals and implements, combined with lack of profitability of farming in general. For the smallholder farmer this has further been exacerbated in that the promotion of draft animal technologies has been more or less exclusively associated with the growing of maize which, for political reasons, has been the worst hit crop in terms of producer price.

On the other hand, credit programmes, in addition to their management and organisation problems, also suffer economic problems. Loan interest rates only go up to 50%, while inflation is well over 100%. This means that, in a given period, the lender makes a loss, even with all the loans recovered. This is especially so for medium-term loans; ox package loans are normally medium term.

This problem is complex, especially when factors that influence interest rates on one hand, and inflation on the other, are taken into consideration, particularly in Third World countries where inflation is very high and unstable.

Agricultural marketing infrastructure is another factor that can in itself greatly motivate farmers to adopt draft animal technologies. Apart from the supply and distribution of inputs, the farmer should have the purchasing power (probably through credit) to acquire the inputs. The use of purchased inputs is closely linked with the availability of credit (Francis, 1988).

On the other hand, the farmer should be able not only to sell his or her produce, but to sell it at economically competitive prices. Because of the marketing arrangement and incoherent price policies that prevail in Zambia, what could have been the farmers' profit ends up in other peoples' pockets (middle men, consumers). Hence the farmer remains with no capital to re-invest in the farm, let alone repay the loans.

An agricultural technology transfer programme should ensure marketing efficiency. Apart from giving farmers a good price for their produce, better transport and handling facilities, cutting out some intermediaries, etc, are prerequisites. The broader aim should be to give farmers "power" to negotiate a fair price for their produce.

Policies

National agricultural policy has greatly influenced the advancement or non-advancement of the agricultural industry in Zambia. A major factor has been the pricing of agricultural produce and associated inputs. Unfavourable price ratios have rendered farming generally unprofitable.

One crop seriously affected has been maize. This is the crop that most small-scale farmers are growing, and so promotion of draft animal technologies has, consciously or unconsciously, been based on this important (staple food) but unfortunately commercially unprofitable crop.

In transferring animal power technologies we should be aware of the implication and consequences this might have on the community and its people. It is very possible that the consequences could out-weigh the advantages in using animal power. For instance, in cropping systems, destumping becomes essential (labour demand); it entails integration of crop and livestock farming and this may create tensions—increased plowed area, hence increased planting, weeding and harvesting jobs, etc.

Finally, it is increasingly being noted that factors hindering promotion and adaptation of animal power technologies lay primarily in the socioeconomic, cultural and political areas rather than in the technical elements of the technology. In particular, because the supply of implements is very limited, farmers have to take any implement that is available, with little regard to its quality, construction, etc.

Animal power technologies, like any other agricultural technology, should be appropriate to the beneficiaries or users, and directly address the problem they are meant to solve.

Summary

For an animal draft power technology transfer programme to be effective, and to ensure increased agricultural production through appropriate and sustainable use of animal traction, it should fully involve the beneficiaries. The designing, planning and implementation strategies should fully acknowledge and address the situation and circumstances of the beneficiaries' reality.

Factors such as farmers' ability to understand and use the technology, management and organisation of agricultural credit schemes, training of both extension staff and farmers, organisation of the extension system, economic and political factors, etc, need serious consideration.

Agricultural and overall economic policies in Zambia have not been favourable for the farmers to appreciate and adopt more efficient and effective means of production.

The extension system has been more oriented to the delivery of technical messages (some of which even the extension workers themselves do not fully understand), with little or no regard for the needs and aspirations, let alone the reality, of these farmers.

Particularly for Zambia, there are broadly two main classes of farmer to which technology needs to be transferred. For those in the northern half of the country, strategies that stimulate and facilitate introduction of the technology could be most appropriate, while in the south the need is to improve the efficiency and effectiveness of the technology. However, each farming system should be assessed individually; for some farmers in the south, although they are traditional cattle keepers, the use of animals for draft is just as new a concept as it is for those in the north.

References

Francis P A, 1988. Ox draught power and agricultural transformation in Northern Zambia. *Agricultural Systems* 27:35–49.

Roling N, 1988. *Extension science: information systems in agricultural development*. Wye Studies in Agricultural and Rural Development. Cambridge University Press, Cambridge, UK.

Transfer of animal traction technology to farmers in the North Western Province of Zambia

by

Christian Löffler

Socioeconomist, Animal Power Technology Project (Zambia)
Oekotop Ltd, Bingerstraße 25a, D-14197 Berlin, Germany

Abstract

This paper presents the case study of the introduction of animal draft power in the North Western Province of Zambia within the framework of an Integrated Rural Development Programme (IRDP) sponsored by the German Agency for Technical Cooperation (GTZ). Following a brief analysis of the natural and socioeconomic conditions in North Western Province, the paper highlights the specific oxenisation approach of IRDP, which combined individual ownership and joint use of work oxen. Special attention is paid to the methods applied during the implementation of the work oxen component in order to make this technological innovation socially and economically viable. Finally, empirical data from various monitoring surveys are presented and analysed to give an assessment of the impact of the IRDP Work Oxen Project in North Western Province.

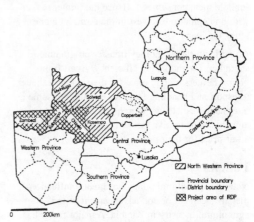

Figure 1: Map of Zambia, showing the North Western Province and IRDP programme area (CATAD, 1988)

Regional characteristics

Natural environment

The North Western Province of Zambia is a plateau region at an altitude of 1200–1500 m, which is covered by a thick layer of Kalahari sands and which merges in the east into the Barotse Plain along the upper Zambezi. The homogeneous topography of the plateau region is interrupted by scattered, shallow linear depressions (dambos) following the major drainage lines. The climate is moderately tropical with five humid months and an annual rainfall well above 1000 mm. The predominant soils are highly leached, ferralitic sandveldts, but there are numerous pockets of fertile alluvial/wetland soils. Except for the treeless, grass-covered dambo areas, the natural vegetation is a dry tropical forest (Miombo woodland).

Large parts of North Western Province are infested with tsetse flies. Only Zambezi District, in the extreme west of the province, is largely tsetse-free: this is the only area where ownership of cattle is traditional.

Socioeconomic conditions

The infrastructure of North Western Province is very underdeveloped. The only important access road runs from the economically important Copperbelt Province (Figure 1). The distance from Zambezi (the old colonial provincial capital of Balovale) to the Copperbelt is 700 km. Transport, communications and banking facilities are very poor. Even to supply the area with basic commodities is very difficult.

Following the upswing of copper extraction in the Copperbelt since 1930, North Western Province has been a reservoir of migrant workers for the mines and urban centres. For several decades, this selective population drain has been destabilising the rural communities in social and economic terms. Since the mid-1970s, the fall in the international demand and price for copper has badly affected the socioeconomic situation in North Western Province. Today, 90% of the population depend on subsistence farming (farm sizes average 1–2 ha), supported by fishing, hunting and occasional employment as the major sources of cash income. Farmers generally cultivate the land using axes and hoes in various shifting cultivation systems summarised by the term *chitimene* (Schultz, 1976).

The key constraint for these subsistence farmers is the lack of access to inputs and markets, which prevents them from making better use of their productive potential and from earning the necessary minimum cash income (CATAD, 1988). The linear design of the formal transportation system in Zambia denies easy economic and physical access to the majority of the rural population. This can be a decisive factor in discouraging subsistence farmers from producing cash crops (Fincham and Markakis, 1980; Müller, 1986).

With an average population density of 2.6 inhabitants/km^2, North Western Province offers abundant land resources for the extension of smallholdings. However, the key area along the major road from the Copperbelt has experienced a decrease in the duration of the fallow period. Such a decrease, which corresponds with an increase in land-use intensity, can be regarded as a decisive precondition for the adoption of a new agricultural technology (Pingali, Bigot and Binswanger, 1987; Strubenhoff, 1988; Schmitz, Sommer and Walter, 1991).

Integrated Rural Development Programme

The Integrated Rural Development Programme (IRDP) in North Western Province started as a project sponsored by the German Agency for Technical Cooperation (GTZ). It was launched in Kabompo District in 1978 and expanded to Zambezi and Chizela (now Mufumbwe) Districts in 1980; it provided technical assistance until 1990. The

programme area, covering nearly 50 000 km, has approximately 125 000 inhabitants. The overall goal of the IRDP was defined as improving the living conditions of the majority of small-scale producers, mainly by increasing their productivity and production (Rauch, 1986). In terms of regional planning, IRDP aimed to maximise the use of local resources, in order to reduce dependence on external inputs and markets by creating self-sustaining, locally integrated trading and economic circuits (Rauch and Redder, 1987). The entire programme comprised 19 sector components (rural crafts, beekeeping, rural water supply, etc) with a special programme for farmers below the credit standing of national institutions (1 ha).

The basic function/strategic approach of the IRDP can be summarised as two complementary elements (Rauch, 1987a; CATAD, 1988):

o promoting the social organisation and technical equipment of target groups in order to strengthen their self-help capacity and to articulate and meet their needs and interests effectively

o establishing small-scale producer-oriented service systems which can be institutionalised by providing adequate support to existing service institutions.

For the agricultural component of IRDP this meant, first of all, establishing rural depots or trade centres for agricultural inputs and outputs; these centres can

Photo 1: Transporting grass with a prototype ox cart manufactured by the small-scale equipment section of the IRDP (the wooden wheeled cart design was replaced by carts fitted with roller bearings and pneumatic tyres)

Photo: Christian Löffler

be accessed directly by farmer groups using ox carts and by servicing institutions using motorised transport.

Approach of the Work Oxen Project

The proposal of the foreign project planning team to foster the mass introduction of animal draft power for transport and plowing purposes encountered massive resistance from the district administration, which favoured establishing a tractor-hiring station for around 300 advanced/emergent farmers (Rauch, 1987b). Decisive for the approval of IRDP's Work Oxen Project was the intervention of national authorities that were interested in stopping rural–urban migration patterns and achieving regional self-sufficiency in food production.

The following setup was established for the Work Oxen Project: young steers were bought from Zambezi District and transferred to a work oxen training centre in Kabompo District, where two-week training courses were conducted for farmers. Bodies and frames for ox carts were manufactured from local timber in rural craft centres. Plows, wheel rims and second-hand tyres were obtained from suppliers in the Copperbelt. The major bottleneck, however, was the inadequacy of axles. Because no axles were available when the Work Oxen Project began, IRDP assessed various types of simple axle, including some using wooden block bearings (Photo 1), which did not prove popular. It introduced some carts with axles made from locally available water pipes and plastic bushes. These axles were not very successful; they wore out quickly, and replacements were difficult to obtain. IRDP then imported car axles and roller bearings until the Small-Scale Equipment Section of the project was able to obtain and test various axles from Zambian manufacturers, which were responding to an increasing national demand.

Rukandema (1986) estimated that the minimum farm size for the introduction of a work oxen system (oxen, plow, ox cart) in North Western Province is 6 ha. But the average farm size of smallholders in the project area is 1–2 ha, including both subsistence and cash crop fields. From the very beginning, therefore, the task of the Work Oxen Project was to discover how animal draft power could be introduced in a way that would be viable both economically and socially. Because experience from previous development projects had shown that communal ownership of work oxen and implements was unlikely to be successful, IRDP decided to try an approach that combined individual ownership of work oxen with their joint use within a group of farmers (group approach).

There is a risk inherent in such an approach. The aim of the IRDP was to make animal draft power technology available to everyone, but because adopting animal draft power generally depends on a certain minimum level of available (family) labour, only the upper stratum of the rural population might be able to do so. Thus, this group approach might initiate a process of social segregation, creating a class of rural capitalists operating at the expense of fellow farmers, either by forcing up hiring charges for oxen and implements or by completely denying contract services. The task of the Work Oxen Project thus became one of finding a way to implement the individual ownership/joint use system in such a way that all farmers might benefit from animal draft power technology on a sustainable basis. The measures adopted to meet this aim are described in the following section.

Methodology of animal draft power dissemination

Selection of the ox owner

The members of each farmer group applying for a work oxen package (or part of the entire package) had to select a loan recipient. Following approval of the loan by IRDP the selected ox owner had to sign a contract which obliged him to provide plowing and transport services to the members of his farmer group. Failure to provide adequate services at reasonable hiring charges could lead to the withdrawal of the loan package. Cohesion of the farmer groups and elements of social control among the local communities were supposed to secure the ox owners' contract services beyond the term of the loan.

Selective mechanisation of farm operations

In cooperation with the Cooperative Union, the parastatal service institution in North Western Province, it was decided not to provide planters/weeders to loan applicants. It was reasoned that the ox owner would thus not be able to increase the size of his own farm because of labour shortages during subsequent field operations.

Close monitoring of the Work Oxen Project

In order to supervise the impact and side effects of this oxenisation model, IRDP commissioned three major monitoring surveys during the implementation of the Work Oxen Project. The first followed the pilot phase of work oxen introduction (Mack, 1984). The second was conducted during the first marketing season fully deploying ox carts, including the subsequent plowing season (Löffler, 1987). And the third covered a complete agricultural year in order to provide a systematic database for the evaluation of the Work Oxen Project (Löffler, 1989).

Empirical results

Transport component

Ox carts have been used increasingly to transport maize (the major cash crop) to the marketing centres (Photo 2). The figures in Table 1 illustrate the increase between 1986 and 1989 which reflects a boost of agricultural production in the project area. The slightly decreasing share of the hired service to fellow farmers shown in Table 1 was due to the gradual expansion of the ox owners' cash-crop area. Nevertheless, the share of hired service during the two monitored marketing seasons, corresponding to five to six fellow farmers served, clearly indicates the widespread impact of ox-drawn transport on farmers' access to rural depots. However, the potential of ox-drawn marketing in the project area, estimated at up to 300 bags per ox cart, was not yet realised in 1988 (Löffler, 1989).

The development of the total yearly transport performance is another indicator for the gradually increasing relevance of ox carts for local transport requirements. For the agricultural year 1988–89 the average number of transport days per ox cart was 120, compared to 75 days in 1986–87 (Löffler, 1989). This dynamic development is mainly due to the increasing assignment of ox carts for the internal transport tasks of rural households, such as harvesting, collecting firewood, etc (Photo 3; Harrison and Howe, 1989).

Regardless of this increasing status of carts within the economy of rural households, two studies (CATAD, 1988; Löffler, 1989) suggested a restrictive loan policy for the further distribution of ox carts in

Photo 2: Transport of maize sacks by ox cart in Zambezi District

Photo: Christian Löffler

Table 1: Marketing performance of ox carts

	1986	1989
Average marketing capacity (bags of maize per cart per season)[1]	65	125
Hired service (%)	60	52

[1] 1 bag = 90 kg
Source Löffler (1989)

1989–90. These proposals were based on tremendous price increases for the loan package (especially for ox carts), which were caused by an aggravating inflationary trend of prices in Zambia. The IRDP feared that there was a finite limit to the local demand for ox cart services which, together with limits to raising hire charges, might prevent new ox cart owners from generating sufficient income to repay their loans. Thus, additional ox cart loans were limited to certain areas, where the forecast demand for ox-drawn carts to transport maize had not been met.

In retrospect, this approach turned out to be controversial as demand for ox-drawn carts was greater than that forecast. The liberalisation of the marketing system for agricultural produce in 1989–90 provided additional business opportunities and stimuli for ox cart owners (eg, inter-district trade with maize) or revived traditional trade routes for the exchange of food products (eg, maize flour for dried fish).

However that may be judged from today's point of view, this controversy clearly shows the dependency of (regional) project planning on imponderable external factors, whose actual impact cannot be predicted.

Plowing component

Work oxen are widely used for plowing (Photo 4) and their plowing potential seems to be fully utilised, considering the specific regional conditions under which animal draft power technology was introduced (tsetse-infestation, poor animal health, etc). Table 2 shows the impact of plowing with work oxen in the project area.

Table 2: Plowing performance of work oxen pairs/ox owners

	1986/87	1988/89
Total area plowed per pair (ha)	6.8	6.5
Number of farmers served per pair	10	7
Average farm size of ox owners (ha)	1.5	2.0

Source: Löffler (1989)

Photo: Christian Löffler

Photo 3: Transporting firewood in an ox cart in Kabompo District

Multiplying the average number of farmers served per pair of oxen by the total number of loan packages (510) shows 3570 farmers had access to plowing services in 1988–89 (Löffler, 1989). As individual ox owners apparently served fewer farmers in 1988–89 than in 1986–87, it was suggested that ox owners might be reducing their contract services after they had completed their loan repayments. This hypothesis was rejected, for ox owners plowing for at least the fifth season in 1988–89 still provided 52% of their total plowing performance as contract service, compared with 54–58% for the categories below five seasons (Löffler, 1989).

The analysis of the relations between ox owners and fellow farmers revealed poor cohesion of the artificial farmer groups created—group membership was not a major determinant in the provision of contract services. Generally, the decisive factors for contract services turned out to be determined by complex, traditionally evolved systems of social obligation among relatives and friends. Some traditional relationships had changed to allow cash payment for hired services.

Disaggregated by gender, the figures of the Work Oxen Survey 1988–89 indicate that only about 5% of the work oxen loan recipients were women and that only 20% of the total contract performance of all ox owners was provided for women. In comparison to the participation of women in IRDP's agricultural project (around 30%) this means that women's benefits within the Work Oxen Project were clearly neglected until 1989–90, when special

promotion measures for female ox owners were initiated.

Considering the average cash crop area of ox owners during the last season before receiving work oxen (1 ha), most (about 80%) of ox owners have been doubling the cash crop area. This upper limit was clearly related to the availability of family labour and to the attractiveness of cash crop farming in 1988–89, which restricted the supply of hired labour for planting and weeding. Only about 20% of the ox owners equipped with loan packages by IRDP have been expanding their cash crop area at the expense of providing plowing services for their fellow farmers in 1988–89 (Löffler, 1989).

As the average plowing charges in both 1986–87 and 1988–89 corresponded to the market value of one bag of maize, it seems that contract services were generally provided without exploitative tendencies.

Final assessment

There have been some problems with IRDP's Work Oxen Project. For example, fellow farmers have complained about the unsatisfactory contract services provided by the ox owners, especially in terms of timeliness of plowing. The main beneficiaries of the introduction of work oxen in the project area have been the ox owners themselves. Moreover, the *de facto* ownership/control of work oxen by women was neglected until the final stage of the project. However, considering the widespread impact that the introduction of work oxen has had in

Photo 4: Plowing dambo soil, Chizela District, North Western Province

the project area, IRDP's individual ownership/joint use approach can be regarded as a success. When a wide range of farmers and representatives of the district administration were asked about the sustainable impact of IRDP projects, the general feeling was that the introduction of animal draft power has been the most welcome innovation of the IRDP, but that a work oxen package loan should be available to every farming family.

References

CATAD, 1988. *The sustainability of the impact of the Integrated Rural Development Programme (IRDP), North Western Province of Zambia*. Centre for Advanced Training in Agricultural Development (CATAD), Technical University, Berlin, Schriftenreihe des Fachbereichs 116, Berlin, Germany. 283p.

Fincham R and Markakis J, 1980. *The evolving structure of Zambian society*. Edinburgh, UK.

Harrison P and Howe J, 1989. Measuring the transport demands of the rural poor: experience from Africa. *GATE* 1/89:3–6. German Appropriate Technology Exchange, GTZ, Eschborn, Germany.

Kurbjuweit D, 1989. "Ihr bildet Kapitalisten heran". Ein deutsches Entwicklungsprojekt bekämpft wirksam die Armut auf dem Lande. *Die Zeit* 22/89:46.

Löffler C, 1987. *Work oxen utilization survey*. Integrated Rural Development Project in North Western Province (IRDP/NWP). German Agency for Technical Cooperation (GTZ), Eschborn, Germany. 84p.

Löffler C, 1989. *Work oxen survey 1988/89*. Integrated Rural Development Project in North Western Province (IRDP/NWP). German Agency for Technical Cooperation (GTZ), Eschborn, Germany. 83p.

Mack R P, 1984. *The impact of the introduction of work oxen utilization within the frame of the IRDP/NWP*. Integrated Rural Development Project in North Western Province (IRDP/NWP). German Agency for Technical Cooperation (GTZ), Eschborn, Germany. 51p.

Müller H, 1986. *Oxpower in Zambian agriculture and rural transport. Performance, potential and promotion*. Edition Herodot Socioeconomic Studies in Rural Development No. 65, Rader Verlag, Aachen, Germany. 151p.

Pingali P, Bigot Y and Binswanger H P, 1987. *Agricultural mechanization and the evolution of farming systems in sub-Saharan Africa*. Published for World Bank by Johns Hopkins Press, Baltimore, Maryland, USA. 216p.

Rauch T, 1986. Dezentralisierung, Bauern und Staat in Sambia. Erfahrungen bei grundbedürfnisorientierter regionalplanung in einer ländlichen region. *Zeitschrift für Wirtschaftsgeographie* 3–4/86:52–71.

Rauch T, 1987a. Sambia: Modell Kabompo. Entwicklungsprojekte für die Ärmsten im ländlichen Raum. *GTZ Info* 4/87:23–27. GTZ, Eschborn, Germany.

Rauch T, 1987b. Schwierigkeiten und Chancen bei der Umsetzung armutsorientierter Entwicklungsprogramme. Beispiel Sambia. *Journal für Entwicklungspolitik* 2/87:75–93.

Rauch T and Redder A, 1987. Möglichkeiten und Grenzen der Umsetzung des Konzepts kleinräumiger Wirtschaftskreisläufe im ländlichen Zambia. Beispiel Nordwest-Provinz 1980–1986. *Die Erde* 118:127–141.

Rukandema, M, 1986. *An economic assessment of proposed introduction of animal draught power in Solwezi, Kasempa and Mwinilunga Districts, North Western Province of Zambia*. Miscellaneous Paper 1. Report for North Western Province Area Development Project and Food and Agriculture Organization of the United Nations (FAO), Rome, Italy. 25p.

Schmitz H, Sommer M and Walter S, 1991. *Animal traction in rainfed agriculture in Africa and South America*. Vieweg for German Appropriate Technology Exchange, Eschborn, Germany. 311p.

Schultz J, 1976. *Land use in Zambia. Part I. The basically traditional land use systems and their regions*. Africa Studies 95. IFO-Institute for Economic Research, Munich, Germany. 208p.

Strubenhoff H W, 1988. *Probleme des Übergangs von der Handhacke zum Pflug. Eine ökonomische Analyse der Einführung der tierischen Anspannung in Ackerbausystemen Togos*. Kiel, Germany. 150p.

Photo: Christian Löffler

Experiences with improving animal traction technology in Kaoma District, Western Province of Zambia

by

H G Kamphuis[*]

Adviser, Western Province Animal Draft Power Project
Department of Agriculture, PO Box 910067, Mongu, Zambia

Abstract

Kaoma District in Zambia's Western Province has better soils for crop production, but a smaller cattle (and oxen) population, than other districts. Farmers in this district are more commercially oriented than those in other districts, but they have less experience and knowledge of animal draft power. The Animal Draft Power Project is currently concentrating its activities in Kaoma District.

Training activities are closely linked to the availability of oxen, implements and spares, and have concentrated on ox-training courses and the use of primary and secondary tillage implements. Farmers in the district are encouraged to form groups, to improve the availability of animals and implements. The use of ridgers for weeding has gained popularity among the farmers.

Agricultural extension officers in the district lack clearly defined extension messages. There is a need to improve farm management advice to farmers. Rural transport in the district also needs to be improved.

Introduction

Cattle keeping is fairly traditional in Zambia's Western Province; the first cattle were introduced some 300 years ago. Within the agricultural system, people in the province rely heavily on cattle for manure, draft power for plowing and, to a lesser extent, transport. Oxen have been used for plowing in the province since the 1930s.

Although cattle keeping is traditional in most parts of Western Province, regional differences occur (Table 1). Most cattle are found in the Zambesi plains area (to the west of the province) where grazing areas are better and larger than elsewhere in the province. In Kaoma District, to the east (see Map 1), which is a relatively new settlement area for farming, cattle keeping and the use of oxen for farm work are a relatively recent phenomenon. There are several reasons for this: the indigenous inhabitants, as well as most of the settlers, have little or no experience in cattle keeping; grazing is

---
[*] *Subsequent address:*
RDP Livestock Services, PO Box 523, 3700 AM Zeist, The Netherlands

scarce (the district has fewer dambos/river valleys than the rest of the province); and the eastern part of the district is infested with tsetse flies. Thus, while about 30–40% of farming households in Western Province as a whole own cattle, only 10–15% of households in Kaoma District do so (Beerling, 1991).

On the other hand, Kaoma District has better soils for agricultural production, and higher, and better distributed, annual rainfall, than other districts. And it is in this district that the more commercially oriented farmers of the province are found (some 90% of the marketed maize production is grown in Kaoma District).

About 16–18% of the province's cattle population are oxen, but about one-third of the oxen are not trained for farm work (Corton, 1988). Trained oxen are generally only used for plowing and for transport (mainly using sledges).

The provincial Animal Draft Power Project is currently concentrating its activities in Kaoma District. Various aspects of these activities are presented in this paper.

Present situation in Kaoma District

Although Kaoma District has favourable conditions for crop production, several bottlenecks inhibit expansion of agricultural activities. A major part of the district's population consists of settlers from other parts of the province, or from other provinces, who have limited experience and knowledge of the use of animal draft power. The number of work oxen in the district is quite low, and not sufficient to meet demand. And the supply and distribution of ox-drawn implements and spares is inadequate. Because of these bottlenecks, coupled with low producer prices, high prices of input (such as fertiliser) and the shortage of seasonal and medium-term loans, farming in the district remains a marginal enterprise.

Despite the present economic difficulties, however, farmers want to improve and expand their agricultural production for the market rather than remain in, or return to, subsistence levels of farming, and to this end they are keen to invest in knowledge and equipment (van Rootselaar, Kamphuis and Muma, 1991).

The approach of the Animal Draft Power Project

The Animal Draft Power Project actively promotes and supports sales of oxen and animal draft power implements and spares to farmers through various channels. By increasing the availability of oxen and implements in the district, the project aims to promote more efficient use of animal draft power, involving also other techniques like weeding. The activities the project is undertaking or planning in the district include:

○ short mobile courses, focusing on the methodology of ox training and the proper use of plows and weeding implements

○ demonstrations of the use of ox-drawn cultivators and ridgers (Photo 1), and issuing farmers' groups with these implements on a trial basis for one season

○ support for input supply activities (in December 1990 an oxenisation revolving fund for oxen, implements and spares was established under the auspices of the Kaoma District Cooperative Union)

○ short mobile blacksmithing courses (follow-up support will be given in form of the loan of materials and basic tools to trained blacksmiths).

Results

During the past few seasons many farmers and extension staff have received training in animal draft power technology. Nearly all agricultural extension staff in the district have attended a residential course

Map 1: Western Zambia showing district and provincial boundaries

on animal draft power. Since they received little such training during their formal education, this has certainly increased their knowledge and confidence; many of them only started to implement animal draft power extension activities after attending the course. These extension officers are further supported by the Animal Draft Power Project with transport (bicycles), and are being involved as much as possible in various project activities in their areas.

Table 1: Cattle, crop areas and populations by district, Western Province, Zambia

	Kaoma	Kalabo	Lukulu	Mongu	Senanga	Sesheke	Total
Total cattle	23 678	106 154	77 307	99 904	168 189	71 575	**546 807**
Total oxen	5 072	18 134	8 564	16 324	26 639	12 318	**87 051**
Trained oxen	(3 380)	(12 100)	(5 700)	(10 900)	(17 800)	(8 200)	**(58 000)**
Human population	112 747	101 410	51 016	142 213	135 210	64 901	**607 497**
Households	(22 500)	(20 200)	(10 200)	(28 400)	(27 000)	(13 000)	**(121 300)**
Trained oxen per household	(0.15)	(0.60)	(0.56)	(0.38)	(0.66)	(0.63)	
Area under crops (ha)	22 726	12 151	10 558	19 935	13 703	17 785	**96 858**
Trained oxen/ha	(0.15)	(0.99)	(0.54)	(0.55)	(1.30)	(0.46)	

Figures in brackets are project estimates
Due to low cattle population, number of trained oxen in Kaoma District might be higher
Some 12% of the population in the Western Province live in the six district capitals.
Numbers of households are estimated from district populations divided by 5 (average household size)
Sources: Department of Agriculture (1989); Central Statistical Office (1990); Schoonman (1991)

Farmers are eager to attend animal draft power extension activities. As well as ox training, farmers are particularly keen to learn the proper use of ox-drawn implements, especially weeding implements; as a result, the use of ridgers for weeding purposes is becoming quite popular in the district. Since 1987, several mobile ox-plowing courses have been conducted for women. A recent study on the impact such courses (Hocking, 1991; 1994) concluded that women who apply plowing skills themselves benefit both in sociological terms and, indirectly, through enhanced economic benefits to the household. Those who attend a course but have no access to oxen still benefit in sociological terms. Female farmers want more courses organised specifically for them. These courses should include such topics as ox handling and management, yoking and unyoking of oxen, plowing and weeding with oxen.

In December 1990 the Animal Draft Power Project established an oxenisation revolving fund under the auspices of the Kaoma District Cooperative Union (KADICU). It was expected that this would improve the supply, and especially the distribution, of oxen, implements and spares through the cooperative system. But the operation of this fund is constrained by several factors:

○ relations between KADICU and the affiliated societies appear to have deteriorated. KADICU is buying oxen, implements and spares (mainly implements and spares), but so far is only selling them in Kaoma township; it has not yet entered into an agreement with any local society for distribution

○ KADICU did not given enough publicity in the rural areas of the district to the availability of ox-drawn implements and spares in Kaoma Boma

○ KADICU has, at present, no transport of its own.

Therefore, once farmers have attended a mobile animal draft power course, the project is currently trying to implement follow-up activities through the ex-trainees, who are encouraged to organise themselves as farmer groups. The main aim of these groups would be initially to improve the availability and supply of implements and spares in their areas. Once organised, they are expected to express their requirements as a group to KADICU and other input supply institutions. Alternatively, farmers could decide to channel the supply of implements and spares through a local entrepreneur or blacksmith (who would then receive full back-up support from the farmers in his area). If KADICU is unable to secure appropriate transport to supply the implement and spares, the Project itself will offer transport (and charge KADICU a hiring fee). However, the project will encourage farmer groups to develop their own transport capacity, possibly by offering ox cart loans to farmer groups or to individual members within a group.

The stimulation of farmer groups has started recently. Some groups appear promising, but no clear results can yet be reported.

Constraints on implementation of Animal Draft Power Project activities

Despite the efforts by the Animal Draft Power Project to increase participation of farmers in developing a more sustainable system of input supply by organising them into groups, most farmers still believe that the government should provide them with all essential services (inputs, marketing systems for crops, credit, etc). For some time, the government has provided most of these services through the cooperative system; each ward was expected to organise its own cooperative society. Because the cooperatives are mainly top-down organised (rules and regulations are dictated by the government), farmer participation has been low.

Even in the present situation, where the government is no longer able to provide all the essential services, farmers still tend to wait for government help. For too long, farmers had (and often still have) the opinion that "the government should provide" and that "whatever comes from the government is free of charge".

Photo 1: Demonstration of a weeder in Kaoma District

"Improving animal traction technology"

Agricultural extension officers are supposed to play an important role in agricultural development, as they are the only nearby source from which farmers can obtain advice on agricultural practices. Their present effectiveness is, however, questionable. One reason is that they do not have clearly defined extension messages. The main message to farmers at the moment is simply to increase production of cash crops, which many farmers in Kaoma District are trying to do by plowing more land; but this only creates a labour problem, especially at weeding time. In addition, fertiliser application is often reduced. As a result, yields are often only one-third or less of what could be expected under proper management (current average maize yield is 1800–2250 kg/ha). In addition, farmers are not advised on farm management practices—planning in relation to available inputs and human resources, cost benefit calculations, etc.

In the present situation of relatively low producer prices, high costs of farm inputs and the effects of the high inflation, many farmers depend each year on a seasonal credit to carry out their cropping plan. Currently, the LIMA Bank and the CUSA (Credit Union and Savings Association) are the main providers of credit (some 125 million Kwacha for 1991/92 season, equivalent to about US$ 3 million). Both the LIMA Bank and the CUSA depend on the government for funding.

The Animal Draft Power Project has conducted a substantial number of residential and mobile training courses and field demonstrations. Although farmers have gained knowledge through these, they can only put this knowledge into practice if they can obtain the required inputs (oxen, implements, spare parts). Therefore, training activities are closely linked to the existing input supply infrastructure (which should be improved at the same time).

Rural transport is underdeveloped in Kaoma District. One reason for this is the lack of incentives to farmers to invest in rural transport. In the past, the cooperative system provided most of the inputs (fertiliser, implements, etc) near to the farmers and maize was bought for a gazetted price at rural depots. An improved supply and distribution system for ox-drawn implements, spares and other inputs, as well as a better marketing system for farm produce, can only be attained if rural transport is improved. The number of ox carts (and oxen) should be increased, but currently, the price of an ox cart is beyond the reach of most farmers.

References

Beerling M L, 1991. *The advantage of having cattle*. Department of Veterinary and Tsetse Control Services, Mongu, Zambia, and RDP Livestock Services, Zeist, The Netherlands. 177p.

Central Statistical Office, 1990. *1990 Census of population, housing and agriculture: preliminary report*. Central Statistical Office, Lusaka, Zambia. 20p.

Corten J J F M, 1988. *Productivity of cattle in Western Province*. Department of Veterinary and Tsetse Control Services, Mongu, Zambia. 93p.

Department of Agriculture, 1989. *Final crop forecasting data 1989/90*. Department of Agriculture, Mongu, Zambia.

Hocking C, 1991. *The impact of mobile ox-plowing courses for women: a study in Kaoma East and in areas surrounding the Lui River valley, Western Province, Zambia*. MSc Thesis. Department of Agriculture and Environmental Science, University of Newcastle-upon-Tyne, UK. 69p.

Hocking C, 1994. The impact of mobile ox plowing courses for women in the Western Province of Zambia. In: Starkey P, Mwenya E and Stares J (eds), *Improving animal traction technology*. Proceedings of Animal Traction Network for Eastern and Southern Africa (ATNESA) workshop held 18–23 January 1992, Lusaka, Zambia.

van Rootselaar G H, Kamphuis H G and Muma A K, 1991. *Internal mid-term project review: identification of follow-up projects and recommendations for the remaining project period*. Western Province Animal Draft Power Project, Department of Agriculture, Mongu, Zambia, and RDP Livestock Services, Zeist, The Netherlands. 106p.

Schoonman L, 1991. *Livestock census figures, Western Province 1990*. Department of Veterinary and Tsetse Control Services, Mongu, Zambia. 16p.

A note on animal draft power in Kabwe Smallholder Development Project, Central Province, Zambia

by

A Mkandawire

District Agricultural Engineer (Kabwe North and South)
Ministry of Agriculture, PO Box 80434, Kabwe, Zambia

Abstract

The Kabwe Smallholder Development Project in Central Province, Zambia, has been set up to help increase food security, production, level of income and the general standard of living of small farmers. The project has organised farmers into groups, mobilised and extended extension services, encouraged animal traction and livestock development, and studied ways of improving rainfed agriculture. The main economic activities of people in the project area include farming, fishing, charcoal burning, and local shops and services. The use of animal draft power is widespread throughout the project area, and is increasing slowly; animals are used for many agricultural operations, and for transport. Some of the functions of the project are to provide loans for the purchase of animal-drawn implements, to test implements and to demonstrate and promote animal traction in agriculture through plowing contests.

Introduction

Much has been said about the vital role animal draft power plays in the development process of the rural sector in Zambia and abroad. There is overwhelming evidence that animal traction will go a long way toward alleviating the problems that small-scale farmers experience in tillage, crop establishment, on-farm transport and even public transport in remote areas.

Successful promotion of animal draft power depends on several factors including the availability of land, animals, veterinary services and appropriate credit. It also depends on local culture, environmental conditions, producer price/cost ratio, the skill of rural blacksmiths and the competence of extension services. Most important of all, whatever resources and services might be available, the success of animal traction technology will largely depend on whether the farmer *wants* to adopt, *is able* to adopt and *knows how* to adopt the technology.

Kabwe Smallholder Development Project (KSDP) covers an area which includes both Kabwe Rural District (Kabwe South District) and the whole of Kapirimposhi (Kabwe North District) in the Central Province of Zambia. This project involves around 35 000 smallholder farming families living in an area of 35 000 km^2.

The overall goal of KSDP is to contribute towards increasing the food security and production of small-scale and emergent farmers. This will improve the self-sufficiency, level of income and general standard of living of smallholder farmers in the intervention area, and will contribute toward improving national food security.

To realise this goal this project has:

- organised smallholders into groups
- mobilised and motivated district extension services
- extended extension services to cover information on inputs, marketing and credit
- provided advice to the District Veterinary Services
- encouraged animal traction and livestock development
- investigated improvements to local rainfed farming systems
- developed a monitoring and evaluation system.

This paper deals specifically with what KSDP is doing in the project area in relation to animal draft power.

Village economic systems in the project area

The geographical position and environment of an area greatly determine the social and economic activities of the village community. The principal economic activities of people in the KSDP area include farming, fishing, charcoal burning, village commerce (shops) and local services (eg, grinding mills). Fishing is common around lakes and rivers, such as the Lukanga swamps, the Kafue River and the Mulungushi dams. Fishing provides households with a small income, depending on available family labour and the proximity of a fishing area. Charcoal burning can produce a steady income depending on proximity to roads and the availability of transport to take the charcoal to urban centres. Small village shops are common; they sell basic items such as paraffin, candles, matches, clothing and spare parts for bicycles. Sugar, salt and cooking oil are rare commodities. Some villagers have grinding mills, but constant breakdowns and lack of space are common problems. Hunting and the collection of wild fruits and mushrooms from the bush allow poorer families to raise some income.

Farming plays a major role in the village economies. Most villagers view farming primarily as a source of food for the family. Traditional farmers either sell surplus agricultural produce or exchange it for family necessities. Small-scale and emergent farmers are starting to undertake commercial production on a larger scale.

Role of animal draft power

The use of animal draft power is widespread throughout the project area and is increasing slowly.

Oxen are the main draft animals but a few farmers use cows and donkeys for draft purposes. Animal draft power is used to a varying extent for land tillage (plowing), seedbed preparation (harrowing), crop establishment (planting), secondary cultivation (weeding and ridging) and transport (farm inputs and outputs, fire wood, water, etc). Animal power can play a major role in all these operations, helping to alleviate human labour constraints.

One major constraint among smallholders in the KSDP area has been that of transport. Draft animals are used to pull ox carts in almost all the villages. Ox carts provide transport for all village economic activities: for example, traffic on the Lenje road consists mainly of ox carts loaded with charcoal, agricultural produce, fish and the villagers themselves. Most villagers hire ox carts to take their produce to town markets or to the main roads.

Public transport is rarely available and ox carts give the villagers an alternative means of transport, even though travel is very slow and it may take days to reach a destination.

KSDP animal traction programme

In order to develop animal traction in the area, KSDP provides loans for the purchase of animal-drawn implements, undertakes trials of animal traction implements and holds plowing competitions.

The programme of trials is carried out in association the Magoye Animal Draft Power Research and Development Programme and the Palabana Animal Draft Power Training Programme. The plowing contests are held annually with the main aim of demonstrating, through farmer competitions, the importance of plow setting and handling. They also serve to demonstrate new or more systematic soil tillage techniques.

The project identified lack of transport and tillage implements as particularly acute problems facing smallholders in the area. While farmers have access to other lending institutions, these provide seasonal loans for inputs like seeds, fertilisers and hire of labour. The project therefore aims to provide medium-term credit to smallholders for the purchase of animal power equipment and ox carts. The project's loan scheme is administered through the Zambia Cooperative Federation Finance Service Department (known as ZCF–FS). Also operational in the area is a small pilot loan scheme related to the field cultivation trials. This scheme, run by the Magoye Animal Draft Power Research and Development Programme, provides loans for the different types of cultivators and ridgers being evaluated.

Transfer of animal traction technology in Luapula Province, Zambia

by

S L Lubumbe

Provincial Animal Husbandry Officer, Department of Agriculture
Luapula Province, PO Box 710072, Mansa, Zambia

Abstract

A three-year pilot oxenisation project has shown that there is great potential for adoption of animal traction technology in Luapula Province of Zambia. The main constraint is the shortage of work oxen—the result of the lack of a cattle-keeping tradition in the province, the lack of a provincial breeding herd to provide steers, and the population's appetite for beef which leads to the slaughter even of work animals. An Animal Draft Power and Cattle Development Project is underway with two major objectives: to ensure an adequate supply of steers for training into work oxen; and to develop the peasant cattle industry in Luapula Province up to a stage where steers for work oxen can be obtained locally, thus ensuring the sustainability of animal draft power technology.

Introduction

Luapula Province in Zambia ranges in altitude from 900 to 1500 m and has annual rainfall of 1000–1500 mm. At least 80% of the population are engaged in agriculture and the production of food crops. The traditional hand hoe tillage practices have meant that the total cultivated land area has remained small, and production of maize, the staple food, is not sufficient to meet the provincial demand. As a result maize grain has to be brought in from other provinces. Animal traction technology offers a means of improving agricultural practices and increasing food crop production. This paper describes efforts to introduce this technology into the province.

Background

Cattle rearing is not a tradition in Luapula Province, and so pioneers of the oxenisation drive had to deal with a number of socioeconomic constraints to the introduction of animal draft power technology among small-scale farmers. These constraints included:

- non-availability of a provincial base for steers
- the high cost of transporting steers from distant places, which meant that only a few steers could be brought into the province at any one time

- the high demand for beef in the province, which meant that the beef industry took all the available steers from among the small (10 000 head) provincial cattle population
- the prevailing low regard for cattle herding as a job, which meant that few people were interested in adopting cattle keeping, even for draft purposes
- tsetse infestations in northern parts of Zambia
- non-availability of suitable credit facilities to assist progressive small-scale farmers to acquire work oxen
- non-availability of ox-drawn implements and spare parts.

Faced with these constraints the Catholic mission used its breeding herd at Lubwe and Chibote mission stations in Samfya and Kawambwa Districts, respectively, to introduce animal draft power to the rural population, beginning in the early to mid-1970s. The mission organised rural households into what were referred to as Family Farming Schemes, and gave each group of about 10 households a pair of oxen almost free of charge. This system of introduction was not generally successful: losses of trained oxen were high, mainly as a result of poor management.

During the same period the Department of Agriculture established a breeding herd of cattle at the Ox-Supply Centre in Mansa District: this was to be a source of steers for sale to farmers in the province. However, the breeding herd proved to be too small and it could only supply a few steers annually to the farming community. Furthermore, by the early 1980s the Zambian Government could not supply adequate veterinary services to maintain the herd. As a result, productivity of the herd was very low, and the project achieved little progress.

Provincial Oxenisation Pilot Project

In early 1983 the Integrated Rural Development Programme (IRDP), funded by the Swedish International Development Authority (SIDA), initiated the Provincial Oxenisation Pilot Project.

The main objectives of the pilot project were to evaluate the prospects for adoption of animal draft power technology among small-scale farmers in Luapula Province, and to devise a systematic way of introducing work oxen to the rural population.

Implementation

Implementation of the Provincial Oxenisation Pilot Project involved:

- construction of the Lubwe ox-training centre in Samfya District
- establishment of a revolving fund for use in the purchase of steers for training into work oxen
- procurement of steers and ox-drawn implements from any corner of the country
- careful selection of small-scale farmers from all districts for inclusion in the animal draft power annual training programmes
- carrying out annual internal evaluations of the impact of the animal draft power pilot project on the farming community of the province
- provision of credit to selected farmers who lacked the financial resources to purchase oxen and ox-drawn implements.

The project lasted three years and a total of 250 small-scale farmers were trained under the close supervision of the Provincial Animal Husbandry Officer, who also carried out the annual internal evaluations.

Evaluation

The following conclusions were drawn from the annual evaluations of the project:

- more than 50% of farmers trained were able to increase their cultivated area from the previous 1 ha to almost 10 ha after obtaining oxen in the first season
- farmers with other money-making business ventures found little time to use their oxen for crop production and were thus not able to prepare more than 2 ha of land for planting
- farmers who obtained oxen through loan facilities used their oxen almost solely for transportation in order to earn enough money to pay back their loans in the shortest possible time. The animals therefore needed to be retrained in the second, and even third, year for land cultivation.
- farmers who sent their hired labour to animal draft power training courses rather than attend themselves generally failed to use the oxen after the hired hand left the farm
- the non-availability of replacement steers in the province was a discouraging factor for farmers

who experienced disease problems with their oxen, as the project had no reserve funds to cover accidental loss of steers
- inadequate veterinary support in the districts was another factor contributing to the failure of some farmers, as essential drugs and chemicals were not always available to farmers when required
- veterinary staff in the districts lacked transport to reach farmers in remote corners of the province
- farmers who did not purchase ox carts when they started to use oxen for crop production usually found themselves not being able to haul their extra produce to storage or market.

On the whole it was concluded that animal draft power technology was highly adoptable among the small-scale farmers of Luapula Province, as evidenced by the ever-increasing demand for participation in the training programme. The pilot project could only meet 20% of the annual provincial demand for more than 250 work oxen.

Animal Draft Power and Cattle Development Project

At the conclusion of the IRDP Oxenisation Pilot Project in 1986, the experiences gained were used in formulating the Animal Draft Power and Cattle Development Project. Implemented with the financial support of the Finnish International Development Agency (Finnida), the short-term objective of this project was to supply steers for training into work oxen on an annual basis and to ensure their availability to farmers for increased agricultural production. The long-term aim was then to develop the peasant cattle industry in Luapula Province up to a stage where steers for work oxen could be obtained locally, thus ensuring the sustainability of animal draft power technology. Training of farmers in animal draft power technology was to be decentralised to Farmer Training Centres.

Implementation of the Animal Draft Power and Cattle Development Project involved five institutions.

Department of Agriculture

Two sections of the Department of Agriculture are involved in the project.

The Animal Husbandry Section has been responsible for acquiring steers for work oxen ever since the inception of the provincial oxenisation programme. Its role in the new project was to oversee the training of these steers and their proper introduction to small-scale farmers, as well as the training of the few cattle keepers in the province in improved management practices.

The Agricultural Engineering Section was jointly involved with the Animal Husbandry Section in the training of work oxen and small-scale farmers. It was also to look into the training of village artisans and blacksmiths in the hope of establishing service groups for the ox users in the villages; and to oversee the local fabrication of ox-drawn implements.

Department of Veterinary and Tsetse Control Services

Two sections of the Department of Veterinary and Tsetse Control Services were involved in the project.

The Animal Health Section was charged with providing timely and dependable veterinary services to cattle farmers in the province.

The Tsetse Control Section was charged with providing an early warning system, closely monitoring the tsetse population in the province and devising methods of controlling the tsetse fly.

Mansa rural dairy

The rural dairy in Mansa District is run by Zambia Agricultural Development Limited. Its role in the project was to establish a breed herd of Boran type cattle which would be maintained separately from the dairy herd. This breed herd was to be that long desired provincial base to provide both breeding

stock for the peasant industry and steers for training into work oxen.

Chimengwa farm

The Luapula Cooperative Union was charged with the rearing of steers purchased by the project up to trainable weights. Thus Chimengwa farm was to be developed for efficient finishing of steers with the use of improved pastures.

Zambia Cooperative Federation–Finance Services

Under the Cooperative Credit Scheme the cooperative was charged with the organisation of loan packages for selected farmers before they underwent training in animal draft power technology.

Future aims

Much work still needs to be done to increase the population of cattle in Luapula Province and subsequently to satisfy the provincial need for work oxen. The project has met a lot of stumbling blocks hindering the fast development and attainment of its goals. One of the long-standing problems limiting the growth of the peasant cattle industry is the high demand for beef. This has led to the loss of even work oxen, not to mention the many pregnant cows that are slaughtered every year in the province. The project has therefore taken on additional responsibilities in trying to promote the production of other species of animals such as sheep and goats, so as to reduce the slaughter pressure on cattle.

Transfer of animal traction technologies in Zambia through on-farm programmes

by

Roelof A Meijer [*]

Coordinator, Animal Draft Power Research and Development Programme, PO Box 11, Magoye, Zambia

Abstract

This paper describes the approaches that the Animal Draft Power Research and Development Programme follows in its on-farm programmes, which aim at promoting the diversification of animal draft power techniques as well as formulating alternative animal draft power based tillage systems. The topics of these programmes are highlighted, and some related activities—establishment of sales agents, training of extension staff and regional cooperation—are discussed. Institutions based in other countries and involved in the introduction, diversification or intensification of the use of animal power could benefit from this particular Zambian experience.

Introduction

The Animal Draft Power Research and Development Programme (ADPRDP) has been operating since mid-1987 (initially it was called a project but since 1991 it has been referred to as a programme). Its general objective is to increase and secure agricultural production in Zambia through further development and introduction of animal draft technologies.

To achieve this objective, the ADPRDP has been focusing on the following activities:

o testing and development of animal-drawn implements
o applied research on animal draft power based soil tillage and cropping systems
o on-farm testing and farming systems research programmes
o establishing close cooperation with other national and regional institutions working on animal draft power.

Because very little information that could readily be translated into extension messages was available at the start of the ADPRDP, the emphasis of the work programmes in the first two years was on testing and development work and applied tillage research. The results obtained from these programmes have led to a continuously increasing shift from

information gathering to information dissemination through extension programmes.

The distinct variation in the status of animal traction use in different areas of Zambia, and the fact that constraints on its implementation differ from area to area, demand a flexible, non-uniform approach by ADPRDP's programmes.

The areas where animal traction has been in use for the longest time are Southern and Western Provinces, traditional cattle-keeping areas. In Southern Province in particular, farmers often possess a wide range of animal draft power implements, such as several plows, harrows and cultivators, a planter and an ox cart. In Central, Lusaka and Eastern Provinces the situation is more mixed: in some areas the use of animal traction has been well established for many years, while in others the technology has only recently been introduced. In the Copperbelt, North Western, Luapula and Northern Provinces animal traction is generally a new technology, whose use is steadily increasing (Starkey, Dibbits and Mwenya, 1991). In those areas where animal traction is a new concept, plowing and, to a lesser extent, transport are its main applications. For many farmers, animal-drawn cultivators, ridgers and planters are novel implements; planting is generally done by hand, and most farmers use either hoes or their plow for weeding.

Applied research highlights

The major constraints that Zambian farmers face in using animal draft power for soil tillage are (ADPRDP, 1991):

o time and energy bottlenecks at the beginning of the rainy season (seedbed preparation) and during the crop growing season (weeding)
o poor availability of properly designed and constructed tools for plowing, seedbed preparation, weeding and planting.

On-station and on-farm research programmes on tillage systems using animal draft power have so far focused on alternative primary tillage systems

[*]*Subsequent address:*
Paddepoelsweg 1, 6532 ZG Nijmegen, The Netherlands

(direct ridging, tie-ridging and ripping) and weeding techniques (using ridgers and cultivators). The major conclusions from this research (ADPRDP, 1991) can be summarised as follows:

º under specific regional and management conditions, certain primary tillage systems (such as direct ridging and ripping) can be alternatives to plowing, but further adaptive research at the farm level is needed to formulate feasible and acceptable systems

º animal draft power based weeding techniques, especially ridging and re-ridging, are very effective under diverse conditions. However, these methods are scarcely used at present in large parts of the country, so awareness should be created and farmers' acceptance monitored. Moreover, few appropriate weeding implements were available in the past and so their manufacture and distribution should be encouraged.

On-farm demonstration programmes

As a logical follow-up to the soil tillage research programmes, an increasing number of regional activities are being carried out by the ADPRDP at farm level. Demonstrations play a major role in these activities, the objectives being to:

º encourage the diversification of animal draft power techniques through promoting proven animal draft power technologies

º formulate alternative animal draft power based tillage systems through on-farm adaptive research

º train extension staff and actively involve them in animal draft power extension and development programmes.

ADPRDP's demonstration programmes focus on:

º systems and implements which are already known in some areas, but need to be further extended in other regions: an example is the use of ridgers and cultivators for weeding

º alternative systems (and related implements) that need further adaptive research and development in the regions before they can be extended on a wider scale. Major attention is given to direct ridging, and location-specific attention to direct planting, tie-ridging and ripping, as alternatives to plowing for reduced time and energy requirements, improved timeliness of operations and better soil and water management.

Weeding systems demonstrations

Competition by weeds is still one of the major yield-limiting factors in small- and medium-scale farming in Zambia.

As a follow-up to previous research into weeding methods and tests of weeding equipment, pilot demonstrations of weeding methods aiming at effective weed control and reduced work times were held in the 1990/91 season at seven locations in Southern and Western Provinces; various ridgers and cultivators were compared, as weeding implements, to a standard mouldboard plow. The demonstrations, in which more than 350 farmers participated, were greatly appreciated by farmers and cooperating extension officers. In view of this success, the ADPRDP decided to conduct demonstrations on a larger scale during the 1991/92 season: 10 areas were selected in seven provinces. By the end of the 1991/92 season weeding demonstrations had been conducted at approximately 30 locations.

Approach

Locations for the demonstrations are selected in conjunction with local organisations, mainly regional agricultural development programmes. The pilot demonstrations indicated that these organisations can have an impact in virtually all areas where animal traction is being used. However, in order to make most efficient use of its limited resources, the ADPRDP presently restricts the demonstration programmes to areas were effective local cooperation has been established.

The demonstrations are carried out in close cooperation with such "local counterparts". Extension personnel are responsible for selecting farms on which to hold the demonstrations, arranging dates for the demonstrations, and taking care of all practical arrangements, such as inviting farmers, providing refreshments, etc.

The implements demonstrated comprise five makes of ridger (two locally manufactured and three imported) and two makes of cultivator—all animal-drawn weeding implements that are (or at least were, when the demonstrations were planned) sold commercially in Zambia. The demonstrations thus not only introduce new concepts to farmers who are not (yet) using such equipment for weeding, but also allow comparisons to be made between the two weeding methods (cultivating and ridging) and between the different makes of equipment.

Execution

Each demonstration starts with an explanation of its objectives, followed by an introduction to the different implements (names of parts, adjustments, etc) and related tillage practices.

An extension worker then demonstrates the use of each implement in a field with a crop that needs weeding, after which the farmers are encouraged to try out each implement themselves. After the actual demonstrations, the implements' quality and performance, as well as the farmers' preferences, are discussed extensively, and a classification of the implements (best to worst) is determined by vote. Participating farmers are also asked to comment on the organisation, execution and content of the demonstration.

An immediate demand is often created for certain implements, and as they are not readily obtainable in most areas, these are made available to participating farmers after the demonstration; to date a total of 450 cultivators and ridgers have been distributed in this way. Farmers are given two options for obtaining an implement of their choice: they can either buy it outright, by paying the ex-factory (or ex-importer) cash price immediately; or they can pay a deposit (10–20%) and enter into a contract to settle the full amount (ex-factory price at the moment payment is completed) before a specified date.

Feedback of results and follow-up are an important aspect of the demonstrations. ADPRDP staff make regular visits to all regions, and extension personnel are issued with special forms on which record farmers' demand for all demonstrated equipment. At the end of the season the information gathered is made available to implement manufacturers and importers.

A workshop is held for all extension staff directly involved in the season's demonstration programmes. The purpose is to review the achievements of the past season, and to formulate recommendations for the demonstration programme for the following season.

On-farm adaptive research

Initial approach

In the past, the ADPRDP selected farmers for its on-farm research activities through local extension personnel who had been briefed on the planned programmes. At the beginning of the season, ADPRDP staff would then give explanations and, if necessary, brief demonstrations to each selected farmer. This procedure had its drawbacks: because of this complete involvement of ADPRDP staff, the number of participating farmers and the number of selected regions had to remain relatively small;

furthermore this method of selection often led to disappointing levels of farmer enthusiasm and participation.

New approach starting with the 1991/92 season

Problem identification and planning of the research programme are, as before, based on region-specific demands and results obtained so far. The programmes focus on tillage practices (direct ridging, ripping, direct planting, split-ridging, tied ridging) and related implements as alternatives to conventional plowing, the aims being to reduce time and energy requirements, to improve timeliness of tillage and planting operations, and to achieve better soil and water management in regions prone to erosion, in low-rainfall areas, or in areas where waterlogging occurs.

Selection of locations is generally determined by region-specific constraints and subsequent requests, which generally originate from the extension service or agricultural development programmes.

Participating farmers are selected through small-scale on-farm field days during which the techniques are demonstrated. The approach to implementing and executing these demonstrations is identical to that of the weeding demonstrations.

The application of these techniques and implements by participating farmers is encouraged by offering them the use of the implement(s) of their choice for the duration of the season. At the end of the season, farmers can either buy the implement at the prevailing factory price, or they can return the implement to the ADPRDP.

Monitoring and evaluation of these applications, using record sheets and questionnaires, is carried out in close cooperation with extension staff and regional development programmes.

Feedback of results translated into clear-cut recommendations adapted to the requirements of the different target groups is an essential goal of the research effort.

At the conclusion of the 1991/92 season, a workshop was held for all extension staff directly involved in the season's programmes.

If after one or more seasons the investigated techniques prove to be successfully accepted by farmers, that particular adaptive research activity will evolve into a more widely spread demonstration programme.

Programme topics

Direct ridging

The direct ridging programme is a follow-up to several research programmes the ADPRDP has executed on ridging as a primary tillage practice. This research indicated that direct ridging (ridging without plowing) can be a viable alternative to plowing: a considerable reduction in work times for primary tillage allows earlier planting, and weeds can be controlled effectively by re-ridging (Meijer, 1992). However, its suitability in various regions (and thus under different agroclimatic conditions) and its practical value to farmers need to be further investigated through on-farm programmes.

This was the largest primary tillage programme in the 1991/92 season, with 14 demonstrations in five provinces and a total of 124 ridgers handed out to farmers.

Tie-ridging and ripping

The tie-ridging and ripping programme originates from the soil and water conservation tillage trials conducted in Lusitu (Southern Province) for the past three years. They are an addition to the direct ridging programme in three out of six locations, and thus the three alternatives investigated are direct ridging, tie-ridging and ripping.

Tie-ridging shows definite advantages over plowing. Run-off is reduced, and so water conservation is improved and there is less erosion. Land preparation takes less time, thus allowing earlier planting. Weed control (by re-ridging) is very effective. Ripping has potential as a "last resort option" when rains start late: land preparation takes very little time and can be done before the rains, allowing a farmer to dry-plant. However, weed growth on a ripped field will be abundant, and run-off and erosion are potential hazards (Meijer and Chelemu, 1990). As with the direct ridging programme, the practical applicability of tie-ridging and ripping in various regions, and farmers' acceptance of these techniques, are further investigated through this on-farm programme, which involves nine demonstrations in three provinces, using 60 ridge-tiers (two ADPRDP prototypes) and more than 70 rippers (two commercial makes).

In addition to the above two main programmes, small-scale region-specific demonstrations are carried out in certain areas.

Sales agent programme

During the pilot demonstrations held in the 1990/91 season, it was found that the awareness created among farmers through these demonstrations often led to an acute demand for one or more of the demonstrated implements. Although, of the equipment demonstrated, the tie-ridgers and all but one model ripper are manufactured, or at least marketed, in Zambia, only a few, if any, implements are available in sufficient numbers in rural areas.

Several factors contribute to this poor availability:

o logistic problems of manufacturers/importers (eg, acquisition of foreign exchange, procurement of raw materials, sub-capacity production levels)

o the tendency to manufacture on order only, without the establishment of a network of sales points

o malfunctioning of marketing channels.

The second and third factors, especially, are responsible for the present situation whereby, if a demand exists in a particular area, little response can be observed from the manufacturer/importer. Retailers (sporadic in most rural areas) have to recognise such a demand and place a firm order before most manufacturers/importers will take any action.

In view of the above, it was decided to combine the demonstration programmes with the establishment of equipment sales points and agents in most locations. Manufacturers were approached to supply such agents (any private entrepreneur can qualify) with their equipment and spares on a "pay when sold" basis. One local manufacturer, Lusaka Engineering Company, agreed to supply 300 implements (with a value of close to 2 million Kwacha, approximately US$ 20,000) on such conditions, and also supplied 30 implements free of charge for use in demonstrations. The Lusaka-based African Farmers' Enterprises is supplying 100 implements on a "pay when sold" basis. In addition, the ADPRDP and the counterpart organisations are supplying quantities of all other demonstrated implements and their spares on the same basis. It is hoped that, after this initial support, these local agents can continue to operate on a sound economic basis and thus alleviate the present shortage of animal draft power implements and spares, while simultaneously providing a market outlet to manufacturers/importers.

Provincial cooperation and training

When one considers the scope of the on-farm programmes the ADPRDP is presently carrying out, it is obvious that these can only be executed successfully if the extension services and provincial and district agricultural development programmes are closely involved with their implementation.

In the first half of 1991, discussions were held with these local counterparts with a view to formulating the outlines of the on-farm programme and to selecting participating staff. An important criterion in this selection was previous participation in the regular training course of the Palabana Animal Draft Power Training Project.

In September 1991, the ADPRDP organised a specific follow-up training course for all regional staff (40 in total) involved in the programme. Each area was represented by a supervisor (often a district agricultural engineer) and one extension worker from each location where demonstrations were to be held. The course aimed at providing the participants with all necessary knowledge and skills to carry out the demonstrations programme in their areas without major involvement from the ADPRDP. Course subjects included lectures on primary tillage and weeding practices, a lecture on the planning and execution of on-farm demonstrations and an extensive explanation of the demonstrations and sales agents programme. Through field practicals, participants were made familiar with all the animal draft power equipment involved. Towards the end of the course, the participants had to organise and execute a field demonstration for invited farmers. Finally, individual discussions on logistic matters were held with each group representing an area. Apart from ample background information, the course syllabus contains practical guidelines and checklists for the organisation and execution of the field demonstrations.

In five out of the 10 areas, regional development programmes are either partly or completely funding their part of the demonstrations programme and providing logistic support. In the other areas, the ADPRDP supplies the implements and provides the supervising extension staff with a budget for expenses for such things as fuel and spares, bicycles and allowances.

Conclusions

The generally high attendance of farmers, and their active participation during the demonstrations (both primary tillage and weeding), indicate that the demonstrations are an answer to a widely existing need. Not only do the demonstrations offer the farmer the opportunity to view new techniques and compare different implements, they also offer a platform for discussions (among themselves and with extension and project staff) on a wide range of subjects related to animal draft power.

The active and enthusiastic cooperation from extension staff demonstrates that their close involvement in such programmes can strengthen their motivation and performance. It is felt that the combination of training on animal traction subjects, as provided by the Palabana Animal Draft Power Training Project and the follow-up on-farm programmes described above, can act as a catalyst to boost the introduction, intensification and diversification of the use of animal traction.

The keen interest of regional development programmes and their subsequent commitments for support (financial, logistic and personnel) indicate that within these programmes a distinct need exists for the type of expertise provided by the ADPRDP.

The establishment of sales agents is not an easy matter; selection has to be done carefully and constant monitoring is necessary. Good planning is required to get equipment and parts to the right place at the right time and procurement is hampered by irregular stocks and ever-increasing prices.

The keen interest of farmers in obtaining demonstrated equipment, their readiness to pay deposits and the number of farmers that buy implements on the spot, prove that a great demand for such equipment exists. It also indicates, however, that farmers desperately need access to credit facilities. Although confident in their ability to complete payment, many farmers have stressed that late payments of crop proceeds by the cooperatives (frequently six months or more after delivery of the crop) could make payment before the set deadline very difficult.

References

ADPRDP, 1991. *Course on regional demonstrations*. Animal Draft Power Research and Development Project (ADPRDP), Magoye, Zambia. 63p.

Meijer R A, 1992. *Ridging as a primary tillage practice*. Animal Draft Power Research and Development Programme (ADPRDP), Magoye, Zambia. 14p.

Meijer R A and Chelemu K, 1990. *Lusitu soil and water conservation tillage trial: season 1988–1989*. Animal Draft Power Research and Development Project (ADPRDP), Magoye, Zambia. 16p.

Starkey P H, Dibbits H J and Mwenya E, 1991. *Animal traction in Zambia: status, progress and trends*. Ministry of Agriculture, Lusaka, Zambia, in association with IMAG-DLO, Wageningen, The Netherlands. 107p.

Role of the Farm Implements and Tools (FIT) project in the transfer of animal traction technology

by

Hans Helsloot[*]

Farm Implements and Tools (FIT) Section, TOOL Consultancy Department
Sarphatistraat 650, 1018 AV Amsterdam, The Netherlands

Abstract

The Farm Implements and Tools (FIT) project—a joint venture by the International Labour Office (ILO) and the Dutch non-governmental organisation TOOL—is concerned with the transfer of animal traction technology, particularly the promotion of small-scale animal-powered farm implements and food processing devices in developing countries. A study was carried out to investigate the feasibility of local manufacturing of animal-drawn implements in northern Tanzania. The study was undertaken jointly with Camartec (Centre for Agricultural Mechanisation and Rural Technology), a Tanzanian organization with testing facilities and experience with product development. The demand for ox-drawn implements in the three regions surveyed is enormous. A local workshop was selected to start up manufacturing, with the support of a Dutch and a Zambian manufacturer. Camartec supports the workshop, assisting the adaptation of the technology to suit local requirements.

The FIT Project

The International Labour Office (ILO) and the Dutch non-governmental organisation TOOL have started a collaborative project with the overall objective of promoting the development, production and use of improved farm implements and tools, and food processing devices. The project, called the Farm Implements and Tools (FIT) project, is funded by the Government of The Netherlands.

The objectives of the FIT project are to:

o strengthen local capacity for the promotion of farm implements and food processing devices
o improve the flow of technological information
o strengthen local capacity for research and development.

In order to fulfil these objectives, the project aims to:

o develop various improved tools and implements, and establish rural manufacturing units producing such items
o set up efficient and appropriate institutional mechanisms, organised through government agencies, non-governmental organisations or the private sector, to promote the local development, production and marketing of improved tools and implements for the agricultural and food processing sectors.
o develop local documentation centres, capable of collecting, processing and disseminating technological information among small-scale producers of appropriate tools and implements, making use of the experiences of others, rather than developing new technologies themselves
o produce publications about successful technologies, to make experiences available to others (food packaging for the local market has been selected as one of the subjects).

Beneficiaries

The project's direct beneficiaries include artisans (individuals or groups), cottage workers, cooperatives and small-scale producers, involved in the production of tools and implements for the agricultural and food processing sectors. Indirect beneficiaries include users of agricultural tools and implements and food processing devices. Rural women, who are traditionally involved in these types of activity, are an important category of indirect beneficiaries.

South–south exchange

The project tries to avoid duplication of efforts in different areas. This is a waste of funds and energy. Therefore, exchange of technology between southern countries is stimulated wherever feasible. Technological information (research methodologies, questionnaires, technologies, etc) is exchanged between the southern countries, trade between southern countries is promoted, and training is carried out in neighbouring countries wherever practicable.

Country activities

The project started in 1991 and has so far initiated activities in Benin, Burkina Faso, Ghana, Niger,

---
[*]*Subsequent address:*
Havensingel 70, 5211 TZ Den Bosch, The Netherlands

Tanzania and Zambia. From September 1992 the project aims to be active in other countries as well.

In Tanzania the project is involved in the several activities, including:

○ a survey of the need for technical assistance in the small-scale equipment sector in the Arusha, Moshi, Singida and Shinyanga Regions

○ assistance to Camartec (Centre for Agricultural Mechanisation and Rural Technology, based at Arusha) in order to stimulate the local manufacture and development of small-scale implements and tools for the agricultural and food processing sectors (including the development of a documentation centre, strengthening research and development capacity and training staff to carry out consultancies)

○ a feasibility study on manufacturing ox-drawn farm implements (plows, ridgers, harrows, planters and weeders) in Mbulu District.

Technology transfer to a local workshop in Tanzania

Mbulu District is part of Arusha Region in the north of Tanzania. Most of the people in the district are involved in rain-dependent mixed farming. Main crops grown by smallholders are maize, beans, cotton, wheat and coffee.

The Mbulu District Rural Development Programme asked the project to investigate the feasibility of establishing the production of ox-drawn farm implements in the district. The study was carried out in collaboration with Camartec, a Tanzanian centre for agricultural mechanisation: two engineers from Camartec were given on-the-job training in the different aspects of introducing animal traction technology.

The study investigated the market size for these implements as well as the feasibility of establishing a production capacity in one of the workshops in the district.

Market survey

Ox plows are common in many areas of Tanzania. Other ox-drawn implements are rarely found.

The total expected sales of ox plows for the 1991/92 season in Arusha, Shinyanga and Singida Regions are almost 13 000 per year. The genuine demand for ox plows exceeds this number considerably, because every major sales outlet indicated that it would have sold more if the supply had been greater.

The purchasing power of the farmers in the regions concerned is quite high. The profitability for the

farmers of using one or more of the ox-drawn implements is also quite high. Lack of efficient credit schemes is not expected to hamper the purchase of implements.

The plows actually available on the market are very cheap. The plows to be introduced will cost more, but they are of better quality. (This has been confirmed in several places in Tanzania, by farmers as well as testing institutes.) It is expected, however, that not all farmers will be prepared to pay more for higher quality.

Most of the farmers are not aware of the existence of ox-drawn tillage implements other than the plow. Therefore, although it was found that an enormous potential demand exists, the communicated demand is still low and hence the agricultural extension services will have to play a substantial role in the transfer of the technology.

Local manufacture will initially be of plows, ridgers, harrows, planters and weeders. Market trials will indicate to what extent there is a genuine demand for each of these implements.

Rumptstad – Lenco

Lenco is an engineering company in Lusaka, Zambia, manufacturing plows and ridgers of the Rumptstad type, ox carts and hammermills. The FIT project has stimulated collaboration by Lenco and the workshop in Mbulu District for the following reasons:

○ Lenco has gathered a lot of experience with development, production and distribution of the Rumptstad implements

○ the modifications made to the plow by Lenco and Rumptstad to adapt it to Zambian requirements are probably interesting for Tanzanian farmers as well

○ Lenco can supply its implements cheaper than Rumptstad can, and is very interested in exports

○ Tanzania and Zambia are promoting trade between themselves through the regional organisations SADCC (Southern African Development Coordination Conference) and PTA (Preferential Trade Area)

○ Lenco can supply better training to the staff of the workshop in Mbulu.

Local manufacturing

One of the workshops supported by the Mbulu District Rural Development Programme was found to be very suitable for manufacturing the implements. This workshop will start with the assembly of 200 implements in 1992: these will be used for demonstrations and market trials.

Demonstrations

Mbulu District has 21 wards and in each ward an innovative farmer, involved in the agricultural extension network, will be offered the use of a full set of implements, ie, plow, harrow, ridger, planter and cultivator, on his or her fields (a total of 105 implements). This should make these farmers, as well as their neighbours, aware of the existence and use of such implements. The farmers' judgements and suggestions for improvement of the implements will be monitored.

Market trials

The remaining 95 implements will be used for market trials. In the second year it is planned that 350 implements will be manufactured, and the results of the market trials will be used to determine how many of each type of implement will be made, and the market prices. In the third year 700 implements could be manufactured, the numbers of each implement type being determined by the sales levels in the preceding year.

Step-by-step

A step-by-step process will be used to establish implement manufacture by the workshop. Developing local manufacturing in this way keeps down the initial investments and the financial risks involved, and also guarantees product quality during production start-up.

In the first year the workshop will only assemble (bolt together) implements using parts manufactured by Rumptstad or Lenco. The reason for this is that it is of utmost importance that implements used for demonstrations and market trials are of good quality. An employee of Rumptstad will go to Mbulu to train workshop staff in the assembly of the implements, and also to train workshop staff and extension workers in how to use and operate the implements. Camartec will also be involved in the training.

In the second year, operations such as cutting, drilling, bending, welding, grinding, painting, etc, will be done by the local workshop. Some of the workshop's employees will go to Lenco in Zambia for training in these skills. (This is much better than sending workshop staff to Rumptstad in The Netherlands, because the manufacturing process in The Netherlands is much more capital intensive. In addition, it is cheaper to send people to Lusaka than to The Netherlands, people in Lusaka speak English and Zambia does not differ greatly from Tanzania.) The jigs needed for production will be supplied by Lenco or Rumptstad. Machinery can be ordered from Rumptstad, Lenco or a local supplier.

In the succeeding years, the local workshop will gradually take over all the manufacturing processes. Local subcontractors will have to be found for hardening the soil-touching parts and for casting some iron parts for the planter. Camartec will use its testing facilities and experience in product development to help the workshop to locate suitable subcontractors, able to deliver good quality for a reasonable price. Also, quality control of these parts will be done in collaboration with Camartec.

Following an evaluation by the Dutch Government, the FIT project will concentrate its future activities in just two countries, Kenya and Ghana, in order that its resources are not spread too thinly. More information about the FIT project can be obtained from:

TOOL (Attn FIT Project)
Sarphatistraat 650
1018 AV Amsterdam, The Netherlands
Tel: + (31 20) 6264409; Fax: + (31 20) 6277489

ILO–ENT/MAN (Attn FIT Project)
4 Route des Morillons
CH 1211 Geneva 22, Switzerland
Tel: + (41 22) 7997633/6242. Fax: + (41 22) 7988685

Photograph opposite
Members of a women's group using a two-shaft cart designed for a single donkey, Tanga, Tanzania

---

Improving animal traction technology

Photo: Paul Starkey

Animal-powered transport

Improving animal-based transport: options, approaches, issues and impact

by

Mary Anderson and Ron Dennis

IT Transport Ltd, The Old Power Station, Ardington, Near Wantage, Oxon OX12 8QJ, UK

Abstract

The use of draft animals for rural transport is an important complement to their use in agriculture. The movement of agricultural and subsistence goods is a major burden in time and effort for rural households. The majority of movements take place at farm and village level, often by walking. The use of animals can improve the efficiency of transport, alleviating constraints on farm productivity and aiding agricultural development. However, the potential role of animal-based transport is still largely unrealised in eastern and southern Africa.

This paper discusses the options for animal-based transport. Carts have the greatest potential for improving rural transport although smaller farmers may not be able to afford them. There is a large unsatisfied demand for carts in the region resulting from problems in production, primarily the limited availability of materials and components, particularly good quality wheel–axle assemblies. The issues involved in improving the production of carts are considered and an integrated approach is recommended to improve the supply of materials and critical components to rural workshops which would construct and assemble carts. It is anticipated that this would develop an effective infrastructure for supply and maintenance of carts and provide carts to farmers at minimum cost.

Affordability and profitability of animal-based transport are key issues in its wider dissemination. Experience from many parts of Africa suggests that the availability of credit facilities is of great importance to successful dissemination programmes. The issue of access to transport facilities by women is of major significance in improving the impact of these programmes.

Introduction

Recent years have witnessed increased dissatisfaction with conventional approaches to rural transport planning in developing countries. Growing evidence points to the existence of a significant off-road transport burden undertaken by rural households. At the same time the economic crisis set ever tighter limits on budgets for the construction and maintenance of roads and for the import of motor vehicles. As a result of these trends, increasing attention is being focused on the exploration of alternative options for addressing rural transport problems. Animal-based transport is increasingly seen as having high potential in this respect, particularly as a complement to the use of draft animals in farming systems.

This paper summarises the main issues of animal-based transport and the role it could play in alleviating the transport burden of rural households in eastern and southern Africa. In particular, it identifies ways in which the production and dissemination of animal-drawn carts could be improved. In another paper in these proceedings, the same authors consider some technical aspects of cart design (Dennis and Anderson, 1994).

The role of animal-based transport

Transport needs

Conventional transport planning has often overlooked the importance of transport needs at the farm and household level in rural areas. Transport projects have tended to focus on the provision of roads for motorised vehicles. While roads and motor vehicles can play a vital role in connecting rural centres to larger markets, planners are increasingly realising that the "road and motor vehicle" approach has little impact on the daily transport needs of most rural households in Africa. Most rural travel takes place "off-road", usually on foot. Recent surveys, in Ghana and in Makete District in the south-west of Tanzania, show that over three-quarters of the time and effort spent on transport are devoted to movements around the household and fields. Trips to the market, grinding mill, health facilities and other places outside the village represent less than 25% of the annual transport effort in these areas (Barwell and Malmberg-Calvo, 1988; Howe and Zille, 1988).

Data from the Makete surveys showed that the typical household in this area spent on average more than 2500 hours per year on local transport for subsistence and agricultural purposes (Figure 1; Barwell and Malmberg-Calvo, 1988). This transport burden fell disproportionately onto women, who spent an average of 30 hours a week on local transport, compared with an average of only 10 hours a week for men. These figures are by no means unique. Studies undertaken in Ghana and in Tanga Region of Tanzania reveal similar transport burdens and a particularly heavy burden on women, in terms of both time and load-carrying effort. Other studies (Kaira, 1983; Curtis, 1986) have also shown that the transport of water, fuelwood and other goods for subsistence needs imposes a heavy burden on rural households in many parts of Africa.

Often the only means of moving goods around the farm or village is by headloading, which is slow and inefficient, and can cause spinal injuries and other health hazards (Dufaut, 1988). Animals offer a more efficient way of moving goods over short distances: pack animals and carts have a higher carrying capacity than humans, and can therefore move large loads in fewer trips (Table 1). At seasonal labour peaks, animal-based transport can help to alleviate time constraints on agricultural production and domestic activities. More efficient transport can also facilitate other income generating activities and can potentially bring social or health benefits, particularly to women, by alleviating the burden of moving firewood and water.

Animal-based transport cannot match the speed or carrying capacity of motor vehicles, but it can offer other advantages. For example, rural households can afford it; pack animals and carts can operate on lower quality tracks and paths than motor vehicles; and animals do not require imported fuel. In any case, most farmers rarely need to move loads of more than 1000 kg. In these respects, animal transport provides an attractive "intermediate" option between headloading and motorised transport.

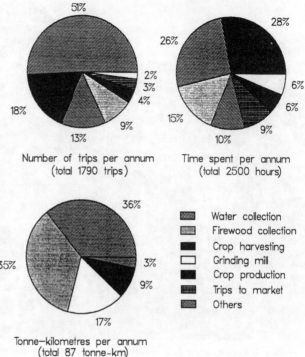

Number of trips per annum
(total 1790 trips)

Time spent per annum
(total 2500 hours)

Tonne–kilometres per annum
(total 87 tonne-km)

Water collection
Firewood collection
Crop harvesting
Grinding mill
Crop production
Trips to market
Others

Figure 1: Travel pattern of a typical sampled village in Makete District, Tanzania

Status of animal transport in Africa

Animal transport has been a major feature of traditional economies in many parts of Asia, South America and, until relatively recently, Europe and North America. In India, Sri Lanka and many parts of South East Asia, bullock carts, buffalo carts and sledges play an important role in rural areas. India has around 15 million animal-drawn carts (Photo 1), which transport an estimated 1500–1800 million tonnes of goods per year. This far exceeds the 300 million tonnes of goods transported annually on the Indian railway system (Srivastava, 1989).

In Ethiopia, Sudan and North African countries, donkeys, horses, oxen and even camels have been

Table 1: Comparison of typical loads and speeds of some transport systems

Means of transport	Load capacity (kg)	Typical speed (km/hour)	Load carrying capacity (tonne–km/hour)
Human (headloading)	25	4	0.1
Donkey (pack load)	50	5	0.25
Ox cart	1 000	4	4
Two wheel tractor	1 000	10	10
Tractor/trailer	3 000	20	60
Truck	10 000	50	500

Photo 1: Bullock carts in India. Animal-drawn carts could play as vital a role in Africa as they already do in Asia

Photo: IT Transport

used as means of transport for centuries. Ethiopia has a population of about 6 million oxen, 7 million horses, mules and donkeys, and a million camels (Goe and Abiye Astatke, 1989). The most important feature of animal transport in Ethiopia and neighbouring countries is the use of donkeys to carry packs and horses to pull carts.

Elsewhere in Africa, traditional use of animals for transport is rare. In Kenya and Tanzania only the Masai tribes traditionally use donkeys as pack animals. Wooden animal-drawn carts have been used traditionally in Madagascar, which was influenced by Asian and Arabic trade, but not in other parts of eastern and southern Africa. Animal-based transport was introduced to some other parts of the region during the colonial period, in conjunction with draft animal power for agriculture. In parts of southern Africa, including Botswana, Zimbabwe and parts of Mozambique, use of pack animals and carts has become well established since their introduction earlier this century.

Elsewhere in the region, animal transport is still relatively rare: the total number of animal carts in Africa is estimated to be around 700 000. According to some estimates, for every 10 African farmers who use draft animals for agriculture there is only one who owns a cart (Dawson and Barwell, 1993).

These figures suggest that there is significant under-utilisation of animal power for transport in Africa.

Animal transport in farming systems

Animal-drawn transport can form an important component of an animal traction farming system, complementing animal tillage in many ways. Some of these are outlined below.

Crop harvesting

The use of animal-based transport, rather than inefficient headloading, to move harvested crops from the fields can help reduce labour constraints at harvest time. Animal-based transport has also been observed to reduce post-harvest losses from pests by allowing timely removal of harvested crops from the fields (Scheinman, 1986; Dawson and Smith, 1990). In areas of insecurity (such as parts of northern Uganda) the speedy removal of crops from the fields may also help to reduce theft of the harvest.

Crop marketing

Animal-based transport can play a vital role in transporting surplus produce to marketing depots. Transport for marketing is becoming increasingly important in countries such as Tanzania and Zambia, where policy-makers are beginning to limit the role of inefficient central marketing boards. While giving farmers more choice in selling their surplus, these policies often give farmers more responsibility for the cost of transporting their surplus to market. In this situation, farmers without efficient transport may market their surplus through visiting traders who operate as entrepreneurs. Various studies have observed that animal carts can enable farmers to get higher prices for their crops, since the farmer can sell directly to market and avoid paying margins to traders (Scheinman, 1986; Malmberg-Calvo, 1992). Müller (1986) also observed that ox carts enabled farmers to reach the market from a radius of 5–15 km, while headloading did not extend beyond a radius of 3–5 km from the market.

Farm inputs

The side benefits of animal traction can be increased if animal manure is used as a fertiliser. A study in Tanzania (Kjaerby, 1989) found that manure was generally only applied to food plots near the household, apparently because the manure was laboriously transported by women in small baskets. However, some farmers who owned carts or sledges were beginning to apply manure in larger quantities to land of low fertility further from the homestead. Greater use of manure by cart owners, with anticipated benefits in terms of yields, was also noted by Scheinman (1986). Animal-based transport can also facilitate the collection of fertiliser and other farm inputs from distribution depots. A study of animal cart use in Kenya noted that fertiliser use was higher among animal cart farmers (Smith and Dawson, 1989).

Transport of implements

Animal-drawn sledges can play an important role in limiting damage to animal traction implements while moving them between the household and fields. Use of sledges to transport plows is common even among farmers who own carts, not only in parts of Africa but also in parts of Asia such as the Philippines.

Year round use of animals

Transport demands tend to be highest in the dry season, when harvesting and marketing are undertaken, and when farm inputs are collected for the next growing season. Studies in Tanzania (Shetto and Kwiligwa, 1988) and Zambia (Müller, 1986) have shown that animal carts are intensively used for agriculture over at least four months of the year, and may be used for other purposes throughout the year. In contrast, use of draft animals for plowing rarely exceeds a season of four to eight weeks per year. The extended use of draft animals for transport

can bring benefits by reducing the tendency for animals to forget their training between plowing seasons (Soko, 1990).

Agricultural constraints

The use of animals for transport may have negative, as well as positive, effects on farming systems. Two particular constraints which farming systems may demonstrate are nutrition and financial risk.

Nutrition

Animals which are being used year round for transport work need more food than animals which are only worked for a few weeks of the year for plowing. This may cause problems if there is a shortage of dry season grazing, or if animals do not spend enough time grazing to meet their energy requirements. Where grazing is a constraint, farmers are beginning to use crop residues to supplement feeding for their animals (Kjaerby, 1989). There is scope for complementarity, as animal-based transport can be used to transport groundnut hay and other fodder residues from the field to the household.

Risk

Investment in animals and transport equipment increases the financial risks faced by farmers. The ability of farmers to repay loans on transport equipment depends on the overall profitability of the agricultural system, which is in turn affected by price and other risks associated with the marketing of cash crops. In a marginal system farmers may not be willing to increase their risk exposure despite apparent benefits.

Loss of animals through theft or disease is a risk affecting animal traction farmers in general. Donkeys tend to be less prone to theft than oxen because they have little or no meat value. However, high losses have particularly affected schemes in Malawi and Tanzania where donkeys were introduced as pack animals to farmers who were not familiar with the health or care of these animals. It is important that measures are taken to minimise these risks through training or extension support.

Non-agricultural benefits

Rural transport surveys in Kenya (Smith and Dawson, 1989), Mbeya, Tanzania (Shetto and Kwiligwa, 1988), Zambia (Müller, 1986) and Zimbabwe (Dawson and Smith, 1990; Gaidzanwa, 1991) show extensive use of animal-drawn carts and sledges for non-agricultural purposes. Some of these applications are directly income generating, but others generate benefits by reducing human effort or releasing time for other purposes. While these non-cash benefits are more difficult to quantify, they are nonetheless real.

Transport services

Animal carts are relatively expensive, and beyond the reach of poorer farming households in most parts of Africa. Most studies of animal cart use have observed transport services and vehicle and/or animal hire markets in operation. This has two important effects: first, it makes the benefits of cart use available to a wider group; and second, it generates income for cart owners, in cash or in kind. It is still fairly rare for non-owners to hire animals and/or carts to transport goods which are not income generating, so most hiring arrangements relate to agricultural transport. The importance of rental income for the profitability of transport investments is discussed further below.

Fuelwood and water

As explained above, the collection of fuelwood and water is often the biggest transport burden for rural households in terms of time and effort consumed. Use of animal-based transport by owners to collect firewood for subsistence is not uncommon, with a few large loads replacing small daily ones. The use of carts and sledges to collect water is less common, depending on whether the people responsible for the collection (usually women) have access to animal-drawn transport. It also depends on the accessibility of the water source to such transport, the distance involved and the availability of a suitable drum to carry water. Müller (1986) found that some cart owners in Zambia still preferred to use sledges to transport water, apparently due to ease of loading and lower risk of spillage.

Traditionally, firewood and water collection tend to be the responsibility of women, so the use of animal-based transport for these tasks is dependent on the level of control which women have over the means of transport. Several studies have observed that young men and boys within a household often control the household cart or pack animal and may assume responsibility for wood collection and other "women's" tasks. Anecdotal evidence suggests that women value the social aspects of water and firewood collection, an additional factor affecting the use of transport in these activities.

Careful interpretation is needed in relation to wood and water transport statistics. A survey of ox cart use by Shetto and Kwiligwa (1988) found that 25–50% of carts were used for firewood collection and 50–90% were used to carry water, but that most of this wood and water was not destined for

domestic use but was being transported by men for use in making bricks.

Grinding mill

The transport of maize or other grain to the grinding mill is a time-consuming task for women in many parts of Africa. Animal-based transport can help to remove some drudgery from these tasks, but this again depends on women's access to the means of transport. It also depends on the size of load which needs to be transported, since frequent trips to the grinding mill with small loads may be required to avoid deterioration in stored flour (Urasa, 1990). Some women overcome this problem by combining their small loads with those of neighbours and sharing a means of transport to the mill.

Other income generating activities

Several studies have observed the use of animal-based transport for transport intensive income generating activities. These include brick making, which tends to be a male activity, and beer brewing, which tends to be the province of women. There are some examples, still fairly rare, of cart owners using their vehicles to operate as traders in firewood and other materials (Dawson and Smith, 1990).

Construction

Another activity for which animal-based transport is commonly used is the transport of materials for house construction (Müller, 1986; Shetto and Kwiligwa, 1988). Scheinman (1986) observes that rental income from cart hire is often used to pay for home improvements, so that the cart plays a dual role in generating income and transporting the materials. The causality of such observations is difficult to prove, but they illustrate the way in which animal-based transport can facilitate other activities.

Pack animals

Characteristics

Donkeys, horses, mules and camels can be used to carry substantial loads on their backs, unlike cattle which cannot bear loads on their spines. Donkeys have many useful characteristics, being cheap, hardy and suitable for many types of terrain including hills and dry areas. A further advantage is that women's use of donkeys rarely poses the same cultural or social barriers as women's use of oxen, so donkeys can often help to lighten women's transport burden.

When loaded, donkeys walk at a rate of 3–4 km/hour; trotting is faster but can only be maintained over moderate distances (2–5 km). The load which can be safely carried by a donkey depends on the size of the animal and the type of terrain. It is not uncommon to see larger animals carrying 70–80 kg over flat terrain, but in hilly areas this has to be reduced. A general rule is that the load should not exceed about one-third of the donkey's body weight, so maximum loads of 50 kg or less may be appropriate for smaller animals. This compares with typical human headloads of 25–35 kg.

Animal care

While donkeys are used extensively as pack animals in North Africa, Botswana and the Masai areas of Kenya and Tanzania, their introduction to Malawi, Zambia, Zimbabwe and other parts of easernt and southern Africa is only just beginning. There is considerable potential for wider use of donkeys in eastern and southern Africa but many farmers are not familiar with the use of donkeys for transport or agriculture (Scheinman, 1986). The introduction of donkeys to a new area requires careful extension support, particularly in training farmers about donkey care and health (Jones, 1990). Animals which are moved between different regions should also be carefully screened for infectious diseases, as animal losses from disease have been a serious problem in several donkey projects (Barwell, 1991).

Design of harnesses and packs

The technology used to attach packs is relatively low cost and simple, and can often be made from locally available materials such as leather, rope, cloth and wood. The University of Nairobi in Kenya has undertaken considerable work on the design and manufacture of donkey harnesses. The Institute of Agricultural Engineering in Zimbabwe has also published a manual on donkey use which covers harnessing in some detail (Jones, 1991). A good pack harness for a donkey should have three straps (belly, breast and rear), and straps should be well padded to avoid sores. The load should be supported by the back on either side of the spine and should not sit directly on the spine itself.

The design of the pack or panniers themselves depends on the type of load to be carried. The simplest pack for agricultural produce and other low density goods consists of one or two sacks tied over the donkey's back, connected by ropes over padding. Baskets or panniers, attached on either side, are useful for bulky goods and can generally be made from local materials. In Ethiopia and Sudan, pack animals are used to carry large water bags made from canvas or goatskin which are slung over the animals' backs (Curtis, 1986). Alternatively, a wooden frame can be used to carry heavy goods such as water cans, fuel cans or construction materials (Photo 2).

Flexibility can be achieved by using a wooden saw-buck saddle to which a number of different

Photo 2: Donkey with water containers on a pack saddle

Photo: IT Transport

types of loads can be attached. As shown in Figure 2, the saw-buck design is small, light and simple to make. Saddles of this type have been used traditionally on horses, donkeys and even yaks in Asia and the Americas.

Sledges

Characteristics

Ox-drawn (and in some areas camel-drawn) sledges can be used to drag loads of 150–350 kg at speeds of 2–4 km/hour, depending on the terrain. Sledges are difficult to pull and have a low capacity, limited range and poor efficiency compared to carts. They are believed to cause erosion of paths and for this reason have been banned in some countries (eg, Zimbabwe). The load is usually unprotected from vibration and dust.

Despite these drawbacks, sledges play a vital role in some areas of Kenya, Tanzania, Zambia and other countries. They can be made by local artisans or farmers, requiring few skills and readily available materials—little more than a suitable Y-shaped piece of wood and a rope or chain attachment. The low cash cost means that almost all ox-owning farmers can afford a sledge, even when a cart is well out of reach. They can also be used on very sandy soils which can be difficult for some wheel designs. Farmers who have access to a cart sometimes still use a sledge for certain tasks, such as transporting the plow to the fields without damage and transporting water barrels without problems of cart loading and spillage.

Sledge design

Details of a typical African sledge are shown in Figure 3: the basic design may be developed by building a load-carrying platform on the Y-shaped runners. The performance of this type of sledge has been evaluated by Immers (1988), who measured a tractive force of approximately 50–60% of the load on sandy surfaces (this would be about two to three times larger than for a wheeled cart). A significant

Basic - forked branch from a tree   Modified - with load platform

AFRICAN TYPE SLEDGES

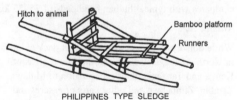

Hitch to animal

Bamboo platform

Runners

PHILIPPINES TYPE SLEDGE

Figure 3: Examples of animal-drawn sledges

proportion of the drag is due to the wide frontal area of the Y-type runner and it would seem that drag might be reduced by using parallel runners. However, tests by Immers (1988) showed that there was no reduction in drag since the reduced frontal area was offset by increased sinkage of the runners. Another problem with parallel runners is that an elevated load platform is needed to avoid contact with the track between the runners: an example is the "Cebu" sledge which is widely used in the Philippines (Figure 3).

It appears that there is a conflict in the best type of runners for different terrains: for firm surfaces the need is to reduce friction and parallel runners are probably best whereas for soft surfaces such as sand the need is to reduce sinkage and a Y-type runner or runners with increased contact area are best. It seems that there may be some potential for improving sledge design to reduce draft requirements and the inherent low cost of sledges may justify some development work in this area. Any research effort involving sledges should also examine ways of minimising damage to terrain by low-cost improvements to the design of sledges or the paths and road crossings which they use. For example, in north-east Zimbabwe sledges have been modified into crude two- or four-wheeled carts by the addition of small wooden wheels which are made by the farmers themselves.

Animal drawn carts

Two-wheeled carts

Most carts pulled by draft animals in Africa have one axle with two wheels (Photo 3). Carts have a high efficiency and capacity relative to pack animals and sledges: an ox cart can carry 600–1000 kg, while a donkey cart can carry about 300–500 kg.

Figure 2: A versatile harness for pack animals

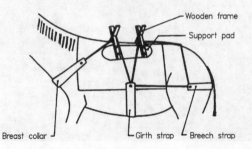

Wooden frame

Support pad

Breast collar   Girth strap   Breech strap

Compared to sledges, ox carts are easier to pull and have a greater range (up to 25 km a day).

Drawbacks of the two-wheeled cart are its high cost compared to pack and sledge technologies, and the relatively complex technology of wheels and bearings. Some types of wheels and bearings can be made from local materials, but there are usually trade-offs in terms of local availability, efficiency, cost and reliability. Careful maintenance is required, and the availability of spare parts in rural areas is often a problem. A further consideration is that carts can only be used on roads and relatively wide tracks and they are not well-suited for used in hilly terrain.

Four-wheeled carts

The use of four-wheeled animal carts is rare outside the commercial farming sector. These carts are generally larger, carrying up to 2000–3000 kg, and are usually pulled by a team of oxen or horses. They put less strain on the animals because the cart is balanced and hence avoids the downward force exerted on the animals by a two-wheeled cart.

However, the cost of a four-wheeled cart is generally more than double that of a two-wheeled cart, because of the need for a second wheel–axle set and for a swivel axle at the front for steering. Given this high cost, the use of four-wheeled carts is likely to be restricted to high load applications in farming, mining, transport services or other sectors. Nevertheless, some organisations do produce four-wheeled carts, including Camartec, (Centre for Agricultural Mechanisation and Rural Technology), Arusha, Tanzania.

Photo 3: Steel-wheeled cart. Steel rimmed wheels may be preferred in areas where punctures are frequent

Cart design issues

A two-wheeled cart is basically a very simple vehicle and in an ideal situation would probably comprise an axle having wheels with pneumatic tyres and rolling contact bearings, a steel chassis and a sheet steel or wooden body (Photo 4). However, in most African countries the design and construction of carts is considerably more complicated because of restricted access to materials and components, limited manufacturing resources, severe limitations on affordability of carts by rural households, and a limited infrastructure for repair and maintenance of carts. A fairly wide range of options is therefore needed to meet different situations. Some of the available technologies and issues are discussed in detail in the companion paper of Dennis and Anderson (1994) and the publication of Barwell and Hathway (1986).

Features of good cart design

A well-designed cart is one which performs as efficiently and reliably as possible within the

Photo 4: Two-wheeled ox cart with pneumatic tyres

Table 2: Average towing capacity of a pair of oxen for different cart designs

	Earth roads		Rutted sand	
Cart design	1 in 20 gradient	1 in 10 gradient	1 in 20 gradient	1 in 10 gradient
Pneumatic tyres and rolling contact bearings	1880	1150	750	600
Rigid tyres + plain bearings[1]	1300	910	490	420
Rigid tyres + plain bearings[2]	750	600	375	330

[1] *This assumes good quality bearings which are properly lubricated and allow no significant wheel wobble*
[2] *This assumes poor or worn bearings which are inadequately lubricated and allow considerable wheel wobble (tests in Ethiopia by Kebede and Bekele (1990) indicate that poor bearings and substantial wheel wobble can more than double towing resistance)*

constraints of affordability and acceptability to rural households. Important features of good design are:

○ **efficient performance**: this depends mainly on the wheel–axle assembly—the wheels should have low rolling resistance and the axle bearings low friction

○ **smooth operation**: it is recognised that smooth operation has a beneficial effect on the performance of animals (O'Neill, Hayton and Sims, 1989) and therefore it is desirable to minimise impact or fluctuating loads transmitted from the cart. This may be achieved by using pneumatic-tyred wheels or by introducing some cushioning into the suspension or hitch assembly of carts with rigid-tyred wheels. Little work appears to have been done so far in the latter area

○ **low cart weight**: since the draft effort available from the animals is relatively low it is important not to waste it in towing unnecessary vehicle weight. It has been recommended that the weight of ox carts should not exceed 200 kg (FAO, 1972). Upper limits for donkey carts may be 100 kg (single) and 150 kg (pair)

○ **reliability**: this implies a robust, durable construction requiring minimum maintenance and repair. Of particular importance are low wear of bearings, reliable performance of critical components such as wheels and avoidance of failures or deterioration of frame and body members

○ **affordability**: it is likely that material and component costs account for over 50% of cart cost, possibly up to 80% in smaller workshops. It is therefore important to use materials efficiently and as far as possible to use low-cost materials which are readily available. Distribution costs may also be relatively high for centrally produced carts and manufacturing strategies should be devised to minimise these.

It is clear that these desirable features involve conflicting requirements, especially the need to achieve good performance and reliability while minimising the weight and cost of materials and components. The achievement of efficient designs which are also affordable and acceptable is therefore a considerable challenge.

Performance and design

Combining the data on rolling resistance of tyres and friction in bearings, estimates can be made for performance of different cart designs for various operating conditions (Table 2). The estimates are for the total load that can be towed by a pair of oxen producing a draft effort of 150 kgf (1500 N). The weight of the vehicles must be subtracted from the figures in the table to obtain load capacities. The table clearly shows the benefits of good cart design and the need to minimise the weight of the cart. Since the average towing capacity of a donkey is only about 25% of that of a pair of oxen the criteria of good design and low cart weight are even more critical for donkey carts.

Two important issues for cart performance are the weight of the cart body and the choice of technology for the wheel–axle assembly. Wheels with pneumatic tyres and rolling contact bearings are often preferred by users because they offer significantly less rolling resistance than the lower technology rigid wheels with plain bush-type bearings. The maintenance requirements of these technologies also differ: on the one hand, users may have problems with punctures of pneumatic tyres, particularly in areas where repair facilities are scarce or punctures are particularly frequent; on the other hand, rolling contact bearings require much less routine maintenance and lubrication than plain bush-type bearings.

Approaches to cart production

Technology choice for animal carts cannot be made purely on the basis of optimum performance. Other important factors must be taken into account, including:

- ○ farmer preferences
- ○ nature of terrain and types of load transported
- ○ cost and affordability
- ○ sustainability of supply of materials and components
- ○ reliability and ease of maintenance.

This is not an exhaustive list but it indicates that a comprehensive approach must be taken, embracing demand, marketing, production, distribution and maintenance as well as performance. The three main approaches which have been followed to date are outlined below.

Informal sector/scrap

The carts most commonly found in many parts of eastern and southern Africa comprise a scrap wheel–axle assembly, with a rough wooden or scrap steel cart body made by local farmers or artisans.

Advantages: These carts are evidently popular with farmers. The use of scrap pneumatic tyres and roller bearings makes the carts easy to pull on rough surfaces, despite cart bodies which are typically quite heavy. The cost is often 30–50% of commercially produced carts, depending on the cost of the scrap axle. These carts can be made using local skills and materials, provided scrap axles can be found.

Disadvantages: The limited supply of scrap axles often constrains the number of carts which can be made by the informal sector. This is particularly marked in countries where scarcity of foreign exchange has restricted car and truck imports over many years. Another drawback of this approach is the poor availability and lack of standardisation of spare parts.

Aid sector/local materials

Many aid organisations, and some inventive artisans, have focused on minimising the imported materials and skills required to make their cart designs. Over the 1970s and 1980s, Camartec in Tanzania, Kasisi and Katapola in Zambia and many other "supported" organisations have experimented with different designs. These carts tend to use wooden or simple steel wheels, with bush bearings made from wood or other materials

Advantages: These carts can be made mainly from local materials, with low requirements for steel and

other imports. The cost of production is generally low (40–50% of commercial cart cost), but there are exceptions to this rule. The carts tend to be fairly robust and are not susceptible to punctures.

Disadvantages: Farmers have not taken up these carts in any great numbers, particularly those with wooden wheels. This may be due to the poorer performance and lower load capacity of these carts and to their old fashioned image. While most materials are locally available, good carpentry skills are required to make bearings and wheels of adequate quality. Bearings also require regular greasing and maintenance.

Commercial/central

In some West African countries, and to a lesser extent Malawi and Zimbabwe, there has been large-scale production of carts by centralised producers in the private or public sectors. These carts generally have roller or ball bearings and pneumatic tyres. They may be produced fully assembled, with sheet steel or wooden bodies, or in kit form to be assembled by rural workshops. Local assembly reduces the cost of transporting the cart from the factory.

Advantages: Many farmers prefer roller bearings and pneumatic tyres. Cart quality is usually higher than that of locally produced carts but this is not always the case.

Disadvantages: These carts tend to be more expensive than other types of cart, particularly when distribution costs are included. Centralised manufacturers in eastern and southern Africa rarely have well developed supply and distribution networks, so it is often difficult for rural farmers to purchase a cart and to obtain spares.

Comparison of approaches

The introduction of carts appears to have been fastest in those countries which have focused on centralised production of good quality carts. Since the 1950s the number of carts in Senegal has reached over 100 000, due largely to the success of the lightweight cart manufactured by the Sismar (Siscoma) factory. This cart has roller bearings and pneumatic tyres. This represents almost one cart for every two plows or cultivators. Similar penetration can be seen in Zimbabwe and in Mali (over 100 000 carts), Burkina Faso (about 40 000 carts) and Malawi (around 20 000 carts) (Starkey, 1989a).

The introduction of carts has been much slower in Tanzania and Zambia, where aid-supported "local material" carts with rigid wheels and bush bearings have had more prominence. The ratio of carts to

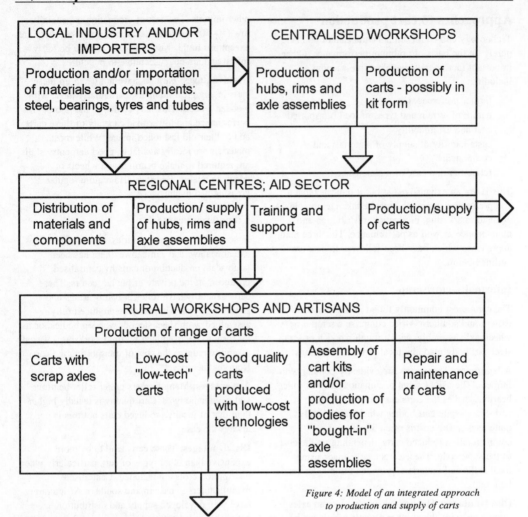

Figure 4: Model of an integrated approach
to production and supply of carts

plows/cultivators in Zambia is estimated to be roughly one to 10 (Starkey, Dibbits and Mwenya, 1991). There is little evidence of farmer acceptance of wooden-wheeled carts, and it is evident that most carts use scrap pneumatic-tyred wheels.

This difference in cart introduction rates cannot be explained purely in terms of technology choice, but must be understood within the general economic and policy conditions prevailing in these countries. The overall profitability of agriculture, the status of infrastructure and distribution systems, the existence of rural repair workshops, and the level of extension support are only some of the factors affecting the demand and supply of carts. The centralised production of good quality carts is unlikely to be successful on a large scale unless supply and distribution systems are effective in reaching rural areas. The ready availability of credit schemes has been a particularly important factor in the success of

centralised cart production in West Africa, since credit support has helped to create a large-scale effective demand for carts.

Suggested way forward

The way forward for cart production in eastern and southern Africa appears to be a combination of the above approaches. The aim is essentially to create better links between centralised manufacturers, aid workshops and informal sector artisans. There should almost certainly be more than one type of cart design in production, but each sector should focus on producing the components or playing the role for which it is best equipped (see Figure 4). Suggested roles are discussed below.

Role of large-scale commercial sector

There is an evident demand for an increased supply of pneumatic-tyred wheels with roller bearings. In the short term, this could be met by importing second-hand axles and wheels, but a longer-term solution could be to establish centralised local production of wheel axle assemblies or hub units incorporating imported bearings (following the example of SKF Zambia). It is not yet clear how successful or economic SKF's initiative will be compared to imported hubs.

Centralised production of complete carts would be able to meet a larger proportion of the market if commercial producers improve their distribution and spare part networks. Distribution costs could be further reduced by producing the cart in kit form for assembly by local workshops.

Role of aid sector

The aid sector could play an important role in strengthening provincial depots or workshops to act as centres for the distribution of materials and components (including wheel–axle–hub units) to smaller rural workshops. These provincial centres could also provide training and support to blacksmiths and artisans. There is also likely to be a role for these workshops in producing components and/or carts based on lower technology roller bearing hubs, axles and split rim wheels. However, research, monitoring and sharing of results is still needed to assess farmer acceptance of these products.

Some continued development and testing of cart designs is still required, such as experimentation with puncture-proof cushioning for rigid wheels. However, it is vital that researchers in the aid or government sectors seek and listen to feedback on their designs (eg, farmers' unenthusiastic response to solid wooden wheels in Tanzania and Zambia). Attempts to maximise the use of local materials, or minimise the cost of carts, should not be followed dogmatically if the resulting designs are not acceptable to farmers. A flexible approach to cart design is likely to be more successful, combining some centrally produced or imported components with local resources where appropriate.

Credit and extension support for cart users and producers is another important role for development projects and the government sector. This is discussed in more detail below.

Role of informal sector

Small workshops in the informal sector are well suited to production of carts from scrap wheel–axle assemblies, and to the assembly of carts from kits purchased from large-scale manufacturers or aid workshops. Neither of these activities requires sophisticated tools or skills, except possibly welding.

As an alternative to purchasing cart kits or components, small workshops can manufacture some types of carts themselves. Rigid wheel and some split-rim wheel with pneumatic tyre technologies require only basic skills and low cost tools. Bush bearings can be made by small workshops which have good carpentry skills, but roller bearing hubs generally require investment in a lathe. Such components could still be purchased by small workshops from commercial or provincial workshop centres.

The role of small rural workshops in the production or assembly of animal carts, supported by training and spares distribution services from provincial workshop centres, should create a network of workshops capable of undertaking local repairs on the carts. These workshops are often in a better position than central producers to recognise and respond to the needs of the local community.

Integrated approach to cart production

Some aid organisations which are attempting to create better links between centralised manufacturers, and workshops and informal sector artisans, focusing on improving the supply of pneumatic wheel and roller bearing components and spares to small rural workshops, include:

○ Animal Power Utilisation project in Malawi (Ashburner, 1989)

○ North West Integrated Rural Development Project in Zambia (Soko, 1990; Starkey, Dibbits and Mwenya, 1991)

○ Mbeya Oxenization Project in Tanzania (Shetto and Kwiligwa, 1988, Starkey, 1989b)

○ Driefontein/Institute of Agricultural Engineering/Intermediate Technology Development Group training programme in Zimbabwe.

It is hoped that the approach advocated here will lead to the following outcomes:

○ a general improvement in the construction and availability of carts and supply of these to rural communities at the lowest possible cost

○ an integrated approach to production incorporating manufacture of carts and cart components

○ an improved supply of materials and components to artisans and small workshops to develop local construction and assembly of carts

○ development of an effective infrastructure for the supply, maintenance and repair of carts.

Socioeconomic aspects of cart dissemination

So far this paper has examined the potential role of animal-based transport in farming systems, the technical options for animal-based transport, and detailed issues relating to the design and production of animal cart. This final section will look in some detail at the economic and social impact of animal-drawn carts on farming households, and the implications for wider dissemination of animal-based transport.

Purchase cost

Animal carts vary widely in price according to type and to the general economic situation in each country. Comparisons of costs of carts between countries are difficult due to varying exchange rates (official and shadow). High quality commercial carts tend to be fairly expensive: the Animal Power Utilisation Project in Malawi supports the purchase of two-wheeled carts from Petroleum Services for around 3000 Malawi Kwacha, which is equivalent to over US$ 1000 per cart (Barwell, 1991). In most countries carts produced from scrap by artisans cost substantially less than commercial carts: in Zambia carts based on scrap axles can be bought for 15–20 000 Zambian Kwacha (ZK), while a commercially produced cart costs at least ZK 45 000 (representing a range of approximately US$ 150–450).

Carts produced by development organisations vary according to design and possible subsidy. In Tanzania, carts produced by Camartec sold for 50–60 000 Tanzanian Shillings (TSh), which is approximately equivalent to US$ 200–260 while TSh 30 000 (US$ 130) was the price for some aid-project carts (Brewis, 1992). There are examples of development projects having higher production costs than centralised workshops, due to costly designs and lack of economies of scale. These cost differences tend to be masked by price subsidies and, to a lesser extent, by easier and cheaper distribution of carts compared to central producers.

Throughout eastern and southern Africa, the cost of wheels, tyres and axles is a major element of the cost of a cart. Scrap wheel and axle assemblies have become increasingly difficult to find and have risen steeply in price in many countries. In 1989, a report for the North West Integrated Rural Development Project in Zambia found that more than 55% of the cost of its ox carts was attributable to the wheel–axle components (Soko, 1990); in the case of artisan-produced carts this percentage may well be higher.

Constraints to demand for carts

At these prices, ownership of a cart is still beyond the reach of many rural households. In areas where agricultural potential is poor, where crop prices are low, or landholdings are small, cart ownership may not be achievable for any but the wealthiest farmers (Becker, 1984; Malmberg-Calvo, 1992). Credit support will improve the affordability of carts to poorer farmers, but there are still likely to be some situations in which a poor farmer cannot afford to service a cart loan. Cheaper means of transport such as pack animals, sledges and bicycles may be more appropriate for ownership by such households. However, poorer households may be able to hire a cart from wealthier neighbours to meet their peak transport demands.

In areas of higher agricultural potential, where landholdings reach 4 ha or more, cart ownership can be both profitable and attractive despite the high cost (Dawson and Smith, 1990). There appears to be an unsatisfied demand for animal carts in many areas but it is unclear whether this demand remains unsatisfied because of supply constraints, lack of access to credit or a combination of these factors. Supply constraints, particularly shortages of wheels and axles, are often cited as the main factors which limit wider dissemination of carts (Harder, 1989; Dawson and Smith, 1990), but perceived demand for carts may be "latent demand" which will be translated into effective demand only if credit facilities are made available to overcome cashflow problems.

Profitability analysis

Several attempts have been made to assess the profitability of cart ownership, with widely differing results. There are examples from Kenya and Tanzania of carts paying for themselves within one or two cropping seasons, through hire income or savings on motorised transport costs (Scheinman, 1986; Smith and Dawson, 1989). Similar findings have been reported in the Mansa area of Zambia (Starkey, Dibbits and Mwenya, 1991) and in West Africa (Harder, 1989). However, other analyses have found that investment in an ox cart appears less profitable than other elements of an ox traction package (Löffler, 1989).

These inconsistencies partly reflect differences between the overall profitability of agriculture in the areas under study: the returns to cart ownership are likely to be higher in productive agricultural areas with good infrastructure. Differences are also partly due to lack of consistency in the treatment of costs: some analyses allocate animal as well as equipment costs to transport, while others assume no incremental cash cost if animals are used for transport as well as tillage. Where animal costs are attributed to transport, some analyses of cart costs do not allow for appreciation in the meat value of oxen over their working life. Most analyses omit benefits of cart use which do not directly generate cash, and some omit all uses with the exception of crop marketing. Assumptions on hire income also differ widely in their optimism or pessimism. Drawing together these different approaches, a thorough analysis of the economics of animal-drawn carts should consider the following:

Costs:

∘ cash cost of cart purchase or annual depreciation

∘ annual cart maintenance costs

∘ a proportion of the cost of animal purchase (with allowance as appropriate for risk of animal loss, and for appreciation in resale value)

∘ a proportion of animal maintenance costs (generally low in cash terms, except if additional feeding costs are significant).

Benefits:

∘ savings on hire payments for transport of own goods

∘ generation of income by hiring cart to other households

∘ value of time saved through more efficient transport (if reinvested in agriculture, domestic or income generating activities)

∘ possible reduced losses from crop deterioration, pest damage or theft through timely transport of harvested crops

∘ possible increases in producer prices by direct sales to market

∘ possible profits from trading activities using cart.

In most cases it is found that the profitability of animal cart purchase is highly dependent on the market price for cart hire.

Hire markets

In many parts of eastern and southern Africa there is an active hire market for animal carts. Households who cannot afford or do not own a cart can often hire or borrow a cart from neighbours from time to time. The timing of use may not be ideal, as the cart owner usually has first priority during the peak harvest season, but hire arrangements do allow more households to share the benefits of cart use.

Hire arrangements are most commonly observed for trips which involve some element of cash generation, particularly those related to marketed

crops. The data given in Table 3 were collected in a village in northern Zambia where only two households in 42 surveyed owned ox carts (Airey and Barwell, 1991):

Hire charges may vary according to season, distance travelled and trip purpose. Payment may be in the form of mutual obligation or cash, depending on the social relationship between the cart owner and borrower. In Zambia charges of 100 Kwacha (ZK) per 100 kg bag have been quoted for the transport of maize during the peak harvest season (equivalent to about US$ 1 per bag or US$ 8–9 per cartload). Further reports from Zambia (Starkey, Dibbits and Mwenya, 1991) suggest that farmers are paying 10–15% of the value of their maize crop to hire an ox cart for a few kilometres. Much lower hire charges of ZK 20 (US$ 0.20) per load have been quoted for off-season tasks such as firewood collection.

Supply and oversupply

The importance of hire markets for cart profitability has led to some concern over "saturation" of the market for carts. One argument for saturation is that the rental market will tend to become less profitable as cart ownership levels rise, since hire charges may fall due to oversupply. Conversely, demand for cart services is likely to increase as hire becomes cheaper. The implications for cart profitability depend on the elasticity of demand to price, and it is difficult to predict where the equilibrium level for cart ownership would be in any given case.

An analysis by Löffler (1989) suggested that there was already an oversupply of carts in the North West Integrated Rural Development Project area in Zambia. This analysis was based on calculations of the size of cart fleet required to market all the maize surplus during the peak agricultural season. Löffler (1989) identified some crucial assumptions which underlie this analysis: that all farmers have equal access to carts in the "fleet"; that all owners are motivated to hire out their carts to the specified extent; and that other cart uses such as crop

Table 3: Uses of ox carts in a village in northern Zambia

Purpose of trip	Percentage of households using cart
Carry harvested crops from field	41
Collection of fertiliser	18
Collection of seeds from depot	6
Firewood collection	2
Water collection (source nearby)	0

harvesting do not conflict with crop marketing during the peak season.

Even if these assumptions were found to be justified, the methodology used in this type of analysis does not allow for the possibility that some cart purchases may be motivated by broader benefits such as the value of time and effort saved through more efficient transport. Further, cart purchase may still be profitable for new entrants even though the cart fleet is theoretically just large enough to transport all the marketed maize. The perceived utility of carts is demonstrated by high levels of ownership in parts of West Africa and of southern Africa: in Senegal it is not uncommon to find ratios of one cart to every two households (Starkey, Dibbits and Mwenya, 1991), and similar levels are observed in some parts of Zimbabwe (Dawson and Smith, 1990). The market for carts will ultimately depend on a number of factors including the cost of carts and draft animals relative to their perceived utility, the levels of disposable income and the availability of credit support.

Credit

As discussed above, animal carts are relatively expensive purchases which poorer farmers may not be able to afford. If the problem is one of limited cashflow, rather than intrinsically poor profitability, then credit assistance may be effective in encouraging dissemination. Evidence from Malawi, Zimbabwe and West Africa suggests that the widespread dissemination of carts is closely linked with the success of government credit schemes for carts (Dawson and Smith, 1990). Supply constraints may also respond to credit initiatives, since producers will be reluctant to develop cart production on a large scale unless they are confident of effective demand, which is often dependent on credit support.

There is evidence that investment in transport equipment may, in some areas, be more profitable than investment in animal traction for agriculture: Starkey (1989a) observed a Malawi farmer who found it profitable to hire his cart and oxen out for transport, while he paid hired labourers to work his own fields. Such evidence of profitability again suggests that carts should be given a high priority for credit assistance.

Some animal traction projects, such as Mbeya, have been reluctant to stimulate demand for carts by offering credit while cart supply cannot satisfy existing demand (Harder, 1989). Others, such as the North West Integrated Rural Development Project in Zambia, initially have offered credit for a complete package including oxen, tillage implements and cart but have changed their credit policy due to supply shortages and high costs for carts. This project now attaches lower priority for cart loans, with loans not being given for an ox cart until a farmer has already invested in a pair of oxen and a plow (Löffler, 1989). Low prioritisation of credit for carts may be appropriate in the short term, in areas where supply constraints are particularly serious. In the longer term such strategies are likely to limit the potential economic benefits from wider cart ownership: the best solution to a supply shortage is surely to improve supply rather than restrain demand.

It should be remembered that the provision of credit does not in itself improve the profitability of investment in animal-based transport equipment. Even if credit is available, there are likely to be some farmers for whom investment in a cart would not be feasible. Some animal traction credit programmes use landholding requirements as a shortcut to assess feasibility: the government agricultural credit system in Malawi, for instance, only lends to farmers holding more than 2 ha (Barwell, 1991). Such rules can become too rigid, effectively excluding poorer farmers and many women from buying carts, even if they would be able to repay loans from hire income. Credit schemes need to take a more flexible approach to the profitability of transport investments, and to investigate mechanisms such as group ownership which could reach poorer farmers and women.

Impact on women

It cannot be automatically assumed that women will benefit from the introduction of animal-based transport. As noted above, households which do not own animals or a cart are less likely to pay hire charges for subsistence transport than for income related agricultural transport purposes. This means that carts are not commonly hired for the transport of wood and water, which often are a major burden on women's time and effort. Even in households which own animal carts, women's access to the carts and other "intermediate" means of transport is often limited (Gaidzanwa, 1991).

As noted above, the introduction of animal transport has in some cases resulted in men assuming responsibility for fuelwood collection or other tasks traditionally performed by women (Doran, 1990; Urasa, 1990). This shift of responsibility is generally in women's interest, but it remains the case that women tend not to have direct control over the means of transport. In some cases, men's assumption of responsibility for water supply and other services has meant that women lose control over income or become liable to service charges (Howe, 1989). Women's access to, and control over, animal carts is discussed by Doran (1994).

Given the high proportion of local level transport which is undertaken by women, and the constraints which this imposes on women's time during peak agricultural seasons, ways must be found to reach women more effectively. There are a number of possible ways of improving women's access to, and control over, animal-based transport. These include work with women's groups; credit assistance targeted at women; education campaigns to break down taboos against women using simple means of transport, as have been successfully implemented in Burkina Faso and Ghana; and wider use of donkeys, which are regarded as "women's animals" in some parts of southern Africa. In some cases it may be more effective to address women's domestic transport burden by other means, such as non-transport interventions to improve access to essential supplies of water and firewood (eg, water pumps, village woodlots).

Conclusions and future directions

Animals can provide an affordable means of reducing the significant burden faced by rural households in transporting agricultural and subsistence goods at village level. The efficiency of animal-based transport relative to human headloading can increase the productivity of agriculture and other income generating activities. Integration of animal-based transport with animal draft farming systems offers many synergies, particularly in harvesting, marketing and transport of farm inputs, although the use of animals for transport may increase their nutrition needs.

This paper has argued that animal-based transport can make a substantial contribution to rural development in eastern and southern Africa and justifies special consideration in animal draft projects. It has focused particularly on the technical and socioeconomic issues related to carts, pulled by oxen or donkeys. Nevertheless it has emphasised that ox-drawn sledges currently serve a vital function for poorer farmers and that donkeys could be much more widely used as pack animals than they are at present. In many situations the most efficient option for animal-based transport is the two-wheeled cart, offering good performance and high carrying capacity, but at a cost significantly higher than the alternative options.

Carts can offer significant benefits and income generating opportunities in many circumstances, and can act as important catalysts for rural development. Use of carts is adversely affected by supply constraints, high cart prices and cashflow problems. The approach advocated here is a two-part strategy of addressing both supply constraints and cashflow constraints, putting a high priority on credit schemes where cart ownership is intrinsically profitable. Dissemination strategies should be designed so that women and poorer farmers are not excluded.

Some important points have been made in relation to future research and project work:

○ policy-makers and project planners should be encouraged to appreciate the importance of local-level transport, and the role which animal-based transport can play

○ wider use of donkeys should be encouraged, for pack-carrying and donkey carts. Projects should share experiences on the introduction of donkeys into new areas

○ sledges should not be discouraged while carts remain unaffordable to many poor farmers, unless there is an overwhelming case against their use on the grounds of soil erosion

○ a flexible approach to cart design and production is needed which is responsive to the local preferences and financial resources of farmers. Localised manufacture or assembly should be encouraged but, where necessary, this should be integrated with centralised or regionalised manufacture of some components such as wheel–axle assemblies

○ to support this approach, a major effort is needed to improve the supply of materials and components to workshops involved in production of carts and cart components. This will need to include the importation of some components such as rolling contact bearings

○ credit schemes for carts should be given high priority, to translate "latent demand" into effective demand and help to justify large-scale production

○ efforts should be made to improve women's access to and control of animal transport, or to address their transport needs through accompanying interventions.

This paper has tried to show that there is no universal formula for the improvement of animal-based transport, in terms of cart design, credit policy or dissemination strategy. Instead, there are learning processes which communities, producers and projects go through in reaction to the changes in their particular circumstances and objectives. The learning process can be speeded up by communicating lessons learnt in other projects, and by developing careful methodologies for testing new ideas. A good example of shared learning has been the cart testing programme at Magoye in Zambia (Dogger, 1990), which has provided the region with a useful database on the performance of different designs of animal-drawn carts under controlled conditions. It has also demonstrated the importance of well-structured methodologies to involve farmers in the testing and evaluation process. Similar initiatives are needed to evaluate and share information on other aspects of policy and project design, including the assessment of demand, provision of credit and the involvement of women. Ongoing communication of lessons learnt through research, testing and project experience is the most effective way to improve both technical and socioeconomic aspects of animal-based transport in the region.

Acknowledgement

This paper was prepared by staff of IT Transport with funding provided by the Overseas Development Administration (ODA). Considerable assistance was provided by Paul Starkey in the preparation of this paper, in terms of his insights and experience and access to his resource library.

References

Airey A and Barwell I, 1991. *Interim analysis of first village-level survey in Zambia.* Rural Travel and Transport Project, Sub-Saharan Africa Transport Programme. Report 307. IT Transport, Ardington, Oxon, UK. 145p.

Ashburner J, 1989. *Study concerning equipment manufacture, supply and distribution for draught animal power utilisation in Malawi.* Food and Agriculture Organization of the United Nations (FAO), Lilongwe, Malawi. 159p.

Barwell I, 1991. *Pilot integrated rural transport project, Malawi.* Report 308. IT Transport, Ardington, Oxon, UK.

Barwell I and Hathway G, 1986. *The design and manufacture of animal-drawn carts.* Technical memorandum prepared for the International Labour Office (ILO) and UN Centre for Human Settlements (HABITAT). IT Publications, London, UK. 72p.

Barwell I and Malmberg-Calvo C, 1988. *Makete Integrated Rural Transport Project. The transport demands of rural households: findings from village-level travel survey.* Report 192. IT Transport, Ardington, Oxon, UK. 147p.

Becker H, 1984. *Principles of mechanisation: economic aspects of oxen-mechanisation in Liwonde Agricultural Development Division.* Field Development Services Volume 10. Liwonde Agricultural Development Division, Liwonde, Malawi. 35p.

Brewis A, 1992. *Wheels Tanzania: report of visit to the Arusha, Dodoma and Singida Regions in December 1991.* Report 315. IT Transport, Ardington, Oxon, UK. 27p.

Curtis V, 1986. *Women and the transport of water.* IT Publications, London, UK. 47p.

Dawson J and Barwell I, 1993. *Roads are not enough: new perspectives on rural transport planning in developing countries.* International Forum for Rural Transport and Development Occasional Paper. IT Transport, Ardington, Oxon, UK. 70p.

Dawson J and Smith A, 1990. *Low-cost wheel production and dissemination in Zimbabwe: results of survey of scotchcart ownership and hire characteristics and survey of rural workshops.* Report 263. IT Transport, Ardington, Oxon, UK. 30p.

Dennis R and Anderson M, 1994. Improving animal-based transport: technical aspects of cart design. In Starkey P, Mwenya E and Stares (eds), *Improving animal traction technology.* Proceedings of first workshop of Animal Traction Network for Eastern and Southern Africa (ATNESA) held 18–23 January 1992, Lusaka, Zambia. ATNESA in collaboration with Technical Centre for Agriculture and Rural Cooperation (CTA), Ede-Wageningen, The Netherlands.

Dogger J W, 1990. *Final report ox cart testing activities: August 1987–July 1990.* Animal Draught Power Research and Development Project, Magoye Regional Research Station, Magoye, Zambia, and Institute of Agricultural Engineering (IMAG-DLO), Wageningen, The Netherlands. 40p.

Doran J, 1990. *A moving issue for women: is low-cost transport an appropriate intervention to alleviate women's burden in southern Africa?* Gender Analysis in Development, Sub-Series 1. University of East Anglia, Norwich, UK. 83p.

Doran J, 1994. Transportation by women, and their access to animal-drawn carts in Zimbabwe. In Starkey P, Mwenya E and Stares (eds), *Improving animal traction technology.* Proceedings of first workshop of Animal Traction Network for Eastern and Southern Africa (ATNESA) held 18–23 January 1992, Lusaka, Zambia. ATNESA in collaboration with Technical Centre for Agriculture and Rural Cooperation (CTA), Ede-Wageningen, The Netherlands.

Dufaut A, 1988. Women carrying water: how it affects their health. *Waterlines* 6(3):23–25.

FAO, 1972. *Manual on the employment of draught animals in agriculture.* Food and Agriculture Organization of the United Nations (FAO), Rome, Italy. 249p.

Gaidzanwa R, 1991. *Low-cost rural transport in Zimbabwe.* United Nations Development Fund for Women (UNIFEM), Harare, Zimbabwe. 20p.

Goe M and Abiye Astatke, 1989. Development of draught animal power systems in Ethiopia. pp. 69–79 in: Hoffman D, Nari J and Petheram R (eds), *Draught animals in rural development.* International Research Symposium, Cippanas, Indonesia, 3–7 July 1989. Australian Centre for International Agricultural Research, Canberra, Australia.

Harder J, 1989. *Report of the Credit Consultant to the Mbeya Oxenisation Project, Mbeya, Tanzania.* Mennonite Economic Development Associates, Winnipeg, Manitoba, Canada. 56p.

Howe J, 1989. *Social and economic impact of carts and wheelbarrows on women.* Report for United Nations Development Fund for Women (UNIFEM). Report 204. IT Transport, Ardington, Oxon, UK. 54p.

Howe J and Zille P, 1988. *The transport demands of small-farm households in Africa: a synthesis of IT Transport research.* Report 169. IT Transport, Ardington, Oxon, UK. 36p.

Immers L H, 1988. *Possibilities for improvement of intermediate transport means in the Western Province of Zambia.* Delft University of Technology, Delft, The Netherlands. 52p.

Jones P, 1990. Overcoming ignorance about donkeys in Zimbabwe: a case study. pp. 311–318 in: Fielding D and Pearson R (eds), *Donkeys, mules and horses for tropical agricultural development.* Colloquium held 3–6 September 1990 at Edinburgh, Scotland. University of Edinburgh, Scotland, UK.

Jones P A, 1991. *Training course manual on the use of donkeys in agriculture in Zimbabwe.* Agritex Institute of Agricultural Engineering, Borrowdale, Harare, Zimbabwe. 81p.

Kaira C, 1983. *Transportation needs of the rural population in developing countries.* Institut für Regionalwissenschaft der Universität Karlsruhe, Germany.

Kebede A and Bekele D, 1990. Improvement of transport capacity of donkey carts. *Draught Animal News* 12:17–20. Centre for Tropical Veterinary Medicine, University of Edinburgh, Scotland, UK.

Kjaerby F, 1989. *Villagisation and the crisis: agricultural production in Hanang District, Northern Tanzania.* CDR Project Paper 89.2, Centre for Development Research (CDR), Copenhagen, Denmark. 78p.

Löffler C, 1989. *Work-oxen survey 1988/89: final report.* Integrated Rural Development Programme, NW Province of Zambia. GTZ, Eschborn, Germany.

Malmberg-Calvo C, 1992. *Intermediate means of transport: women and rural transport in eastern Uganda.* Working Paper 3: Rural Travel and Transport Project. World Bank Sub-Saharan Africa Transport Programme. Report 317. IT Transport, Ardington, Oxon, UK. 65p.

Müller H, 1986. *Ox-power in Zambian agriculture and rural transport: performance, potential and promotion.* Socio-Economic Studies on Rural Development, Volume. 65. Institut für Rurale Entwicklung, Gottingen, Germany.

O'Neill D, Hayton S and Sims B, 1989. Measurement of draft animal performance. pp. 264–271 in: Hoffman D, Nari J and Petheram R J (eds), *Draft animals in rural development.* International Research Symposium, Cipanos, Indonesia, 3–7 July 1989. Australian Centre for International Agricultural Research, Canberra, Australia.

Scheinman D, 1986. *Animal draft use in Tanga Region: a descriptive and analytical study assessing the implications of past, present and future Kilimo and TIRDEP involvement.* Tanga Integrated Rural Development Programme (TIRDEP), Tanga, Tanzania. 237p.

Shetto R and Kwiligwa E, 1988. *Survey of ox cart production and use in Mbeya Region.* Mbeya Oxenization Project, Mbeya, Tanzania. 69p.

Smith A and Dawson J, 1989. *ITDG animal cart project, ActionAid Kenya.* Report of field visit to Kenya, July 1989. Report 263. IT Transport, Ardington, Oxon, UK. 31p.

Soko D L, 1990. The impact of the oxenization programme in the North-Western Province of Zambia. pp. 452–454 in:

Starkey P and Faye A (eds), *Animal traction for agricultural development.* Proceedings of the Third Workshop of the West Africa Animal Traction Network held 7–12 July 1988, Saly, Senegal. Technical Centre for Agricultural and Rural Cooperation (CTA), Ede-Wageningen, The Netherlands.

Srivastava N, 1989. Research on draught animal power in India. pp. 53–60 in: Hoffman D, Nari J and Petheram R (eds), *Draught animals in rural development.* International Research Symposium, Cippanas, Indonesia, 3–7 July 1989. Australian Centre for International Agricultural Research, Canberra, Australia.

Starkey P, 1989a. Animal-drawn transport in Africa. *GATE: questions, answers, information 1/89:13–18.* GTZ, Eschborn, Germany.

Starkey P, 1989b. *Mbeya Oxenization Project 1989 Evaluation: observations on the research, development and extension components of the Mbeya Oxenization Project, Tanzania.* Mennonite Economic Development Associates, Winnipeg, Manitoba, Canada. 15p.

Starkey P, Dibbits H and Mwenya E, 1991. *Animal traction in Zambia: status, progress and trends 1991.* Institute of Agricultural Engineering, Wageningen, The Netherlands, and Ministry of Agriculture, Lusaka, Zambia. 103p.

Urasa I, 1990. *Women and rural transport: an assessment of their role in sub-Saharan Africa.* Rural Travel and Transport Project, Sub-Saharan Africa Transport Programme. Infrastructure and Rural Works Branch. International Labour Office (ILO), Geneva, Switzerland. 61p.

Improving animal-based transport: technical aspects of cart design

by

Ron Dennis and Mary Anderson

IT Transport Ltd, The Old Power Station, Ardington, Near Wantage, Oxon OX12 8QJ, UK

Abstract

Transport of goods in rural areas in Africa is carried out mainly on foot, imposing a major burden on rural households in terms of both time and effort. Animal-drawn carts can considerably reduce this burden and so improve the productivity of small farmers, but their use is still quite limited. Poor availability and/or high cost of materials and components both constrain production and cause wide variations in the design and quality of construction of carts. One means of improving the quality of carts is to increase awareness of good design practice and of design features that have proved successful in practice. This paper reviews the various issues of cart design and compares some of the available options. It attempts to establish a sound technical base for cart design. The paper concentrates on design of two-wheel carts for oxen and donkeys.

Introduction

Surveys indicate that up to 90% of travel in rural areas involves transportation of goods and that a large portion of this is done by head, back or shoulder carrying. Transport therefore imposes a considerable burden on rural people in both time and effort and limits the efficiency and output of small farmers. For the foreseeable future it seems that the main option for reducing the transport burden will be to increase the use of non-motorised means of transport such as bicycles, handcarts and animal-based transport.

Animal-drawn carts have about 40 times the load carrying capacity of human porterage (see Table 1) and can make an important contribution to improving rural transport. Their use varies greatly from country to country and also regionally within

countries. The main reasons limiting wider use of carts are their high cost compared to rural incomes and lack of credit facilities to support their purchase. Technical and cultural factors also impose limitations. The main technical constraint is usually the lack of access to suitable materials or components needed to produce reasonable quality carts, but poor design and/or construction methods may also limit the supply of carts which are acceptable to rural households.

A cart is basically a simple vehicle and in an ideal situation the construction would comprise a welded steel frame, pneumatic-tyred wheels running on roller bearings and a sheet steel or wooden body. However, there will often be constraints on the use of the most suitable materials or components of construction due to high cost and/or lack of availability. Compromise solutions therefore have to be adopted and a fairly wide range of cart designs exists to suit the available and affordable resources in different locations.

The quality and performance of carts varies widely and there is considerable scope for improving the overall standard of design and construction. A first step is to increase the level of awareness of good design practice and of design features which have been proven successful by experience. With this in mind this paper reviews the various aspects of cart design and compares the different design options which are available. It attempts to establish a sound technical base for cart design. Particular attention is given to wheels and axles which have the greatest

Table 1: Comparison of typical loads and speeds of some transport systems

Means of transport	Load capacity (kg)	Typical speed (km/hour)	Load carrying capacity (tonne–km/hour)
Human (headloading)	25	4	0.1
Donkey (pack load)	50	5	0.25
Ox cart	1 000	4	4
Two wheel tractor	1 000	10	10
Tractor/trailer	3 000	20	60
Truck	10 000	50	500

"Improving animal traction technology"

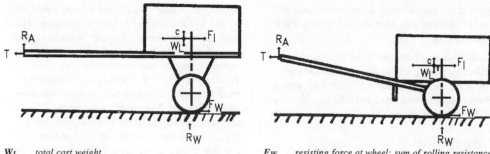

W_L total cart weight
F_I inertia force
T tractive force
R_A vertical reaction from animal
R_W vertical reaction from wheel

F_W resisting force at wheel: sum of rolling resistance and bearing friction
c centre of gravity. This should be close to the wheel axis to limit downward forces on the animal and as low as possible for stability

Figure 1: Basic configurations of animal-drawn carts

effect on cart quality and performance and are also the major problem for small-scale cart producers. The information presented is based on professional experience and tests on wheels and bearings carried out by IT Transport. The paper concentrates on two-wheel carts pulled by oxen and donkeys, as most carts in rural Africa are of this type. The paper briefly reviews all aspects of cart design, but it does not tackle the closely related topic of harnessing.

Basic design factors

Cart capacity

Capacity must be matched against the draft effort available from the animals. It is generally recognised (eg, Goe and McDowell, 1980) that the average draft effort of a pair of oxen is about 9–11% of their combined body weight, ie, a total effort of 90–170 kgf. Allowing an overall resistance factor of 0.1 for wheel resistance, bearing friction and gradient, and an average draft of 130 kgf (1300 N), the limit on total cart weight is about 1300 kg, giving a load capacity of around 1000 kg: most carts are designed for an 800–1000 kg capacity.

The average draft capacity of a donkey is about 15% of its body weight giving a draft effort of 30–50 kgf (300–500 N). On the same assumptions as above, the average total weight of a donkey cart should be about 400 kg for a single donkey or about 700 kg for a pair of donkeys. This should give a cart capacity of 250–300 kg for a single donkey and 500–550 kg for a pair of donkeys.

The load capacities given in Table 1 are for well designed carts operating on reasonably firm surfaces with medium gradients. Animals can exert much higher draft forces for short periods of time, but if carts have to operate continuously on soft or sandy

surfaces or on hilly terrain then load capacities will need to be reduced

Overall layout of cart

Carts consist basically of a wheel–axle assembly, a chassis or frame, a load platform or body and a drawpole. The major feature governing layout is the orientation of the drawpole and the resulting height of the cart body. The two basic configurations are illustrated in Figure 1.

A tilted drawpole allows the body of a cart to be lowered by about 40 cm. The resulting lower centre of gravity of the loaded cart is an important benefit to stability, particularly when operating on slopes, and makes the cart easier to load. The rear end of the drawpole may conveniently be attached via a bracket to the axle of the cart.

The other important aspect of layout is the balance of the cart, which affects the vertical load which has to be supported by the animal(s). The load an animal can pull is several times greater than the load it can carry. If the proportion of a cart load that has to supported ("carried") by the animals is increased, less energy and effort will be available for the more efficient work of pulling the cart. The trend of higher supporting loads reducing overall transport efficiency seems to have been confirmed (see O'Neill, Hayton and Sims, 1989) although it does not yet appear to have been quantified.

An upper limit of vertical load of 20 kg has been suggested (FAO, 1972). This requires that the centre of gravity should be about 7 cm in front of the axle for a typical laden cart in which the distance from axle to hitch point is 300–350 cm. Although farmers are unlikely to have the time or inclination to worry about such precision when loading their carts they should check that the vertical load on the animal(s) is not excessive if they want the animal(s) to work to full capacity.

In India an attempt was made to overcome the problem by placing a third wheel (castor) at the front of the cart to eliminate the load on the animal. However, this increases cost and reduces stability of the cart and it has not caught on.

Choice of wheels

The efficiency and reliability of a cart depend largely on the design and performance of the wheel–axle assembly. The acquisition or construction of this assembly also constitutes the main problem for workshops involved in cart production, and is often a major bottleneck for smaller workshops. The cost of the wheel–axle assembly is likely to constitute between 40 and 70% of the production cost of the cart.. In the following sections, aspects of wheels, tyres, hubs, bearings and axles are discussed, but ideally these components should be considered as part of an integral assembly.

Types of tyres

Pneumatic tyres provide important benefits over rigid tyres in terms of cushioning impacts to give a smoother ride and having a lower rolling resistance for a similar sized wheel. However, they are prone to puncturing which can be a major disadvantage in some situations.

Figure 2: Comparison of rolling resistance on different road types of pneumatic and two sizes of rigid tyres (illustrative information from various sources presented as draft force (in Newtons) needed to overcome rolling resistance for wheel load of 1000 kgf or 10 000 N)

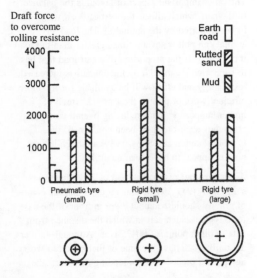

Rigid tyres include rims of steel wheels, steel tyres around wooden wheels and solid-rubber tyres. Their main advantages are that they can be made by small workshops and artisans using locally available materials, they are cheaper to make, and maintenance costs and problems are less than for pneumatic tyres. However, high impact loads from rigid tyres cause discomfort for the towing animal(s), may cause damage to the goods being carried, and generally accelerate wear and tear of cart components so that carts need to be more robust and therefore heavier. A further disadvantage is the damage they may cause to roads.

Figure 2 shows a comparison of the rolling resistance of pneumatic and rigid tyres on a number of surfaces. It is seen that to have the same rolling resistance, rigid tyres should be roughly twice the diameter of pneumatic tyres. Large wheels of this diameter, 1.2–1.5 m, are seldom found in African countries but are standard on carts in Asian countries such as India and Bangladesh. Rigid-tyre wheels on African carts are generally 0.7–0.9 m in diameter, which makes the carts more difficult to pull and reduces load capacity.

Although farmers generally recognise the benefits of pneumatic tyres they may sometimes choose rigid-tyre wheels because of reduced maintenance, especially the absence of punctures, or because of their lower cost and local availability.

The supply and cost of pneumatic tyres may sometimes be problems for cart manufacturers, particularly for smaller workshops. The latter often use scrap tyres which are usually badly worn and therefore very susceptible to puncturing. The specifications for tyres for carts are less demanding than for higher speed vehicles and it is possible that cheaper, lower grade tyres could be produced specifically for carts. Starkey (1989) reports the use of reject tyres in West Africa but there appear to have been few other innovations on this topic. This may be worth further investigation.

Wheels for pneumatic tyres

Car and truck wheels have rolled rims and pressed centres. Their high strength-to-weight ratio is achieved by forming sheet steel into relatively complex profiles which have high structural strength. The expensive equipment needed for this is only economical for high volume production and is generally not suited to non-industrialised countries.

Simpler forms of wheels for pneumatic tyres can be produced locally on less costly equipment, but these need to use thicker material to retain strength and therefore tend to be heavier. For example:

○ Camartec in Tanzania has developed a wheel comprising two halves hot-pressed from 3 mm steel sheet which are bolted together with a rolled rim welded in between. This manufacturing method is suited to centralised production of wheels in larger, well equipped workshops. Camartec also produces fabricated split-rim wheels, with rims formed on a rolling machine

○ IT Transport has developed a low-cost technology for producing split-rim wheels in which a hand-operated bending machine is used to produce good quality rims (Dennis, 1990). This manufacturing method is suited to small to medium workshops and for production levels of up to 500 wheels a year.

Split-rim wheels are made in two parts which bolt together from either side of the tyre. They therefore have substantial benefits for use on carts as tyres can be easily fitted and removed using only a spanner: the inner part of the wheel can in fact be left mounted on the axle.

Rigid-tyre wheels

Two common types of wooden wheels are produced:

○ wooden disc wheels are formed by cutting a disc from a sandwich structure of wooden planks. They are the simplest form of wheel to construct but are heavy and inefficient. However, they are suitable for very basic carts because they can be made by local artisans or farmers from readily available materials using hand tools

○ wooden spoked wheels are considerably more complex to make and require good carpentry skills. Spoked wheels were commonly used on carts in many countries in the past and are still widely used in some Asian countries. However, high-grade wood and good wheelwright skills are needed to produce good quality wheels. These are not generally available in African countries and the spoked wheels produced tend to be fairly crude and smaller in diameter than traditional cart wheels so that they do not perform well and have poor appeal for cart buyers.

Wooden wheels should have steel or rubber strip tyres fitted to protect the rims and the wood needs to be adequately protected against adverse environmental conditions. Even so, these wheels are susceptible to distortion and cracking of the wood and from deterioration and loosening of joints under repeated impact loads. However, it seems likely that wood will continue to be used for very low cost disc

wheels and in locations where steel is not readily available.

Steel wheels comprise rims formed from flat steel bar, 8–12 mm thick and 70–100 mm wide, joined to a hub by welded-in steel spokes. Rims may be formed by rolling (equipment is not widely available), by bending around a former or by blacksmithing techniques: the latter method requires considerable time and effort and may result in poorer quality rims. A common problem of these wheels is fatigue fracture at the welded joints: for instance, Shetto and Kwiligwa (1988) reported that 50% of the steel wheels in their survey had suffered fatigue failures. The problem could be overcome by a better understanding of the structural design of the wheel: the flat bar rims in particular are heavy and structurally inefficient. Another problem is that when operating on sandy surfaces, the rims tend to pick up sand and deposit it on the hubs, greatly accelerating wear on the bearings.

Steel wheels tend to have more appeal to cart buyers than wooden wheels and are quite widely used, particularly in regions where puncturing of pneumatic tyres is a serious problem. They could be improved by better structural design to reduce weight and failures and by a wider use of simple equipment to produce good quality rims.

Puncture-proof tyres

Because pneumatic tyres offer considerable benefits to cart performance, but punctures are a major source of concern to cart owners and buyers, there could be potential for some form of puncture-proof tyre which offers some degree of cushioning but with a much reduced risk of puncturing. The following are some possibilities which might be considered.

○ agricultural tyres with increased tread thickness are much less prone to punctures but are not foolproof. This type of tyre should be considered in any move towards producing special tyres for cart wheels

○ the standard method for puncture proofing "off road" vehicle tyres is to fill them with urethane foam. This is 100% effective but is costly and would rely on imported materials so that it is unlikely to be appropriate for cart wheels

○ some attempts have been made to fill tyres with sawdust but it is difficult to compact it adequately and ingress of water turns it into a heavy, soggy pulp

○ the increased concentration of carts in certain regions may act as an incentive to establish puncture repair workshops. This could be a partial solution but punctures will still result in considerable "down time" of carts, particularly for farmers working in more remote areas

° various experiments are being carried out on the use of non-inflated rubber tyres which are stiffened by mechanical means. The Technology Development and Advisory Unit (TDAU) of the University of Zambia has patented the "flexiwheel", which uses sections of scrap tyres mechanically supported or bolted in place around a wooden disc. Early results are encouraging, but the wheels are very heavy—75 kg for one wheel (Vroom, 1994).

Puncture proofing is an area where further development and testing are required.

Bearings

The basic principles and arrangements for supporting axles are illustrated in Figure 3. The bearings have to support both vertical and side loads from the wheel. Side loads from cornering will be quite small on carts but those from impacts against potholes, ridges, rocks, etc, may be up to 15% of vertical loads (Dennis, 1990). They exert a leverage effect on the wheel which increases with wheel size and to combat this the effective length of the bearing should be as large as possible. This has an added advantage in reducing the freedom of the wheel to "wobble". In bush bearings, side loads tend to concentrate wear at the ends of the bearings leading to increased wheel wobble which aggravates the problem, the combined effect leading to accelerated wear of the bush.

Rolling contact (ball and roller) bearings

Rolling contact bearings provide smooth precision running with negligible friction and wear, high reliability and low maintenance, provided they are properly mounted, lubricated and protected against ingress of sand and dirt. However, they must be imported, and are therefore relatively costly and not always readily available. Also, if imported bearings are fitted to locally-made hubs and axle, these must be accurately machined, necessitating access to a lathe.

The bearings most commonly used on carts come from scrap hub assemblies from motor vehicles. These may give problems if they are approaching the end of their operating life and finding replacement bearings of the same type may be very difficult. Some better equipped workshops also produce machined hubs incorporating imported bearings. This seems to be a viable approach which should be developed as it could allow standardisation on a few sizes of bearings, hopefully leading to reduced costs and improved availability.

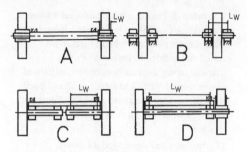

Lw effective bearing length (length resisting side load and wheel wobble)

A   wheels rotating on stub axles attached to an axle beam. This is the simplest and most common arrangement

B   two live axles rotating in bearing blocks located either side of the wheels. This requires a more extensive cart frame and is seldom used

C   two live axles rotating in bearing blocks attached to an axle beam. This has significant advantages in minimising the effects of wear (the bearing wear and resulting wheel wobble may be only about 10% of that for the bush arrangement A). However, the bearings are more difficult to align and bearing friction may be greater

D   a single live axle with one wheel fixed to the axle and the other free to rotate. The latter wheel only rotates on the axle when the cart is not moving in a straight line so wear in the bushes should be substantially reduced. This arrangement has some advantages over C: although it has been suggested for use on carts it is not known if it has actually been tested

Figure 3: Basic arrangements of wheel–axle assemblies

Taper-roller and deep-groove ball bearings are the most appropriate types because of their ability to support both radial and axial loads.

Taper-roller bearings have the higher load capacity and are commonly used in hubs of motor vehicle wheels. However, they are fitted in two parts which must be carefully adjusted to give the correct tightness of the bearing. A good degree of skill and care is therefore needed in assembling the hubs.

Deep-groove ball bearings are single piece bearings which require axial location in the hub but not adjustment. They are cheaper than taper-roller bearings and can be obtained sealed and pre-greased for life, which is a useful advantage. Because of the point contacts of the balls the bearings are more susceptible to damage from impact loads, but providing they are adequately sized and spaced apart in the hub they should perform quite satisfactorily.

Locally made rolling contact bearings may offer a satisfactory, intermediate alternative which is cheaper and more readily available than imported

Table 2: Typical values of bearing pressure (P) and "PV" factors for various materials

	P (kg/cm^2)	PV $(x10^4 \, kg/m/s)$
Bronze	350	14.5
Cast iron	500	11.0
Hardwood	140	3.6
Unfilled nylon	70	1.1

bearings. Roller bearings with unhardened rollers and races have been used on carts in India and are at present being investigated at the Development Technology Unit, University of Warwick, UK (Oram, 1994) and also by IT Transport. They appear quite promising but can only support radial loads so that additional thrust washers are needed. A cup and cone type of ball bearing (similar to a bicycle axle arrangement), using hardened balls and case hardened races, is being developed by Camartec in Tanzania: this supports both radial and axial loads.

Plain bearings

Plain bearings involve sliding contact between the bearing and axle so that both friction and wear are substantially higher than for rolling contact bearings. Their advantages are that they are cheaper and can be made from locally available materials.

The design of these bearings is based on allowable values of bearing pressure, P (kg/cm^2), and "PV" factor, where V (m/s) is the sliding velocity between bearing and axle. Typical values for cart bearings are P = 10 and PV = 1.2. Allowable values for some bearing materials are given in Table 2.

These design data indicate that bronze, cast iron and hardwoods should be satisfactory for cart bearings but plain nylon is very marginal. However, the performance of plain bearings is very much dependent on proper lubrication and the exclusion of abrasive materials, and bearing materials which should be satisfactory may perform very poorly because of inadequate attention to these two factors.

The materials commonly used for plain bearings in industrialised countries are bronze and polymers. A wide range of low-wearing polymers are available but they are relatively costly and would need to be imported for use on carts. Materials which are locally available and have been used on carts include:

o **phosphor bronze**: this is a relatively hard material and it is recommended that axles are case hardened. Bushes need to be machined on a lathe

o **cast iron**: this is cheaper than bronze and does not perform quite so well. Other comments are the same as for bronze

o **mild steel**: mild steel bearings running on steel axles are very prone to seizure and should be avoided. In general, identical or similar pairs of materials should not be used. If steel is to be used then either the bearing, the axle or, preferably, both should be case hardened

o **hardwoods**: these are suitable bearing materials and are still used in some particularly dirty conditions in industrialised countries. Hardwood is best used in the form of oil-soaked bearings and, because of its higher wear rate, in a live axle arrangement which should have a life at least 5 to 10 times longer than wooden bushes used in a hub assembly. Significant advantages are that good quality bearings can be produced without a lathe and that they are cheap and can be readily replaced.

The performance of plain bearings used on cart wheels has been very variable. Dogger (1990) cites bronze bushes which wore out completely in less than one year, while Müller (1986) quotes a case of hardwood bearings in a live axle arrangement lasting more than 12 years. Although different operating conditions may partially account for variations in performance the major factors are undoubtedly attention to lubrication and protection against ingress of sand and dirt. The two main areas for improving performance of plain bearings are therefore:

o improved methods of lubrication, particularly in terms of retaining lubricant in the bearing for longer periods to avoid the need for regular lubrication (which experience shows is rarely carried out)

o improved shielding or sealing of bearings to prevent the ingress of sand and dirt.

Friction and wear in bearings

Data on the friction and wear of common types of bearings are shown in Figure 4: they are obtained partly from the literature and partly from testing carried out by IT Transport.

Friction data are presented in terms of the draft effort needed to overcome bearing friction for a cart with a wheel load of 10 000 N (or 1000 kgf). This is obtained from the expression:

$$Draft \ effort = \frac{f \, W \, d}{D}$$

where f is the coefficient of friction, W is load (1000 kgf), d is axle diameter (assumed 50 mm) and D is wheel diameter (assumed 700 mm). The expression indicates that the draft effort needed to overcome bearing friction gets smaller as the wheel diameter increases. Bearing wear may also be smaller because the rotational speed of the wheel will decrease, but this will be counteracted by the increased effect of side loads on the wheel.

Figure 4 shows that the draft effort is:

○ negligible for rolling contact bearings

○ 100–120 N for lubricated bushes, representing 7–10% of available draft from a pair of oxen

○ 150–200 N for lubricated wooden bearings in a live axle assembly or 10–15% of available draft (higher than bush bearings because of increased load at the outer bearing and greater problems in aligning the bearings)

○ 300–400 N for unlubricated plain bearings or 25–35% of available draft (note the substantial penalty for inadequate lubrication).

Wear of rolling contact bearings is usually negligible (provided abrasive materials are excluded); deterioration tends to be due to surface failures such as pitting. The wear rate for bronze, used as the reference base for plain bearing materials, is roughly equivalent to 1 mm depth of wear of the bush bore in 10 000 hours (but the wear of the axle may be three to four times this value if it is not case hardened). Field experience and preliminary tests by IT Transport suggest that if sand gets into the bearing, wear rates will increase by up to 50 times.

Selection of bearings

The following is a rough order of preference for selecting bearings for best performance and durability:

○ commercial rolling contact bearings are the best choice if they are available, affordable and the workshop has access to a lathe

○ locally made rolling contact bearings seem promising, but further testing is needed. A lathe is desirable but it may be possible to construct roller bearings from standard sizes of pipe and round bar

○ bronze or, more likely, cast iron bushes with case hardened axles. The bushes need to be machined on a lathe

○ hardwood bearings used in a live axle arrangement

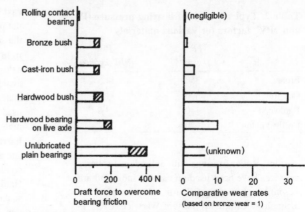

Figure 4: Comparison of friction and wear for various types of bearings. Data are based on draft force required to overcome a bearing load of 10 000 N (or 1000 kgf) and are indicative for good quality bearings, adequately lubricated and sealed against ingress of sand and dirt

○ other low cost alternatives as they are developed and proven.

In all cases the bearings must be adequately lubricated and sealed or shielded against the ingress of sand and dirt.

More detailed information on design of bearing/axle assemblies is given by Thoma (1979) and IT (1994).

Frame and body

The size of the cart body should be compatible with its capacity and intended use. Making the body too large is wasteful in terms of increasing the cost and deadweight of the cart, and may encourage overloading. The width is set within limits by the wheelbase which should be standardised at about 1.4 m. Dimensions of ox carts are generally in the range 1.1–1.3 m wide by 1.8–2.2 m long. Donkey carts should be smaller and lighter: for example, a cart for a single donkey might be 1–1.2 m wide and 1.4–1.6 m long.

The cart frame must support the body and transfer the load from the floor area into the axle supports. A typical frame layout is illustrated in Figure 5: it may

Figure 5: Layout of a cart frame

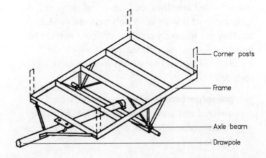

be constructed from steel or wood. A welded steel frame is the most effective design and the simplest to construct, depending on the availability and affordability of suitable steel sections. In construction of wooden frames, care is needed to make joints which effectively lock members together and prevent them from vibrating loose under constant impact loading. The corner uprights may be fitted with brackets to provide for fitting of extension panels for the sides and/or ends of the cart.

Careful attention needs to be given to the design of the body to avoid excess material and weight. Fully enclosing the body can add considerably to its weight. For example, sheet steel bodies commonly used on carts in Zimbabwe weigh roughly 70 kg; a body made from 25 mm thick wooden planks would weigh about 50–60 kg. These represent substantial contributions to the total weight of the cart so careful consideration should be given to the need for a fully enclosed body. Other factors which need to be considered are whether the side and/or rear panels should be removable or hinged to allow easier loading and unloading of the cart, and whether a tipping body is needed. Steel bodies are the more durable, but equipment is needed to cut and fold the sheets: thin sheet material may need folded ribs in the panels to increase rigidity. Wooden planks are widely used for agricultural carts and should be quite adequate, provided appropriate grades of timber are used and properly treated to prevent deterioration from pests and the environment. A wooden body is easier to construct and allows greater flexibility in body design.

Drawpoles may be made of wood or steel pipe. Pipe of the required size is relatively costly so wooden poles are commonly used where they are available. The latter should be attached to the frame with U-bolts: holes should be avoided at the front fixture as they would introduce a point of weakness at the most critical section of the pole. Shetto and Kwiligwa (1988) report that failures of wooden drawpoles are common; 80% of farmers in their survey reported failures, in some cases as many as three a year. Abuse appears to be a common cause for failures, for instance allowing the drawpole to drop to the ground. If this is the case it may be worthwhile considering the addition of legs to the front of the cart which strike the ground just before the drawpole.

In general, carts in rural Africa are too heavy and consideration needs to be given to improving designs by removing excess material. As a comparison, the ox cart produced in Senegal by the Sismar (Siscoma) factory, having a load capacity of 1000 kg, weighs 190 kg, whereas similar capacity carts in Zambia and Zimbabwe often weigh 250–300 kg. It seems that there should be some scope for weight reduction on the latter carts.

Brakes

Carts for use in hilly regions should be provided with adequate braking systems which ensure safe operation. The braking system should control the cart going downhill and, if necessary, hold the cart to allow the animal(s) to rest when going uphill.

Two very simple braking systems are:

○   a pole attached to the cart which can be levered to drag against the ground

○   animal braking, in which a strap attached to the harness or a crossmember attached to the drawpole restrains the cart against the hind quarters of the animal(s). This is only effective for heavier animals and only works when the cart is going downhill.

These systems are fairly crude and unsatisfactory.

A braking system acting on the wheel or axle would give greater safety. These comprise a friction pad, shoe or band which is forced against the rim of the wheel or against a drum or disc fitted to the wheel or axle (for live axles). To be effective, the friction member should act at as large a radius as possible and have a good area of contact on a surface which is unlikely to get wet. The options include:

○   braking against the outside of the tyre. This provides the maximum radius of action but is not very effective in wet conditions and will cause increased wear of pneumatic tyres

○   friction pads acting against the inside of the wheel rim, if it is wide enough, or against a drum attached to the wheel or axle. This reduces the radius of action but provides a better braking surface

○   a band brake, for example, a leather strap, acting around a drum attached to the wheel or axle.

The simplest form of friction brake comprises a bar, fitted across the cart and free to slide in guides, which has friction pads at each end and is pulled against the wheel or drum by a hand lever. A good lever ratio (eg, 10:1) should be provided and the pulling mechanism should equalise the forces at each end of the braking bar. Pieces cut from scrap tyres may be used as friction pads. A ratchet or stops should be provided to allow the brake lever to be locked on. Further details of braking systems are given by Barwell and Hathway (1986).

Suspension

A suspension is seldom used on carts, or on any farm vehicle. It would be of little use on carts with pneumatic tyres but could provide some benefits for rigid-tyred carts in cushioning impacts and possibly reducing rolling resistance on hard bumpy surfaces. To be effective the suspension must provide good springing involving a reasonable vertical displacement of the body relative to the axle at full load (possibly 20 mm or more). The simplest approach is to use scrap leaf springs from motor vehicles but these are likely to be in short supply. If rubber springs, cut from scrap tyres, are used then some ingenuity will be needed to provide the required vertical springiness at the axle mounting while retaining adequate constraint in the horizontal plane. This is an area in which some development and testing may be justified in conjunction with work on puncture-proof tyres.

Conclusion

This paper has reviewed the design and construction of two-wheel animal-drawn carts. It is clear that the main problem in producing good quality carts, particularly in smaller workshops, is the procurement or construction of suitable wheel–axle assemblies. Scrap axles from motor vehicles are a useful resource but their supply is often too limited to sustain cart production. Secondhand axle assemblies may sometimes be imported but this does not seem a sustainable solution, or in the best interests of developing local capabilities for manufacture and maintenance of carts. A more appropriate approach may be to develop some specialisation in wheel–axle manufacture in certain workshops and to standardise on certain materials and components so that these are more readily available at reasonable costs.

References

Barwell I and Hathway G, 1986. *The design and manufacture of animal-drawn carts*. Technical memorandum prepared for the International Labour Office (ILO) and UN Centre for Human Settlements (HABITAT). IT Publications, London, UK. 72p.

Dennis R A, 1990. A wheel manufacturing technology for rural workshops. *Appropriate technology* 17(3):9-12.

Dogger J W, 1990. *Final report ox cart testing activities: August 1987–July 1990*. Animal Draught Power Research and Development Project, Magoye Regional Research Station, Magoye, Zambia, and Institute of Agricultural Engineering (IMAG-DLO), Wageningen, The Netherlands. 40p.

FAO, 1972. *Manual on the employment of draught animals in agriculture*. Food and Agriculture Organization of the United Nations (FAO), Rome, Italy. 249p.

Goe M R and McDowell R E, 1980. *Animal traction: guidelines for utilisation*. Department of Animal Science, Cornell University, New York, USA. 83p.

IT, 1994. *Making wheels: a technical manual*. IT Publications, London, UK.

Müller H, 1986. *Ox-power in Zambian agriculture and rural transport: performance, potential and promotion*. Socio-Economic Studies on Rural Development, Volume. 65. Institut für Rurale Entwicklung, Gottingen, Germany.

O'Neill D, Hayton S and Sims B, 1989. Measurement of draft animal performance. pp. 264–271 in: Hoffman D, Nari J and Petheram R J (eds), *Draught animals in rural development*. International Research Symposium, Cipanos, Indonesia, 3–7 July 1989. Australian Centre for International Agricultural Research (ACIAR), Canberra, Australia.

Oram C, 1994. Low-technology, roller-element bearings for animal-powered transport and equipment. In Starkey P, Mwenya E and Stares J (eds), *Improving animal traction technology*. Proceedings of first workshop of Animal Traction Network for Eastern and Southern Africa (ATNESA) held 18–23 January, 1992, Lusaka, Zambia. ATNESA in collaboration with Technical Centre for Agriculture and Rural Cooperation (CTA), Ede-Wageningen, The Netherlands.

Shetto R and Kwiligwa E, 1988. *Survey of ox cart production and use in Mbeya Region*. Mbeya Oxenization Project, Mbeya, Tanzania. 69p.

Starkey P, 1989. Animal-drawn transport in Africa. *GATE—Questions, Answers, Information* 1/89: 13–18. GTZ, Eschborn, Germany.

Thoma G, 1979. *Low-cost transportation*. Arbeitsgemeinschaft für Entwicklungsplanung, Munich, Germany. 63p.

Vroom H, 1994. Rural transport in Zambia: the design of an ox cart which can be produced in rural areas. In Starkey P, Mwenya E and Stares J (eds) *Improving animal traction technology*. Proceedings of first workshop of Animal Traction Network for Eastern and Southern Africa (ATNESA) held 18–23 January 1992, Lusaka, Zambia. ATNESA in collaboration with Technical Centre for Agriculture and Rural Cooperation (CTA), Ede-Wageningen, The Netherlands.

Design, adaptation and manufacture of animal-drawn carts

by

Josef Wirth[*]

Institute of Production Innovation, University of Dar es Salaam, PO Box 35075, Dar es Salaam, Tanzania

Abstract

Animal-drawn carts can meet many of the transportation needs of a small farmer. This paper describes some designs and details of animal-drawn carts that have been promoted for more than 20 years. Information is based on the experiences of the author with appropriate technology organisations in Tanzania and Ghana. Drawings are provided of several designs of cart and bearings, some suitable for manufacture in local workshops. Production methods are also discussed.

Introduction

The most important implements for a farmer using draft animals are the plow, followed by the inter-row weeder. But the use of these implements is seasonal, and if a farmer wishes to make use of his draft animals all year round, the cart is the really important item. A cart owner can make considerable income from hiring out the cart for haulage of goods.

It is not easy to make a durable ox cart at a price that a small-scale farmer can afford. Carts can be made using wheels and axle assemblies from old cars, but the supply of these components is not nearly enough to meet the demand for ox carts. There is a need, therefore, to design bearings and axle–wheel assemblies that can be made by any local craftsmen with average skills.

The following analysis is based on the author's experience with carts while working at the Tanganyika Agricultural Machinery Testing Unit (TAMTU), Arusha, Tanzania (1968–76), the University of Science and Technology, Agriculture Engineering Department, Ghana (1976–85) and the Institute of Production Innovation (IPI), Dar es Salaam, Tanzania (1985–92).

*Josef Wirth was tragically killed in a car accident in Tanzania in 1992

Designs for ox carts suitable for manufacture by rural artisans

Design of a suitable bearing

The biggest problem encountered when designing a suitable axle–wheel assembly for an ox cart is finding a suitable bearing. Such a bearing should be:

○ simple to manufacture
○ extremely durable
○ resistant to rough treatment
○ easy to maintain, repair or replace
○ reasonably priced.

Experience has shown that a very suitable combination of bearing materials is a mild steel shaft running in an oil-soaked hardwood bearing.

The hardwood bearing can be made as a prismatic wooden block or as a cylindrical wooden bush (Figure 1). The wooden block bearing is the easiest to manufacture; making the cylindrical wooden bush needs more skill or, preferably, a lathe.

African mahogany is a suitable wood for this purpose, as is wood from the trees known locally as *mvule, loliondo, panga panga* and *mtundu*. The wood must be well seasoned and dried. Artificial drying can be carried out in a solar drier, provided it can produce temperatures of around 60–80°C: this process takes about two weeks.

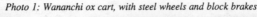
Photo 1: Wananchi ox cart, with steel wheels and block brakes

Photo: TAMTU, Arusha

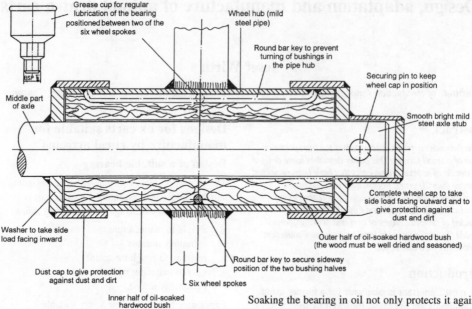

Figure 1: Standard cylindrical wooden bush bearing

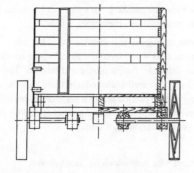

Soaking the bearing in oil not only protects it against water, but also gives it some emergency lubrication, which is important if the farmer does not grease the bearing frequently.

Test of bearing performance

The two types of bearing mentioned were tested on a drum type test rig. This rig simulated an ox cart travelling on a rough road at a speed of 9.3 km/hour (slightly high due to the second-hand components available for manufacture of the rig) for a total travel distance of 4000 km, running over about 5 million obstacles. This test was made in 1973 by TAMTU in Arusha, Tanzania. (TAMTU has since become Camartec—Centre for Agricultural Mechanisation and Rural Technology—also based at Arusha.)

The measured wear was less than 1 mm of the bearing's diameter, despite the fact that lubrication

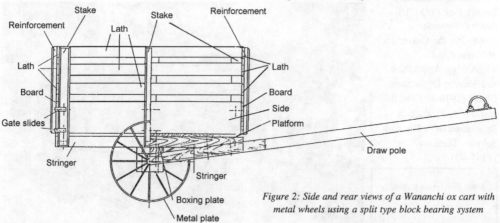

Figure 2: Side and rear views of a Wananchi ox cart with metal wheels using a split type block bearing system

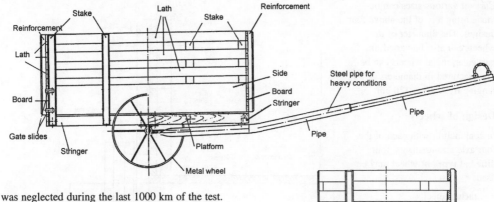

was neglected during the last 1000 km of the test. The load on the bearing was 365 kg.

One cart made by TAMTU was called the "Wananchi" ox cart (see Photo 1 and Figure 2). One such cart made in 1969 was still in good condition in 1976. It was used on stony roads in the Lekuriki area in Arusha Region. A wooden bush rail axle cart (*Afromosi* bush bearings: Figure 3) showed very little wear after five years of use in a village in northern Ghana.

Over the years, field observations have shown that the bearings do wear considerably, especially if they are not well made or if unsuitable timber is used. Some carts seen during a tour of Iringa Region in 1986 showed serious damage or failure of the bearings due to poor manufacture and the wrong choice of material.

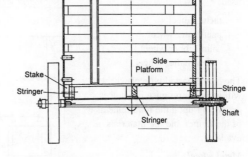

Figure 3: Rear and side views of an ox cart using a rail axle and wooden bush bearing system with metal wheels

Figure 4: Wananchi ox cart block bearing system

Design of axle–wheel arrangements

Based on the two types of bearings mentioned above, four different axle–wheel systems have been designed:

- ○ Wananchi ox cart block bearing system
- ○ symmetrical wheel block bearing system
- ○ wooden bush stub axle system
- ○ wooden bush rail axle system.

These four bearing systems, and ox carts built around them, are shown in Figures 2–8.

Each system has its advantages and disadvantages which make it more or less suitable for different applications.

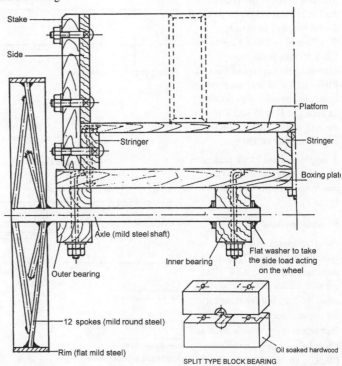

Carts of various sizes can be made using any of the above four designs. The diameter of the wheels can also be varied; in particular, metal wheels can be manufactured in diameters ranging from 80 to 120 cm.

Design of wheels

In conjunction with each of the four axle arrangements, four different types of wheel may be used:

○ metal wheel
○ pneumatic wheel
○ solid rubber wheel
○ "mbaomatic" wheel.

The diameter and type of wheel will be a compromise of choices depending upon the requirements of the farmer and the materials available.

Metal wheel

The metal wheel (Figure 9) will be the choice if the cart is to be used in remote areas with no puncture repair facilities. Metal wheels for travel on sandy soil will have wider rims. The size of the flat bar that is bent to form the the rim will have to be 80 x 10 mm to 120 x 12 mm (to 150 x 16 mm at the most) depending on the size of the cart. Rims of 10 x 10 mm are good for small donkey carts. For normal ox carts flat bars of 100 x 12 mm are well suited. Recommended wheel diameter is 750 mm.

A simple wooden block brake can easily be incorporated into the construction of the cart (see Photo 1).

Pneumatic wheel

Pneumatic tyres will usually come from old cars. Tyres from a passenger car ("175 x 14" size) are suitable for donkey carts and small ox carts but for most carts the larger wheels used on a four-wheel drive vehicle such as a Land Rover or a Land Cruiser ("7.50 x 16" size) are preferred.

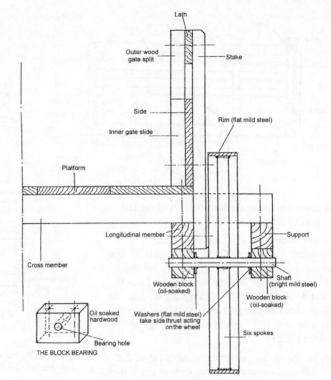

Figure 5: Symmetrical wheel block bearing system

Figure 6: Wooden bush stub axle bearing system

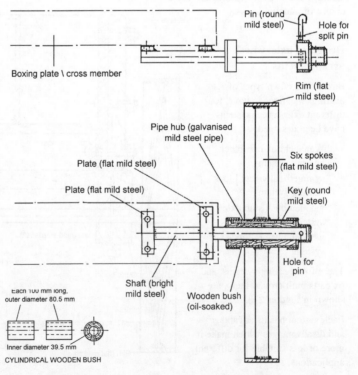

Usually, old tyres are more readily available than old rims. The design of a rim suitable for local manufacture is shown in Figures 10 and 11.

Solid rubber wheel

Solid rubber wheels seem to be the answer for ox carts. Only a few carts have been made with these wheels, but the experience so far is positive. On sandy soil, solid rubber wheels have no advantage over metal wheels. On stony roads, solid rubber wheels will not make the noise associated with metal wheels, but they also will not give the suspension effect of pneumatic tyres. Unfortunately, solid rubber wheels are quite expensive and are not available locally. A compromise wheel can be made by cutting out the middle part of an old car tyre and fixing it to the rim of a metal wheel.

One prototype ox cart with a solid rubber wheel is still in use at the Mbeya Rural Craft Workshop after about 12 years.

"Mbaomatic" wheel

The name "mbaomatic" is derived from "mbao" (Kiswahili for timber) and "matic" (from pneumatic, as the tyre from a pneumatic wheel is used for the lining). This wheel (designed by George Macpherson) consists of a wooden disc made of three pairs of planks (2–3 cm thick) nailed together crosswise and cut into a circular shape (Figure 12). This wooden wheel disc is covered with an old car tyre of suitable size (eg, an old Land Rover tyre).

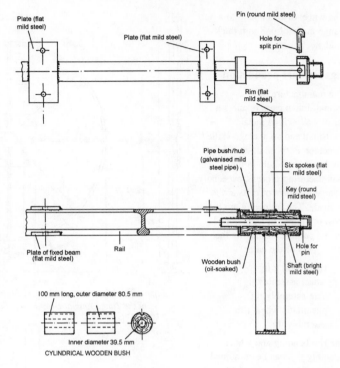

Figure 7: Wooden bush rail axle bearing system

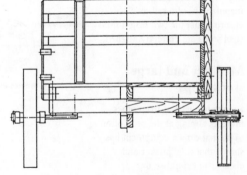

Figure 8: Side and rear views of an ox cart using stub axles and metal wheels

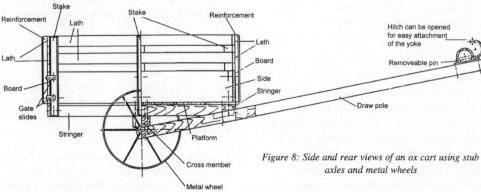

The wheel disc is bolted to a hub flange made of 6–8 mm thick mild steel plate.

Jigs for cart production

The manufacture of animal-drawn carts requires a fairly well-skilled metal craftsman and an average-skilled carpenter. Purpose-designed jigs can be of great help in the manufacturing process, especially if large numbers of carts are to be made. The following are the most important jigs developed for the purpose of making the metal parts of the carts:

○ rim bending jig
○ wheel assembly jig
○ axle assembly jig
○ pneumatic wheel rim assembly jig.

The rim bending and wheel assembly jigs can be combined into one (Figures 13 and 14) and will allow the manufacture of an accurate metal wheel.

The axle assembly jig is less important, but it is useful in the manufacture of a rail axle for ensuring that the two bright mild steel stubs are correctly aligned.

Medium and large workshops

Experience gained from other projects aiming at the promotion of animal-drawn equipment has shown that it is quicker and cheaper to centralise the manufacture of ox carts or related items in one or a few workshops, depending on the size of the project area.

In West Africa, several countries have large workshops producing carts. The Arcoma production organisation in Burkina Faso has two main workshops, one in Ouagadougou and one in Bobo Dioulasso. These two workshops produce carts and plows for the whole country and even export some items to neighbouring countries. Similarly, a workshop in Tamale in northern Ghana

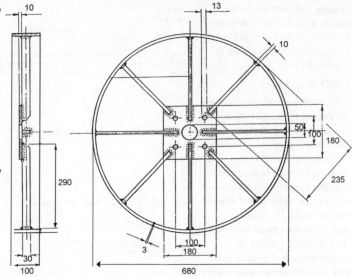

Figure 9: Replacement metal wheel designed for a pneumatic tyred cart of the Tanga Animal Draft Power Project (dimensions in mm)

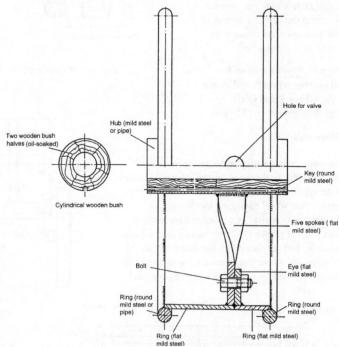

Figure 10: Rim for pneumatic tyre

produces equipment for the whole of the Savannah Region of Ghana. Senegal has the large Sismar factory. These workshops all produce carts with roller bearings and pneumatic tyres.

There are several advantages of such centralised production. Experience has shown that at least the manufacture and supply of equipment in sufficient quantity and quality can be guaranteed with this arrangement.

For quick and measurable success it is better to go for centralised production. Attempts to achieve a widespread introduction of animal-drawn carts through decentralised production have had limited success.

However, given the necessary efforts, it is certainly possible to cover a demand by decentralised production. Local production has the advantage of encouraging local repair and maintenance services.

The Institute of Production Innovation (IPI) in Tanzania has designed two animal-drawn carts, one small and one large (Figures 15 and 16), for production in a central workshop. Both are equipped with pneumatic tyres. The wheel hubs run on roller bearings (Figure 17) and the basic frame of the cart is made of metal sections welded together. Timber is used for the draw poles and the platform.

Raw materials

Under the economic circumstances prevailing in Tanzania it is cheaper for an aid project to import raw materials than to depend on local supply. This is a very unusual situation. The main reason is that the unfavourable exchange rate makes local purchases from officially converted foreign currency very expensive.

For example, in the late 1980s, a piece of mild steel plate suitable for the floor of an ox cart cost 975 Tanzanian Shillings (Tsh) at the National Steel Corporation in Tanzania. The same sheet metal imported through aid channels would cost only about Tsh 650. Wooden planks of equivalent area cost Tsh 1152 at that time.

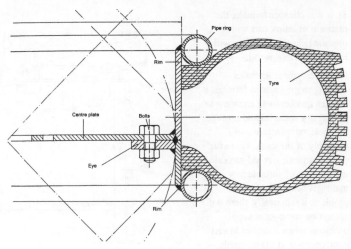

Figure 11: Detail of rim for pneumatic tyre

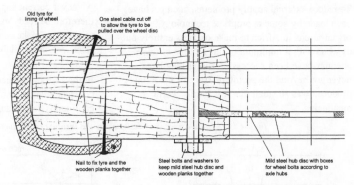

Figure 12: Replacement "mbaomatic" wheel designed for a pneumatic tyred cart of the Tanga Animal Draft Power Project

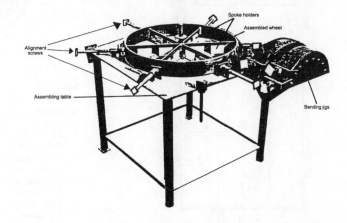

Figure 13: Combined wheel assembly and rim bending jig

So it was cheaper to make the platform of an ox cart with imported sheet metal than with locally available wood.

For development agencies wishing to get carts to farmers, it is often quickest and cheapest to import raw material and arrange the local manufacture and assembly of the carts. However, once that particular aid has dried up, the lack of suitable raw materials becomes a major problem. Realistically, there will always be some local supply problems when it comes to cart components and the desirable objective of strict reliance on local materials may prove very difficult to follow.

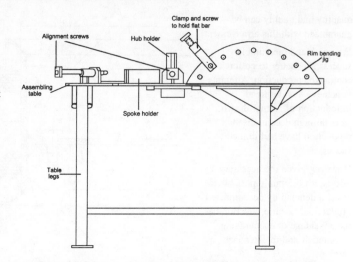

Figure 14: Side view of combined wheel assembly and rim bending jig

To reduce external supply problems, attempts have been made by some appropriate technology organisations in Africa to make ox carts entirely out of wood with a minimum of nails. None of these attempts have been successful. Either they have never got beyond the prototype stage or the number produced was so small that it is hardly worth mentioning.

Cart manufacturing enterprise that are not in a position to do their own importation have to rely on whatever current supplies are available. They must therefore be ready to adjust their designs frequently so they can make use of the materials, bearings and steel sections available.

In the case of reliance on local material supplies, a constant adaptation to available supplies requires continuous design adaptation efforts. If a workshop

Figure 15: Animal-drawn cart designed by the Institute of Production Innovation

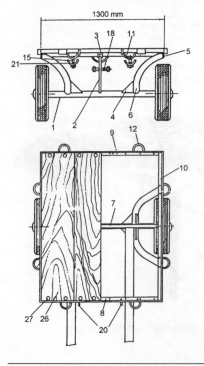

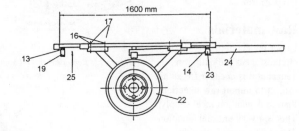

KEY

1	Axle	14	Donkey draw-bar bolt
2	Support	15	Pole clamp bolt
3	Flange	16	Bolt to fixed platform
4	Reinforcement	17	Square washer
5	Flange parts	18	Ox pole bolt
6	Platform support	19	Ox pole clamp
7	Middle traverse	20	Draw hook
8	Front traverse	21	Donkey pole clamp
9	Rear traverse	22	Pneumatic wheel
10	Longitudinal member	23	Donkey pole holder
11	Bolt support	24	Donkey draw bar
12	Pole eye	25	Ox draw pole
13	Ox draw-bar bolt	26	Wooden plank
		27	Cup head bolt and nut

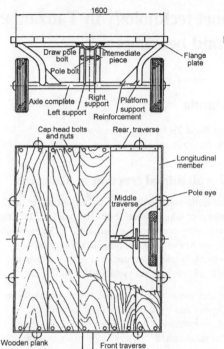

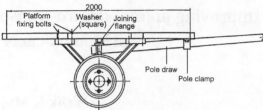

Figure 16: Three views of the Institute for Production Innovation's large animal cart

cannot do this, that would be one of the jobs to be done by a permanent consultant to the workshop.

Further information

Further information and technical drawings of many suitable cart designs are available from IPI (PO Box 35075, Dar es Salaam, Tanzania) and Camartec (PO Box 764, Arusha, Tanzania).

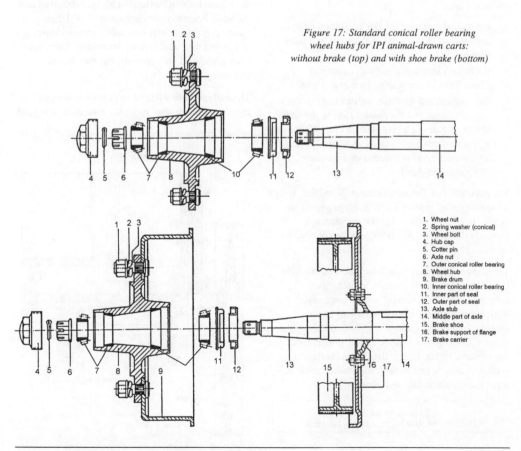

Figure 17: Standard conical roller bearing wheel hubs for IPI animal-drawn carts: without brake (top) and with shoe brake (bottom)

1. Wheel nut
2. Spring washer (conical)
3. Wheel bolt
4. Hub cap
5. Cotter pin
6. Axle nut
7. Outer conical roller bearing
8. Wheel hub
9. Brake drum
10. Inner conical roller bearing
11. Inner part of seal
12. Outer part of seal
13. Axle stub
14. Middle part of axle
15. Brake shoe
16. Brake support of flange
17. Brake carrier

Improving animal-drawn transport technology in Tanzania: work on ox carts and bearings

by

Felix K Mujemula[*]

Centre for Agricultural Mechanisation and Rural Technology (Camartec)
PO Box 764, Arusha, Tanzania

Abstract

This paper gives background information on animal traction in Tanzania and the type of animal traction equipment in use. It then describes research and development work done on the wheel bearings for animal-drawn carts, and describes some advantages, disadvantages, failures and successes in the course of development of different types of bearings. The main objective of this work is to make available to the farmer a locally made, good quality, durable and affordable product.

Introduction

Tanzania covers an area of 945 000 km^2 in three climatic zones:

- the coastal belt north of Dar es Salaam, with an annual rainfall of 1000–1900 mm in two rainy seasons
- the Lake Victoria region, with rainfall of 750–1000 mm per year uniformly distributed
- the northern and southern mountain areas, the central plateau and the coastal zone to the south of Dar es Salaam, where rainfall (750–1200 mm a year in mountainous areas, and 250–750 mm a year elsewhere) is concentrated between December and April.

The population of Tanzania is about 24 million, with an annual growth rate of 3.7%. Average population density is 25 people/km^2, but the population is unevenly distributed. About 90% of the population are peasants.

The country has about 10 million hectares of arable land; about six million hectares are actually cultivated, and the cultivated area is increasing. Agriculture is greatly diversified owing to the special climatic and geological characteristics of the country. Crops grown include cotton, coffee, sisal, tea, tobacco, wheat, rice, maize, beans, millet, potatoes, cassava, groundnuts, sunflowers, sesame, sugar cane, cashew nuts and bananas.

[*] *Subsequent address:*
PO Box 464, Usa River, Arusha, Tanzania

Use of animal traction in Tanzania

The cattle population in Tanzania is estimated at 12 million of which which about 10% are used for draft work. They are unevenly distributed in Shinyanga, Tabora, Mwanza, Mara, Singida and Arusha Regions. Donkeys are used to a limited extent as pack animals and, occasionally, for pulling carts.

Ox cultivation was introduced in the country some 50 years ago by settlers from southern Africa, almost extensively by the use of the single-furrow, steel mouldboard "Victory" plow. This type of plow is still the main implement; more than 250 000 of them have been manufactured by local factories and the annual demand is estimated at 20 000. Few harrows, planters, inter-row cultivators or ridgers are in use, but their numbers are increasing. Carts have been introduced only recently, but their use is increasing rapidly.

The multipurpose wheeled toolcarrier is almost unknown in Tanzania. In 1960 a toolcarrier designed

Figure 1: Wananchi ox cart, with wooden block bearings

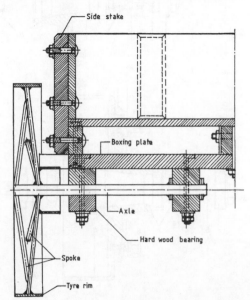

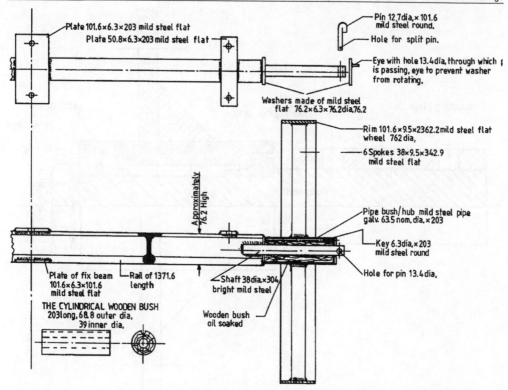

Figure 2: Wooden bush rail axle system (dimensions in mm)

Figure 3: Locally made rim for tyre

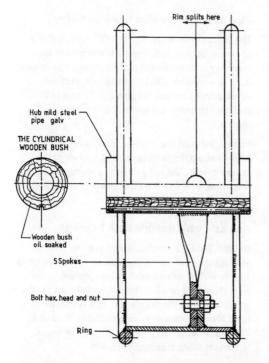

by the National Institute of Agricultural Engineering was tested at the Tanganyika Agricultural Machinery Testing Unit (TAMTU) and a modified prototype was developed. Due to a lack of an appropriate draft animal power extension service this implement was not tested extensively and its acceptance by farmers has been neglibible.

Problems with animal traction

Although the use of animals in agriculture represents a great advance over the use of the hand hoe, some farmers are still opposed to using their animals for draft work. Extension service staff are trying to educate these farmers on the advantages of having their animals trained, and actually offer such training free of charge. Even in areas where animal-drawn implements are in common use, animal power is not used for all agricultural operations; major bottlenecks are in weeding (inter-row cultivators are not common) and in harvesting and processing the crops. Ox-drawn planters and inter-row cultivators and simple threshers and hullers are gradually being introduced in an effort to solve these problems.

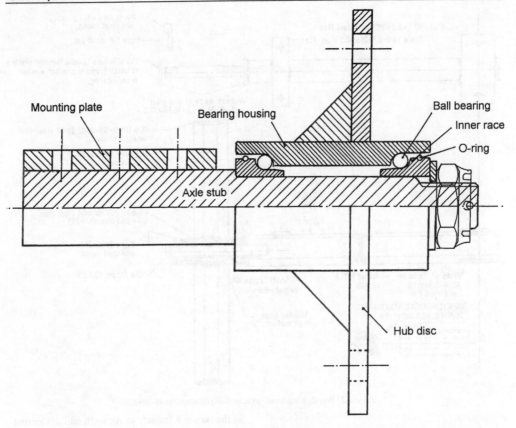

Labels on figure:
Mounting plate
Bearing housing
Ball bearing
Inner race
O-ring
Axle stub
Hub disc

Figure 4: Ball bearing hub

Rural transport and ox carts

Rural transport is a major bottleneck for the Tanzanian farmer. The introduction of ox plows has enabled farmers to increase their crop production, but they are still faced with the problem of transporting their produce from the field to the homestead and from the homestead to market. This need for rural transport has led to the development of the ox cart.

Ox carts were first used in Tanzania in the early 1960s when local artisans tried to copy imported carts found on settlers' farms. The basic raw materials for making the carts were scrap front or rear car axles which still had their original wheels with pneumatic tyres. But because the supply of scrap car axles was limited, few carts could be made. (Such carts are, however, still being made in urban areas where scrap car axles are available; they are mainly used as hand carts.) The lack of suitable axles led to the development of axles made from locally available raw materials.

Pipe axle with wooden block bearings

The first axle developed by TAMTU consisted of a 75 mm steel pipe with a metal wheel on one end revolving in two wooden block bearings which were fixed to a wooden 50 x150 mm plank. Further development changed the pipe to a 38 mm steel shaft, but still with the hardwood block bearings (Figure 1).

Further tests and use of these block bearing carts brought about the development of, and eventual change over to, the rail axle with a shaft welded on either side with wooden bush bearings in a wheel hub revolving round the shafts.

Rail axle with wooden bush bearings

In 1968 TAMTU developed, and put into production, a rail axle with metal or pneumatic tyred wheels with wooden bush bearings pressed in the hubs (Figures 2 and 3). The standard chosen for the wheel was the 16 inch split rim; this is the size of Land Rover tyres which are plentiful in Tanzania. The rim is deliberately split to obviate the use of tyre levers when repairing punctures.

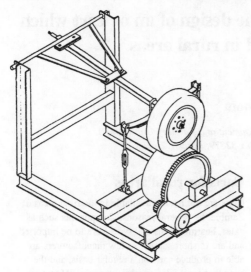

Figure 5: Wheel bearing test rig

Wooden bush bearings do have some disadvantages:

○ they wear out very fast if they are not greased (and farmers rarely grease them)

○ bearings are replaced by knocking the new one in with a hammer, and this sometimes smashes the bush

○ farmers tend to use any wood that is readily available instead of the recommended hardwood; softer wood wears even more rapidly.

The advantages of these bearings, however, are that they are cheap, are easily replaced and require very little maintenance.

Rail axle with ball bearings

In response to an increasing demand for bearings with less friction, the design department of the Centre for Agriculture Mechanisation and Rural Technology (Camartec) developed a new axle assembly to incorporate a simpler and lighter 16 inch split rim and a hub on ball bearings (Figure 4).

The stub axle bearing system is similar to that of a bicycle, but considerably bigger. The original design used 6 mm balls, as used in the rear hub of a bicycle; these could be bought from local shops and were relatively cheap. However, tests showed that these bicycle balls could not withstand loads higher than 500 kg, and so they were abandoned in favour of SKF class 3 balls. The whole hub, including the hardened bearing races, is manufactured in the Camartec workshop.

It is interesting to note that encouragement for this development was found in old engineering books. We reasoned that if it was possible to manufacture satisfactory ball bearings as early as 1923, it must be possible for us to produce such bearings using design methods of that time. These bearings cannot be loaded as highly as modern bearings, but they fully satisfy our needs for a maximum load of 1000 kg.

It may be argued that this development was unnecessary because imported bearings could easily be bought locally. But imported bearings cost over 10 times as much and are meant for larger loads and higher speeds.

Although an ox cart with the new ball bearing hub system costs 25% more than a cart with the old wooden bush stub axle system, the advantages to the farmer justify the increased price and the farmers are prepared to pay more.

Future plans

Tests to check the performance of the new bearings are being carried out on Camartec's test rig (Figure 5). This can simulate various road conditions, such as "moving" at 5 km/hour over a bumpy surface with a load of 300 kg, or being pulled by a tractor, with a load of 500–1000 kg. These tests have covered "a distance" of more than 500 km, and results so far are encouraging.

Finally, Camartec would be interested to hear the experiences of researchers in eastern and southern Africa who are currently doing work on rural transport, particularly on bearings.

Rural transport in Zambia: the design of an ox cart which can be produced in rural areas

by

H Vroom

Project Engineer, Technology Development and Advisory Unit (TDAU)
University of Zambia, PO Box 32379, Lusaka, Zambia

Abstract

Ox carts can be regarded as the most suitable means of transport in rural areas. The problem with the ox carts manufactured in Zambia is that they are too expensive and are not available in the (remote) rural areas. Ox carts should therefore be produced in the rural areas using, as much as possible, locally available materials; this will also facilitate repair and maintenance.

The University of Zambia's Technology Development and Advisory Unit has designed an ox cart especially for rural production. The design uses wood as the basic raw material wherever possible, and has no imported parts. The cart has wooden bearings, which can be manufactured easily and have surprisingly low friction and wear rates. Flexi-wheels use the flexibility of rubber to provide good shock-absorbing characteristics. They cannot be punctured. The process of testing and improving the present design is continuing, based on the experience gained from carts already produced.

Introduction

Zambia's rural areas could easily grow enough food to feed the whole country. A major constraint to achieving such self-sufficiency is the shortage of transport to bring agricultural produce from remote rural areas to the urban centres, as well as to supply the rural areas with farm inputs and other basic needs.

Although motor vehicles can be used for transport between collection points and towns, their use in the rural areas is not economical. They are very expensive to buy and maintain because they, and their spare parts, have to be imported and paid for with foreign exchange. Also, roads in the rural areas are very poor, so breakdowns are frequent, and repairs are extremely costly and time-consuming.

Animal power can provide the solution to the transport problem in the rural areas. Sledges are useful for short-range transport, but for transport over longer distances—between the agricultural areas and the collection points—ox or donkey carts are the only viable answer.

Carts for rural areas

Carts are not readily available in the rural areas of Zambia, for several reasons. Components such as axles, bearings, rims and tyres have to be imported and are in short supply, so few manufacturers are able to produce carts on a regular basis, and the ones that are made are very expensive. Moreover, manufacturers of ox carts are concentrated in Lusaka and other cities, and transporting assembled carts to the rural areas is expensive because they take a lot of space. Thus only commercial and progressive emergent farmers can afford to buy carts. Another problem is that spare parts are not readily available, and difficult repair jobs can only be done by the manufacturers or by well-equipped workshops; this makes maintenance difficult, and so the reliability of carts is rather low.

The high demand for ox carts can therefore only be partially met. Only people in the areas close to the manufacturers and a few distribution points can obtain ox carts, while those in the more remote areas, where the need for this kind of transport is much more urgent, have to do without.

Producing ox carts locally, in the areas where they are needed, could provide an answer to the supply problem. This is already being done by some local artisans who use old car suspensions and/or pick-up bodies to build ox carts (Photo 1). However, there are very few broken-down cars available in the rural areas—not nearly enough to cater for the demand for ox carts. Furthermore, such local carts may be poorly designed and badly balanced, which places a considerable burden on the oxen. In addition, repair jobs to carts based on pick-ups often require welding and spare parts which are not available in the rural areas—the high costs and the hassle of repair work result in many carts being abandoned.

What is required is a more systematic approach to the design and local production of ox carts. The Technology Development and Advisory Unit (TDAU), an autonomous unit of the Department of Mechanical Engineering of the University of

Photo 1: Ox cart made locally from an old pick-up

Zambia, works in partnership with aid organisations to give technical assistance in the testing and redesigning of equipment to suit Zambian conditions. TDAU has designed a basic cart that can be made with locally available materials and parts (Figure 1).

The advantages of the type of local manufacture required for the TDAU cart are clear: the cart will be cheap to produce, easy to maintain and repair, and available where the demand for this kind of transport is the greatest. Furthermore, carts can, to some extent, be custom-made according to the particular requirements of the local farmers.

TDAU is also providing support and training to local workshops and craftsmen who will make these carts. In its Rural Workshop Programme, TDAU is helping carpenters and blacksmiths to equip their workshops and upgrade their skills by offering tools on a hire-purchase basis, giving advice on technical and managerial matters and organising training courses. TDAU may enter into joint cart production arrangements with local manufacturers.

Design of the TDAU ox cart

The TDAU ox cart has been designed to be:

○ affordable for the small-scale farmer
○ highly reliable and durable
○ easy to maintain and repair with locally available materials and limited tools and spares
○ easily manoeuvrable, with low draft force requirements

The cart has three main functional parts—the cart body, the suspension and the wheels—and the design choices for each of these parts are discussed in the following sections.

Cart body

A cart body can be made entirely of steel, of a steel frame with wooden boards or entirely of wood. The choice of material for the TDAU cart body was dictated by local availability: very little scrap metal is available in the rural areas, while wood is plentiful. Wood was therefore chosen as the basic material, with steel being used only to reinforce critical joints.

The body of the TDAU ox cart is made of thick boards of local timber, which are strong and durable although rather heavy. The boards are painted with old engine oil, to protect them against water and attack by ants, and hence to ensure a long life-span. Very few steel parts are used, so the cart body can be made by any capable carpenter. Experience to date with this cart body has been good.

Figure 1: The TDAU ox cart with flexi-wheels

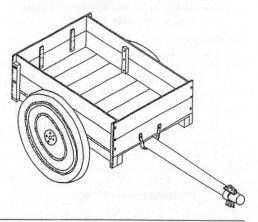

Suspension

A two-wheeled ox cart is more suitable for use in rural areas than a four-wheeled version, because of simplicity of construction, manoeuvrability and price.

A suspension comprises a shaft and bearings mounted on some sort of subframe. For the bearings, a choice had to be made between roller bearings or plain bearings.

Roller bearings are the common choice for ox carts produced in a factory. They have a low friction coefficient (0.005 unsealed) and, if properly greased and sealed, can have a long life-span in a harsh environment. Their life-span is, however, affected by their sensitivity to impact loads which are quite heavy on ox carts. The roller bearings produced in Zambia (with imported, expensive steel) are of questionable quality; satisfactory bearings must therefore be imported ready made, so they are expensive and not readily available as spare parts. For all these reasons, roller bearings are not the best choice for an ox cart produced and used in the rural areas.

Plain bearings are less sensitive to impact loads, but have higher friction coefficients and need a lubrication system. They can be made of various materials, most of which are not very satisfactory for use in rural areas: PVC or bronze bearings wear too fast in harsh environments, and metallic bearings running against a mild steel shaft cause excessive wear on the shaft. Furthermore, bearings made of these materials cannot be repaired, but have to be replaced as a unit. So none of these bearings is a suitable choice for a rural ox cart.

TDAU chose plain wooden bearings (Photo 2) made of local Mukwa (hardwood) timber. The bearing blocks can be easily manufactured by any carpenter, with little training, so they are cheap. Fitted with grease-pots, their friction coefficients and wear rates

Photo 2: Plain wooden bearing used on the TDAU ox cart

are surprisingly low (friction coefficient < 0.2, see Figure 2). Split bearing blocks were chosen because, when these get worn, they can be restored to almost new condition simply by replaning.

A shaft could also be made of wood, but TDAU's experience with wooden shafts have not been good: they are not capable of absorbing the impact loads typical of ox carts, and because they run in a wooden bearing block they wear rather fast, and then break. So TDAU chose mild steel as the shaft material, this being the cheapest alternative. Mild steel is strong and, in combination with the wooden bearings, has a long life-span. TDAU decided to use a "live shaft" system construction (Photo 2) as this facilitates manoeuvring. However, production of these shafts requires jigs and welding, so regrettably they will probably have to be manufactured in an urban workshop and supplied to the small rural workshops together with the grease-pots for the bearings.

Wheels

Land Rover rims and tires are the common choice for ox cart wheels. Pneumatic tyres have low draft requirements (if properly inflated) and excellent shock absorbency, but they puncture easily, and in rural areas a puncture can keep a cart out of use for days.

Wooden or metal disc wheels (spoked or solid) could be made locally. However, they are heavier and their lack of shock-absorbency results in frequent breakages of wheels and other cart parts, and discomfort for the oxen.

TDAU has designed a compromise solution, the flexi-wheel, which consists of an old rubber tyre clamped on a wooden disk. Rubber has good shock-absorbing characteristics, but the great advantage of these wheels is that they cannot be punctured. Old truck-tyres are the best choice

Figure 2: Friction coefficient in relation to bearing pressure (ie, bearing load/bearing area) for dry and lubricated wooden bearings

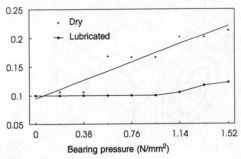

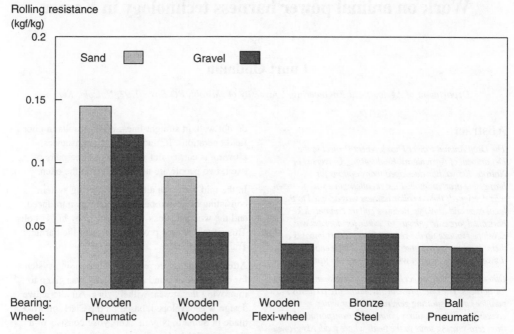

Figure 3: Rolling resistance for different wheels and bearings
(rolling resistance was calculated as draft force in kgf divided by load in kg)

because their size creates good roll-over characteristics: the cart rolls over uneven places in the road instead of bumping into all the holes and depressions. This reduces the necessary pulling force and the burden on the oxen. The major disadvantage, however, is the high weight of these wheels which can be 65–100 kg each depending on the diameter, materials used and configuration.

The results produced so far with the flexi-wheels have been very encouraging: there have been no punctures, and the shock absorbency and rolling characteristics have been good. In comparative tests on a sandy surface, the rolling resistance (draft force/total load) for the combination of flexi-wheels with wooden bearings was 0.075 kgf/kg compared with 0.030 kgf/kg for the combination of pneumatic tyres with roller (ball) bearings (Figure 3). The good rolling characteristics of the big flexi-wheels largely compensates for their extra weight and the friction of wooden bearing blocks.

As yet insufficient data are available to predict the life-span of these flexi-wheels, but it is hoped to study several different flexi-wheel designs in the near future.

Adaptability of the TDAU ox cart

The standard design of the TDAU ox cart, with a hardwood body, wooden bearings and flexi-wheels, can easily be adapted to suit locally available materials and manufacturing possibilities, the particular local conditions and customers' specific requirements. For example, the body could be made from another kind of wood or have different dimensions. Land Rover wheels could be used instead of the flexi-wheels.

Conclusion

The design of the TDAU ox cart is still being improved, but it can already be produced mainly with locally available materials by a carpenter and blacksmith in a rural area. Only a few parts, such as shafts, grease-pots and some wheel parts, would have to be supplied by a better equipped (urban) workshop.

Therefore the TDAU ox cart can be part of the solution to the transport problem in the rural areas of Zambia.

Work on animal power harness technology in Kenya

by

Luurt Oudman

Department of Agricultural Engineering, University of Nairobi, PO Box 30197, Nairobi, Kenya

Abstract

The Draft Animal Power Development Project in the Department of Agricultural Engineering, University of Nairobi, Kenya, has developed many options for harnessing draft animals. First an alternative yoke for oxen was developed; then a collar harness was adapted to the local oxen and donkeys. Because collars can only take horizontal forces lengthwise, a saddle for donkeys was developed to take up the vertical forces a cart imposes on them; it comes with a breeching strap which enables the donkey to brake the cart when it is going too fast.

Other work by the project has been on developing panniers for donkeys. The ones presently available are a canvas pannier for transporting general goods or water containers, a canvas slurry pannier for transporting slurry from zero-grazing units to the fields where fodder is grown, and a steel frame saddle with hooks for attaching metal baskets or bundles of fodder grass.

Yokes

Since the first introduction of ox cultivation in Kenya early this century, the harnessing system has hardly been changed. Double withers yokes (also known as neck yokes: see Photo 1) are common: they are cheap and easy to construct. Generally farmers use a long wooden pole with sticks through it to separate and link the animals. The centre of the yoke has a ring or U-bolt to which implements can be attached by a chain. This kind of yoke is seldom adapted to the shape of the withers (base of the neck) and the contact area is very small, thus creating a lot of pressure on the animal's skin which in turn leads to discomfort and even injury. Oxen are steered using verbal commands with the help of sticks. If the animals are not properly trained they do not walk in straight lines, which results in poor field operations. If, under these circumstances, plowing is carried out with two or three pairs of oxen, two people are needed to guide the oxen.

In the mid-1970s an alternative steering system consisting of nose ropes and reins was introduced, and the wooden sticks were replaced by big U-bolts. This system is now promoted through the Farmers Training Centres.

After studying improvements of harnessing systems for oxen in Africa and Asia, priority was given to improving the present withers yoke. An alternative design was developed, based on the Clarkson Yoke, made in Samaru, Nigeria. This yoke consists of a smoothly finished square piece of timber about 125 cm long, 10 cm wide and 10–15 cm thick.

The areas of the yoke which bear on the animals are 75–90 cm apart and contoured to the shape of the oxen's necks. The yoke is kept in position by two loops made of conduit pipe or round bar which are angled forward to clear the animals' throats and are adjustable by means of spring pins. Not only is the new yoke contoured to the shape of the neck, which provides a much larger contact area, but the shaped areas are also covered with pads made of canvas filled with tail hair. The "improved" yoke does not cost much more than the traditional one in terms of materials, especially when traditional wooden sticks (also known as skegs, skeis or staves) are used instead of round bars, but does take more time to make (Dibbits, 1985).

Collar harness for oxen

It took a long time before there was any progress in the development of collar harnesses for oxen (and donkeys). Lack of experience with this type of harness, and lack of documentation about existing designs. caused the slow start. The old harness-making tradition in Europe was transferred from father to son and was therefore never recorded.

First, two collar harnesses made in Germany were borrowed from the Department of Agricultural Engineering of Egerton College (now Egerton University). These collars were designed for humpless oxen and were unsuitable for the zebu

Photo 1: Double yoke built at University of Nairobi

Photo: Luurt Oudman

"Improving animal traction technology"

*Photo 2: Collar harness for oxen
(note the use of nose-rings)*

breeds in Kenya. However, a study of them revealed a great deal of information about the unwritten technology. Mr W L Micuta, of the Bellerive Foundation of Geneva, Switzerland, assisted in the construction of the first two collar harnesses: he derived his knowledge from harness makers in that country (Micuta, 1985).

The collar harness (Photo 2) consists of the collar itself and accessories such as a hump strap, a back strap, a tail strap, draft traces, a swingle tree, a double tree and a bridle or halter. The collar consists of a left and a right hame, upper and lower hame straps to keep the two hames together, shoulder pads to protect the animal's shoulders from rubbing by the hames and a neck pad to keep the collar at the right height. The straps are all adjustable to fit the most common sizes of draft animals. The draft traces conduct the draft force from the hames to the implement through a swingle tree. The swingle tree allows the collar to move slightly with the shoulders of the animal when it is walking. These movements are important to prevent the collar rubbing on the animal's skin. If a pair of animals is employed, a double tree or evener is also used to balance the forces of the two animals.

The lumber strap, back strap, tail strap and side strap combination suspends the draft ropes, mainly to prevent the ropes from becoming entangled with the legs of the animal while it is working (Ogweno and Oudman, 1990). The halter consists of a number of straps and rings; reins are connected to these rings to enable the ox to be steered from behind. Oxen which do not respond to a halter with a tight nose strap should be ringed. The reins are then extended to the nose-ring. Gentle pulling of the nose-ring is usually enough to steer the oxen.

The departmental oxen, which were trained using the traditional yoke, accepted the collar harness immediately. The harnesses have been used at the university for several years, but they have not yet been widely adopted by farmers in Kenya.

Collar harness for donkeys

The first development in the attempt to improve the harnessing system for donkeys was the construction of a few breast bands. However, the breast of a donkey slants and a breast band does not fit properly, as it does on horses. Although not ideal, a breast band could be used for light work, such as pulling a light cart; it is not considered suitable for heavy work. Therefore, further attention was given to the development of a collar harness which would enable farmers to use donkeys for cultivation in light and medium-heavy soils.

The first collars for donkeys were constructed in 1983. Thereafter, the departmental donkeys were trained and the collars were modified based on the experiences with our own donkeys and those of farmers.

The donkey collar (Photo 3) has the same parts as the ox collar: the differences are only in size and shape. The bridle looks like the ox halter extended with a bit and two mouth plates. Donkeys, like horses, have an open space in the mouth where a bit can fit. A bridle with such a bit is a very useful part of the harness when it comes to training donkeys and for easy control after training. The collar and the bridle are sufficient for pulling agricultural implements, but for pulling a cart a back-saddle and a breeching strap are needed. The back-saddle with its girth and shaft-holding straps takes up the downward, and sometimes upward, loads of the shafts. The breeching strap allows the donkey to apply a braking force comfortably and efficiently whenever the cart tends to run into the donkey.

Photo 3: Collar harnessing system for donkeys

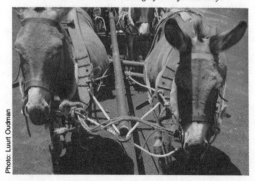

Photo 4: Two donkeys with collar harnesses pulling a wagon. The wagon has drum brakes on the rear wheels while the donkeys can brake with their breeching straps

Photo 5: Four donkeys pulling a cart. The rear ones have a collar and a saddle. The front ones have only a collar

Such a complete harness which satisfies the principles of efficiency and comfort is not cheap to make, in terms of materials or labour. A harness for carting (collar, saddle and accessories) presently costs 950 Kenyan Shillings (Ksh). This includes the cost of materials with an additional 30% of the material cost attributed to labour. By comparison, a pair of plowing collars for two donkeys costs KSh 850 and a pair of collars for oxen KSh 1250. (At time of writing in January 1992, the value of the Kenyan Shilling was about KSh 33 = US$ 1.)

If two donkeys are needed for a cart, because of steep terrain, the cost of harnessing doubles. The second donkey can only work effectively if it is harnessed in the same way as the first. This means that the cart should be provided with three shafts and that both donkeys should wear a collar and a saddle, at a cost of KSh 1900.

The same donkeys in front of a wagon require a harnessing system costing KSh 1000, as a plowing set is needed plus two breeching straps. These breeching straps are attached to the collars and the collars are attached in turn to a ring at the front end of the pole which steers the wagon. If the wagon tends to overrun the donkeys, the pole will pull at the collars (by means of nylon ropes which are slackened when the animals pull) and the donkeys are thus able to resist that pull with their breeching straps (Photo 4). The same applies to oxen, at a harnessing cost of KSh 1400.

If four donkeys are needed in front of a cart (Photo 5), the principles for cart and wagon harnessing as outlined above can be combined. The rear donkeys are harnessed in the regular way as for a two-donkey cart. To accommodate the front donkeys properly, the centre shaft should be extended by a pipe which slides into the shaft for about 50 cm and is secured by a pin. This pipe has a

ring at the front end to which the collars of the front donkeys are attached by means of nylon ropes. These donkeys are equipped with breeching straps attached to the collars only, but no saddles. While pulling is done with these collars through traces, swingle trees and a double tree attached to a hook under the pipe right in front of the coupling with the centre shaft, braking is also possible with the same collars and the attached breeching straps. This solution is rather expensive on harnessing (KSh 1900 + KSh 1000 = KSh 2900). For oxen the expense would be KSh 3500, comprising KSh 2500 for two plowing sets and KSh 1000 for two ox saddles.

Panniers

Project work on developing panniers for transporting goods, water and slurry is continuing.

A canvas pannier is undergoing tests at missions in remote areas for transporting goods and water. It is basically a strong, weatherproof canvas cloth spread across the back and sides of a donkey. The cloth has a pocket at each end for carrying assorted goods or water containers. The pockets have been reinforced with leather strips. Underneath the cloth, and stitched to it, are pieces of leather with straps for fastening the pannier to the animal.

The slurry pannier (Photo 6) is made of the same material, but it has a few extras for easy loading and unloading. The slurry is scooped into a square wooden box which has a metal screen for collecting straw and other coarse material which could clog the drain pipe. It then drains into 40 litre closed pockets on either side of the donkey. The pockets taper at the bottom into short canvas hoses which conduct the slurry through PVC elbows into a PVC pipe which has a hole halfway along its length (Photo 7). A second, shorter pipe with a similar hole is put

Photo: Luurt Oudman

Photo: Luurt Oudman

Photo 8: Steel frame saddle pannier on a model donkey

Photo 6: Slurry panier to transport slurry from the stable to the field

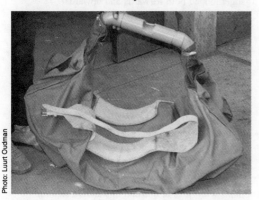

Photo: Luurt Oudman

Photo 7: The slurry pannier upside down to show the saddle part and the two concentric PVC pipes which regulate the flow

around the first one. With this arrangement the flow of slurry can be regulated by rotating the outer pipe to change the alignment of the two holes.

The slurry pannier is intended for farmers with a zero-grazing unit. If they own (or can hire) a donkey and a slurry pannier they can conveniently take slurry to the field where the fodder is grown. It is recommended to prepare furrows along the rows of Napier grass ahead of time. When the donkey is led through these furrows, the slurry can be dropped in them without spillage. The nutrient losses will be minimal if the furrows are closed within a few hours after application of the slurry.

The third pannier would also be of interest to the zero-grazing farmer. It consists of a steel frame saddle with two hooks on either side (Photo 8) to which metal baskets can be attached for carrying groceries or other goods from the market. Also, bundles of fodder can be attached to the hooks and transported from the field to the zero-grazing unit. The full potential of this pannier is yet to be discovered.

References

Dibbits H J, 1985. *Animal draft power development project. Progress Report 1*. Department of Agricultural Engineering, University of Nairobi, Nairobi, Kenya. 36p.

Micuta W, 1985. The Swiss Collar, a harness for developing countries. *Agriculture International* 37(4):130–135.

Ogweno S and Oudman L, 1990. *Step by step guide to making collar harnesses*. Department of Agricultural Engineering, University of Nairobi, Nairobi, Kenya.

A note on a donkey harnessing problem and innovation in Zimbabwe

by

Peta A Jones

Teaching and Consultancy Services, Private Bag 5713, Binga, Zimbabwe

Abstract

The only animal-drawn cart available to ordinary farmers in Zimbabwe (the two-wheel, single-shaft "scotchcart") is not suitable for use with two harnessed donkeys: the cart has a long draw pole designed to be pulled by an ox yoke. There are no attachments to allow the donkeys to draw from the cart itself. Moreover, because the cart has only two wheels, a poorly distributed load can force the shaft down, placing great weight on the donkeys' necks. As a result, efficiency can be reduced to such an extent that a third donkey is needed, making the whole thing lop-sided and awkward.

A new method of harnessing donkeys to the cart is described in this paper. It uses a breast band harness on the hind quarters of the animal in addition to the breast band over the chest; this second harness acts as both breach strap and saddle. Chains from this harness are then attached to swingles and eveners at both back and front.

This new harness is cheap and easy to make, and should dramatically improve the donkeys' performance. This innovation has yet to be fully tested by farmers, but it is hoped that it will be accepted quickly and subsequently widely adopted by donkey owners.

The problem

An ordinary farmer in Zimbabwe currently has access to only one kind of animal-drawn vehicle—the two-wheel, single-shaft "scotchcart" (Figure 1). This cart is designed for oxen. Some models are smaller than others and could be used by smaller animals such as donkeys but even these are basically "ox carts" not "donkey carts". Most have little or no provision for a pulling point in the middle of the front of the cart. Often they only have hooks at the outside front corners, with bars running from these corners to a point some distance up the shaft. The shaft, or disselboom, ends with a metal gadget looped both forwards and upwards (Figure 1). Most scotchcarts are modified in some way by their users.

For donkeys, the farmer again has access to only one type of harness, mass-produced to a standard size (although two sizes are sometimes available) and made of strips of rubberised canvas machine or conveyor belting, bolted together (Photo 1). The only way to adapt this harness is to move the bolts, but making big enough holes in the belting is extremely difficult without proper tools, and most farmers do not try. When the belting breaks, it is mended with wire.

Chains with rings at one end in standard size for donkeys are also widely obtainable, but the design of the scotchcart does not seem to lend itself to any easy attachment of two harnessed donkeys. The usual solution is to attach the donkeys to the front of the shaft by the centre of a shared wooden yoke under their necks, linked over their necks by a belt (Photo 1). The cart is pulled by chains attached—in four places for two donkeys—to a single pole wired

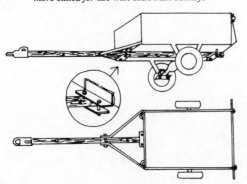

Figure 1: Standard Zimbabwe "scotchcart" more suited for use with oxen than donkeys

Photo 1: An example of "the problem": the common and inefficient system of harnessing donkeys to "scotchcarts" in Zimbabwe

Photo: Paul Starkey

"Improving animal traction technology"

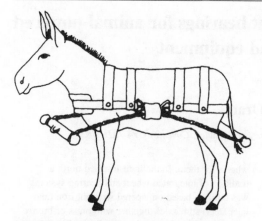

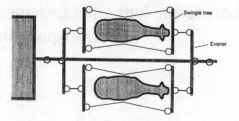

Figure 3: System of arranging swingle trees and eveners for cart pulling

Figure 2: Donkey harnessed with a breast strap and with a second breast strap used as a breech strap, both fitted with swingles

by the farmer at right angles to the shaft and firmly to the front of the cart. Very often, three donkeys are used abreast, so the whole thing becomes lop-sided, with two donkeys on one side of the shaft, and only one on the other.

As the cart has only two wheels, the level of the front of the shaft depends very much on the distribution of the cart's load, and the weight on the donkeys' necks can be considerable, reducing their efficiency to such an extent that a third donkey is often required. In addition, the carts are used without a breech band to take the weight of the cart on down slopes: the yoke takes it all. Only a donkey's patience could endure all this.

Aside from the obvious effect on the donkeys, it does not take sophisticated instruments to detect that the whole thing is awkward and inefficient. The donkeys strain and stumble, even with an empty cart.

Solutions

One might recommend harness and collars whose production is well within the capability of village technology (Jones, 1991). However, farmers are not looking for radical changes and farmers themselves are not necessarily skilled craft workers. Even if they were technically competent in the skills of collar production, they would have little time to make what they need.

A compromise needs to be sought between what is known, what is easily obtainable, and what is most comfortable for the donkey and can thus lead to greater efficiency. The criteria should obviously be ease of contrivance, speed of contrivance and cheapness.

A method developed by the author and a neighbour involves using a breast-band harness on the hind quarters of the donkey in addition to the one over the chest. The one at the back then acts as both breech strap and saddle, although it lacks a girth (see Figure 2). This does not seem to be much of a problem at the moment; perhaps at some later stage a saddle-girth arrangement could be suggested, which would also solve the problem of the crossing chains against the animal's sides. At the moment, a simple hessian sleeve is the proposed solution for this: this seems uncomplicated and appears to work well.

Additional swingles and an evener are, of course, correspondingly required at the front (Figure 3). There is nothing difficult about these, they are the same as those required for the back. The real problem is finding a part of the cart on which to attach the back evener.

Transferring the technology

Given the dramatic improvement in the donkeys' performance, and also the availability of the materials and technology, it is hoped that donkey owners will adopt the method widely and quickly. The extra expense is minimal—not more than 20 Zimbabwe dollars (≈US$ 4) a donkey at current prices—and would soon be recouped as a result of the increased efficiency.

The drawings included in this paper are to be incorporated into an extension leaflet for wide distribution. The donkey manual (Jones, 1991) will also be updated. A short video illustrating this harnessing technology has been made and enquiries about this may be addressed to the author.

Reference

Jones P A, 1991. *Training course manual on the use of donkeys in agriculture in Zimbabwe*. Agritex Institute of Agricultural Engineering, Borrowdale, Harare, Zimbabwe. 81p.

Low technology rolling-element bearings for animal-powered transport and equipment

C E Oram

Development Technology Unit, University of Warwick, Coventry CV4 7AL, UK

Abstract

Conventional bearings used in animal-powered machinery have been of two types: either plain boundary-lubricated bearings made of wood or brass running on steel shafts, or high technology rolling-element bearings made from vacuum degassed steel and imported from the industrialised nations of the "north". Both types have been found to be wanting in ease of manufacture and use, availability and cost, or longevity and maintenance.

Work carried out in the past 10 years at the University of Warwick suggests that cheap and relatively easily manufactured rolling-element (anti-friction) bearings can be made from common materials such as cold-rolled steel bar, malleable-iron water pipe and plywood. Present indications are that these bearings can have lives well in excess of those required for typical animal carts and indeed for many other applications as well.

One advantage of such bearings is that, apart from some raw material, all manufacturing could take place in the country and, in many cases, the locality of use. In most countries of the "south" today, difficulties with foreign exchange are crucial to the success of new technologies, and retaining labour costs in the locality of use can be highly beneficial. In many situations the costs of moving parts, and in particular the costs of obtaining and fitting bearings, are a major component of the final cost of the product. In some cases as much as 40% of the net price to the manufacturer can be attributed to bearings. Clearly the profitability of manufacturing and operating carts, implements and machinery will be influenced by these high costs. Re-inventing the wheel, or at least the rolling-element wheel bearing, promises to result in substantial reductions in net vehicle or implement operating costs. This paper outlines some of the thinking behind the University of Warwick Development Technology Unit's work in this area and some of the tests and experiments that have been conducted by it.

Introduction

The history of the animal cart is an old one and today a very large number are in use worldwide. The largest concentrations are found in the Indian subcontinent and efforts are being made to spread the extensive use of animal traction to most African countries as well.

An historical problem for all carts has been the provision of bearings and, to a lesser extent, the wheels for them. In the industrialised north a tradition of integrated wheel and bearing systems was built up based on tapered wrought iron (and later steel) stub axles together with brass or bronze bushes mounted in wooden wheels (Sturt, 1943). These tapered bearings allowed the running clearance to be adjusted by varying the wheels' axial positions on the axles using washers and wedges. Although these systems were quite successful there was interest in reducing both the wear and the friction of the bearings of animal-drawn vehicles, both from the point of view of reductions in maintenance and from considerations of the fatigue of the animals used. The advent of commercial rolling-element bearings in the early part of this century (such bearings were developed and introduced primarily for factory use) eclipsed plain bearing systems and replaced them within only a few years. The advantages of the new rolling bearings were their low friction, particularly on starting, and their low wear and long life. These bearings made it possible, for the first time, to "fit and forget".

In the intermediate technologies intended for Third World countries, problems with the provision, installation and maintenance of conventional rolling-element bearings are well known. While the costs of deep-groove ball races of the sizes fitted to, say, the Land Rover, are tolerable in Nigeria or Kenya, in many other countries even these sizes are expensive and difficult to obtain.

Use of conventional rolling-element bearings in Third World applications generates further problems during design and manufacture. Careful design may be required to avoid early bearing failure through misalignment and bearing fight. Another problem concerns the accuracy with which the bearing seats and housings can be made in a workshop of limited capacity and operator skill level. Conventional bearings are lifed on the basis that they are mounted on shafts and in housings that control their running clearances. For example, a 50 mm shaft should be finished to an accuracy of perhaps 0.05 mm. This is on the limit of what can be achieved by a good operator with a single point tool in a good lathe. The author has personal experience, in one African country, of 115 mm shafts, made from galvanised water pipe, which were not only not round but which were tapered and in error by about 0.35 mm on diameter after being worked on by a good operator on a good lathe.

What is required is a bearing that is not much more difficult to manufacture than a wooden bearing installation and yet can function for long periods when badly misaligned and poorly lubricated. Animal cart bearings do have some easy features: loads are reasonably modest, and speeds are slow by comparison with many other bearing applications. Also, much higher wear can be tolerated than is commonly possible in conventional applications, so the criterion of bearing failure can be relaxed. (In the present work "failure" means jamming that cannot be rectified by cleaning and relubrication.)

The issue of the place of manufacture is important and has implications for the effective cost of many animal-based technologies. Many authors (Starkey (1988), for example) have detailed the difficulties experienced by emergent farmers with inappropriately designed equipment manufactured overseas, or in some distant location. These authors make clear the point that local design and manufacture enable more effective communication between manufacturer and customer and more ready modification of poor design and repair of existing equipment.

The author became aware of the difficulties in using conventional rolling bearing while working in Botswana in 1982. He carried out a short research project (Oram, 1983) based on the idea that rolling-element bearings made of less than ideal materials might be adequate in some circumstances. He had made pantograph bearings from mild steel in the 1970s and there were other precedents for alternative materials. Some industrial castors and wheelbarrow wheels have rolling-element bearings of low-carbon steel, and the UK company Bearings Non Lube Ltd has been making rolling-element bearings from thermoplastics for some years for many industries including food and photographic process applications. Races of these bearings are made of polyacetyl, and balls of stainless steel, glass or nylon. The races are often moulded to include some other component, for example, a wheel or roller, with the bearing. The author's tests were made on bearings of black mild steel plate and bright drawn round bar. Bearings were of 160 mm inner race diameter with 20 mm diameter rollers 19 mm or so long; loads were up to 7 kN; and

speeds were about 150 rpm. The test was terminated after about two million revolutions by jamming caused by conflict between axially and radially disposed rollers, a crossed roller format of orthogonal rollers and races having been erroneously used.

Since that time a number of other students (Godden, 1986; Austin, 1987; Mascia, 1989) have worked on alternative rolling-element bearings, including crossed roller bearings, needle roller bearings, a cylindrical roller thrust bearing, bearings consisting of steel strip tyres on wooden backings and bearings with wooden races only. Results of tests on such bearings have been encouraging. Even at high loadings on the edge of plasticity, bearings have survived for periods adequate for animal-power applications and in most cases tests have been suspended because of the time taken for testing, rather than because the bearing failed. The author thus believes that these bearings merit further attention and may offer the solution to some bearing problems.

The present approach marks a change from a conventional approach to bearing provision, namely using highly selected materials, to one of using only those materials that are more readily available and to accepting that performance will be adversely affected. Although it would be possible to investigate and promote the use of modest hardening processes, for example, case hardening of the bearing components, pressure for this has been resisted because it is felt that problems will arise with quality control during such processes; and in any case additional work such as this is unlikely to be cost-effective in terms of the potential material saving.

Conventional bearing approaches

Conventional bearings used for vehicle wheels reflect the choice open to designers of most machinery: use either plain bearings or anti-friction or rolling-element bearings.

Plain bearings are used in two operating modes: either as directly rubbing bearings where intimate contact is made between the bush and the shaft throughout operation or, with higher speeds and in the presence of a suitable lubricant, the load may be carried by a viscous film which completely separates shaft and bush. Under the latter conditions no wear takes place. This latter mode of operation is called hydrodynamic and unfortunately usually requires conditions which cannot be met in animal transport applications. At intermediate speeds contact may exist and thus wear can occur.

Plain bearings exhibit high friction at start and at low speed but may have effective friction coefficients lôwer than those of anti-friction bearings at high speeds when operating in the hydrodynamic mode. They are capable of accepting a small amount of permanent misalignment and inaccuracy in manufacture and assembly by both plastic deformation and wearing in or "running in". They are not good at tolerating loss of lubricant but may have lubricant supplied fairly reliably over a long period by porous bushes or other absorbent material in the vicinity. Careful choice of materials for the shaft and bush is necessary to ensure that operation in the rubbing mode does not result in "pick up" of one surface by the other, ie, localised welding of one surface to the other which can cause very rapid wear. It is usual to make shafts of a hardish material such as steel and bushes of softer material such as white metal (an alloy of lead and tin) or brass. Because of the generous area of contact between shaft and bush they are tolerant of shock and abuse, even with modest material quality.

Wooden bearings have a special place in animal transport bearing technology and have been, and are being, investigated for this application. Intermediate Technology Transport Ltd and the Technology Development Advisory Unit in Zambia have carried out investigations into timber selection and oil impregnation. Difficulties have been expressed regarding timber selection, wear and dirt and lubricant sealing, but some organisations are happy with their performance. Conventional rolling-element bearings have characteristics complementary to those of plain bearings. They are tolerant of interruption in lubricant supply and have low friction throughout the speed range. They are not good in situations of shock and misalignment and never "wear in" so that a misalignment set during manufacture or assembly is present throughout the life of the bearing. As stated above they depend for their running clearances on their fit onto the shaft and into the housing and are especially vulnerable to tight fits in conjunction with misalignment and axial loads. A notable trend in the automotive area is the adoption of "integrated hub bearing" configurations such as those used on the Fiat Panda and the Saab 9000 series passenger cars where, under particular space pressure, both outer and inner bearing races have been extended to provide bolted fixing points to the suspension system and to the wheel hub. These integrated systems reduce assembly costs and the dangers of bearing fitting. One company has introduced the Fiat Panda bearing for animal-drawn carts with mixed success.

Stress analysis of rolling-element bearings

Hertz was the first mathematician to devise an analytical basis for determining stresses in the contact areas of "higher pairs" or nonconformal surfaces. He developed expressions for both compressive stress and shear stress which show that shear stress reaches a maximum of 0.304 of the maximum compressive stresses at a depth of 0.78 times the contact strip half width (for parallel cylindrical bodies). Maximum compressive stress is given by:

$$\sigma = \left(\frac{F}{\pi L} \times \frac{\dfrac{1}{r_1} + \dfrac{1}{r_2}}{\dfrac{(1 - v_1^2)}{E_1} + \dfrac{(1 - v_2^2)}{E_2}} \right)^{\frac{1}{2}}$$

Transforming this equation to show the maximum roller load when yield stress is reached gives:

$$F = \pi L \sigma_y^2 \left(\frac{\dfrac{(1 - v_1^2)}{E_1} + \dfrac{(1 - v_2^2)}{E_2}}{\dfrac{1}{r_1} + \dfrac{1}{r_2}} \right)$$

The half width b of the contact strip is given by:

$$b = \left(\frac{4F}{\pi L} \left[\frac{\dfrac{(1 - v_1^2)}{E_1} + \dfrac{(1 - v_2^2)}{E_2}}{\dfrac{1}{r_1} + \dfrac{1}{r_2}} \right] \right)^{\frac{1}{2}}$$

where:
σ is compressive stress
σ_y is compressive stress at yield
v is Poisson's ratio
F is roller load
L is roller length
r is roller radius
E is Young's modulus or material stiffness
The subscripts denote the two materials.

Examination of these equations shows that roller load at the point of plasticity rises with the square of material hardness (or yield stress) and inversely as material stiffness. Table 1 shows the load to just produce plasticity and the contact strip half width for a range of candidate bearing materials. The effect of Young's modulus is striking in the case of polyacetyl bearings where the low stiffness allows relatively large contact areas and low stresses. Clearly, permissible loads on intermediate technology roller bearings are very modest by

Table 1: Alternative bearing materials and bearing loads

Material	Young's modulus (MPa)	Compressive yield stress (MPa)	Poisson's ratio[1]	Roller load[2] at three times yield stress (N)	Contact strip half width at yield (mm)
Bearing steel	210 000	1 850	0.29	10 049	0.10
Mild steel	210 000	350	0.29	360	0.02
Galvanised water pipe	210 000	195	0.28	112	0.01
Aluminium	70 000	200	0.36	335	0.03
Brass	100 000	400	0.33	960	0.04
Wood	20 000	50	0.45	67	0.02
Polyacetyl	3 000	65	0.35	832	0.24

[1] For wood this is heavily dependent on orientation: average figure taken from Beaver (1986)
[2] For 25 mm diameter shaft and 10 mm diameter rollers each 10 mm long

comparison with those that may be applied to bearings made of conventional bearing steel. As a comparison, conventional roller bearings for 25 mm shafts have static ratings of about 10 000 N, and ball bearings a static rating of about 4000 N. Notwithstanding the greatly reduced potential loading, reasonable loads can be carried provided enough race area is available. This may not be too difficult (see the bearings shown in Figures 1 and 2). In essence we are replacing small bearings of good material with larger ones of poorer material.

No discussion has so far been made of multiple roller contact. Manufacturing accuracy in conventional ball and roller bearings allows loads, both radial and axial, to be carried by more than one rolling element. Stribeck, in the middle of this

century, and those after him, assumed that all rolling elements in a thrust bearing, or half of them in a radially loaded bearing, carried load (Allan, 1945; Barwell, 1979). This situation is not likely with intermediate technology rolling-element bearings where manufacturing accuracy is low. A roller would be completely unloaded by making it smaller than the others in the set by a small fraction of the dimensions shown in the last column of Table 1. Nevertheless it is probable that more than one element is under load at any instant, simply from considerations of kinematic stability. Observations of test bearings at Warwick indicate that three rollers normally support the load. There is an argument that in intermediate technology bearings a certain amount of "running in" or plastic deformation could take place so that the outer race might become a

Figure 1: Proposed low technology rolling-element bearing hub for carts using old rims of the Land Rover type

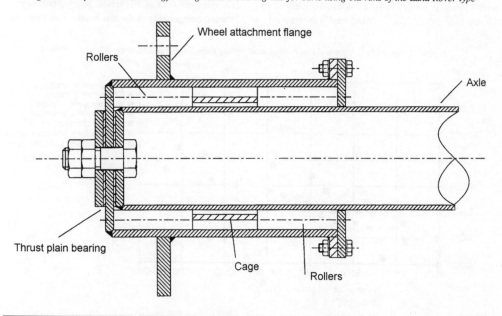

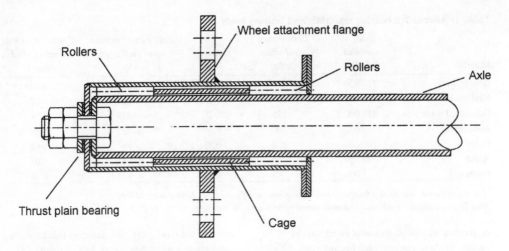

Figure 2: Proposed low technology rolling-element bearing for passenger car rims

better fit to the roller profile. This effect might well improve misaligned operation also.

All work in the present programme has centred on the use of cylindrical roller bearings because of both ease of manufacture and the low potential load carrying capacity of intermediate technology ball bearings.

Intermediate technology rolling-element bearings

Experimental work at Warwick

Figure 3 shows data from a series of tests by Mascia (1989). Experiments were conducted on bearings with 26 mm diameter shafts and with nominally 10 mm long rollers. The imposed load was obtained by spring balance and was maintained at 500 N throughout all tests except those with a caged bearing on which the load was 400 N because the caged rollers were only 8 mm long. Rotational frequency was maintained at 500 rpm in nearly all tests. Wear in these tests, in which race stresses probably approached yield for most of the time, was about 2 microns/million revolutions when using free machining mild steel obtained in the UK, except for the anomalous test with the full cage, when the rate of wear was very high. No pursuit of this anomaly was made because it was thought that little use would be made of cages in low technology anti-friction bearings.

In some early tests in this series, pick-up between locating components in the test bearings and loss of

Figure 3: Wear of experimental low-carbon steel rolling element bearings (Source: Mascia, 1989)

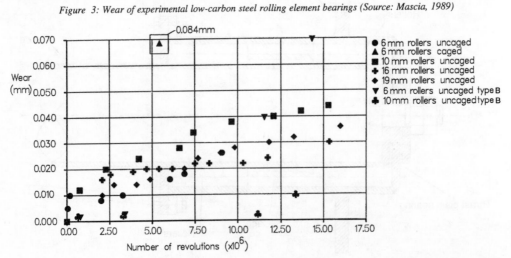

lubricant resulted in the races being polluted with large amounts of steel swarf. The "Type B" bearing cited in Figure 3 contained brass washers to prevent this pick-up.

A figure of 15 million revolutions required for bearing life was arrived at by assuming that a cart travels 20 km daily for 200 days per year over a 10 year life.

Other work has included tests on naked wooden outer races and outer races of wood with 1.6 mm and 3 mm steel surfaces. In one such test an outer race of 200 mm diameter carried a load of 40 kN for 1000 revolutions and although it sustained some damage this was essentially exaggerated by flaws existing before tests started.

A bearing made of parallel discs of 18 mm birch plywood, to a total axial length of about 110 mm, successfully carried a load of about 3.5 kN for many hours as part of an animal-powered gear experiment. Its use illustrates the ease with which a solution can be obtained with intermediate technology bearings. No other solution was readily possible using conventional bearings.

Provisional designs

Figures 1 and 2 show cross-sections of provisional designs of wheel hub for carts using wheels from passenger cars or four-wheel drive vehicles such as Land Rovers. Radial load is carried by small diameter rollers of almost needle-roller proportions, disposed in two separated bearings to cater for the out-of-plane moments arising from cornering or running on cambered roads. Plain bearings cater for axial loads in both cases for simplicity. A small volume of oil should be able to lodge in the hubs to provide long-term lubrication. Not shown in either Figure 1 or 2 is any form of dirt or oil seal. Leather will probably be used in proposed tests in Nigeria.

A major constraint, especially with the hub intended for use with the car rims, was the overall diameter of the hub. Passenger car rims have only a small hole about 60 mm in diameter in their middle to accept the hub and it is preferable to position the rim in the middle of the hub axially in order to equalise load on the two bearings. Alternative configurations, able to cope with small wheel holes, are possible but are a little more complicated to construct and will not be investigated in the present programme until proven necessary. To date all designs have used steel components throughout. Testing of these hubs has already started.

Other uses of low technology rolling-element bearings

Other applications include hand carts and pedal-powered farm and urban vehicles for transporting passengers and goods on farms or in towns. Such bearings could also be used in crop processing machinery, wind turbines, water pumping turbines and hydropower plants. Another application that the author has been working on is stationary animal-powered gears for water pumping, crop processing and the like. This requires large torques.

Further work

Much further work is required. All designs to date have been in steel and have involved machining of either races or rollers or both. A suggestion by Hawkins (1992) is to fabricate the outer race from strip or wire around a former and freeze the final assembly by welding or other means. This might allow serious production of bearings for slow speed use without any machining and would thus enlarge substantially the number of potential manufacturers. It is envisaged that one major advantage of such bearings would be the possibility of local manufacture so that repair of hardware would be more readily achievable and better contact and feedback between manufacturer and customer possible.

Table 1 suggests that materials other than steel, in particular components of brass, wood and possibly aluminium, might make good candidates for further work. A second material to avoid steel-on-steel contact would be beneficial, since this contact causes friction and wear in existing designs. Some slip is inevitable in all rolling contacts under load and there are many points where incidental and irregular contact takes place and pick-up is potentially possible.

Work is necessary to carry further the investigation of steel tyres or races mounted in wooden backings or structures. Work completed so far suggests that this approach may be successful; it would certainly save substantial amounts of steel. Again races of plywood have performed satisfactorily in some light duties on animal engine pulleys; this could be taken further.

Work is also required on dirt/abrasive material tolerance and wear. To date all bearings have been fairly clean and have run with oil or grease most of the time. Some use of vegetable or cooking oil has been made but this and anti-oxidant additives could be investigated.

In some countries large numbers of scrap motorcycle wheels are used. These wheels have bearings which may well be damaged during removal from the machine or during use on the cart. Light motorcycle (eg, Honda 200 cc) wheels usually have integral brake drums of steel cast into the aluminium hub. These brake surfaces may make adequate bearing surfaces.

Research is under way at Warwick on a number of these issues and some results are published in the MSc thesis of Umara (1992).

Conclusions

Present bearing technologies using either locally made wooden bearings or rolling-element bearings imported from industrialised countries have shortcomings: in the case of the former, bearing life may be short; and in the latter case foreign exchange and skilled labour supply may be a problem. Rolling-element bearings made from materials usually fairly readily available may be able to fill the price/performance gap between these two bearing choices. Preliminary work undertaken over the past 10 years in the Development Technology Unit in the UK suggests that this technology deserves further investigation.

References

Allan R K, 1945. *Rolling bearings*. Pitman, London, UK. 401p.

Austin M, 1987. *The development of a simply manufactured crossed roller bearing for animal drawn carts in Zambia.* Third Year Undergraduate Project Report. Department of Engineering, University of Warwick, Coventry, UK. 110p.

Barwell F T, 1979. *Bearing systems, principles and practice.* Oxford University Press, Oxford, UK. 565p.

Beaver M B, 1986. *Encyclopaedia of materials science and engineering.* Vol 7. Pergamon Press, Oxford, UK. pp. 5417–5418.

Godden P, 1986. *Simply manufactured crossed roller bearings: their design for use in animal drawn carts in Zambia.* Third Year Undergraduate Project Report. Department of Engineering, University of Warwick, Coventry, UK, 110p.

Hawkins A M, 1992. *Animal power units for developing countries.* MSc Thesis. Department of Engineering, University of Warwick, Coventry, UK, 150p.

Mascia A, 1989. *The analysis and testing of low carbon steel roller bearings for use and manufacture in developing countries.* Third Year Undergraduate Project Report. Department of Engineering, University of Warwick, Coventry, UK, 100p.

Oram C E, 1983. *Mild steel cylindrical roller bearings for developing countries and alternative technologies.* Third Year Undergraduate Project Report. Department of Engineering, University of Warwick, Coventry, UK. 202p.

Starkey P H, 1988. *Perfected yet rejected: animal-drawn wheeled toolcarriers.* Vieweg and Sohn, Braunschweig, Wiesbaden, Germany, for German Appropriate Technology Exchange, GTZ, Eschborn, Germany. 161p.

Sturt G, 1943. *The wheelwright's shop.* Cambridge University Press, Cambridge, UK. 236p.

Umara B, 1992. *Transportation in Nigeria and the development of intermediate technology rolling element bearings.* MSc Thesis. Department of Engineering, University of Warwick, Coventry, UK. 200p.

Photograph opposite
Logging with oxen in a forestry plantation in Malawi

"Improving animal traction technology"

Improving animal traction technology

Diversifying operations using animal power

Improving the efficiency of an animal-powered gear to meet the requirements of different machines

by

K Dippon[*]

Institute for Agricultural Engineering, University of Hohenheim (440)
Postfach 700572, 70593 Stuttgart, Germany

Abstract

The use of animal traction as an energy source for agricultural operations is one step in the mechanisation of agriculture in developing countries. An animal-powered gear, based on a double-friction wheel transmission, can be used to drive various machines (cereal mill, rice huller, oil press, etc). Based on the torque and speed requirements of these machines, and the power available from typical draft animals in Africa, the University of Hohenheim, Germany, has carried out research to determine the optimal configuration of the power transmission to achieve the best efficiency for a given combination of animal and machine. Using a 100 mm rough friction wheel with a pressing force of 500 N, an efficiency of more than 90% was obtained.

[*]*Subsequent address:*
Philippine-German Coconut Project
PO Box 297, 8000 Davao City, The Philippines

Objectives

The "Documentation, improvement and dissemination of animal-powered technology" project, sponsored by GATE (German Appropriate Technology Exchange, a division of the German agency for technical cooperation—GTZ) has introduced animal-powered machines in some West African countries (Burkina Faso, Mali, Niger, Senegal, Sierra Leone) and in Zambia (Franzke, 1991; TDAU, 1990). These machines should be used for mechanising agricultural operations in remote areas.

Most project activities focus on the use of animal-powered gears in cereal grinding mills (Photo 1) and water lifting devices. Using animals as a "motor" for cereal mills should relieve women of the strenuous work of pounding and reduce the time they spend each day making flour: to produce

Photo 1: An animal-powered mill being pulled by a horse in West Africa

Photo: Klaus Dippon

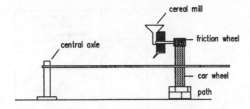

Figure 1: Drive unit of the animal-powered gear

the weekly flour requirement of a typical Zambian rural household takes about two hours of pounding a day (Löffler, 1990). The aim of the project is not to introduce animal traction where it is unknown, but to encourage the use of existing animals.

In Africa 90% of the draft animals are used for soil tillage (Busquets, 1986). Because this is a seasonal operation the animals only work for 40 days a year, on average. If animal traction is known and practised, the introduction of animal-powered gears allows animals to be used for longer periods, which should improve the economics of animal keeping.

The construction of the disseminated animal-powered gear is well adapted to rural conditions in developing countries. Most of the components are obtained from the local market, the only ones imported being high quality bearings which reduce frictional losses and guarantee continuous operation. Skilled local blacksmiths and craftsmen are capable of manufacturing the power transmission, and even the grinding stones of the cereal mill will be made locally in the near future.

Optimisation of the power transmission

Based on the analysis of the working performance of the actual model of the animal-powered gear and the intention to drive other machines with this system, one has to think about the most suitable friction wheel combination. Figure 1 is a general sketch of the drive unit of the animal-powered gear.

By changing the diameter, material and surface of the friction wheel, one can influence the main parameters (speed and transferable torque) of the power transmission depending on the pressing force between the two wheels. This was the main idea behind subsequent investigations at the Institute of Agricultural Engineering of the University of Hohenheim, Germany. The main aim was to identify at a given power (animal) the best combination for a specific case. Furthermore one should be able to give some information about the highest efficiency which can be achieved when operating a machine at a known speed and torque.

Test unit

To obtain realistic results, a copy of the animal-powered gear now in use was fabricated. It was powered by a tractor test unit which already existed on the camp of the institute. The animal-powered gear was mounted to the pivot of the tractor test unit. They were connected by a rope with integrated load cell. A torque transducer was attached to the output axle of the friction wheel. Next to this, a brake was placed to simulate the loading of the

Figure 2: Test unit for an animal-powered gear

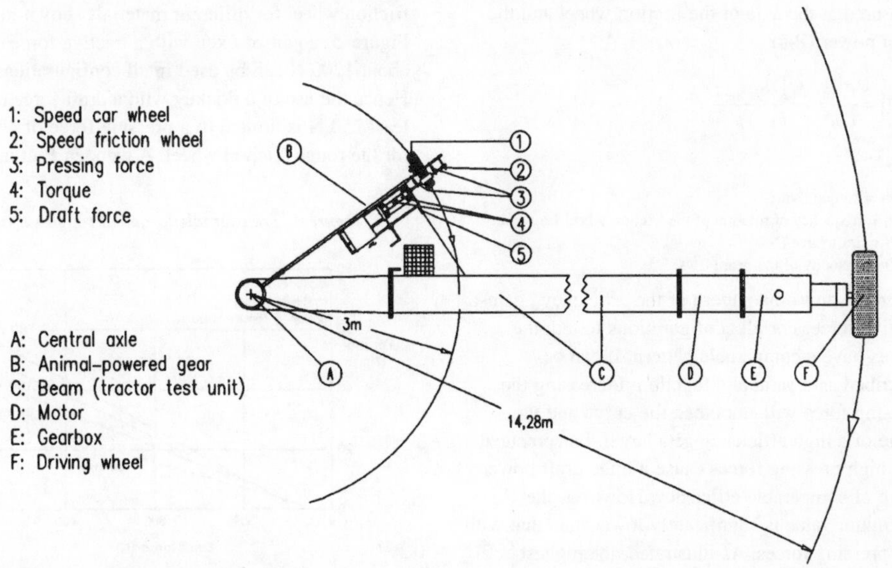

1: Speed car wheel
2: Speed friction wheel
3: Pressing force
4: Torque
5: Draft force

A: Central axle
B: Animal–powered gear
C: Beam (tractor test unit)
D: Motor
E: Gearbox
F: Driving wheel

3m

14,28m

power transmission. Between the axles of the wheels another two load cells were installed to measure the pressing force between them. The speed of the wheels was measured using two generators mounted on the axles of the wheels. All tests were carried out at a velocity of 1.1 m/s of the tractor test unit beam. Construction and arrangement of these components are shown in Figure 2.

Parameters investigated

The tests are based on the parameters listed below:

○ surface (smooth, rough)
○ diameter of friction wheel (60, 80, 100, 120 mm)
○ friction wheel material (steel, wood)
○ pressing force (300, 500, 1000, 1500, 2000 N)

Starting from the 120 mm friction wheel used in the actual animal-powered gear only smaller diameters were tested. Mounting wheels with smaller diameters will increase the speed available for the attached machine and also cause a smoother running at a reduced loading. The pressing force is directly proportional to the transferable power and was investigated in a range typical for animal traction.

During the test the brake was tightened continuously until the friction wheel slipped on the car wheel. All data were collected with an analog data logger and afterwards evaluated by suitable hard- and software.

Results

The most important parameter which characterises the power transmission is its efficiency. It is determined as the quotient of the power (P_{ab}) measured at the axle of the friction wheel and the input power (P_{zu}):

$$\eta = \frac{P_{ab}}{P_{zu}} = \frac{M_d \cdot n_{fr} \cdot 2\pi}{F_z \cdot V_R}$$

where:

M_d = torque (Nm)
n_{fr} = frequency of rotation of the friction wheel (revs/min)
F_z = draft force (N)
V_R = velocity of the beam (m/s)

Figure 3 shows the pattern of the efficiency against tractive force. For all configurations tested, the curves have a comparable pattern. It can be described as a parabolic function. Increasing the pressing force will smoothen the curve and the range of a high efficiency gets larger. For practical use, high pressing forces cause a huge draft power range of comparable efficiency. However, the maximum value is significantly lower than that with low pressing forces. As illustrated, the highest

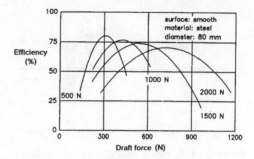

Figure 3: Efficiency of the 80 mm friction wheel at different pressing forces

efficiency of 81% for an 80 mm friction wheel at 500 N decreases to 69% at 2000 N pressing force.

Regarding the influence of the surface, one notices that the efficiency of rough surfaces is on the average 10 to 15% higher than the other ones. The maximum value of 92% was measured for the rough 100 mm friction wheel.

Taking into account all parameters, the 100 mm wheel shows the best efficiency.

If different machines should be powered, one has to consider the different torque requirements. As shown in Figure 4, the main difference in the curve pattern of torque against draft force for different diameters is the gradient of the straight line. In general the bigger the diameter the higher the gradient. The pressing force has no influence on the gradient but determines the maximum value of the transferable torque.

The best efficiency at a sufficient torque is worthless if the animal cannot provide the required draft force. Considering the pattern for the 100 mm friction wheel for different materials shown in Figure 5, a pair of oxen with a tractive force of about 1200 N can be used in all configurations. Hence the use of a donkey with a draft force of at least 250 N is limited to a pressing force of 450 N for the rough friction wheel. A wooden friction

Figure 4: Transferable torque at rough surface

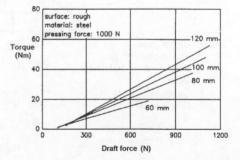

Table 1: Friction wheel combinations for a donkey with 250 N tractive power

	Diameter (mm)	Pressing force (N)	Efficiency (%)	Torque (Nm)	Frequency of rotation (revs/min)	Draft force (N)
Smooth surface						
1	60	500	64	3.9	303	217
2	100	500	84	9.1	182	225
3	100	300	71	7.1	182	198
4	120	300	75	5.4	152	124
Rough surface						
5	60	500	81	5.3	303	214
6	60	1000	81	6.7	303	226
7	80	500	89	6.5	227	293
8	120	500	77	12.8	152	251
Wooden surface						
9	60	500	79	6.8	303	284
10	60	1000	74	6.2	303	286
11	100	500	87	8.0	182	193

wheel increases the pressing force to 700 N; using smooth friction wheels, one can apply a pressing force of more than 1000 N.

Concerning the practical use of this investigation, it is possible to select the best friction wheel based on the measured data. For this selection the power of the animal has to be known.

As an example, Table 1 shows all the friction wheel combinations investigated for a donkey with a tractive force of 250 N. For a supposed torque requirement of the machine of 7 Nm at a speed of 300 revs/min, combinations 1, 5, 6, 9 and 10 are valid. Taking into account the efficiency, the only practicable solutions are combinations 5 and 6.

Normally, the measurement of the pressing force in remote areas is not possible. Using a spring balance or people of different weights standing on the pivot mounted machine to adjust the pressure are simple

methods to get information with a sufficient accuracy of the real pressing force.

Conclusion

The investigations have provided information on how to achieve the most efficient power transmission. The greatest efficiency was obtained with a 100 mm rough friction wheel. The most efficient pressing force depends on the draft force provided by the animal.

Acknowledgements

The author would like to thank all the students of the University of Hohenheim who were involved in the investigations.

References

Busquets E, 1986. The power gear makes it worthwhile to keep draught animals. *GATE Questions, Answers, Information* 4/86:13-16. GTZ, Eschborn, Germany.

Franzke M, 1991. *Project progress report from 01.03.91 to 31.07.91.* GATE/GTZ, Eschborn, Germany.

Löffler C, 1990. *Introduction of animal-powered grinding mills in Zambia 1990. Preliminary Report.* Oekotop GmbH, Berlin, Germany.

TDAU, 1990. Project progress reports. *TDAU Newsletter* Vol 2 (2). Technology Development and Advisory Unit (TDAU), University of Zambia, Lusaka, Zambia.

Figure 5: Draft forces of the 100 mm friction wheel at the highest efficiency

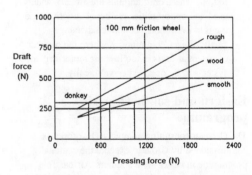

Experience with the introduction of animal-power systems in Zambia

by

Hans Drechsel[1] and Christian Löffler[2]

[1] *Project Coordinator, Animal Power Technology Project (APTP), Private Bag RW 37X, Lusaka, Zambia*
[2] *Project Liaison Officer, Oekotop GmbH, Binger Bingerstraße 25a, D-14197 Berlin, Germany*

Abstract

Animal-power stationary machines, such as mills, pumps, presses and threshers, potentially have many advantages over motor-driven systems. For example, they use locally available renewal energy sources (oxen or donkeys), they have low investment, operating and maintenance costs, in local currency, and they can be manufactured and repaired locally. For the past few years the German Appropriate Technology Exchange (GATE) has been trying to promote the use of animal-powered grinding mills in rural areas of Zambia. Although the technical aspects of technology transfer posed no problems, experience to date shows that rural women prefer to have their maize processed by motor-driven hammer mills wherever these are available, and regard animal-power mills as old-fashioned. Also, animal-powered mills are very often not competitive in economic terms. The prospects for the dissemination of animal-powered grinding mills are therefore very limited, and their operation can only be cost-effective in extremely remote and/or inaccessible areas where fuel prices are far above the national average.

Introduction

In 1984 the German Appropriate Technology Exchange (GATE), a department of the German Agency for Technical Cooperation (GTZ), initiated a programme for the "Documentation, Improvement and Adaptation of Animal Power Systems". The programme has been operating in West Africa (with a regional centre in Senegal) since 1984, and in eastern and southern Africa (with a major base in Zambia) since 1990. (A third regional programme has been operating in South America, mainly Bolivia, since 1990.)

In the context of this programme, animal-power systems are defined as technical devices which use the muscle power of draft animals to drive stationary machines such as mills, pumps, presses and threshing machines. These systems have been playing an important role in agriculture for centuries in various societies in Europe and North Africa. In many regions of Africa, however, they are unknown, despite their potential contribution to the mechanisation of agricultural smallholdings which

mainly depend on hand-operated tools for food processing and water lifting.

Ambitious motorisation programmes, launched to substitute for these labour-intensive hand operations, have been failing in many rural regions of Africa because the machinery is cumbersome and because fuel and spare parts are both scarce and expensive. But for the past two decades the use of animal draft power in Africa has been increasing, and so the basic idea of the GATE programme is to promote animal-power systems as an intermediate solution for the technology gap between manual and motor-driven technologies.

Animal-power technology is seen as having the following advantages over motor-driven systems:

o   use of locally available, renewable energy sources (oxen, donkeys) which are often seasonally underutilised
o   low investment, operating and maintenance costs
o   import dependence is low, because components can be manufactured and repaired locally
o   low maintenance requirements and easy to handle at village level
o   designed for a small number of users in rural areas, thus contributing to a decentralised satisfaction of basic needs.

Based on these features, the primary target regions for animal-power systems are:

o   remote rural areas and/or thinly-settled regions where obtaining fuel and spare parts is difficult
o   regions where draft animals are already widely used and opportunities are being sought to use them to even more economic advantage
o   small villages/communities where the number of potential users is too low for motor-driven systems to be operated economically.

Eastern and southern Africa programme

The German consulting company Oekotop was commissioned by GATE to execute the regional programme in eastern and southern Africa. This

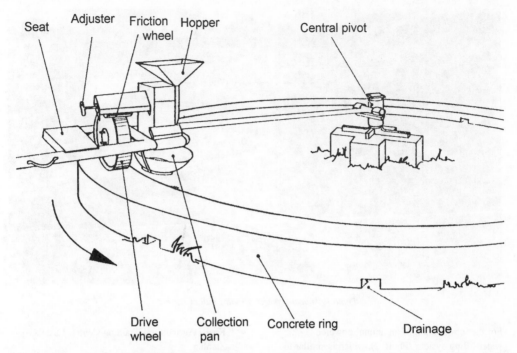

Figure 1: Diagram of the animal-powered grinding mill. One or two draft animals move in a circle and set a drive wheel in motion on the concrete ring. The rotational force is transmitted to a friction wheel connected to a shaft. This drives one millstone against another with the grinding unit

programme started as the Animal Power Technology Project (APTP), with a one-year pilot phase in Zambia followed by a two-year dissemination phase (1991–92) covering also the Mbeya region across the border in Tanzania. Results from the pre-feasibility studies led to the decision to focus on the promotion of three different types of animal-power systems: grain mills, water-lifting systems and oil presses. The introduction of animal-powered grinding mills (Figure 1 and Photo 1) was given top priority, as the availability of local grinding facilities became a crucial bottleneck for the rural population in Zambia during the structural adjustment programme in 1990.

Technical aspects of technology transfer

The APTP has been using two approaches to transferring animal draft power technology from West Africa to eastern and southern Africa: both aim at producing local prototype animal-power systems which are adapted to local needs and manufacturing facilities.

For the introduction of animal-powered grinding mills, APTP imported the West African prototype which had been developed for sorghum processing

by a Belgian engineering company in cooperation with Senegalese craftsmen. This prototype had to be tested to determine its basic suitability for maize processing, and it was assumed that it would have to be modified, depending on the on-station test results and the availability of materials at local production units in Zambia.

For the test and modification programme, APTP cooperated closely with two research and development centres and with various potential manufacturers having different production equipment and levels of staff training. Experience so far shows that only well-equipped or medium-scale engineering companies are able to manufacture animal-powered grinding mills independently. Production of these systems is therefore restricted to urban/peri-urban areas, thus disqualifying the assumed advantage of decentralised local manufacturing.

The entire procedure from the first assembly of the imported prototype to the completion of the local version of an animal-powered grinding mill took about 12 months. The most time-consuming part of this procedure was the multiple feedback between field tests and local manufacturers.

Photo 1: Animal-powered grinding mill in Zambia

For the introduction of an animal-powered water-lifting system (Photo 2), which is similar to the traditional "Delou" in North Africa and called "Bidon verseur", APTP chose another approach. Due to its simple technical design and its status of dissemination in West Africa, APTP requested a direct transfer of know-how to Zambia. Within a four-week consultancy the project engineer of the West African Animal Power Systems programme passed on his experience to the Technology Development and Advisory Unit of the University of Zambia, Oekotop's major counterpart in research and development. The consultant produced a Zambian prototype for testing and copying.

Both approaches to technology transfer from one African region to another proved to be feasible. Generally, the first approach (import of a prototype) is cheaper and advantageous for the on-going adaptation of implements, but it takes much more time. The second approach (import of know-how) is faster, but much more expensive in terms of financing the short-term consultancy of an expert.

Institutional aspects

APTP cooperates with a wide range of institutions and organisations at local, national and international level. They can be divided into counterparts for technology adaptation and technology dissemination.

The major cooperation partners for the adaptation process are:

○ Agricultural Engineering Section, Ministry of Agriculture, Lusaka, Zambia

○ Kasisi Agricultural Training Centre, Lusaka, Zambia
○ Technology Development and Advisory Unit (TDAU), Lusaka, Zambia
○ Institute for International Cooperation, Vienna, Austria
○ Mbeya Oxenization Project, Tanzania
○ Project Consult, Königstein, Germany (Regional Animal Power Systems programme, West Africa, Dakar, Senegal)
○ Institute for Agricultural Engineering, University of Hohenheim, Germany.

For the dissemination of animal-power systems APTP has established contacts with more than 30 institutions ranging from non-governmental organisations which implement local projects (eg, Africare, Village Industry Service) to international organisations such as ILO (International Labour Office) and UNIFEM (United Nations Development Fund for Women) mainly sponsoring comprehensive development programmes.

The overall response to the introduction of animal-power systems in Zambia was positive at both levels, largely because of the evident failure of motor-driven systems as a solution for the bottlenecks of smallholder production in remote rural areas. Nevertheless, quite a number of institutions expressed their scepticism concerning the viability of animal-power systems in economic and socio-cultural terms.

When faced with a decision on whether or not to adopt this new technology, local projects and

Photo: Hans Drechsel

Photo 2: Animal-powered water lifting system of type "Bidon verseur" in Zambia

sponsoring institutions adopted a policy of wait-and-see, which can last up to two years from the first inquiry to the final decision. Clearly, early dissemination of a new technology can only be achieved by high financial and material inputs, ie, pre-financing quite a number of demonstration units.

Acceptance by the target groups

Rural women, the major target group for food processing technology innovations in Zambia, usually know two alternatives for maize processing (Löffler, 1991):

○ pounding by hand with mortar and pestle, which is extremely arduous and time-consuming (60 hours per month)

○ using a hammer mill, which can also be arduous as women may have to walk long distances to the mill.

Women show a strong preference for using hammer mills whenever there is one within a distance of up to 15 km, even though they have to pay a grinding charge. Hammer mills have been setting standards and aspirations in terms of output and consumption patterns even in remote rural areas without hammer mills. The costs and outputs of animal-powered grinding mills and hammer mills are compared in Table 1.

A similar preference for hammer mills is shown by potential entrepreneurs. As the distribution of hammer mills was frequently subsidised by 50% until early 1990, these mills turned into "money machines" as soon as the rural population in Zambia was cut off from maize meal sources following the structural adjustment policy. In order to cushion these negative effects of the structural adjustment, more hammer mills were built in rural areas in 1990/91, usually without considering local requirements and preconditions. These circumstances have obviously been reinforcing the demand for hammer mills, even in small communities.

To summarise, the rural population is crying out for hammer mills, which are seen as the only desirable (modern) grinding technology. Animal-powered grinding mills are regarded as an old-fashioned technology whose output is far too low in comparison to hammer mills. This means that animal-powered grinding mills will be accepted only where hammer mills cannot be installed or run economically.

Economic efficiency

One of the basic assumptions governing the introduction of animal-powered grinding mills in rural areas has been that an animal-power system can compete with motor-driven mills at locations with a low consumer potential (Priewe, 1989). Experiences in Zambia have shown that this assumption is not valid in all regions.

Based on relevant empirical input/output parameters for animal-powered grinding mills and hammer mills in 1990, and the assumption that government subsidies would continue to be cut in 1991, it was calculated that hammer mills and animal-powered grinding mills would have equal break-even charges in 1991 (Löffler, 1991).

Table 1: Comparison of animal-powered grinding mills and hammer mills

	Hammer mill	Animal-powered mill
Retail price 1990 (ZK)	200 000	50 000
Retail price 1991 (ZK)	300 000	100 000
Average output rate (kg/hour)	200	20
Average break-even charge per tin (ZK)	30–40	40
Average charge per tin (ZK)	30–35	20–25

All prices in Zambian Kwacha
(US$1 = ZK90 in December 1991)
1 Tin = unit of 20 litres of maize (15–17kg)

Generally this prognosis did not prove true, because:

○ prior to the presidential and parliamentary elections in 1991, subsidies for hammer mills were extended or re-introduced

○ animal-powered grinding mills were affected by a disproportionately large increase in the production price, as mass production and large-scale stock-keeping for hammer mills proved to be less susceptible to the tremendous increases in production costs in 1991

○ on-station output results for animal-powered grinding mills could not be completely reproduced under village conditions

○ daily and weekly hours of operation of animal-powered grinding mills were lower than expected, mainly due to lack of draft animals.

In fact, the arithmetical break-even charges for animal-powered grinding mills sharply increased in 1991, from 30 to 40 Zambia Kwacha (ZK) per 20 litre tin, while the average hammer mill charge stagnated at 30–35 ZK (US$ 1=ZK 90 in December 1991). Thus animal-powered grinding mills are generally neither competitive nor cost-covering, if the installation and operation of a hammer mill is feasible in the same location. So the operation of animal-powered grinding mills only can be cost-covering and competitive with hammer mills in extremely remote and/or inaccessible areas where fuel prices are far above the national average.

Constraints to the dissemination of animal-power systems

Apart from the above-mentioned economic and socio-cultural obstacles to the introduction of animal-powered grinding mills, other factors also limit the viability and dissemination of animal-powered systems. For example, remote rural areas often do not have sufficient trained draft animals to operate additional animal-power systems, even during seasons when draft animals are under-utilised on other work. Also, using animal draft power for food processing and water lifting often clashes with the traditional, gender-specific division of labour. Men usually have the right of disposal over draft animals and use them for their specific field of work. Thus, the access of women to draft animals still depends on the approval of men.

Conclusions

Because of the macro-economic conditions in Zambia and for a wide range of technology-specific reasons, the prospects for the dissemination of animal-powered grinding mills are very limited. Considering all site-specific requirements for the operation of animal-powered grinding mills, there are hardly any locations which fully meet the various preconditions for these systems. Because the operation of animal-powered grinding mills is generally not viable in economic terms without subsidies, in the final analysis the promotion of animal-powered grinding mills becomes a decision of general principle concerning conflicting objectives: economic viability of a technology versus its potential to alleviate poverty, improve food security and ease the workload of women in selected rural areas.

References

Löffler C, 1991. *Introduction of animal-powered grinding mills in Zambia 1990: framework conditions and a discussion of alternatives for local maize processing*. Oekotop GmbH, Berlin, Consultancy report prepared for GTZ, Eschborn, Germany. 120p.

Priewe J, 1989. *Die Wirtschaftlichkeit angepaßter Technologien in Entwicklungsländern*. German Appropriate Technology Exchange (GATE), GTZ, Eschborn, Germany. 113p.

Animal traction technology for logging in Zambia

by

Christopher Kalima

Logging Superintendent, Zambia Forestry and Forest Industries Corporation (Zaffico)
PO Box 21871, Kitwe, Zambia

Abstract

The introduction of tractors and trucks in the forestry industry in Zambia has not been successful. These machines are capital (foreign exchange) intensive, and the country lacks the necessary infrastructure and trained manpower to maintain and repair them. The Zambia Forestry and Forest Industries Corporation (Zaffico) has therefore been studying the use of animal traction technology to supplement tractor power and hence cut costs. It has found that four pairs of oxen can do the work of one tractor, but because the investment and operating costs of oxen are much lower than those of tractors, oxen can be 10 times more cost-effective than tractors. The move to animal traction brings other benefits to the rural sector. Zaffico hires oxen from farmers, thus creating income-generating work for the farmers. And the local people therefore have a vested interest in protecting plantation trees from forest fires for which, previously, they were partly responsible. Research and development efforts on improving animal traction technology are continuing, and include the design of new implements for log skidding and ox-drawn transport.

Background

In the second half of the 20th century countries in eastern and southern Africa enjoyed the fruits of their political struggles (in the form of independence), and anticipated economic independence for their peoples. Many lives were sacrificed in the pursuit of this goal. But the question being asked today is: has the quality of life of the people of this region actually improved in comparison to what it was before independence? If the answer is yes, then bravo. If the answer is no, what went wrong?

After attaining political independence, the governments of the day became pre-occupied with establishing large industries. They were in a great hurry to catch up with their former colonial masters. They believed that large industries were essential to their socioeconomic development and hence to the improvement of the quality of life of their peoples, by providing jobs and involving them in production activities.

Effects of industry-led development

Because the industries were set up in or near urban centres, the much dreaded rural–urban drift ensued. The urban areas are now overpopulated, and local councils do not have enough money to provide the necessary services and amenities. The rural areas, on the other hand, have not only remained underdeveloped but have now been deprived of their able-bodied young men and women; even the ones that have stayed in the rural areas are only waiting for their chance to drift. Therefore, instead of benefiting the rural areas by way of the "trickle-down" effect, large industrial set-ups have further weakened their intended beneficiaries.

This bitter experience should teach us that any society is only as strong as its weakest components. Countries in eastern and southern Africa are only as strong as their poor rural populations, regardless of the large industries in their cities.

Possible solutions

Although there are several possible practicable solutions that can benefit the rural population socioeconomically, improved animal traction technology is the "locomotive power" in rural socioeconomic development. In its current state, animal traction technology is of little significance to the betterment of the intended beneficiaries. This notion is proved by efforts that have been made in the past decade to substitute the technology with mechanical power in the form of farm tractors and other diesel and petrol engine powered machinery. The region lacks the necessary infrastructure and adequate trained manpower to maintain and repair the machines, and most of machines have not lasted for their expected economically productive lives. As these machines are capital (foreign exchange) intensive, the main result of their purchase by the poor countries in the region has been an increase in foreign debt.

This has led to below-capacity production levels in industry, and agricultural produce not being collected from rural areas or being collected at huge cost which the regional economies cannot afford.

Improved animal traction technology is a solution which the rural population can afford, manage, improve upon and sustain. The people can use it to bring in required inputs and deliver products to market. And they can generate income by hiring out their draft animal power to others.

The case study of Zaffico

The ongoing research and application of animal traction power at Zambia Forestry and Forest Industries Corporation (Zaffico) demonstrates the practicability of this technology, even in a non-traditional application in Zambia. In this large state enterprise, local people are participants in their own development as well as in that of the Corporation and the nation.

The management and expatriate development agency staff of Zaffico realised that industrial forestry, and concern for the protective function of forests, was an answer in itself to people's needs. Forest fires were rampant in the Corporation's tree plantations. The local people, being partly responsible for these destructive fires, were of no help as they did not realise the monetary benefit that could be obtained from the trees growing on the plantations.

Protection of the plantation trees was a big expense for the Corporation. To buy fire-fighting equipment required foreign currency, which was not readily available. The cheapest solution was to enlist the cooperation of the local people in protecting the trees from fires.

This was not all. The trees needed tending and harvesting, and the timber needed to be transported to the processing plants. Tractors and trucks were made available through World Bank loans and the Finnish International Development Agency (Finnida). But this solution was short-lived. As a result the processing plants were forced to run at lower than installed capacity levels.

In February 1988, Zaffico embarked on trials of animal traction technology with a view to supplementing tractor power and hence cutting costs. The target of the Corporation was to have 20% of harvesting capacity carried out by animal power. Several implements were improvised and tried, but much progress was made with the secondment by Finnida of a wood harvesting specialist from Ekono-CTS consultancy. This expert advised on tree harvesting using locally available resources, as was done in Finland before the tractor came on the scene.

The Ekono-CTS team also designed a sledge (the Kite sledge) which has been modified to suit local conditions and the needs of the users. This is a very important point as it is not easy or cheap for manufacturers to make special changes for a handful of users in one small far-away corner of the world.

With the introduction of the Kite sledge the proportion of trees harvested using animal traction rose to 90%. This represents 450 m^3, or 400 tonnes, of timber daily.

Zaffico does not own oxen but hires them from farmers, who are paid monthly according to the work done.

Competitiveness of animal traction technology

The improvement in technology made oxen competitive with tractors. Whereas a four wheel drive tractor can skid 80 m^3 of round timber to a loading area in eight hours, a pair of oxen can skid 10 m^3 in four hours. Therefore four pairs of oxen can do the same work as one tractor. But the operating costs of the two power sources are vastly different; tractors are capital intensive (in foreign exchange) while oxen are labour intensive and do not cause a drain on hard currency. In fact, overall, oxen were found to be 10 times more cost-effective than tractors.

Some of the advantages of animal traction over tractors are shown in Table 1.

Further research and developments

Zaffico, Finnida and Ekono-CTS are continuing their research and development efforts aimed at further improving animal traction technology. These efforts include the design of new implements for, for example, log skidding and ox-drawn transportation.

Trials are underway on log transportation over short distances. The aim is to reduce down-time due to trucks getting stuck in the mud after heavy rains or being damaged by the poor roads. The money saved on repair and maintenance of trucks by using animal traction over short distances can be used for long-distance transportation of raw materials to processing plants (saw mills). The reduced use of spare parts and fuel will also provide savings of foreign exchange.

Conclusion

Instead of neglecting animal traction technology, the people of eastern and southern Africa should remove it from the back yard and improve and develop it, as

Table 1: Advantages of animal traction technology over tractors

	Forest tractor (4x4 75 kWP)	*Ox pair*
Purchase price	Expensive	Low cost
Purchase currency	Foreign currency	Local currency
Economic life (years)	5	7
Actual productive life (years)	2–3	4
Resale value	Lower (scrap)	Higher than purchase price
Resource requirements	Capital intensive in hard currency for purchase, repair and maintenance	Labour intensive. Creates more jobs
Technological requirements	Fully dependent on foreign technology	Uses local skills. Implements can be locally designed and produced
Replacement	Replacement only by purchase, mostly through loans from abroad	Replacement by purchase in local currency or breeding
Environmental effects	Can cause damage to environment	Environmentally sound

it is the real "locomotive" to rural socioeconomic development.

The system works well when local people are allowed to work independently and to negotiate their contract fees in line with operating costs incurred. This gives people a sense of pride in their work.

People should not be coerced to work; they should be attracted to the work by seeing the economic benefits that result from participating. Zaffico and Finnida should play a supportive rather than a management role. The added wealth generated, and the employment created, reduce the impoverishment of people outside the large industry-led development programmes.

An appropriate choice of foreign experts can produce beneficial results. In the Zaffico case study, the expertise provided by the Finnida wood

harvesting specialist and by the Ekono-CTS team is far-reaching and long-lasting.

The aid agency workers could easily have chosen to introduce modern wood harvesting technology in line with the industry-led theories of development which, although they can produce quick results, cannot be sustained by an economy with limited reserves of hard currency. Instead the most appropriate technology was selected, and more than 400 jobs were created. With more improvement on the chosen technology, more jobs will be created by way of implement design and manufacture in the rural areas.

Farmers can purchase their inputs without resorting to high-interest loans. Improved animal traction technology is the locomotive to rural socioeconomic development. What is outdated technology for the developed countries has produced results in Zambia, establishing a base for future development.

A note on the use of donkeys for rural road maintenance in Tanga Region, Tanzania

by

René Fischer[*]

Project Manager, Tanga Draft Animal Project, PO Box 228, Korogwe, Tanzania

Abstract

Donkeys are being used to haul gravel for road maintenance work in Tanga Region, Tanzania. The scheme has helped to accelerate the adoption of animal traction technology in the region. For farmers living close to the roads, this work provides sufficient income to finance the purchase of carts which can be used later for other agricultural and transport work.

Introduction

The Tanga Draft Animal Project is introducing the use of draft animals in the north-east of Tanzania where there is little tradition of using animal power. When the project started in 1981, it only promoted the use of oxen in farming systems, and adoption was slow. Diseases and animal losses were the major problems at that stage. More recently, the project has changed its approach and has achieved greater success. One change has been the promotion of donkeys, particularly for transport.

Use of donkeys

Donkeys proved a very interesting alternative to oxen. They are liked by farmers who do not own cattle and have no cattle husbandry experience. They are particularly important where animal draft power is exclusively used for transport. Donkeys seem more hardy than cattle and are able to survive local conditions without intensive care.

Adoption rates for donkeys did not increase substantially until a suitable design of donkey cart was produced locally. Modified ox carts were cumbersome to construct and use. The donkey cart introduced was based on one used at Mbita Mission near Kisumu, Kenya.

Donkey-drawn gravel haulage

The latest and most sophisticated development is the use of animal-drawn carts to haul gravel for road maintenance.

---

[*]*Subsequent address:*
René Fischer, PO Box 5047, Tanga, Tanzania

For the farmers involved, this work gives substantial income in a comparatively short time; lack of credit facilities is not a problem because carts are issued to farmers on loan and can be paid for within a few months. Compared to crop production, transport yields immediate income and, apart from business sense, little technical information is required to perform well.

The Tanga Draft Animal Project established a first trial site in 1989, in cooperation with the local Rural Road Maintenance project and with the assistance of an ILO (International Labour Office) specialist in labour-intensive road maintenance and construction. These trials made use of experience gained from a similar scheme in Kisii, Kenya (Illi, 1987). Farmers enter contracts to carry gravel from the quarry to the road. A road supervisor allocates plots for excavating gravel and makes sure the gravel is spread correctly on the road. The farmer is responsible for the whole operation, including excavation, loading, carrying and spreading the gravel on the road, and is paid at a fixed rate per standard trip (0.4 m^3 of gravel). An example of the rates paid is given in Table 1.

Table 1: Payment rates for gravel haulage in 1990 (with approximate US$ equivalent)

Hauling distance (m)	Maximum trips per day (number)	Payment per 0.4 m^3	
		(TSh)	(US$)
0–499	24	125	1.40
500–999	14	150	1.70
1000–1499	10	175	2.00
1500–1999	8	200	2.20
2000–2499	7	225	2.50
2500–2999	6	250	2.80
3000–3499	5	275	3.00

Road maintenance

Roads are between 4 and 4.5 m wide. A layer of loose gravel approximately 15 cm thick is spread over the whole width of the road. This requires 675 m^3 of gravel per kilometre. No special

---

Table 2: Summary of roads regravelled using animal-drawn carts and amount paid to cart-contractors

	Road distance maintained	Volume of gravel	Amount paid to contractors	
Road section	(km)	(m³)	(TSh)	(US$[1])
Korogwe to Mashewa	2.4	1434	447 305	5 000
Kwameta to Dindira	7.9	3619	1 246 216	14 000
Maguzoni to Mnyuzi	12	6480	6 269 000	31 000

[1] *US$ equivalent is very approximate. The exchange rate during the time has moved from 90 TSh to 330 TSh = US$ 1.00*

equipment is used to compact the gravel: normal traffic is sufficient to achieve compaction, except during a long dry period when the gravel is completely dry. Examples of the some of the roads maintained in Tanga Region using donkey carts are given in Table 2.

Advantages and constraints of animal-drawn gravel haulage

Provided there are suitable quarries within a short distance of the road, using animal power to haul gravel for road maintenance has several advantages over mechanised haulage. For example:

- the cost of animal-drawn haulage is considerably lower than that of tractors and trailers or tippers and wheel loaders
- the foreign exchange component of total costs is very low (13%), comprising only the cost of an inspection vehicle
- people living along the road earn substantial amounts of money from maintenance work
- the money spent on road maintenance finances the purchase of carts which are then available as vehicles for transport or future maintenance work.

Piles of gravel transported by animal-drawn carts in Tanga Region, Tanzania

Photo: René Fischer

Photo: René Fischer

Unloading gravel from a donkey cart

There are, however, a few possible minor constraints. Gravel must be available a short distance from the road; the maximum hauling distance is about 2 km. Due to the payment structure shown in Table 1, farmers preferred many shorter runs to fewer longer hauls. The people living along the road have no control over the work; although they compete with the road administration for earnings from road work, it is the road administration that makes the decisions.

Conclusion

The use of animal-drawn carts has helped to accelerate the adoption of draft animal technology in Tanga Region. The regular and intense use of animals on road maintenance work has a considerable publicity effect and carts issued to contractors on loan are paid for within a few months through a scheme of deductions from the contract payments. Experience has shown that it is possible to finance one cart for every kilometre or so of road gravelled.

Reference

Illi W, 1987. *Study on hauling of gravel for routine maintenance by animal-drawn carts*. Intermediate Report 2 (Technical Report). Minor Roads Programme, Ministry of Transport and Communications, Kisii, Kenya. 54p.

The potential for animal power in small-scale mining in southern Africa

by

K C Taupitz

Mining Adviser, SADCC Mining Coordinating Unit
Small-Scale Mining Subsector, c/o GTZ, Private Bag RW 37X, Lusaka, Zambia

Abstract

The use of animal power in small-scale mining in southern Africa may be seen as an alternative to expensive mechanical equipment. However, for environmental and legal reasons, the only animals suitable for mining work are donkeys (or perhaps mules), and these animals do not have sufficient power for most mining and ore processing operations. Nor can the use of whim-type animal powered gears overcome this deficiency. These animals can, however, be efficiently used for surface haulage of ore, overburden or supplies, as load carriers in gemstone mines, as pack or riding animals, and for pulling trains of mine cars underground, and their use for this work should be promoted.

Introduction

About 80–90% of all mines in the SADCC (Southern African Development Coordination Conference) countries are small-scale mines which together produce 10–20% (by value) of each country's mining production. (In this context "small-scale" means a production level of up to 100 000 t/year in the case of open cast mining and 50 000 t/year for underground mining.) The exceptions are small-scale gemstone mines in Zambia and Lesotho, which contribute about 25 and 80% by value, respectively.

Small-scale mining provides jobs (some part-time) for 70 000–100 000 people. About one-third of all employees in the SADCC mining sector work in small mines.

Some small-scale mines rely entirely on manual labour; the miners are often local farmers who use mining to supplement their incomes in seasons when little agricultural work is being done. Other mines use mechanical equipment to greater or lesser degrees. But engines and motors, and the fuel (or electricity supply) to run them, are expensive. For these latter mines, animal power may seem to offer a cost-effective alternative. However, a closer look at the practices and power requirements of mining shows that the potential for adoption of animal traction is limited.

Choice of power animals

Unlike farmers, miners do not have a wide choice of draft animals, for various reasons:

- the environment in many mining areas is not suitable for farming or ranching (dry, barren land with very scarce animal feed resources, or widespread tsetse infestation): many animals simply cannot survive in these areas
- in many countries, larger animals cannot be kept on mining claims because farmers have sole grazing rights on communal or state lands
- some mines are located in game parks or safari reserves where domestic animals are not permitted.

Where environmental or legal conditions are favourable, farmer-miners or farmer-contractors can use their own oxen or horses. And full-time miners could hire such animals from local farmers. But for most miners, the only practical draft animal is the donkey (or perhaps the mule, but this has so far not been very popular in Zambia).

Mining practices

The power requirements of mining practices are rather high in comparison with the power that can be generated by draft animals. For example, the power needed to crush and grind ore to a size suitable for mineral extraction, or limestone to agricultural lime, is some 5–20 kWh; drilling holes requires about 0.7–1 kWh/m; and pumping 1000 litres of water up 50 m over a distance of 200 m takes 2.4 kWh. By comparison, a donkey can generate only about 0.25 kW during six to eight hours of continuous work, an ox or a mule about twice this power, and an horse only about three times this power. Clearly, the use of animal power for these operations is not an efficient alternative to mechanical equipment.

Animals could be used for hoisting, but again their power output is not sufficient. For example, in a vertical shaft, a span of two donkeys can lift a load of only 60 kg by direct pull, or 120 kg using block and tackle; typical capacities on an incline are 85 kg at 45 degrees or 150 kg at 15 degrees. Such gross weights are too small for practical application.

Whim-type animal-powered gears and runner-wheel gears could be used to make better use of the limited power obtainable from draft animals. For example, in the past, horse whims have been used for hoisting operations in Europe and North America. A simple American design, which could be used in southern Africa, has a sweep length of more than 4 m (5–7 times the drum radius, to avoid gears). One mine donkey could therefore lift about 180–200 kg gross (150 kg net) at 0.1–0.12 m/s. Unfortunately, these capacities are not very useful, and the costs per kWh are quite unfavourable compared to a small diesel engine which has 10 times the power output (Table 1).

In general, therefore, the small amount of power obtainable from donkeys is not really interesting to the miner, bearing in mind the high energy requirements for most mining and ore processing applications.

Haulage and transport

Although donkeys cannot be used cost-efficiently for many mining operations, they can be valuable sources of power for haulage and transport work.

Surface haulage and transport

In Zimbabwe, many small mines use two-wheeled carts pulled by two oxen or five donkeys to take ore from the mine to the mill or to fetch supplies. On a good level (or slightly downhill) road up to 2 tonnes net load can be transported, although in more hilly areas (common in most mining districts), loads should be limited to about 1 tonne to avoid over-exerting the animals. Daily outputs of 12 tonne-km (6 t over a distance of 2 km) would be normal.

A tractor and trailer would, of course, have a much greater work capacity, probably at a lower cost per unit output. But for transporting small quantities of materials a tractor would be under-utilised and hopelessly uneconomical.

Small carts (0.6–0.7 t net load), pulled by two donkeys, could be used in open cast mines to haul ore to the mill or overburden to the dump. Outputs of 2.5–4 tonne-km per shift can be expected under average open cast mine conditions—equivalent to the work of three to four men using wheelbarrows. A disadvantage is that donkeys would not be able to work on gradients greater than about 5%, compared to 8–12% for motorised haulage.

Table 1: Comparison of the estimated costs of running an animal-powered gear and a diesel engine

	Animal gear (US$)	Dieisel engine (US$)
Capital outlays		
Engine or animal gear	800	3500
Donkeys (4)	400	–
Total outlay	**1200**	**3500**
Daily operating costs		
Driver	10	–
Animal feed	6	–
Fuel	–	13
Lubricant	negligible	1
Maintenance	1	1.50
Total operating costs	**17**	**15.50**
Daily depreciation		
Engine or animal gear	0.32	2.80
Animals	0.32	–
Interest	0.29	0.84
Total depreciation	**0.93**	**3.64**
Total daily running costs	17.93	19.14
Energy produced (kWh/day)	5	50
Cost per kWh output	3.59	0.38

In the past, prospectors have used donkeys and mules as means of transport, and these animals could still be used today as pack animals, especially in mountainous areas where there are no roads for wheeled traffic. For example, for many gemstone mines, the daily output of a few kilograms of unprocessed stone could easily be carried by mule or donkey to the central processing facilities. Also, supervisors and maintenance personnel could use these animals to carry themselves and their tools from a central plant or workshop to the individual small mines and diggings.

Underground haulage

The use of horses or mules to pull trains of mine cars (tubs) has a long tradition in the USA and Europe. An American textbook from 1941 says: "For duties below 200 mineral-ton-miles per day, it has been claimed that no mechanical system can compete with animal haulage".

In southern Africa, haulage distances underground are generally short (20–200 m) and best suited for hand tramming. Only in the chrome mines of the northern sector of the Great Dyke (Zimbabwe) are adits (tunnels) of several hundred metres common. In these mines, one donkey (adits are too narrow for two animals) could pull a train of 3 x 0.8 t (net) mine tubs at a speed of 0.7 m/s. For a 400 m adit, the productivity of one donkey could equal that of two to three hand trammers.

Other applications

In corundum mines in northern Transvaal, animal power is used for washing corundum (dissolving out softer impurities) in rotating 400–500 litre drums half filled with stone and water. The drums have a horizontal axis, the ends of which are hitched to the drag chain of a span of four oxen. The drum is then rotated by the oxen pulling it over the ground, like a roller, until the corundum is sufficiently clean.

This principle could be applied more generally: a pair of donkeys should be able to rotate a 200 litre drum, with a load of 80–100 kg stone or ore.

Conclusions and recommendations

Donkeys can be used efficiently for surface haulage of ore, overburden or supplies, as load carriers in gemstone mines, as pack or riding animals, and for pulling trains of mine cars underground, and their use for this work should be promoted. However, whims and other arrangements to covert donkey power into rotating energy cannot be recommended, because the energy requirement of even small-scale mining are too high.

Photograph opposite
Four oxen in northern Namibia pulling a sledge carrying wood

Improving animal traction technology

Country experiences and constraints

Development and transfer of animal traction technology in Ethiopia

by

Kebede Desta

Head, Agricultural Implements and Equipment Division, Rural Technology Promotion Department
Ministry of Agriculture and Environmental Protection, PO Box 62347, Addis Ababa, Ethiopia

Abstract

Development and transfer of animal traction technology is the key to technological development of Ethiopian agriculture, avoiding the inefficiencies of existing practices which restrict yields and work output and also increase the time needed for seedbed preparation and sowing. The modified Getema plow provides an illustration of how animal traction can improve efficiency: seedbed preparation with this implement takes only about 25 hours/ha, compared with the 160 hours/ha needed to achieve a similar quality of land preparation with the local maresha; *and wheat yields from plots plowed with the modified Getema are twice those obtained from plots plowed using the local* maresha. *The common* maresha *is an inefficient and inadequate tool for land preparation as the seedbed produced is of poor quality. In the absence of sowing equipment, broadcast seeding is widely practised, resulting in inefficient use (poor positioning and spacing) of seed.*

Introduction

Ethiopia is a large country with a surface area of 1.22 million km^2 and a human population of 52 million. The country has the largest livestock population in Africa, and the ninth largest in the world.

Agriculture (defined to include crop and livestock production as well as forestry) is the mainstay of the economy; it engages over 85% of the population and accounts for about half of GDP and nearly 90% of exports.

Although about 80 million ha (65% of the land area) are considered suitable for agricultural purposes, only 13 million ha are actually used for agriculture, and only about half of this area is used for crop production in any one year. Almost all cropping is rainfed and of a subsistence nature; the major crops are teff, barley, wheat, maize and sorghum. The total annual production from the cultivable area is about 6.5 million tonnes—an average yield of only 1 t/ha. This low productivity is mainly attributable to the primitive traditional methods of cultivation, which have remained unchanged for centuries.

Review of existing practices

The *maresha* ard is cheap to produce using local skills and materials, and is light enough (11 kg) to be carried easily to and from the fields, or dragged along the ground behind the oxen. The wearing parts have a life of about five years and so the operating costs are low. Seedbed preparation can take up to six passes of the *maresha,* depending on the type of crop to be sown, and this may require up to 150 ox-team–hours/ha. Seed is normally broadcast by hand but occasionally maize is planted in rows using a rope as a marker. Teff seed, because of its small size, is driven into the ground by walking animals over the field.

Weeding is mainly done by hand (a time-consuming operation), except in robust crops like maize where the plow is driven through the crop. Ministry of Agriculture trials have shown that hand weeding consumes 140 labour-hours/ha but that yield increases of up to 40% can be obtained as a result of weed control. Harvesting is done with a sickle, and threshing is carried out either by hand beating or by animals trampling the crop. The threshed straw is removed with a forked stick which is also used for winnowing. The mixture of grain/chaff is partially winnowed in the field and then sacked and taken to storage by pack animals.

Improved farm implements

Several private and governmental organisations are concerned in the development, import and manufacture of agricultural implements in Ethiopia.

Almost 100 different types of agricultural implement are used for soil preparation, crop handling, transport, storage and other agricultural operations in Ethiopia. Of these, 21 are animal-drawn plows; eight of them have been locally tested and developed, but little improvement work has been done on the others.

An extensive programme of development and testing of a range of harrows, planters, threshers, carts, seed cleaners, grain storage systems and other equipment was undertaken locally by the Arsi Rural Development Unit (ARDU), the Institute of Agricultural Research (IAR) and the Rural Technology Promotion Department (RTPD). Most of the implements either did not perform satisfactorily or were not promoted to the farmers. Those that did promise success, and were further developed, manufactured, tested and distributed to farmers by RTPD, are described below.

Getema *mouldboard plow*

The *Getema* mouldboard plow was developed by RTPD based on the French *Ebra* model. It is simple to manufacture and the results of field tests were encouraging. Following suggestions from farmers, the plow was modified by replacing the two handles by a single one and the pulling chain by a wooden beam. Provision was also made for depth control. Up to 1991, 768 plows had been produced, and 665 units had been distributed to farmers and governmental and non-governmental organisations.

The main advantage of this plow is that it can prepare a good quality seedbed in less than one-sixth of the time needed using the local *maresha* (25 *vs* 160 hours/ha). The main disadvantage is that it requires a much higher tractive effort than the *maresha*, particularly in heavy black clay soils.

Harrow

The ARDU harrow, a triangular wooden frame with 18–24 steel spikes, was modified by providing a handle on the frame to control the movement of the animals and the working depth. As a result, a fine seedbed can be prepared much faster than with the earlier model. The new harrow also has better seed covering characteristics, and is cheaper, than the old one. It has been widely accepted by farmers.

Planter

A prototype batch of ox-drawn maize planters has been produced; trials are still underway.

A row planter and a seed drill have been imported. Tests on farmers' fields show that neither implement improves labour productivity compared to broadcasting by hand, but both increase production.

Weeding

Ministry of Agriculture research data show that good weed control can increase crop yields by up to 40%. Farmers are well aware of the weed problem, and make considerable efforts to overcome it. An animal-drawn weeder, which should reduce the time needed for weeding, is still on trial.

Rural transport

Manual transport of seed, fertiliser, farm tools, market produce, etc, between fields, the home and the market is tiresome and inefficient and absorbs unacceptable amounts of rural women's time. To alleviate these problems, comprehensive efforts have been made to develop, manufacture and distribute horse, ox and donkey carts as well as wheelbarrows. The carts, of which 1100 have been distributed in different parts of the country, have wooden or metal frames and either metal wheels or 16-inch pneumatic tyres.

Constraints to development and transfer of animal traction

The main technical and socioeconomic constraints that limit the development, manufacture and widespread adoption of improved implements and equipment are:

- identifying and developing farm implements that are best suited to the needs of the farmers
- shortage of raw material (steel) and spare parts due to lack of foreign exchange
- lack of technical skilled manpower
- limited purchasing power among smallholders
- lack of coordination between government and other organisations engaged in developing, manufacturing, marketing and promoting animal traction
- the prevalence of tsetse flies in lowland areas and also lack of strong draft animals
- shortage of transport, and hence limited opportunities to visit farmers' fields
- limited training facilities for both extension agents and farmers
- inadaquate infrastructural development.

Conclusion

Development and transfer of animal traction technology is taken to mean the application of animal-drawn implements (improved plows, harrows, planters, cultivators and rural transport) in the agricultural production process, with the aim of promoting labour and land productivity. Ethiopia has recently given due attention to development, manufacture, distribution and promotion of improved animal draft technology. The estimated six million smallholders use primitive tools and implements which are also in short supply. Thus there is a potential to increase labour and land productivity by using better improved agricultural implements.

Animal traction technology in Malawi: potential and constraints

by

M L Mwinjilo*

Senior Lecturer, Department of Agricultural Engineering, Bunda College of Agriculture
University of Malawi, PO Box 219, Lilongwe 3, Malawi

Abstract

Soon after independence in 1964 the Government of Malawi embarked on tractor mechanisation in two areas of the country; the enterprise was a failure due to low utilisation. The government then changed its policy to promoting the use of draft animal power. Malawi's economy is based on agriculture, which makes the largest contribution to GDP, with the smallholder subsector accounting for the bulk of it. Animal draft power has the potential to increase agricultural production by overcoming labour limitations. The promotion of draft animal power is, however, constrained by small land holdings and a shortage of draft animals, implements and spare parts. Although credit is available to individual farmers, those with smallholdings (ie, the majority) have difficulty in obtaining it because they are deemed not to be viable risks. The promotion of the use of cows for draft could go some way towards improving the availability of draft animals.

Introduction

Malawi covers an area of 11.8 million ha, 20% of which is water. In mid-1988 the population was estimated at about 8 million, with almost 85% of the people living in rural areas and deriving their livelihood from farming. A preliminary analysis of the 1987 census suggests an annual growth rate of 3.5% over the 1977–87 period, implying that the country's population will double in about the next 21 years (Economic Intelligence Unit, 1988). The age distribution of the population is such that 19.5% of the people are less than five years old and 44.6% are below the age of 15. The population density ranges from 10 to 292 people per square kilometre with a national average of 85 people per square kilometre (Statistics, 1987).

With few exploitable mineral deposits, Malawi's most valuable resource is land. Because of the favourable climate, the land is potentially highly productive, with the result that agriculture is the

Subsequent address:
Senior Lecturer
Faculty of Agriculture and Natural Resources
Africa University, PO Box 1320, Mutare, Zimbabwe

backbone of the Malawi economy, accounting for 34.4% of Gross Domestic Product in 1991. The agricultural sector is declining because of faster growth in other sectors, but still accounts for the highest proportion of export earnings (90% in 1991) and wage employment (46% in 1988), apart from employing the majority of the population (85%) residing in rural areas, who derive their livelihood from farming (Planning, 1991).

The agricultural sector

Malawi's agriculture is dualistic, production being derived from two subsectors—estates and smallholders.

The estate subsector farms freehold or leasehold land, mainly under private management, and produces estate-type crops (burley and flue-cured tobacco, tea, sugar, tung oil and macadamia nuts) which constitute the bulk of Malawi's exports, accounting for some 90% of agricultural export earnings. Occupying 6.7% of the land, this subsector is administered through the Ministry of Agriculture, but largely through specialist departments and organisations.

The smallholder subsector comprises some 1.3 million farm families occupying over 80% of the land which they hold under a customary tenure system. Smallholder farmers operate mainly at subsistence level and supply the bulk (85%) of the country's food requirements. Maize, the dominant crop, is grown on 75% of cropped land; groundnuts, root crops, cassava and pulses are also planted in significant quantities. Fire-cured and sun/air-cured tobacco, hybrid maize and cotton are the main cash crops. Farm size averages 1.1 ha, with 55% of farms being smaller than 1.0 ha and 95% being smaller than 3.0 ha. This subsector accounts for about 80% of total agricultural output (World Bank, 1987).

Smallholder production is achieved almost entirely with the aid of family labour. Although labour is not considered a constraint for most farmers, labour shortages do occur during land preparation and harvesting periods on relatively larger holdings. Levels of technology use are very low; virtually all cultivation is done by hand hoe. Only 4.9% of households own draft animals, only 3.5% own animal-drawn plows and only 2.0% own animal-drawn ridgers. The use of improved packages is also low; in 1980 only 6.3% of households applied fertiliser (MoA, 1984). Very few farms have adequate storage facilities, and significant post-harvest losses occur. The majority of farmers have very low cash incomes, estimated at 300 Kwacha in 1984/85 (US\$ 1 ≈ 5 Kwacha), of which about 80% was from crops and livestock and 20% from off-farm activities (World Bank, 1987).

Agricultural development strategy

Because of the overwhelming importance of the agricultural sector, the Government of Malawi has adopted a development strategy which gives priority to improving agricultural productivity, with the aim of:

∘ maintaining self-sufficiency in food staples
∘ diversifying production
∘ expanding agricultural exports
∘ improving rural incomes.

The estate subsector has been left largely in private hands, with government assistance limited to providing a favourable investment climate. This has involved considerable transfer of customary land to estates in areas suitable for production of flue and burley tobacco, moderate tax levels and a deliberate low wage policy (Spurling et al, 1982).

In the past, attempts were made to improve smallholder productivity through restricted but expensive and management-intensive integrated development projects based on four intensively settled and potentially highly productive areas. These projects were the Lilongwe Land Development Programme and the Lakeshore Rural Development Project in Central Region, both of which commenced in 1968; the Shire Valley Agricultural Development Project in the Southern Region, which started in 1969; and Karonga Rural Development Project in the Northern Region, which began in 1972. In other traditional farming areas there was a gradual improvement of extension, land husbandry and farmer training, augmented by special activities and programmes, such as ox training and dairy development (MoA, 1984).

In the mid-1970s, with the realisation that the expensive major projects could not be replicated throughout the country within a reasonably short period, the concept of a National Rural Development Programme (NRDP) emerged. The

NRDP was formulated to provide a more extensive level of service, through relatively less capital intensive rural development projects than the major projects, to the whole smallholder subsector within a 20-year period. The programme was designed to increase smallholder production levels by expanding and increasing the efficiency of delivery systems, with particular emphasis on agricultural services such as extension, credit, marketing and input supply (MoA, 1977).

For planning and implementation of the NRDP, the country is divided into eight Agricultural Development Divisions (ADD): Karonga and Mzuzu in the Northern Region; Kasungu, Lilongwe and Salima in the Central Region; and Liwonde, Blantyre and Ngabu in the Southern Region. The ADDs are divided into two to five Rural Development Projects (RDP) which are in turn divided into Extension Planning Areas (EPA). The EPAs are supposed to have similar natural resources such as soils, topography, temperature and rainfall, and hence are used as basic units for planning purposes. The Ministry of Agriculture is the parent ministry responsible for planning, implementing and administering the NRDP.

Some experiences with smallholder mechanisation

From independence in 1964 the government accorded great importance to improving rural incomes. As the major occupation in rural areas was agriculture, and as labour shortage appeared be the main factor limiting agricultural production, the government adopted policies to increase smallholder production by introducing mechanisation packages. A tractor hire service for cotton farmers was introduced in one district in 1965–67, but it was a failure: high charges compared with those for hired labour, and delays in providing the service because of poor logistical planning (the service radius was larger than was practicable), led to low utilisation rates, and the service was uneconomic. At the same time, aerial spraying of cotton was also introduced. This too was unsuccessful because of high hire charges and farmers' unwillingness to cooperate with their neighbours for ease of spraying. Around 1967 the government abandoned its mechanisation approach and shifted to promoting the use of draft animals, mainly oxen (Gemmill, 1971).

A German-aided project, the Central Region Lakeshore Development Project, had a farm mechanisation unit at its inception in 1968, with the responsibility of providing tractor hire services to settlers in rice schemes within the project area. For a number of reasons, mainly the cost of tractor hire, the policy of providing tractor cultivation was modified to only providing the service to open new rice land for smallholder rice groups for the first two years, after which they were expected to acquire work oxen for land preparation. The policy was successful between 1973 and 1978, but the rapidly increasing cost of fuel and spare parts raised the hire charge to a level beyond the reach of many farmers, and the demand for the service is now virtually nonexistent. It was later decided to phase out the tractor hire service, and emphasise the promotion of ox cultivation (Mwinjilo, 1985).

To facilitate ox cultivation the government established ox-training teams and centres throughout the country, and instituted the provision of draft animals and implements on credit, with a repayment period of three to seven years.

Potential for draft animal power use

Oxen are the main source of animal draft power. Cattle are found in all districts of the country, although they are absent in some areas with high population pressures and tsetse infestations.

About 13% of households own cattle but only about 5% own oxen (MoA, 1984). A survey of the use of animal draft power (Mwinjilo and Kasomekera, 1989) showed that the major uses were tillage, transport of farm produce and other goods and transport of water (in that order). The relative importance of these different operations varied from area to area. The survey also showed that, on average, 62% of owners of draft animals hired out their animals for plowing, 18% for ridging/weeding and almost all for transport. The use of animal draft power is therefore not restricted to owners of draft animals. Use of draft animals for weeding is limited because there is no weeder/cultivator on the market in Malawi suitable for weeding between ridges; weeding is therefore a major constraint on relatively large holdings.

Mwinjilo (1987) reported that lack of farm power was limiting smallholder crop production because labour requirements were inadequate during critical periods (planting, fertilising and weeding). But the use of draft animals and animal-drawn implements reduced crop labour requirements; this resulted in improvements in labour productivity which, coupled with improved inputs, led to improved land productivity through improved yields.

Constraints to increased use of animal draft power

Draft animal power is not yet very widely used in Malawi. The major problems put forward include limited land availability, poor access to credit, inadaquate supply of equipment and spare parts, and animal diseases (Mwinjilo and Kasomekera, 1989; Mwinjilo and Ng'ong'ola, 1990).

Land is a major constraint to the majority of farmers due to population pressure, which is reflected in the distribution of holding sizes. The 1980 National Sample Survey indicated that 24% of households farmed less than 0.5 ha, 55% less than 1.0 ha and only 5% more than 3.0 ha (Statistics, 1984). Most smallholder farmers have low incomes and so cannot buy draft animal power packages with their own funds. The government has credit facilities for the purchase of such packages, but these are available only to individuals who can show ability to service the loan. It is estimated that a farmer needs to farm at least 3 ha in order to be able to service a loan package for draft animals and implements. Thus only 5% of households would qualify for government credit to purchase a draft animal power package.

The supply of draft animals is limited because of competition with the demand for beef. This has resulted in the government's Department of Animal Health and Industry being the main supplier of oxen from its few livestock centres. Distribution outlets for implements and spare parts are located mainly in urban centres and major rural centres, which are far apart. Even in these centres, low turnover rates of these items make them very unattractive lines to stock. Farmers therefore often have to travel long distances to buy implements and/or spare parts.

Tsetse infestation and trypanosomiasis are prevalent in some areas of Malawi. Vaccination against the disease is available, but farmers cannot afford to vaccinate whole herds. In one area there are frequent outbreaks of foot and mouth disease; because this is the major cattle rearing area of the country, these outbreaks have had a devastating effect on the supply of draft animals.

Conclusion

The potential for increased use of animal draft power exists in Malawi as long as measures can be taken to overcome the identified constraints. Nothing can be done to increase the sizes of land holding, but group ownership of draft animal power packages would ensure a large serviced area and therefore assurance of loan repayment. Credit administrators have indicated their willingness to lend to groups but they are cautious because their own performance is measured by levels of repayment.

There is also a need to look at different types of equipment suitable for different areas of the country and various cropping systems. With increased use of draft animal power, turnover of spare parts would increase and distributors would be more willing to stock these items.

Finally, the use of cows for draft work could help to increase the supply of draft animals, especially for cattle owners who do not have oxen. Research on the implications of using cows for draft work is urgently needed.

References

Economic Intelligence Unit, 1988. *Malawi: country profile 1988–89*. World Microfilms Publications, London, UK.

Gemmill G T, 1971. *Tractor hire services: a case study*. Research Bulletin of Bunda College of Agriculture, (University of Malawi), Lilongwe, Malawi. Vol 2.

MoA, 1984. *National rural development programme: Policies, strategy and general features*. Ministry of Agriculture (MoA). Government Printer, Zomba, Malawi.

Mwinjilo M L, 1985. *The role of smallholder mechanisation in the national rural development programme: a case of Salima Agricultural Development Division*. Paper presented at National Workshop on Rural Development and Agrarian Change in Malawi, held 30 December 1985 – 5 January 1986, Bunda College of Agriculture (University of Malawi), Lilongwe, Malawi.

Mwinjilo M L, 1987. *Farm power and mechanisation for smallholder production systems in Malawi*. PhD Thesis. Silsoe College, Cranfield Institute of Technology, Silsoe, UK.

Mwinjilo M L and Kasomekera Z M, 1989. *Survey of animal power utilisation in Malawi*. Report submitted to FAO Project UNDP/FAO MLW/86/002 Animal Power Utilisation. Food and Agriculture Organization of the United Nations (FAO), Rome, Italy.

Mwinjilo M L and Ng'ong'ola, 1990. *An investigation of the constraints restricting the uptake of medium-term credit by smallholder farmers in Malawi*. Report submitted to the Smallholder Agricultural Credit Administration, Ministry of Agriculture, Lilongwe, Malawi.

Planning, 1991. *Economic report 1991*. Office of the President and Cabinet, Department of Economic Planning and Development. Government Printer, Zomba, Malawi.

Spurling A, Nelson R, Nyberg S, Senganalay C, Warnaars C, Vasur E and Shams H, 1982. *Malawi: smallholder fertilizer supply and policy project*. Report of an appraisal mission which visited Malawi in September/October 1982. World Bank, Washington DC, USA.

Statistics, 1984. *National sample survey of agriculture 1980/81 (customary land in rural areas only)*. National Statistical Office. Government Printer, Zomba, Malawi.

Statistics, 1987. *Malawi statistical yearbook 1985*. National Statistical Office. Government Printer, Zomba, Malawi.

World Bank, 1987. *Malawi: smallholder agricultural credit project (IDA/IFAD Credit)*. Staff Appraisal Report 6886-MAL. Southern Africa Department, Agriculture Operations Division, World Bank, Washington DC, USA.

Improving animal traction technology in Malawi: some recent investigations and trials

by

Darwin Dodoma Singa

Commodity Team Leader (Agricultural Engineering), Department of Agriculture Research
PO Box 158, Lilongwe, Malawi

Abstract

Research on farm machinery in Malawi is now directed towards smallholder farmers who are responsible for the bulk of agricultural production in the country. Most smallholders operate at the subsistence level and practise hand-tool farming because motorised mechanisation is technically and economically beyond their reach. Also, imports of tractors and fuel into Malawi are restricted in an effort to conserve foreign exchange reserves. A similar situation is found in most of eastern and southern Africa. This paper describes some of the efforts of the Agricultural Mechanisation Research Programme to develop the use of draft animals as an efficient source of agricultural power. The emphasis that has been placed on the use of animal-drawn implements for crop production and farm transportation is also indicated.

Introduction

The low productivity of land and labour contributes to the poor achievements in food production and economic performance seen in eastern and southern Africa and other developing regions. Greater emphasis on animal-drawn equipment for smallholders should improve labour and land productivity without the drain on foreign currency reserves associated with tractor use and oil imports. The use of different sources of animal power and associated mechanical innovations could help improve timeliness of agricultural operations, which is particularly important in a country like Malawi which has unimodal rainfall (Singa, 1984).

Options for animal power for Malawi

The choice of draft animal species in any area has to be based on technical principles as well as on socioeconomic and environmental factors.

The size of animals influences draft provision. Small animals are able to develop a greater gross efficiency than large animals because their power/weight ratio is smaller. Working speed of animals in relation to loading capacity is a factor that needs to be taken into consideration when choosing animal species for transport work. Table 1 shows a range of speeds and draft capabilities for different animals.

Horses are not suitable draft animals for smallholder farmers in Malawi as they are not resistant to local pests and diseases. They also require complicated harnessing systems.

Water buffaloes do not necessarily need water to wallow in: they can survive and work in many tropical areas, including semi-arid zones. They may be suitable for rice-producing areas, but they are unlikely to be as well adapted as local cattle.

In terms of overall animal power suitability in the environmental conditions prevailing in Malawi, and in the light of management and feeding limitations, it has been recommended that emphasis be placed on oxen and donkeys, with the possibility that water buffaloes be assessed in rice areas.

Donkeys are being recommended in Malawi particularly for transport as they are quicker than oxen. Some 45 donkeys have been imported into Malawi from Botswana for crossbreeding with the local animals. A donkey cart is being manufactured by the local Petroleum Services Company.

Evaluation of draft animal equipment

Malawi is now self-sufficient in domestic manufacture of all ox-drawn implements.

Over the past three decades the Farm Machinery Research Team of the Ministry of Agriculture has been engaged in research, development and coordination of appropriate technologies with special emphasis on the use of animal power. Assessments have been made on different sources of oxen and donkeys and their associated field and farm transportation equipment. Field trials have also been conducted, and recommendations made.

Multipurpose toolframe

In recent years a highly promising multipurpose toolbar has been developed and tested: it is now being made by Agrimal, the local implement manufacturing company. Attachments currently

Table 1: Estimates of draft capacity of several species at low and high speeds

Animal	Mature weight (kg)	Low speed			High speed		
		Speed (km/hour)	Draft (N)	Power (kW)	Speed (km/hour)	Draft (N)	Power (kW)
Horse	500	2.4	630	0.46	4.0	500	0.53
Ox	450	2.4	640	0.46	4.0	450	0.53
Buffalo	650	2.4	910	0.61	3.2	650	0.61
Camel	430	3.5	640	0.61	4.0	480	0.53
Elephant	2900	2.0	2300	1.29	–	–	–
Dog	32	5.4	90	0.08	8.4	30	0.06

Source: After Goe and McDowell (1980)

available are a plow, a ridger and a groundnut lifter. Work on a planter, cultivating tines, weeding sweeps and a clod crusher is underway.

The toolbar with plow and ridger costs about 35% less than two single-purpose implements. This is important as it has been found that the lower the capital and operating costs of the animals and equipment, the higher are the chances of successfully introducing animal traction (Starkey, 1986).

Animal-drawn planters

In 1969 and 1970 the Farm Machinery Unit (FMU) of the Ministry of Agriculture investigated four types of ox-drawn planter. Two were proposed attachments to the National Institute of Agricultural Engineering (NIAE) wheeled toolcarrier, and the third was part of a human-powered toolbar designed for planting maize: none of these proved to be appropriate, and they were not recommended. The fourth, a "Safim" design manufactured by Agrimal, was recommended for planting maize and soy bean: it was, however, not suitable for groundnuts because it damaged the seed. Only this planter reached the farmer.

A double-row ridge planter attachment to the toolbar was designed and tested by FMU from 1982 to 1985. It plants on two ridges per run, placing a seed 3–5 cm deep every 30 cm. The planter comprises two drive wheels (which move in the furrow), two hoppers and seed plates, an opener and a cover. Following the final stage of development, Agrimal and Lilongwe Sheet Metal have been approached as possible manufacturers.

Rice planter

A four-row rice planter was tested by FMU in 1975. The tests showed that it would have limited appeal

to farmers because it was complex, with many parts that needed frequent maintenance, and its use would have required extensive training in operation and care. However, use of the machine could reduce farmers' seed costs by about 60% because broadcast seed is sown at approximately 110 kg/ha while the average seed rate recorded for the machine was only 43 kg/ha.

Harnessing

In Malawi, zebu oxen are usually harnessed in pairs with withers or shoulder yokes. Single yokes are rarely used. Use of a single yoke was investigated at Bunda College of Agriculture in 1977 and at Chitedze Agricultural Research Station from 1984 to 1987. The results were encouraging in terms of power provision and operational efficiency in field work (especially for weeding, where it is difficult to use a pair of animals when crops—such as late maize—are tall).

Ox carts

The Farm Machinery Commodity Team is currently working on a single-animal ox cart constructed mainly of wood to reduce weight and cost. Hardwood is used for load-bearing components, while the main body is made of softwood. The wheels are positioned in the centre of the cart body to allow the loading pressure to act on the wheels rather than on the animal's neck. The dissel booms are made from light poles, also to reduce weight. The animal pulls are between the two poles which have a yoke in front. The loading capacity of this cart is about 500 kg. The estimated cost is about 400–600 Malawi Kwacha (when US$ 1 ≈ MK 2.8). It is easy and cheap to maintain because it is made with locally available materials..

Animal power in forestry

A recent study of log extraction (skidding) with oxen in Malawi showed that oxen skidding is technologically, economically and socially superior to skidding with tractors (Solberg and Skaar, 1987). Research is continuing on many aspects of oxen logging, including the work organisation and the skidding equipment used.

Field cultivation trials

Plowing, harrowing and ridging

Trials were conducted at Bunda College in 1976 to compare traditional hand cultivation with ox plowing and ridging, and with plowing, harrowing and ridging, for cultivation of maize.

The overall results were not statistically different (except for soil aggregate size), but plowing, harrowing and ridging produced the best seedbed (with 56% of the soil aggregates less than 4 mm in diameter), led to higher germination percentage, resulted in the lowest soil compaction, and gave the highest grain yield. Hand cultivation produced the best ridge stability.

A wooden clod breaker was made and tested, and reported to work adequately. Work conducted by Salima Agricultural Development Division in 1980 using a steel roller with cast iron ballast weights was abandoned because the cost was prohibitive.

Weed control

Weed control and crop response to alternative cultivation systems and subsequent weeding methods using ox-drawn equipment on maize and groundnuts were studied from 1981 to 1984. Results showed that:

- tine cultivation provides less residual weed control. Cultivators (deep-tine) have higher draft requirements than plows
- although ridge formation requires extra labour there are substantial labour savings in ridge planting, particularly when animal-drawn implements are to be used for weeding: ridge planting is faster than flat planting in straight lines
- weeding with an animal-drawn cultivator (tines and sweeps) is only effective when the soil has average moisture and weeds are small
- if soil is well-plowed, it makes no difference to yields if planting is on ridges or on flat land
- ridger weeding on flat-planted crops provides good banking systems and saves labour
- only two weedings are required, that is, up to the time maize reaches ox-shoulder height

- groundnut lifting using animal-drawn implements is easier when the crop is grown on ridges
- crop performance for flat plant/flat weed plots kept on deteriorating over three years of trials. Poor root extension was noticed under such conditions.

Based on these results, the following recommendations can be made.

Where residual weed control and proper soil tilth are required, a mouldboard plow should be used instead of deep tines or a chisel plow. Deep tines and front tines can only be used where drainage is required and weeds are not a problem in land preparation (for example, on an old field with no residual weeds). The animals should be strong as these implements require high power.

Although planting on ridges is faster than planting on flat land, initial ridge-making requires a lot of labour.

Ridging is appropriate where the slope of the land would lead to erosion. Otherwise, for maize and groundnuts, flat planting on well-plowed land requires less labour and leads to superior yields.

A ridger is recommended for weeding flat-planted crops (grown in straight lines) because it requires less labour, and achieves simultaneous earthing-up.

Weeding with a cultivator saves time but this should only be done when weeds are small and the soil is not too wet. When crops are gown on ridges, hiller blades should be used.

Minimum tillage can be safely practised only for three years, after which the land should be fully plowed again. During the three years all recommended inputs should be applied; otherwise the crop will be badly affected during the last two years, compared to normal tillage.

Groundnut lifting

Between 1968 and 1970 FMU carried out trials on the use of blades and shares for lifting groundnuts. These trials showed that a curved blade mounted between supports spaced at 600 mm was the most suitable implement for this work: the blade penetrates the ridge effectively, but has a low draft requirement.

A modification to this design was made by the FMU in 1982. This has additional advantage of circular legs which enable the lifted groundnut haulms to slip off easily during the lifting operation. This implement is being manufactured by Agrimal as one of the attachments to its toolbar.

References

Goe M R and McDowell R E, 1980. *Animal traction: guidelines for utilization*. International Agricultural Development Mimeograph 81. Department of Animal Science, Cornell University, Ithaca, New York, USA. 84p.

Singa D D, 1984. Sources and utilization of animal power and equipment for Malawi's agricultural sector. Unpublished paper summarised (pp. 32–34) in: *Report of a networkshop on draught power and animal feeding in Eastern and Southern Africa held Ezulwini, Swaziland, 4–6 October 1983*. Networking Workshops Report 2. CIMMYT (Centro Internacional de Mejoramiento de Maíz y Trigo) Eastern and Southern Africa Economics Programme, PO Box 1473, Mbabane, Swaziland. 93p.

Solberg B and Skaar R, 1987. *A technical and socioeconomic study of skidding with oxen in Malawi*. Agricultural Development Report 5. Norwegian Centre for International Agricultural Development (Noragric), Agricultural University of Norway, Aas-NLH, Norway. 104p.

Starkey P H, 1986. Introduction, intensification and diversification of the use of animal power in West African farming systems: Implication at farm level. pp. 97–117 in: Starkey P H and Ndiamé F (eds) *Animal power in farming systems*. Proceedings of Second West Africa Animal Traction Networkshop held 19–25 September 1986 in Freetown, Sierra Leone. Vieweg for German Appropriate Technology Exchange, GTZ, Eschborn, Germany. 363p.

Improving animal traction technology in northern Namibia: past experience and apparent needs

by

D K Morrow

Ministry of Agriculture, PO Box 788, Grootfontein 9000, Namibia

Abstract

The social turbulence associated with a long civil war brings about wide-ranging alterations to cultural traditions and practices. In northern Namibia, the use of animal traction for crop production was severely affected by the recent war. The subsequent introduction of subsidised tractor plowing services is unlikely to bring about long-term benefits for the rural communities. Such services are not sustainable and have failed throughout Africa. However, some means of tractive power must be made available in order to raise the level of crop production and the standard of living of small-scale farming families in northern Namibia. Such communities require timely and adequate tractive power for primary land preparation and subsequent cultivation and weeding. The power source must be readily available and fully sustainable and must involve appropriate technology which the small-scale farmer can both adopt and adapt.

A project proposal covering several interrelated development problems has been submitted to the National Planning Commission for approval and funding. The project, based on testing and dissemination of animal traction, includes the training of oxen and their handlers, the development of farming systems based on animal traction and the establishment of small agro-industries to repair and manufacture equipment. Credit facilities to support such developments are also envisaged.

Background

For a variety of historical reasons, some going back almost 100 years, the northern districts of Namibia have suffered from severe economic and administrative neglect. As a consequence little development has taken place in Owambo, Okavango and Caprivi. (The names of the northern administrative regions of Namibia have recently changed—Okavango used to be known as Kavango. The old area of Owambo corresponds broadly with the new regions of Omusati, Oshana, Ohangwena and northern Oshikoto—see Figure 1.)

With population densities doubling over the past 30 years, the existing natural resource base has been both over- and under-exploited. The situation varies from location to location and can be well illustrated by considering two factors closely related to future progress in animal traction technology.

Animal health protection systems have been systematically applied in the three regions for many years, and these have led to more animals surviving to maturity. Unfortunately, these measures have never been supported by corresponding efforts to improve animal husbandry and management techniques. Thus, as the cattle population has risen, overgrazing has become more and more severe, resulting in progressive degradation of the fragile ecosystems. Unsustainable overgrazing now exists over the greater part of Owambo, especially over the central spine and western parts; all along the Okavango river within a variable belt of 5 to 10 km from water; and around the flood plains and seasonally flooded areas (*molapos*) of Caprivi. As the population densities of livestock, principally cattle, and humans are greatest in Owambo and much less so in Caprivi there exists a broad continuum of degradation from east to west. Compounding this has been the absence of any crop research programme designed to benefit the communal farmers of the far north.

Two ancillary factors have reinforced this situation: first, the political decision to regard these northern districts, principally Owambo, as sources of migrant unskilled labour, thereby justifying the administrative policy of benign neglect; and second, of more direct influence on the use of animal traction, the existence of a protracted civil war for independence. Once again, in general terms, the effects were most severe in Owambo, but localised concentrations of cultural degeneration can be observed over the entire area.

The existence of a large military force dispersed over the three districts for about 25 years was not entirely unwelcome by the local populace. The presence of such a force, substantially made up from tribal/ethnic territorial forces, meant that a constant supply of uncommitted cash was freely available, leading to many employment and enhanced trading opportunities which were enjoyed by the locals. Hand in hand, however, went the destruction, modification and moulding of cultural values and practices.

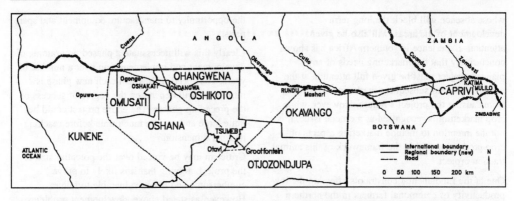

Figure 1: Map of northern Namibia showing the new administrative regions. The old region of Owambo referred to in the text is the central northern area between Okavango and Kunene. It corresponds broadly with the new regions of Omusati, Oshana, Ohangwena and northern Oshikoto

One such practice, which was virtually eliminated in many areas through these socioeconomic forces, was the use of animal traction for land preparation. For example, during the period 1986–89, the author did not see a single example of animal traction in Owambo. The situation in Okavango and Caprivi was more variable, but the shortage of animal traction was also evident there, albeit to a lesser extent.

Tractor hire schemes

A further factor undermining the use of animal traction in the north was the introduction of subsidised farming services in Caprivi and Okavango, although to the author's knowledge this was never the case in Owambo. These services were instigated by the pre-independence territorial ethnic administrations. While Caprivi maintained its service after independence, Kavango (now Okavango) curtailed operations in 1988. In 1991, the new government introduced a blanket subsidised service for the three regions, although the availability of tractors and equipment to provide a timely service for both large and small communal farmers leaves much to be desired.

Subsidised plowing services have been provided by governments throughout developing Africa, but in no single instance have they proved themselves sustainable. Indeed, the fact that they are subsidised means they are non-sustainable. No long-term benefits have ever accrued to a communal community from such services since sooner, rather than later, the services have been withdrawn because of shortages of foreign exchange. Animal traction suffers from their introduction and so communities face disastrous consequences on their withdrawal. As a result, food production levels eventually

decline to terminal volumes lower than the pre-mechanisation status quo.

Another unavoidable, if not inevitable, result is that the larger, wealthier personages with economic and hence political weight tend to monopolise the available services and secure greater benefits. The smaller-scale farmers tend to obtain the service later in the season with many farmers being unable to benefit due to the inadequacy of the service.

Associated with the agricultural scenario outlined above is an extension service which is poorly educated, inadequately qualified and lacking in experience, and with no message to impart to the small-scale farmer.

It was a Roman general who once said *ex Africa semper aliquid novi* [there is always something new from Africa] yet in northern Namibia our experiences relating to animal traction are unlikely to produce anything different from that experienced elsewhere on the continent.

Project proposal

The difficulty with starting to solve current development problems is that rarely can one tackle one problem at a time. A plethora of problems has to be tackled in concert since they have a network of interlocking connections. With this in mind an animal traction development project has been submitted to the National Planning Commission, with a request for an initial budget allocation of 450 000 Rand (about US$ 180 000).

The essence of the project is to address those needs of the small farmer which are recognised as being the primary factors restricting agricultural productivity within the region. In addition, those non-farm activities which can make a valid contribution to such productivity increases, and whose absence will block the long-term development of the areas, will also be given attention. Experience in southern Africa has shown conclusively that the marketing needs of any planned project must be given full attention at the outset to prevent subsequent marketing constraints from causing the project's failure. However, while crop marketing is recognised as a crucial issue, it is not the intention to include marketing aspects of crop production within the framework of this animal traction project.

One of the fundamental constraints affecting the low productivity of communal farmers in the northern territories of Namibia is the extremely low availability of trained ox teams with handlers and appropriate technology for use in land preparation and crop cultivation. The only ox-drawn implement freely available is an all-metal plow, first manufactured more than 60 years ago. It is identical to that available elsewhere in Africa. The vast majority of field tasks are carried out with manual labour which means that land preparation is always delayed until the onset of the rains, crops are inevitably planted late and the subsequent cultivation/weeding of crops is usually inadequate. This scenario is further compounded by the shortage of available labour, as those left to work the farms are generally the older parents or, in too many cases women and younger children who are not attending school. Many men go to the major urban centres in an attempt to gain employment but salary remission is usually irregular and unreliable and may cease altogether. This cycle of activity locks the communal farmer into an inescapable circle of poverty.

It is intended that the project should become involved with several agricultural and agriculture-related activities relating to animal traction. In the initial phase there will be testing of implements and related research. New and improved cultivars of existing crops (mainly millet, sorghum, groundnut and maize) will be tested using a farming systems approach to small-scale farmer problems. New crops will be introduced along with alternative cropping techniques such as intercropping. A training phase will be included as soon as possible to produce qualified trainers who in turn should produce trained teams of oxen with competent handlers. Trials of on-farm cropping systems will take place using equipment already found to be acceptable to the farmers. Thereafter it is planned to introduce blacksmith training programmes. These will aim to produce a trained cadre of local artisans capable of carrying out repairs to existing equipment. Some more gifted artisans may be given

the opportunity to manufacture equipment and spare parts.

Clearly this will necessitate a phased programme of development and implementation over a number of years. The speed with which each new phase is introduced will depend on the degree of success of the preceding phases. The entire project could be quite large and require much time before reaching its final dimension.

Criticism may be voiced over the potential size of the project, arguing that it is likely to prove cumbersome and hence vulnerable to failure. However, as stated above, development problems can rarely be solved in isolation. Small-scale farmers operate their farms as a unit, dealing each day with problems which have social (family), economic and agronomic dimensions. To solve farmers' problems frequently involves solving community problems first, or at least at the same time.

Proposed project actions

Testing of equipment

The testing of equipment will take place at two centres—the Mashare Government Farm, east of Rundu in Okavango, and an unspecified site outside Katima Mulilo in Caprivi. No adequate research facilities were ever established for Caprivi and the Ministry of Agriculture is currently finalising the acquisition of 100 ha of land donated by a local tribal authority. The actual testing will be carried out within the framework of a variety of crop production systems, not only to demonstrate the usefulness or otherwise of specific pieces of equipment but also to demonstrate the productivity of new (unknown to local farmers) crops and improved cultivars of known crops.

Training of oxen and handlers

Almost simultaneously an unassociated centre is to be created, along very simple lines, to train pairs of oxen, owned by communal farmers, in the recommended cultivation activities using the improved equipment. Courses will initially be for a planned four-week period and the trainee handlers will be accommodated on site. It may be necessary for the centre to provide transport for the trainees' animals if the distances are too far for the animals to walk. All costs of training will be carried by the Ministry of Agriculture.

Farming systems research

Farming systems research (FSR) will be introduced to the research centre as early as possible but this may not occur until the second year of operation.

Group discussion activity will take place with local extension officers and with interested farmers; the intention is to have combined groups, as far as possible, in order to build links between the two groups via the research activity. Depending on the progress achieved in the second and third activities/phases, FSR will be introduced to on-farm trials, but must depend on the degree of trust and cooperation which can be established among the centre, the extension service and the farmers.

Training for field repairs

In time, should the previous three activities progress satisfactorily, it will be desirable to have local entrepreneurs with some skills in blacksmithing and welding to carry out running repairs on the equipment. Final details of this stage will depend on the rate of breakage (which may be minimal) and the availability of a pool of existing artisanal skills, which will vary from place to place. Where necessary, organisations outside the project may provide the specialised training. Existing non-governmental organisations (NGOs) already provide such training in other areas, and the project may persuade these NGOs to arrange periodic training opportunities in Okavango and Caprivi.

Establishment of local manufacture

Local entrepreneurs will be given training in the manufacture of the approved range of equipment.

Credit

Credit will only be offered to people where the opportunity for success is considered good and where the potential for credit repayment is favourable. In this regard, the supply of trained cattle and approved animal traction equipment to individuals or small groups is considered an acceptable risk. The provision of tools, jigs and basic working materials to small-scale entrepreneurs should also merit credit, the loan being secured by tools, working materials or finished goods. In both these examples, if credit is not repaid, repossession by the credit institution should lead to minimum loss being incurred. On the other hand, if the technology is transferred successfully, repayment of loans should be straightforward with the improved level of productivity envisaged.

A possible (and quite optimistic) timetable for project implementation over a four-year period is presented in Table 1.

Table 1: Timetable for project implementation (assuming ideal conditions)

Year	Description	Project involvement
1992	Import equipment	P
	Establish research centre	P
	Prepare credit facilities and procedures	O
1992	Establish training centre	P
1992/93	Establish FSR programme	P
	Organise farmer discussion groups	P
1993/94	On-farm FSR programme	P
1994	Train local people to do field repairs	O
1995	Train and establish local entrepreneurs to manufacture equipment	O
1993 onwards	Make credit facilities available	O
1993/94 onwards	Integrate extension and development personnel in an outreach programme	O

P = Project activity. O = Non-project activity

A note on promoting an ox cultivation strategy for Uganda

by

A A Okuni

Agricultural Engineer, Ministry of Agriculture, Animal Resources and Fisheries
PO Box 236, Tororo, Uganda

Abstract

There is a need to develop a suitable strategy for animal power in Uganda. The promotion of tractors does not seem appropriate since they are expensive and have many disadvantages. Ox cultivation has many advantages for smallholder farmers. Several of the constraints to animal traction could be solved by government action, including more attention to relevant research, training and extension.

Introduction

Developing countries such as Uganda need to improve the efficiency of their agricultural production. Mechanisation offers a means of achieving this, as an alternative to hand tool technologies which are time-consuming, laborious and offer little scope for opening new land to cultivation. But what is the most appropriate source of power for mechanisation—tractors or draft animals?

Tractor problems

Tractors have several serious disadvantages, including:

o high capital and operational costs, in foreign exchange
o high depreciation of equipment
o lack of supporting infrastructure in most production areas
o farmers' lack of technical knowledge and skills
o shortage of spares for imported machinery
o major operational problems on small fields.

Animal traction

Compared with tractors, animal traction has many advantages:

o oxen and ox-drawn implements are cheaper than tractors and tractor equipment
o oxen appreciate and have a high salvage value
o oxen are more suitable in the small, fragmented fields common in Ugandan farming systems
o livestock are an existing resource in the country, ripe for exploitation

o "fuel" is available locally in the form of arable grazing land

Constraints to animal traction

Ox cultivation technology has been in existence for a long time but it has not yet been fully adopted. Reasons for this include:

o difficult topography in some areas
o cultural factors and traditions
o tsetse fly in some areas
o farmers' poor economic standing and lack of access to credit facilities
o farmers' lack of technical know-how and training
o complicated land tenure system and fragmented land usage
o lack of properly trained extension staff to promote the programmes.
o lack of local facilities and workshops for making, repairing and maintaining suitable implements and spares.

Possible government action

The government could take action to overcome many of these problems. First steps towards a wider adoption of animal traction technologies might include:

o conducting research into animal traction and small-scale technologies, and extending these technologies to farmers, for example, through mobile ox cultivation workshops
o providing training and demonstrations for farmers and their animals, local blacksmiths, extension staff, etc
o reviving ox cultivation competitions
o identifying workshops for draft animal implement repair programmes
o liaising with scientific institutions and scientists in other countries to keep abreast of current developments in animal traction technology.

Animal draft power in Zambia: constraints to development and possibilities for improvements

by

E Mwenya[1], W N M Mwenya[2] and H J Dibbits[3]

[1] *National Draft Animal Power Coordinator, Agricultural Engineering Section*
Department of Agriculture, PO Box 50291, Lusaka, Zambia
[2] *Department of Animal Science, University of Zambia, PO Box 32379, Lusaka, Zambia*
[3] *Institute of Agricultural Engineering (IMAG-DLO), Mansholtlaan 10–12*
Postbus 43, 6700 AA Wageningen, The Netherlands

Abstract

This paper discusses some of the constraints to increased use of animal traction technology in Zambia. Most smallholder farmers in cattle-keeping areas have the skills necessary to train and handle their work animals, but this is not the case in non-cattle-keeping regions where animal traction is a new technology. In all areas, poor producer prices do not provide farmers with enough income to invest in animals and implements. Nor are existing credit facilities adequate to overcome this problem. The government's 1985 five-year investment plan, aimed at improving the use of animal traction, covers such areas as research and development, training, implement supply, and information and documentation.

Introduction and background

In common with most other countries in eastern and southern Africa, agricultural mechanisation in Zambia is mixed. All forms of farming power (human, animal and tractor) are available, but the extent of their use is determined by traditional background, economy and availability.

Traditional background has played a major part in the development of farm mechanisation in Zambia. The southern part of the country, comprising Southern and Western and parts of Central and Eastern Provinces, has a long history of cattle keeping, and farmers here are familiar with the training of draft oxen and the handling of some ox-drawn implements: they have been using oxen for their farming operations since the 1930s when white settler farmers started coming into the country. These farmers used animal traction on their own farms with the help of local labourers, but the spread of the technology to Zambian smallholder farmers was quite limited. Moreover, farming is not a traditional occupation in some regions, and people's preferences for other occupations, such as hunting, fishing and mining, slowed the rate of adoption of animal traction. In other areas, however, the technology spread rapidly.

In 1985 the government decided to encourage the use of animal draft power technology as a means of increasing agricultural production. A five-year animal draft power investment plan was drawn up (MAWD, 1985), and several programmes were initiated, some in conjunction with the donor community, others run solely by the government.

Present status of animal draft power

Cattle are the principal source of animal draft power in Zambia. The technology relies mainly on oxen, although recently cows have been used to a small extent. Local indigenous breeds are used in cattle-keeping areas. Where there are few cattle, there have only been limited transfers from areas of cattle surplus due to veterinary restrictions and high transport costs. The use of other animals, such as donkeys, is minimal, but could increase as farmers start to believe that donkeys can survive adverse conditions, such as drought, better than cattle.

About 240 000 draft animals with 120 000 animal-drawn mouldboard plows, 30 000 ridgers, 20 000 cultivators, 60 000 sledges and 30 000 carts were in use in Zambia in 1990 (Starkey, Dibbits and Mwenya, 1991). The plow is clearly the most popular implement, mainly because plowing is the main activity in parts of the country where animal power is used. However, many farmers also use their plow for preparing ridges and for inter-row weeding, even when ridgers are available; some farmers consider the ridger to be too heavy for the animals and the operator, especially when turning at the ends of the fields, while others prefer a plow because it is cheaper than a ridger. However, the use of ridgers is increasing, particularly on crops such as groundnuts. Ridging is a common practice in maize fields during the first weeding.

Animal power distribution

The distribution of animal power in Zambia varies between and within provinces (Starkey, Dibbits and Mwenya, 1991: see Map 1 and Table 1). Southern, Eastern, Central and Western Provinces, where animal traction has been used for many years, have higher cattle populations than other provinces, and about 8–10% of the cattle are trained for work. By contrast, in areas where the cattle population is lower and animal traction has been introduced only recently, far fewer (3–4%) of the available cattle are trained; in these areas government intervention has been necessary to facilitate animal training.

About half of the country's trained oxen are located in Southern Province, which also contains about half of the national cattle population. Although not all farmers own oxen, in some areas about 90% of farmers use draft animals for cultivation and transport. The highest concentration of trained oxen is found in Monze District (30 000) followed by

Table 1: Cattle population and trained oxen distribution in Zambia, 1991

Province	Cattle population	Number of trained oxen	% trained oxen
Southern	1 081 200	105 000	9.7
Eastern	273 600	32 500	11.9
Lusaka	89 500	5 200	5.8
Central	483 400	40 900	8.5
Northern	102 600	3 600	3.5
Luapula	10 800	500	4.0
Copperbelt	65 000	2 400	3.7
North Western	59 400	2 000	3.5
Western	512 800	50 000	9.7
Total	**2 678 300**	**242 100**	**9.0**

Map 1. Schematic presentation of the numbers and distribution of work oxen in Zambia.
The numbers of work oxen are represented by circles. The size of each circle is approximately proportional to the number of trained oxen in that area. The shaded areas on the map are considered to be of relatively high tsetse challenge. The map also indicates broad rainfall zones by giving the approximate positions of the 1200 mm and 700 mm isohyets
Source: Starkey, Dibbits and Mwenya (1991)

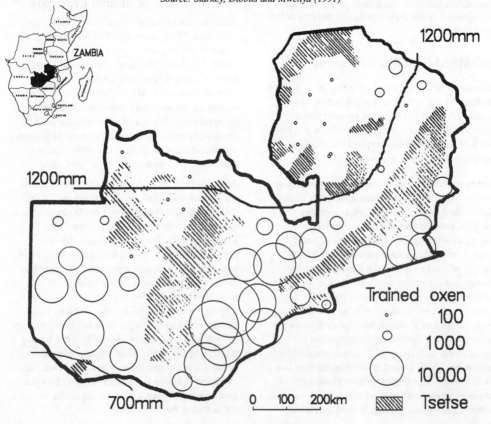

Namwala (18 000) and Kalomo (15 000). In these areas most farmers train their own animals.

Constraints to increased use

The present state of use of animal traction is far from optimal. Constraints to the increased use of this technology include:

∘ the poor state of the national economy

∘ low producer prices

∘ inadequate credit facilities

∘ lack of technical knowledge by most farmers and extension workers

∘ inadequate research and demonstration of animal traction technology

∘ poor supply and marketing of animal traction implements.

Most promoters of animal power technology in Zambia, and the farmers themselves, agree that poor producer prices, especially for maize, the major crop grown by smallholder farmers, is one of the main factors contributing to farmers' inability to adopt animal traction technologies. Growing maize appears not to be profitable. Use of such technologies as animal draft will only be attractive to smallholder farmers if they are paid handsomely for their produce, as this will enable them to increase their financial resources and undertake investment in animals and implements.

Inadequate credit facilities are another constraint to increased agricultural production by animal traction farmers. Although financial assistance has been provided by some lending institutions, such as Lima Bank, Zambia Cooperative Federation Finance Services and some commercial banks, support has not been adequate and there is evidence that many farmers have had to rely on their own resources to purchase inputs, including animal-drawn implements.

Lack of technical know-how by some extension workers and farmers, mainly in areas where animal traction is being introduced, but also in traditional animal traction areas, is yet another constraint to the spread of this technology. The technical training of extension workers in smallholder mechanisation techniques seems inadequate to enable them to advise smallholder farmers effectively. Until recently the agricultural education and training curricula at technical colleges and the university have included little on animal traction. As a result, graduates from these institutions lack skills in animal traction technology and are not very useful to farmers who have no knowledge of how to train and manage draft animals, and how to operate the animal traction implements.

Poor distribution of animal traction implements is generally agreed to be another hindering factor to improving agricultural production through the use of draft animals. Manufacturers and importers of

Plowing in Southern Province of Zambia

Photo: Paul Starkey

animal traction implements are concentrated along the railway line between the Copperbelt and Livingstone (see Map 2) which covers only some parts of four of the nine provinces. The distribution networks of these organisations are mostly based on provincial cooperative unions which are located mainly in the provincial capitals. These unions are supported by district unions which are in close contact with farmers and are expected to know their farmers' needs. Although the district unions may know what is needed, they often cannot satisfy the need because the provincial union does not have adequate stocks of implements or inputs or cannot distribute the stock because of financial or administrative deficiencies. Supply of spare parts is another problem: most Cooperative Managers seem to concentrate on provision of complete implements rather than on spares.

Cattle diseases have also played a major role in determining the level of use of animal traction technology. Constant outbreaks of diseases, particularly in Southern, Western, Central and Eastern Provinces, have reduced the numbers of animals available for work, and consequently some

farmers are wary of investing in cattle (including oxen) because of the economic risk. However, cattle diseases are less prevalent, and so have not yet posed a big threat, in areas where animal traction is a new introduction.

Proposed solutions to constraints

Increased use of animal traction will depend largely on the positive growth of the national economy, and especially on reductions in inflation and interest rates. With reduced interest rates, coupled with a free market economy, farmers will have the incentive to invest in animal traction.

The 1985 five-year investment plan contained several solutions to animal traction constraints, especially in the areas of research and development, training, implement supply and information and documentation. The investment plan has been implemented since 1987. Sufficient research results are not yet available in a form that extension workers can understand and take to the farmers. The Magoye Animal Traction Research and Development Project worked on equipment testing and the development of tillage systems. Formal test

Map 2: Zambia showing districts and provinces and the "line of rail" from Livingstone to Lusaka and the Copperbelt

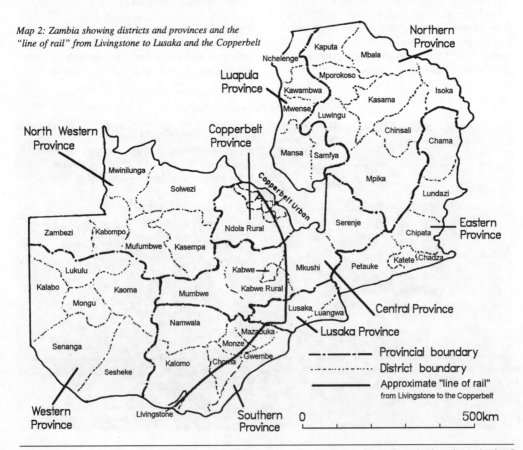

Oxen pulling grass mower at Palabana Animal Draft Power Training Centre, Zambia

Photo: Paul Starkey

procedures for animal-drawn carts and animal-drawn plows have been established and test results have been communicated to the manufacturers for improvements in design.

The Palabana Animal Draft Power Training Project has developed an animal traction technology training curriculum for agricultural development staff (suitable for governmental and non-governmental organisations). Several in-service courses have been conducted for extension workers. An outreach programme has been developed to support trainees and provide technical advice to other animal traction institutions.

In order to improve the information and documentation situation, a National Animal Draft Power Coordination Unit was established in the Department of Agriculture. The unit's main activities include animal traction problem identification, setting of priorities to support policy makers, and providing technical advisory services.

On the question of poor supply of animals, it has been suggested that small, privately owned breeding herds be established in areas with low cattle populations. This solution is believed to be more sustainable than the transfer of animals from areas with surplus cattle. This idea is already being implemented in Luapula Province using Finnish technical cooperation (Finnida). Private traders are being encouraged to specialise in the purchase of young steers for sale.

Trypanosomiasis, and tick-borne diseases such as East Coast Fever, are the major cattle diseases in Zambia. Some measures to control the tsetse fly population through the use of insecticides, and tick-borne diseases by regular dipping, are being undertaken by the Department of Veterinary and Tsetse Control. However, the government's

introduction of a dipping fee has discouraged some farmers from treating their animals. Farmers seem not to understand the economics of the government's move, and so proper farmer education should be intensified if the situation is to improve.

The problem of implement supply and distribution could be minimised if private traders realise the profitability of the animal-drawn implement business. What is needed is coordination between the various importing and manufacturing organisations and the establishment of an efficient distribution network.

Conclusions

The majority of farmers (80–90%) in most parts of Zambia are smallholders who cannot afford to own a tractor or use tractor hire services for their agricultural work. Animal traction has been acknowledged by many to be very relevant to these farmers, and will continue to provide the best alternative for farm mechanisation. Although the technology has been confined mainly to cattle-keeping areas, efforts are being made to extend this important innovation to areas in which animal draft use has not been a tradition. In both cases application of the technology has some limitations. Unless issues suggested in this paper are tackled effectively, improving animal traction technology in Zambia will be a very slow process and will depend largely on farmers' own ability to invest.

References

MAWD, 1985. *Animal draft power*. Investment Plan Task Force, Planning Division, Ministry of Agriculture and Water Development (MAWD), Lusaka, Zambia. 159p.

Starkey P H, Dibbits H J and Mwenya E, 1991. *Animal traction in Zambia: status, progress and trends*. Ministry of Agriculture, Lusaka, Zambia, in association with IMAG-DLO, Wageningen, The Netherlands. 105p.

Animal traction technology in Niger and some implications for Zambia

by

Fred Kruit

Animal Draft Power Research and Development Project, Private Bag 173, Woodlands, Lusaka, Zambia

Abstract

A feasibility study on the use of animal traction in Sahelian (low rainfall) farming systems was undertaken in Niger, West Africa. In one area where animal traction had been used previously, but abandoned, on-farm research was executed and farmers were given training, loans and implements. In another area, where animal traction was still used, village studies were carried out to discover how farmers make animal traction profitable. The results could be of interest and value to the low rainfall areas of eastern and southern Africa.

Introduction

The extent of animal traction use in West Africa seems to be determined by the climate:

- in the Sahelian zone (roughly 200 to 600 mm annual rainfall) there is hardly any use of animal traction because this zone is thought to have low agricultural potential (and hence low or non-existent profitability)

- in the Savanna area (600–1200 mm annual rainfall) use of animal traction is generally widespread

- in the Forest area (more than 1200 mm annual rainfall) there is again hardly any adoption of animal traction, mainly because shifting cultivation systems do not allow its easy introduction, and because disease problems have kept cattle populations low.

A similar relationship between climatic zone and animal traction use is seen in eastern and southern Africa. Therefore, experiences of animal traction use in West Africa could be of interest to eastern and southern Africa.

At the beginning of the 1980s, the Food and Agriculture Organization of the United Nations (FAO) wanted to find out about the possibilities of using animal traction in the Sahelian zone. Niger was chosen as the project country because its agriculture depends on this zone; other "Sahelian" countries concentrate their agricultural activities in the non-Sahelian south. The research was taken over by SNV (a development organisation based in The Netherlands) in 1988, and concluded in 1991.

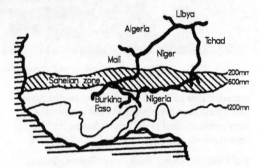

Figure 1: West Africa showing Niger and Sahelian zone

Characteristics of Niger

Climate and population

The southern part of Niger (200 x 1500 km) lies within the Sahelian zone (Figure 1). Annual rainfall is 200–600 mm; the rain falls during a short (three to four month) wet season, but is very irregular and unevenly distributed. This region is home to most of the country's 7.25 million population, 85% of which depend on traditional agriculture for their livelihood. Between this zone and the vast desert in the north is a pastoral transition zone, where nomads roam with their large herds of cattle.

Poverty

Niger is a very poor country. It is land-locked (1000 km from the coast), has a population growth of 3.1%, and has experienced food deficiencies since 1970. Per capita GNP was only US$ 200 in 1985, even though the local currency (FCFA) is fixed to the French Franc. The national economy depends almost entirely on uranium mining in the north. Export of cattle is important in the south but is generally an unofficial activity.

Topography

The terrain is generally flat, with sandy soils which form crusts after rainfall. Extensive use is made of all possible agricultural land. Almost all of the natural vegetation and rich topsoil have disappeared as a result of high human and cattle population

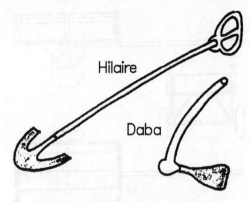

Figure 2: Traditional weeding tools in Niger

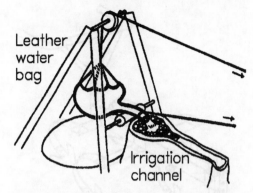

Figure 3: A "delou" in Niger. This is a traditional device
that uses animal power to lift water from deep wells

densities and of water and wind erosion. Land degradation has become a major problem during the past few decades. Also, the disappearance of vegetation has led to a decline in rainfall over the past 100 years.

Agriculture

An average family consists of six to eight persons with 3–5 ha of land and some animals. The land is farmed extensively, without any inputs, and most farms are barely self-sufficient. Hand tools are used for weeding (Figure 2): the "hilaire" (push hoe) in the pure sandy areas and the "daba" (hoe) in the areas with crusty soils, which are relatively more fertile.

Traditionally, tillage by hand hoe is only undertaken in some small areas with clayey soils, in combination with cash crops.

The main crops are pearl millet (75% of all crops grown; mean yield 300 kg/ha), sorghum and cowpeas (mainly as an intercrop). Yields have declined within the past few years, although total production has increased slightly as agricultural land has been extended. Some income is obtained from the sale of crops and animals, the hire of transport (animal-drawn carts), commercial activities (among the Haussa tribe), seasonal work at the coast and, in some areas, the growing of cash crops.

In the past, nomads grazed their cattle on the stubble fields of farmers after harvest (and so provided manuring) in exchange for millet. Because of the extension of cropped land, fewer grazing areas are now available for the cattle of either the nomads or the villages.

History of animal traction in Niger

For centuries, farmers in the north have had efficient ox or camel operated water-lifting devices above

their wells (Figure 3), to irrigate small gardens in the desert oases (de Beus and Kruit, 1989a; 1989b). In the south, animal traction was first introduced in the 1950s to stimulate the production of the cash crops (cotton and groundnuts) in some areas. In the 1970s, after independence, a country-wide loan scheme was established and several regional rural development projects promoted the use of animal traction in some regions by providing training to young farmers. Five local factories were established to meet the future demand for implements and carts, made of steel imported from Europe. Local cooperatives took care of distribution.

However, by the end of the 1980s, animal traction had still not been adopted in most of Niger, for the following reasons:

○ the "trickle-down" theory did not work: most of the young "farmers" sent for training were outcasts from the villages and did not have any influence

○ farmers could only obtain the whole animal traction package (UCA—unite de culture attelée), which included an *Arara* frame with plow, a cultivator (Figure 4), a ridger, a groundnut lifter, an ox cart and two oxen

○ farmers were not trained properly on how to use the different implements, some of which were, in any case, not appropriate for their specific soil types

○ spare parts were not available at the local cooperatives and farmers had to buy them from the factories

○ insufficient attention was given to the combination of animal traction with organic or chemical fertiliser to improve yields

○ donkey traction was not promoted at all, although large numbers of donkeys were already used for transport (carrying loads on

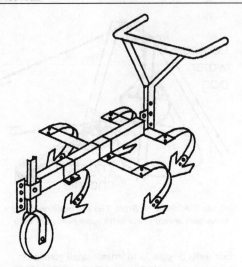

Figure 4: "Canadian" cultivator mounted on Arara frame

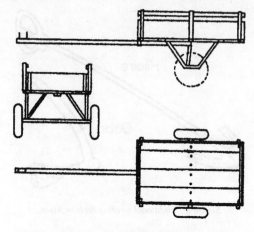

Figure 5: Cart design of the type widely used in West Africa, being based on a fixed solid steel axle, roller bearings and imported wheels and tyres

their backs). Farmers believed that only oxen were appropriate for animal traction

° cash cropping (cotton and groundnuts) suffered from the declining rainfall and international market prices. Only in irrigated areas and in some valleys (with heavier soils) can cash crops still be grown and in these areas implements and carts are still used

° the loan scheme had to be stopped in 1982; repayments were falling seriously behind because of the high costs of the loans and the inefficiency of the scheme

° during severe drought years (especially 1984) equipment was sold to Nigeria. Without the loan scheme, farmers were not able to repurchase the factory implements.

Around 1990, ox and donkey carts (the "West African type", Figure 5) became very popular, mainly because hiring out transport was a good source of cash income. In some areas farmers had to pay tax when they used carts for commercial purposes other than their own agricultural activities.

Only one local factory (in Tahoua) still produces Arara equipment (with steel purchased from Europe with a loan)—mainly plows for the irrigation projects along the Niger river. Farmers use the plow as a ripper: they turn it sideways so that only the point is used to break up the heavy soil. Some cotton fields are ridged. Weeding is mostly done by hand hoe, because the proper use of a cultivator is not well known.

In the rainfed agricultural zone of Niger, animal traction is applied to any great extent in only one area—the Maradi Department. Around 1980,

extension by a regional rural development project had a great impact in this area. Although a lot of equipment was sold to Nigeria during the drought of 1984, local workshops continued to make improved copies of existing implements and carts, using cheap steel purchased in Nigeria.

Feasibility study: animal traction in rainfed agriculture in Niger

In the period 1984–91, research on rainfed agriculture in Niger was carried out by FAO and SNV to see if there was any potential for animal traction within Sahelian farming systems. A feasibility study was carried out in villages of Maradi Department to discover how farmers make animal traction profitable (Löwenberg-de Boer, Abdoulaye and Kruit, 1991). In Tahoua Department, where animal traction equipment was sold after 1984, on-farm research was undertaken and farmers were provided with training, loans and implements (Kruit, 1991).

Tahoua Department

In this area, total production was increased by extending the cropping area. The limit of extension has now been reached and in most areas yields have decreased considerably. Furthermore, much natural vegetation has disappeared as a result of population pressure and overgrazing. Topsoil has been removed by wind and water erosion, leaving bare hard soil, in some places already revealing the rocky layer. Old farmers in Niger still remember the country being covered by medium-sized trees on rich loamy soils. Today, only shrubs and sand or rocks are left, out of

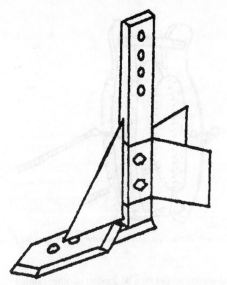

Figure 6: Ripper tine "Konni" to be mounted on an Arara *frame*

which it will be very difficult to recreate productive agricultural land.

The following advantages of animal traction for crop production were found in the area:

○ tillage breaks the crust and causes better rain infiltration and water conservation

○ weeding can be done quickly and at the right time. Also the crop can be thinned on time, which influences yields considerably.

These are not spectacular results, but under Sahelian conditions they can be important. Up to now, organic or chemical fertiliser has been applied only in the valleys where water is adequate and cash crops are cultivated—cotton, onions in small gardens and, recently, "dolique", a bean species planted after rains have stopped. In rainfed agriculture the use of fertiliser was too risky: if rainfall is low, the crop will burn, while without fertiliser it will still yield something.

Improved tillage through animal traction makes more rainwater available for the crop and a small application of fertiliser or manure will be possible. In this way cropping systems can be intensified. Although marginal in terms of profitability, this improvement could mean survival to a lot of farmers.

The implement promoted by the project for ox traction was the five-tine spring-cultivator (*Arara*, Figure 4) available from the Acrema factory nearby. It could be used for cultivating (breaking the crust and working in fertiliser) and weeding. Because crusts are quite heavy and soils are rocky in places,

a solid rigid-tine cultivator would have been better, but this is not available in Niger.

The project also developed a ripper tine (Figure 6) which can be used to make furrows in degraded land. Crops, grasses or trees can then be grown to reform the agricultural land, especially in combination with small contour dikes which capture rainwater running off. Farmers also used the ripper tine to plant crops quickly on crusty soils.

The ridger was not promoted in Sahelian agriculture: timely sowing is important and the risk to farmers of waiting for a second shower is too high. Furthermore, ridging is quite intensive and needs a lot of fertiliser in combination with rain to produce well.

One clear observation was that although ridging promoted a good initial plant stand, yields were poor when no fertiliser was applied. Ripping has the opposite effect: the crop develops slowly, though very uniformly, at first, but at shooting it suddenly develops very quickly, producing large grains, even without fertiliser. An explanation might be that roots catch the descending layer of water and nutrients later in the season.

The project strongly promoted donkey traction, because it is much cheaper than ox traction and affordable by a small farmer. Ox traction, including ox carts, will mainly be used by wealthier farmers to cultivate a large area but this would also speed up land degradation. Furthermore, small farmers who gain cash by weeding for rich farmers will lose this source of income and could even give up farming because of a lack of sufficient suitable land. Also, if a lot of farmers use oxen, not enough fodder will be available in the area.

Five different donkey cultivators were promoted in Niger, but none of them was really appropriate. The project has proposed two new types of donkey cultivator (Figure 7) and a harness design being assessed in Burkina Faso (Figure 8).

Because soils are relatively heavy in the area, good factory-made implements are needed, which are relatively expensive. Farmers in these areas need medium-term loans to be able to buy solid implements. The loans can be paid back slowly through the small income-generating activities mentioned above. However, the combination with a cart will cease to be highly profitable when a lot of farmers start using them, because the opportunities for hiring out carts will then decrease.

Training of animals does not present problems: traditionally farmers have kept oxen and donkeys and trained them for transport purposes.

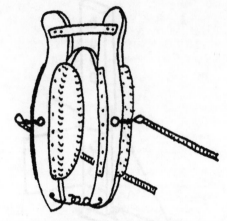

Figure 8: Donkey harness being promoted in Burkina Faso

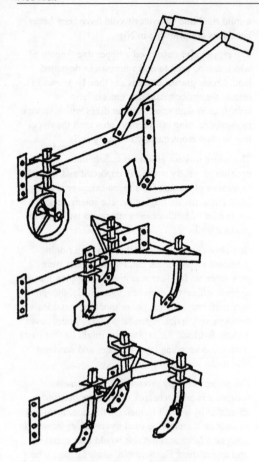

Figure 7: Donkey weeder "Konni".
Basic frame with lifter (top), triangle addition (middle),
"Simone" frame (bottom)

After this animal traction research, a follow-up SNV project—Projet participatif pour le renforcement des institutions villageoises pour le développement de l'agriculture à Tahoua (PRIVAT)—started to intensify agricultural systems in the area by creating village loan institutions to enable male and female farmers to buy inputs themselves (Narua et al, 1990). Another aspect of this new project is extension of research messages.

It was very clear that farmers were not aware of the possibilities of animal traction. After extension and training by the project, some farmers in the research villages started reusing old discarded equipment; others purchased implements with a two-year loan given by the project.

Maradi Department

In Maradi Department the project wanted to find out how farmers make animal traction profitable; this

knowledge would then be applied in other rainfed agricultural areas in Niger.

Initial project assumptions on animal traction use

At the outset it was thought that the profitability of animal traction arose from three main areas: use of animal traction for transport, cattle breeding and cash cropping. However, the project found that these reasons were not as important as expected.

Transport: It had been thought that only the cart was really profitable; that farmers use implements only because the transport animals were available. However, in most villages, the first implements were obtained before the first carts. Although the combination of ox carts with ox-drawn implement was quite common, small farmers mainly used only donkey implements without carts.

Cattle breeding: It had been thought that if farmers bought young oxen, they could sell them within five years at a high profit. However, farmers normally only sell oxen when they have a direct need for cash or if the animals are old, weak or ill. Cattle are seen more as a part of the farm investment which also has running costs (fodder), and will not be as profitable as originally thought.

Cash crops: It had been thought that animal traction depended on the presence of a real cash crop. Certainly, in cash crop areas, up to 100% of the farmers used animal traction, but even in areas with subsistence agriculture, up to 50% of farmers did so.

Farmers' systems of using animal traction

Well-provided extension by a former rural development project made the farmers aware of the possibilities of animal traction.

To raise total crop production, it was still possible in the area to extend agricultural land. The average yield per farm normally remained the same. Enough grazing land was still available for nomads and the village cattle, so fodder costs could be kept low.

The small local workshops reacted to the demand for implements and carts by producing improved copies of existing designs, made from cheap, poor quality steel and scrap purchased in Nigeria. Farmers were able to buy this cheap material without a loan.

The "non-economic" aspect of easing drudgery also proved to be important. Children take care of draft animals after work, but their weeding task is lightened considerably. Since women in most areas do not do weeding, their only benefit from animal traction would be increased food production.

Farmers in this area are beginning to complain that yields are decreasing because extension of cropping land is no longer possible. Their first reaction is to start growing cash crops again, especially souchet and pure cowpeas (high yielding variety). The latter need insecticides to produce well, which is difficult to obtain through the cooperatives.

The situation is similar in Tahoua Department: farmers will have to apply organic or chemical fertiliser to stabilise production. It will be interesting to see if the extension of the former project on the use of fertiliser will have its desired effect, such that farmers will "automatically" apply it. The carts will play an important role in transporting cheap chemical fertiliser from Nigeria and manure from villages to the fields.

Figure 9: Donkey weeder widely used in Maradi area. improved from existing models by farmers. Ox weeder is based on Arara *groundnut lifter*

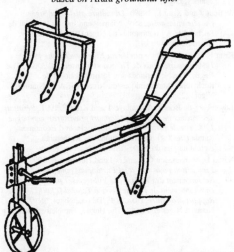

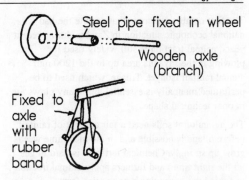

Figure 10: Simple wheel–axle system used in Maradi area

Implement type, manufacture and repair

The most popular implement is the groundnut lifter for oxen, or a small one for donkeys (Figure 9), used for weeding. The blade is set to a steeper angle to act like a ridger. Two passes have to be made between two crop lines (about 1 m apart). Few farmers have a three-tine cultivator to break up the crusty soil. Camels are also employed.

Because steel quality is bad, implements are not very solid and are badly aligned. A lot of cash and time is wasted on repairs, especially of the lifter blade which has to be changed many times each season.

The simple iron wheel is replaced by a wooden one with an axle of steel pipe and a piece of wood (Figure 10), which proves to be very effective.

The Super-Eco seeder, copied and produced by a factory in Niger, is still used to plant cash crops, including groundnuts, cotton, cowpeas (monocrop) and "souchet" (a plant which forms small bulbs).

Repair and some production of implements is carried out by local blacksmiths trained by the former project. Almost all blacksmiths want a generator for welding; at present they have to travel to larger villages to repair and assemble implements, which is expensive in terms of time and money.

Local workshops producing these simple implements could be of use for the sandy areas where simple, cheap tools (groundnut lifter) are sufficient for weeding. For areas with crusty soils, such as Maradi, solid factory implements on loan will be more profitable in the long run.

Some reflections on the different situations in Zambia and Niger

It is difficult to compare the situation in Zambia with that in Niger, for the climatic zone in Zambia (700–1500 mm) starts where it ends in Niger.

The first notable feature is that despite the bad national economic situation in Zambia during recent years, animal traction is still widely used for plowing in the savanna area up to the 1200 mm annual rainfall isohyet. Tillage, which used to be performed manually is essential, but many plows are in poor technical shape.

The agricultural soils need a fair amount of rainfall before tillage is possible and in the meantime weeds grow up strongly. Chemical fertiliser is hard to get (at the right time) and farmers apply animal traction to extend their cropping area to raise farm production. Furthermore, labour is scarce through a high rate of urbanisation, which makes mechanisation inevitable.

One of the main problems seems to be the scarcity of expertise, machines and good raw material to produce proper implements locally. With a better economic situation this could be improved: unlike Niger, good quality steel can be purchased nearby (South Africa).

On the other hand, ox carts are not very widely used, possibly because they is of low economic profitability to farmers. Good designs and spare parts are not available and locally made carts are expensive. Maybe with new government policy they will become profitable, especially for transport of fertiliser and harvest surpluses, and proper designs could be introduced.

In Niger with its dry climate, cattle disease is not a big problem. In Zambia it is a real threat, especially in areas with a high cattle population. This could mean that farmers could be interested in donkey traction, with lower risk.

One concern is careless use of the land, as animal traction is seen as a way of cultivating a greater area. Generally speaking, there is enough space and vegetation available in Zambia, but there are dangers in the high potential agricultural areas, where population density also is high. Here, the use of animal traction to raise total production through extensification (without intensification through fertiliser use) could mean severe land degradation, yield decline and erosion. The environmental effect may be worsened by herds of small ruminants and wood cutting for charcoal for the urban population. This effect can already be observed in certain regions in Zambia, eg, in the Gwembe Valley and Zambezi escarpment.

Only the south valley of Zambia (700 mm rainfall) can be compared with Niger, and care should be taken to ensure that farmers apply animal traction properly, ie, non-intensive tillage (cultivator or ripper) in combination with small applications of fertiliser. In the north of Zambia (1500 mm rainfall), it will be very difficult to introduce animal traction on a large scale (in many high rainfall areas of Africa animal traction does not exist because of the problems mentioned earlier). Ridging by animal traction could be carried out in areas where ridges are already made traditionally by hand.

More farming systems research should be carried out to find out how animal traction could be more effectively utilised or introduced in Zambia.

Conclusion

Experiences from Niger show that animal traction, especially ox traction, has up to now been used only to extend cropping area to increase total production. The process of land degradation through erosion is speeded up by animal traction, in combination with devegetation by pressures of the human and animal populations.

The only way this process can be stopped is to combine animal traction with organic or chemical fertiliser as a means of intensifying production. Research has shown that animal traction improves water storage in the soil, so low levels of fertiliser can be applied, which previously would have been too risky within Sahelian farming systems. Furthermore, donkey traction for small farmers should be promoted so as not to enlarge the gap between them and wealthier farmers.

References

de Beus J and Kruit F, 1989a. *La culture attelée au Niger: étude des possibilités d'application.* SNV, Niamey and Institut National de Recherches Agronomiques du Niger (INRAN), Niamey, Niger. 74p.

de Beus J and Kruit F, 1989b. *La culture attelée au Niger: enquête villageoise.* SNV, Niamey and Institut National de Recherches Agronomiques du Niger (INRAN), Niamey, Niger. 32p.

Kruit F, 1991. *La culture attelée au Niger: recherche 1989 et 1990, Départements de Tahoua et Maradi.* SNV/DGIS, The Hague, The Netherlands and Institut National de Recherches Agronomiques du Niger (INRAN), Niamey, Niger. 120p.

Löwenberg-de Boer J, Abdoulaye T and Kruit F, 1991. *Résultats des travaux de recherche (Rapport provisoire): campagne 1990, site de Birni N'Konni.* Département d'Economie Rurale (DECOR), Institut National de Recherches Agronomiques du Niger (INRAN), Niamey, Niger.

Narua D, Mahamadou O, Lamers J and Huizinga B, 1990. *Proposition pour un Projet Participatif pour le Renforcement des Institutions Villageoises pour le Développement de l'Agriculture à Tahoua (PRIVAT). Rapport provisoire.* DDA/DDP, Tahoua, Niger; SNV, Niamey, Niger and DGIS, The Hague, The Netherlands. 51p.

Index